The Oxford Conspirators

THE OXFORD CONSPIRATORS

*A History of the Oxford
Movement 1833–45*

BY

Marvin R. O'Connell

THE MACMILLAN COMPANY

COLLIER-MACMILLAN LTD., LONDON

Library of Congress Catalog Card Number: 68-31279

FIRST PRINTING

The Macmillan Company
Collier-Macmillan Canada Ltd., Toronto, Ontario

Printed in the United States of America

FOR

RICHARD O'CONNELL (1904–1959)

ERAT VIR JUSTUS

Contents

Preface

IT may have been presumptuous for one who is not an Englishman to have written a book about something so peculiarly English as the Oxford Movement. I was moved to the attempt primarily because it seemed to me to be such a very interesting story. Yet it was a story hard to unravel, moving as it did through a social and intellectual milieu now gone from England as well as from the rest of the world. Although I read hundreds of books of varying quality on the subject, I never found one that supplied a straight narrative account of the Movement intelligible to me and my generation. My modest object has been to fill that gap.

I have tried to rely mostly on contemporary sources, published and unpublished. My readers may see for themselves what I have used by consulting the notes to the text. The amount of such material is so vast and varied that some of my criteria of selection may appear arbitrary. My chronological rule of thumb, for example, eliminated for my purposes Newman's *Loss and Gain* and *Difficulties of Anglicans* on the grounds that both these works were commentaries too close upon the events and, incidentally, too directly polemical in intent. The *Apologia*, on the other hand, filled as it is with correspondence from the 1830s and 1840s, I have used without hesitation. But obviously no judgments of this kind can be considered definitive.

Writing a book is the best way to find out that no man is an island. Among the many pleasant debts I have accumulated I should acknowledge first of all the one I owe to the Louis W. and Maud Hill Family Foundation and to its Executive Director, Mr. A. A. Heckman, for a grant which enabled me to do archival research in England. My spokesman with the Foundation was that most eloquent of advocates, Bishop James P. Shannon. My thanks must go as well to the Warden of Keble College, Oxford, and to the Principal of Pusey House, Oxford, for allowing me to study the papers under their jurisdiction. Similarly, I am grateful to the

Fathers of the Oratory in Birmingham, and especially to Fr. C. S. Dessain, whose courtesy and helpfulness to wandering students of Newman have become part of a living legend.

I have employed the resources of many libraries, including notably the New York Public Library, the Library of the University of Minnesota and the St. Paul Seminary Library. I am particularly indebted to the Superintendent of the Reading Room of the British Museum, London. And it is not too much to say that this book could not have been written without the constant and cordial aid of Fr. Clyde Eddy and his staff at the O'Shaughnessy Library, the College of St. Thomas. A special word of thanks must be offered explicitly to Mrs. Geraldine King.

My judicious friend, Fr. Henri DuLac, read a good part of the typescript and made several valuable suggestions. So did Mgr. Philip Hughes, whose comments, however, I did not find until after his recent death. The genesis of this book really goes back a decade and more to the long conversations about Newman I used to have with this beloved mentor as we took our leisurely automobile drives across the bleak landscape of northern Indiana. I recall conversations as well, which were all too brief, with Fr. Alphonse Chapeau at St. Mary of the Angels in Bayswater and with Mr. David Newsome of Emmanuel College, Cambridge.

I am deeply grateful to my dear friends Dr. and Mrs. James Ryan, who pondered the effect of every word and who suffered with me through every phase of composition.

My warm thanks are due finally to Mrs. Kathleen Boyd, who typed the manuscript with astonishing patience and efficiency, and to Miss Elizabeth Bartelme of The Macmillan Company, who made it possible for a dream to become a reality.

MARVIN R. O'CONNELL

St. Paul
May 20, 1968

PART I

Prelude: To 1833

CHAPTER 1

Farewell to the Tories

"THINGS are still in a bad way down here," wrote Richard Hurrell Froude from Devon in January 1831. "The labouring population, as well as the farmers, seem thoroughly indifferent to the welfare of the parsons and squires; and this does not seem at all to depend on their situation in respect to poverty or the way in which they have been treated." Froude's father was a parson—an archdeacon, in fact—with considerable landed property in the vicinity of Dartington. He owned a threshing machine which his sons guarded through several worrisome nights lest the mob should come and destroy it. Then, much to the pugnacious Hurrell's disappointment, the archdeacon decided to dismantle the machine. "I have now made up my sage mind," said Hurrell, "that the country is too bad to deserve an established church."[1]

At about the same time, in Gloucestershire, Froude's former mentor and close friend, John Keble, was attempting to stem the tide of agrarian riot in his own neighbourhood. On one exciting afternoon he stood astride some farm machinery and tried to cajole a hostile crowd of labourers out of their intention to wreck it. "The truth is," he said later, "their sufferings last winter were extreme in many cases. . . . I am not without hope that our [gentry and farmers], having been thoroughly frightened, will allow us to teach them a little more sympathy with the labourers than they have generally chosen to show."[2]

The Oxford Movement, which was founded by Keble and Froude, dealt with eternal verities and values, but it happened at a certain time and in a certain place. So far as we can reconstruct it more than a century later, we see that it could not have emerged in any other locale or at any other moment. The English nation, the English Church, the University of Oxford: these three shaped the Movement, and during its brief passage these three, to borrow a phrase from the New Testament, were peculiarly one. Nation, Church and university were so intertwined with one another

[3]

that what affected one affected the others as well. When, as Dean Church put it, "Mr. Newman made up his mind to force on the public mind, in a way which could not be evaded, the great article of the Creed—'I believe one Catholic and Apostolic Church,' "[3] the consequences were felt up and down the land.

Of all the religious institutions in the world, only the Church of England could have been mother to the Oxford Movement. And similarly only the university which gave it its name could have provided the Movement with all its leaders and most of its rank and file. Finally, the condition of English society between Waterloo (1815) and the passage of the great Reform Act (1832) determined the lines which, the wisdom of hindsight allows us to say, the Movement was bound to take.

Those were restless years, filled with economic dislocation and political uncertainty. As the dumb, inert masses began to stir, many old and treasured English habits suddenly appeared threatened. The steam engine was transforming the face of the earth. New social doctrines proclaimed the humanitarian ideals of the French Revolution. Agitators urged highly abstract schemes to alter the national structure and thus promote the greatest happiness of the greatest numbers. Meanwhile, unemployment skyrocketed and riots broke out as workers tried to destroy the machinery which, they thought, deprived them of jobs. More than once it seemed that the specter of civil war was just over the horizon.

The men who lived through these times did not of course grasp their full significance. They felt the winds of change blowing, but they seldom appreciated the direction or velocity. The members of the ruling class reacted with various degrees of enlightenment, and the Oxford Movement was part of that reaction.

I

In those days England was a greener, more spacious place than it is now. Less than a third as many people occupied the same area, and most of them, as yet, led a rural life outside what Blake called the "dark, satanic mills." In 1820, the year King George III died, it took the fastest coach seven hours to travel from London to the seaside pleasure palaces at Brighton. But few had time or money for the trip, with a four-pound loaf of bread costing a shilling and the ordinary workman seldom earning more than ten shillings a week. Nobody dreamed then that a weekend in Brighton would one day be a commonplace within the means of shopgirls and clerks with the modest price of a railroad ticket. The genteel tourists of 1820 would have been pained and perhaps shocked at the idea of a proletarian litter of paper cups and cigarette stubs along their favourite beaches. For in those days the diversions of sand and sun and sea breeze, like most other diversions, were reserved for the great folks of the land, like the Prince Regent, who built his vast and hideous pavilion at Brighton, and enshrined in it, so the delicious rumours went, all sorts of obscenities.

King George III had gone quite mad long before he died, and the monarchy, which his upright life had for a time delivered from the universal contempt to which his ancestors had brought it, had sunk to a new low in popular esteem thanks to the immorality and stupidity of his children. The Prince Regent now became King George IV, but under new title or old he remained as ever a monument to self-indulgence, a bad son and a faithless husband, gross, vulgar and mean. Thackeray observed that he was not really a man at all, but only "silk stockings, padding, stays, a coat with frogs and a fur collar, a star and blue ribbon, a pocket handkerchief prodigiously scented, one of Truefitt's best nutty brown wigs reeking with oil, a set of teeth and a huge black stock, under-waistcoats, more under-waistcoats, and then nothing."[4]

The time had passed when kings could have much direct effect, for good or ill, upon the life of the nation. But George IV's viciousness and extravagance, like everything the sovereign did and was, possessed symbolic importance. They demonstrated how deep was the chasm separating the haves from the have-nots. While the First Gentleman of Europe (a title George valued inordinately) stuffed himself with the finest jellies and the most delicate *pâté de foie gras*, while he guzzled his claret and port and fondled Lady Conyngham and won or lost thousands of an evening at cards, hunger stalked many parts of his three kingdoms of England, Scotland and Ireland. It took a wiser man than he to discern not only the tragedy but also the danger in that sour discontent which wrapped the British people round like a wet blanket.

There were plenty of measurable reasons to explain that discontent. Only five years before at Waterloo in Flanders, the British, led by the noble and unflappable Duke of Wellington, won by a whisker the decisive battle in the greatest war the world had ever seen. It had taken a quarter of a century and the united efforts of all the great powers in Europe to bring revolutionary France to her knees, and it could be argued that even that would not have been enough if Napoleon Bonaparte, the heir of the Revolution, had not pushed his luck too far. The struggle, hard as it had been, seemed at the time quite worthwhile. Englishmen of all classes agreed, in a vague sort of way, that the Revolution was a wicked, foreign thing, and that Old Boney, though smart for a foreigner, was wicked too.

But the cheers for the returning heroes had hardly died away before anguished cries for social change were raised on every side. The end of the war brought a short, deceptive boom and then an increasingly severe depression. The stimulation of the economy through military expenditure ceased at the same moment that foreign orders for British manufactured goods suffered a sharp reduction. Prices fell steadily and this aggravated the slump, for people will not buy today if they think they can buy more cheaply tomorrow. Nor will they invest to expand industrial plants when they are haunted by the fear that today's borrowed capital will have to be repaid tomorrow at an increased cost in real goods. The result was widespread factory cutbacks and shutdowns. Unemployment reached calamitous proportions when 400,000 veterans of the Napoleonic wars were loosed on the already glutted labour market. The price of grain, and hence of bread for the table, was falling too, but not fast enough to save a large proportion of the labouring classes from a life of bare subsistence. There was no relief for them, except from capricious charity and the almost medieval provisions of the Elizabethan Poor Law.[5]

The spoils of war have a way of turning to dust in the victors' hands, but the hard times after Waterloo reflected something deeper than an ordinary postwar deflation. There was a dramatic shift going on in the economic life of the nation and, indeed, of the whole Western world. Steam-driven machinery was about to alter the habits of a thousand years. This painful process took a long time to accomplish; it began long before 1820 and would continue for generations after. It brought with it dislocation and insecurity and unconscionable greed. It threw up ugly cities and ghastly sweatshops in which women and children were systematically maimed in the name of an abstract economic theory. It scarred the countryside with slag heaps and blinded the eye with industrial haze. And it provided ordinary people with comforts and leisure beyond the wildest dreams of their ancestors.

Nothing can instruct us better than the Industrial Revolution about the mixed character of the human condition. Good mingled with bad, cruelty with enlightenment. But one thing is eminently clear: The Industrial Revolution pulled up roots a thousand years old. It radically changed the way men lived and the way they thought. It altered their basic habits and shifted their sense of values. It substituted the assembly line for the workshop, the tenement for the cottage. It ended forever the rural orientation which Western men and women had taken for granted for as long as they could remember; it ended forever that England which George Eliot described as "swelling hills, muffled with hedge-rows and long meadow grass and thick corn," crowned by "some homestead with its long length of barn and its cluster of golden ricks," or by "some grey steeple looking out from a pretty confusion of trees and thatch and dark-red tiles."[6]

The distress of the English commons found its outlet in riots which sputtered across the country during the years after Waterloo. They were spontaneous, uncoordinated outbreaks of violence, dumb protests of men whom unseen forces had deprived of work and hope. Power looms and other machinery were smashed, monster meetings held, petitions drawn up. There were attempts by a small articulate minority to organize these demonstrators into a class movement. Agitators appeared at workmen's rallies wearing red revolutionary caps, sporting the tricolour and shouting the cant phrases of 1789. But for the most part the crowds did not respond to the impassioned pleas for class solidarity. Abstractions did not appeal to them. The men wanted jobs, not slogans, and so far they hated only the machines.

In August 1819 a huge protest meeting was held in an open space called St. Peter's Field, near Manchester; the crowd of fifty or sixty thousand people was well behaved, but when the town magistrates tried to arrest an agitator, there followed a scuffle, then a nervous charge into the crowd by some mounted hussars, and then a scene of wild, unreasoning panic which left eleven dead and four hundred injured. The Peterloo Massacre, as this tragedy came to be called, caused a wave of revulsion all over the country, but it did not lead to a new Declaration of the Rights of Man and the Citizen, it did not lead to that organized indignation which is the heart of revolution. The dull, mute anger of the English commons remained, for the moment at least, like the rumble of distant thunder, ominous of a storm yet to come.

II

The shadow of Peterloo fell darkest over the small, tightly knit English ruling class. Not many of them were as insensitive as the Prince Regent, who sent his hearty congratulations to the Manchester magistrates immediately after the massacre. Most of them still had enough of the *grand seigneur* in them to contemplate with horror the picture of cavalrymen galloping with swinging sabers into a crowd of unarmed civilians. But they had an equal horror of democracy. English gentlemen, who traditionally prided themselves on their happy relations with the lower orders, were now heard to refer to "the swinish mob." They had a vivid (and perhaps overdrawn) notion of the excesses of revolutionary France, and throughout the decade after the death of George III they lived with the uneasy memory of the Reign of Terror. Nervously they shuttered up their town houses and looked to their firearms. They listened to and half believed rumours that wild Jacobins were poised to seize London or to blow up the houses or Parliament.

The catastrophe which haunted the dreams of English gentlemen never happened, and one of the main reasons why was that the ruling class learned to bend and therefore did not break. Reform of political and economic institutions, gradual but real, preempted a violent revolution. It would be a mistake, however, to think of reform as a program precisely thought out beforehand. It was rather a long muddling from crisis to crisis. It was a slow and painful process for all concerned, and no one knew quite where it would end. It was instinctual rather than theoretical. It had none of that abstract logic which puts into their proper categories all possible future contingencies. It appalled the social engineer and the French constitutional lawyer. But it worked. English society evolved into the era of the common man, not without injustices indeed or inconsistencies or even violence, but without that peculiarly intense savagery which is evoked in the name of abstractions. And the old ruling class escaped falling before that most beguiling abstraction of all, the classless society; it maintained itself and continued to rule, although it gradually expanded itself to include more of the nation at large.

In 1820 political power rested, as it had since time immemorial, with those who controlled the land. In England this meant in effect that a few thousand families were represented in the two houses of parliament, provided officers for the army and navy and bishops for the state Church, sent their sons to the two universities, and dominated the chief positions in the civil service and in the professions. The rural nature of this aristocracy was modified more in England than elsewhere, because for a long time commercial endeavour had created wealth together with agriculture. The English gentleman, therefore, was not necessarily a farmer, though he usually was, and his cousins certainly were. More commonly, if he were a banker or a shipowner, he was a farmer, too, with a country estate which he probably regarded as his proper habitat rather than as just another investment.

The gentlemen who ruled England were divided into Whigs and Tories. These party designations went back to the seventeenth century when the aristocracy had split over the issue of excluding a Roman Catholic heir apparent from the royal succession. Those who opposed the exclusion of the prince were contemptuously nicknamed Tories (a term originally referring to a group of Irish Catholic agitators), and generally speaking their descendants came to be regarded as the court party, while the Whigs were identified with the parliamentary interest. By 1820, however, this distinction, whatever its original validity, had lost any practical political meaning. Someone compared the parties to two coaches lumbering along side by side; they occasionally spattered mud on each other, but even so they were following the same road, at about the same pace, and headed for the same destination. The members of the caste, in other words, had much more in common with each other, whichever party they belonged to, than they had with the unwashed multitude.

Whig and Tory did, however, represent two discernible traditions within the ruling class, though it is impossible to draw the line sharply. Many of the differences depended on habit and heredity, upon family connections which stretched back generations, rather than upon any carefully drawn principles. But basic to the assumptions of 1820 were the struggles of the seventeenth century, which had pitted cavalier against roundhead, the Episcopal Church against the Puritan Congregation, the king against the parliament. The Tories in some sense were descendants of the cavaliers; they were the English country gentlemen par excellence who were committed to the defense of those foundations of rural "merrie England," the crown and the Church. The Whigs, on the other hand, represented, again with qualifications, the Puritan tradition. They were the more cosmopolitan group of the two, reflecting more completely the alliance and intermingling of the country gentry and the urban financiers which had developed during the seventeenth and eighteenth centuries. They tended to distrust bishops and to exhibit a more militant and radical Protestantism. The Age of Enlightenment had, to be sure, diluted the religious enthusiasms of an earlier time, but the tension still existed within the Anglican Communion in terms of a Tory High Church versus a Whig Low Church. In short, the two parties, despite their common class consciousness, stood for two different points of view about government and religion and economics, points of view which survived the coming of democracy in the modern Liberal and Conservative parties.

The time was still indeed a long way off when Gladstone and Disraeli would have to compete for power through persuasion of a large electorate. As George IV began his reign, English political life thrived in the atmosphere of a posh, exclusive club. The aristocratic families, Whig and Tory, for the most part effectively controlled the workings of the immensely complex and restricted franchise; only a handful of the 658 seats in the House of Commons could be said to be free of their influence. Politics was a game which only gentlemen had the leisure and, so the common opinion went among gentlemen, the wit to play. And they played at it as fiercely as they played at dice, the way the parliamentary giants of the preceding generation had taught them: Sheridan and Burke, Charles James Fox and the younger Pitt.

But within this rickety party structure the forces of change found a voice. Among the Whigs there was an inheritance of liberalism which had long lain dormant but which by 1820 was experiencing a new birth. The great Whig families—like the Cavendishes, the Russells, the Howards—had been weaned on liberal sentiments. The Glorious Revolution of 1688—that practically bloodless coup which had dethroned the Stuart dynasty and had debunked forever the theory of the divine right of kings—had been peculiarly their victory, and the Bill of Rights, imposed the next year on the new king, had been their document. Whig fervour for libertarian causes had languished during the several generations that the party had controlled the government, but the tradition of aristocratic liberalism, at least in theory, was maintained.

Then the Whigs found themselves in the wilderness of opposition. By 1820 they had been out of power for more than thirty years. The Tories, thanks to the incomparable skill of Pitt and the not inconsiderable help of George III, fashioned an ascendancy which seemed destined to endure

forever. The crisis brought about by the French Revolution and the war
with Napoleon strengthened the Tory government's hand, and even after
Pitt died and the king went insane the Tories stayed comfortably in
power. As long as the war lasted any talk of liberty, equality and fra-
ternity was suspect, and the Whigs—the party of 1688—found the revolutionary tag a definite handicap.

Once the war ended, however, and the country's economy sank into
severe depression, the political atmosphere changed. The Whigs were
neither more nor less idealistic than other people. They sensed that
reform of political and economic institutions might be now not only a
cause but an issue. The clamour from below, most eloquently symbolized
by Peterloo, might be mobilized to overturn the Tories. The Whigs themselves were gravely divided over precisely what reform should involve and
how far it should go. It is doubtful that more than a few of them had
any democratic ideas. But they had two great advantages. They were
more attuned than their opponents to the economic factors which were
remaking the country; and, secondly, they could appeal to that tradition
of liberalism to which they had always given at least lip service. It had
been, for instance, a Whig magnate, the immensely wealthy and eccentric
Duke of Norfolk, who, even before the war ended, had given this toast
at a public banquet: "To our Sovereign, the People."[7]

The Tories, for their part, were peculiarly vulnerable. The Industrial
Revolution, as it created new wealth and hence new centers of power,
undermined the Tory position more than it did the Whig. The country
gentry, those squires and parsons who were the backbone of the Tory
party, were more deeply committed to the ancient ideal that political
authority resided solely in the ownership of land. With their almost
exclusively rural interests, the Tories came to be increasingly identified
with the unpopular artificial support of grain prices called the Corn
Laws. High-priced bread, the Whigs charged, was the only policy of the
Tory government.

To some extent the charge was true. Despite many differences of detail
among the leaders, the Tories became the party of the status quo, and had
the Whigs possessed sufficient cohesion themselves and an alert, attractive
leader, they would have brought the government down long before they
did. As it was, the Tories stayed in power till 1830, but when they collapsed, the wreckage was complete.

III

The Tory Prime Minister in 1820 was the Earl of Liverpool, a man
said to be so conservative that had he been present on the first day of
creation he would have prayed "Dear Lord, let us not disturb the chaos."

The only bona fide national hero was a Tory too, though the Duke of Wellington, victor of Waterloo, in some sense enjoyed supra-party regard. For all his pluck and loyalty to his sense of duty, the Duke had too limited an intelligence to grasp complicated issues. Tory intellectual talent was for the most part concentrated in two men whose ambition and mutual hatred brought them once to the dueling ground and permanently hampered their effectiveness. One was George Canning, the brilliant, unscrupulous, spellbinding orator, the darling of the House of Commons; the other was the Viscount Castlereagh, a cold, ruthless Irishman, with administrative gifts of a high order, whose accomplishments as Secretary for War and Foreign Secretary had made his the dominant voice in Tory councils. In the popular mind Castlereagh, not the lackluster Liverpool, represented the cabinet, and so Castlereagh became the target of the pamphleteers who flayed the government for its repressive measures against lower-class agitation after Waterloo.

> I met murder on the way [wrote Shelley]
> He had a mask like Castlereagh,
> Very smooth he looked yet grim,
> Seven bloodhounds followed him!

In 1822, Castlereagh in a fit of depression cut his own throat. Five years later Liverpool was incapacitated by a paralytic stroke, and within a few months, after a brief premiership, Canning died. This left Wellington alone of the old guard to hold the Tory fort, but the Duke, who had proved himself in Spain and Belgium one of the world's ablest defensive tacticians, was shortly to have his position outflanked and overrun.

One Tory leader, emerging to the front rank in 1820, deserves special notice. Robert Peel, though only thirty-two, had already sat in Commons for more than a decade and had served with distinction in the difficult post of Chief Secretary for Ireland. The son of a wealthy Lancashire cotton tycoon, Peel wore his Toryism on his sleeve. His dedication to the interests of the old order earned him the right, after 1817, to represent in Parliament that Tory stronghold, the University of Oxford.[8]

The relentless pressure of events rather than the blows of their opponents finally brought the Tories down. To be out of power at that moment was itself an advantage to the Whigs, but to have been out so long had left them scarred with dissensions and schisms. As it turned out, they could muster barely enough unity to seize the opportunity when it came. They were an unlikely group of reformers.

The titular head of the party was Earl Grey, a patrician to his fingertips, "an aristocrat both by position and by nature," as he put it himself. Grey, unlike Wellington, was ready to bow to the inevitable, and that spelled the difference between the two men. There were, to be sure, Whigs to the left of Grey, like the versatile and impetuous Henry

Brougham, but his outspoken liberalism sounded, even to his close friends, more opportunistic than genuine. Young Lord John Russell, frail and thin, his reedy voice hardly audible in House of Commons debates, stood for a carefully restricted measure of reform. And there was the shrewd, cynical, indolent Viscount Melbourne, a man bored by public life and by almost everything else, who never bothered to hide his disdain of his colleagues or his countrymen. What these men sought was a solution, once and for all, to the troubles which had led to disasters like Peterloo. They certainly never intended to initiate the evolutionary process which would end with universal suffrage and the graduated income tax. But they held a tiger by the tail, and, quite beyond their intention, they ushered in the era of the common man.

IV

The popular discontent was, as we have seen, basically an economic thing, sprinkled over by liberal political doctrine drawn from various sources. During the 1820s it crystallized into two key issues: Catholic emancipation and parliamentary reform. Once the remaining civil disabilities affecting Roman Catholics were removed, and once the House of Commons became more genuinely representative, the differences between the people and aristocracy might be settled. So at any rate went the widespread conviction.

Neither of these issues was new. Since 1800, when the separate Irish parliament had been suppressed, Ireland incorporated into the United Kingdom, and one hundred Irish members brought into the Commons at Westminster, leading politicians of both parties had urged that the remnant of the old penal laws against Roman Catholics be revoked. Men as diverse in their political philosophy as Castlereagh and Brougham had at one time or another supported emancipation. But George III, a fervent and narrow Protestant, had adamantly refused to give his sanction, and time after time bills granting Catholic emancipation died in Parliament. In his stand the king sensed accurately English public opinion, which was overwhelmingly opposed to any concessions to popery. George IV shared his father's views on this question, though for no discernible religious reasons; in doing so he perhaps sought a scrap of approval for himself amidst the almost universal hatred.

In any case, the issue had little practical significance in England or Scotland, where Roman Catholics had withered to a tiny, ostracized minority. But in Ireland it made all the difference, and now, after 1800, when Irish representatives sat in the expanded British parliament, its ramifications were bound to be felt throughout the United Kingdom. The Tories, on the whole, supported the king in opposing emancipation, while the Whigs generally favored it. What neither side grasped adequately was that emancipation was more a political than a religious question. It was part, really, of the larger Irish problem, which, in turn, presented in its most dramatic form the confrontation of the masses with the aristocracy. In Ireland the misery of the people was more pronounced than anywhere else in Great Britain, and the alienation of the haves from the have-nots took on added intensity because of racial and religious hatred.

As far as parliamentary reform was concerned, it too had had a long history. In 1793, Grey, then a rising young Whig politician, had called for the abolition of pocket boroughs and rotten boroughs—towns, that is, which sent members to Commons even though the towns had ceased to exist or had become the property—in the pocket, so to speak—of some private interest. He attacked the muddle of unrepresentative constituencies which denied the existence of the prosperous middle classes and turned every election into an orgy in bribery. But 1793 was the year the French Revolutionaries executed their king, and reform became then and for many years afterwards a dangerously radical idea.

One of the most glaring abuses was the unevenness of the franchise. A property qualification existed for voters in all parts of the United Kingdom, but it worked with a singular lack of consistency. Scotland, for example, with a population of about two million, sent forty-five members to the House of Commons, of whom thirty-six represented the county or rural (as opposed to the borough or city) constituencies. These thirty-six were returned by 2405 electors (or hardly more than .1 per cent of the population), who owed their right to vote to the fact that they held land liable to a tax of forty-five shillings on lists drawn up in the thirteenth century. As might be imagined, the electors stayed securely under the thumb of the local aristocrats. In England the property qualification was slightly lower—forty shillings—and the number of electors somewhat larger. The English counties differed widely in the number of electors, who, in a few places, exhibited some independence. On the whole, however, it is safe to say that the aristocratic families controlled the English county constituencies, though they often had to go to considerable trouble and expense to do so.[9]

Ireland, "that cloud in the west" as Mr. Gladstone was to call it in later years, presented a different picture altogether. Here, as in England, the county vote went with a holding of land taxed at forty shillings or more a year. But the Irish forty-shilling freeholders (as they were called) were much more numerous than the English, so numerous, in fact, that in some counties the franchise was extremely wide.[10] Actually, these freeholds existed only on paper; they were legal fictions created by the aristocratic landlords, who simply dictated their tenants' votes when election time came round. Since voting took place quite publicly, it was easy for the landlord to discover which of his tenants had voted against his wishes and to deal with them accordingly. And this was only one sordid aspect of the Irish land tenure situation.

During the years immediately after the Union of 1800, the Irish electors meekly voted as their landlords directed. The sixty-four county constituencies routinely returned to Westminster the candidates chosen by the Protestant aristocrats. Yet even as they trooped obediently to the polling places, the Irish masses held a pistol to the head of aristocratic privilege. Because of the peculiar Irish electoral system, a genuine and strictly legal popular movement was possible. In the struggle with the aristocracy, the masses' only strength lay in their numbers, and only in Ireland, with its tens of thousands of forty-shilling freeholders, could a legal wedge be driven into the privileged classes' parliamentary bastion. What had to come first, of course, was organization; until the Irish peasants found a voice and a program, their single advantage would go for nothing. Daniel O'Connell and his Catholic Association filled that need; thanks to them the pistol was cocked.

V

So it was that Catholic emancipation and parliamentary reform linked together to make *the* popular cause. However much the Englishman and the Scot disliked the Irish peasant's religion, the Irish peasant had the vote. The religious barrier to public life had to come down, if the larger popular cause were to succeed, because an Irish electorate, choosing freely, would not elect a Protestant to the office of dogcatcher of Drogheda. The persecution of Catholics which dated back to Queen Elizabeth's time had gradually given way to a set of civil disabilities called, simply, the penal laws, the last relic of which was that mechanism of exclusion which kept Roman Catholics out of public life by demanding of members of Parliament and officers in the military and civil services an explicit disavowal of Catholic belief and practice. The penal laws had practically eliminated Catholicism from England and Scotland. But the Irish masses had remained stubbornly Roman Catholic, five or six million strong.

O'Connell's accomplishment was to mobilize a whole people who had no resources except their own brutish poverty and their hope for a better life.[11] And, thanks to the miscalculation of their landlords, the vote. Through twenty years of agitation which stopped just short of rebellion, through many mistakes made and lessons learned, O'Connell forged his series of Catholic Associations into a tough, efficient political organization. He was the soul of it himself. His bulky, floridly handsome figure, dressed in a blue coat with a black velvet collar, yellow waistcoat and white trousers, appeared everywhere in Ireland during those years. He never stopped, he never rested. It was as if the air he breathed was less vital to him than the touch of the Irish people. His powerful voice thundered out from thousands of platforms that the Irish must become men, that they must stand and fight—not with guns, indeed, for then they would lose, then they would be shot down by the troops (and this, he said, was what the bigots wanted), but with their unity, their numbers and the justice of their cause. For financial support he turned to them, the people, and they responded with their pennies, which swelled into thousands of pounds a year. This was the famous Catholic Rent, collected after Mass on Sunday, under the supervision of the parish priest, from the poorest people in Europe. "King of the beggars," someone dubbed O'Connell, but the contemptuous nickname backfired.

The moment of truth came for this civil rights movement in the summer of 1828 when a parliamentary by-election was held in County Clare. The Tory incumbent—an able, amiable Protestant landlord named Fitzgerald, who had consistently championed Catholic emancipation—came home to campaign as a matter of form. He found, to his dismay, that his opponent was none other than O'Connell himself. "I am qualified to be elected and to be your representative," he told the electors of Clare. "It is true that as a Catholic I cannot and of course never will take the oaths at present prescribed to members of Parliament; but the authority which created these oaths—the Parliament—can abrogate them. And I entertain a confident hope that if you elect me the most bigoted of your enemies will see the necessity of removing from the chosen representative of the people an obstacle which would prevent him from doing his duty to his king and to his country." He went on to quote the objectionable oath which called the Mass and invocation of the Virgin Mary idolatry. "Of course I will never stain my soul with such an oath; I leave that to my honorable opponent. He has often taken that horrible oath; he is ready to take it again and asks your votes to enable him so to swear. I would rather be torn limb from limb than take it. . . . Return me to Parliament and it is probable such blasphemous oath will be abolished forever."[12]

The election was no contest. The forty-shilling freeholders, drilled into their best, most sober behaviour by the Catholic Association, overwhelmed Fitzgerald's supporters among the gentry by more than two to one. A wildly exultant crowd of sixty thousand heard the result on July 5, 1828, and sent O'Connell off to Dublin on his triumphal march. Delirium seized the whole country. In Dublin O'Connell paused long enough to tell the cheering crowds, "What I now say I wish to reach England, and I ask: What is to be done with Ireland? What is to be done with the Catholics? They must either crush us or conciliate us. There is no going on as we are; there is nothing so dangerous as going on as we are."[13] Then he set out for London and the bar of the House of Commons, "the chosen representative of the people," who would not be allowed to take his seat.

The news of the Clare election traveled ahead of him. "All the great interests broke down and the desertion has been universal," wrote Fitzgerald to Robert Peel. "Such a scene as we have had! Such a tremendous prospect as opens before us!" Peel by this time was Leader of the House of Commons and Home Secretary in the Tory cabinet headed by Wellington. As Home Secretary he headed the department charged with the internal order of the kingdom, and he knew, with statistical accuracy, how close Ireland stood to revolution. One word from O'Connell and the fires would be lighted from Bantry to Ballycastle. Peel scribbled on the bottom of Fitzgerald's letter, "A prospect tremendous indeed."[14]

In the months which followed the popular victory was consolidated. O'Connell did not indeed take his seat, but the Wellington-Peel government, faced with no other alternative, agreed to introduce Catholic relief legislation in the next session of Parliament. On March 5, 1829, Peel, in a four-hour speech, explained to the Commons the reasons for the government's change in policy. It was said to be the best speech he ever made. "The House was crammed to suffocation and the lobby likewise. The cheering was loud and frequent and often burst upon the impatient listener without."[15] What self-mastery this performance demanded of Peel can hardly be appreciated. O'Connell, the sweating demagogue, vulgar, ostentatious and extravagant, represented all that was philosophically and personally repugnant to the fastidious Robert Peel. As for George IV, he whimpered to the end that acceptance of emancipation would break his coronation oath and defame the memory of his dead father (the same old man he had treated so shabbily when alive). But when Wellington told the king, in effect, that he must do his duty or he, Wellington, would resign the premiership, George's resolve crumbled, and he contented himself with an impotent curse. "O'Connell! God damn the scoundrel," said his Britannic majesty.[16]

VI

From a less exalted personage, and in more restrained language, came a similar judgment. "That the anti-Catholic party," wrote John Henry Newman to his sister, "who have by far the majority of number, should have been betrayed by its friends suddenly, craftily, and that the government should have been bullied by Mr. O'Connell into concessions, is most deplorable."[17] Newman was then a young Fellow of Oriel College, Oxford, and he could do little but regret O'Connell's victory. But he and his friends had it in their power to punish another leading actor in the Catholic emancipation drama.

Robert Peel was a member of Parliament for the University of Oxford. When, after the Clare election, he found it necessary to alter his long public position on the emancipation question, he was required, both as a gentlemen and by the unwritten mysteries of the British Constitution, to seek a new mandate from his constituency. The by-election took place late in February 1829, and Peel was defeated. He took what consolation he could from the fact that most of the "talent" of the university voted for him: fourteen out of twenty professors, for example, thirty-eight out of forty members of Parliament and all the noblemen.[18] But most of the Oxford electors were parsons and they poured into Oxford from their country parishes to vote against a traitor to the Church. Newman was active in the anti-Peel campaign, which moved him to his first act of political passion. "I am sure," he said, "I would have opposed Mr. Peel had there been only just enough with me to take off the appearance of egotism." He rejoiced that the bulk of the resident electors and a majority of Oriel had voted with him. "We have achieved a glorious victory. It is the first public event I have been concerned in, and I thank God from my heart both for my cause and its success. We have proved the independence of the Church and of Oxford."[19]

That remained to be seen. Meanwhile the tide rolled on. Another constituency was found for Peel, and the Tory government rammed emancipation through the Commons and Lords. Wellington carried on, as he conceived it his duty to do, but he could not see that the inevitable consequence of Catholic relief involved at least a measure of parliamentary reform. He had alienated the ultra-Tories by giving in to the Irish; he now alienated the moderate elements in the party (who were appealing with some success to Peel's instincts for political survival[20]) by refusing to consider even minimal reform. The Tory death agony was dragging itself out, but not for much longer.

A general election was held in the summer of 1830, necessitated by the death, to nobody's grief, of King George IV. In the midst of the poll, the rebellion of Paris workers called the July Days erupted to drive the Bourbons out of France for good. The July Days made a tremendous impression in England. The question they raised was obvious: If Frenchmen could overturn a reactionary government in three days, why could not Englishmen do the same? The Tory majority dwindled by thirty seats. Then, in the autumn rioting broke out in the rural areas of southern England. It was heedless, uncoordinated violence, as had so often disturbed England since Waterloo, but to most people, with the recent Irish and French examples at hand, the threat of revolution seemed imminent. At that moment the Duke of Wellington chose to speak his mind. In a November speech before the House of Lords, the bluff old Duke said that in his opinion parliamentary representation was perfect as it stood. A few weeks later, after Brougham moved a consideration of reform, the government chose to resign over a minor defeat rather than to face the issue.

The Whigs at last came back to power. They were hardly less shattered by recent events than the Tories. Earl Grey kissed his sovereign's hands (those of another of George III's disreputable sons, the Duke of York, now King William IV) and formed a cabinet made up almost entirely of Whig aristocrats. That did not matter, however; the writing was clearly on the wall. The only issue was reform. By March 1, 1831, the government submitted its bill for the reform of the House of Commons. Everyone was surprised by its far-reaching character. In one swoop the bill regularized the franchise. It wiped out 168 seats of the rottenest boroughs and created 108 new constituencies, mostly representative of the new urban communities. All in all, it was a very liberal measure, far more liberal than anyone had expected. It reflected the realities of the situation. Though it denied the vote to the working classes, it did enfranchise their middle-class allies. It represented a substantial change and as a result it effectively silenced the most radical agitators, who had proclaimed that the Whigs would do no more than make a gesture towards reform.[21]

The struggle to pass the reform bill took more than a year. Throughout that time tense excitement seized the country and the Parliament house itself. Sir Robert Harry Inglis, victor over Peel in the Oxford election of 1829, faithfully represented his constituents' convictions in the matter by leading the opposition to the bill in Commons. He argued that the present state of the British Constitution could not be improved upon. He pointed to the able men who had sat in Parliament for the rotten boroughs and who, under another system, might never have had an opportunity for public service. On the night of March 2, 1831, the young Whig member for Calne, Thomas Babington Macaulay, rose to reply. "It is said the system works well. I deny it," said Macaulay to the honourable member for the University of Oxford. "I deny that a system works well which the people regard with aversion." As for able men representing rotten boroughs, "It is true that many distinguished persons have represented places of this description. . . . Every form of government has its happy accidents. Despotism has its happy accidents. . . . If there were a law that the hundred tallest men in England should be members of Parliament, there would probably be some able men who would come into the House by virtue of this law." As he concluded his speech, Macaulay made an appeal to his colleagues which they remembered for many a long day. "Save property, divided against itself. Save the multitude, endangered by its own ungovernable passions. Save the aristocracy, endangered by its own unpopular power. . . . The danger is terrible. The time is short. If this bill should be rejected, I pray to God that none of those who concur in rejecting it may ever remember their votes with unavailing remorse, amidst the wreck of laws, the confusion of ranks, the spoliation of property, and the dissolution of social order."[22] Three weeks later, the bill passed its second reading by a majority of one, secured only by the solid support of the government by O'Connell and his Irishmen. But in April, the Whigs were defeated in committee. They reacted by forcing the king to dissolve Parliament.

The general election which followed was fought on the Whig slogan "The Bill, the whole Bill, and nothing but the Bill," and it resulted in a large Whig majority in Commons. In June, the government introduced its second reform bill, substantially the same as the first. It passed the Commons with a comfortable majority in September, only to be thrown out by the Lords after five days' debate. If the twenty-one bishops who opposed it had instead voted for it, the second reform bill would have passed by a majority of one.

The Lords' defiance of public opinion determined that the decisive act of the drama should take place in the streets. Monster meetings, harangued by radical agitators, were held all over the country. Within days after the Lords' vote became known, riots broke out in the north of England. And in Bristol a mob sacked the mayor's house, broke into the prisons, and, significantly, burned down the bishop's palace.[23]

The violence proved enough. In December 1831 the government began again. The third reform bill contained a few concessions to the Lords and aimed at gaining the votes of those who were not prepared to see blood spilled over the rotten boroughs. There followed much hemming and hawing, but the last resistance of the Lords sputtered out when it was made clear to them that Grey was ready to dilute the opposition by creating fifty new peers, or a hundred if necessary. Their lordships, shaken by the howling mob and completely routed by the thought of democratizing their own sacred precincts, passed on its third reading the bill reforming the House of Commons. It was June 4, 1832.

VII

The Reform Act proved to be, much to the surprise of the Whigs who sponsored it, not an end but a beginning. In the years after 1832 the process of reshaping British attitudes and institutions has gone on, and it continues even to our own day. Among the institutions most profoundly affected was the Church of England. Some of those who lived through the tumults of 1828–32 rejoiced that the changing times should bring about changes in the old ecclesiastical order. As Charles Greville, that busy man about official London, wrote in his diary:

It is remarkable that attacks, I will not say upon the Church, but upon Churchmen are now made in both Houses with much approbation. The Oxford parsons behaved so abominably at the election [which Peel lost in 1829] that they have laid themselves open to the severest strictures, and last night Lord

Wharncliffe in one House and Murray in the other commented on the general conduct of Churchmen at this crisis with a severity which was by no means displeasing except to the bishops. I am convinced that very few years will elapse before the Church will really be in danger. People will grow tired of paying so dearly for so bad an article.[24]

Others sensed the same danger, though they judged it in a different light. At Oxford, Newman's friend Hurrell Froude pondered the events which had reached their climax with the passage of the Reform Act. To his mind they represented neither progress nor the acceptance of the inevitable, but rather an act of desertion of the Church by those who should have defended her. It was not that Froude despised a widened franchise or failed to sympathize with the economic plight of the lower orders. As a matter of fact, he hardly thought of such things at all. To him the crucial issue went beyond political categories to the supernatural, where Acts of Parliament have no relevance. A surrender to the humanitarian was a betrayal of God, who had warned the children of Israel not to put their trust in the power of Egypt. Complicating Froude's vision was the not very accurate notion that England had once enjoyed an idyllic state in which the supernatural priorities had been universally recognized. He put his thoughts into a sonnet; not a very good sonnet, indeed, but one with an apt title. He called it "Farewell to Toryism."

> 'Tis sad to watch Time's desolating hand
> Doom noblest things to premature decay:
> The feudal court, the patriarchal sway
> Of kings, the cheerful homage of a land
> Unskill'd in treason, every social band
> That taught to rule with sweetness, and obey
> With dignity, swept one by one away;
> While proud Empires rule in fell command.
>
> Yet Christian! faint not at the sick'ning sight;
> Nor vainly strive with that supreme decree.
> Thou hast a treasure and an armory
> Locked to the spoiler yet: thy shafts are bright:
> Faint not: heaven's keys are more than sceptered might;
> Their guardians more than king or sire to thee.[25]

CHAPTER 2

The Church by Law Established

LORD Grey prided himself upon his devotion to facts. He had been born and raised in the atmosphere of sweet reason which historians have called the era of Enlightenment, and his reaction to any dogmatism but his own was a sniff of his aristocratic nose and the back of his aristocratic hand. In the course of the debate in the House of Lords on the second reform bill, the Earl in his flat monotone informed the Anglican bishops of the facts. He warned them that their continued opposition to the measure might well prove their own undoing. To his mind this was the ultimate argument. No other consideration weighed as much as the survival of the aristocracy, and the bishops were part of that aristocracy. Surely they could understand that their position, their fortunes and perhaps their necks depended upon an accommodation with the disgruntled nation. But it seems that the bishops remained oblivious to the noble Lord's facts. When the division came, on October 8, 1831, only two bishops voted with the Grey government, seven abstained and twenty-one voted against. The Prime Minister noted wryly that had the episcopal nays been yeas, the bill would have passed.

All was quiet for a day or two, except that Brougham, Lord Chancellor in Grey's government, as he rode in his carriage from Downing Street to Berkeley Square, was mildly heckled by what Greville called "a very poor mob." In the Lords, Grey, still smarting, got into a heated argument with Bishop Henry Phillpotts, whose Toryism was so high as to be virtually out of sight, while "Brougham from the wool-sack, in a strain of the bitterest irony and sarcasm, but so broad as to be without the semblance of disguise, attack[ed] the bench of bishops." None of this, however, was crucial. Aristocratic gentlemen often were sarcastic towards one another within the private club which was the House of Lords. But at the end of October the nation spoke with a voice and a tone unmistakable. A wave of popular rioting spread from Bristol across the southwest.

Troops had to be called out once more, and Greville heard that hundreds of bodies, cut down by the dragoons' sabers, littered the roads outside Bristol.[1] Nevertheless, before order was restored, the Bishop of Bristol saw his palace go up in smoke to the mob's chant of "The Bill, the whole Bill, and nothing but the Bill."

Eight months later the third reform bill became law, and the lord bishops and the clergy generally had reason to take uneasy stock of their situation. It appeared to them grim indeed. "Things go on at such a rate," wrote John Keble from his remote Gloucestershire parsonage, "that one is quite giddy. . . . Anything, humanly speaking, will be better than for the Church to go on in union with such a state."[2] With the wisdom of hindsight we may judge that Keble and his colleagues were unduly pessimistic, that they took too dark a view in likening their position to that of the Gallican clergy in 1792. England was not France. There never occurred in England that persecution and spoliation of the Church which marked the progress of the French Revolution. But to those who lived in the midst of the uproar prior to and immediately after the passage of the Reform Act the Church of England appeared to have reached a particularly delicate and vulnerable moment in her long history, and many churchmen—perhaps most of them—were convinced that Armageddon was just around the corner.

I

It had taken a long time and many adventures to bring the Church of England to this critical moment. In 1832 she was the living record of all that had ever happened to her. Her character reflected the shifting currents of a thousand years, and men and events long forgotten had left the permanent stamp of their conflicting influences upon her spirit. It was as though she had absorbed everything and missed nothing, as though she were a vast, many-mansioned house whose shape and colour depended upon the eye of the beholder. Like a good mother she could match the moods of her different children. She wore with equal grace the spiraling gothic of the Middle Ages and Christopher Wren's sumptuous baroque. But for most of her children her dearest shrine was some small, graystone village church, with a gaunt tower which went back to Norman times and a bell which tolled away the generations of birth and death, set in the midst of a tangle of headstones, green shrubbery and red flowers.

The Church of England appeared to be Catholic and Protestant and Erastian,[2a] all rolled into one. She enfolded in her ample embrace people whose theological opinions were contradictory and people who had no theological opinions at all. Her divines were careful scholars, bibliophiles and pedants, polite controversialists who always spoke in calculated understatement and who seldom if ever had an original thought. Her piety, which she gently encouraged but did not insist upon, was austere and self-effacing, a kind of spiritualized amalgam of those qualities which every patriotic Englishman imagined were peculiarly his birthright.

For those whose tastes were Protestant she had the Thirty-nine Articles.[3] These statements of Anglican orthodoxy had been drawn up during the Reformation era, and they represented the anti-Roman reaction of the time. Even so, they were purposely vague on some matters, so that, for example, though they committed one to a denial of Roman transubstantiation, they left room for a belief in some permanent corporeal Presence of Christ in the Eucharist. The Book of Common Prayer, on the other hand, with its ancient chants and lessons rendered in lilting cadences reminiscent of Shakespeare or Donne, enshrined the older Catholic tradition. There the sacramental principle prevailed, and the liturgy which the Prayer Book inculcated seemed to be viewed as a good work no less than the Roman Mass. Yet the Anglican Protestant, who abominated good works, still used the Prayer Book and put his own construction on the meaning of the words.

Nobody minded that. Anglicanism represented somehow the reconciliation of the irreconcilable, of the Protestant and the Catholic, of justification by faith alone and the power of the sacraments. Every clergyman swore to the Thirty-nine Articles and immediately began to use the Prayer Book to conduct services. It was presumed that intellectually he came down somewhere in between. Meanwhile, the Church called her children to calm, rhythmic worship where the Deity was encountered with decent English moderation. She provided sermons for every inclination—sacramental, fierce Calvinist or bland rationalist—delivered at great length by a clergyman with a wife, ten children and five hundred pounds a year, who nevertheless never preached without dressing up in the costume of a medieval monk. What he said mattered very little; everyone knew that somehow it would all come out even in the end. Meanwhile, one could have one's blood moderately stirred by listening to a crashing Handel oratorio or to a delicate motet by William Byrd, either of which, if properly performed, could touch a reasonable man's heart with the prospect of an encounter one day with a reasonable God.

This was the Church of England which Lord Grey and his friends thought worth saving. When that eminent statesman pleaded with the bishops to take a realistic position on the reform bill, when a little later he warned them to put their houses in order or he would do it for them, he spoke from the heart as a gentleman and a Christian who was genuinely concerned for the welfare of religion. His colleague, Viscount Melbourne, who would succeed Grey as Prime Minister a few years later, expressed their common point of view when he said that no one had a higher regard for Christianity than he, Melbourne, so long as it did not presume to meddle in gentlemen's private business. These great Whig reformers (and a large part of the nation with them) took it for granted that the Church was a public utility. The Church's doctrines and liturgy answered needs of the people which no other agency could satisfy. Good order, patriotism, local government, education, charitable works, indeed a whole range of civilizing activities had been the Church's province for generations. The Church was, in short, an integral part of that phenomenon lovingly called the Establishment, and she was worthy of public trust and support, unless of course she should allow dogmatism, mysticism or some other abstraction to interfere with the performance of her real duties.

Lord Grey had reason to expect, on simply partisan grounds, that the clergy would resist his program of reform. The clergy was overwhelmingly Tory. Indeed, one wag had described the Church of England as the Tory party at prayer. Many ecclesiastical offices, including all the bishoprics and a good number of the choicest deaneries and canonries, were direct appointments of the crown, and for forty-five years before the Grey ministry came to power in 1830 the Tories had enjoyed almost uninterrupted control of government patronage. What is more, at least half the parish clergy owed their situations to the Tory country gentry. The alliance of squire and parson had in most localities political as well as social significance.

But the alarm and resistance of the clergy went beyond mere partisan politics. No institution reflected that rural England, now fast passing away, as did the Established Church. Her constitution, her finances, and above all, the character of her personnel were rooted deep in the past. There was a charm in this, to be sure; there were elegies written in country churchyards and tributes paid to a simple pastoral Christianity. But by 1832 economic realities were cutting the ground from under this placid scene. Peasants no longer (if they ever had) danced happily and chastely around a maypole next to the village church, while the squire, the parson and their good wives sat watching and sipping tea under the shade of a great oak. More likely the peasants of yesterday were the urban poor of today, with not enough to eat and no church to worship in and no clergyman in sight. Or perhaps they were the rural proletariat, who, when they danced, did so around the threshing machinery they had just set on fire, and who thought nothing of God and bitterly regarded the clergy as part of an exploiting class. If 1832 means anything, it marks the collapse of Toryism, considered not as a political regime but as a way of life. The clergy of the Established Church, who knew no other life, found it a particularly tense and dangerous moment.

It was widely known that once parliamentary reform was out of the way, it would be the Church's turn. Lord Grey and, when they formed their governments, Viscount Melbourne and Robert Peel meant reform of the administration and finances of the Church. They were not concerned with her teaching, or at least so they said. The question of course was whether the state, in presuming to reform the Church, was not by that very fact intruding into the area of doctrine. The statesmen, however, with the massive evidence of ecclesiastical abuses before them, shrugged off the point as irrelevant. And the nation at large was inclined to agree.

II

The Church of England, to put it mildly, was an administrative chaos. Her basic division was into twenty-six dioceses spread across England and Wales. (In Scotland, the state-supported Church was Presbyterian, and in Ireland, though technically connected to the Church of England, the Establishment for all practical purposes was a separate entity.) Dioceses were subdivided into archdeaconries (though a very small diocese might have but one). The archdeacons were parsons appointed by the bishop, for whom they acted as liaison officers with the rest of the clergy. Otherwise their office was largely ceremonial, although a bright young man on the rise often started his climb as an archdeacon.

The dioceses differed vastly in size and population; York, for example, covered 5300 square miles and had nearly a million and a half people, while Ely measured only 858 square miles with a population of about 125,000. The boundaries of the dioceses went back to feudal times, as did a patchwork of enclaves and an archaic system of mixed or interrupted jurisdictions. Thus the area subject to the Archbishop of Canterbury was split in two by the Diocese of Rochester. Or, to cite the most extreme case, the Diocese of Bristol included the city itself but not the county in which it was located (the County of Gloucester, with the exception of Bristol, was co-terminous with the Diocese of Gloucester); instead the County of Dorset belonged to the Diocese of Bristol, even though Dorset was divided from Bristol by two counties (Devon and Wiltshire) and by two dioceses (Salisbury and Bath and Wells).[4]

Each diocese was ruled by a lord bishop who had been elected by the cathedral chapter. The right of election was a faint echo of the ancient practice of choosing bishops by the will of the local Christian community, expressed by those clergy who staffed the cathedral church. During the Middle Ages both kings and popes had endeavoured to nullify the chapter's electoral function, and by 1832 it had long been a legal fiction. The members of the chapter—the dean and canons, as they were called—were bound under the severest penalties to elect the nominee of the crown, and they unvaryingly did so. The very existence of the chapter, however, indicates how tentative was the bishop's rule within his own diocese. The chapter was an independent corporation over which the bishop had no real control. Over the centuries it had secured its own endowment and had become a self-perpetuating body, whose revenues were often very considerable. The chapter had for generations ceased to serve the cathedral church in any but the most perfunctory manner, so that in 1832 the dean and canons were perhaps the purest examples of sinecurists, which word might be loosely interpreted as clergymen without a care in the world.

The cathedral chapter was only one compartment in a maze of corporations, vested interests and independent property rights which confronted the bishop in his diocese. The principle of controlled administration rests ultimately upon the control of personnel, and this is precisely what the bishop lacked. Of almost twelve thousand ecclesiastical offices in the Church of England, the bishops had the power of appointment over less than fifteen hundred. In other words, nine out of ten clergymen assumed their posts and enjoyed their status without reference to their bishop, except for a brief formality at the beginning of their tenure when the bishop automatically conferred on them their spiritual jurisdiction.[5]

Anglicans called an office in the Church a "living"; they regarded it primarily as a species of private property. It involved certain strictly religious duties, of course, but conceivably those duties might change in character over the years (as they had during the excitement of the Reformation), while the endowment which supported the office went on forever. For that endowment was the land itself and it outlasted the transient fashions of theology and politics. The clergyman's legal position was expressed in the phrase "the parson's freehold," which meant that once he entered into his office he had the same practical right to the income of that office as a landlord had to rent from his tenants. Income attached directly to the office, to the "living," no matter who held it or how he had obtained it. Indeed, it mattered little, as far as his legal position was concerned, whether he gave any service for it or not. At the turn of the eighteenth century, there was a parish in Wiltshire with neither church nor parsonage nor parishioners, but with income of three hundred pounds a year. Whenever the living fell vacant, a tent was set up on the spot where the church had once stood; here the new appointee was formally inducted into office and began to enjoy the fruits of his nonexistent charge.[6]

The income of a living came chiefly from two sources: from investment in real estate which had accumulated over the centuries, and from a variety of extra charges called tithes which from time immemorial had been collected from the faithful for the support of religious persons and property. These latter in the Ancient Church had been a general and rather informal collection of foodstuffs and the like, but as the parochial system developed they had hardened into a kind of local tax, attached directly to agricultural produce, whereby the landholders had to pay a certain percentage of the value of their crop to the parson. Tithes eventually came to be considered as truly personal property as the real estate whose rents supplied the holder of the living with the rest of his income.

This method of church finance was rooted deep in England's long rural past and by 1832 it had become a legal jungle where only the boldest ecclesiastical lawyers dared to tread. The process had begun even before the Normans came. Throughout the Middle Ages ecclesiastical institutions—monasteries, friaries, colleges, universities as well as dioceses and parishes—had been founded and gradually endowed. The right to tithes had been little by little secured. From the beginning the system had displayed a combination of altruism and shrewd self-interest. A feudal lord would found a parish for the use of his retainers and set aside some acres for the support of a priest. A hundred years later the lord's great-grandson might decide that the living would provide an ideal haven for his ne'er-do-well brother-in-law. Two principles can be seen here simultaneously at work: once the parish was founded it was both sacrilegious and impolitic to discontinue it; but the decision as to who would enjoy the living belonged to the man who had endowed it and to his descendants unless the right were freely given up.

The religious orders during the Middle Ages contributed to the complexity of the system. The large monastery was in effect a corporation, made up of ecclesiastics, self-governing and self-perpetuating, itself endowed with real estate. But it might increase its income by founding a parish in its neighbourhood and staffing it with one of the monks; then the monastery would collect the tithes, and the monk, who said Mass for the people in the parish, would be supported by the monastery, which had to support him in any case. Or perhaps the monastery would hire a secular priest for the parish and pay him a stipend pegged low enough to assure the monastery a profit. Thus had arisen the distinction between rector and vicar. The rector of a parish was entitled to all the tithes, while the vicar (i.e., a priest who substituted for the rector) received about one third of the tithes. In fact, the monastic corporation in this situation was itself the "rector." Or again, the monastery might buy a parish outright from a lord in need of ready cash; the parish would continue as before, but the monastery would enjoy a modest but permanent profit on its investment. What the monasteries could do, other ecclesiastical corporations could do as well, and did: Cathedral chapters, convents of nuns, colleges at Oxford and Cambridge all became proprietors of church livings.

All this was immensely complicated, and there were a thousand local differences in the way the system worked. But one thread of consistency could be found running throughout the fabric: he who paid the piper called the tune. The right to choose the ecclesiastical personnel lay with the proprietor, whether a corporation or an individual. The suppression

of the religious orders at the time of the Reformation had given a wrench
to the system but it had not altered it essentially. The monastic property
which Henry VIII confiscated, including a multitude of endowed and
tithe-collecting parishes, fell to various hands. Some small portion of it
stayed with the crown, but most of it went to those ecclesiastical corporations which survived (like the cathedral chapters) or to individual
families among the gentry or to favourites of Henry VIII or simply to
men shrewd enough to seize a good investment possibility when they saw
it. So it was that the bishop in 1832 headed a diocese staffed by clergymen
half of whom were chosen by various lay proprietors, perhaps 10 per cent
by the Prime Minister, including often the dean of the chapter and many
of the canons, another 30 per cent by, say, Eton Preparatory School, one
or more Oxford colleges and his own chapter, and about one tenth by
himself.

This pattern of appointment explains why the clergy fit so snugly into
the Establishment, why, indeed, the Church herself was often designated
by that very word. The landed aristocracy, the same people who had the
vote and sat in Parliament, who could afford to buy commissions in the
military services, who sent their sons to the two universities and monopo-
lized the secular professions—the landed aristocracy also controlled the
clergy. Or, to state the matter perhaps more exactly, the clergy themselves were gentlemen; they were members of the ruling class. If they were
not, there was no point in being a clergyman, or at least there was no hope
of making a decent living in the Church. Charles Darwin went to Cambridge in the 1820s with the intention of becoming a clergyman. This
did not mean that he had any particular interest in things religious.
Rather it was the result of a process of elimination: politics bored him,
the thought of an operating room sickened him, he was too frail for the
army. What was left for a gentleman's son but the Church? One wonders
what might have happened had he not discovered the magic of zoology
at Cambridge.

The educational standards set for the clergy were appallingly low. All
candidates for ordination had to hold degrees from Oxford or Cambridge,
but neither university offered any specialized training for the prospective
minister or for that matter any formal theological course at all. At
Cambridge no student was ever asked a divinity question in examination
during his three or four years' residence. Having once passed the
childishly simple entrance examination, he could, if he chose, advance
immediately to clerical status. Oxford examinations did include one question in Christian doctrine asked just before the student was given his
degree. Nobody could remember a time when the most superficial answer
did not suffice. It is true that the bishop or his delegate examined the
candidate before ordination, but this too had become an empty formality.
"A few minutes' conversation or examination," wrote a critic of the

system in 1809, "which either good nature or pity or interest or careless-
ness, or all together, may render very slight, can never make the [bishop]
thoroughly acquainted with the literary, much less with the moral, character of the intended minister."[7] The idea of reforming clerical education
or of founding something akin to the theology faculties in continental
universities was raised only to be dismissed. A clergyman must be first
of all a gentleman, and so he must receive the same education which
other gentlemen received. If he wanted to putter about with theology
after ordination, in the same spirit that other men cultivated roses or
collected bugs, that of course was his own concern.

A clergyman's financial reward could be very handsome if he had the
right connections. But because the accumulation of endowment and tithes
differed from place to place and because of changes in the value of
Church property over the centuries, there was no discernible consistency
in clerical income. One parson might receive three hundred pounds a
year and his neighbour three times as much, even though their duties
were exactly the same. During the years before the passage of the Reform
Act, the total income of the Anglican clergy was estimated at about
3,500,000 pounds a year, though this figure, in an era careless of statistics,
is at best tentative. It would be fanciful in any case to try to compute the
average clerical remuneration, since livings differed in value so much
from one another.[8]

Pluralism and its companion evil absenteeism flourished in this lush
atmosphere. Of 10,500 parochial livings available in 1827, about 4500
were held in combinations of two or more. This meant that one parish
was not serviced at all or else it was attended to by a low-paid curate, with
the vicar or rector taking the lion's share of the income for himself.
Corporations indulged in this practice as well as individuals. The cathedral chapter of the Diocese of Carlisle, for example, held one parish
which returned an income of more than a thousand pounds a year; the
curate who did the actual parochial work received eighty pounds a year.
In 1831, 2268 individual clergymen held two or more livings; of these,
352 held three, 57 held four and 3 held five. In some cases this practice
could be explained by the fact that the small income from one living made
two a necessity for livelihood. Yet of the 2268 pluralists 643 held livings
each of which was worth in excess of two hundred pounds annually and
711 held two of which one was worth that much.[9]

Yet there were plenty of impoverished clergymen. During the late
eighteenth century in the Diocese of Oxford (outside the city itself)
there were eighty-six livings below the value of fifty pounds, or 45 per
cent of the total number.[10] For clergymen in these situations the normal
avenue of relief came through the government agency called Queen
Anne's Bounty, which was a fund, augmented by Act of Parliament, used
for capital grants to the poorer clergy and for disbursements for con-

struction of parsonages. But Queen Anne's Bounty was a stopgap which never was intended to go to the root of the trouble and which, there-fore, could do little to promote the Anglican ideal of a resident parson and his family in every parish.

Episcopal incomes displayed the same wild divergence as those of the lesser clergy. The twenty-six bishops enjoyed a total annual revenue of more than 180,000 pounds, which works out to an average of about 7000 pounds. As a matter of fact, two bishops received more than 20,000 pounds a year, three between 10,000 and 20,000, and five between 5000 and 10,000. The other sixteen trailed off from there down to the Bishop of Exeter, who made barely 1500 pounds a year, a good deal less than many a pluralist parson. And yet Exeter was one of the larger dioceses, with a population of 800,000 people. In contrast, the Diocese of Win-chester, considerably smaller than Exeter in area and about the same size in population, brought its bishop an income of more than 10,000 pounds, while his brother of Ely, whose flock amounted to less than a quarter of Exeter's, enjoyed 9000 a year.[11]

With this irrational system of appointment and reward, the wonder is that the clergy of the Church of England were not a great deal worse than they were. Theologically illiterate, constantly exposed to the tempta-tion of careerism, they nevertheless proved themselves to be, on the whole, a body of decent and conscientious men. The numerous exceptions only proved the rule. If they had a besetting sin, it was idleness. There was simply very little for them to do. Again, there were exceptions, but for the most part a clergyman's obligations were fulfilled by a service on Sunday (or possibly two services), and whatever else he did was deter-mined by his own taste in the matter. A tradition of amateur scholarship existed among the Anglican clergy, and this no doubt occupied the minds of many and kept them from less decorous activities. But the scholarship itself was never very remarkable, for the narrow university training they had received gave the clergy few of the tools necessary for serious intellectual work.

The bishops tended to be respectable but lackluster men. Appointed by the crown (which in effect meant by the Whig or Tory cabinet), they were mostly political hacks or careful, inoffensive men who could be counted upon to cause no trouble. Advancement from a poor to a rich diocese depended upon a bishop's good odour with the politicians, and having climbed this far up the slippery ladder of preferment he was not likely to ruin his chances to go higher by criticism of the established order. The bishops usually possessed the proper academic credentials—doctor of this or professor of that—but these meant next to nothing at a time when the universities had become intellectual wastelands. Above all, if a bishop wished to prosper, he had to be free of the taint of religious enthusiasm; in fact, it was often preferable if he concentrated his interests in some gentlemanly pursuit other than religion. There was as much fact as fiction in Trollope's candidate for the bishopric of Barchester, who was "an eminent naturalist, a gentleman most completely versed in the knowledge of rocks and minerals, but supposed by many to hold on religious subjects no special doctrines whatever."[12]

The clergy was not so obtuse as to fail to see some of the faults of the ecclesiastical system, but they were unequipped to do very much about them. They placed great stock in the freedom which the financial support from endowment and tithes gave them. Though they might admit instances of corruption—parsons and bishops alike intriguing for promotions to better-paid livings or indulging in pluralism—they maintained that even these failures were better endured than to depend upon the free-will offerings of the faithful. They pointed at the ministers of the dissenting sects—the non-Anglican Protestants—who had to toady to their congregations in order to secure bread for the table. The Anglican parson, on the contrary, could preach the unadorned gospel without fear of economic reprisals. Whatever the truth of this in theory, the fact was that the parson often discovered he had nobody to preach to at all. His economic independence tended to separate him from the people in his parish, except for the squire and the other members of the gentry, upon whom, of course, he was dependent. And with his own church standing empty, how could he appreciate the need for new churches in the urban areas where the mobile population was settling in such great numbers? As he walked serenely between the high hedges which separated the church from the parsonage, was he likely to ponder the fact that in London there were only 150,000 church seats for more than a million and a half people?[13]

III

John Keble suggested radical surgery to cure the ills of the Church. His solution—the separation of Church and state—might seem to us an eminently sensible one. If indeed the nation had so altered its constitution between 1828 and 1832 that the Church could no longer identify with it, then the Church should go her own way and perform her own function without reference to the nation. This sounds plausible enough in the abstract, and it is precisely the solution which most Western peoples have adopted in their pluralist and largely non-Christian societies. But to his own contemporaries Keble's proposal appeared far too extreme, and Keble himself, though he continued to advocate separation for some years, found that his most intimate associates did not agree with him and ultimately he gave up the idea. There is something ironic in the fact that while less outspoken leaders of the Oxford Movement abandoned the Established Church in disgust or despair, Keble remained a pillar of it to the end.

The plain fact was that English life and the English Church were too much mixed up together to make Keble's suggestion workable. The nation and the Church had, so to speak, grown up together. They reacted upon each other in a thousand ways. They were what they were because of the shared experience of a common history. The average Englishman might be hazy on his catechism and mildly anti-clerical, but the Church had always been part of his life. If her somewhat equivocal formularies failed to engage his mind (and this was true for some but by no means for all), he still sensed that his personal roots were intertwined with hers. He linked her in his mind with those other things which made England uniquely what it was: the crown, the Parliament, the sanctity of property, freedom under the law. Whatever her faults the Church of England was a far cry from the tyranny of Rome or Geneva which prevailed in dark and foreign lands. It may be possible to discuss certain abstract ecclesiastical and secular "realms" which exist side by side and only intrude upon one another in a third abstract area called "mixed." But in 1832 such a discussion would have led nowhere. The Church's part in every phase of English life would disappear only when the essential ingredient, a generally explicit if ill-defined acceptance of the Christian revelation, withered away. That day would come, but it had not come yet.

Meanwhile, if the application of abstract categories would not do, still something had to be done. The realities of English life were changing, and the Church, so much a part of those realities, would have to change too. From this distance it is hard to appreciate how bitter a pill this was for the clergy to swallow. We can look back and point to this or that event—to the introduction of steam-driven machinery, for instance, or to the passage of Catholic emancipation—and wonder how any intelligent person could have failed to grasp what was happening around him. Of course those who lived in the midst of the events did not have our advantage. The process which we can trace with precision was for them a jumble of apparently contradictory elements. What we neatly (and no doubt approvingly) describe as the Dawn of Industrial Democracy the clergy of the Established Church in 1832 saw as a painful series of threats and alarums.

The movement for reform of the franchise was, in their view, the first line of the anti-Church forces, and the repeal of the Test and Corporation Acts, in 1828, seemed to them the signal of worse things to come. These statutes, which went back to the seventeenth century, aimed at excluding from public life not only Roman Catholics but also non-Anglican Protestants by making yearly reception of the Eucharist according to the rites of the Established Church a condition of office under the crown and of membership in a municipal corporation. In other words, by law no one save a formal Anglican could take part in either national or local government. The fervour which produced this legislation, however, did not last, and a wonderfully English compromise was worked out whereby members of Protestant sects—all lumped together in the terminology of the times and called Dissenters or Nonconformists—received their civil rights without denying the theoretically exclusive position of the Established Church.

The Test and Corporation Acts remained on the books, but every year Parliament passed an Indemnity Act which excused Dissenters from complying with them. This procedure satisfied nobody completely and everybody somewhat, and it was maintained until the 1820s when the Whigs, led by Lord John Russell, moved for repeal as part of their larger program of parliamentary reform. The crucial battle over the matter came in 1828. Wellington's Tory cabinet—three members of which were Presbyterians—opposed Russell's motion for repeal on the plea that sleeping dogs should be allowed to lie. The compromise worked well enough and should be let alone. The Irish dogs were what Wellington and Peel had in mind for they knew that repeal of the Test was only the prelude to Catholic emancipation. But Russell had the votes, so that the government had to accept repeal, save what face it could and wait with apprehension for the next act of the drama.

Churchmen had to accept repeal too, and the next year they had to accept Catholic emancipation. They did so with little grace and much foreboding. The removal of the Test and Corporation Acts from the statute books made no practical difference at the moment, but it was an immensely important and ominous precedent. Churchmen saw it as the first break in the dike. From now on Protestants who spurned the Anglican Communion—and in some cases blasphemed it—would sit in the nation's legislatures and perform the king's business. They had in fact done so for a long time by virtue of the annual Indemnity Act; but then they had acted by privilege and exception, and now they acted by right. Part of the king's business was the government of the Church, and so, churchmen argued, those who formally stood outside the Church would formally shape the Church's destiny.

The almost hysterical opposition of the Anglican clergy to Catholic emancipation was rooted in the same fear. It was bad enough to have a Methodist debating Church measures; it was beyond endurance to think that one day Daniel O'Connell, the champion of popery, might cast the deciding vote on a matter affecting the Church of England. In 1829 the Roman Catholics joined the Dissenters on the parliamentary benches. And bad as that was there were yet worse possibilities. Dissenters at least were Protestants, Roman Catholics at least were Christians. Might not the day come when Jews and pagans and agnostics would determine the Church's liturgy or discipline or even her doctrine?

This is why the clergy resisted what seems to us the enlightened and in any case inevitable policy of the parliamentary reformers. This is why the parsons rejected Peel in the Oxford by-election of 1829 and why the bishops battled all three reform bills to the bitter end. These men were probably less bigoted than the generality of their countrymen and certainly they had no natural preference for a narrow and corrupt franchise. But the Establishment was their life, and the creation of what Keble called a "godless parliament" seemed to them a much graver crisis than the possibility of an Irish rebellion. It is likely that they did not appreciate the pressures under which the politicians laboured, but given their circumstances and habits of mind they could hardly be expected to do so. And given their professional commitment, they necessarily viewed the drift of events with special alarm. On the lowest moral level they found their privileges and financial security threatened. On the higher plane where most of them operated, it was a matter of losing their personal and professional fulfillment as the anointed servants of a Christian nation.

IV

Lord Grey and his colleagues agreed that England was a Christian nation in the sense in which the eighteenth century (the good old days of their own youth) understood that term. Indeed, they might have said that the Church was the nation, viewed in its religious aspect. But other men had other meanings for the phrase, and here was the crux of the problem. Grey remembered (and inevitably romanticized) a golden era when bluff country parsons, staid and portly bishops and even remote university dons did their duty as Englishmen without fussing over dogmatic niceties. They had known their place, these ideal ecclesiastics of an earlier time, and it puzzled Grey when he discovered that their successors did not know theirs.

In what sense then could England in 1832 be called a Christian nation? Grey had his answer, and as far as he was concerned the events of 1828–32 did not materially affect it. The nation, in response to the overwhelming pressures of public opinion, had altered its constitution, and the Church —in her status as a kind of solemn adjective—had done the same.

There were, however, plenty of alternate definitions offered by a great variety of people, some of whom were prepared to go along with Lord Grey and others not. All could agree that England was indeed still Christian in the sense that a large majority of the nation maintained some connection with institutional Christianity, though it had to be admitted that for many the connection was exceedingly feeble. It was also true that a majority of Christians were Anglicans, but nobody was ready to cite any statistical evidence of this, least of all the parsons who looked at the empty benches in their churches Sunday after Sunday.

There had emerged since the turn of the century a generally higher regard for public morality and "serious religion" than had prevailed before, when Hogarth had found the inspiration for his art in Gin Alley. No bishop in 1832 would follow the example of his eighteenth-century predecessor in defining the sacrament of Confirmation as "a totally un-objectionable ceremony." But if the old deism had lost its appeal, there had appeared other anti-Christian movements to take its place. Neither the highbrow disciples of Bentham and James Mill nor the ever-growing masses of urban poor had much time for the Christian covenant.

Amidst the confusion of voices raised to define "Christian nation" by non-Anglican Protestants, utilitarians, Romantic poets and budding socialists (and once in a great while by a stray Roman Catholic), the Anglicans offered a babel of their own. The Established Church tradi-tionally supported two parties, like the good, decent English aristocracy with which she was so closely associated. But by 1832 the old parties had splintered and the points of view had multiplied. The Church had become the victim of all the compromises she had been forced to make. Bitter sarcasm and exclusiveness tended to make rational discussion within the Church very difficult. In 1832, Thomas Arnold, Headmaster of Rugby and a boyhood friend of John Keble, published a pamphlet in which he offered his solution to the Church's troubles. Without ever having seen Arnold's effort, John Henry Newman, when told about the pamphlet, dismissed it icily by saying, "But is Dr. Arnold a Christian?" Later on Arnold would have his revenge on Newman for that remark. More important, however, than any personal animosity, and leaving aside (for the moment) the admittedly radical nature of Arnold's proposal, was the fact that these two clergymen of the Established Church, similar in background (both Oxford men and Fellows of Oriel) and equally dedi-cated to educational and moral reform, were divided so deeply that they could hardly carry on a civilized conversation.

As much as most Englishmen disliked abstractions, the truth was that the Church of England in 1832 was foundering because of a theory. The venerable idea that the civil and ecclesiastical communities should be convertible had turned into a ghost to haunt churchmen at every turn in the road. It may have been true once that the citizen was automati-cally the communicant as well, though the fact of the matter is surely debatable. But it was no longer so in 1832 and had not been for a long time.

V

The rise of the modern state and the religious divisions initiated by the Protestant Reformation combined to put an end forever to the medieval ideal of Christendom in which the believer, by reason of his

Baptism, possessed citizenship in the Christian community. The first stage of this process was the fragmentation of the older ideal into a group of little "Christendoms." In England this meant that the Anglican Communion—the Church of Christ in England—was to be the ecclesiastical home of every Englishman. National sovereignty would thus be shored up by religious allegiance, and vice versa. At least, this was the modification of the theory as worked out through the sixteenth century by Henry VIII, Elizabeth I and their advisers. They intended not to obliterate the old idea but to limit it to a nationalist setting. There would still be, as the Aristotelians put it, only a logical distinction between citizen and communicant. In reality every Englishman would be both the one and the other—but a citizen of what King Henry VIII called "this imperial realm," not of a larger Christian commonwealth.

So was born the Royal Supremacy. On its practical side it aimed to bring the administrative and financial business of the Church under the ultimate control of the government, and for the most part it proved to be a workable and more or less popular policy. Its theoretical foundations, however, were not so satisfactory. The forces loosed by the Reformation, deep feelings of total religious commitment, did not fit easily into the Erastian compartment. Queen Elizabeth made the system work more successfully than anyone else, and she had no end of trouble with it. She created a Church as broad as possible, so that all factions might find a place in it. Catholic forms of worship and ideas of sacramentality mingled with Calvinist notions of grace and predestination. Episcopal structure of government was maintained, but now, of course, without the general supervision of the papacy. Instead hard-eyed lay-statesmen kept a firm hand on the clerical estate. No one was perfectly comfortable with the arrangement, but most people could live with it even if they picked all sorts of abstract holes in the fabric. The queen, for her part, insisted that her subjects go to church, that they demonstrate a minimal religious conformity. If they did not, she was prepared to pauperize them, torture them or even kill them. Those few Roman Catholics and puritans who would not adjust their consciences to accept the queen's grand consensus could expect no mercy from her. And they received none. Elizabeth's famous remark—that she would not, even if she could, look into her subjects' hearts to see what they believed—should not be interpreted as expressing a contempt for doctrine. It was rather a statement of the loftiest Elizabethan doctrine of all, that lesser dogmas and loyalties must serve the interests of the nation.

All might have gone well for this Elizabethan settlement had the Reformation been simply a protest against Rome or a crusade to purify the medieval Church of abuses. Then presumably statesmen and reformers might have got together like sensible men and constructed a tidy little English Christendom, working out among themselves whatever compromises seemed best. Indeed, this may well have been the way Lord

Grey, with his youthful remembrances of the placid eighteenth century, read the history of the sixteenth. A somewhat watered-down version of Elizabeth's Erastianism was the foundation of his own ecclesiastical policy. Though he and his colleagues were not prepared, as Elizabeth had been, to use force to accomplish religious uniformity, they shared the old queen's order of priorities: The Church must be judged in the last analysis upon her performance of her national functions.

The Protestant movement, however, was an affirmation, not a denial. It had system and purpose. It went beyond political categories, deeper than any Erastianism, and it called to men of all rank and none. It opened a crack in the Christian consciousness, which no pretense or artifice could close. Queen Elizabeth, that matchless political artist, had painted over the crack with good, stiff nationalism, and to a degree she managed to make the English people forget the crack was still there. But it was. Her successors, the Stuart kings of the seventeenth century, were not so skillful or lucky as she, and they reaped the whirlwind of religious passion. What Lord Grey was perhaps not equipped to see was that while Elizabeth had made the Church of England permanently Erastian, the struggles of the seventeenth century made her just as permanently Catholic and Reformed.

There is a deep and abiding irony here. In order to create a truly national Church some agent had to be employed to get rid of Rome. The reformers fulfilled this function in cooperation with the statesmen. Each group had something to contribute: the one provided the muscle of political power and the other gave to the nation a new, un-Roman philosophy of life. The alliance succeeded in sending the pope and his minions packing, and then, about the time Queen Elizabeth died, it fell apart. The reasons are not hard to see. Protestantism thrived and spread because it was more than protest. It possessed immense energies which spilled over into every area of human activity. The reformers had a spiritual vision which transcended any of the petty considerations of this world. They demanded a selflessness as complete as any ancient desert ascetic's, a loyalty far above patriotism, and in return they offered a new creation, fashioned by justice and holiness and truth. So long as the spirit moved them, they could never be content with political posturing.

"Protestant" is a particularly unfortunate word because of its negative connotation, and "Reformed" is not much better. But they are all we have and so we must make the best of them. What then did the Protestant vision involve? First of all, it presented a viable alternative to what had formerly been the accepted view of the human condition. It was gloomy, to be sure, with its insistence upon the radical corruption of human nature, but it countered this with its idea of the Christian vocation as a total surrender to God in Christ, whose death upon the cross had loosed upon evil men a flood of healing grace. The unique instrument of this redemption, as far as human beings were concerned, was the act of faith. For the Protestant every word of the famous Pauline formula rang with urgency. "The just man lives by faith." But faith, according to the Reformed view, ought never be confused with intellectual assent. Faith rather meant the acceptance of Christ as one's personal saviour, the acceptance of the fact that the Son of God has died for me as an individual, and in so doing has left me free of the debts of sin and punishment which were (and are) my natural deserts. This, said the Protestant (whether Lutheran or Calvinist or any other variety), is what the biblical revelation is all about. And any religion worthy of the name must be geared to making faith and its consequences operative in the individual and in society.

All of this might be stated differently and no doubt more completely. But enough has been said to make clear that men and women who seriously saw their lives in the perspective of this first breathtaking decision would not suffer compromise gladly. They could not have anything but contempt for the political tinkerings of the Lord Greys of this world. It is not too much to say that Protestantism was a radical movement. It struck at the roots of ideas long accepted and cherished. The reformers would not be shunted aside by minor matters. Or, to put it perhaps more accurately, they judged all matters, great and small, in the light of their unique insight into the gospel. They confronted the world with its own wickedness. They stated the abstract problem of evil in the concrete terms of sinful people who, unwashed in the blood of the Lamb, were hurtling with every breath towards a richly deserved eternity of pain, from which no earthly work could save them. Protestantism offered an explanation of and a solution to the basic riddle of human existence. No human being escapes the anxious burden of sin and guilt (whatever names he gives to them), and here was a system of beliefs and practices which guaranteed to the elect not only deliverance but certain victory. Little wonder that Protestantism aroused the enthusiasm it did, and left the deep mark it did upon the Church of England.

Protestantism, however, made its impact through its appeal to the individual, not through a monolithic organization. Though Protestants might agree upon the primacy of justification by faith alone, there remained plenty for them to quarrel about. It had ever been so, even in Martin Luther's first reforming days at Wittenberg. The issue might be infant Baptism or the Real Presence in the Eucharist or any number of other matters. Whatever it was, Protestants did not refrain from hurling anathemas at each other as zestfully as they did at papists. So it was also in England, with one significant difference. Elsewhere in Europe the presence or threat of Roman Catholicism provided the Protestants with a constant target, with a rule, so to speak, against which to measure each other. The Calvinist, for instance, damned as a crypto-papist the Lutheran who believed in Christ's literal presence in the Holy Eucharist. The

Anabaptist, for his part, consigned to perdition all the other Protestants who practiced the deadly Roman corruption of infant Baptism. But in England, by the time Queen Elizabeth died (1603), the pope had gone for good and Roman Catholicism had been reduced to an ever-shrinking and ever more impotent minority. And so, when the basic intellectual challenge to Protestantism came in England, it came not from Rome, not from the revivified theology of the Council of Trent, but from a home-bred, non-Roman version of Catholicism.

VI

It was a grand vision, this Catholicism without the pope. It was austere, dignified, intellectually respectable. It stood above the vulgar exhibitionism, whether of the German or Italian variety, which has traditionally made the Anglo-Saxon writhe with embarrassment. In one sense, it was a reactionary movement. Those who subscribed to it did so at least in part to protest what they considered the excesses of the Reformation. But it was a two-edged sword. English Catholicism also claimed to cut the Church free of Roman corruptions. For these English Catholics, the Protestant *Weltanschauung* was too simple, too ready to bend facts to fit its dismal theory of human wickedness. Romanism, on the other hand, they found too rich a mixture, the original revelation too much clouded over by human fancy and encrusted with superstitious practices. Protestants based their position upon their special reverence for Scripture, but in reality they picked and chose among the sacred texts and blithely discarded any which conflicted with their preconceived notions. Roman Catholics harped upon the glories of the Christian tradition, but in reality they had let the Bishop of Rome obscure and degrade that tradition. Anglo-Catholics argued that it was one thing to get rid of the pope and quite another to substitute the infallibility of Geneva for that of Rome. Richard Hooker, the premier architect of Anglo-Catholicism, dismissed what he judged to be two kinds of fundamentalism in a line of withering sarcasm: "Two things there are which trouble greatly these later times, one that Rome cannot, another that Geneva will not err." Neither to Rome nor to Geneva would these English Catholics go, and their theologians of the seventeenth century—dubbed collectively the Caroline divines, though many of them, including Hooker, lived before the reign of Charles I—put together a wonderfully attractive alternative, a middle way, a Via Media.

There are considerable semantic difficulties in grasping the Anglo-Catholic position. The word "Catholic," even when stripped of the adjective "Roman," suggests meanings which no Caroline divine could accept. (The difficulty in terminology was felt during the seventeenth century when writers freely applied "Catholic" to the Church but hesitated to use it of themselves.) And "Via Media" might seem to mean a sort of compromise between extremes, as if, in order to achieve it, one mixed a bucket of Protestant yellow with Roman blue and ended up with a pale Anglican green. In this sense indeed Lord Grey and his colleagues in 1832 did understand the term, seeing the Church of England as a glorious middle way which took a doctrine here and a practice there and arrived finally somewhere in between. Genuine Anglo-Catholics, however, never saw their ideas in such a light. They rather thought of themselves as the direct spiritual descendants of the great Christian teachers of the third and fourth centuries—the Fathers of the Church—through whom ultimately they were related to the apostles and to Christ himself. This is what they meant by following a middle course, since both Protestants and Roman Catholics, in their different ways, had forsaken the straight path and wandered off on detours of their own invention. In England, however, there were no Roman Catholics to speak of after the sixteenth century, and so what intellectual debate there was among religious groups centered in the opposition between Protestants and Anglo-Catholics. As a matter of fact there were not three choices open to the Englishman of the seventeenth century, only two. And precisely at this point we can understand how slippery a phrase Via Media can be. If we think of it simply as a halfway house between extremes, we shall fail to judge it for what it really was: a positive, dynamic, exclusive system, offering doctrine for doctrine a different interpretation from the Protestant one of Christian revelation. In theory, Anglo-Catholicism navigated between Rome and Geneva. In fact, and in the construction of the modern Anglican Communion, it stood foursquare against Geneva.

We believe in the "holy, catholic Church," said the Caroline divines, and they took the words directly from the article of the ancient Christian creeds. The Church of England to their mind had to be the manifestation, in this particular time and place, of primitive Christianity. Times changed, of course, and so did details; but in all essential matters the Church must be what it was in apostolic times. And so they placed their theoretical and practical hopes in that institution which stretched back beyond Luther and the other reformers, beyond (as they saw it) the papacy, and which had survived the tinkering of the politicians in Queen Elizabeth's days. The episcopate for the Caroline divines was the cornerstone upon which the whole ecclesiastical edifice rested. It was the latest link in the chain which bound the contemporary Christian to the apostolic college and to Christ himself. The politicians might consider the bishops simply administrative officers of the crown, Protestants might look upon them as superintendents of religious activities. To the Anglo-Catholics, their bishops were the angels of the churches, the successors of the apostles, the divinely instituted teachers and sanctifiers of the Christian people. Real spiritual power flowed from them and their works.

This episcopalian bias (if we may call it so) involved the Anglo-Catholics automatically in a sacramental system. The unbroken succession of bishops from the apostles down to the present could be verified only in terms of one generation passing its power visibly to the next, by means of some kind of external rite. Anglo-Catholics did not rigidly confine sacramental action to seven airtight compartments; this, they said, was a papist superstition. But clustered around the two great sacraments—Baptism and the Holy Eucharist—was the whole life of the Church, itself the greatest sacrament of all, the most striking outward sign of inward reality. At this point stood the great divide between Catholic and Protestant. For the Protestant a sacrament was a symbol of faith or a means of exciting faith; it had its value only in such a context because faith alone was a really significant religious act. The Catholic answered that certain formal, external actions did produce an unseen grace, not indeed independently of faith but in conjunction with it. The sacrament did in fact regenerate and bring God's favour to the communicant. Not so, said the Protestant, for this notion of sacrament made of it precisely the good work which, according to basic and unanimous Protestant teaching, sinful man was incapable of. As was always the case in the Protestant-Catholic argument wherever it appeared in the sixteenth and seventeenth centuries it boiled down ultimately to the opposition of faith to good works (in this sacramental rather than in the moral sense) as instruments of justification.

This same fundamental issue divided Protestants from Roman Catholics, whose answer was roughly the same as that of the Caroline divines. It is no wonder then that Protestants habitually suspected and accused Anglo-Catholics of papist leanings. This is why English Catholicism since it parted company with Protestantism on the deepest level, the level of justification, acted as the unique agent in England crystallizing Protestant opposition. The Roman-inspired Counter-Reformation went to pieces owing to the success of the Elizabethan persecution and to the wretched quarrels between the Jesuits and the seculars. But the English Counter-Reformation was something else. As far as the dedicated Protestant was concerned, there was little to choose between them.

The Anglo-Catholics, therefore, who agreed with the Romans on many basic points, had to take care to keep their skirts clean of all unnecessary Roman stain. They rejected as so many innovations such things as the sacrificial character of the Eucharist, Purgatory, indulgences, invocation of the Virgin and the saints and, needless to say, the primacy of the pope. None of these doctrines, they argued, was primitive, nor were certain practices like clerical celibacy, monasticism, or auricular confession, though these latter purely disciplinary measures may have had their uses at certain times. Everything necessary for salvation is to be found in Scripture, but Scripture, they said, could only be understood in the setting of the Primitive Church. The early Fathers were in the best position to judge what the ideal of the Christian Church should be and to distinguish between the essential and the accidental aspects of the Christian vocation. Approximation insofar as possible with the practice of the Fathers was the Church's task in every age. And Christians would have to be intellectually satisfied with the accumulation of historically probable arguments, because fundamentalist infallibility was as elusive as a handful of sunlight, whether chased by a German romantic waving his Bible or by an Italian friar with a papal decretal up his sleeve.[14]

VII

Catholic, Protestant, Erastian; the sacramental system, justification by faith alone, administrative control of the Church by the state. Here are the three ingredients which came together to form the permanent texture of the Church of England. How they would be related to one another, how one or the other would predominate would be settled only after all three had passed through the fiery furnace of the seventeenth century. For several tense generations Anglo-Catholics and Protestants battled it out toe to toe for the soul of the nation, or, to put it another way, for the right to define in what sense England would be a Christian nation. When the end of the struggle came, with the Glorious Revolution of 1688, it was clear that both doctrinaire sides had lost and that the Erastians, those who held by the Elizabethan principle of live and let live, were the only winners.

Religion, to be sure, played but one part in a drama which moved on several levels. It can best be described perhaps as a long constitutional crisis over royal prerogative versus parliamentary ambition, with various other political, economic and psychological factors swirling around the central issue. But there is little doubt that religious fervour gave the fighting a tone, a single-mindedness and, it must be admitted, a savagery reserved for holy wars. In the course of it England experienced much worth remembering: the gallant wrongheadedness of Charles I, the charming and sophisticated debauchery of Charles II, Prince Rupert and his cavaliers, the grim genius of Oliver Cromwell, and, most remarkable of all, John Milton, full-time pamphleteer and part-time poet. In 1688 the parliamentary magnates in a brilliant coup threw over the last Stuart king, James II, and set up in his place the Dutchman, William of Orange. The change in personnel in Windsor Castle, however, meant less than the establishment of the aristocracy's domination over the throne. As for the man in the street, he was content to salute the end of the power struggle and the uncertainties connected with it by raising his glass: "To the immortal memory of good King William III, who saved us from slavery, popery, and wooden shoes."

Most Englishmen would have been hard put to it to define just what form of slavery they had escaped or how wooden shoes figured into their deliverance, especially since the new king came from Holland. But they agreed about one bitter lesson they had learned: If the Catholic and Protestant systems were taken seriously, they became dangerous; they became a threat to the public peace because they were based upon contradictory first principles. The masses of the people, weary of religious war and never much interested in ideological matters anyway, were quite prepared in 1688 for a solution which would take neither too seriously. Perhaps good Queen Bess had had after all the right idea. England could be a truly Christian nation only if the leading edges of Catholicism and Protestantism were blunted. The times called for flexibility, and the statesmen of 1688 had plenty of that. They pointed out that though raw Catholicism and Protestantism could never live together in peace, Elizabethan Erastianism could live with either or both, provided the two philosophies did not press their differing points of view too much. The Church of England then could offer something for everybody. For the Protestants there were the Thirty-nine Articles of 1563, good, solid Protestant statements, with just enough vagueness to allow a man with Catholic sympathies to swear to them in good faith. And for the Catholics there was the pre-Elizabethan Book of Common Prayer, with its lofty sacramental sentiments dear to Catholic hearts and yet, with a shift of emphasis here and there, not unpalatable to the Protestant, unless, of course, he was some sort of fanatic.

To be neither Catholic nor Protestant, but to sound like and look like either or both: this was the genius of the Anglican Communion as the eighteenth century began. It was as though an eleventh commandment had been added to the decalogue: Thou shalt not adopt extreme opinions. Ladies and gentlemen of good breeding might follow their own tastes in the matter, and the common people might be safely left to follow the taste of their parson. One would quote the Prayer Book, another invoke the Articles, but neither should do so in a tone calculated to upset the other. In this quiet, tolerant, cultivated fashion the Church of England could work out her destiny as the religious home of all Englishmen. Competition could be left to High Church versus Low Church, instead of the dangerous Catholic versus Protestant, and it could then be seen as part of the political balance of the nation. High Churchmen tended to be Tories, Low Churchmen Whigs. They differed as little as the political parties did over matters of substance. A High Churchman held a loftier view of the Church's political prerogatives, while a Low Churchman was more open in his acceptance of rationalism. But neither of them laid claim to any enthusiasm for religion as such, and so generations could grow up (as Lord Grey did) without having the faintest interest in those issues over which their ancestors had bloodied the ground at the battle of Marston Moor. Meanwhile, Catholicism and Protestantism wrapped themselves in their long white beards and fell fast asleep. When Queen Anne died (1715), the royal Georges came over the sea from Hanover. As they shuffled through their largely ceremonial duties in the company of their fat German mistresses, they provided the perfect symbol of the religious temper of their time: They always stood up when they heard Handel's Hallelujah Chorus.

Catholic and Protestant loyalties, however, did not quite die during the long night of the eighteenth century. They may have been reduced to harmless and not very deeply felt formalities within the Established Church, but outside the pale of official orthodoxy they survived. In the chapels of the Dissenters—Presbyterians, Moravians, Baptists, Quakers— old-fashioned Protestantism continued to be preached, though with considerably less fire as the century of Enlightenment wore on. The Caroline divines found descendants of a sort in the Non-Jurors, so called because they refused to swear the oath of allegiance to King William in 1688. Eight bishops and about four hundred clergymen took this difficult path, which led to their loss of office by Act of Parliament and to their social ostracism. The Non-Jurors maintained a kind of shadow-Church for some decades, though they exercised very little direct influence and by the end of the eighteenth century they had been pretty well absorbed back into the Establishment.

VIII

These were dim sparks indeed, hardly discernible next to the massive and imperturbable apathy of the Established Church. And yet they combined in a curious way to start up the old fires once more. In 1728, John Wesley, a twenty-five-year-old Anglican clergyman and Fellow of Lincoln College, Oxford, read a recently published book entitled *A Serious Call to a Devout and Holy Life*. The book made a deep impression on young Wesley. Written by a Non-Juror named William Law, it was a simple and yet vigorous statement of the traditional Christian spirituality, emphasizing especially the daily need of the moral virtues, mental prayer and ascetical exercises. Soon Wesley gathered around himself a small group of earnest people who shared with him a dissatisfaction with the religious listlessness of the time and a horror of contemporary moral standards. He found very little sympathy in Oxford, where he and his friends were soon dubbed contemptuously the Holy Club and the Bible Moths. Opposition, however, never stopped Wesley, as he was to prove again and again during his long life. He came into contact eventually with various dissenting groups—notably the Moravian congregation in London— through which he was introduced to the writings of Martin Luther and brought finally to conversion. From that glorious moment on, Wesley determined "to promote as far as I am able vital practical religion and by the grace of God to beget, preserve and increase the life of God in the souls of men."

Wesley's active career of evangelization lasted half a century, and during those years he demonstrated what organizational genius mixed liberally with courage and a warm and generous personality could accomplish. He was tireless in his cause; he crisscrossed the British Isles on horseback dozens of times, averaging at one period eight thousand miles a year. The first circuit rider himself, he inspired a whole troop of followers to carry the message of simple faith and methodical piety everywhere that the English language was spoken. He even went across the Atlantic to Georgia, to bring the gospel to the indentured servants who made up a large part of the colony's population. But his outspoken opposition to gin and the slave trade cut short his American mission. At home, Wesley's allies included the spellbinding orator George Whitefield, and his own brother, Charles Wesley, whose prodigious hymn-writing—he turned out more than five thousand hymns altogether—brought the Wesleyan brand of Protestantism to the lips and hearts of people everywhere.

For this, essentially, is what Wesleyanism was, a Protestant revival. John Wesley himself would have preferred to work within the Established Church, and to the end of his life he regarded himself as an Anglican clergyman. His gospel, however, won small welcome with the ecclesiastical powers, whether High or Low, and he soon found the churches closed to him. He cheerfully moved his meetings to the town green or to a nearby field, and more than one English village church stood empty while the crowds flocked to hear John Wesley or one of his Methodist preachers and to be moved by the sweet, simple message. "Dear friends, brothers and sisters, whom I love as those for whom my Lord has died, I know what this great blessedness is; and because I know it, I want you to have it too. I am poor like you: I have to get my living with my hands; but no lord nor lady can be so happy as me, if they haven't got the love of God in their souls."[15]

The impact of Wesley's fervent, selfless crusade is hard to overestimate. He left behind him an organized Methodist Church, whose adherents at the time of his death (1791) numbered in the tens of thousands. He breathed new life into the other dissenting and nonconformist sects, which increasingly adopted his system and method, while still maintaining their individual identities. And as far as the Established Church was concerned, though Wesley's fervour perplexed and finally eluded her, she felt his influence profoundly. Her genuinely Protestant character, lethargic from generations of indifference and disuse, awoke with a start. Anglicans who could not sympathize with some of Wesley's eccentricities—in the 1780s he began to "ordain" his own ministers—nevertheless heard his call to a serious religion and to a disciplined and elevated moral life. It was like the old sixteenth-century reformers come again, and there arose within the Anglican Communion those fathers of the Victorians, the Evangelicals, who were to give a new and noble meaning to the phrase Low Church, and who included in their ranks at one time or another not a few of the nineteenth century's greatest names: Macaulay, Gladstone, Newman, Manning and Wilberforce.

The founder and sustainer of the Evangelical movement within the Church of England was William Wilberforce.[16] From the moment of his conversion as a young man, Wilberforce dedicated all his energies to the promotion of the Protestant gospel and, more specifically, to those charitable works which, according to classical Protestant theory, should grow out of the committed man's faith. The influence of Wesley upon Wilberforce and indeed upon all the Evangelicals was deep, but they achieved what Wesley had failed to achieve, the rescue of the Established Church from the indifferentism and rationalism which had disfigured her through most of the eighteenth century. Their views and Wesley's were hardly distinguishable except that they had perhaps a loftier notion of the state Church's role as the evangelizer of the English people. And of course they had the immense advantage of having had Wesley go before them, like a precursor up and down the land, preaching the simple Bible Christianity which they quite frankly shared with him.

Wesley was still active when, in 1780, the twenty-one-year-old William Wilberforce first went into Parliament. He kept his seat in Commons for forty-five years, during which time he formed a close friendship and political alliance with the great Tory, William Pitt the Younger, and held his own with such parliamentary lights as Burke, Charles James Fox, Canning and the young Palmerston. Wilberforce's single-minded devotion to good causes wilted the most cynical politicians. He fought first for the abolition of the slave trade, and when this was accomplished (1807) after repeated rebuffs, he carried the fight for the abolition of slavery itself, which became a reality a few months after his death (1833). Humanitarianism, however, was not the moving power in Wilberforce's activities. He struggled against slavery for the same reason that he spent a large part of his fortune to send Bibles to savages all over the world and to support Christian education for the working English poor: these were his responses to the serious call to a devout and holy life.

A kind of Evangelical ghetto grew up at Clapham, near London, where Wilberforce and his family settled in 1797. The neighbourhood eventually became filled with like-minded and wealthy Anglicans— Grants, Stephens and Macaulays, among others—who worshiped together at Clapham Church and who came to be called the Clapham Sect. This informal group was never very large, but it exerted an influence far out of proportion to its size, due mainly to its dedication, its cohesion, its financial resources, and Wilberforce's leadership and political connections. The atmosphere at Clapham was strict but not stuffy. The bonds of affection were close and the conversation sprightly, though novel-reading and other frivolities were frowned upon. The members of the Sect, who considered their wealth and influence a sacred trust, spent the greater part of their day on long devotions and hard work. Some little Claphamites grew restive under this severe if not uncomfortable regime, and when the opportunity came they quite readily gave up Clapham for more relaxed environments.[17] Most of them, however, did not forget that they had witnessed a remarkable revival and had lived among truly remarkable men. "From that little knot of men," wrote Lord Macaulay, who had grown up in Clapham, "emanated all the Bible societies and almost all the misisonary societies in the world. The whole organization of the Evangelical party was their work. The share which they had in providing means for the education of the people was great. They were really the destroyers of the slave trade and of slavery."[18]

IX

William Wilberforce's own sons eventually left Clapham and embraced religious views different from those of their father. Three of them became Roman Catholics and a fourth a more or less High Church bishop. Yet they did not feel that they had deserted their father's principles. Writing eighteen years after his father's death, Robert Isaac Wilberforce explained his conception of the impact of the Evangelical Movement:

The Church was roused to her plain duty of instructing her children and converting the heathen; the gospel was again heard in our pulpits; the sacraments were more duly administered; the clergy ceased to be men of pleasure. Such was the great work which was going on in all parts of the country during the first quarter of the present century. It was a work which consisted not so much in introducing new principles as in giving effect to old ones. There was no change in the Church's position which required a modification of her laws, but the increasing demands of a more earnest age called for the alteration in her manners. The clergy began to feel and preach the gospel—the laity to believe and obey it—but what else had ever been the duty of either? There was no new creed laid down, nor any fresh principle promulgated; but that slumber was broken which rendered all principles indifferent. The controversies which prevailed at that day were about feelings, not doctrines—dispositions, not opinions—earnestness, not orthodoxy. The whole movement, in short, was not objective but subjective; it did not aim at establishing facts which have an external existence to our minds, such as the Holy Trinity, or the inspiration of Scripture; its end was the increase of that earnestness which is admitted on all hands to be necessary for salvation.[19]

That "increase of earnestness" with which he had been bred at Clapham had given Robert Wilberforce his first impetus towards doctrinal Catholicism. He saw no conflict between the two; indeed, to his mind they fulfilled each other. However that may be, this much is certain:

With the reawakening of the Protestant character of Anglicanism, its old rival came awake too. In some circles the Caroline divines began to be read seriously again, and the Non-Jurors were converted from outcasts into heroes. If one listened carefully, one could hear again earnest talk about sacramentality, apostolic succession, and even about the Real Presence.

This Anglo-Catholic renewal, never so strong as its Protestant opposite number, curiously reflected many of the Evangelical Movement's accidental features. For one thing its leader also was a layman, a London wine merchant named Joshua Watson.[20] Its center was at Clapton, also a London suburb, where Watson bought a house in 1811. Pundits delighted in the play of words made possible by the Clapham Sect and the Clapton Sect. Yet Watson was no William Wilberforce; he was a retiring man who never exerted in the country at large any very pronounced influence. But he shared nevertheless many of Wilberforce's fundamental attitudes; like Wilberforce, he devoted his energies and his considerable fortune to the promotion of his own brand of Anglicanism. Watson's philanthropies, like Wilberforce's, concentrated upon the support of the colonial Church and misisonary activity generally. He founded the National Society for the religious education of the English poor, and he subsidized the quarterly *British Critic*, which from 1811 became the chief organ of Anglo-Catholic opinion. The Evangelicals tended to identify themselves with and send their sons to Cambridge University. Watson and his friends did the same with Oxford. One of the most distinguished Oxonians of the 1820s was Charles Lloyd, who had been Robert Peel's tutor and who was named in 1827 Bishop of Oxford. Lloyd was a close friend of Watson's, whom he called "the best layman in England." The compliment, if perhaps exaggerated, still was understandable.

X

The old ecclesiastical parties did not die out with the double revival led by William Wilberforce and Joshua Watson. They simply had to make room for new arrivals. By 1832 there were discernible four instead of two distinct groupings within the Church of England. The Tory parsons who made up the old High Church party—the High and Dry as it was often derisively called—continued to flourish. So did their Whig rationalist counterparts, the eighteenth-century Low Church party. But now added to these were the Evangelicals and the Apostolicals, representing genuinely Protestant and Catholic interests respectively. Inevitably the convenient terminology "high" and "low" began to be used of Apostolicals and Evangelicals.

Inevitable too was conflict among these bedfellows. But first they had to survive a moment of common danger. Early in 1833 Lord Grey's cabinet introduced in Parliament its Irish Church temporalities bill. This legislation was the government's first tentative step towards general Church reform. It was shrewdly conceived in that it chose the ground where corruption was the greatest and where English public opinion was least likely to be aroused. Technically the Church of Ireland was united to the Church of England, but in fact it possessed control of its own administration and finances, subject of course ultimately to Parliament. The income of the Irish Church from endowment and tithes amounted to about 775,000 pounds a year. Its jurisdiction was exercised by four archbishops and eighteen bishops. It was really a shadow-Church, because it served hardly 10 per cent of the Irish population, the overwhelming majority of whom were stubborn Roman Catholics. The existence of the Irish Church, with its endowment in Irish real estate and especially with its tithes charged against the production of the poverty-stricken Irish peasantry, was a constant source of trouble. Lord Grey simply recognized the facts of political life (as Wellington and Peel had had to do at the Catholic emancipation crisis) when he proposed to suppress ten Irish dioceses, appropriate their revenues, and to refashion the whole financial structure of the Church of Ireland.[21]

With the exception of a few of the old Whigs, the English clergy closed ranks against this latest and, as they judged it, worst act of aggression against the Church. They could hardly have chosen poorer ground upon which to fight. The Church of Ireland was a deformity and they knew it. Yet, the government's proposal involved a principle which, if more generally applied, would affect every clergyman. If he were concerned simply with his own financial security and social status, the bill threatened him, because someday a hostile Parliament might decide to suppress his office and confiscate his endowment. If he viewed the Church as a spiritual entity (and both Evangelicals and Apostolicals did in their different ways), then the government's attack upon the Church of Ireland was a tearing of the seamless garment of Christ. It was then a matter of unwarranted interference by the secular arm. And in either case clergymen sensed that behind the sleazy Irish business the forces of evil had gathered for the final assault upon the Church. In the end the government modified some of the provisions of its bill, but the suppression of the ten Irish dioceses stood, and on August 15, 1833, the bill became law. John Keble fumed in private at this "godless parliament,"[22] and in public he accused not only the Grey cabinet but the king, Lords, Commons and people of England of what he called an act of national apostasy. Fittingly enough, his platform for this charge was the University Church in Oxford.

CHAPTER 3

"Dominus Illuminatio Mea"

THAT tireless traveller and chronicler of Anglo-Saxon institutions, Alexis de Tocqueville, first visited Oxford in August 1833. He fell at once under that spell which Oxford casts even upon a casual tourist who walks up the High Street from Magdalen Bridge, past Oriel College and St. Mary's to Carfax corner, and then turns down St. Aldate's towards the massive pile of Christ Church. "Oxford," Tocqueville wrote, "is now one of the most remarkable towns existing in Europe."[1] He admired the gothic lines of the college buildings, their walls of butter-yellow stone gleaming in the late-summer sun. He soon discovered a charming combination of physical uniformity and diversity: each college had its central courtyard, with the deep green of the finely manicured grass set off by the blaze of snapdragons and poppies; and around the courtyard rose the college buildings to two or three stories where masters and students lived up the several staircases and where, at some focal point, the hall or dining room, library and chapel were located to serve the needs of the whole academic community.

Yet the working out of this consistent pattern differed from college to college; Oriel's double courtyard, for example, surrounded on all sides by masonry, appeared small and cramped when compared to the broad sweep of Worcester's green, which had its own lake circled by weeping willows. And though Oxford was a city of spires, no two spires were alike. If, as was likely, Tocqueville walked across Christ Church Meadow on a clear, cool August evening he could see stark against the sky Merton's square tower and, behind it, Magdalen's spiraling one; and from Tom Tower, at Christ Church itself, he could hear the great bell strike precisely 101 times at precisely fifty minutes past nine. "One's first feeling in visiting Oxford," Tocqueville said, "is of unforced admiration for the men of old who founded such immense establishments to aid the development of the human spirit."[2]

I

The first glow of enthusiasm, however, did not last. "When one examines things closely and gets below the surface of this imposing show, admiration almost vanishes and one sees a host of abuses which are not at first sight obvious." The archaic practice of ringing the bell in Tom Tower at the same time every night might have served Tocqueville as a symbol: Christ Church, when it was founded early in the sixteenth century, had 101 members, and so the bell rang that many times to call the Christ Church residents home and to signal the closing of college gates all over Oxford. This quaint custom continued long after it had ceased to have any significance, which would not have mattered had the university kept pace with the times in other ways. It decidedly had not. "The principal study," wrote Tocqueville, "is that of Latin and Greek, as in the Middle Ages. I should see no harm in that if the studies of the nineteenth century had been added to those of the fourteenth. But that is only done very incompletely." The natural sciences, he observed, received only trifling treatment in the curriculum, and modern languages were banned altogether. He might have added that the theology and philosophy which had adorned the university in earlier times had also been abandoned. "Dominus illuminatio mea" was the motto of the university, but one may doubt that the Lord was pleased to be held accountable for the dim light shining in the Oxford of 1833.

The medieval ideal of teaching everything teachable had frozen into teaching only what had been taught before or teaching nothing at all. Tocqueville was horrified to learn that Oxford enjoyed six months holiday every year. Yet even less intellectual work was done in term time when the young gentlemen were in residence, for then those few among them who wanted to study were distracted by the wine parties and general indolence of their peers. The colleges of the university were heavily endowed and immensely rich, but Tocqueville estimated that "a hundredth of the cost" could maintain "a university much richer in talent and more useful than present Oxford." And what of the future? "Oxford at the present time is menaced with reform. Thus all the secondary abuses upon which the aristocracy leans are falling. After its fall will England be happier? I think so. As great? I doubt it."[3]

The English university system, as much an aristocratic preserve as Parliament or Church, was soon to be confronted by the new forces of industrial democracy. Tocqueville judged that in the long run the reform of Oxford (and Cambridge) would prove to be a good thing. But he was not indifferent to the cost. The aristocratic society had made England a great power and the universities had been an integral part of that society. The very characteristics which rendered Oxford a third-rate university— the narrow classicism, the snobbishness and high jinks of upper-class students, the closed character of its society, the deadening indifference of many teachers—also made the place an ideal training ground for empire builders' sons. Here future cabinet ministers mingled with future bishops and generals. Here the contacts were established which would be solidified later on in Parliament or at Whitehall or even in far-off India. At Oxford friendships were entered into which would last a lifetime, and aristocratic students met their classmates' aristocratic sisters whom they would marry and establish in new homes where the next generation of little aristocrats would be born. Never mind if the students seldom studied and the masters seldom taught. Oxford provided the English ruling classes with the mettle which won the battle of Waterloo.

Or at least so gentlemen earnestly believed. Oxford, the bastion of Toryism and High Church, was part of the mystique of "merrie England." Cambridge might lean towards liberalism in politics and even dabble with Evangelicalism, but never Oxford. Robert Peel, Oxford's most distinguished son and the university's representative in the House of Commons, lost his seat when, in 1829, he weakened on the issue of Catholic emancipation. Oxford would not be trifled with. And yet Oxford, during that August of 1833 when Tocqueville strolled with guidebook in hand from college to college, faced a threatening future armed only with weapons which had grown rusty with age.

II

There had been a tradition of scholars in residence at Oxford for more than six centuries.[4] The medieval university had grown up in the lively market town up the Thames from London and in a corner of the sprawling Diocese of Lincoln. Neither king nor bishop was too close for comfort or too close to curb the exuberant spirits who came to Oxford to learn and teach. In the beginning the university was simply another guild of masters and apprentices, distinguished from other guilds only by its educational objective. A degree was a license to teach. It signified a proficiency in the liberal arts analogous to the skill, gained after long years of training, of a master craftsman in silver or leather. Little if any distinction was drawn at first among titles like Master, Professor or Doctor, though Bachelor was a term reserved to young men, still on a kind of probation, not unlike the position of a journeyman in the craft guilds. The important thing was to bring together those who had learned something and those who had not, and to put them together for a period of time in the hope that knowledge would thus be passed on.

The University of Oxford, then, was a very simple operation in its early days. It had no buildings or property. The teaching process took place in rented rooms, and for solemn functions, like the granting of degrees, the whole university gathered in the Oxford parish church of St. Mary the Virgin. The university was not a place one could point to; it was not a campus. It was rather a corporation, a group of people bound together by a common interest. This essential character had not changed by 1833.

In the beginning Oxford students found what board and lodging they could in the town. The stories abound of the harsh conditions under which these pioneers lived, of the squalid rooms, the cold and dampness, the badly prepared food when there was food at all. Gradually, masters began to rent space which they sublet to undergraduates, who would then come together to live and study under some general supervision. Here, in these undergraduate halls, life was by no means soft, but at least the basic idea of the university as a community of scholars was better maintained.

Towards the end of the thirteenth century—about fifty years after the founding of the university—the all-important collegiate system began to develop. The first three colleges—University, Balliol and Merton—were all founded about the same time and were typical in their character. In each case a benefactor provided an endowment in land which would support a certain number of men who would otherwise be unable to pursue their studies. Between 1262 and 1274, for example, Walter de Merton made over to the Oxford community which bore his name an estate in Surrey, the income from which gave the members of Merton College the means of basic sustenance. There was no money left over to provide luxuries; the members of the college lived with Spartan simplicity, in rooms with earthen floors, glazed windows and unplastered walls. Each college had its own statutes, but all of them followed the same general pattern. One of the members was elected head of the college, with a variety of terms employed to mean the same thing; Oriel College had its Provost, Magdalen its President, Balliol its Master and so on. The other members took turns acting as bursar or man of business, whose duty it was to superintend the college's endowment and to see to the mundane details of the house. The statutes of the particular college determined the manner in which new members should be chosen to replace the dead or departed; often conditions were imposed by the founder restricting nominees to a certain locality (a particular county, for example), but even though limited by restrictions like this, members still retained the right of final election.

All these arrangements were calculated to free the fellows—as members of a college soon came to be called—from financial worry and to provide them with a congenial atmosphere for the research which was their real business. To be elected fellow of any college a man had to be a Bachelor; he had to have spent, in other words, seven years already in the university and to have gained his arts degree. Only then was he judged ready to advance to the higher studies of theology, law or medicine. A college was a place for advanced scholarship, not for instruction. The fellows followed a common regimen which included eating together and participating as a group in religious services (there was always at least one priest among them). One or another of them might teach in the university, but this was not the normal practice. They were men dedicated primarily to individual study, and their common life, with its emphasis on matters intellectual, was meant to serve as mutual stimulation and aid.

But little by little, during the late Middle Ages, the character of the colleges began to change. Undergraduates came to be accepted into the colleges where they took up residence while they followed courses in the university. This system developed very slowly, and at first only the best-born youths could take advantage of it. The undergraduate residents were gradually sorted out into three groups: first, the Gentlemen Commoners or Fellow Commoners, who paid a high fee to share the college's common facilities, like the library, chapel and dining room where these sons of noblemen and knights sat at the fellows' own table; the Simple Commoners, who made up the bulk of the undergraduates and who paid about half as much as the Fellow Commoners; and finally the Servitors, who were scholarship students. Only the Servitors, of course, received income from the college foundation; the other undergraduates paid for the privilege of living in residence and thus added to the college's revenues. During the reign of Queen Elizabeth undergraduate residence in a college or hall became a statutory condition for university matriculation. The effects of this were far-reaching. The college became henceforth an institution of teaching as well as a research center, and the undergraduate hall was transformed into a kind of second-class college—that is, a college with undergraduates but no endowment. New officers had to be found among the fellows to meet this new condition: a dean to supervise undergraduate discipline and tutors to engage formally in instruction.

Oxford thus emerged as a group of independent corporations—the colleges and halls—within the framework of the larger university corporation. If a man were designated, say, a Fellow of All Souls College, Oxford, it meant that he belonged to two corporate structures: to the university and to his own college. The university gave final examinations, granted degrees and provided general lectures through officers now called Professors. The colleges, however, were supposed to do the day-to-day job of drilling and instructing which prepared the undergraduate for his degree. Nevertheless, the university and the colleges remained in another sense indistinguishable, because the same people—whether undergraduates or fellows or professors—made up both.

University and colleges were from the first clerical institutions. Undergraduates and masters alike wore the academic gown which signified that they enjoyed the special status granted to priests or to those who technically were advancing towards the priesthood. During the Middle Ages this had given the academic community a considerable advantage in disputes with the Oxford townsmen, because clerics were subject to the Church courts and hence escaped the harsh penal provisions of the civil law. What applied to individuals applied to the institutions themselves. The university and the colleges, as ecclesiastical establishments, stood apart from and independent of the feudal countryside and the municipal organization. Conflicts between gown and town were frequent and occasionally bloody, but the academics won most of them. They had on their side the bishop, they could appeal as well as their opponents to the king, and, as a final trump, they could expect a sympathtic hearing from the pope. The Reformation of course eliminated this last advantage and brought the Church courts under the general supervision of the crown. But by that time the university's corporate independence had been established beyond challenge. In any case the shopkeepers of Oxford, however much they disliked the arrogance and rowdiness of the students, had to face the hard economic fact that they needed the university more than the university needed them.

III

During its first century and a half the university accumulated those judicial and financial rights which, guaranteed in charters issued by bishop, king and pope, ultimately formed its constitution. A whole language grew up to describe the organs which the university employed to govern itself. The Masters of Arts, first of all, were considered the responsible and mature members of the university who should therefore make all important decisions. The M.A.'s were divided into regents and non-regents; the regents were those actually engaged in university business or, to be more specific, those who presided over (regens, or one who rules) the formal disputations which amounted to examinations. The non-regents were all other M.A.'s, whether resident in Oxford or not, who had maintained connection with the university. The regents tended to be younger men, because the duty of presiding at disputations normally fell only to an M.A. for the first five years after receiving his degree.

The two legislative assemblies of the university developed on the basis of this division. Congregation was composed of regent M.A.'s and hence was dominated by the junior members of the university; it dealt mostly with minor matters and with those things formally academic, like the granting of degrees. Convocation, which included all M.A.'s, regent and non-regent, was the university's real ruling body. Its function was to enact, repeal and amend statutes. Nothing of any consequence could be accomplished without Convocation.

The university's chief administrative and judicial officer was the Chancellor. By 1350 he had to be a Doctor of Divinity or a Doctor of Civil Law, which meant in effect that he had been a member of the university for at least twenty years, since doctoral degrees could not be earned in any less time. The Chancellor was elected by Congregation and confirmed by the Bishop of Lincoln. He presided over both assemblies. His wide judicial powers brought under his jurisdiction all members of the university, privileged persons (university servants, for example) and mixed cases (involving, say, an undergraduate and a townsman). He could punish by fines, imprisonment and even excommunication. The Chancellor was assisted by two Proctors who were elected by the Masters of Arts for one-year terms. They took care of much routine business and were charged with maintaining university discipline. The Proctors were probably the most ancient administrators in the university, and since they represented the M.A.'s directly while the Chancellor was strictly speaking the bishop's officer, they retained certain presidential rights even after the Chancellor's position had evolved. Most notably, the Proctors, if in agreement, could veto legislation of the two assemblies.

When Tocqueville visited Oxford in 1833 he found this primitive structure pretty much intact. There had been indeed refinements, shifts of emphasis here and there, additions of various kinds. Mighty events like the Reformation and the civil wars of the seventeenth century could not fail to leave an imprint upon the university. Most of the changes which had taken place, however, tended to confirm rather than replace or even broaden the medieval ideal. We have already seen Tocqueville's severe judgment of the effect of this upon the quality of Oxford education. As far as the numbers of the university community were concerned, there had actually been a decline. In 1833 there were nineteen colleges, but hardly more than fifteen hundred undergraduates. And, to Tocqueville's mind, the fire and colour and intellectual zestfulness which had filled the medieval university's lecture halls and had spilled over into the streets of the town, had given way to a mindless, respectable formalism.

IV

By 1833 one seed planted in the Middle Ages had reached full flower: the colleges completely dominated the university. This had come about in part because of undergraduate residence in the colleges and the consequence that whatever education a young man received he received it in the college, except for an occasional university lecture. And whatever loyalty he had to Oxford, or whatever good times he remembered later on, these too he associated with Trinity or St. John's or Merton. There was an economic factor at work, too. Over the centuries the extent and value of the colleges' endowments had increased vastly while the number of fellowships had remained more or less constant. As a result, a fellowship carried with it an income which brought not only leisure but great comfort. Also a fellow could implement his revenue by engaging in private tutoring for which he charged a fee, and, if he were lucky, he might combine his fellowship with one of the twenty or so university professorships which possessed their own handsome endowments. The professors were chosen in various ways, some appointed, others elected. But the fellows were the real aristocrats of the university; "dons" they were called, and donnishness—a combination of arrogance, remoteness and a condescending *noblesse oblige*—was a quality the fellows cultivated and a right everyone else grudgingly granted them. Understandably enough, fellowships were eagerly sought and nepotism was common. Less common was a concern on a fellow's part to impart knowledge to the mind of a raw young undergraduate.

The constitutional development of the university reflected this growth of collegiate influence. The two assemblies of Congregation and Convocation remained as before, but now matters for their formal consideration had to be proposed by the Hebdomodal Board, so called because it met once a week. This body was also called the Board of the Heads of Houses, because it was composed of the chief officers of the colleges and halls and was presided over by the Vice-chancellor, himself inevitably the head of a college. (The Chancellorship was now an honorary position, usually held by some prominent public figure; in 1834 the Chancellor was the Duke of Wellington.) The Board included as members the two Proctors, who now also represented collegiate interests. They were no longer, as in former days, elected by the university at large; instead they were chosen from among the fellows of the colleges in a prearranged order. The Proctors, however, retained the old privilege of veto over the acts of Convocation, and in this perhaps the colleges' domination of the university was most strikingly demonstrated.

The formal religiosity of Oxford had survived the Reformation, although the free and easy eighteenth century had considerably diluted it. Undergraduates were required to subscribe to the Thirty-nine Articles of the Established Church twice during their academic careers. They also had to receive the Anglican Eucharist at certain times stated by statute. These procedures effectively barred Dissenters and Roman Catholics from the university, but they do not seem to have turned the students into sturdy Anglicans. Chapel attendance, said Tom Brown,

is regular enough, but I don't think the men care about it in general. Several I can see bring in Euclids and other lecture books, and the service is gone through at a great pace. I couldn't think at first why some of the men seemed so uncomfortable and stiff about the legs at morning service, but I find that they are the hunting set and come in with pea-coats over their pinks and trousers over their leather breeches and top boots, which accounts for it. There are a few others who seem very devout and bow a good deal and turn toward the altar at different parts of the service. These are the Oxford High-church school, I believe; but I shall soon find out more about them. On the whole I feel less at home, I am sorry to say, at present in the chapel than anywhere else.[5]

Indeed, the religious temper of Oxford was such that an articulate minority pressed for the abolition of subscription to the Articles, while the whole community was alarmed by the casual way the students mingled drunkenness with reception of the Eucharist. Nor did the university's Anglicanism always appeal to the most gifted undergraduates. The historian Gibbon, while a student at Magdalen, reacted against the system by becoming, for a time, a Roman Catholic; and Shelley, a generation later, was expelled for writing a pamphlet in praise of atheism. Perhaps this sort of lapse was due at least in part to the sorry level of instruction which prevailed in the university pulpit. One undergraduate recalled in later years hearing a university sermon which dealt with Abraham under the threefold aspect of patriarch, father of the faithful, and country gentleman.[6]

Oxford's clerical character also had continued down into the nineteenth century. Most of the fellows were clergymen or planning to become clergymen. What struck Tocqueville as especially curious was the fact that the fellows were celibates, as their medieval predecessors had been, even though the Anglican Church of course did not demand or even encourage celibacy of her ministers. Yet the practice was not so strange in the light of the college's function as a kind of house of studies, an idea to which Oxford clung stubbornly. And the celibacy requirement had a further pragmatic advantage in that it guaranteed a reasonable turnover among the fellows. Normally a man served as fellow for a few years and then, at the time of his marriage, took a parish living from some patron who, often as not, was the college itself. As a result, Oxford's permanent academic society consisted of fellows who for one reason or another chose not to marry, and the Heads of Houses who, technically, were not fellows and therefore could marry. Between these two groups fell the university professors, some of whom were at the same time fellows, and some not. John Keble, for example, was for many years Professor of Poetry and Fellow of Oriel. When he married in 1835, he had to resign his fellowship but not his professorship.

Oxford in its spirit, tradition and personnel was very much High Church. The Evangelicals were hardly more than a small if growing minority within the university. What opposition there was to the Tory and High Church ascendancy came from a group of able but heavily outnumbered liberals, the intellectual forebears of the anti-dogmatic Broad Churchmen. Although the lines cannot be strictly drawn, these were the men, generally speaking, who favoured Catholic emancipation and parliamentary reform and who agitated for the abolition of religious tests in the university; they were the "talent" who voted in vain for Peel in the by-election of 1829.

The preponderance of High Church opinion in Oxford possessed an eloquent symbol in Christ Church, which was at the same time a bishop's seat and the largest, richest and in many ways the most influential college in the university. Henry VIII, who had founded both the college and the diocese, bound the two together so that the college chapel was also the cathedral of the Bishop of Oxford, and the dean of the cathedral chapter was also the head of the college. Moreover, several university professorships had attached to them the dignity (and the income) of canonries in the chapter. Thus, Edward Pusey was Professor of Hebrew and Canon of Christ Church for more than fifty years. It should be noted in passing that Christ Church, to emphasize its unique position, never called itself a college, though for all practical purposes it was. For the same reason, Christ Church's foundation supported students rather than fellows; the title was different but the office was precisely the same.

V

If the education offered by the University of Oxford was bad in 1833, a short time earlier it had been a great deal worse. For all Tocqueville's censures reform had actually been going on for more than a generation. How far the university had to come even to reach the stage of which Tocqueville was so critical can be seen perhaps in Edward Gibbon's famous description of his fourteen months spent as an undergraduate at Magdalen in the middle of the eighteenth century:

They proved the most idle and unprofitable of my whole life. . . . The fellows . . . of my time were decent, easy men who supinely enjoyed the gifts of the founder; their days were filled by a series of uniform employments: the chapel and the hall, the coffee house and the common room, till they retired weary and well-satisfied to a long slumber. From the toil of reading or thinking or writing they had absolved their conscience; and the first shoots of learning and ingenuity withered on the ground. . . . The silence of the Oxford professors, which deprives the youth of public instruction, is imperfectly supplied by the tutors. . . . The first tutor into whose hands I was resigned appears to have been one of the best of the tribe. . . . But his temper was indolent; his faculties, which were not of the first rate, had been relaxed by the climate, and he was satisfied, like his fellows, with the slight and superficial discharge of an important trust.[7]

Gibbon's complaint was not unique, and by the end of the century the outcry, both inside and outside the university, had risen to a pitch that could no longer be ignored. The root of the problem lay in Oxford's examination procedure. Since everybody in the university knew that the examination which preceded a degree was an empty formality, the undergraduates, with rare exceptions, did not bother to study, nor the professors to lecture, nor the tutors to instruct. Lord Eldon, who later became chancellor in a series of Tory governments, told of his own experience.

An examination for a degree at Oxford was a farce in my time. I was examined in Hebrew and in history. "What is the Hebrew for the place of the skull?" I replied, "Golgotha." "Who founded University College?" . . . "King Alfred founded it." "Very well, sir," said the examiner, "You are competent for your degree."[8]

Whether or not Lord Eldon embroidered the story to contribute to afterdinner jollity, it is still perfectly credible. Examinations often were supervised by the regent M.A.'s whom the candidate himself chose from among his drinking companions. Instead of the public examination, in which the medieval schoolmen had reveled and which was still required by university statute, the exercise usually took place in some dark, out-of-the-way room, as a tedious prelude to a festive meal, with the new graduate playing host to his examiners.

In a university where the legendary association of King Alfred with one of the colleges could pass for history, something had to be done. In 1800, something was done, and Oxford started up the long road towards intellectual respectability. That year the university approved the revolutionary Examination Statute. Modified and amended over the next quarter century, the statute eventually cut through accumulated abuses by establishing a board of public examiners sworn to take their duties seriously and to set aside all fear and favour. No candidate for a degree could present himself to the board until the thirteenth term after his matriculation, and he had to certify that he had previously witnessed the examination of others. The test had to occupy at least three hours. It was to include both written and oral parts, with the latter predominating. Utmost publicity was to be given to the examination process.

Besides reforming the simple pass examination, the statute also introduced an honours system. It provided that twelve candidates a year could be presented to the whole board of examiners in order to determine whether their attainments called for special recognition from the university. The material covered in an honours examination did not differ from that of a pass, but in extent and thoroughness it differed a great deal. One of the early honours candidates "was tried for two days successively and during four hours each day, before a most crowded audience in Divinity, Ethics, Rhetoric, Logic, Mathematics, Natural Philosophy and the chief Latin and Greek classics."[9] The results of the honours examinations were published in terms of First, Second and Third Class. The First Class included those "worthy of some eminent commendation";

in the Second Class list were placed alphabetically the names of those who had done well enough to show "laudable progress"; while in the Third Class were listed those who had simply failed to attain the distinction of First or Second. The Third Class men passed of course, and took their degrees, but they earned no special notice; and with that genius for apt colloquialism which students have displayed in all times and places, Oxford soon dubbed Third Class standing as "under the line," that is, it appeared on the honours list below the line which appeared after the last Second Class name, and it was, by implication, beneath the formal notice of the university.

The provision which restricted the honours candidates to twelve seemed hardly necessary at first. In 1802, the first year the statute took effect, only three students tried for honours. In 1803 there were four candidates, in 1804 three, and in 1805 only one. Little by little, however, the practice caught on, and as it did the whole tone of the university began to rise. In 1807 an important modification was introduced whereby a candidate could present himself to the School of *Litterae Humaniores* (roughly equivalent to a department of classical languages) or to the School of Mathematics and Physics (which tested primarily for proficiency in Euclid and Aristotle). Honours could be sought in either school or, if the candidate thought himself up to it, in both. In 1808 Robert Peel of Christ Church graduated with a Double First and Richard Whately of Oriel with a Double Second.

It was fitting that Christ Church and Oriel should have been the first colleges to have distinguished themselves in both the schools, because the Dean of Christ Church and the Provost of Oriel had been the leaders of the group which pushed through the Examination Statute and then made it work. Their reform efforts had obviously extended to their own colleges as well as to the university at large. Yet the Examination Statute, for all the good it did, marked only a beginning. The M.A. degree, which the reformers had hoped to include in the Statute, continued to be awarded on the basis of time spent in Oxford, rather than for intellectual merit. It was not unknown for a young man to work hard for honours, secure a fellowship and an M.A. and then lapse into lazy eccentricity for the rest of his academic life. Moreover, the reform introduced into the university was vertical rather than horizontal. It toughened the demands made upon the student of the Greek and Latin classics, and since everybody in Oxford was engaged in classical studies, it consequently raised the general level of the university.

Nevertheless, Tocqueville's criticisms of Oxford education still stand. He complained not that the classics were taught badly but that only the classics were taught—and in the term "classics" he included, reasonably enough, the mathematics of Euclid and the physics of Aristotle. One can only guess at the measure of his horror had he visited Oxford in 1800

instead of 1833. In any case, the statute had not touched the problem of
Oxford's narrow curriculum. This was particularly evident in the sorry
state of the natural sciences. The Prince Regent established Professorships of Mineralogy (1813) and Geology (1818), but the scientists could
do little to stir undergraduate enthusiasm when their subjects were not
covered in any examination. They operated at a constant disadvantage;
their endowment was small, they lacked suitable accommodation and
apparatus, and they faced complete indifference from university officials.
In 1817, the Professor of Chemistry appealed for an expansion of his
facilities, which were housed in a damp lower room of the Ashmolean
Museum. The Vice-chancellor responded by graciously offering to let the
chemist share the janitor's kitchen and use the common pump.[10]

VI

The Examination Statute had no doubt lessened but it had not eliminated the idleness of Oxford undergraduates and fellows who, whatever
their good intentions, could spend only so much time and energy in
parsing Greek verbs. When Tom Brown matriculated at the fictional St.
Ambrose's College, his reaction was boyishly unequivocal. "First and
foremost," he reported, "it's an awfully idle place, at any rate for us
freshmen. Fancy now. I am in twelve lectures a week of an hour each:
Greek testament, first book of Herodotus, second Aeneid, and first book
of Euclid. There's a treat! two hours a day; all over by twelve or one at
latest, and no extra work at all." Tom found that the material covered
in lecture was about the same as fifth form—that is, next to last year—
in prep school, and he thought the construing so bad as to "make your
hair stand on end."[11] Tom's three years at Oxford did indeed make him
a man, but it was no intellectual adventure.

Robert Peel's Double First Class stood as a goal to be matched and a
dream to be achieved. The honours system, however, touched directly
only a handful of the B.A. degree candidates, who averaged during the
years after Waterloo between two and three hundred a year. And it was
precisely the man capable of honours who felt most cramped by the
narrow Oxford curriculum. "I am wretchedly deficient in the knowledge
of modern languages, literature and history," wrote William Ewart Gladstone to his father in 1830; "and the classical knowledge acquired here,
though sound, accurate and useful, yet is not such as to complete an
education."[12] Gladstone, then an undergraduate at Christ Church, idled
away the first half of his university career, then turned to his books with
that relentless concentration of which he was always capable, won his
Double First, and went on to follow Peel to the heights of political accomplishment.

Perhaps, in the long run, the Examination Statute's real impact was in that it made study at least as respectable as riding, boxing and rowing. If so, it was the necessary first step in creating a great university. Frivolity still held its own, but studiousness was no longer laughed at. Henry Edward Manning came up to Balliol in April 1827; he was awestruck by Oxford at night; "the streets and colleges by lamplight seemed a fairy land." Manning, his biographer continues, "rode and boxed like the Christian gentleman of the time." His pink silk riding breeches were the wonder of his friends. But he read too, like a demon, and helped turn an informal debating society into the Oxford Union.[13] He took his First in classics in 1830, and moved on, with his strange combination of restlessness and calculation, to become ultimately archbishop, cardinal and champion of the working class.

A few years earlier, a shy and awkward boy named Frederick Oakeley matriculated at Christ Church. Long afterwards he remembered how unhappy he had been as an undergraduate, how out of place he had felt among the Christ Church fast set with their wine breakfasts and their effete manners. He recalled that the rules of the game demanded that the host deprecate the good things at his table while he urged them on his guests. " 'This ice,' said the host, 'is atrocious, perfectly beastly.' Then after a short pause, 'My dear fellow, do take some of it.' " Yet Oakeley was aware, at Christ Church and later as a Fellow of Balliol, that amidst the prevailing indolence and affectation there was growing up a seriousness both intellectual and religious. The latter he credited to the increasing number of Evangelicals who came to Oxford instead of Cambridge.[14]

Gladstone was an Evangelical, but more remarkable and more a tribute to Oxford's gradually changing character was the fact that William Wilberforce, after his eldest had fallen into eccentricity and dissipation at Cambridge, sent his other sons to Oxford. Samuel, Robert and Henry Wilberforce all matriculated at Oriel College and all of them succeeded brilliantly. The presence of the Wilberforces was evidence that earnestness was what interested the Evangelicals and that they considered doctrinal differences with the High Church of secondary importance. There was plenty of earnestness at Oriel. Among that college's fellows were Edward Pusey, soon to be Professor of Hebrew, and John Keble, Professor of Poetry and already an Oxford legend. And there was a tall, thin, deadly earnest young man named John Henry Newman.

CHAPTER 4

Oriel

ON Holy Saturday, April 6, 1822, at ten o'clock in the morning, eleven young men gathered in the hall of Oriel College. They had come to compete through five days of examinations for two vacant fellowships. Included among the candidates were some of Oxford's most brilliant recent graduates. To be Fellow of Oriel was "the great object of the ambition of half the Bachelors of Oxford," and the man who became one was well on his way to success in any profession he should choose. Talent flowed towards Oriel in those days as though by the laws of gravity. An Oriel fellowship was a prize beyond all others in the university, because indeed of the handsome income attached to it, but more importantly because, as one awestruck observer expressed it, "in point of character it was immortality."[1] Oriel had reached such eminence by the simple expedient of awarding its fellowships on the basis of merit. Of more than five hundred college fellowships in the university, only a handful were unrestricted and "open" to all comers, and almost all of Oriel's were of this kind. In other colleges, most fellows, by terms of the foundation or later endowment, had to be taken from a certain locality or from among those who had been undergraduates in the same college. At Oriel the race went to the swift and the strong. This was why his friends had shaken their heads sadly when John H. Newman, B.A. of Trinity College, had announced his intention to stand. For Newman, only a year before, had suffered something close to a nervous collapse in the Honours Schools and had finished Third Class, under the line. He was not unaware of how bold his step appeared. "Who indeed will not rightly wonder," he wrote to his mother, "at the audacity of him, who, being an under-the-line himself, presumes to contend with some of the first men in the university for a seat by the side of names like Keble and Hawkins?"[2]

The Oriel examination[3] was always part written, part oral. The first day was invariably spent on a translation from English to Latin and an English essay on some classical theme. Once the candidates assembled in the hall they could remain until it was too dark to write, but no examinee could return to the hall once he had left. There was a blazing fire, but candles were not allowed. Newman wrote for nine hours that Holy Saturday, translating a piece of literary criticism from the *Spectator* and composing an essay based on a line from Cicero. On Easter he went to church and received the Sacrament and spent the rest of the day fretting over the results of the day before. On Monday morning he joined the others back in the hall where he was confronted with a Latin essay to write and twelve mathematical and philosophical questions to answer. Newman's mathematical background was stronger than that of the other candidates, and this should have been his easiest test. Instead he found it impossible to concentrate, and much of the day was lost as he paced up and down the hall trying to relieve the nervous tension and to ease his throbbing head. By dusk he had answered only five of the questions.

Next morning, though still very nervous, he felt somewhat better and he was able to answer nine of the ten questions in logic. In the afternoon one of the junior fellows called him out of the hall and took him up the corkscrew staircase which led to a large room over the Oriel gate. Here Newman faced the assembled Fellows of Oriel, gathered around a table with pen and paper in front of them. The oral part of the examination occupied that Tuesday afternoon and continued Wednesday and Thursday. The fellows were courteous but grave. As Newman translated at sight nine Greek and Latin passages (Thucydides, Aristotle, Euripides, Aeschines, Euripides again, Juvenal, Cicero, Lucretius and Pliny), there was no sound in the room save Newman's high-pitched voice and the scratching of pens upon paper. When each session was completed, the provost kindly dismissed him, and a junior fellow, chatting amiably all the way about the weather and other trivialities, led the numbed candidate down the winding stairs and out into the spring sunshine.

If the Oriel examination was an ordeal for the candidates, it was a rigorous exercise for the fellows too. They knew what they were looking for: They wanted men to share their common room who were capable of "good Latin, good Greek, good English and good sense." A candidate need not have read even as much as necessary to distinguish himself in the Honours Schools. It was not breadth so much which Oriel sought— that could come in time—but depth. The key part of the examination was that held on the first day, the translation of English to Latin prose and the English essay. Seldom did a man fare well in the judgment of the fellows if he did not shine in those two papers. The whole body of fellows corrected the papers in a most minute fashion, going over them sentence by sentence. "It was not easy for a crammer or loose scholar or mere fine writer to slip through the meshes."⁴

On Tuesday afternoon, just after Newman had finished the first ex-cruciating experience of the orals, three Oriel fellows went over to Trinity to make discreet inquiries about the young bachelor's character and antecedents. The reason for this expedition was that Newman had greatly impressed the examiners by his Holy Saturday performance, despite his own misgivings of Easter Sunday. His Trinity friends were jubilant. His undergraduate tutor immediately sent for Newman, and though he could tell his former pupil nothing directly, yet by his smiles and winks and encouraging if obscure remarks—and with the help of the early supper of lamb cutlets and fried parsley which he made Newman share with him—he gave the despondent candidate the impression that all was going exceedingly well.

By late Thursday afternoon, however, the examination at last over, the doubts returned, and Newman, sitting wearily in the Oriel hall, looked up and saw in the stained glass window the motto "Pie repone te." This admonition, to rest securely in the Lord, took hold of him, and a strange sense of peace enveloped him. That night he wrote in his journal, "Thank God, I am now going to bed, and have been very calm the whole evening. How can I sufficiently praise Him. Before I look at this book again, it will be decided."

Friday morning, the calm still persisting, Newman was playing his violin in his lodgings on Broad Street when the provost's butler arrived. Following protocol, the butler said that he had disagreeable news: Mr. Newman had been elected Fellow of Oriel, and his presence was required at the college immediately. Newman, with that sensitivity which always characterized him, thought the butler was being impertinent, and so, continuing to saw away on his fiddle, he answered abruptly that he would be along presently. The butler left, scratching his head at this angular new don; but the moment he was out of sight, Newman threw down his violin, snatched his gown in wild exultation, and ran down the stairs and out into the street. That night he told the tale simply in his journal. "Friday, April 12. I have this morning been elected Fellow of Oriel. Thank God, thank God."[5]

I

So the last and the greatest of the protagonists of the Oxford Move-ment entered the sanctuary of Oriel. All the others had come there be-fore him, those who would be his friends and colleagues and those who would be his fiercest enemies. There would be still others—Frederic Rogers, Thomas Mozley, Richard Church—who would come later and play their parts. And the mutual influences of all these brilliant men would in the end make Oriel and the Movement inseparable entities.

Oriel College[6] owed its foundation to one Adam de Brome, Rector of the Oxford parish of St. Mary the Virgin in the early fourteenth century. De Brome was a favourite of King Edward II, whom he served as almoner and Clerk in Chancery. His relationship with the king proved crucial for Oriel, because as proprietor of St. Mary's Edward, thanks to de Brome's persuasion, bestowed upon the college the parish itself as a key part of its endowment. With the various properties accumulated by de Brome, plus the parish, the House of Blessed Mary the Virgin in Oxford supported a provost and ten fellows, all of whom were to be Masters of Arts and all but three of whom were to study theology. The three exceptions might devote themselves to the canon and civil law. It was, like all colleges down to the sixteenth century, a center for advanced students rather than a place for undergraduate instruction. The college site was across the High Street from St. Mary's Church. Here the rectory house stood, and at the southwest corner was a tenement called, for reasons nobody could remember, La Oriel. The college's nickname was in common use a generation or so after its founding.

Oriel's earliest endowment consisted of house property in Oxford and three parishes, including St. Mary's. Extensive landholdings in Berkshire and Oxfordshire fell to the college during the fifteenth century, and these were used to establish eight more fellowships. But the most significant piece of Oriel endowment remained St. Mary's. The college as rector drew tithes and offerings from the parish, and it occupied the rectory house, which ultimately developed into St. Mary Hall, an undergraduate residence dependent upon Oriel. Besides this, the bonds between college and parish were such as to make St. Mary's a kind of collegiate church. The fellows, for example, enjoyed extra income from holding chantries attached to St. Mary's—endowments, that is, to support priests who offered Mass for deceased persons. The college hired a vicar to see to the parochial duties; after 1583 the Vicar of St. Mary's was invariably a Fellow of Oriel. Finally, St. Mary's Church had always been the formal meeting place of the university, which had no buildings of its own; conferral of degrees, religious and academic festivals all took place at St. Mary's, and this lent Oriel a certain amount of prestige.

The coming of undergraduates into residence altered Oriel's placid pattern of life to some degree, although the number of such intruders was never very large. In 1822, the year Newman was elected fellow, the undergraduates totaled about seventy-five.[7] Four of the fellows acted as tutors, while another was dean. And some of the junior fellows had to live outside the college; Newman, for instance, did not take up residence in Oriel until four years after his election. The undergraduates followed a course not markedly different from those in other colleges; they were carefully segregated along class lines, they studied as little as possible. They learned to act like gentlemen, to hold their liquor and to construe a little Greek. They were friendly, lazy and full of high spirits. Meanwhile, the college went the way of other colleges. It gloried in its former members, among whom were Sir Walter Raleigh and Bishop Butler, and it slipped deep into the moral and intellectual lethargy of the eighteenth century. Dons led increasingly comfortable and idle lives, content with their superficial scholarship. Then, in 1781, John Eveleigh was elected provost.

Dr. Eveleigh[8] was not the sort of person with whom one usually associates significant movements of reform. He was a quiet man, gentle, self-effacing, colourless even, when compared to some of the academic eccentrics of his time. And yet it was due to him more than to anyone else that the Examination Statute of 1800 became a reality. His persistent efforts in behalf of university reform had their most direct effect in Oriel itself. Under his headship the tone of the college improved to the point that Oriel undergraduates were among the first to distinguish themselves in the new Honours Schools. But more important still, Provost Eveleigh swept away all restrictions on Oriel fellowships and thus opened the golden era of the college's history. The talented men who thronged the Oriel common room during the first third of the nineteenth century gratefully remembered Eveleigh (in the words of one of them) as "a man to bring down a blessing upon any society of which he was a member."[9]

Eveleigh died in 1814, rich in the honours of Oxford, where he was in old age a venerable figure, "with his large wig, his slow and solemn gait, his mild but melancholy countenance."[10] His successor as provost was his own protégé, and a man as unlike Eveleigh in personality as one could imagine. Edward Copleston[11] was neither mild nor melancholy. A B.A. of Corpus Christi College, Copleston's election as Fellow of Oriel in 1795 was really the inauguration of Eveleigh's new order, because the vacant fellowship was supposedly reserved for a Wiltshire candidate and Copleston, only nineteen at the time and a Devonshire man, was elected notwithstanding. The choice proved epoch-making. Copleston was a genuine if narrow scholar: His published lectures on the nature of Latin poetry became the standard text for tutors all over Oxford. More remarkable, however, was his prowess as a teacher. He worked his students hard during the years he was himself a tutor in Oriel (1797–1810) and his lectures became famous or infamous, depending on one's point of view; one dejected undergraduate said that Copleston's demands had turned Oriel into a prison house, while another swore that he would "limp upstairs on one leg" if necessary, so as not to miss the fascinating Copleston in action.[12]

"The more I think on it," Copleston once said, "the more I am convinced that to *exercise* the mind of the student is the business of education rather than to pour in knowledge."[13] This sentiment came to be more and more the criterion of Oriel scholarship. Copleston demanded from his students first of all precision, and thanks to his dialectical ability, and to his overpowering presence, he usually got it. Though he had been closely associated with Eveleigh in establishing the honours examinations and had been himself one of the first university examiners, he grew as the years passed increasingly impatient of what he called "the quackery of the schools." To his mind the real purpose of the Statute was evaded if candidates simply crammed as many authors as possible in order to dazzle the board momentarily into granting First Class Honours. Indeed, by the time Newman was elected fellow, Oriel almost prided itself upon not choosing candidates who had done well in the Schools; Newman's under-the-line standing did him no particular harm in Copleston's eyes. Newman, the provost remarked candidly, "was not even a good classical scholar, yet in mind and powers of composition, and in taste and knowledge, he was decidedly superior to some competitors who were a class above him in the schools."[14]

Copleston stamped the Oriel of his time with the idea that breadth of knowledge was a dangerous thing. There were of course disadvantages as well as advantages to this point of view. Someone observed that the Oriel common room "stank of logic," that the fellows, even in their small talk, were up to their ears in slashing dialectic. Copleston was pleased to think that he and his associates concentrated their energies upon first principles rather than in the desultory discussions which distracted men who had read too much and thought too little. But at the same time Oriel men were often accused of being "unlearned," that is, of failing to keep abreast even within the narrow confines of their classical studies. They thought a great deal, argued a great deal more, but they read very little. It was a valid accusation. One after another the Oriel men who had felt Copleston's influence—Newman not excepted—displayed a finely honed intellect which nevertheless remained strangely closed to new ideas.

Copleston himself sinned less in this regard than did many of his Oriel disciples. Actually he was a wide-swinging individual whose immense vitality saved him from the narrowness which he unintentionally encouraged in others. Vicar of St. Mary's at twenty-four, university Professor of Poetry at twenty-six, Provost of Oriel at thirty-eight, Copleston personified the Oxford which emerged out of the reforms of 1800. One undergraduate remembered him long afterwards as "the most substantial and majestic and, if I may say so, richly-coloured character within my knowledge of Oxford."[15] He received the significant compliment of having others imitate his gait and manner. An outspoken Tory, and a great friend of Canning, Copleston held forth on the complexities of political economy—he wrote several memorable pamphlets on the subject—with as much confidence as he parsed a Latin verb. He was inordinately proud of his physical strength, and he boasted in his old age how, during the French wars, he had been a captain of the Oxford Volunteers.

And even after he stopped playing soldier, he walked prodigious distances every day to keep his legs strong. Copleston's masculine vigour sometimes spilled over into insensitivity and even rudeness; more than one of his colleagues felt the lash of his tongue. But even when angry his deep, rich voice kept its cadence and the words he spoke reflected his passion for precise expression. Wellington made him Bishop of Llandaff in 1828, and Oxford no longer saw his well-groomed, black-suited figure striding purposefully along the High Street. Neither town nor university was quite the same without him.

II

Some men regarded Copleston as a curiosity, others thought him a heroic figure. To Richard Whately[16] he was a kind of idol. The youngest son of a Surrey clergyman, Whately was a frail, shy boy when he matriculated at Oriel as an undergraduate in 1805. His childhood had been a lonely time of solitary reading and long tramps through the southern English countryside. He never afterwards lost his taste for outdoor activity, and the wonders of nature never ceased to fascinate him. His health improved too, and the delicate child grew eventually into a big, powerful man, an avid fisherman and hunter whom friends nicknamed the Bear.

What sun and air and exercise did for Whately's body, Copleston did for his mind. Copleston was Oriel tutor during Whately's undergraduate days, and the young pupil fell headlong under the superb teacher's spell. Between the two of them there developed a singular sympathy. Copleston saw in the quick wits of the younger man an ideal dialectical instrument, while no one took closer to heart than Whately did Copleston's dictum that "exercise of the mind" was the essence of education. In 1808, Copleston was quite satisfied when Whately came out of the honours examination with a Double Second. Many years later Whately summed up his undergraduate career by recalling that no thrill was comparable to Copleston's quiet remark, "That is well, Mr. Whately; I see you understand it."[17]

Whately, who wanted nothing more than to be Copleston's other self, stood for election to an Oriel fellowship in 1811. He also began to display that vein of eccentricity which was to be the delight of Oxford for a generation and which, in time, made him an even more famous academic character than Copleston had been. To prepare for the Oriel examination he retired to the Isle of Wight for some concentrated reading. The island's peace and quiet, however, proved to be not enough. He decided he could read more if he made two days out of one. Accordingly, he rose every morning at three, worked till noon, and then, with the curtains drawn, popped back into bed. He got up again three or four hours later and studied until ten. With twice as much time, he observed solemnly, a man can get twice as much done.

Whether or not due to this odd schedule, Whately was elected Fellow of Oriel in 1811, and so became Copleston's colleague. He maintained his association with the college for ten years. He went to chapel there and often dined in hall, but most of the time he kept lodgings in the town, where he tutored undergraduates privately. He used to lecture stretched out full length on an enormous sofa, "with a pipe in his mouth, the atmosphere becoming denser and denser as he puffed." His pupils found that he tended to be digressive but that he was always entertaining and that he followed strictly the Copleston tradition of putting mental agility ahead of mere information. "Shall I form your mind," he asked one of them, "or shall I cram you for a First?" A general complaint was that as a teacher Whately was excessively repetitious. When reminded that he had made the same point in the same way the day before, he would shrug and remark that really he had nothing else to say, and in any case fundamental truths were worth repeating.

Whately's strongest subject was the formal logic of Aristotle, which he supported by English Aristotelians like Bishop Butler and Francis Bacon. Significantly, he read little else. "My own learning," he wrote in his journal, "is of a very singular kind, being more purely elementary than anyone's I know. I am acquainted with the elements of most things, and that more accurately than many who are versed in them, but I know nothing thoroughly except such studies as are intrinsically of an elementary character."[18] He thought himself to be "one of the few teachers who could train a young person of retentive memory for words without spoiling him." Here indeed was the image and likeness of Copleston. It was about the time when Copleston was provost and Whately a young fellow that people began to speak of the "Oriel School" and of the members of the Oriel common room as the "Noetics" (from the Greek word for mind). The terms indicated little except a devotion to debate and to Aristotle's methods of rational inquiry, but that, given the state of the university at the time, was quite a lot.

Whately's religiosity during these years also bore the mark of Coplestons' influence. He became a clergyman almost as a matter of course, as most other dons did, but the change in status affected the tenor of his life very little. He "regarded High Church and Low Church as equal bigotries," and by Low Church he meant the Evangelicals. Too deep a commitment, Whately thought, led to partisanship. He considered himself a Bible Christian, but in the sense of an eighteenth-century Whig who found biblical maxims uplifting. He had no understanding of and no interest in the old controversy over sacramentalism versus justification by faith alone which was beginning to reappear. He preferred to save his dialectical weapons for other, more significant matters. In this attitude he echoed Copleston, who, when asked by a young don about the propriety of undergraduates' taking the Eucharist, replied, "I beg you will not put such an idea into their minds. I am persuaded the question never occurs to them."[19]

Whately married in 1821 and so had to resign his fellowship. He remained in Oxford for a year, still taking private pupils, and then, in 1822, he took the living of Halesworth in Suffolk. He lived there for three years, but the damp climate proved unhealthy for his delicate wife, and by 1825 he came back to the more congenial atmosphere of Oxford. (It is worth noting that he did not give up his parish when he left it.) He was appointed Principal of St. Alban Hall, an undergraduate residence near Merton which had fallen on evil days. Whately descended upon the lazy and fun-loving students like a whirlwind, and soon St. Alban presented to the Oxford world a new face of propriety and industry which astonished everyone. Whately himself did much of the tutoring, as usual from a sofa and a cloud of tobacco smoke.

Most of Whately's published works date from the 1820s. He wrote various undistinguished religious tracts, including an anti-Roman pamphlet or two. Of permanent importance were his *Logic* (1826) and *Rhetoric* (1828). These both began as encyclopedia articles and developed into very influential books which helped keep alive the Aristotelian revival in Oxford even after Copleston and Whately had left.

Of more immediate interest, however, was a little book which Whately published anonymously in 1826. *Letters on the Church by an Episcopalian* contained six essays on the Church-state problem as it appeared to Whately in the years just before the Catholic emancipation and Reform Acts. The position he advocated in them was certainly not typical of Tory Oxford, but it influenced some of the highest Oxford Tories of all, as we shall see.

In substance Whately flatly called for the separation of Church and state. He brushed aside, first of all, the standard argument that the Church continues in her relationship to secular governments the polity of ancient Israel. The Old Testament, he argued, was "the system of secular government by the Lord, sanctioned by the rewards and penalties of this life." Religious crimes, under such a system, were treason and sedition since Church and state were convertible and Jehovah directed both. Not so with the institution founded by the suffering Messiah. His kingdom is not of this world. There exists a vast difference between the Old and New Testaments in this regard. Religious offenses under the New Testament can be punished by God alone, and no coercion in matters of religion can be allowed. Neither Protestants nor Roman Catholics have properly grasped this principle, said Whately. If Protestants have persecuted less, it has been usually for the wrong reason. "It is quite as much an act of *injustice* though of far less *cruelty*, to *fine* a Socinian [a Unitarian] as to burn him."

What then is the Church, and what kind of authority does she wield?

The Church, answered Whately, is "a society or body-corporate . . . of divine institution," based upon the apostolic succession—an "unbroken succession down to the present day." Whately of course did not mean to introduce here a sacramental theory, which to him was nonsense. He spoke rather "of that decency and good order . . . distinctly enjoined by St. Paul." And for the sake of good order it was necessary that an ecclesiastical polity have control over its membership. "The *lowest* interpretation (and I think the right one) which can, with any shadow of reason, be put on the expressions of the 'keys' and 'the remission and retainment of sins' is that spiritual governors may, at their discretion, admit men within the pale of the visible church, exclude offenders from it, and restore them on submission."

The alliance between Church and state in England, Whately went on, should be done away with, because "one of the two communities must resign its independence and submit to be governed by the supreme head of the other." The Articles do not call the king the "Head of the Church" but rather state the king's secular government over clergy and laity alike. Defender of the Faith, then, has no meaning or perhaps an all-inclusive meaning, for the crown serves the Jews in the same way as it does the Christians. The Articles do indeed link the British king to "the godly princes" mentioned in Scripture. But, said Whately, this refers not to the kings of Israel but to monarchs like Cyrus and Darius "under whose auspices the temple was rebuilt and the sacred vessels restored. This is certainly not the most obvious interpretation, but may nevertheless be the true one. In a case of such manifest ambiguity I cannot pretend to decide."

Whately's whole argument in *Letters by an Episcopalian* turned upon his distinction between "alliance" and "establishment." An alliance between Church and state, he maintained, was bad for both. It put clergymen into politics—bishops in the House of Lords, parsons acting as local magistrates—and it put politics into religion. An establishment, on the other hand, guaranteed the stability of the Church and contributed to the common good of the nation. By establishment Whately simply meant Church property. And in drawing this distinction he was trying to set at rest the fears of churchmen who, however much they favoured separation of the Church of England from the state, feared that such a move would involve the confiscation of endowment and the cancellation of tithes. Whately pointed out that this need not be the case. The Church's right to tithes and endowment "is founded (like that of individuals to their [property]) in *possession*. There are many landholders whose titles would not bear looking into if they were made to rest on a justification of every step by which they had been originally acquired and subsequently transmitted." The Church does not, in other words, hold her property by suffrance of the state any more than other corporations do. So separate the state from the Church, and leave the Church her property, and you will end "the profanation of Christ's kingdom by that *double usurpation*, the interference of the Church in temporals and of the state in spirituals."[20]

Whately offered in his book what seemed to him a straightforward and sensible solution to one of the great social problems of the time. He little dreamed that his ideas would be pondered by others and become the starting points of theories which he would abhor. But the whole plan of separation, the notion of excommunication, the use of a less than obvious interpretation of the Articles, these were pregnant ideas, and men, who had heard them first from Whately as they walked together around Christ Church Meadow, would, before many years passed, get a great deal more out of them than Whately had put in.

That was still in the future, however. Meanwhile, Whately went from triumph to triumph. In 1825 he took the degree of Doctor of Divinity. In 1829 he was elected university Professor of Political Economy, which gave him a platform from which to lecture the nation on his ideas of parliamentary reform. He suggested, for instance, that everybody be given one vote and the rich be given two, three, four or even more votes apiece, in order to guarantee the stability of the aristocracy. He walked every day through Oxford, a large, shaggy man followed by a pack of dogs whom he amused by throwing sticks for them to fetch and bring back to him. He became the terror of Oxford hostesses because of his gargantuan appetite and his loud and repetitious monologues, which he delivered "swinging, plunging and shifting on his seat while he talked." On one such occasion "an ominous crack was heard; a leg of the chair had given way; he tossed it on the sofa without further comment, and impounded another chair."[21]

In the autumn of 1831 Lord Grey appointed Whately Archbishop of Dublin. There was consternation in some circles, mild amusement in others. Bishop Phillpotts of Exeter spoke against his appointment in the House of Lords, while one of Whately's Oriel colleagues wrote lightly that it would indeed be difficult to call the new archbishop "his grace."[22] But from Grey's point of view Whately was an obvious choice. He was a liberal in politics and theology. Moreover, the Anglican primacy of Ireland, a difficult post under any circumstances, was particularly so in 1831. It demanded a tough man, and Whately assuredly was that. One last bit of comedy had to be played out before Whately assumed his new duties. It was discovered on the eve of his consecration that he was still the absentee parson of Halesworth, a place he had neither seen nor thought about for almost seven years. Legally he could not hold an Irish bishopric and an English parish at the same time, and so his consecration had to be delayed while he divested himself of the latter. Perhaps his failure to do so on his own initiative says much about the Church of England in 1831.

III

Lord Grey's letter appointing him to Dublin reached Dr. Whately at Rugby in Warwickshire, where he and his family were paying their annual visit to the Thomas Arnolds. Headmaster of Rugby public school since 1828, Arnold[23] represented another stream of English intellectual and religious life which flowed out of Oriel during the years between Waterloo and the Reform Act. Arnold was part Noetic indeed, as his deep friendship with Whately, so different from him in so many ways, might indicate. But he was part moral reformer too, a man of fiery purpose whose mind fed upon Aristotle while his heart warmed to the stirring phrases of Thucydides.

Arnold came to Oriel by way of Winchester and Corpus Christi. He was born on the Isle of Wight in 1795. His father, a customs inspector, died when Thomas was only six years old. He spent most of his childhood away from home, first at a grammar school in Wiltshire, and then, from his twelfth to his sixteenth year, at Winchester Public School. Winchester, like Eton, Harrow, Rugby and the rest, was a privately endowed preparatory boarding school staffed by clergymen. It was called public not in the sense that the government subsidized it, but because it prepared boys for entry into one of the universities and hence ultimately for public service. At Winchester young Arnold endured the poor teaching and savage hazing which characterized the pre-reform public schools. He read pretty much what he pleased—mostly history and geography. And though he entered furiously into the sports of the place and made several lasting friendships, his contemporaries remembered him as something of a loner. It was not that he disdained his school fellows; rather he seemed removed from them in basic sympathy, as though his real interests lay elsewhere. As a result he appeared to them distant, formal and somewhat abrupt.

When he came to Oxford in 1811 as a scholar of Corpus Christi College, he brought his rather beligerent disposition with him. He brought too the bad intellectual habits which his indifferent masters at Winchester had done nothing to discourage. He worked only by fits and starts; he took upon himself ambitious academic projects which, once started, he soon grew tired of and deserted for something else. Yet the raw intellectual power was there, though often hard to discern beneath the impulsiveness and the long periods of moody inactivity.

Arnold was fortunate that he came to Corpus at the particular moment he did. Its administration was relaxed to an extreme. The tutors did little and the president did nothing at all; his regime, one of Arnold's friends recalled, was "mild and inert rather than paternal."[24] The undergraduates filled the vacuum themselves. Left more or less to their own educational devices, they read and debated their way into a prominent place in Oxford life. Corpus was a small college—never more than twenty undergraduates in Arnold's time there. They were also the youngest body in the university and one of the closest-knit. Most of the academic high life and hard drinking passed them by. Corpus was the ideal environment in which Tom Arnold's earnestness could grow and prosper.

Corpus when Arnold arrived was dominated by John Keble, then in his last year as an undergraduate, and John Taylor Coleridge, the poet's nephew, who though older than Keble was academically a couple of years behind him. Keble and Coleridge, close friends themselves, set the tone and pace of the little community. It was a tone of good scholarship —as Oxford understood scholarship in those days—and deep High Church piety. For Arnold it was quite a change from the mindless, brutally regimented and pagan atmosphere of Winchester.

Three years at Corpus Christi changed Thomas Arnold, mostly for the better. He learned to work hard and consistently. He curbed his temper and his impulsiveness. The give and take with his peers, discussing the classical authors and the great political events of their own times, smoothed many of his rough edges. Mental discipline came hard to Arnold, but come it did. The small, genial world of his college gave scope to his high principles, his idealism, his warmheartedness. He was a little Whig in a nest of little Tories, and there were times when he battled them one and all until wearily and happily he went off to bed ready to take up the fight again the next day. He became Keble's warm friend, and as for Coleridge, he said later in life that he owed more to him than to any living man. In 1814 Arnold took his B.A. with a First in classics.

The next year he stood for an Oriel fellowship. Copleston had just become provost, and Whately and Keble were junior fellows. It was Whately who persuaded the other fellows, as they pondered the examination results, that Arnold's paper, despite some "crudities," showed more promise of development than those of his smoother competitors. So Arnold won a place in Oxford's most prestigious common room. He found there in some measure the same intellectual *esprit* as had prevailed on a lower level among the undergraduates at Corpus: free-swinging and incisive debate, good humour and the widest possible freedom. Arnold followed Whately's example and tutored privately while pursuing his own studies in the Oxford libraries. As a teacher he proved worthy of the Copleston tradition, with an added dimension of moral earnestness which the older Noetics could seldom muster. And as a student he justified Whately's confidence; historical studies and Aristotle combined to make a graceful scholar out of the stiff and angular boy.

The religious temper of Oriel, however, was different from Corpus, for Keble's influence was minimal, while Copleston and Whately, with their "a plague on both your houses" attitude towards High and Low Church alike, usually carried the day. Arnold followed them into their un-doctrinal liberalism and never swerved from it for the rest of his life. But it was to his old friend Keble that he turned when he was stricken by religious doubts which troubled him off and on during most of his time at Oriel. Keble's advice was sound and sensible and had nothing of partisanship about it. He recommended that Arnold take a country living where he could continue at the same time the tuition work he did so well and enjoyed so much. "I am inclined to think," Keble wrote a mutual friend, "[that Arnold will] cure himself not by physic, i.e. reading and controversy, but by diet and regimen, i.e. holy living. In the mean-time what an excellent fellow he is. I do think that one might safely say, as some one did of some other, 'One had better have Arnold's doubts than most men's certainties.' "[24a]

Arnold followed the advice. He took orders in the Church of England in 1819, married a clergyman's daughter the following year, and settled in a Thames-side village where he divided his time between slight parochial duties and the tuition of seven or eight boys preparing for the university. These years saw Arnold's character reach its full ma-turity. He moved with ease, all the nagging insecurity of his youth apparently gone. His pupils remembered him as a little above middle height, spare but vigorous. His slightly projecting lower lip and his deep-set eyes beneath strongly marked brows gave him a stern look. He cared nothing for art and science, and he was completely tone deaf. He gloried in the beauties of the countryside, especially flowers. "Flowers are my music," he would say. And with his blissfully happy marriage as a constant support, he found his real vocation in the intellectual and moral training of pre-university boys. His success in this hazardous work was well known in 1828 when, thanks in large part to the recommenda-tion of his old friends at Oriel, he was named Headmaster of Rugby.

That legendary figure, Arnold of Rugby, lies outside the scope of these pages, except insofar as his influence was felt in the Oxford of the 1830s through the boys who came there from Rugby. How deep that influence was may be hard to calculate, but it is certain that no boy who listened to Arnold's famous Sunday afternoon sermons ever forgot him.

We couldn't enter into half that we heard; we hadn't the knowledge of our own hearts or the knowledge of one another; and little enough of the faith, hope and love needed to that end. But we listened . . . to a man whom we felt to be, with all his heart and soul and strength, striving against whatever was mean and unmanly and unrighteous in our little world. It was not the cold, clear voice of one giving advice and warning from serene heights to those who were struggling and sinning below, but the warm, living voice of one who was fighting for us and by our sides, and calling on us to help him and ourselves and one another. And so, wearily and little by little, but surely and steadily on the whole, was brought home to the young boy, for the first time, the meaning of his life: that it was no fool's or sluggard's paradise into which he had wandered by chance, but a battle field ordained from of old, where there are no spectators, but the youngest must take his side, and the stakes are life and death.[25]

The same high moral enthusiasm which left its imprint upon public school education also guided Arnold when he ventured into the larger field of public controversy. Early in 1833 he published the long pamphlet on church reform which occasioned Newman's scathing rhetorical question, "But is Dr. Arnold a Christian?" The remark was unkind as well as unfair, because no one could question the sincerity of Arnold's Christian devotion as he understood it. And yet one can also understand the horror which his solution to the Church's troubles produced on all sides. It could be argued that if Arnold had his way there would be no Christian Church at all.

Principles of Church Reform begins with the argument that Church establishment is "essential to the well-being of the nation." Dissent impairs the effectiveness of the Establishment, and "now, from peculiar circumstances, threatens its destruction." Persecution is "wicked and impossible," but there remains "the true but hitherto untried way to extinguish it by comprehension. . . . Different tribes should act together as it were in one army and under one command, yet should each retain the arms and manner of fighting with which habit has made them most familiar."

History, Arnold continued, displays a permanent dilemma afflicting the Christian community: the unavoidability of religious disagreements and at the same time the disastrous consequences of these disagreements. "Is it not then worthwhile to try a different system? And since disunion is something so contrary to the spirit of Christianity, and difference of opinion . . . so inevitable to human nature, might it not be possible to escape the former without the folly of attempting to get rid of the latter?" What Arnold proposed was a "thoroughly united, thoroughly Christian" church, which would "allow great varieties of opinion, and of ceremonies, and of forms of worship according to the various knowledge and habits and temples of its members, while it truly held one common faith, and trusted in one common saviour, and worshipped one common God." Arnold thought that only Quakers, Unitarians and Roman Catholics would be left outside his giant umbrella, and even they might be prompted to give up their silly notions if confronted with a genuinely national Church.[26]

Arnold was stunned by the howls of protest which his pamphlet caused, even among his close friends. To him doctrines and sacraments were matters of taste; what was essential to Christianity was a personal devotion to Christ which exhibited itself in manly and honourable conduct.

Anything else seemed to him priestcraft or revivalism. In 1833 the Church appeared on the edge of doom, with her enemies about to destroy and pillage her. What could be more sensible than a great act of "comprehension" which would do away with petty differences, or rather preserve them within a larger framework, and thus save the Church for the battle with unbelief? What Arnold in his enthusiasm evidently failed to see was that to most Anglicans his program itself was unbelief. Arnold's scheme, wrote a prominent churchman to John Keble, "is one of the most unsound and dangerous pieces of theology which we have seen for years. I *know* from actual testimony that it is doing dreadful mischief among the higher classes."[26a] Arnold's old friend had sorrowfully to agree.

IV

Nobody criticized Arnold more severely for his tract on Church reform than did the Provost of Oriel, Edward Hawkins.[27] Typically, he stated his objections plainly and directly to the author. Your pamphlet, he wrote to Arnold, shows that it was prepared "with haste and without consideration"; you have held forth "on subjects which you have not studied and do not understand" and "which are not within your proper province." Hawkins never pulled his punches, even when a close friend was involved. And Arnold, who owed his appointment to Rugby at least in part to Hawkins' influence, was neither the first nor the last man to feel the sharp edge of the provost's candour.[28]

Edward Hawkins was a few years Arnold's senior. The eldest of a Gloucestershire parson's thirteen children, he came up to St. John's College, Oxford, in 1807, the year after his father died. Nothing much has been recorded of Hawkins' childhood, except that he once saw Lord Nelson being cheered by a crowd and noted how the old sea dog enjoyed the adulation; and that the Hawkins children once burned in effigy a radical member of Parliament from their constituency, much to the satisfaction of their Tory parents. For the most part, however, young Edward was a sober boy and an industrious student, whose naturally serious disposition was intensified when, at seventeen, he became the chief support of a widowed mother and nine surviving brothers and sisters.

In 1811 Hawkins won his Double First Class in the Honours Schools, and two years later he was elected Fellow of Oriel. His association with the college was destined to last nearly three quarters of a century. With the steady income and the leisure which the fellowship provided him, he began to prepare himself for ordination and a career as a theologian. His reasons were quite frankly pragmatic. He wanted very much to be a lawyer, but his first concern remained his mother and family, and he knew that a clerical career in Oxford—especially as a don at Oriel—would render swifter and surer financial return than (as his biographer delicately expressed it) "the problematical rewards of the Bar."[29]

Hawkins was accordingly ordained sometime before 1818. He became a college tutor the next year, and in 1823 Vicar of St. Mary's. The legal texture of his mind showed itself in all his activities. He was a solid, conscientious, exact, but never a brilliant teacher. He was on good terms with all the members of the common room, but he seldom entered into the theoretical debates which interested most of them. He was a practical man, a man of business, at heart a man of the law. At St. Mary's he found plenty of congenial work to do. The church had been for a long time physically run down; Hawkins restored it. University functions held in St. Mary's had become times of chaos during which nobody, from the Vice-chancellor on down, knew where to sit or what to do. Hawkins, who could not abide confusion of any kind, changed all that and introduced a new respect for propriety which made everything run smoothly and thus contributed to everyone's comfort. Hawkins also established a carefully regulated schedule of parochial services—a rather full one, given the temper of the times. For good measure he instituted the Sunday afternoon service at which the vicar himself usually preached.

Hawkins, in short, was a man who liked order and decorum and who was willing to go to the trouble to secure them. He was somewhat humourless, perhaps a little too literal to follow the drift of Whately's more subtle quips; but he was not unpleasant. His courtesy was genuine, if rigid, and he tried to be considerate in a clumsy sort of way. He found no piece of work too tedious for his attention, no sum of money too small to be scrupulously accounted for, as the merchants in the High Street learned from their dealings with him. His habitual bluntness, while it sometimes irritated his colleagues, yet earned him their respect. He chose his positions carefully, and planned his life the same way. Once he made up his mind, Edward Hawkins never budged, and he left no doubt as to where he stood.

Late in 1827 came the most important moment in Hawkins' life. Copleston was promoted to the bishopric of Llandaff. Arnold and Whately had left Oriel years before, and so there were only two candidates seriously proposed as the new Provost of Oriel. Both Keble and Hawkins wanted the post, but Hawkins wanted it more. Keble had some personal and family reasons for hesitating, while Hawkins' situation was just the opposite. Moreover, Keble determined that there should be no divisive contest: If the fellows unanimously chose him, he would accept; if not, he would withdraw. Hawkins, on the other hand, was prepared to canvass for the majority of votes if necessary. Ironically, it was John Newman and Edward Pusey who did most to prevent Keble's election.[30] They loved and reverenced him, but they were afraid he was not shrewd or tough enough to be a competent provost. For his part, Keble kept the discussion on a bantering level; at one point he suggested the office be divided, with Hawkins doing the work and himself receiving the income.

By Christmas it was clear to Keble that he could win the prize only by waging a strenuous campaign for it, and this he refused to do. He wrote a light and gracious letter to Hawkins in which he retired from the race, while explicitly maintaining that he did not do so out of any feeling of inadequacy.

I say this because I don't want to have it imagined that I am eaten up with a kind of morbid mistrust of myself; and also in order to prepare you for a little amicable discussion as to the principles of university discipline, with which you may expect to be regaled when next I have the pleasure of seeing you. Not that I think there is any great difference between us; I am sure we used always to agree very well on those as well as on most other matters, and so I dare say we always shall.[31]

Keble proved to be a good loser and a very poor prophet.

In one sense Edward Hawkins' personal life began with his installation as Provost of Oriel in February 1828. Up to that moment his chief concern, the object of all his calculations, had been his duty to his mother and his younger brothers and sisters. Now with his greatly increased income—attached to the provostship were a canonry in Rochester Cathedral and a parish living in Essex—he could satisfy his family obligations and still live a little for himself. He must have thought, that summer, of the old saying that all things come to him who waits. He proposed to his childhood sweetheart, and she accepted him. They were both in their late thirties.

The story is told that as part of his ceremonial induction as provost Hawkins had to go out of the college into Oriel Street and then be received formally at the college gate. Accordingly, the gate was closed and the fellows gathered just inside. A knock was heard. The dean advanced a step and called out, "Quis adest?" expecting to hear the prescribed answer, "Edwardus Hawkins hujusce collegii Praepositus." But instead of Hawkins' strong and decisive tones, a tremulous feminine voice was heard. "Please, sir, it's me, the college washerwoman." And so the gate swung open to receive an aged lady who carried a basket of clean linen between the double file of gowned fellows.[32]

There may have been an omen in the untimely appearance of the washerwoman (if indeed the story is true). Hawkins' administration lasted more than fifty years and witnessed the steady decline of Oriel. The decline was slow and much of it can be traced to factors outside Hawkins' control. Yet, though no one could have guessed it in 1828, the new provost's competence was itself partly responsible. Once he took power he displayed that tragic flaw of narrowness which afflicted in different ways almost all the Oriel men of his time. His strict sense of justice hardened into intolerance. His candour became more and more an occasion for petulant outbursts against anyone who disagreed with him.

His respect for tradition gradually deteriorated into a permanent state of reaction. Perhaps all this would have happened to Eveleigh and Copleston if they had had to face the trials Hawkins did. But they were luckier than he, and Hawkins, as a result, never quite achieved the level of eminence in the university that they had enjoyed. For years every vacant bishopric gave rise to the rumour that Hawkins would be appointed. But he never was. Instead, the short, slender figure of the provost, with his fussy passion for formal dress and his eighteenth-century manners, beguiled several generations of Oxford men. Old East Wind, they called him, because of his formidable reputation as a disciplinarian. Only a very few were allowed to see the real human being beneath the martinet. Yet even the people who blamed him for his coldness and for what his enemies called his bigotry had to admit that he gave his all to Oriel and that he served his college the very best he knew how. The spark of greatness was simply not in him. Newman, who was in a better position than most to weigh the good in Hawkins against the bad, wrote when they were both old men, "I can say with a full heart that I love him and have never ceased to love him."[33]

With regard to matters intellectual and religious, Hawkins' watchword was caution. He made no stand until he was sure of his ground. He was born Tory and High Church and he always remained so, but like his friends Arnold and Whately—good Whigs both of them—he considered it ungentlemanly and un-Christian to press mysterious matters too far. He had no time for Caroline divines or for Wesley. Take no excessive positions was his advice to younger men; if you weigh your words carefully you will never say anything you will have to be sorry for later. Hawkins was an Establishment man through and through.

A certain amount of literary production was expected from a don, and so, dutifully, Hawkins did it. In the mid-1820s he published a four-volume edition of Milton's poetical works. The most notable thing about it was a footnote in which Hawkins explained why he thought Milton was an Arian. Because of the profession he had chosen, it seemed proper (and Hawkins was always proper) that the bulk of his publications have something to do with religion. Accordingly, he produced a manual of piety, some rather tedious tracts and lectures and a great many sermons.

Whately used to say that the majority of preachers aimed at nothing and hit it. Hawkins' fault was of a different kind. He tended to practice a species of pulpit overkill. What most people remembered about his sermons was their numbing length. His native caution led him into an exhaustive, often pedantic statement of his point which was consequently lost for many in an avalanche of words. Yet there was nothing wrong with his aim, and he always knew what he was talking about.

Hawkins was still a young don when, on May 31, 1818, he preached perhaps the most influential sermon in his career. As usual it was too long, but it showed to good public advantage Hawkins' sound sense and practicality. His subject was what he called "unauthoritative tradition." The problem he aimed at was indeed a practical one: "Why," he asked at the beginning, "are many of the Christian doctrines so *indirectly taught* in the Scriptures?" This must pose a serious obstacle to Bible Christians (and of course Hawkins assumed that Anglicans were Bible Christians). Many people are simply unaware of the problem, while others "suppose particular doctrines to be directly asserted in texts, which in fact only imply and assume them."

The answer to this difficulty, said Hawkins, will clarify the relation of the Scriptures to the Church. It does not seem unreasonable that the mysteries of Christianity should be presented to our minds in a way analogous to the teaching of any other subject. Even when subjects have been treated in the most exact and systematic order in some book or other, "we seldom even then commit such treatises into the hands of others . . . without some oral, some preliminary view of the contents of the work. . . . Now exactly such an aid and guide may surely be found in *tradition,* the traditions conveyed from age to age by the Church in general. . . . Common experience and common practice seem to declare that some assistance of the kind is *needful* and *reasonable,* why may not this assistance have been designed for us from the first—as from the first *in fact* almost every Christian has been by such aid introduced to Christianity?"

In other words, "to speak generally . . . the Church should *teach* and the Scriptures *prove* the doctrines of Christianity." The New Testament itself is witness to priority in time of the spoken word. Take, for example, the fifth chapter of Romans in which St. Paul treats the doctrine of original sin. "Throughout the chapter the consequences of Adam's transgression are not taught but rather assumed by the apostle as already known to his readers in order to argue from them to the corresponding extent of the gracious consequences of Christ's atonement."

Hawkins distinguished sharply between tradition as he spoke of it and the same word as used by Roman Catholics. "Their error consisted in claiming an authority for tradition equal or even superior to that of the Scriptures themselves." On the contrary, tradition "has often been corrupt and must be by its nature liable to corruption and therefore fallible." So Hawkins employed the qualifying "unauthoritative" to set out exactly what he meant. Yet he maintained just as strongly that there is a presumption in tradition's favour which cannot be prudently ignored. "Any uninterrupted tradition indeed of any given doctrine brings with it a reasonable *presumption* in its behalf. This it were most uncandid not to allow."

As might have been expected from a man of Hawkins' temper of mind, the sermon had an explicit recommendation as a conclusion. It will in the long run do little good to distribute Bibles indiscriminately to naked Hottentots or English coal miners unless formal instruction precede this good work. "The Scriptures . . . although a sufficient rule of faith . . . appear incomplete for teaching the faith according to the sense of the [English] Church exhibited in her practice; and unauthoritative tradition seems required in general to introduce men to the records of salvation."[34]

Among those who filed out of St. Mary's after Hawkins had finally finished was young John Newman, only seventeen and still an undergraduate at Trinity. When asked about the sermon he mentioned its length and then turned the conversation to other matters. Still, Hawkins' ideas lingered in his mind, and as that rarity in the Oxford of those days, an Evangelical, they disturbed him. The Bible was all-sufficient and yet in some subtle way it wasn't. He puzzled over the apparent contradiction a good deal, and a year later, when Hawkins' sermon appeared in print (inevitably somewhat enlarged), he bought a copy and studied it. He must have found this passage especially intriguing. "We perceive that traditions may be contradictory to the Scriptures and then we allow them no further than as they coincide with the dictates of reason; or they may be supported by the sacred writings, and then we respect them as the original sentiments of the first believers—as derived indeed from the true and only authority."[35]

V

If Newman admitted his intellectual debt to Hawkins, and never ceased to love him, even when the two of them were at odds, the case was far different with another of the old Oriel Noetics. Renn Dickson Hampden[36] received none of that chivalrous treatment which lightened the religious controversies of the 1830s and 1840s. To his enemies he was a *bête noire*, an unmitigated villain; to his allies—he had no friends—he proved an embarrassment or a puzzle. It is perhaps not often enough stated that Newman and Hampden differed over personal as well as intellectual matters. They were at one time or another rivals for office in the university and for influence within Oriel. Even so, Newman managed better than his friends to keep his attacks leveled at Hampden's ideas rather than his person. In substance Newman accused Hampden of promoting religious skepticism, and he was probably right. The irony is that the most familiar picture of Hampden is that drawn by Tom Mozley, Newman's brother-in-law and once his fervent disciple. Mozley wrote his memoirs when he was a blind old man and far more skeptical than Hampden had ever been; yet he could not, even over the distance of fifty years, shake his hatred for Hampden, whom he described as "the most unprepossessing of men . . . not so much repulsive as utterly unattractive. . . . [His] face was inexpressive, his head was set deep in his broad shoulders and his voice was harsh and unmodulated. Someone said of him that he stood before you like a milestone and brayed at you like a jackass. It mattered not what he talked about; it was all the same, for he made one thing as dull as another."[37]

Nothing in Hampden's appearance or in his quiet and inoffensive manner can explain such animosity. Perhaps what Mozley dredged up from his memory was Hampden as a symbol or Hampden as a spoiler of Mozley's own youthful dreams. However that may be, there is really very little to tell about Hampden before 1832. He was born in the West Indies in 1793, the son of a military officer stationed there. At seventeen he came to Oriel as an undergraduate, and at twenty he won a Double First. The next year, 1814, he was elected Fellow of Oriel, but he kept his fellowship only for a brief time. In 1816 he was ordained and married. He held several country curacies and eventually settled in London, where his considerable means allowed him to live in quiet style and to cultivate his intellectual tastes.

He came back to Oxford in 1829, acted as an examiner in the Schools, and in 1833 was appointed Principal of St. Mary Hall. With this last achievement Hampden took his place in the university power structure as a Head and member of the Hebdomadal Board. It was at this time too that he met Blanco White, a Spanish refugee and ex-Roman Catholic priest who had settled in Oxford and had been made an honourary member of the Oriel common room. White[38] was a gentle, tortured soul, who hungered for acceptance and security and never found either. He was a curiosity for most Oxford men, though he found a bond with some of them in music. "Music," said Tom Mozley, "was Blanco White's chief solace for he could almost forget himself when listening to Beethoven."[39] Several of the younger Oriel dons used to quiz him about Roman Catholicism. But for Hampden, White was a source of more specific information. The two of them were often closeted privately so that the Spaniard could tell the Englishman what he knew about scholastic philosophy. Hampden, who studied his Aristotle as carefully if not as noisily as Whately, had for years been interested in scholasticism, and he had already written several long articles and one book on the relation between philosophical science and revelation.

Hampden did not cut an impressive figure. He was a short man, with black hair which grew straight back from a sloping forehead. His eyes were dark and his complexion swarthy. Someone, searching desperately for a compliment, remembered that he had nicely shaped feet. He was extremely reserved. Even as a boy his school fellows had called him "Old Hampden." Once, at an Oxford dinner party, he amazed the lady who sat next to him by saying not one word in the course of the evening. Later, when he became a bishop, he set something of a record by sitting in the House of Lords for eighteen years without giving a single speech.

R. D. Hampden had no charm or sparkle, but this did not mean he was the vicious and stupid man his enemies made him out to be. They also accused him of living luxuriously off the fat of the Church. He was indeed a pluralist and he did live well, yet no better than Hawkins and Whately, who were pluralists too. Given the state of the Church and society in those days, the epicure charge against Hampden falls to the ground. The average Oriel don was not without his comforts. Hampden was an obstinate man, and sensitive; but even Newman cannot be absolved from these faults. As far as his native intelligence was concerned, the charges made against it came mostly from men far less intelligent than Hampden.

In 1832 Hampden was named Bampton Lecturer for that year, and with this prestigious appointment both his troubles and his triumphs began. John Bampton had been an eighteenth-century Canon of Salisbury who left an endowment for eight lectures to be delivered annually at St. Mary's, Oxford, on the general subject of defense of the Christian faith. Hampden delivered his lectures on "The Scholastic Philosophy considered in its relation to Christian Theology." They made no particular stir when they were given. Attendance at them was good, and Hampden published the first of three editions of them the following year (1833).

The outcry against the Bampton Lectures came, as we shall see, a few years later. But this would seem to be the best place to dismiss the most common charge raised then. It was said that Hampden did not know what he was talking about, that his reasoning was murky and confused, and that his arguments made no sense. The truth really was that his audience did not know what Hampden was talking about. The University of Oxford knew literally nothing about a long list of matters, including scholastic philosophy. When they heard his lectures, or read them later, Oxford men simply could not understand them. All they knew for sure was that they disliked Hampden's conclusions very much indeed, and on this they based the assumption that Hampden must be stupid. Such a stance was even easier to take for the great mass of their confreres who had not bothered to hear or read the lectures.

The theory advanced by Hampden may have been wrong, but he argued it clearly, persuasively and without dissimulation. It deserved a better answer, especially in an academic community, than the cries of outraged piety which greeted it. Eventually it received several very able answers, but in the meantime Hampden had been made a martyr by those whom Arnold called "the Oxford malignants." In an emotion-charged atmosphere little room was given for serious discussion of the issues.

And the issues raised by Hampden were crucial. He attacked the whole of traditional theology, he cut creeds and articles adrift from their scriptural moorings and he put the sacramental system in the same class as primitive magic. His purpose, as he stated in the first lecture, was to "show how the intellect of man has insinuated its own conclusions into the body of revelation in the course of its transmission, and [has] modified the expressions by which the truth is conveyed."

Hampden saw scholastic philosophy as "preeminently a record of the struggle which has subsisted between the efforts of human reason on the one hand to assert its own freedom and independence; and on the other hand the coercion exercised over [human reason] by the civil or ecclesiastical powers." The first stage in its development was the gradual ascendancy of the Latin over the Greek clergy, most significantly in the rise of papal power. The impact of the Fathers of the Western Church was the same, like St. Ambrose: "He united the inflexible religion of Athanasius with the practical dexterity of the man of the world"; or St. Augustine, who made his mark by his "shrewdness and versatility in the management of the Church," which "was daily becoming a more complex machine, more unwieldy to ordinary hands." Hampden also drew the contrast between Greek and Latin monasticism: the Oriental withdrew to be alone, "to luxuriate in the dreary and melancholy loneliness of his meditations," while the Westerner "sought solitude as a means of acting more forcibly on the busy scene of society."

The mind speculates, and the Church, in the hallowed name of Tradition, incorporates that speculation into her official teaching. This compromise between freedom and authority is what created scholasticism as Hampden understood it. One should not be surprised, he said, that where this temper of mind prevails—as in the medieval universities—one finds a combination of "moral disorder" and "mental coercion." Hampden was unequivocal in his condemnation of the sort of theology which rises out of the scholastic system: "That speculative logical Christianity which survives among us at this day . . . has been in all ages the principal obstacle, as I conceive, to the union and peace of the Church of Christ." Buy why should "logical" theology be such an obstacle—especially when the logic was that of Aristotle, which Hampden admitted was the "strongest, best discipline of the mind?" Hampden's answer was the key to his whole argument. "The Scripture intimates to us certain facts concerning the Divine Being; but conveying them to us by the medium of language it only brings them before us darkly, under the signs appropriate to the thoughts of the human mind." This works well for moral exhortation, because from it we learn in language we understand "both how to feel and how to act towards God." But the same approach "is altogether inadequate in point of science. The most perfect reasonings founded on the terms of theological propositions amount only to evidences of the various connections of the signs employed." And that, said Hampden, is all. What we have at the end is a "vast apparatus of technical terms" which have meaning only in relation to each other. "It will appear that whilst theologians . . . have thought they were establishing religious truth by elaborate argumentation they have been only multiplying and arranging theological language."

What tradition then has accomplished is the setting up of "idol-abstractions. . . . The signs have been converted into things." For as was, immediately clear Hampden did not restrict scholasticism to the schools of Paris in the thirteenth century. To him it was a much more sweeping term, which included any human agency at all. The Nicene Creed and the *Summa Theologica* were for Hampden on an equal footing: "Arguments proposed originally as answers to an opponent, and availing properly only as solutions to particular objections . . . were applied as grounds of evidence for the establishment of the truth universally." No human words or signs can express what God is, or what his relation to man is. One may make formal statements on these subjects, but the words will have no relation to the realities. Take, for example, the mystery of the Trinity: "The principal if not *the only difficulties* on the doctrine of the Trinity arise from metaphysical considerations— from abstractions of our own mind, quite distinct from the proper, intrinsic mystery of the holy truth in itself."

So quite simply what Hampden maintained was that "the restless impatience of the human mind" had been imposed upon the Christian community by "the arbitrary determinations of spiritual authority." That imposition may historically have been the work of Catholics or Protestants; it mattered little, because in either case it was scholasticism, the ignoble mixture of freedom and coercion. Scholasticism has effected "the disparagement of Revelation as a code of moral discipline and the exaltation of theology in the sense of a theoretic science." Can there then be anything called strictly religious doctrine? Only, said Hampden, in a negative sense. Creeds, articles, formularies have all been necessary at one time or another to give theoretical denial to theoretical challenges to Scripture-facts. The Arian, for example, employed certain technical language to deny the Scripture-fact of the Trinity. The Nicene Creed responded by setting out a defense of the Scripture-fact by using the same technical language. "As records of opinion," Hampden said of the ancient creeds as well as the modern articles, "they are essentially variable. It is no impeachment of their truth to regard them as capable of improvement." There is an analogy between dogmatic theology and political institutions, Hampden said at the end of his last lecture. "Were all men just the social instincts would develop themselves, without the artificial methods of civil government. So were all the humble disciples of Christ, Christian sentiment would speak in its own accents and not be constrained to learn the foreign tongue of technical theology." Formal statements of doctrine then—and this would include the Church of England's Thirty-nine Articles—have some social value and significance.

"The anathemas of creeds and councils can only be justified on this ground. They are the penalties of social religion."[40]

When he had finished his series, the mild-mannered Bampton Lecturer went back to his quiet pursuits. Nobody much noticed at the time. But Renn Dickson Hampden had set the fuse in a bomb which, when it exploded, would shake the foundations of the Church of England and the University of Oxford.

VI

Not far from where the streams of the Coln and the Leach flow into the upper Thames, about twenty-five miles straight west of Oxford, lies the little Gloucestershire village of Fairford. Here, as the nineteenth-century began—at the moment when Ireland was incorporated into the United Kingdom and the University of Oxford passed its Examination Statute—lived a clergyman named John Keble. He was an absentee parson who served the parish of Coln St. Aldwyn two or three miles away. Mr. Keble, with his wife and five children, preferred to live in the ancestral family home in Fairford. It was the house in which Mr. Keble had been born and in which, just short of his ninetieth birthday, he would die.

The elder of his two sons was also called John.[41] Only one intimate picture emerges from John Keble, Jr.'s childhood: it shows a small boy reading a Latin grammar which he holds in one hand while he bounces a ball off the garden wall with the other. Those who described this scene used to point out that the boy seemed able to work and play at once quite satisfactorily. In some measure this was to be the story of John Keble's life.

The Kebles of Fairford were a remarkably happy family. The parson and his good wife and their children—Elizabeth, John, Tom, Sarah and the beloved baby, Mary Anne—followed a regular and genial round of activities which centered in their deep and mutual affection. Their world was a small one. They were removed a long way from the fashionable bustle of London and even farther from the new, raw, urban centers springing up in the Midlands and the North. The most exciting event of their day was the arrival of the mail coach which stopped at the inn on its way from Cirencester to Cheltenham. The only life they knew, and the only life John Keble ever wanted, was the slow, rural, joyful one of the pre-industrial English countryside. It was a pattern of life more reminiscent of Charles I than of George III.

Mr. Keble was a Tory and a High Churchman, and he taught his children to be the same. His creed leaned heavily upon the Caroline divines and the Non-Jurors, and he mourned the martyrdom of King

Charles. Yet, though he was an educated man (sometime Fellow of Corpus Christi College, Oxford) and, as all the neighbourhood knew, a deep thinker, he did not press his Anglo-Catholicism to its logical extreme. Indeed, he had never really had it challenged, for in all that west country people of every class were High Church; and if they were not, Mr. Keble simply closed his eyes to them. He did not question a man's right to differ with him; he refused, however, to be drawn into the difference. He sought out his own and found solace and comfort with them. He had no antipathy for outsiders; he just had nothing at all to do with them.

Nor did he listen to those with fanciful ideas of social reconstruction. Some people are gentlemen, he would say, and some are not; and gentlemen are meant to rule and others to obey. That is what God intended or else he would not have permitted it to happen. But, he would add, a gentleman, to justify his privileges, must be upright and honourable, never harsh or unjust. For God loves all Englishmen, whatever their station. One's reverence must be practical: a man must do his duty and stand where he has been put, for God does nothing to his children without purpose. And so a man must revere God's holy name, and all that He has made; and a man must be good to the poor, loyal to his friends, his country and his king.

It was often noticed and remarked upon that the younger John Keble, after he had grown up, never lost his boyish characteristics. As he tumbled across the lawn with his nieces and nephews—he never had any children of his own—someone was sure to say that Uncle John appeared to enjoy himself more than all the other children. This was a large part of Keble's immense charm. In a very real sense, however, Keble never did grow up. He put his roots down deep in Fairford and into all that Fairford meant, and he never really left. He did indeed in middle age exchange a Gloucestershire parsonage for one in Hampshire, but this was only a matter of geography. Spiritually Fairford and Hursley were different aspects of the same reality.

This does not mean that Keble failed to grow intellectually or emotionally, or that he could not adapt to altered circumstances. He met many steep challenges in his lifetime, and he faced them all like a man. No one suffered sharper pangs of separation and bereavement than Keble. And yet, at the same time, he never ceased being the boy who bounced the ball off the garden wall. He had learned from his father, and in the warmth of his first home, the ideals of manhood and Christianity, and he could never accept anything different. If they were attacked, he would resist with all the strength at his command, and then he would withdraw to a small circle of intimates. He had a host of friends, but except for Pusey and Newman (who were special cases), they were the friends of his boyhood or former pupils or people who lived near his parsonage. The man closest to him by far was his brother, and it was typical of him that when he finally married he chose his brother's wife's sister.

He hated to leave Fairford (and later Hursley) for any reason. When necessity brought him to London or even to Oxford he could not wait to leave again for home. Someone described him as the sun of the little world he lived in, that ever-shrinking little world which turned its back on the momentous events of the nineteenth century and pretended they hadn't happened. It is perhaps not too much to say that Keble was the last of the Caroline divines and the Non-Jurors; and the best of them. With Newman's secession to Rome and the collapse of their common hopes, Keble was aghast; he felt, he said, "as if the spring had been taken out of my year." Even so, the thought of taking a similar step never crossed his mind. As he had learned from his father, a man must stand where he has been put.

John Keble, Sr., prepared his sons for the university himself and thus prolonged their stay in happy Fairford. John Jr. went up to Oxford and matriculated at Corpus Christi College early in 1807. He was not quite fifteen years old. Little Corpus was as ideal for Keble as it proved to be, a few years later, for Arnold. The college was small enough to provide the intimate setting in which Keble was always at his best. He made many firm friends at Corpus, J. T. Coleridge especially. Thomas Arnold, as we have seen, came to Corpus in Keble's last year there; their ill-starred friendship was solidified later on at Oriel. Keble never seemed to study much as an undergraduate. He went to dances and parties, wrote poetry, and engaged in those endless discussions for which the Corpus under-graduates were famous. When the time came, in 1810, to go into the Honours examinations, many of his friends wondered if Keble were really ready. He was. He won a Double First at the age of eighteen.

During Easter week 1811, Keble, in company with Richard Whately, was elected Fellow of Oriel. Although he was a don for almost twenty-five years, Keble never found Oriel the congenial place that Corpus had been. He spent as little time there as possible, except for the few years he was tutor, and even then he was off to Gloucestershire whenever he could. There was little sympathy between him and the Noetics. He was too con-servative in politics and religion for their liberal tastes. Yet he remained on good terms with all of them: with the argumentative Arnold, with the silent Hampden, who passed briefly through the common room like a specter, even with the rude and boisterous Whately. Tom Mozley, who belonged to a younger Oriel generation, wondered what they talked about when they were all together, because Keble then and throughout his life lost his temper easily when pressed in debate.[42] And debate was the lifeblood of a man like Whately, more important, indeed, than any conclusion debate might lead to. In any case, they made no impression intellectually upon Keble, nor he upon them. Perhaps Keble's long absences from Oriel provided a solution to a ticklish social situation.

Only once did Keble consider giving up the country life for a full-time academic career, and that was when it appeared he might be elected

Provost of Oriel. By that time—1827—the character of the college had changed. Most of the Noetics—Copleston and Whately, Arnold and Hampden—had gone and had given place to dons much more to Keble's taste—E. B. Pusey, for example, and two of Keble's former pupils, Robert Isaac Wilberforce and Richard Hurrell Froude. But even then Keble, as we have seen, gave way to Hawkins in the election. The spell of the country and the hold of his family proved too strong.

It had never crossed Keble's mind to follow any other profession than that of his father. He was ordained in 1815, and for the next eight years he served as curate several small parishes in the neighbourhood of Fairford. These pastoral burdens were not very heavy. Keble carried them with the help of his brother Tom (by now also a clergyman) even while he was tutor in Oriel, from 1818 to 1823. Then, in 1825, a former pupil of Keble's came into an unexpected inheritance which included patronage of the parish of Hursley, near Winchester in Hampshire. The young squire offered the curacy to Keble with the added assurance that the living would be his once the ailing, absentee vicar died. Keble accepted.

His first stay at Hursley was destined to last hardly a year. And it was a time when the accumulation of private sorrows reached a climax. Keble fell in love with the younger sister of a friend. He was thirty-two; she was eighteen, and though ready enough to flirt harmlessly with her brother's ancient friend, certainly not ready to marry him. Even though she refused him, Keble accepted Hursley, with its substantial income and new parsonage, in hopes that she might change her mind. She did not. Some years earlier his sister Sarah had died, and then his mother. His sister Elizabeth fell prey to an excruciatingly painful disease which resulted ultimately in the amputation of a leg. Then, in the autumn of 1826, his sister, darling Mary Anne, the charming and irrepressible, "my little wife" as Keble fondly called her, suddenly died too. It was as though a dark cloud had overshadowed the once gay, witty household at Fairford. Old Mr. Keble was nearly eighty, increasingly feeble and far too much to handle for his surviving daughter, with her wooden leg. Tom Keble was now married and about to embark on his own clerical career. And so it was up to John Keble to come home to Fairford and to take care of his father, his sister and the little parish at Coln St. Aldwyn.

Keble's lost love was reproached often by her friends for having rejected him. "He is such a good man," they said. The poor girl answered on one occasion, "Yes, but he is such an *ugly* one." In her understandable annoyance she rather overstated the facts. Keble's appearance in these years was not so much ugly as undistinguished. He was short, with a tendency to stoop. He dressed carefully and he was abreast enough of the fashions of the day to be considered something of a dandy by Oxford undergraduates. He had a solid Gloucestershire face with a strong jaw line, a large mouth and wide brow. But what people remembered most about him were his eyes and his smile. Indeed, when he smiled, his face was transfigured with a unique radiance, with a genuine goodness which nobody except perhaps girls of eighteen could resist.

All the troubles of Keble's middle life did not dim that smile. His attachments—especially that to his brother—became stronger, his personal religion deeper. It was the Anglo-Catholic religion of the Prayer Book which his father had taught him and which now, partly because of the restless, anti-religious agitation of the 1820s and partly because of his own study and reflection, became dearer to him than ever. His practical reverence had always centered in the Prayer Book, in its rhythmic cadences and restrained observance of the fasts and feasts of the liturgical year. Now, not long after the death of Mary Anne, he gave to the world the poetic expression of his meditations.

No one was more surprised than Keble at the fantastic success of *The Christian Year*. The book went through ninety-two editions in its author's lifetime and became a devotional staple to several generations. It is important to emphasize the devotional character of *The Christian Year*. "Next to a sound rule of faith," wrote Keble in the preface, "there is nothing of so much consequence as a sober standard of feeling in matters of practical religion. . . . The object of the present publication will be attained if any person find assistance from it in bringing his own thoughts and feelings into more entire unison with those recommended and exemplified in the Prayer Book." Keble meant these words quite literally. He did not write poetry for poetry's sake.

Indeed, there are those who would say that Keble did not write poetry at all, that he rather wrote verse for God's sake. Though the judgment sounds harsh, or even sardonic, Keble himself would not have objected to it. He subtitled the book, "Thoughts in verse for the Sundays and Holydays" and that is exactly what they were. Wordsworth is said to have liked them (he knew and liked Keble very much), and Thomas Arnold, no special friend to the Prayer Book, hailed "the richness of poetry which they exhibit and which I never saw paralleled." But then Thomas Arnold was tone deaf; he had not a note of music in him, and neither had Keble. The writing of poetry to the Oxford generation to which Keble and Arnold belonged was a matter not of inspiration but of intellectual exercise. Everybody wrote poetry in this sense; they filled reams of copybooks with it. Keble had been writing poetry since he was a small boy, in the same spirit as he had been working mathematical problems. After all, his Double First demonstrated proficiency in mathematics and literature. Certain rules of proportion had to be learned, certain classical authors had to be imitated, and the result, after years of exercise, was a ready wit and a quick pen.

None of this is said to denigrate Keble's work. *The Christian Year* is in its way a beautiful book and a reflection of Keble's uniquely beautiful spirit. But it must be judged by its author's own norms. What Keble set out to do was to provide a thoughtful commentary in verse to the

Prayer Book. He succeeded admirably. Judged by strictly literary criteria, however, *The Christian Year* was no more than a minor achievement to brighten the wasteland between Keats and the young Tennyson.

What is of more interest to these pages is the fact that *The Christian Year* and its success made Keble overnight a national figure. To all those Anglicans who loved the Prayer Book and thought that it was threatened, Keble's book was not so much a consolation as a challenge. And in the struggles which lay just over the horizon, the reputation of Good John Keble was to play a very large role indeed. As one reads his meditation for the Feast of the Conversion of St. Paul, one cannot but wonder whether Keble had, by some intuition, an inkling of those struggles to come.

> Ah! little dream our listless eyes
> What glorious presence they despise,
>   While, in our noon of life,
> To power or fame we rudely press—
> Christ is at hand, to scorn or bless,
>   Christ suffers in our strife.[43]

VII

It was in a discussion over a few fragile lines of Greek poetry that Keble first met the man whose name was destined to be linked so closely to his own. Edward Bouverie Pusey[44] of Christ Church appeared in the Oxford Honours Schools at Easter 1822, when Keble was one of the examiners. "I never knew," Keble observed later, "how Pindar might be put into English until I heard Pusey construe him in his examination."[45] Pusey won his B.A. on that occasion with a First Class in classics. A year later he was elected Fellow of Oriel.

Pusey, like Keble, was a member of the country gentry, though his place in the hierarchical structure was several cuts higher. He was born in 1800 at Pusey House in Berkshire (there was a village nearby, also called Pusey), a couple of hours horseback ride from Oxford. His father was the youngest son of a viscount, and his mother the daughter of an earl and the widow of a baronet. Edward, the second of their nine children, never lacked social connection or financial resources. Mr. Philip Pusey was fifty-two when he married, twenty-four years older than his wife, and he was a martinet. A Tory of the Tories, he classed Whigs and atheists together as the enemies of mankind. His many years as a bachelor prepared him admirably for the role of domestic autocrat. As Pusey's biographer guardedly described it: "When [his children] were young, his reserved habits made the boisterous society of children unwelcome to him; and they had taken their own line when they were old enough to be his companions."[46] It is significant that when he first had an opportunity to express an independent political judgment, Edward Pusey chose the Whig side, in direct opposition to his father.

Lady Lucy Pusey was a tall, slim, rather remote person who affected the manners of an eighteenth-century drawing room. She conformed herself to the rigid standards of her husband, even to the point of reading every day, a practice which she despised. Dutifully, at the prescribed time she opened her book and kept it open until the watch, set carefully by her side, told her she could turn to something more congenial. All her life—she lived into her ninetieth year—she was a stickler for the decorum of her girlhood: "She rarely or never would lean back in her chair, and she used to say that to stoop was the mark of a degenerate age."[47] She could only marvel at her brilliant son and his passionate love for books. After he had become famous, she would point out the corner of the garden at Pusey where Edward sat daily during the summer of 1822 studying a thick volume of the Fathers of the Church; Mr. Pusey had given him a complete set as a reward for his First Class. Next to him was a tub of cold water into which he would plunge his head whenever he got drowsy.

The secret of Pusey's success was his industry. In preparation for his honours examination he read up to sixteen or seventeen hours a day and became, as he put it ruefully himself, "a reading automaton who might by patience be made into a human being." He was much less clever than his older brother Philip, and since the two boys were drawn together in a household where their father kept himself at a distance and their mother was occupied by the younger children, Edward learned early that he would have to scramble to keep up. Scramble he did, and all his life. Mr. Pusey did not begrudge his sons the finest possible education. In hopes evidently that they might one day be civilized enough to deserve their father's company, they had the best private tutors and five years at Eton before they went to the university.

Shortly before he entered Christ Church in January 1819, Edward Pusey fell in love. It was not the normal puppy love which afflicts most youngsters of eighteen, though everybody, especially Pusey's father, thought it so at the time. Her name was Maria Catherine Barker. She was pert and pretty, and she came from a distinguished Gloucestershire family whose seat was not far from the Keble home in Fairford. Pusey had seen her only a few times, but it was enough for him to decide that there could be no one else for him. "I was no free agent," he wrote to her later, "after I had seen you. . . . Everything has been the necessary consequence of that."[48] Mr. Pusey saw no necessary consequence of his son's adolescent attachment. At first he ignored it and then he forbade it to continue. He did not, however, take into account his son's dogged persistence—a mistake many others would make in their relations with

Edward Pusey. In this instance the young lover pined away, torn by alternating hope and despair, for nine years. Then he got his way.

A naturally shy disposition, a voracious appetite for work and a longing for Maria combined to make Pusey at Christ Church a more or less gloomy recluse. Though he played a good game of chess, athletics bored him. He turned instead to his books. His religious life at this period was exact, though hardly deep. His moral life was blameless. He indulged as an undergraduate and for some years afterwards in what he later called "Byronism." The spell of Lord Byron's poetry caught many of Pusey's generation, but it was not the sensualism nor even the matchless music of the verse which fascinated Pusey. He enjoyed its morbidity.

The extreme force and beauty of Byron's poetry combined with a habit of deep and, in some degree, morbid feeling, which had always, more or less, a shade of gloom, induced us to give our assent to and even in some measure exult in feelings of whose full extent we were either at the time unaware, or at least against which we half, and but half, shut our eyes. . . . The Byronist, though encircled by the purest air, with the golden sun, full of joy and pleasure, gleaming in the bright blue sky will fix his eye on any speck of mist which he sees crouching near the horizon, and gaze on it till it swell and seem to fill heaven and earth. To a real Byronist a pure blue sky is a dull insipid thing.[49]

Without Maria no sky could be blue enough.

This "Byronism" did not affect Pusey's religious faith or his moral habits, but it did become for a while his world view. He read Scott's novels with a Byronist eye, so that the heroines were always Maria and the tragic heroes himself. He confided in his only close friend at Christ Church, Richard Jelf, whom he had known at Eton, his conviction that evil might perhaps be more interesting than dangerous. Jelf did his best to cheer up his friend and to some extent succeeded, but a spirit of gloom was to haunt Pusey all his life.

A combination of events turned Pusey from Byron to religion. The first was a long correspondence he had with an Eton friend who, while living on the Continent, lost his faith. With his usual industry, Pusey trotted out at enormous length the whole apologetic apparatus, only to find that his friend refused even to read it. It was a simple lesson that Pusey learned, but a profound one; a man believes what he wants to believe, and if his moral sensitivity is dull all religious arguments will fall on deaf ears.

The expanded horizons which came with his Oriel fellowship in 1823 led Pusey further away from Byron. His association with the radiantly religious Keble and Newman was partly responsible for this. Also the famous thrust and parry of the Oriel common room played its part, but in an unexpected way. Pusey was never fast on his feet. Any of the old Noetics could have chopped him into mincemeat in debate, and the same was true of the younger generation of dons. But Pusey took refuge in a quality none of them had, a tremendous capacity for the accumulation of facts. Pusey was unique among the Oriel men of his time in the vastness of his reading, the kind of thing Copleston called "quackery." Whatever the provost thought of it, Pusey habitually took his stand, with his feet firmly planted, on facts which nobody else had heard of. Much to their chagrin, the dons of Oriel, with all their dialectical expertise, often found him immovable and invulnerable.

But to Charles Lloyd more than to anyone else belongs the credit of rescuing Pusey from the half-dreams of his youth and bringing him into intellectual maturity. Lloyd had been for many years a Student (i.e. Fellow) of Christ Church, where Pusey as an undergraduate had first known him. In 1822 he was appointed Regius Professor of Divinity, which, as the title suggests, was a crown appointment. Lloyd was an Anglo-Catholic, a close friend of Joshua Watson and other members of the Clapton Sect. He had once tutored Robert Peel at Christ Church and had remained close to that rising Tory politician in the intervening years. This relationship had done his cause no harm when the Tory government filled the divinity chair. Lloyd was an able scholar, a superb teacher, and, moreover, he had a streak of hard practicality in him which made him a good physician for moonstruck youths.

Pusey began attending Lloyd's lectures in May 1823, just after his election at Oriel.[50] They were, strictly speaking, private lectures, but few public ones were so well attended. Lloyd never sat down as he talked. He walked around the room, wrapped in a long coat that looked like a dressing gown and waving a coloured pocket handkerchief, "a necessary accompaniment of his habits as a professed snuff-taker." He delivered his material with the greatest verve and yet always with perfect clarity and order. His favourite expression was "D'ye see?" with which he punctuated any point he was trying to make. He also used a kick in the shins for emphasis. "I suppose," he might say to one of his hearers with a friendly kick, "I suppose you have been taught from your cradle upwards that it is a special duty of a Christian to abuse Roman Catholics." Then, with another kick, he would add, "That, d'ye see, I hold to be a mistake." Lloyd continued his lectures after he became Bishop of Oxford in 1827, and the only noticeable change in his manner was that he hung his episcopal wig on a peg near the door before he started to speak.

After faithfully attending Lloyd's lectures for two years, Pusey had compiled a vast and elaborate set of notes and gained a new sense of what an academic vocation could be. He had always intended, without thinking much about it, to become a clergyman—his older brother was reserved for a political career—but it was the intellectual excitement of Lloyd's lecture room which caused him to consider combining religion and study for life. Pusey admired Lloyd especially for his thoroughness, a characteristic which appealed to Pusey's temperament. "Lloyd taught us not so much the full meaning of the Holy Scripture as how to study it." The professor usually covered only a few verses in his lecture, but he examined them from every historical and linguistic angle available to the admittedly limited English scholarship of the time. On his side Lloyd could not but be flattered by Pusey's devotion and impressed by his industriousness and flair for languages.

One day Lloyd said to Pusey, "I wish you would learn something about those German critics." This suggestion ushered Pusey into what might be called the last phase of his youth. The critics to whom Lloyd referred made up that group of German Protestant theologians, located at various universities, who were in the process of creating a new rationalist school of theology. Oxford knew nothing of Germany; indeed, it was said that in the whole university only two men could read the German language. Perhaps Lloyd saw in Pusey's relentless approach to study a Teutonic quality which might make him competent one day to oppose a German wave of unbelief. In any event, Pusey set himself to learn German with a tutor, and in June 1825 he left England for Germany. During the next two years Pusey spent about fifteen months visiting various German universities. He met Schleiermacher and Neander and formed friendships with several young, rising theologians.

Pusey was alternately appalled and fascinated by what he found in Germany. As Lloyd suspected, unbelief was all around, but it was combined with an intellectual sophistication beyond anything Pusey had dreamed of. He sensed how unready England was for the kind of scriptural criticism which abounded at the German universities. Of special interest to him were the linguistic studies upon which much of this criticism rested. Pusey made a momentous decision. He would study Hebrew and the other Oriental languages—Arabic, Syriac and the rest—which formed a complement to Hebrew. Then, he reasoned, and only then, the rationalist Germans could be met on their own ground.

As it turned out, Pusey never did do battle with the German critics. His controversies were destined to be of a different kind and to be almost entirely with his own countrymen. Indeed, Pusey's German adventure almost immediately landed him in hot water at home. In 1825 a Cambridge man named Hugh James Rose published a series of sermons in which he violently attacked the "abdication of Christianity" which, in his judgment, was in process among German Protestants. Rose's indictment was sweeping and not overly subtle, and Pusey, who was in Berlin when a German translation of Rose's work appeared, decided to write an answer. He did not so much disagree with Rose's general conclusions as he did with the reasons Rose advanced. Also Pusey objected that Rose's scatter-gun approach wounded the orthodox as well as the rationalist theologians. The result was a long, tedious and often acrimonious controversy during which appeared Pusey's first serious theological work, *An Enquiry into the Theology of Germany*.[51] These two volumes were characteristic of all Pusey's later work: They were long, immensely learned, and murkily written. English critics immediately seized upon what seemed to be a rationalist definition of scriptural inspiration. In his second volume Pusey attempted to explain his meaning and only managed to confuse everyone further. Even his friends found the book obscure. "It is sadly deformed with Germanisms," Newman confided to his sister Harriet. "He is wantonly obscure and foreign—he invents words. It is a very valuable sketch and will do good, but will be sadly misunderstood."[52]

Pusey came home from Germany in mid-1827, and though he was tempered by literary controversy and alarmed over the future of Christianity, the thoughts at the top of his mind were still of Maria Barker. Maria's father died in 1827 and this seemed to soften Mr. Pusey's opposition to the match. There was, however, still the question of finances, for Edward Pusey's personal income came from the fellowship at Oriel, which he would have to resign if he married. To the surprise of all, Mr. Pusey relented still further and agreed to supply his son with an income through which he could marry and still carry on his intellectual work.

The arrangement has a curiously modern ring. On June 1, 1828, Pusey was ordained a deacon in the Church of England and eleven days later, with his friend Richard Jelf officiating, he and Maria Barker were united in marriage.[53] For nine years he had struggled for her, for eleven years he was destined to keep and cherish her; and when he lost her, it was for him a catastrophe beyond all reckoning.

But at this moment fortune was still kind to Pusey. In the middle of 1828 the Regius Professor of Hebrew died, and Lloyd, now Bishop of Oxford and confidant of the Wellington-Peel government, secured the appointment for Pusey. Along with the chair went a handsome income, a house and a canonry in Christ Church. Lloyd had quizzed Pusey about some of the more obscure passages in *German Theology* and had been satisfied of his protégé's orthodoxy. Others in Oxford were not so convinced, but no one could deny that Pusey was eminently qualified for the post from an intellectual point of view—and this was something one could rarely say about crown appointments to academic offices. In quick succession between November 1828 and January 1829, Pusey was ordained priest, installed as Canon of Christ Church and formally took up his duties as the King's Professor of Hebrew in the University of Oxford.

So Edward Pusey, not yet twenty-nine years old and already famous, financially independent and blessed with the presence of the only woman he ever loved, entered upon the office he was to hold for more than half a century. The dreams of Byron were gone, and sharp conflicts were just around the corner. But this was a blissful time for the young professor and his beautiful bride. Pusey often recalled when he and Maria, at the end of their honeymoon in the Lake Country, stayed at Badger Hall in Shropshire and how he preached his first sermon in Badger Church. The text was from the twelfth chapter of Hebrews: "Follow peace with all men and holiness, without which no man shall see the Lord." In his search for holiness, Edward Pusey was to find most of the time not peace but a sword.

VIII

Discussion raged for some years before 1832 over the proposed parliamentary reform bill and what it might mean to the nation and the Church. One day in the Oriel common room, that hot center of dialectic, the subject received a rather unusual treatment. "As to the Franchise," said one of the young dons as he draped his lanky frame over a chair, "the most sensible qualification would be submitting to a previous flogging; no one would vote without being in earnest about it." The speaker was a tall, very thin man in his late twenties, who stooped when he stood up and whose delicate features were set off "by penetrating grey eyes, not exactly piercing, but bright with internal conceptions, and ready to assume an expression of amusement, careful attention, enquiry, or stern disgust, but with a basis of softness."[54]

His name was Richard Hurrell Froude,[55] B.A. of Oriel College (with a Double Second in the Honours Schools) in 1824, Fellow of Oriel in 1826, and priest of the Church of England in 1829. Those who heard the quip about franchise reform laughed heartily, as they so often had occasion to do when Froude was in good form. There may have been, however, a bit of uneasiness in their manner too, for one could never be sure when Froude's savage wit might be directed at one's own foibles. Yet, as Tom Mozley remembered it, those around him "would rather writhe under his most cutting sarcasms than miss their part in the workings of his sympathy and genius."[56] All his conversation was punctuated by the hacking cough of incipient tuberculosis.

Froude came from Dartington, in the midst of the moors of Devon, where he was born in 1803. His father was Rector of Dartington and an archdeacon to the Bishop of Exeter, a High and Dry Tory parson of the old school who rode to hounds, collected rare books and ruled the country round about his rectory like an Old Testament patriarch. Archdeacon Froude spurned subtleties of all kinds; he accepted both the Thirty-nine Articles and the Prayer Book with no sense of inconsistency. Hurrell— he seemingly never used his first name—was the eldest of the archdeacon's eight children; his youngest brother was James Anthony, the future historian. He grew up to be a strong rider and bold sailor, and he had the quick intelligence of his father, with something also of his mother's delicacy and imagination.

Hurrell Froude went up to Oriel from Eton in 1821. Keble was tutor then, and from their first meeting until Froude's death fifteen years later the closest bond existed between the two. It was not just the relationship between the cultivated teacher and the gifted but raw pupil as was the case, say, with Lloyd and Pusey. Keble had a magic way of making a younger man comfortable, of instructing and yet befriending him, of drawing out the essential human person from the muddle of adolescent ambition, passion and insecurity. Froude's native gift for slashing repartee assured him of success at Oriel. And Keble did nothing to discourage his pupil's impulsive wit. He tried instead to temper it with serious scholarship—in the Oxford sense—and with a deep, personal religion.

The results of Keble's treatment were somewhat mixed. Froude did indeed, under Keble's tutelage, become an intensely religious young man. But he rushed at what seemed to him the conclusions of Keble's premises in a way that startled the older man. When Keble mourned over the sad state into which England had fallen, Froude's response was, "I am afraid I must confess that the only war I could enter into with spirit would be a civil war."[57] And Keble's position that the English Prayer Book continued the practice of the early Christian ages was expressed by Froude with disconcerting directness: "The Reformation was a limb badly set—it must be broken again in order to be righted."[58] In the midst of the agrarian unrest of 1831 (which was severe around Dartington) Froude concluded, "I have now made up my sage mind that the country is too bad to deserve an established church."[59]

The flippant remark, the contempt for posturing, the straightforward condemnation of abuses, all these gave evidence of one side of Hurrell Froude's nature. There was another, darker side. In January 1826 he began to keep a journal and to jot down random thoughts, a practice he continued for three or four years.[60] These revelations draw a far different picture from the one of the clever don who made frivolous and sarcastic remarks in the Oriel common room. They reveal a frightening introspection, an avid concern to unravel action from motivation so that the soul itself might be laid bare. Another striking feature of them is their self-absorption. There is no hint in them of compassion for others; there is only an obsession with self-improvement or self-contempt over repeated failures which borders on the morbid. There runs through them a pathetic concern for the trivial. On November 23, 1826, in a conversation with a friend, Froude "could hardly tell what to do and dropped imperceptibly into a style [of speech] which I am sure was quite inconsistent with all my feelings and the conduct I aim at. Now I feel certain that it would be wrong to let any one know these; yet it is worse to be ashamed of them."[61]

He raged at himself over and over for a lack of discipline. "Was disgustingly ostentatious at dinner in asking for a china plate directly [i.e., right away—in the college hall meat was served on pewter], as I had finished my meat. I did it on purpose too, that others might see I ate so much less than they did."[62] He took on horrendous fasts, sometimes not eating anything until nine in the evening. He also frequently slept on the floor in order to be uncomfortable. But nothing seemed to calm the tortured spirit. He observed in April 1826, just after his election to an Oriel fellowship, "I am happier than I ever was at Oxford, . . . but that is not saying much."[63]

One should take care to read no more into these expressions (which, after all, were never meant for the public eye) than is in them. In the first place Froude was a very young man when he wrote them, restless and romantic, standing on the edge of life, seeking, as most young men do, a sense of completion and fulfillment. "If a man must fall in love," he said wistfully, "it should be in the reverential way of Sir Kenneth in *The Talisman*."[64] There is a moment in life when the unstained heroes of Scott strike a young man as more real than his own flesh and blood. Moreover, Froude wrote his journal and random thoughts under a peculiarly dark personal cloud. He had come into the possession of some of his mother's papers shortly after her death. In reading them he discovered that she considered him, despite his many gifts, to have been inconsiderate of her and cold and demanding towards the other members of his family. There was an element of truth in what she said: Froude, a compulsive perfectionist, was always hard on others, and especially on his family. But the same drive towards perfection made his mother's criticisms strike him with particular force. He admits once to crying violently over them.

Keble then had taught Froude to know himself, but Keble had not intended the exercise should reach such painful lengths. This phase had pretty well passed by 1829, and Froude after that date no longer felt it necessary to record his reasons for self-loathing. Yet throughout the remainder of his life there remained two Hurrell Froudes: the hard-riding, tough-talking, hater of sham and pretense; and the small boy, unsure and afraid, calling out wordlessly to his mother through a perpetual dark night of the soul. One wonders what bluff old Archdeacon Froude made of it all when he read this curious line from his son, written in 1823: "I think the more I see of Keble the more I get to like and admire him; in everything but person and manner he seems so very like my mother."[65]

The alliance with Keble, whatever its psychological implications, channeled some of Froude's energies and tempered some of his fears. Above all it gave him a cause. Froude became a fire-eating Anglo-Catholic. He poured scorn upon Evangelicals, High and Dries, and liberals alike with lofty impartiality. When he was first coming to know Newman, he cheerfully labeled him a heretic. When accused of extravagance and rash judgment, he replied, "Catholic enthusiasts may be hated but they never can become ridiculous as the Methodists are."[66] "Keble is my fire," he said on another occasion, "but I am his poker."[67] He was ready to light up the sky with a Catholic revival which would burn up the sluggishness and hypocrisy of English religious life, and, perhaps, purge away some of his haunting doubts about himself. He delighted in saying favourable things about Roman Catholicism, because he knew nothing would shock Englishmen more. "I never could be a Romanist," he said once. "I never could think all those things in Pope Pius' creed necessary to salvation. But I do not see what harm an ordinary Romanist gets from thinking so."[68]

Froude got his first serious look at Roman Catholicism in the winter of 1832–33, which he, in company with his father and Newman, spent traveling in Italy. The occasion for the trip was the condition of Froude's lungs, which had become a cause of concern to his family and friends. Keble assured him that he would come home a better English Churchman than when he went away. If he meant by this that Froude would be disenchanted by what he saw in Italy, the prophecy was quite correct. He was not disturbed much by what other Englishmen considered idolatry. "I cannot make up my mind," he wrote, about devotion to the Virgin and the saints. The gross immorality, as he judged it, of three quarters of the population seemed to him a worse idolatry. "The Christian system all over Europe" is tending towards dissolution, he reported. "The same process which is going on in England and France is taking its course everywhere else; and the clergy in these Catholic countries seem as completely to have lost their influence and submit as tamely to the state as ever we can do in England."[69] When in Rome he talked to the rector of the English College, an Anglo-Irishman named Nicholas Wiseman, about the possibilities of ultimate reunion. It was an idle conversation, but even so Wiseman, though polite, made it clear that Rome had no terms for Canterbury but unconditional surrender. "So much for the Council of Trent," Froude wrote to Keble, "for which Christendom has to thank Luther and the reformers. [Newman] declares that ever since I heard this I have become a staunch Protestant, which is a most base calumny on his part, though I own it has altogether changed my notions of the Roman Catholics and has led me to wish for the total overthrow of their system. I think the only topos [starting place] now is the ancient Church of England, and as an explanation of what one means, Charles the First and the Non-jurors. When I come home I mean to read and write all sorts of things for now that one is a radical there is no use in being nice."[70]

Froude came home early in the summer of 1833, pale and thin and still coughing, but cheerful and ready for battle. He had not long to wait. His words were still razor sharp; when asked about the caliber of the members of the new reformed Parliament, he answered, "Fancy a gentleman not knowing Greek!"[71] But the Tory old guard received no more comfort from this newly radical Oxford don than the vulgar middle class. "What fun it is to be living in such times as these! How could one now go back to the times of old Tory humbug?"[72]

CHAPTER 5

Newman

"I MEAN to ally myself to him in a close league and put as much mischief into his head as I can."[1] So observed Froude with his customary vigour. The head into which he intended to put the "mischief" belonged to John Henry Newman, whom Froude on first acquaintance suspected of being a heretic. Heresy for Froude was a blanket term which applied to anybody who did not hold Froude's own fervent Anglo-Catholic views. He at first thought Newman might be an Evangelical or else a liberal, like Whately, and either of these positions was anathema to him. As a matter of fact, Newman, by the time Froude came to know him well, had already experienced both and was committed to neither. He was ripe, so to speak, for Keble's influence. "Do you know," asked Froude shortly before his death, "the story of the murderer who had done one good thing in his life? Well, if ever I was asked what good deed I have ever done I should say I had brought Keble and Newman to understand each other."[2]

This remark had the genuine Froude ring to it. It was jaunty and clever, and still at the same time it revealed that dark strain of self-doubt which always troubled him. Certainly there was a good deal of truth in it: Froude did indeed provide a bridge between Keble and Newman. But significant as that association may have been, perhaps it was in the long run less important than the relationship between Newman and Froude himself. For Newman was the giant among the men of Oriel. It was he, not the others, who left a mark upon the world. Yet Oxford shaped him and made him what he was, and no one in Oxford had the impact upon him that Froude did. Throughout his long life Newman had a host of close friends, but only Froude approached him as an equal. Not John Bowden, not Rogers or Henry Wilberforce, certainly not Pusey, not even Keble, least of all Ambrose St. John; as dear as Newman was to all of them and they to him, yet none of them, except Froude, escaped a sense of awe in their proximity to Newman's genius. Froude, on the other hand, the playful, irreverent and painfully candid Froude, the passionate seeker of truth, the gay warrior racked by disease and inner doubt, proved a refreshing and healthy exception.

I

Their backgrounds were entirely dissimilar. Newman, two years older than Froude, was born in London in 1801.[3] Mr. John Newman, his father, was a banker who did well enough to provide his family with comfort, security and status—the latter best symbolized by his ownership of a country as well as a town house. Mrs. Newman was as middle class as her husband; she came from French Huguenot stock, and her father had been a prosperous paper manufacturer. Even later, when the clouds of financial distress descended upon them, they were a happy, compatible couple, easygoing, fond of music and the theater. In religion they followed a relaxed, conventional course, going to church regularly and reading the Bible in their home, but committed to neither Evangelical nor Anglo-Catholic views. Their intellectual interests were unpretentious.

John Henry was the oldest of their six children; there followed him Charles, Harriet, Francis, Jemima, and finally Mary, who was born in 1810. Newman, as it turned out, had little joy from his family. He was a dutiful son to his parents, but there never seemed much genuine sympathy between him and them. They were no doubt first startled by his precocity and later on bewildered and often irritated by his intense religiosity. Both his brothers grew up to be wildly eccentric and caused him no little anxiety. His sister Harriet, a talkative, headstrong girl, cut off all communication with him when he became a Roman Catholic and died unreconciled. Newman lavished most of his familial affection upon his baby sister Mary, whose death, when she was only nineteen, was one of the severest trials of his life.

At the age of seven John Henry was enrolled in a private boarding school at Ealing. Here for the first time he displayed that rich and rare combination of gifts which would mean for him a life of lonely eminence. The poetical and the mathematical seldom coalesce in one person. They did in Newman. He possessed a remarkably lively set of senses which remained acute down into his old age. A good ear for music made him a highly skilled amateur violinist, competent to play for his pleasure the quartets of Beethoven (significantly, his favourite composer) and Mozart whenever the rest of an ensemble was available. He was also keenly sensitive to light and colour, and delighted especially in the visual beauties of the sky. The sights of nature were never monotonous to him: "The heavens changed if the earth did not, and when they changed they made the earth new."[4] He had an extraordinary appreciation for flavours and fragrances too; though hardly a tippler, he was always regarded as the best judge of wine in the Oriel common room.

With such a high level of sensual perception it was natural that feeling and imagination should convert the outer world into an inner experience of song and romance. In childhood he "used to wish the Arabian Tales were true: my imagination ran on unknown influences, on magical powers and talismans. . . . I thought life might be a dream, or I an angel, and all this world a deception, my fellow-angels by a playful device concealing themselves from me, and deceiving me with the semblance of a material world."[5] As a boy, early on summer mornings before anybody else was awake he would often lie in bed reading the novels of Walter Scott.

But the poetry did not drive out precision. Newman, boy and man, had a mathematical bent, a strongly logical mind which could measure, balance, penetrate with singular directness. Yet he did not rush headlong at intellectual problems but approached them carefully, analyzing them from every side, often with painful deliberation. No detail escaped his eye. No consequence of his own or someone else's reasoning failed to impress him. Indeed, his remarkable insight into the minds of others —a quality, by the way, which he thought lacking in Froude—worked so well that during his controversies he often explained an opponent's position more clearly than the opponent did himself. Newman was consumed by a passion for accuracy. No one tried harder than he did to state exactly what he meant. Many times this led him into a subtlety which to lesser minds appeared devious. He was capable of exhaustive inquiry, but it never resulted, as it so often did with Pusey, in a vast and unrelated catalogue. The parts and the whole for Newman had to come out even. It was a mathematician's bias, and, in Keble's judgment, it was to be Newman's downfall.[6]

The mathematician and the artist developed together at Ealing and, during the vacations, in London or at the Newman country place at Ham. Young John Henry, his inner self a wondrous balance between *A Thousand and One Nights* and the theorems of Euclid, grew up tall and thin, with gray eyes, a wide, full-lipped mouth, a prominent nose, and thick, fine brown hair which always flopped down over his forehead. He did not care about athletics, but he learned to ride and enjoyed boating on the Thames. He could not swim, though he liked to plunge into the water and feel the shock of exhilaration which followed. He belonged to secret clubs at school, edited boyish magazines, acted in plays. He was a strong-willed youngster and tended to dominate his brothers and sisters and his schoolfellows. When he left Ealing to go to Trinity College, Oxford, in 1817, already everyone expected great things of him.

But before his Oxford career began he had to pass through the first of those spiritual crises which were to mark the progress of his life.

In March 1816, caught in the post-Waterloo depression, Mr. John Newman's bank closed its doors. He and his partners managed to pay off
their depositors, but the failure left them all in a precarious position.
For the Newmans it meant a tightening of the belt while Mr. Newman
sought other employment. He found it managing a Hampshire brewery.
John Henry, meanwhile, was left to spend the summer holidays at Ealing.
Sometime during this summer of 1816 he fell ill, not seriously but with
a high enough fever to cause him discomfort and depression. The sickness together with the uncertainty about the family's fortunes and the
loneliness of separation from home all helped to turn the high-strung
boy's thoughts towards the perennial questions of life, death and purpose.
One of his teachers at Ealing, an Evangelical clergyman named Walter
Mayers, had already impressed Newman by his calm and cultivated faith.
Newman borrowed books from Mayers—all of them more or less Calvinist
—which opened his mind to serious religious influence for the first time.
One of them was the standard Evangelical Church history, an uncritical
book filled with inaccuracies but widely read in the early nineteenth
century. Milner's *History*[7] was like an explosion of light for Newman,
because in it he discovered the Fathers of the Church. It was not just
that his mood made him receptive; in these great Christian thinkers of
the fourth and fifth centuries he found a combination of intellect and
imagination which suited his temperament exactly. Reading the Fathers,
he was to say later, was like music to his mind; they were filled with
melody, rhythm and harmony, joys for the sensualist and the mathematician alike.

The really significant event of these months, however, carried him far
beyond books.

When I was fifteen [Newman wrote in the *Apologia*], a great change of
thought took place in me. I fell under the influences of a definite creed, and
received into my intellect impressions of dogma which, through God's mercy,
have never been effaced or obscured. Above and beyond the conversations and
sermons of the excellent man, long dead, who was the human means of this
beginning of divine faith in me, was the effect of the books which he put into
my hands, all of the school of Calvin. One of the first books I read was a
work of Romaine's; I neither recollect the title nor the contents, except one
doctrine, which of course I do not include among those which I believe have
come from a divine source, viz. the doctrine of final perseverance. I received it
at once, and believe that the inward conversion of which I was conscious (and
of which I still am more certain than I have hands and feet) would last into
the next life, and that I was elected to eternal glory. I have no consciousness
that this belief had any tendency whatever to lead me to be careless about
pleasing God. I retained it till the age of twenty-one, when it gradually faded
away; but I believe that it had some influence on my opinions, in the direction
of those childish imaginations, . . . in isolating me from the objects which
surrounded me, in confirming me in my mistrust of the reality of material

phenomena, making me rest in the thought of two and two only supreme and luminously self-evident beings, myself and my Creator.[8]

II

So John Henry Newman went up to Trinity College, Oxford, a fervent, recently converted Evangelical, surer of his predestined state than of the reality of his own limbs. Some of the accidental features of his first conversion were to pass quietly away, as he remarked in the passage just quoted. At least, those Calvinist features seemed accidental to him. Many Evangelicals, however, concluded that Newman's later activities proved that his youthful experience was not a genuine conversion, presumably because it lacked the permanent and thoroughly Protestant characteristics which had, for example, marked the vocation of John Wesley. However that may be, Newman remained convinced throughout his life that his discovery of the reality of God, in a piercingly direct way, possessed a permanence of its own. He had been a Roman Catholic for almost twenty years when he observed, "What I held in 1816, I held in 1833, and I hold in 1864. Please God, I shall hold it to the end."[9] That "earnestness of heart" which Robert Wilberforce claimed was the real fruit of the Evangelical revival, this, certainly, Newman carried with him all his life.

Trinity in 1817 was not a place frequented by morally earnest young men. The college was famous for indolent and hard-drinking undergraduates and indifferent scholarship. Newman had a difficult time of it at first. The presence in their midst of a serious student who played the violin rather well and who refused for religious reasons to get drunk brought out the worst in some of his collegiate companions. But Newman's cool self-possession and, when the occasion demanded it, his silent stare ultimately proved enough to disconcert his tormentors, who were, after all, more boisterous than mean. In the end he won the respect of all of them and the affection of a good many. He had, however, only one close friend at Trinity, the handsome, amiable John William Bowden, a wealthy youth whose father was a director of the Bank of England. They were inseparable in their college years and close friends until Bowden's death in 1844. Indeed, Bowden was the first of many to play Horatio to Newman's Hamlet.

By the end of his first year the authorities at Trinity knew they had a rare academic specimen in John Newman. They awarded him a nine-year college scholarship, worth about sixty pounds a year. It was not a small sum in those days and to a boy of seventeen it seemed a fortune. The scholarship gave him the satisfaction of easing the financial difficulties at home. It also opened up to him the possibility of a permanent

Oxford life. Newman began to look at the snapdragons that grew on the walls opposite his freshman rooms at Trinity as "the emblem of my perpetual residence even unto death in my University."[10]

The conversion of 1816 had brought with it the ideal of a celibate life. This did not become a practical and settled decision for Newman until 1829, but in the meantime it played a part in the plans he made for the future. During his undergraduate days he pretty well decided to be a clergyman, though at times he felt an attraction for a legal career. (When he was campaigning against Peel in 1829 someone said that he ought to go into politics.) But what kind of clergyman should he be? Anglican foreign missions were then in their infancy and they had a definite appeal. Yet one could not take a wife to some obscure and perhaps dangerous corner of Africa. Another possibility was to be a don in an Oxford college, and this too meant remaining single. And so the calculation went on for some time, with both alternatives involving a devotion to the service of the Church and a detachment from the ordinary bonds of family living.

Meanwhile, he pursued his studies in the relaxed atmosphere of Trinity. Everything interested him. He dabbled in the infant natural sciences, going to lectures in geology and mineralogy and trying chemical experiments on his own. He read the English philosophers, like Hume and Locke. Gibbon's style enthralled him even when he found the historical judgments scandalous. He memorized long passages in the Bible, and of course analyzed Euripides, disentangled Euclid, translated Horace. It was a joyful life for Newman, and it gave as much scope for his mind as was possible in an English university of a century and a half ago. He had his violin, too, and found like-minded friends to play quartets with. He and Bowden edited a comic undergraduate periodical, took long walks and rides together, and solved the world's problems in their endless conversations, as students usually do. It gradually came upon Newman that here, in Oxford, was where he wanted to stay.

The ordinary avenue to an Oxford career passed through the Honours Schools. In 1820, when Newman went up for his examination, all of Trinity was cheering him on and expecting him to be the first of their college ever to win a First Class. Instead he finished off the list entirely in mathematics and under-the-line in classics. What happened apparently was that a combination of badly frayed nerves, religious scruples and a foolish cramming schedule did him in. He had worked up to fifteen hours a day for months before the examination until, at the moment of truth, he was physically and emotionally exhausted. He was called up to the Schools a day earlier than expected; panic seized him, his mind went blank and he was unable to complete the examination. He had prayed that success would not prove an occasion of pride or worldliness to him. His prayer evidently was heard, and Trinity men gloomily concluded that if Newman could not succeed, there was no hope for any of their college.

Newman himself, however, suffered no permanent harm from his failure. Indeed, he entered the Honours Schools a boy and came out a man. Though humiliated and regretful, he engaged in no recrimination and no fruitless excuses. "It is all over and I have not succeeded," he wrote simply to his father, and there was an end to it. He was already showing that tough-fibered resilience which would carry him through many a dark hour in the years ahead. As for the present moment, all was far from lost. He still had his Trinity scholarship. He could earn extra money in private tutoring and help provide for his younger brothers' education. Most important, his confidence remained unshaken: he knew another chance would come. It did at Oriel, two years later. And so, with a brilliant rebound, Newman stood on that April day in the Oriel common room, accepting shyly the congratulations and welcome of the first men in Oxford: Copleston, Hawkins, Pusey's friend Richard Jelf, who had been elected fellow the year before, and then Keble: "When Keble advanced to take my hand," he wrote to Bowden, "I quite shrunk and could nearly have sunk into the floor, ashamed at so great an honour."[11]

III

"In 1822," Newman recalled in the *Apologia*, "I came under very different influences from those to which I had hitherto been subjected."[12] The new influences, however, did not include Keble, who spent little time in Oxford and of whom Newman saw hardly anything before Froude's election as fellow in 1826. Nor did Copleston deal much with the new don; Newman lived outside the college until 1826, and anyway the provost, intent on the nation's economic problems and looking around for a bishopric, found Newman's shy intensity somewhat repelling. With most of the older dons, Newman maintained pleasant but rather distant relations. His first close friend at Oriel was Pusey, elected in 1823. They both had lodgings in the same house, and before long they recognized that they were kindred spirits. For a while they walked regularly together and engaged in long, deadly serious conversations. But Pusey soon went off to Germany and when he returned it was not to Oriel but to marriage and the Hebrew professorship.

Perhaps it was an omen that Newman had been elected to the fellowship vacated by Thomas Arnold, for the significant influence upon him during the first phase of his Oriel life was wielded by two of Arnold's Noetic friends, Whately and Hawkins. Whately had resigned his fellowship the year before Newman's election. He spent the summer of 1822 in Oxford prior to assuming his parish living in Suffolk. During these few months, Newman remembered, "He used to take me out walking and riding, and he used to talk; and thus he was the first person who opened my mind, that is, who gave it ideas and principles to cogitate upon."[13] It must have been a fascinating sight, these two antipodal characters, the loud, florid Whately, wrapped in his pea-green coat, and the shy, skinny Newman, striding together down the High Street, with Whately's inseparable pack of dogs sniffing along behind them. But Whately was more than a talker; he was a great teacher. And Newman learned from him that summer, and again when Whately first returned to Oxford in 1825, all that the master had to teach about Aristotle and the utilitarian beauty of logic.

Whately, while he talked to Newman, was actually composing his book on logic. This was his way, to expound his ideas to a clever student and see what effect they had. He loaned Newman several papers he had written on logical subjects so that their conversations might be more genuinely dialogues. The rubbing of mind against mind was the method he had learned from Copleston and he passed it on to Newman. To Newman, also, Whately intrusted the writing of a few sections of the *Logic* which, when it appeared in book form, contained a graceful acknowledgment of Newman's part in the work.

Whately came back to Oxford in 1825 and became Principal of St. Alban Hall. Newman accepted his offer of the office of Vice-principal. This involved saying public prayers a few times a week for twelve unruly students and helping to put the hall's accounts in order. It might have meant a great deal more, had Newman chosen to take advantage of it, because Whately, now Dr. Whately, had begun his rapid climb up the ladder of ecclesiastical preferment, and he might have taken Newman a long way up with him. But by this time Newman had grown wary of Whately's liberal theology and the events of succeeding years were to make him more so. In 1826 he resigned the post at St. Alban Hall and became tutor at Oriel. Political differences lessened their intimacy and finally religious differences ended it altogether. In 1834 Whately wrote from Dublin suggesting the two of them collaborate in a new edition of "our *Logic*," but Newman declined. The disenchantment appeared complete when Newman remarked in Tom Mozely's hearing "that Whately's *Logic* was a most interesting book, but that there was one thing not to be found in it and that was logic."[14]

Newman's doubt as to whether he should be a don or a foreign missionary was practically settled by his election at Oriel. Accordingly, in June 1824 he was ordained a deacon (he received priest's orders a year later) and shortly afterwards took on the curacy of St. Clement's parish, Oxford. Shortage of money partially dictated this move (St. Clement's paid forty-five pounds a year plus stole fees), but more important was

Newman's conviction that pastoral work was the heart of his vocation. It was under these circumstances that he came to know Edward Hawkins. Hawkins at the time was Vicar of St. Mary's and he did everything he could to help his young colleague. Since they both had parochial responsibilities in Oxford, they often shared the Oriel common room almost by themselves, especially during the long vacations of 1824 and 1825. Hawkins went over Newman's sermons with him and advised him about the mysterious details of parochial administration. And he did more than that. "He was the first," said Newman, "who taught me to weigh my words and to be cautious in my statements. He led me to [a] mode of limiting and clearing my sense in discussion and controversy, and of distinguishing between cognate ideas, and of obviating mistakes by anticipation."[15] Newman developed great respect for Hawkins' practical abilities, and he did not hesitate to support him against Keble in the contest for the provostship in 1827. Unhappily, differences soon after cropped up between them.

IV

Newman succeeded Hawkins as Vicar of St. Mary's in 1828. In six short years at Oriel he had gained a wide experience. He had been parish curate, administrator of a residence hall, tutor in his college, and examiner in the Schools. He had published his first essay—an encyclopedia article on the life and works of Cicero—and, as Vicar of St. Mary's he stood on the verge of his dramatic success as a preacher. Much else of a more personal nature had happened, too. His father died in 1824, and Newman, gazing upon his corpse, wondered if anyone who sees a dead body could be a materialist. Mr. Newman's death put an end to any lingering hopes his son might have had to be a foreign missioner. In the midst of his duties as examiner in the Schools, in 1827, Newman was struck by a severe illness, more or less of a nervous character, which reminded him forcibly of the summer of 1816. A few months later, just after the new year of 1828, Mary Newman suddenly died. Of all the losses he suffered, none of them affected him so much as Mary's death; when he was past eighty the mention of her name could bring tears to his eyes. There is a famous line in the *Apologia* which refers to these events. "The truth is, I was beginning to prefer intellectual excellence to moral; I was drifting in the direction of liberalism. I was rudely awakened from my dream at the end of 1827 by two great blows—illness and bereavement."[16]

Newman's fundamental conviction, a conviction in which he never wavered from its beginning in 1816, was that everything bore upon the relationship between those two luminously self-evident beings, himself

and his Creator. Mary Newman's death was not only a sickeningly personal loss; it was also God's way of delivering her brother from the
preference for intellectual excellence. So at least he believed. It is curious
how many of the people who figured prominently in Newman's life
were to experience something similar. Keble had already felt it with the
death of his own sister Mary Anne. In time Henry Manning would lose
Caroline Sargent and Pusey would watch Maria Barker sink slowly and
painfully into death; and each man would carry the scar of bereavement
to his own grave. Yet somehow Newman's sorrows seemed to have a
depth, an almost cosmic character to them, which other men could not
reach. Perhaps, as the cynic might suggest, this appears to be the case
because Newman talked about his bereavement (or more accurately,
wrote about it), while Manning, for example, kept a tight-lipped, ascetic
silence about his. Or maybe Newman's immense self-awareness made him
feel such things with an intensity which most men escape. More likely
the whole subject is something for the mystics to unravel.

In any case, Newman began his tenure as Vicar of St. Mary's in a
chastened mood. His Evangelical leanings had pretty much passed away,
without, however, lessening in his mind the impression of his original
conversion. He had learned a respect for Whately's mental agility and
Hawkins' shrewdness, but the substance of their respective liberalism
and Toryism had been smothered in the wake of Mary Newman's death.

At Oriel there were new faces and new currents of influence. Froude
had been elected fellow in 1826 and with him another of Keble's favourite
students, Robert Isaac Wilberforce.[17] The brightest of William Wilberforce's sons, Robert wore his famous name with graceful modesty, and
he brought it honours of his own: a Double First in 1824, an Oriel
fellowship two years later, and a constant reputation for solid scholarship.
Among the undergraduates was Henry Wilberforce, Robert's youngest
brother, who, though not on a par with Robert, was intelligent enough
to win a First in classics and a Second in mathematics in 1830. His
friendship with Newman, filled with many stormy ups and downs, began
when Newman was his tutor at Oriel. Another of Newman's students
was Thomas Mozley, a clever, lazy, personable young man from Derby,
who imitated Newman by finishing under-the-line in the Honours Schools
in 1828 and then being elected Fellow of Oriel the next year. Mozley
later married Harriet Newman. Frederic Rogers came up to Oriel from
Eton in 1828. He was afflicted with poor eyesight, but he possessed a
dozen compensating characteristics of mind and spirit. His wit belied his
gentleness and loyalty and his deep intellectual integrity. He took a
Double First in 1832 and the following spring, while Froude (his tutor)
and Newman were traveling in the Mediteranean, he was elected Fellow
of Oriel.

The presence of these young men, and others like them, brought home to Newman the fact that he was now in a position to influence as well as be influenced. How conscious this awareness was remains debatable. At any rate, he saw, however hazily, the possibility of creating at Oriel the ideal of the Christian university, mixing together Keble's lofty religious sentiments, the Copleston-Whately tradition of dialectical learning, and his own unique gift of communication. Without dreaming of the possible consequences, Newman determined upon the reform of the tutorial system. Across his path he found the ponderous, immovable figure of Edward Hawkins.[18]

Oriel maintained four tutors. After 1828 these were Joseph Dornford, Newman, Froude and Robert Wilberforce. Dornford, an eccentric but able don, was the senior and, by a strict interpretation of college statutes, the only tutor, the other three acting as his assistants. In practice, however, this distinction did not apply at Oriel or any other college. Dornford with some reluctance agreed to go along with his three young colleagues in the implementation of Newman's plan. In brief, that plan called for a reassessment of the tutor's position within the college and a new emphasis upon his post as a religious and personal responsibility. Instead of a tutor's merely lecturing a few times a week on certain classical texts to a group of college undergraduates—the customary practice—he should take upon himself the obligation of the direct religious training of the undergraduates assigned to him, and, at the same time, see to their secular instruction in a detailed and personal way. This twofold aspect of the tutor's task seemed to Newman closer to the ideal established in the university statutes, more in harmony with the religious character of the university and with the clerical status of the tutors themselves, and more beneficial to the development of the students' minds.

This latter point, of course, echoed Whately and behind him Copleston; there was little doubt that since the departure of Whately the quality of Oriel instruction had deteriorated to the cramming for Firsts which he and Copleston so much despised. Also, there was not much question that moral and religious subjects had been for a long time left out of Oxford education, despite its ecclesiastical connection. Newman saw education as an encounter between the ripe mind of the tutor and the young, eager, but inexperienced mind of the pupil.

In theory it sounded well enough, but Provost Hawkins was not a theoretical man, especially now that he was the college's chief administrator. It was not that he opposed the Noetic ideal; he was in his limited way a representative of it. Nor did he object to an emphasis upon the undergraduates' religious instruction; he deplored as much as anyone the low moral tone which pervaded the university. The trouble was that like his friend Hampden, Hawkins tended to see religious education as moral training, and he was afraid that a tutor who considered himself a pastor might think it his right to impose Evangelical or Anglo-Catholic views upon his students. And with names like Froude and Wilberforce prominent in the controversy, one can understand the provost's point. In a patchwork of compromises like the Church of England this would obviously be bad administration.

Worse still, in Hawkins' judgment, was the prospect of turning over the college, for all practical purposes, to the tutors. Neither the provost nor the rest of the fellows would have any control over the undergraduates if Newman's plan were adopted. The tutor, not the foundation of Oriel itself, would be the final arbiter with regard to his own students. This would be particularly the case if, as Hawkins feared, the tutors introduced new studies and authors into the old curriculum. Then a man would go up to the Schools as a representative of Mr. X or Mr. Y, his tutor, rather than of Oriel College, the members of which knew nothing of what he had studied. This last threat especially led Hawkins to adopt his stand-pat position and to insist upon the old ways being the best ways. But he also pointed out, with perhaps better justification, that Newman's system depended upon the ability of the tutors. What happened to the undergraduate turned over body and soul to the incompetent tutor? Or what happened to the college if the tutors fell out among themselves?

The new system began to operate in 1829 without Hawkins' knowledge. Strictly speaking, the tutors were within their rights to proceed without the provost's formal approval. When he discovered what was afoot, Hawkins instructed the tutors to revert to the old lecture system. Because of a variety of misunderstandings, this was not done. By the spring of 1830, Dornford had grown very uneasy about the whole matter and he raised it at a college meeting. Hawkins reiterated his demand that the new practices be discontinued. Newman, Froude and Wilberforce refused. But Hawkins had the trump card. Since as provost he assigned undergraduates to their tutors, he simply stopped sending any more to the three recalcitrant tutors. By June 1831 the last of their students had graduated, and bitterness had replaced the old comradely spirit between Newman and Hawkins.

The quarrel over the tuition had many other side effects. Hawkins, faced with three tutors to whom he would send no students, called in R. D. Hampden, now back in Oxford, to come to Oriel and fill the gap by giving lectures. Poor Hampden's style, or lack of it, showed up poorly when compared to the brilliance of Newman, Froude and Wilberforce; but more ominous were the seeds of future animosity which were sown by bringing Hampden, of all people, in to meet the crisis. Robert Wilberforce left Oxford when he ran out of students. Lord Brougham, the Whig chancellor and an old ally of William Wilberforce in the struggle against the slave trade, gave him a parish living in Kent, which he accepted, much to Newman's displeasure, in 1832. As for Newman himself, the quarrel demonstrated how tough and unyielding he could be on what he considered a matter of principle; "flinty" was the word Frederic Rogers used to describe this quality.[19] As the trouble alienated him from Hawkins, so it brought him closer to Froude. They had gone down together, all guns firing; they had neither knuckled under to Hawkins nor accepted favours from Lord Brougham. Though he lived to regret his harsh feelings towards Hawkins, Newman never doubted that his reform plan was right, and he could not but have noticed that with the defeat of the three tutors, Oriel began its slide down to a second-rate position in the university. He would have been less than human if he had not taken some grim satisfaction in that.

V

In his first published work young Mr. Newman of Oriel criticized Cicero for his "want of firmness."[20] That was a fault which the author himself never had. Even so, his poetic and mathematical mind was highly impressionable, and as he celebrated his thirty-second birthday in the late winter of 1833 it displayed the marks of the crosscurrents set up by people he had known and experiences he had had, in London, at Ealing, at Trinity and most of all at Oriel. Some ideas he still kept fresh as they had first come to him. This was especially true of the conversion of 1816, with its conviction that religion was a creed, not a sentiment, and that God's presence was a real, almost a palpable thing. He kept also the intellectual devotion to the writings of the Fathers. Seventeen years of reflection and study had only deepened it, and the association with Keble had lent it the fervour of a grand and gallant cause. Perhaps this was what Froude meant when he spoke of bringing Newman and Keble together. For Newman the bourgeois Londoner, the Ancient Christian Church was an intellectual phenomenon, an abstraction produced by his own mind. But for Keble, his roots deep in the Anglo-Catholic tradition of the English countryside, the Ancient Church was home and warmth, a familiar haven and a friendly beacon.

Other ideas Newman rejected out of hand or else toyed with for a while and then set aside. Among these were Evangelicalism, the liberalism as preached by Whately, and the High and Dry Tory tradition, exemplified, in Newman's mind, by Hawkins after 1831. Yet he had learned an enormous amount from Whately and Hawkins, and not just about the uses of Aristotle or how to deal with Oxford tradesmen. Whately had taught him the essential independence of the Church from the state; he had shown him too how the Thirty-nine Articles might be viewed so that a man of liberal sympathies could accept them. Newman saw the point and changed "liberal" to "catholic." From Hawkins he absorbed the extremely important lesson that the Bible could not be a manual of Christian instruction without the guiding hand of tradition. Hawkins did not arrive at the same conclusion that Newman ultimately did, but he put his young colleague on the track. These were the men, Newman frankly acknowledged, who first opened his mind, and taught him to weigh his words.

He discovered that his words could work magic. His study of Cicero gave him an arresting insight into himself. "In deliberative oratory, . . . great part of the effect of the composition depends on its creating in the hearer a high opinion of the speaker"; Cicero's accomplishment was "to elicit that confidence in him without which argument has little influence." Newman had the ability to create that same kind of confidence in himself, whether as tutor, preacher or counselor. And he came to realize that he could do it with written as well as spoken words. He was no more a poet, in the literal sense, than Keble and yet the verses he wrote possessed a force which Keble's delicate lines lacked. In another early essay, Newman described his theory of poetry, which may help to explain that impact. "A right moral state of heart," he wrote, "is the formal and scientific condition of the poetical mind." He did not mean that a poet must display explicitly a religious bent; the raw materials of poetry are a matter of indifference. But, said Newman, the poet must show that his peculiar kind of originality, the essence of his talent, is "the originality of right moral feeling."[21] Moral probity is the highest expression of the beautiful and the true.

Whately called this essay a Platonic mishmash, but by the time he wrote it—1829—Newman was not much concerned about Whately's opinions. Three years later he cared even less. In 1831 Newman was approached by Hugh James Rose—the same gentleman who had engaged in controversy with Pusey—to take part in a project which Rose was editing called the Theological Library. Newman accepted Rose's proposal to write a history of the councils of the Church. He set to work on the first council, Nicea, and that was as far as he got. Indeed, he hardly got to Nicea, because his researches into the Arian controversy drove him back beyond Nicea to an investigation of the roots of the heresy and the movements of thoughts which had given rise to it. The result was his first book, *The Arians of the Fourth Century*.

This is not the place to analyze Newman's *Arians*. Suffice it to say that it was an able piece of theological and historical scholarship which can be read with profit even now, when the boundaries of our factual knowledge of the third and fourth centuries have been vastly expanded. Of more immediate interest are the indications the book gave of Newman's immediate past and hints to his future. There was, for example, an undisguised slap at Whately: One of the chief causes of the rise of Arianism, Newman charged, was the misuse of Aristotle's "logical system" which "confessedly is [best suited] to baffle an adversary or at least to detect error, rather than to establish truth."[22] And he lashed out too at the whole crowd of liberal heretics (a word he now used in the same sense as Froude). The Christian must give different treatment, he wrote, to

an individual in heresy and to one who is confident enough to publish the innovations which he has originated. The former claims from us the most affectionate sympathy and the most considerate attention. The latter should meet with no mercy; he assumes the office of the Tempter, and, so far forth as his error goes, must be dealt with by the competent authority, as if he were embodied evil. To spare him is a false and dangerous pity. It is to endanger the souls of thousands and it is uncharitable towards himself.[23]

At the time he wrote these words at Oriel, perhaps at the very moment, Renn Dickson Hampden was delivering the Bampton Lectures across the street at St. Mary's.

There was one section of *Arians* which contained a real trumpet blast. Newman took great care to describe the doctrine of "reserve" as he found it in the pre-Nicene Church. Nothing was to be more central to the whole idea of the Oxford Movement, and nothing was to cause the Movement more difficulty in winning acceptance than this notion. Newman understood reserve as a teaching method. Our Lord had said that pearls ought not to be cast before swine, and this statement the Ancient Church had converted into the famous *Disciplina Arcani* (literally, the discipline of the secret). Not everything ought to be said to all people all the time, might be a loose way of stating it. The theologians of the pre-Nicene Alexandrian school (whom Newman championed throughout his book) wrote "not with the openness of Christian familiarity, but with the tenderness or the reserve with which we are accustomed to address those who do not sympathize with us, or whom we fear to mislead or to prejudice against the truth by precipitate disclosures of its details." What this amounts to, Newman continued, is an accommodation of teaching to the condition of the taught. "Those who are strangers to the tone of thought and principles of the speaker cannot at once be initiated into his system."[24] This may sound like good pedagogy and indeed it is, but in the wrong hands it could sound devious and underhanded and not quite truthful and, in the pejorative sense, jesuitical. For the average Englishman, liberal, Evangelical or High and Dry, reserve was to be the great scandal of the Oxford Movement.

VI

Newman, of course, did not know that when he finished *Arians* at the end of 1832. Indeed, he did not yet know there was to be an Oxford Movement. At the moment his attention was focused on his forthcoming trip to the Mediterranean with Hurrell and Archdeacon Froude. It was Newman's first trip abroad. They left shortly before Christmas.

The story of what happened has been told many times, best of all by Newman himself. The climax came in Sicily, where Newman traveled alone and fell gravely ill, to the point that he thought he might well die. In the first days of May 1833 "They gave me over for a week, but my servant said he thought I should get well from the avidity with which I always took my medicine. . . . I gave him a direction to write to if I died (Froude), but I said, 'I do not think I shall. I have not sinned against the light,' or 'God has still work for me to do.' I think the latter."[25]

Or perhaps both. In July he came back to England, thin and drawn, but filled with more vigour than he had ever known. He came back to the England where Grey and Peel ruled the state, and where Whately was an archbishop, and Hawkins was the head of his college. He came back to purify the sons of Levi that they might offer unto the Lord an offering in righteousness. He came back to fight. Thomas Arnold's son Matthew, long afterwards, wrote a few lines which describe Newman perfectly in that breathless moment:

> One of that small transfigured band
> Whom the world could not tame.[26]

PART II

The Transfigured Band
1833–39

CHAPTER 6

July Days

J OHN KEBLE made his careful way through the nave and up the steps of the tall pulpit in the Church of St. Mary the Virgin in Oxford. He set his manuscript on the lectern, took out a pair of spectacles and put them on. Scattered along the benches below him, together with a few academics who had not deserted Oxford for the long vacation, sat the members of the summer Assize Court, the judges, lawyers and functionaries of that circuit court which held sessions every year in all the counties of England. The service they attended was one of the formalities of the circuit, indicating perhaps that ancient preference of Englishmen for legal proceedings which gave at least a gesture towards the divine Lawgiver. The legal gentlemen looked up now at the slight, bespectacled figure, who had been appointed preacher of the day by the university Vice-chancellor, and they heard him read carefully a text from the first book of Samuel. It was Sunday, July 14, 1833, the day, Newman wrote more than three decades later, "I have ever considered and kept as the start of the religious movement of 1833."[1]

And by a pure coincidence, though not without some symbolic interest, it was also Bastille Day.

I

Keble's Assize sermon took him about thirty-five minutes to deliver. From the opening text to the end, he tried to evoke the Old Testament days when the people of Israel had come to the prophet and demanded the establishment of a monarchy. Keble began by quoting Samuel's reply: "As for me, God forbid that I should sin against the Lord in ceasing to pray for you; but I will teach you the good and the right way." This Christian nation, Keble charged, stands in perilous similarity to the

Jews of old who cheerfully exchanged the freedom of God's children for the tyranny of Saul. There are those, unhappily, who, "without any scruple or ceremony," dismiss the lessons of the Old Testament as obsolete. "That portion, in particular, of the history of the chosen people, which drew from Samuel, the truest of patriots, the wise and noble sentiment in the text, must ever be an unpleasing and perplexing page of Scripture to those who would fain persuade themselves that a nation, even a Christian nation, may do well enough, as such, without God and without his Church."

But one cannot so easily escape the consequences of God's Word. "Men must own (what is clear at once to plain unsophisticated readers) that this first overt act, which began the downfall of the Jewish nation, stands on record, with its fatal consequences, for a perpetual warning to all nations, as well as to all individual Christians, who, having accepted God for their king, allow themselves to be weary of subjection to him, and think they would be happier if they were freer and more like the rest of the world."

The signs of this weariness [said Keble] are all around. One of the most alarming, as a symptom, is the growing indifference, in which men indulge themselves to other men's religious sentiments. Under the guise of charity and toleration we are come almost to this pass, that no difference, in matters of faith, is to disqualify for our approbation and confidence, whether in public or domestic life. Can we conceal it from ourselves, that every year the practice is becoming more common, of trusting men unreservedly in the most delicate and important matters, without one serious enquiry, whether they do not hold principles which make it impossible for them to be loyal to their Creator, Redeemer and Sanctifier? Are not offices conferred, partnerships formed, intimacies courted—nay (what is almost too painful to think of), do not parents commit their children to be educated, do they not encourage them to intermarry, in houses on which apostolical authority would rather teach them to set a mark as unfit to be entered by a faithful servant of Christ?

Keble did not mention explicitly that Parliament, the Church's legislature as well as the state's, was now crowded with papists and Dissenters, or that the imminent passage of the Act suppressing ten Anglican dioceses in Ireland—the "Robbery Bill" as he called it in private—demonstrated the government's callous intention to infringe the Church's apostolical rights. But no one could have missed his inferences. "The point really to be considered is, whether, according to the coolest estimate, the fashionable liberality of this generation be not ascribable, in a great measure, to the same temper which led the Jews voluntarily to set about degrading themselves to a level with the idolatrous Gentiles. And, if it be true anywhere, that such enactments are forced on the legislature by public opinion, is apostasy too hard a word to describe the temper of that nation?"

What must churchmen, laity and clergy alike do in these parlous times? They must, said Keble, dedicate themselves to the Church's work of intercession and remonstrance, no matter what happens. They must, in other words, follow the pattern of Samuel, who did not cease praying for his people nor from patiently showing them the good and the right way. This duty is especially incumbent upon public servants like those who belonged to the Assize Court. "Now in proportion as anyone sees reason to fear that such is, or soon may be, the case in his own land, just so far may he see reason to be thankful, especially if he be called to any national trust, for such a complete pattern of his duty as he may find in the conduct of Samuel. That combination of sweetness with firmness, of consideration with energy, which constitutes the temper of a perfect public man, was never perhaps so beautifully exemplified."

It was typical of Keble that he saw the solution of the institutional crisis in terms of the individual's virtue. "After all, the surest way to uphold or restore our endangered Church will be for each of her anxious children, in his own place and station, to resign himself more thoroughly to his God and Saviour in those duties, public and private, which are not immediately affected by the emergencies of the moment: the daily and hourly duties, I mean, of piety, purity, charity, justice. . . . This ought to be felt, for example, as one motive more to exact punctuality in those duties, personal and official, which the return of an Assize week offers to our practice; one reason more for veracity in witnesses, fairness in pleaders, strict impartiality, self-command, and patience in those on whom decisions depend; and for an awful sense of God's presence in all."

As dark as the present moment may appear, Keble concluded, let us take heart. The struggle may be long and lonely, but he who chooses God gains the ultimate victory. "If he be consistent, he possesses to the utmost the personal consolation of a good Christian; and as a true churchman he has that encouragement which no other cause in the world can impart in the same degree—he is calmly, soberly, demonstrably sure that, sooner or later, his will be the winning side, and that victory will be complete, universal, eternal."[2]

II

As John Keble, Fellow of Oriel College and Professor of Poetry in the University of Oxford, left St. Mary's pulpit that July Sunday, he had no idea that he had thrown down the gauntlet before the forces of liberalism. The Assize sermon was a straightforward, even a bold, statement of the contemporary religious crisis, but only hindsight, Newman's in this instance, could have judged it the beginning of a "movement." It

appeared to have had little effect upon the congregation to which it
was preached; of course, public men are not necessarily attentive to
sermons delivered on formal occasions, even when the preacher is a
famous university don and a minor poet besides. Then, too, the Keble
charm, irresistible in small and intimate circles, was never at its most
telling in the pulpit of a large church; and St. Mary's was an especially
difficult place to read in. Thomas Keble, John's younger brother and
lifelong confidant, who was the only one to see the sermon before its
delivery, certainly did not consider it a revolutionary document. His
advice was brotherly and prosaic: John should read in a quick and lively
manner and he should be sure to wear his spectacles.[3]

The sermon, then, was no manifesto. When he returned to Fairford,
Keble arranged to have it printed and circulated, but this was common
practice and it did not indicate that Keble was under any illusions. He
planned to send published copies of the sermon to influential people,
because, as he explained to Newman with more than conventional
modesty, "otherwise, like many of its betters, it will surely pass away as
a dream."[4] Keble entitled the sermon "National Apostasy," and this made
something of a stir. Yet even then Pusey, for one, did not bother to read
the complimentary copy which Keble sent him.[5]

What made the National Apostasy sermon significant far beyond its
substance was the accident of time. The Act suppressing the Irish dioceses
was passing through its final stages during the July of 1833, and the
fears of churchmen had reached their peak. What nobody could have
known at the moment was that never again would the ruin of the
Church of England seem so close as it did in the summer of 1833. High
Church and Low, Evangelicals and Apostolicals, everyone, indeed, except the small minority of liberals like Whately and Hampden, believed
that a point of peculiar peril had been reached. The time had come to
resist. The Oxford Movement—"the religious movement of 1833," to
use Newman's phrase—began as part of a larger struggle, part of a
rallying of all the friends of the Church to a sacred cause which, temporarily, pushed into the background their other differences. That it
survived the particular crisis which gave it birth, that it ceased after a
while to be associated with the general *ralliement* and became instead a
party, is a key to an understanding of the Oxford Movement's later
fortunes. With this qualification, Keble's sermon can be called, as Newman called it, a beginning.

III

During that same ominous July, other English churchmen had decided
upon action. They did not know precisely what action they should take

or what support they could expect. "But in those hours of darkness," one of them recalled, "there were hearts, many hearts, burning with shame and grief for the general apostasy around them."[6] Two of those hearts belonged to Hugh James Rose, editor of a High Church monthly called the *British Magazine*, and to William Palmer, of Worcester College, Oxford, a young Irishman with a considerable reputation for ecclesiastical scholarship. "Rose and Palmer," Keble wrote his brother Tom a few days after the Assize sermon was delivered, "want me to go to Rose's a-visiting, to confer about the Mag[azine], but I really can't give up the time for pleasure and don't think 'twould quite answer for profit."[7] Keble hated to travel and he never left his Fairford fireside if he could help it; and when he wrote his brother, he habitually assumed a light if not a frivolous tone. Yet, granting Keble's foibles, his casual dismissal of this invitation indicates how little of design there was in the beginnings of the Movement, because the meeting, held without Keble at Rose's Suffolk vicarage, during the last week of July 1833, was the celebrated Hadleigh Conference.

The host, the Vicar of Hadleigh, was a man of parts.[8] Thirty-eight years old in the summer of 1833, Hugh James Rose was a clergyman's son who traced his lineage back to medieval Scotland. The Rose family stood high among the gentry of Sussex. Hugh went to Trinity College, Cambridge, in 1813, where he performed brilliantly in classics and a little less so in mathematics. Much to his disappointment he failed to win election to a Trinity fellowship in 1818. A year later he was ordained, married and vicar of a Sussex parish. The real center of his activities, however, remained in Cambridge. For the most part he moved on the edge of university life, giving a series of sermons here or there. He raised a lonely High Church voice amid the prevalent Evangelical and liberal sentiments of most Cambridge men. Above all, he made friends, not only in Cambridge but around the country and with a good many powerful people. Among his intimates were several noblemen, several bishops and the leader of the mild Anglo-Catholic revival, Joshua Watson.

Rose was a tall, thin, slope-shouldered man, with sharp features and a grave, solemn air. He had a good voice and a flair for pulpit oratory. His sermons were memorable if somewhat pompous affairs. One contemporary recalled the authoritative manner and grand intonation with which he read the ten commandments: "it was as if Mr. Rose had been personally commissioned to deliver the decalogue to the congregation."[9] Everyone who met him noticed the lines of suffering which cut deep into his face; from his boyhood Rose suffered from weak lungs and as a man he was ravaged by continuous attacks of asthma.

The turning point in Rose's career was a German holiday his doctors ordered him to take during 1824 and 1825. He was gone for exactly twelve months. Like most Englishmen of his class Rose was wholly ignorant and slightly contemptuous of things German. Germany, after all, was a collection of funny little principalities like Thackeray's Grand Duchy of Pumpernickel whose duke was called His Transparency, whose foreign minister had rooms over the undertaker's parlour and whose army "consisted of a magnificent band that also did duty on the stage" of the opera house.[10] The reality, Rose discovered, was quite otherwise. With regard to his own professional interests he had expected to find among Christian intellectuals a vague but polite and gentlemanly form of Lutheranism, not too far removed, perhaps, from the spirit prevailing in Cambridge common rooms. Instead he found, as Pusey did at about the same time, the theological faculties in the middle of a seething intellectual revolution, with all the excitement and uncertainty attendant upon such moments. Rose may have been stuffy but he was no fool. He did not have to listen long to the disciples of Semler and Schleiermacher to realize that he was in a den of rationalists.

Back in England Rose raised the alarm. As Cambridge select preacher for May 1825, he delivered four lectures in which he castigated the Church in Germany as "the mere shadow of a name." Published the same year under the title *State of the Protestant Religion in Germany*, Rose's views caused an uproar in theological circles both in England and in Germany. As we have seen, there followed an acrimonious controversy between Rose and Pusey which dragged on for several years and left wounds still unhealed in 1833. Few English churchmen were equipped to follow the debate. They knew that Rose said that rationalism was about to swallow up the Church in Germany and that the English were indeed fortunate to possess an episcopal structure and the standard formularies and liturgy which could save their Church from a similar fate. They knew that Pusey said it was all a great deal more complicated than they supposed, and then they lost him in the fog of his incredible prose. But when the successive blows fell—the repeal of the Test Acts (1828), Catholic emancipation (1829), the Reform Act (1832), and finally the suppression of the Irish dioceses (1833)—when, in other words, the liberal attack had been mounted against those very things, the episcopacy not excluded, which Rose had maintained in 1825 could alone protect the Church from rationalism, the debate appeared more academic than before. Whatever the exact nature of the aberrations of German theologians (who, after all, were foreigners), Rose championed old England, the Church and the king, while Pusey had favoured Catholic emancipation and owed his preferment to the traitor Robert Peel. Rose, in short, became predictably a leader of the Church's resistance.

He wore the mantle of a prophet with good grace. His concern was genuine and his gifts considerable. Though cautious, he was warm in his devotion to any good cause. His important connections did not inhibit his candour. He spoke out plainly that the evils of the day were the villainy of godless politicians and the apathy of the clergy. In 1832 he founded the *British Magazine* to combat both. He was from that moment more than ever a rallying point. Newman expressed perfectly the regard which Rose's dedication to the Church of England earned him: Rose was the man "who when hearts were failing, bade us stir up the gift that was in us and betake ourselves to our true Mother."[11]

IV

Rose turned for support to Oxford out of sheer necessity. "I get no help whatever from Cambridge," he complained. "I love Cambridge to my heart; but Divinity is not her tower of strength just now."[12] During the long vacation of 1832 Rose came to Oxford seeking contributors for his new magazine. At Oriel he met Newman and Froude, who were both in residence that summer. Rose had already had some dealings with Newman, since he—Rose—was one of the editors of the Theological Library for which Newman had agreed to write.

Rose received a cordial welcome at Oriel. Newman and Froude both agreed to do whatever they could to help the *British Magazine*, though they told Rose that their projected Mediterranean tour might mean some practical delay. They promised as well to enlist the aid of some of their friends—notably Keble and Robert Wilberforce—in providing a source of regular contribution.

The upshot of this agreement was the collection of edifying verse called *Lyra Apostolica* which appeared in Rose's magazine over the next four years. Newman, later in the autumn of 1832 and just before he and Froude departed for the Mediterranean, explained the idea to Rose.

We propose, if you will let us, on our return to systematize a poetry department for you—which I am sanguine will be above the ordinary run of such exhibitions and may be useful. We shall ask two pages in each number, and shall insert in that space four brief compositions, each bringing out forcibly *one* idea. You will smile at our planning such details, before you have heard a word about it; but if it interferes with any plan of yours, of course we shall take a negative from you very lightly. Our object is to bring out certain truths and facts, moral, ecclesiastical and religious, simply and forcibly—with greater freedom and clearness than in *The Christian Year*. I will not go on to say, with greater poetry. If it answered on trial, we should be content to carry it on *ad infinitum*. It might be called, *Lyra Apostolica*.[13]

The following March Newman sent Rose from Rome the first two numbers of the *Lyra*, which he suggested might appear in the May and June issues of the *British Magazine*. Newman's conditions for publication were precisely stated: "I will make two requests: first, that no poetry from other correspondents should follow the *Lyra* so closely as to seem to come under its title. Next (which your better judgment may decline in granting), that you would put a line of notice before every number of the *Lyra* to signify that 'The editor is not responsible for the opinions contained in it.' This would set us at liberty to speak freely, which might be inexpedient in a known person such as yourself."[14]

Keble did not like the title *Lyra Apostolica*,[15] but eventually he, Wilberforce, John Bowden, and a Trinity College, Oxford, man named Isaac Williams joined Newman and Froude in contributing to the collection. Like *The Christian Year*, the *Lyra* scorned art for art's sake. The poems appeared regularly (and anonymously) in Rose's magazine and later they were published in a separate volume. They were presented to the public "in the humble hope that they may be instrumental in recalling or recommending to the reader important Christian truths which are at this day in a way to be forgotten."[16] The result was verse technically proper, didactic to the extreme and deadly dull.

Newman wrote the majority of the poems, Williams only one or two. Bowden's were perhaps the worst, with such titles as "National Degradation" and "The Religion of the Majority" giving a hint as to their character. Wilberforce's offerings included several complicated treatments of individual writers of the Ancient Church, like Origen, Basil and Clement. Froude managed to get some feeling into his contributions, but Keble for the most part did not reach even the severely limited level of *The Christian Year*. Take, for example, his "Churchman to his Lamp":

> Come, twinkle in my lonely room
> Companion true in hours of gloom;
> Come, light me on a little space,
> The heavenly vision to retrace,
> By saints and angels loved so well—
> My Mother's glories ere she fell.

The "lamp," evidently, meant to convey the idea of the brilliance of the early Church—the "Mother," who now has fallen on bad times. Here is another thrilling stanza:

> Then, hours of prayer in welcome round,
> Far-severed hearts together bound.
> Seven times a day, *on bended knee*,
> They to their Saviour cried; and we—
> One hour we find in seven long days,
> Before our God to *sit* and *gaze*.[17]

Keble was distressed that one Anglican service a week had replaced the once universal daily regimen of canonical prayer. Though one may sympathize with him, yet what comment can one offer about poetry which needs italics to make its point?

V

It was William Palmer[18] who invited Rose to Oxford in the summer of 1832. He too agreed to contribute to the *British Magazine,* not poetry, but a couple of articles on the principles of the various non-Anglican Protestant sects. The articles duly appeared; they were tedious, correct and quite forgettable. Palmer later complained that his articles were widely quoted without acknowledgment.[19]

In a way William Palmer played a genuinely tragic role in the history of the Oxford Movement. As his articles on the Dissenters failed to be properly acknowledged, so, in his mind, his contribution to the defense of the Church of England went virtually ·inrecognized, lost in the glare of Newman's brilliant wrongheadedness. Palmer, the son of a military officer, was born in Dublin in 1803. He took his degree at Trinity College, Dublin, and was ordained an Angelican priest before his arrival in Oxford in 1828. He settled eventually at Worcester College. Not yet thirty when Rose first met him, Palmer nevertheless already possessed a measure of fame. His reputation appeared to be partly based upon the rather vaguely but generally held notion that Palmer had an expert knowledge of Roman Catholic theology, which was one more area of which contemporary English divines were appallingly ignorant. "Palmer knows all about Bellarmine," one don would say to another, and the Irishman's stature would increase another cubit.

More securely, however, Palmer's fame after 1832 rested upon the two volumes he published that year called *Origines Liturgicae,*[20] a careful and workmanlike inquiry into the sources of the Book of Common Prayer. Palmer's thesis, which he supported with a wide quotation and comparison of ancient liturgical texts, was that the English liturgy was in fact what all High Churchmen presumed it to be, a contemporary expression of the forms of worship used in the Primitive Church. Defense of the Prayer Book's integrity was a matter of practical importance in 1832, and so one may assume that Rose was particularly delighted to enlist as one of his writers that rare High Churchman who knew something about it.

Palmer responded to Rose's overtures with enthusiasm. He saw his chance not only to write a few articles for a magazine but to take a leading place in a crusade. Palmer brought Rose to Oriel and introduced him to Newman and Froude, and he must have felt a glow of excitement as he saw himself acting as a bridge between Cambridge and Oxford. Unhappily for him, however, he misread the situation. Palmer possessed a disability which, even had he been more gifted than he was, he could never have overcome. It was neither his humourlessness nor his pomposity nor even his vindictiveness, which latter, by the way, appeared only long years afterwards and under great provocation. Palmer's sin was his nationality. He was an Irishman. He stood outside the Oxford inner circle and no matter how hard he knocked the door was never opened to him. Newman granted in the *Apologia* that in 1833 Palmer "was the only really learned man among us." But, added Newman, "he was deficient in depth; and besides, coming from a distance, he never had really grown into an Oxford man, nor was he generally received as such."21 Keble was not above criticizing Palmer's prose because of its "Irishisms."22 Palmer did not wear the old school tie; he did indeed come "from a distance," from across that infinity called the Irish Sea. The natural snobbery of an academic community, heightened by ancient national bias, foredoomed Palmer to a minor role, even if substantial differences had not arisen between him and the Oriel men. In the end, with the Movement seemingly in shambles, William Palmer was a bitter outsider indeed.

VI

But in July 1833 Palmer, with Rose, took the stance of a prime mover. The invitation which Keble received to Hadleigh came from them both. Keble, as we have seen, predictably refused to attend. "My dear friend," he wrote to Rose,

Mr. Palmer has communicated to me your kind and tempting invitation which I heartily wish it was in my power to accept. Believe me, few schemes would be more pleasant to me, if I was in a condition to indulge in schemes at all. But my father's great age and failing health, and the circumstance that he has no one to be with him in my absence but my sister, who is never well, make me quite a home bird. . . . Nevertheless I would put by everything and come to you if I could persuade myself that I could be of much use in discussions such as you and our friends are meditating; but I know my own deficiency in ecclesiastical learning so well as to be quite prepared to *hear* or *read* with great profit what might pass on such an occasion, but very unequal to *suggest* or *argue* points at the time. And this is really the plain truth, and makes me tolerably sure that altho' *I* should deeply regret missing such a visit as you offer me, your *counsels* will have no great loss.23

Keble wrote this letter on July 16, two days after he delivered his Assize sermon. This was not the last time that his strange combination of indolence and self-doubt was to make him a difficult ally.

Still, Keble did not go unrepresented at Hadleigh. Hurrell Froude traveled down to Suffolk for the conference, and so did another of Keble's former Oriel pupils, the Honourable and Reverend Arthur Philip Perceval.24

Tom Mozley observed years later that Perceval had the "extraordinary idea of the Hadleigh conference as if it were at once a great beginning and a grand finality."[25] Though Mozley perhaps overstated the facts (as he often did) for the sake of effect, Arthur Perceval's career did reach a kind of peak at Hadleigh, and for the rest of his life he gave the impression of one trying to scramble up to the heights and to sit once more in council with the great ones of the land. Unhappily for him, the great ones seldom seemed interested in conferring with him. Like Palmer, once the ball began to roll Perceval had to step aside to make room for those swifter than he. Because of his limited intelligence, he did so with less grace than Palmer, but, for the same reason, probably with less bitterness as well. An enlightening comment on Perceval's impact was John Keble's gentle rebuke to his brother Tom, who could never remember how to spell Perceval's name.[26]

That name, however, was the most socially distinguished of those connected with the beginnings of the Movement. Arthur Perceval, born in 1799, was the youngest son of the second Baron Alden. When he was seventeen he came up to Oxford and Oriel where Keble was for a time his tutor. After he received his degree he was for four years Fellow of All Souls College, until he married in 1825. The next year, Perceval, by this time an ordained priest and Rector of East Horsley in Surrey, reaped the benefit of his social position by being appointed a chaplain to the king. He kept his living until his death, though he was deprived of the royal chaplaincy in the wake of the Gorham controversy in 1850. Perceval mercifully did not record how his High Church ministrations affected those two sturdy Defenders of the Faith and champions of Christian morality, George IV and William IV. But Greville recounts that when their young and respectable niece became queen in 1837, some Evangelicals grew concerned lest Perceval's eloquence might lead Victoria to abandon the Reformation.[27] Bishop Blomfield of London himself preempted the pulpit of the chapel royal for a succession of Sundays to prevent Perceval from taking his preaching turn and thus corrupting the impressionable young queen. Then his lordship fell down and broke his episcopal collarbone, and presumably thanks to this act of God, Perceval got his chance. The bishop might well have spared himself the trouble. The little queen was a more convinced Protestant than any of her bishops, and anyway it would be hard to imagine a girl of nineteen being much moved by the slogans and bombast which were Perceval's rhetorical stock-in-trade.

Duty in the chapel royal occupied Perceval on Sunday, July 21, 1833. On the following Thursday evening, the 25th, he arrived at Hadleigh. As had been the case with Keble, both Rose and Palmer had invited Perceval. On July 10th Palmer had written that he and Rose "proposed a conference of friends on the state of affairs, and to consider of the line [sic] we ought to adopt. . . . There should be some *plan* for continued and vigourous action, so that all should not vanish in smoke." Palmer said that Froude had accepted the invitation, "and he says Keble will also." Newman is expected daily from the Continent, Palmer concluded, "and I hope he will also be there."[28]

VII

So the conference began, at two-thirds strength indeed, since neither Keble nor Newman appeared. The meetings were held in Rose's study, a room at the back of the rectory, looking out over the garden. "Here," Palmer recalled, "we met after breakfast for some hours each day for three days, sitting round the room. Each in succession spoke on the dangers of the Church and the remedies suggested; after which we all expressed opinions. The publication of tracts and other works was much dwelt on, but we could not settle any details."[29]

The informal discussions lasted until Sunday, July 28th. They proceeded under several difficulties. First of all, the four men were not well acquainted and easy, give-and-take conversation was not possible. Rose and Palmer, who knew each other only slightly, did not know Perceval at all. Only Froude had met everybody present, and his sharp, nervous personality was hardly one calculated to smooth the lines of communication. Moreover, as the talk went on, the four did not impress one another very favourably. Froude's habit of indulging in radical talk shocked the more staid Rose and Palmer. Rose, in Froude's judgment, had many splendid gifts, but he was too conservative, too much an Establishment man, "not yet an Apostolical." Froude considered Perceval Apostolical enough, but he struck Froude at the same time as too excitable, undisciplined, and hence unreliable: "Some of the things he says and does make me feel rather odd."[30] Palmer, for his part, considered both Froude and Perceval unlearned and therefore rash; the author of *Origines Liturgicae* was not prepared to accept as his equals these loud, careless fellows who had up to now accomplished nothing.[31]

Another barrier to fruitful action was that each of the conferees came to Hadleigh with a different idea of what the conference was to deal with. Rose intended it to be a chance to explore how his *British Magazine* might serve as an effective weapon against the liberal onslaught. Palmer, on the other hand, felt the occasion suited to the beginning of a wide association of churchmen, who, once organized, could make their voices heard in the highest councils of the kingdom. Froude, in that casual, lounging way of his which was part of his charm and a cause of the exasperation he never failed to arouse, said that he favoured the foundation of another, more Apostolical magazine, which, of course, would have been in competition with Rose's, and that the need of the moment was not to influence the state, as Palmer hoped, but to seize control, by any moral means, of the appointment of bishops. Since it was presumed that Froude could speak for Newman and Keble, his remarks took on an added weight which must have depressed Rose and Palmer.[32]

Perceval also had a tack of his own. As far as he was concerned the chief business at Hadleigh was to discuss his "The Churchman's Manual," which he had begun writing the previous January as an antidote to popery and dissent. This dreary pamphlet with its question-answer format (ninety-three questions and answers, to be precise) had been the occasion for Perceval's first contact with Rose and Palmer. He had sent a copy to Rose, who had shown it to Palmer, and both of them in the spring had written an appreciation of it to its author. Perceval was overwhelmed by attention from such high quarters, and when he was invited to Hadleigh his cup ran over. He brought several copies of the Manual with him, and at least part of the conferees' time was spent in discussing and revising that frail document. It dealt with the grounds of authority in the Church—a spelling out of the preamble to the ordination service and of Articles 23 and 26. One wonders how it could have warranted much discussion; perhaps the conferees were relieved to deal with something concrete, with something so unexceptional that they could agree heartily on it. However that may be, Froude, Perceval noted later, was particularly helpful, and the Manual, although it was not published until the spring of 1834, took its final shape at Hadleigh. Perceval took great pride in the fact that the Manual was the only tract "which was submitted to and received the approval of all immediately concerned in promoting the Theological Movement of 1833."[33] And, he maintained, since his was the first tract "put forth to meet the exigencies of 'the Times,'" it really should have been considered the first of *The Tracts for the Times*. Tom Mozley was not far wrong in judging that for Perceval Hadleigh was "at once a great beginning and a grand finality."

VIII

Except for the approval of Perceval's little catechism, the three days of conferences at Hadleigh did not result in any specific plans. The conferees could agree that the integrity of the Prayer Book and the doctrine of Apostolical Succession had to be defended against the state's aggression, but they were not prepared to say precisely how this was to be done or indeed precisely what they meant by those hallowed phrases. All of them were writers in one sense or another, and so it was easy to agree that some kind of literary campaign ought to be mounted, but again they left the specifics unresolved. Rose was disappointed in his hopes of rallying support for the *British Magazine*, since Froude remained unconvinced. But Froude did agree with Rose that agitation for a lay synod might be an idea worth considering. Perceval favoured the revival of Convocation—the legislative body of the English clergy which had been without power for more than a century—and Palmer, with his heady notions of a grand, nationwide association, talked of the advantages of monster petitions to the crown.

At the end of the discussions, however, Froude confessed himself to be "gloomy" about the whole business,[34] while Rose, to whom speedy action seemed imperative, could not have been less so. Palmer believed that all four men "felt the seriousness of this—the first attempt to combine for the preservation of great essential principles. I know I was myself impressed with the importance of what we were about, but on the whole the result was disappointing; it did not lead to the practical agreement we needed."[35] Only the author of "The Churchman's Manual" appeared satisfied with the Hadleigh Conference. Fittingly, he preached the sermon at the evening service on July 28th which formally ended the conference. The best thing that can be said about the sermon was that it was short. It dealt vaguely with "these troubled times."[36]

Next day Perceval started back to Surrey and Palmer to Oxford. Froude waited another day before he began a round of visits in the Hadleigh neighbourhood. Rose was ill a good part of the next several weeks, and when he wrote to Keble on August 19th he reported of the conference that, if nothing else, "we talked a great deal of good High Church talk."[37] This was a succinct and accurate description of what happened at Hadleigh. There was to be a lot of loose conversation in the years ahead, much of it due to Froude's careless manner of expressing himself, that a conspiratorial plot had been hatched at the conference. Nothing could have been further from the truth. Lofty and unselfish motives had brought together at Hadleigh four men who, whatever their frailties, were never intriguers.

Yet things had not gone very well with them, and Palmer summed up the conferees' frustration: "We had to adjourn the whole matter to Oxford."[38] At Oxford Newman waited, just returned from his brush with death in Sicily and burning with the conviction that there was work for him to do in England.

CHAPTER 7

Tracts for the Times

T HE Church of England, wrote Keble to Newman early in August 1833, "is (as my brother Tom says) like a broken china dish lying on the floor, and 'tis no good to stand moaning around the fragments." With the passage of the Irish Church Act, the old days had gone and would not come back. What lay immediately in the future was disestablishment —which meant, practically speaking, the confiscation of the Church's endowments and the throwing of the clergy back upon themselves—and that was all right with Keble. "As to my own feelings, I think my mind is made up thus far, that I cannot take the Oath of Supremacy in the sense which the Legislature now puts upon it." What good was it to swear allegiance to the king as Head of the Church of Christ in England when the king was controlled by an "infidel parliament"? "I cannot *accept* any curacy or office in the Church," though "I have not made up my mind that I am bound to resign what I have." Meanwhile, the bishops, the clergy's natural leaders, sit absolutely still: "Their lordships," Keble noted wryly, "are so *very* coy."[1]

Yet episcopal sanction, Keble knew, was absolutely imperative. "Will no bishop of them all give us a hint? It would be so *very* much better and more satisfactory to be acting under them, even though one might not always think they gave the wisest orders in the world." Not only the bishops, of course, but the lower clergy too stand bewildered in the face of the liberal onslaught. "Very few of our brethren are yet in the right posture of mind for looking at this question; but," added Keble, "I depend much on the illuminating power of a little wholesome persecution."[2]

The infant party, all of whom shared these fierce, foreboding thoughts, were scattered abroad during the first days of August. Keble was at Fairford, pondering whether he could hold any office in the Church of England. Froude was making his restless way from one southern parsonage to another, all the while trying to stir up the brethren to do something, though he could not tell them what. Rose lay ill at Hadleigh; Perceval had gone home to Surrey, still dazzled by the impression he and his catechism had made at Hadleigh. And William Palmer, gloomy but full of fight, came back to Oxford.

At Oriel he found Newman, who already had reached a momentous decision. "I do not think," he said, "we have yet made as much as we ought of our situation at Oxford, and of the deference paid to it through the country." The center of resistance ought to be here, in the great university which has traditionally given intellectual leadership to the Church. "Are not many eyes looking towards us everywhere, not as masters and scholars but as residents; so that all our acts, as coming from the university, might have the authority of a vote of convocation almost. . . ."[3] Palmer no doubt agreed to this sentiment heartily enough; he did not yet realize that Newman (and Froude and Keble too) did not consider him to be really an Oxford man. Anyway, Palmer was at the moment too preoccupied with his scheme for a nationwide churchmen's association to understand the real drift of Newman's argument. If Newman's principle were accepted, it would mean ultimately that Palmer, the Irish interloper, would be frozen out of leadership in the party, as would the silly Perceval and Rose and his magazine, and indeed anyone not directly connected to the Oriel common room.

This is not to say that there was any calculation in Newman's proposal. He did not mean at this stage to freeze out anybody, certainly not Palmer and least of all Rose. He had not yet even met Perceval. But his eagerness to build upon the Oxford connection inevitably ran counter to the plans Rose and Palmer had formulated. It was, nevertheless, a shrewd judgment. Newman was quite right about the deference Englishmen automatically paid to Oxford. And it showed too the hard core of practicality which Newman possessed. "Now," he said, "no party is likely to be active in Oxford but ourselves, so the field is before us."[4] The movement of resistance, if it were not to end in the air, must have a base of operations, a fortress, so to speak, from which attacks upon the powerful liberals (and they were very powerful indeed) could be launched.

Newman protested later in life that he had no gift for party leadership. In some ways this was true. But it was also true that he always demonstrated an ability without which no leader can succeed: he could grasp the concrete ramifications of a particular position, decide upon it in one way or another, and then stick to his decision. He did precisely this in the August of 1833: We Oxford men, he said, will save the Church "not as masters and scholars but as residents."

I

Keble came up to Oxford on the evening of Monday, August 12th, and the next morning, at Oriel, he met with Newman, Palmer and Froude, who had himself returned only a few days before. Keble learned firsthand from Palmer and Froude what he had already gathered from his correspondence, that aside from the vague plan to fight for the doctrine of the apostolical succession of the bishops and for the integrity of the Prayer Book, the conferees at Hadleigh had agreed upon nothing at all. He probably also had confirmed for him that all had not gone well at the conference, a fact which had already moved him to confide to Newman: "If we Hadleighans could not agree, where *inter quatuor muros* will you find six men to act together?"[5] Evidently Keble hoped the answer might lie within the walls of Oriel, during the hush of the long vacation. At any rate four of the six men sat down there to thrash out if they could a more concrete and specific plan of action.

What emerged from this meeting was a list of six resolutions, the opening manifesto, so to speak, of the Oxford Movement. Predictably, the first of them called for a rallying to the principle of apostolical succession; the next, aimed straight at the Grey government and the reformed Commons, stated that it was sinful to allow interference of non-Church members in matters spiritual; the third said that the Church should attempt to secure a more popular base, insofar as consistent with apostolicity; the fourth was a protest against the separation of Church and state, while the fifth warned of the need for preparation for such an eventuality; and the last resolution asserted the duty to stir up the clergy in these and similar matters.[6]

Unanimous agreement, however, continued to be elusive. Though Newman, Froude and Palmer were willing to go along with the six resolutions as they stood, Keble refused to accept the fourth and fifth, because, he said, the present union of Church and state was in his view sinful and therefore he could not in conscience pledge himself to oppose disestablishment. He might have pointed out that there was an apparent inconsistency between the third resolution, with its appeal to the people, and the fourth, which in effect demanded that the Church keep her aristocratic connection. But Keble was content to say that the resolutions might serve as a starting point, though he reserved the right to raise his objections again.

A day or two after this meeting Froude wrote Perceval to tell him what had taken place. Perceval replied that he agreed with the majority and that he would be happy to subscribe to all six resolutions. The count, then, was four to one, or more likely five to one if Rose were included, since Rose was possibly the last man in England to support anything so radical as disestablishment. But Keble's opinions weighed at least as much as those of the others combined, and so Palmer suggested that for the time being the old reliables—apostolicity and integrity of the Prayer Book—serve as "the principles of the Society." Otherwise, too much wrangling would develop and too much precious time would be lost.[7]

The discussions continued at Oriel in a more or less haphazard way. Keble, of course, fled back to Fairford and appeared in Oxford only occasionally, while Froude towards the end of the month went home to Devon. All of them, however, wrote friends and possible supporters, outlined their basic idea of a society to defend the Church and asked for ideas. In the light of what happened afterwards, it is curious to read Keble's description to his brother of what they were up to. "Palmer, Newman, Froude and Keble," John wrote Tom on August 16th, "have constituted themselves into a committee to write round to their friends and cronies, and know whether they would like to be members of an (anonymous and secret) association for diffusing right principles regarding the apostolical commission of the clergy and protecting the Prayer Book from all profane innovation." If there is any encouragement, "it is proposed for the first thing of all to get up and publish, as *cheap as possible*, an account of St. Ignatius [of Antioch], with extracts from his works, and to follow it up from time to time with other things in the same strain." Once this had begun, the committee would also try to provide something more learned "for the clergy and educated people."[8]

The tenor of the Oriel meeting of August 13, and an indication of the kind of tentative proposals which were advanced, can be seen in some of the musings of Froude. "It is very important," he wrote, "that we all pull together and preach the same thing; at least, if our opinions ever make a noise, it will be so." The wide circulation of cheap publications must be, thought Froude, an essential part of the program. "Could we not by means of our friends and our friends' friends contrive railroads and canals for the diffusion of apostolical knowledge?" And, as usual, his mind raced far ahead of the others so that he could draw a verbal picture of what the tract on St. Ignatius would look like: "[printed] perhaps on handbills, with wood cuts of his martyrdom on the top, and the parts [of St. Ignatius' Epistles] about bishops printed in capitals, perhaps in red letters." Froude had an idea too on how to finance this project. "Such of us as know each other's opinions well and can be sure of never splitting on minor points, may perhaps form a joint stock company to supply means for printing tracts we approve on a large scale. But all this is for a much more advanced stage of our proceedings—only it is well to keep it in view."[9]

II

The six resolutions which emerged from the meeting of August 13th were less important than the unspoken yet unanimous conviction that two steps ought to be taken immediately. The first was the formation of an association or society dedicated to the promotion of "Church principles." This last phrase was a favourite of Palmer's—indeed, with him it became after a while a cliché; it meant roughly the set of opinions based on the apostolic character of the Anglican episcopate and presumably acceptable both to the ordinary Tory High Churchman and also to the more radical Anglo-Catholic. It appeared essential, in the present emergency, that these two be bound together, especially since it was not always clear where the High Churchman left off and the Anglo-Catholic began. When Froude complained about Rose being too "conservative," he meant that Rose was too High Church, too closely linked to the power structure, and therefore little inclined to begin a revolution. Yet not even Froude, upon reflection, was ready to try to do without Rose. The association could provide a common ground for the two groups and thus head off the danger, in Froude's words, of "splitting over minor matters."

The second step was the publication of tracts. This idea chimed in with the sixth of the resolutions, which called for stirring up people to an awareness of the danger the Church stood in and a willingness to do something about it. Such a project had been discussed at Hadleigh but had foundered because Rose understandably wanted his *British Magazine* to be the normal literary channel of Apostolical notions, while Froude, in his infuriatingly abrupt manner, insisted that a more radical publication was necessary. During the weeks immediately afterwards, Keble and Newman convinced Froude to moderate his demands. "I quite agree with you," Keble wrote to Newman, "that Rose's magazine must be supported —unless he actually rats, which I never will believe till I see it." Froude went along with this decision, but reluctantly and not without loud complaints. But Keble knew his man. "As for Hurrell, he is so annoyed just now at his project not being accepted that I count his dissatisfaction for very little."[10]

Froude's view, however, was not so much rejected as compromised at the Oriel meeting of August 13th. What divided him from Keble and Newman was a relatively minor matter of tactics. And though Palmer may have been presumed to speak for Rose, yet he was outnumbered three to one. The meeting determined to support the *British Magazine* but, at the same time and with a good deal more enthusiasm, it also proclaimed the necessity of publishing tracts with more popular appeal. What no one could see at the time was that in this compromise lay the seeds of future disintegration. The same thing was reflected in the inconsistency of the six resolutions. Was the defense of the Church to be a rallying of the Tories, a new and higher dedication to the aristocratic principle in Church and state, now threatened by the Whigs and liberals; or was it to be a genuinely popular movement, making its appeal over the heads of the aristocrats and all their old High and Dry ways to the Christian people themselves? For the moment, evidently, it was to be both; but no one could expect it to be so forever.

This uneasy balance of differing views immediately raised a very practical question: Given the desirability both of an association and of publication, what was to be the relation between the two? Should the association produce the tracts, or should individuals take that responsibility on themselves, even though they might be at the same time members of the association? At first it was tacitly agreed that the association—in some form or other—should be the vehicle of publication. As early as August 5th Newman, referring to the published version of Keble's Assize sermon, remarked to Tom Mozley: "It is excellent. If we had a board, it might be part of its business to insure the circulation of such works."[11] Obviously, such a board would have to agree on the value of a particular work before it would ensure its circulation, and so the principle of joint responsibility figured in Newman's first hazy ideas about publication. Froude and Keble agreed with him in this, and he agreed with them that popular appeal had to be taken into account in any publishing scheme. We must, he said to Mozley, "prepare the *imaginations* of men for a changed state of things."[12]

So the problem took shape. If the association, through some kind of board, controlled publications, what would happen if the members of the board disagreed on the basic question of the people versus the aristocracy? Newman, who was less radical than either Froude or Keble, privately expressed a view abhorrent to Rose and Palmer. "I confess, Tory as I still am, theoretically and historically, I begin to be a radical practically. . . . I, of course, think that the most natural and becoming state of things is for the aristocratical power to be the upholder of the Church; yet I cannot deny the plain fact that in most ages the latter has been based on a popular power." The Church at the time of the apostles, during the crises of the fourth century, in the England of Thomas à Becket rested in fact not upon the aristocracy but upon the people. "I am preparing myself for such a state of things, and for this simple reason, *because* the state has deserted us, and we cannot help ourselves." Newman was not prepared to go all the way with Keble and demand complete separation, "though, I confess, if the destructives go much further in their persecution of us—e.g. if they made Arnold a bishop—I might consider it wrong to maintain that position longer. . . ."[13]

Hugh Rose, ill and far away at Hadleigh, heard nothing of these thoughts nor of the meetings at Oxford held by his friends during that exciting August. But Rose was a shrewd man who knew his way around the ecclesiastical world, and he was a good judge of men as well. Though he could not put his finger directly on the source of it, he must have sensed by mid-August that the program for defense of the Church already was in trouble. On August 19th he left his sickbed long enough to write Keble a long letter urging caution. "I am obliged to hold back more than I like. Not, assuredly, because I care for king or kaiser, prince or prelate, but because the one great object that we all must have in view is this—to *familiarize* men with sound and strong principles. . . ." The liberalizers, "including many of the leading clergy in London," hate the *British Magazine* "where such principles are put forward, and they only want fair occasion to cry me and my journal down as Ultras at once." In order not to give them that occasion, Rose continued, he must be more than circumspect. Perhaps Keble and his friends would label such an attitude "maneuvering and [say] that the bolder and opener course would be better. I can say most solemnly that to me at least it would be the most agreeable and the most natural. But I should have little hope from it." For Rose has learned the hard lesson that

the world is ruled by *seems*, not is, by *words* and *appearances*, not by *things* and *realities*; that if you once give an obnoxious name to a book or a man, *no power* can rescue them, no power can make them sufficient for good. Nothing but *first rate powers* and the *constant* exhibition of them could gain even *attention* for *high principles*, and such exhibition of such powers would not stand against the *interested* cry which would be raised and the *interested* sneer which would be levelled at them: "Very brilliant, very striking, very imaginative, but dreamy, . . . not practical, etc. etc."[14]

There is no evidence that Keble paid any heed to Rose's warning, but perhaps he recalled years later, when the Movement had collapsed, Rose's hauntingly prophetic words: "If you once give an obnoxious name to a book or a man, no power can rescue them."

III

At the time Rose's letter reached him, Keble was trying to draw up a declaration of aims which would satisfy Palmer, Froude and Newman, Rose and Perceval, and, ultimately, all Anglicans of good will. By the end of the month he had finished it and submitted it to his associates for their perusal. Newman endorsed the document enthusiastically, and Palmer, though he had some reservations about the Non-Juring tone of it, accepted it at least as a tentative program for an association of churchmen. The statement was typical of Keble's luminous piety and of his intellectual roots, which lay deep in the Anglican liturgy. The only way of salvation, it began, is "the partaking of Christ's Body and Blood"; the means of doing this has been authorized by Christ himself in "the Holy Sacrament of His Supper." The apostolic succession of the bishops and through them of the lesser clergy is the only guarantee of "the security . . . for the continuance and application of that Sacrament." Under present circumstances in the Church of England, these truths are in danger of being obscured, and thus numbers of Christians are left or tempted to "precarious and unauthorized ways of communion," which amount to "virtual apostasy."

To combat this unhappy state of affairs, "We desire to pledge ourselves one to another, reserving our canonical obedience." Then Keble listed the objectives of the proposed society: to impress "on all committed to our charge a due sense of the inestimable privilege of communion with Our Lord through the successors of the Apostles"; to circulate books and tracts which will "familiarize the imaginations of men" with the succession, and to point out that this is the heritage of the Primitive Church; to encourage daily common prayer and "more frequent participation of the Lords' Supper"; to resist any attempt "to alter the liturgy on insufficient authority"; and finally to make special efforts to inform people about "those points in our discipline which may appear from time to time most likely to be misunderstood or undervalued." Keble concluded by noting that the committee at Oxford had Rev. W. Palmer and Rev. J. H. Newman for its secretaries. "No subscription called for at present but cooperation."[15]

Keble's declaration skirted the crucial issue of the union of Church and state. As Newman explained to Perceval in a covering letter which accompanied a copy of the declaration, "In our society we mean to say nothing one way or the other on the subject." Perhaps in the abstract, he continued, there may be good cause to separate from the state as the Non-Jurors did in the seventeenth century. But pragmatic reasons at the moment call for silence on the matter. "It will be a good thing, as Keble says, to raise our witness in our generation as the non-jurors did; though of course we ought to omit no efforts to be more like serpents and more successful in our good cause than they were."[16]

As far as the other mooted question, Keble's statement seemed to imply that popular tracts would be published under the supervision of the society. At least this was the way Perceval and Palmer understood it. The latter wrote enthusiastically to Rose, who replied favourably but cautiously. "I enter warmly into your plan and feel that, as far as your description goes, no churchman *can* entertain any objection to a society the object of which is to disseminate right views as to the Church and the ministry among our less informed brethren." But Rose wanted more details and he was not prepared to lend his influence until he got them. "I want more distinct accounts of your plans, and, if I had them, should not despair of getting sanction for them."[17]

Palmer was ecstatic over Rose's hint of possible future support. If Rose and all his powerful friends were on their side, Palmer was confident that no one could stand against them. Though he was himself on the scene at Oxford, it would appear that he failed to sense as much of what was happening as did the shrewd Rose off in Suffolk. On the last day of August, Palmer happily told Newman the good news, and added that he had promised Rose that "we should have a committee to revise" the society's various publications before they were circulated.[18] What Palmer did not know was that Newman had already written four tracts, that they were now in the printer's hands, and that their author had no intention of clearing them with any committee.

IV

Newman was bursting with energy that late summer of 1833; he felt stronger, he said, than he ever had since he had come up to Oxford seventeen years before, though in the wake of the Sicilian fever he had temporarily lost his hair. The literary activity of these hectic days reflected his glowing good health. He began the series of patristic studies for the *British Magazine*, which were ultimately published in book form under the title *The Church of the Fathers*. He was also at work on a piece called "Home Thoughts Abroad," which was a kind of dramatic dialogue between two Anglicans, visitors to Rome (as Newman and Froude had been earlier in the year), who discussed the relative merits of the English and Roman churches. England won the imaginary debate hands down, and Rose published it, though not till 1836. And as always Newman was scribbling verse, some of it for mental exercise, but much of it for the *Lyra Apostolica*.

All this work expressed Newman's conviction that, despite Froude's suspicions, Rose and his journal had to be supported. The tracts he wrote late in August, however, were aimed at a larger audience than the *British Magazine*'s limited subscription lists. Newman was prepared to help Rose with one hand, but he wanted the other hand kept free for work which went outside the confines of Tory officialdom. The task of stirring people up—especially the clergy—was not, indeed could not be, congenial to the cautious Rose with his important connections. Newman could appreciate both Rose's position and his unique importance in the political struggle against liberalism. But men like himself, men with lesser responsibilities and reputations, could speak out independently in other ways, he thought, endangering Rose.

The first three Tracts for the Times carry the date September 9, 1833, though it seems the circulation of them had begun a week or so earlier. There was nothing sophisticated about them. They were short, straightforward appeals to the clergy to resist the encroachments of the infidel state. Altogether they totaled less than fifteen pages and could be bought for three pennies. Keble saw them before publication and judged them good but a bit "pompous."[19] They were published anonymously.

Tract Number One[20] was entitled "Thoughts on the Ministerial Commission" and it called upon the clergy to rally to the bishops. "To them we willingly and affectionately relinquish their high privileges and honours; we encroach not upon the rights of the Successors of the Apostles; we touch not their sword and crosier. Yet surely we may be their shield-bearers in the battle without offence; and by our voice and deeds be to them what Luke and Timothy were to St. Paul." For what, after all, supports the clergy of the Church of England? Not the state, which is in the process of de-Christianizing itself, not "temporal honours and substance," which may very soon be taken away. Not popularity either: "Look at the dissenters on all sides of you, and you will see at once that their ministers, depending simply upon the people, become the *creatures* of the people. Are you content that this should be your case? Alas! can a greater evil befall Christians than for their teachers to be guided by them, instead of guiding?" There is, argued Newman, but one prop for the clergy, one strong arm which will not wither, and that is the "grace of ordination. . . . If we trace back the power of ordination from hand to hand, of course we shall come to the apostles at last. We know we do, as a plain historical fact; and therefore all we who have been ordained clergy in the very form of our ordination acknowledged the doctrine of the Apostolical Succession."

The second and third Tracts continued the same theme. In Number Two,[21] Newman made direct reference to the situation in Ireland. "Are we," he asked, "content to be accounted the mere creation of the state, as schoolmasters and teachers may be, or soldiers or magistrates or other public officers?" The government, in suppressing the Irish dioceses, has set aside the definition of the Church which "our divines have ever taken, that there is on earth an existing society, apostolic as founded by the apostles, Catholic because it spreads its branches in every place; i.e. the Church Visible with its bishops, priests and deacons." The state's interference in such a matter can mean the destruction of the Church. "Now what am I calling on you to do? You cannot help what has been done in Ireland, but you may protest against it. You may as a duty protest against it in public and private; you may keep a jealous watch on the proceedings of the nation, lest a second act of the same kind be attempted."

In Tract Number Three[22] Newman pointed to the direction from which the next act of aggression might come. "Attempts are making to get the liturgy altered. My dear brethren, I beseech you, consider with me whether you ought not to resist the alteration of even one jot or tittle of it." The air is full of talk about altering the Prayer Book services; some want them shortened, others want them lengthened. "There are some who wish the imprecatory Psalms omitted; there are others who would lament this omission as savouring of the shallow and detestable liberalism of the day." All this feckless discussion, said Newman, indicates an unstable desire for change. "Were there grievous errors in the Prayer Book, something might be said for beginning, but who can point out any?" Do not be deceived. Even those who advocate changes which they claim to be immaterial do so because "they dislike the *doctrine* of the liturgy. These men of the world do not like the anathemas of the Athanasian Creed." The clergy must be prepared to resist on this front first of all, to protest against any alterations in the Prayer Book. "And should you see that our Fathers the Bishops seem to countenance them, petition *them*. They will thank you for such a proceeding. *They do not wish these alterations*; but how can they resist them without the support of their clergy?"

Newman's rhetorical question went unanswered, though one might have been tempted to suggest that the bishops could and ought to supply leadership to the lesser clergy in the crisis at hand. But it was clear to Newman that they did not intend to do so unless they were pushed to the wall, and, given the tangled jurisdiction within the Church of England which gave so much independence of episcopal authority to individual clergymen, he reasoned that some of the pushing might be done by an aroused body of parsons. He saw his ultimate objective to be the same as Rose's, though his means were very different. While Rose tinkered carefully within the power structure, cornering a bishop here and an influential member of Parliament there, Newman would attempt to exert pressure from underneath, and the end result of both efforts would be, hopefully, the mobilization of the bishops themselves. One wonders what those placid gentlemen made of all this, or what they thought when they read in Tract Number One that "black event as it would be for the country, yet . . . we could not wish [the bishops] a more blessed termination of their course than the spoiling of their goods and martyrdom." The bishops might have been forgiven if they preferred to do their own wishing.

In these first three Tracts Newman laid down what was to become a basic distinction. The Establishment was one thing, the Church of Christ in England was something else. The bishops formed the cornerstone of all Christian endeavour, not because they were mitered lords or officers of the crown, but because they were the successors of the apostles. And so it followed that attacks could be leveled at the old Tory conception of a state-connected Church without touching the essential matter of the bishops' spiritual prerogatives. This is what Newman and his friends meant when they talked about the necessity of building the resistance to liberalism on the people; they were willing to sacrifice the financial and social advantages of the Establishment if, in the process, they could secure a stronger spiritual jurisdiction for the bishops and a clearer manifestation of the clerical character of the Church. Keble put the case in its strongest terms: "Take every pound, shilling and penny, and the curse of sacrilege along with it; only let us make our own bishops and be governed by our own laws."[23] Newman did not go quite so far, at least not yet. A few days before the Tracts appeared he wrote to a friend: "I suppose [the Church] was in a far worse condition in Arian times, except in . . . that there was the *possibility* of true minded men becoming bishops, which is now almost out of the question. . . . I wish the Archbishop [of Canterbury] had somewhat of the boldness of the old Catholic prelates. . . . At the same time, I daresay, were I in high station, I should suddenly get very cautious from the feeling of responsibility. Well, it is a lucky thing to be able to talk; and I think we who can should make the most of it."[24] The first Tracts, in their forthright calls to action and protest, were in a sense Newman's statement of the conditions to be fulfilled if the Establishment and the Church were to continue to live together. If those conditions failed to be met, then the agitation could adopt a more radical line.

V

The publication of the first three Tracts contributed to the growing split between Palmer and Newman. It was not the Tracts' doctrine or even their bellicose tone which disturbed Palmer; he questioned rather their opportuneness and above all their anonymity. He would have preferred that Newman not write at all until the board of revision that Palmer dreamed about became a reality. Or if Newman insisted on publishing, then he should do so over his signature, so that no one would confuse his personal views and his somewhat startling way of expressing them with the program and goals of the infant society. Palmer knew that Newman was called an "ultra" by some clergymen, and that others had found the opening of Tract One—"I am but one of yourselves, a Presbyter"—an odd and disquieting introduction to the resistance movement. If the clerical troops were to be rallied, care must be taken to ensure that sensitivities and partisan loyalties remain unruffled as much as possible.[25]

It is easy to dismiss William Palmer as a fussy little man who did not appreciate the genius with whom he was privileged to work. This may in its measure be true, but it is no less true that Palmer had real grounds for his complaint and that Newman failed to meet his argument. Newman apparently thought Palmer was merely urging greater caution, and so he cited the strong position Rose took in the September 1833 issue of the *British Magazine*: "somewhat violent," was the way Newman happily described it. "I quote him against Palmer," he told Froude, "when the latter preaches about moderation, since he has an especial notion of Rose's prudence."[26] But this hardly answered Palmer's contention. Everyone knew for whom Rose's magazine spoke. For whom did the recently published Tracts speak?

Newman and his friends had agreed with Palmer, Rose and Perceval that an association ought to be formed for the defense of the Church. To make such an association a meaningful reality was the task Palmer had zealously taken upon himself, and certainly at this stage of the proceedings none of the others had discouraged him. Already he had established contacts with the leading High Church forces in the country; with Rose's blessing in his pocket he had been cordially received in that pale shrine of Anglo-Catholicism, Joshua Watson's house in Clapton. Palmer, at the moment the first three Tracts appeared, had reason to be optimistic about the possibilities of a grand, nationwide association, which could effectively mobilize resistance to the liberals.

From the beginning Newman had been skeptical about this heady scheme. But he was prepared to go along with a modification of it, that is, a federation of societies across the country, bound together by the goals they shared but independent of each other in deciding precisely what action to take. As early as September 3rd Newman was speaking of "our society,"[27] by which he meant the Oxford group centered at Oriel, which in turn meant a society controlled by himself, Keble and Froude. Palmer, for his part, agreed to the federation idea, but, as a man often will, he thought of it as he wanted to think of it, emphasizing the federal aspect which, it seemed to him, maintained his preference for a wider association. So, quite consistently, he took the position that if the individual societies were to take a public stance, they ought to take it together, they ought to speak with one voice; and if they were unable to do so, they should remain silent. Only then, Palmer reasoned, would they be heard in the councils of the mighty. This was why he insisted upon a board of revision to issue a kind of imprimatur upon any publication which the Oxford society might wish to circulate; for even though the Oriel men outnumbered him, they could not reasonably keep him off that board. The Oxford society would indeed be the intellectual font of the resistance movement, but with William Palmer armed with a virtual veto power over publications, no one need fear the emergence of any extremist or eccentric ideas. Palmer would protect the principle of joint action.

Newman upset Palmer's careful plans by independently publishing the first three Tracts. When Palmer remonstrated with him, Newman answered by reminding Palmer of the terms of Keble's statement of the association's aims: "We desire to pledge ourselves one to another, reserving our canonical obedience."[28] A clergyman's basic loyalty to his bishop, his "canonical obedience," served Newman as a guarantee of freedom of action. I have pledged myself to you, he told Palmer, but only to the extent that such a pledge does not inhibit me in performing what I judge to be my larger duties as a clergyman. Very well, answered Palmer; but if you think it right to publish without reference to the Oxford society, you should sign your name to the work so that it is clear that you speak only for yourself and not for your colleagues. Otherwise you may, in the public's judgment, commit them to views they are not ready to accept and thus endanger the essential unity of the movement.[29]

Newman never satisfactorily met Palmer's point, and it looks very much as though he wanted to have his cake and eat it too. Certainly his remark at the beginning of Tract Number One—"I conceal my name lest I should take too much on myself," that is, lest I appear presumptuous—was no answer at all. On the one hand, Newman did not want to be restricted by a committee in the subject or style of what he wrote; great things, he often said, "are accomplished by individuals, not by committees; Luther was an individual."[30] At the same time, he could see the advantage of working within the framework of a federation. One of the most perplexing problems about the Tracts was getting them distributed and read, and a chain of local societies was an ideal starting place. The Tracts could be shipped from the printer to the headquarters of a society in Suffolk or Derby, and from there they could be circulated to the parsonages around the countryside.

Still more important was Newman's conviction that resident Oxford men had a special role to play. He wanted to speak out with an authority which was almost that of university Convocation. If he signed his name to the Tracts, they would become just a tiny part of the flood of propaganda which poured from the printing presses every day. But if the anonymous Tracts came out of Oxford, their prestige would be automatically enhanced, as though the university itself were taking a stand.

This was not so devious as it may appear at first glance. On September 8th, Newman wrote to a friend that "we have begun to print tracts."[31] It seems likely that in that first person plural he simply excluded Palmer, not out of spite but out of indifference. Palmer, the Irishman and stranger, had never really been an Oxford man anyway. The "we" meant Newman himself, Keble and Froude, and who better than these three could speak for the resident university in such troubled times?

So Palmer fretted, and Newman loftily insisted on publishing his Tracts anonymously. And if the country thought they expressed the Oxford view, so much the better. Froude egged him on: "We must not enlarge our basis even for bishops," he wrote from Dartington. "I object to anyone whose ear we have not secured, so that our opinions may be the creed of the association."[32] Keble took a playful, and not particularly helpful, line: people will read the anonymous Tracts, he said, because of the fun of guessing who the authors might be.[33]

Not everyone agreed. Pusey, as ever simple as a dove, found the anonymity distasteful if not downright dishonourable.[34] And Samuel Rickards, a former Oriel don and a good friend of Newman's, wrote on September 6th, "As far as my opinion goes for anything, I disapprove of the concealment of names. 'I am small and of no reputation' is an old plea for shrinking, which the best servants of God never liked, and I like it not any better than they did."[35] Such dissent, however, did not change Newman's mind. The Tracts continued to appear anonymously, and Palmer's board of revision never materialized. It was a crucial decision, because it ultimately drove Palmer into silence and then into bitter opposition, and the whole High Church party with him. "They should have borne his name so as not to compromise others," Palmer observed about Newman's Tracts long years afterwards.[36] It was not an unreasonable observation.

VI

During the months which followed, the split between Palmer's and Newman's points of view widened, and as it did the hope of forming a grand alliance of Tories and Apostolicals, joined perhaps by a few Evangelicals, evaporated into thin air. Palmer spent most of his time away from Oxford from the middle of September 1833 till after Christmas. He traveled extensively throughout the country in behalf of the association. The effect of his work was considerable; permanent societies were established in Bath, Bristol, Ripon and elsewhere, and in London he basked in the warm approval of the most powerful High Church clergy and laymen. He was not surprised to discover that these potentates did not much care for the Tracts.[37]

Palmer's absence from Oxford meant that whatever slight chance there may have been that he and Newman could have talked out their differences never came to anything. Newman doggedly followed one line, Palmer another. There was one man who might have healed the breach, but he had gone too far away to be of any service. About October 1, 1833, Hugh James Rose left Hadleigh to assume the chair of divinity in the newly founded University of Durham. This institution was founded by the High Church Bishop of Durham, who wanted to provide for the northern counties a center of ecclesiastical studies which would someday be on a par with Oxford and Cambridge. In the 1830s this was a modest enough ambition, and the immense resources of the diocese of Durham seemed sufficient to bring it about rather quickly. The bishop asked Joshua Watson to persuade Rose to accept the professorship of divinity, and Rose, who had lived so long on the fringes of academic communities, could not resist the offer, despite his poor health and many occupations. Like most new schools, the University of Durham experienced a good deal of distress and confusion during its early years, and

Rose soon discovered that the unfamiliar academic burdens in this strange and raw place were too much for his fragile constitution. He stayed in Durham little more than a year.[38]

Durham lies north of the Tees, not far from the Scottish border, and before the railroads this was a long distance indeed from Oxford. So, as the estrangement between Palmer and Newman grew, Rose was out of touch, absorbed in new duties, and, as always, plagued by bouts with asthma. Whether Rose's presence would have made any difference in the affairs of the Movement, it is impossible to say. Palmer regarded him with a kind of awe, and though Froude and Keble were unenthusiastic about Rose, Newman always liked and respected him. Rose was a much broader man than Palmer, and though he agreed with the latter in principle more than he did with Newman, he possessed enough flexibility to understand that the Oriel dons were in a position to contribute to the common cause in a way in which he and Palmer could not. Also, Rose moved familiarly in those rarefied High Church circles where Palmer was as much an uneasy stranger as he was in Oxford. Palmer panicked when London Tories complained about the Tracts, whereas Rose, if he had been there, might have soothed ruffled feelings. Rose could reassure bishops, Palmer could not. And Newman, for his part, would not so quickly have dismissed Rose's views as he did Palmer's.

All this, of course, is speculation, because by the time he came back from Durham it was too late for Rose to do anything. The line he might have taken, however, appears in a letter he wrote to Newman early in October 1833. "As far as my opinion goes, your Tracts are excellent and *not too strong*."[39] The underscored phrase no doubt was meant to assure Newman that Rose did not share Palmer's alarm. But then if Rose had been on the scene Palmer would probably not have been alarmed either.

Newman naturally rejoiced over Rose's approval of the Tracts, but, sensitive as always to opposition, he needed support of his view from someone closer at hand and closer to his heart. He got it at the beginning of October, when Froude, paler and gaunter than ever, came back to Oxford from Dartington. He stayed at Oriel for three weeks, and during that time whatever doubts Newman may have had, Froude, who only doubted himself, swept them all away. It is significant that Froude was still by his side when, on October 24th, Newman wrote Palmer a long letter. "I do not like the notion of forming a society," he began, "or association even, for many reasons." First of all, there is an "awkwardness" in such a venture without the explicit sanction of the bishops, which, said Newman, we seem most unlikely to get. Moreover, to build up a society is a complicated business for which none of the infant party had any special aptitude or experience. "And further, if we profess an association, we are under necessity of bringing into the government of it men who do not agree with us."

Newman passed lightly over the relation between a society and the publication of tracts, but he did not avoid the issue. If tracts come from a formal body, "it is an assumption of teaching," and thus, in a way, a usurpation of the bishop's office. Besides, a board of revision, which would weigh and carefully correct tracts, would make them "cold and formal and (so to say) *im*personal. An address with much in it which others question, yet coming from an individual mind, has a life about it which is sure to make an impression."

These are some of the reasons why, Newman continued, "I would advocate a less formal scheme; not that I am not eventually for an association, but not till the bishop puts himself at our head in this or that diocese. I would merely exert myself in my own place, and with my own immediate friends, in declaring and teaching the half-forgotten truths of Church union and order to all within my influence." And if Palmer felt that some kind of national effort should be undertaken now, Newman (and Froude) had a concrete suggestion. "Let us . . . draw up a declaration or address to the Archbishop [of Canterbury], an expression of our attachment to the doctrine and discipline of the Church. . . . This very attempt will lay the rudiments of a number of associations, channels of communication will be opened with a most definite object; and whether the attempt succeeds or not, the groundwork of a second future attempt will be laid. . . ."[40]

Newman's letter reached Palmer in London where he had gone to confer with the Tory chiefs. Evidently he read it as though it offered a compromise, which, of course, it did not. The idea of gathering together a monster petition struck a responsive chord in Palmer; he was finding this life of agitation in the company of the very best people quite attractive. And perhaps in his mind's eye he could see already the glittering company at Lambeth Palace, and the grave but benign demeanour of Archbishop Howley as he received the pledge of clerical allegiance from the hand of his humble servant, William Palmer. In any case, Palmer answered Newman enthusiastically. "I write this to beg that you will *without any delay* send up whatever has been drawn up in the shape of an address to the archbishop." Then he happily dropped a dozen names of "men of the right sort from various parts" with whom he had been cavorting. Almost as though it had been an afterthought, he referred to the main burden of Newman's letter: "As far as I can see, it does not seem to be considered at all necessary that there should be at present anything of a more formal organization, but probably by-and-bye we must have one committee in Oxford and another in London."[41] Much was to turn on that vague phrase "by-and-bye," because though the address to the archbishop might serve as a diversion it would do nothing to settle the essential problem whether resistance to the liberals was to be a Tory revival or a rallying of the people.

On October 26th Froude left Oxford, and after spending a few days at Fairford, made his way back to Devon. Both Keble and Newman were appalled at his appearance, and both of them urged him to leave England for the winter. Newman suggested the West Indies; Keble, Brazil. Froude could not but be aware of the gravity of his condition—the rattling cough, the shortness of breath could tell him much, and the worried looks of his friends filled in the rest of the story. With remarkably little resistance, he agreed to leave the field of battle where he felt peculiarly at home. At the end of November he sailed for Barbados. He was gone for almost eighteen months.

VII

Meanwhile, the Tracts continued to come forth. By the end of October three more of Newman's were in print plus one each by Keble, Froude and John Bowden. A simple editorial pattern was established: Newman and Keble both read everything submitted and occasionally changed a word or two for stylistic reasons before they sent the manuscript on to the printer. A depot for the Tracts was set up at Turrill's print and book shop in London, and though Mr. Turrill thought that it would be more economical to produce a weekly Tract-Magazine than to sell the penny Tracts one at a time, Newman rejected this notion, both out of respect to Rose and to preserve the free and spontaneous character of the venture. If a man felt like writing a tract, let him write one, without bothering himself over periodical deadlines. Since each writer paid for the printing costs of his Tract himself, and got back what he could on the sale, Mr. Turrill shrugged his shoulders and perhaps marveled at the prodigal zeal of these well-fixed parsons.[42] (Bowden was the only one not a parson, but he was better fixed than most of them.)

The thrill was fast vanishing for poor Palmer, who had wanted a conservative board of revision and now found that any fellow with a little money could reprint any Tract and leave out or add anything that suited him. No sedate association of important people could survive the freewheeling method Newman had adopted. On November 4th, Tract Number Ten appeared in Mr. Turrill's shop, and it was to cause Palmer many an inward groan. Entitled "Heads of a Weekday Lecture," and written by Newman, the Tract was an imaginary sermon for the feast of SS. Simon and Jude. Most of it was a simple defense of the apostolic office, but in its last paragraph there lay a bombshell. "The day may come," Newman had his imaginary preacher say to his imaginary country congregation, "when the representatives of Christ are spoiled of their sacred possessions and degraded from their civil dignities."[43] Then the ministers of the Church will not be known for their finer clothing or better fare or larger houses, but "as those (if I may say so) who are intrusted with the keys of heaven and hell, as the heralds of mercy, as the denouncers of woe to wicked men, as intrusted with the awful and mysterious privilege of dispensing Christ's Body and Blood. . . ."[44]

Palmer's London friends were aghast at such phrases. Perhaps they could be found in the standard Anglo-Catholic divines, but to say them straight out smacked of Rome and priestcraft and they could spell death to the association and to the petition. None of these people knew Newman, but Palmer was close at hand and they flooded him with protests. Palmer, in turn, complained to Newman that Tract Number Ten could ruin the prospects of the address to the archbishop, which, after all, was Newman's own idea.[45] Samuel Rickards wrote directly to Newman.

Of course I do not quarrel with the expression [i.e. "Christ's Body and Blood" as above] when I meet with it in writers who lived before the controversies introduced into the world upon the subject, through the errors of the Church of Rome; but to use it now, and moreover to use it in a set of tracts which at any rate will be read at first with a good deal of suspicion, and in most instances with a view to ascertain what sort of men write them, and what the real objects of the association are, appears to me nothing less than tossing firebrands into our own work.[46]

Newman shot back to Rickards a letter filled with emphatic underscorings. "*The association has nothing to do with the Tracts.* The latter are the work of Oxford men; Keble, myself and others are answerable for them. . . . It would be highly indecorous in an *association* or *man in office* or of *name* to contemplate the downfall of the clergy; but the very use and meaning of anonymousness is that you say things worth saying in themselves, but not *fit* for you to say."[47] Newman offered to send round a circular explicitly dissociating the Tracts from any association, but Palmer was not satisfied with this. "He goes further and wishes us to stop them. . . . The said Tracts give offence I know, but they also do good; and, I maintain, will strengthen the association by enabling it to take high ground."[48] When Newman pointed out that Rose was doing similar work in the *British Magazine,* Palmer retorted that Rose was known as the editor.[49] And so the argument stood where it had stood two months before.

It was a difficult time for Newman. "Do give me some advice and encouragement," he wrote to Froude, who, on the eve of sailing for the West Indies, replied with his customary vigour. "As to giving up the Tract, the notion is odious. . . . We must throw the Z's [Froude's and Newman's playful code name for High Churchmen] overboard; they are a small and . . . daily diminishing party."[50] It crossed Newman's mind that a possible solution might be to use Keble's name publicly as editor of the Tracts, maintaining anonymity for the individual writers. Then he thought better of it, and on November 17th he told Bowden: "I think that soon I shall advertise them as 'Tracts for the Times, by Residents in Oxford.'" And so he did.

Keble suggested that one way out of the impasse was to get the Tories to commit themselves in tracts, and then everyone would be in the same boat. But on the main issue he stood by Newman.

If you can form an association [Keble wrote to Perceval], or, as I should rather word it, get a knot of people to cooperate with you, . . . why so much the better, and we at Oxford or here [Fairford] might communicate with you without our being bound by each other's proceedings or professions. I am come to the conclusion, and I know Newman agrees, that this is much the likeliest way of getting on. If we are to have a general association we shall be embarrassed with all sorts of cautions, and shall be a year and more settling the first details. Let as many distinct fountains of tracts as may be opened to poison people's minds. We are hardly ripe for anything further at present.[51]

VIII

Meanwhile, Palmer made the cardinal error of promising what he could not deliver. He told the High Churchmen that the Tracts would be stopped.[52] Perhaps he was frightened into such an imprudent step. More likely, he felt that he could reason with Newman once he had convinced him that their common cause depended upon the support of the best people. Whichever is the proper explanation, Palmer threw himself into the work of drawing up a suitable petition to the Archbishop of Canterbury and of securing signatures for it. Immediately there was trouble. The draft which Newman originally sent to London was too strong for Palmer, who cut out of it any reference to "extra ecclesiastical interference," that is, to the parliamentary aggression in the Irish bishoprics matter. Palmer's friends made it even weaker, and when it came back to Oxford it was, to use Newman's word, "uncouth." Drafts went back and forth between London and Oxford until November 8th when Newman wrote: "The address is done today. Such a composition I never saw; we have rewritten each other's (London and Oxford) three times; but now we have made a few alterations *nostro periculo* [dangerous, that is, because the London party might not like them] and have printed it off."[53]

The address to the archbishop, even with the elimination of Palmer's "Irishisms" and other verbal inelegancies and with the changes introduced by Newman without consultation with London, was a pretty bland and general pledge of loyalty to the episcopal principle. Hurrell Froude's father, the blunt archdeacon, thought it "certainly . . . in itself a most unmeaning affair, but people who desire a movement will possibly give it some importance as a first step."[54] For Palmer, however, it was the greatest step of all. He worked tirelessly to make the petition a resounding gesture. His own responsibility in the matter included most of England and Wales, and he crisscrossed the country explaining and exhorting. He ran into all sorts of problems. Some of Palmer's London associates had wanted the inclusion of a statement of confidence in all the bishops in order to avoid jealousies. Rose went so far as to say from Durham that a schism might develop if the bishops other than Canterbury were not mentioned. Others feared that the address might lead to counteraddresses from the Arnold-Whately forces. Palmer found some who criticized the address as a condemnation of all change, while others thought it gave too much scope for change. A few of the bishops did not like the whole business, though none of them condemned it and most let it run its course in their dioceses.[55]

The address was in its way a spectacular success. By the last week in November two thousand clergymen had signed it. At Christmastime Keble spoke of the "heaps" of signatures which had been sent to him from all parts of Gloucestershire.[56] Palmer indeed had overcome differences of opinion, sluggish bishops, petty jealousy (of younger men, he explained later, "undertaking so great a work").[57] In February 1834 his dream came true: Amidst a glittering company at Lambeth Palace, the address was presented to the Archbishop of Canterbury; to it were affixed more than seven thousand clerical signatures.[58]

As it turned out, Palmer's work of stumping the provinces was not quite over. The clergy address sparked the idea of a similar lay address to the archbishop. Snags of various kinds soon appeared in the plan, mostly because the Tory politicians considered a lay address inopportune. Peel did not answer the letter asking his opinion about the proposal, while Wellington said that it might be useful later but not now. Palmer nevertheless found enough distinguished laymen to form a committee, and he was able, as he put it, "immediately to place the committee in communication with zealous and influential laity in seventy of the principal towns and districts of England and Wales."[59]

The lay address marked the final stage of the estrangement between Palmer and the Tractarians (as Newman, Keble and their friends were beginning to be called). The address emphasized the Erastian quality of the Church of England, her dependence upon the state and her rightful place in the Establishment. For those who considered the Tory connection a disaster if not a sin, such sentiments did not go down very well. Palmer was disappointed not in the ideas of the address but with the practical reception it received. Due, he maintained, to bungling by the committee, the address garnered only 230,000 signatures, which were solemnly presented to Archbishop Howley in May 1834. Though his work of agitation and organization ended on a somewhat sour note, Palmer retired from the field satisfied that the goals enunciated at Hadleigh—support for the bishops and for the Prayer Book—had for the most part been achieved.[60] He knew by this time that there was no room for him among the Oriel men, and with quiet good grace he went back to his studies at Worcester College. He would, however, be heard from again, and in the hue and cry over Tract Ninety, in 1841, Newman would have reason to be grateful indeed to him.

IX

But at the beginning of 1834 it was Number Eighteen, not Number Ninety, in the series of Tracts for the Times, which was causing widespread discussion. Called "Thoughts on the Benefits of the System of Fasting Enjoined by our Church," Tract Eighteen was a singularly eloquent statement of the ascetic side of Anglo-Catholicism. It was not eloquent in the literary sense—it was much too wordy for that—but rather in the genuine zeal for the Lord's house which it exhibited. What raised more eyebrows than its contents, however, were the initials printed on its final page: E. B. P., as all the English ecclesiastical world knew, stood for Edward Bouverie Pusey, Canon of Christ Church and Regius Professor of Hebrew in the University of Oxford.

The Tract dealt with several themes which became in time standard Tractarian positions. Pusey emphasized, for example, that revelation called for a corporate or social religiosity which went beyond individual piety. He stressed that forms which produce regularity and exactitude should not be despised as formalism. The practical uses of self-denial include, he insisted, a heightened reflectiveness and a concrete reminder of Christ's sufferings which prepare "the mind for the different solemn occasions which recur in [the Church's] yearly service."[61] In the Prayer Book's fasting regulations, said Pusey, one can find the proper complement for the life of worship. The Prayer Book does not prescribe how a man should fast, and thus avoids Roman subtleties on the matter, but it does insist upon the regular use of self-denial in the Christian's life of communion with God. Nothing could be more in accord with the practice of the Primitive Church. In a short postscript Pusey argued that the neglect of fasting among Anglicans did not amount to its abrogation.

Newman and Keble welcomed Pusey's contribution to the cause not only out of old friendship or from the satisfaction that a slightly liberal lamb had come home again (Pusey, who owed his place in the university to Peel, had supported that statesman in the by-election of 1829). There were other more weighty reasons. "Without him," recalled Newman in the *Apologia*, "we should have had no chance, especially at the early date of 1834, of making any serious resistance to the liberal aggression. But Dr. Pusey was a Professor and Canon of Christ Church; he had a vast influence. . . . He was to the Movement all that Mr. Rose might have been, with that indispensable addition which was wanting to Mr.

Rose, the intimate friendship and the familiar daily society of the persons who had commenced it."[62] And if he could replace Rose, Pusey was worth, in Newman's estimation, a dozen William Palmers.

Pusey had held back at first from open association with the Tracts. He had been ill much of the autumn of 1833, and this explains part of his hesitancy. But the question of the Tracts' anonymity had bothered him too. He soon discovered that Newman's practical sense outweighed his doctrinaire position on that matter. Meeting Newman one day, Pusey, "wrapping his gown round him as he used to do," said, "I think you are too hard on the Peculiars [Evangelicals], as you call them. You should conciliate them; I am thinking of writing a letter myself with that purpose." "Well," said Newman, "suppose you let us have it for one of the Tracts." "Oh no," Pusey answered, "I will not be one of you." But Newman had the measure of his man. "Suppose," he said, "you let us have that letter of yours, . . . and attach your name or signature to it. You would not then be mixed up with us, nor in any way responsible for the Tracts." "Well," said Pusey, "if you will let me do that, I will."[63] So Tract Eighteen received its initials and the Movement a nickname; down to the bitter end the world would most commonly refer to it as "Puseyite."

The break with Palmer and the gradual but distinct drift from Rose were more than compensated for by the adherence of Pusey. Yet, in one sense it amounted to an exchange of a whole group for one individual. By the spring of 1834 it was clear that the Tracts were putting together a party rather than supporting a general rally. Much of the High Church discontent over the Irish Bishoprics Act had moderated. Palmer's addresses had used up much of the anger, and as the danger of imminent disestablishment receded, most of the parsons cooled down. More and more Newman sounded like a party manager. He counted an inner circle, by which he meant himself, Keble and Froude, soon to be joined by Pusey. Then there were, so to speak, the ward organizers, men like Keble's brother Tom; Isaac Williams of Trinity College, who was close to the Keble family and who soon would be Newman's curate at St. Mary's; John Bowden in London; the young Oriel dons and former pupils of Newman, like Frederic Rogers, Tom Mozley and Henry Wilberforce.

Other names soon began to appear in this list, two of them particularly notable. Charles Marriott[64] was elected in 1833 to the Oriel fellowship vacated by Robert Wilberforce. He was a frail man, eccentric in dress and mannerism; undergraduates called him "The Veiled Prophet" because of the black shawls he wrapped around himself and the skullcap perched on his head. They delighted to watch him at solemn functions at St. Mary's, where he invariably fell asleep, and while some distinguished preacher droned on they wagered whether the skullcap would slide off his bobbing head. Marriott used to say that the only preacher who did not put him to sleep was Newman, to whom his devotion was complete. The somnolence was due, however, not to indifference or insensitivity but to his wretched health. He bore this and all his crosses with a dignity which made his Oxford contemporaries call him unhesitatingly a saint. His work for the Movement was wholehearted but unspectacular, and if he had not been so peculiar-looking it is likely no one would have remembered he was there.

Not so Charles Portalis Golightly.[65] A wealthy B.A. of Oriel (1828), Golightly held a parish living for a brief time, and then moved to Oxford where he lived a life of clerical leisure. He was one of the most enthusiastic and outspoken of the Movement's early supporters. In August 1833 he wrote to Newman: "You might safely have assumed that I would most gladly join your society. . . . One of your principles I own I do not like: you protest against doing anything directly to separate Church and state. I would do the same perhaps in ordinary times," but in the light of the Irish Bishoprics Act "it appears to me that the time for separation is come."[66] With these fiery sentiments, Golightly, only half in jest, offered his Oxford house as a refuge from the police when the persecution started. In time he became himself the chief persecutor.

Newman looked for adherents wherever he could find them, and sometimes he grasped too hard. He was especially pleased when Henry Wilberforce told him that Bishop Sumner of Winchester liked the Tracts, and he dreamed that perhaps the bishop would give the Movement his episcopal sanction.[67] What he forgot was that Sumner was the most Evangelical of the whole bench of bishops and that a Wilberforce was welcome to him not for Oxford's sake but because he was a Wilberforce, the son of the greatest Evangelical of them all. Newman also heard that the Duke of Newcastle "has joined us 'in life and death, so that we are true to ourselves,'" and that there were other noblemen and squires ready to lend support. He hoped that William Gladstone might become active, though he thought him perhaps too young.[68] It is not recorded what comfort Newman took from what Rogers told him Christmas week, 1833: "I saw [Henry] Manning in town who wanted to see the Tracts which had come out since those which H. W[ilberforce] showed him, and [I] sent him accordingly to Turrill's."[69]

In Tract Number One, Newman had called upon the clergy of the Church of England to "Choose your side!" He had chosen his, and many of his dearest friends had gone along with him. That choice might involve them all in trouble, or even heartbreak. But in the beginning there was mostly exuberance and youthful exhilaration. "Of course," Newman said to Bowden, "there is much coldness and opposition; . . . but never mind, we will beat them."[70]

CHAPTER 8

A Certain Trumpet

By the end of 1833 twenty Tracts had been published. Reactions were various. The hard-line liberals predictably found them full of "folly" and "intolerance," to use Thomas Arnold's words. The Evangelicals were less ready to make up their minds; some of the Tracts—notably Number Ten, with its reference to the "Body and Blood of Christ"—they thought seriously objectionable, while others, which seemed to call unambiguously for a higher and more serious witness to the gospel, they could not help but like. Keble's association with the writers of the Tracts also softened the Evangelicals' judgments, since Keble's poetry was popular among them.[1] High Churchmen generally approved of what they read, though most of them carefully covered their bets. Dr. Spry of Canterbury, one of William Palmer's Tory friends, was typical. He sent word along to Oxford that he liked the Tracts, indeed, rejoiced in them; but he added that he could not pledge himself to endorse everything he found in them.[2]

One Hampshire clergyman reacted favourably to most of the Tracts, though he thought Number Sixteen weak and Number Thirteen "fanciful in parts." Number Fifteen he judged "a very poor one." Newman must have smiled a little at this last statement, for Tract Fifteen was the only one which Palmer had attempted to write. Several clergymen refused to order Tract Five, because it was written by a layman, John Bowden, who, on the title page, had revealed his lay status but not his name. Still another clergyman commented that the Tracts were excellent, but by no means should laymen be allowed to read them.[3]

Ideas for new Tracts sprang up on all sides. Newman eventually had to write down various "Topics for Agitation" and "Prospective Grievances" which came to his attention. Could Tracts be concocted out of such corrupt practices as laicizing ordained clerics, the suppression of cathedral chapters, allowing patrons to give livings to clergy of suspect orthodoxy, or holding parish meetings in the church building?[4] Only the times could tell.

I

On New Year's Day, 1834, Benjamin Harrison of Christ Church sent greetings to Newman in which he said, among other things, "I assure you, the more I see in this part of the world the more I feel that, without such a stand as you are making on apostolical grounds, all would fall to pieces."[5] And John Bowden, writing the same day from London, also mingled pessimism with congratulation. "Like you, I am not sanguine about your arresting, by your Movement, the flowing tide of innovation, but you are doing your duty; and the Church, if it does fall, I trust will fall with honour." Bowden added as an afterthought a rather unexciting bit of news: "The Duchess of Northumberland was highly delighted with the Tracts."[6]

Newman was not thinking much about great leisured ladies' judgments about the Tracts. He spent New Year's Day correcting proofs for the first volume of his sermons soon to be published, and a few days later he accepted a contract with the Clarendon Press to prepare an edition of the theological treatises of Dionysius, a third-century Bishop of Alexandria. "So you see," he wrote to Bowden, "I have enough to do." The scholarly work involved in a critical edition seemed to Newman doubly valuable; internally it promoted reflection and precision, and externally "such a work gives one a solid influence, built on a foundation which no one can shake, because no one can criticize."[7]

It was vain to hope to avoid criticism, but the Tract party—for so by this time it had become—did find 1834 a year in which its scholarship and its influence grew by leaps and bounds. Between January and November 27 Tracts appeared (Numbers Twenty-one to Forty-seven), together with eighteen cheap reprints of patristic literature. These latter were part of the "Records of the Church," a parallel series to the Tracts, which had resulted from the decision made at Hadleigh to provide at a minimal cost excerpts from the writings of St. Ignatius of Antioch. The series grew to include reprints of other ancient Christian authors, like Justin Martyr and Tertullian.

But whatever the pious reception given these patristic reprints, the original Tracts were what made the real sensation. And rightly so, for taken as a whole the 1834 production was far and away the best of the lot. With a few exceptions they were from a literary point of view crisply and sometimes beautifully written. They employed the varying techniques of straight narrative and dramatic dialogue to great effect. They were still short, pungent pieces, but they were more closely reasoned than their predecessors, contained more substance, and laid down more clearly just what program their authors had in mind. Perhaps this was the result of being freed from the Palmer-Tory chariot, or perhaps it was simply a coming of age.

Though most of them were good, the seven written by Newman himself stood head and shoulders above the rest. It seemed that the delicate mental blend of the mathematical and poetical had by 1834 reached a new level of maturity. Always precise and yet supple, here slashing and there probing, Newman's prose crackled with energy and his argumentation, if sometimes subtle, was nevertheless relentless and controlled. He treated various subjects in various ways. Tract Twenty-one was a simple statement of the New Testament revelation of the need for self-mortification, while Tract Thirty-one, called "The Reformed Church," took a highly rhetorical turn. Newman drew a striking parallel between the state of the contemporary Church and that of the post-exilic Jewish community; he argued that the schisms, partisanships, lack of zeal and many other ills afflicting the Church of England in the 1830s were mysteriously foreshadowed in the days after the Babylonian Captivity. He closed with a flourish: "Let it be remembered that when our Lord seems at greatest distance from his Church then he is even at the doors. Doubtless, when the angel appeared in the temple to Zacharias, the news of a miraculous interposition was as great a marvel to the world at large as if it were now noised abroad of one of our own ministers in the course of his Christian service."[8]

Tract Thirty-three showed Newman in another mood and employing a different approach. The Tractarians' elevated ideas about the role of bishops would remain largely theoretical unless the problems of diocesan structure in the Church of England were faced. Under the title "Primitive Episcopacy," Newman pointed out that in dioceses so vast as York, Chester or London, a bishop could hardly be a spiritual father and a font of Christian life; he was too exhausted by the huge administrative apparatus he had to keep going, to say nothing of his political and social obligations. The problem was not a new one, and various solutions had been advanced in the past. But they had all foundered on the sticky political consideration that more bishops meant more votes in the House of Lords. Newman did not appear to care much about this matter; if it is not feasible to split big dioceses into little ones, why not, he asked, reestablish the office of suffragan (i.e. auxiliary or assistant) bishop, which had the sanction of the Primitive Church and had thrived in England during Queen Elizabeth's reign. Surely, he argued, the Parliament which had just recently suppressed ten Irish sees could create some new English ones or at least some new suffragans without upsetting the political balance. The Tract was a straightforward, matter-of-fact document, which leaned heavily on population charts and quotations from statutes.[9]

He tackled a more theoretical question in Tract Thirty-four. Those who emphasize the doctrinal importance of the practice of the early Christian Church are often confronted with the fact that much of their system has no explicit warrant in Scripture. This, Newman admitted, is particularly the case with rites and customs, which Bible Christians think at best unnecessary and at worst superstitious. Newman's rebuttal to this objection centered in an exegesis of St. Paul to the Corinthians, wherein the Apostle blamed his converts "for not adhering to the *custom* of the Church, which prescribed that men should wear their hair short and that women should have their head covered during divine service; a custom apparently most unimportant if any one ever was." Yet St. Paul imposed it as strictly binding on the Christian community. Newman went on to cite several other similar examples of Pauline practice, and then commented: "These instances, then, not to notice others of a like or a different kind, are surely sufficient to reconcile us to the complete ritual system which breaks upon us in the writings of the Fathers. If any parts of it indeed are contrary to Scripture, that is of course a decisive reason at once for believing them to be additions and corruptions of the original ceremonial, but till this is shown, we are bound to venerate what is certainly primitive, and probably is apostolic."[10] In other words, the Ancient Church presents us with the elaborated system which the apostles established and which St. Paul testified to in his careful, even persnickety instruction about small matters of ritual observance. If, said Newman, rites and customs cannot be squared with Scripture—as is true of Roman Catholicism—then they must be abandoned; but the burden of proof is upon those who assert that the nineteenth century is in a better position than the fourth to say what went on in the first.

Newman wrote Tracts Thirty-eight and Forty-one in the form of a dialogue between "Laicus" and "Clericus." Both Tracts bore the title "Via Media," and together they provide perhaps the clearest and most rigorously reasoned statement of the Tractarian position ever presented. The churchman, argued Clericus, must take his stand on the liturgy and formularies of the Church. What about the Thirty-nine Articles, demanded Laicus? "The Liturgy," replied Clericus, "as coming down from the Apostles, is the depository of their complete teaching; while the Articles are polemical and except as they embody the creeds are only protests against certain definite errors." The Thirty-nine Articles answered the malaise of the sixteenth century and the problems raised by the Reformation; but the Prayer Book is forever.

Laicus responded by pointing out that the Articles have served the Church as a defense against Romanism. Not so, said Clericus. "Be assured of this—no party will be more opposed to our doctrine, if it ever prospers and makes noise, than the Roman party." This was the case in the seventeenth century, and it is the same now. "The glory of the

English Church is that it has taken a Via Media. . . . It lies *between* the Reformers and the Romanists." There is no denunciation of popery in the Articles as harsh as that which the Apostolical English churchman finds on every page of his Prayer Book. The trouble with Rome is not that she speaks reverently of the Primitive Church but that she has ruthlessly corrupted and altered what tradition has passed down to her. The real indictment of her can be found then in the ancient Christian formularies, rather than in a sixteenth-century protest.

"I would do what our reformers in the 16th century did," said Clericus; "they did not touch the existing documents of doctrine," which were preserved in the Prayer Book. "They *added* protests against the corruptions of faith, worship, and discipline which had grown up around them." The attack upon the pure revelation comes now, however, from a different quarter. "I would have the Church do the same thing now, if I could; she should not *change* the Articles, she should add to them; add protests against the erastianism and latitudinarianism which have incrusted them." Liberalism is the enemy of the moment, argued Clericus, and the Protestant element within the Church of England cannot turn back the liberals any more than Romanism can. "A number of distinct doctrines are included in the notion of Protestantism; and as to all these our Church has taken a Via Media between it and Popery."

By "our Church" here Newman meant of course the Church of the Prayer Book, which was the closest possible approximation of the primitive Christian community and with which neither popery nor Protestantism has any genuine harmony—Protestantism, Clericus maintained, "as the religion of so-called freedom and independence, as hating superstition, suspicious of forms, jealous of priestcraft, advocating heart worship; characteristics which admit of a good or bad interpretation, but which understood as they are instanced in the majority of persons who are zealous for what is called Protestant doctrine are (I maintain) very inconsistent with the Liturgy of our Church."[11]

Thus by the middle of 1834 Newman had articulated the point of view which seven years later, in the crisis over Tract Ninety, would break him; that the Church of England was not and indeed could not be Protestant, except in the most superficial sense, and that therefore the Articles must have a catholic interpretation. Thomas Arnold was not wrong in calling the Tractarians the new Non-Jurors. Newman followed Richard Hooker and the other Caroline divines in seeing the Church as a sacramental, grace-dispensing reality, and he was as ready as the malcontented High Churchmen of the 1690s to forswear the state connection. "When the Church," he had Clericus say in Tract Forty-one, "with an unprecedented confidence, bound herself hand and foot, and made herself over to the civil power in order to escape the pope, she did not expect that infidels . . . would be suffered to have absolute disposal of crown patronage."[12]

Like the two Tracts on the Via Media, Tract Forty-five, called "The Grounds of our Faith," also examined the Protestant-catholic tension within the Church of England. It was concerned, however, more directly with what might be termed methodological considerations. There is a tendency within Protestantism, said Newman, with its tenet that Scripture alone proves the faith, "to generate a cautious, discriminative turn of thought, to fix in the mind a *standard* of proof simulating demonstration and to make light of mere probabilities." This attitude owes its existence to the atmosphere of controversy which marked the beginning of the Protestant sects when "various intellectual gifts, such as argumentative subtlety, critical acumen, knowledge of languages, rose into importance and became the interpreters of Christian truth. . . . It followed that in the course of time all the delicate shades of truth and falsehood, the unobtrusive indications of God's will, . . . were rudely rejected; the crumbs from the rich man's table, which faith eagerly looks about for, were despised by the proud-hearted intellectualist who . . . would be content with nothing short of certainty. . . ." This "cold, hard and unimpassioned temper" makes us turn away from the practice of the Church as a guide to our actions, because such practice does not automatically supply a syllogistic proof. Take, for example, the matters of episcopacy and infant Baptism. These two integral parts of Christian life are at best "obscurely contained" in Scripture "and cannot be drawn out from it without a great deal of delicate care and skill. Here comes in the operation of that principle of *faith* in opposition to *criticism*, . . . the principle of being content with a little light, where we cannot obtain sunshine. If it is *probably* pleasing to Christ, let us maintain it."[13]

What Newman recommended in Tract Forty-five was a "true wariness and Christian caution; very different from that spurious caution which ultra-Protestantism exercises."[14] Echoing Hawkins' sermon on unauthoritative tradition of fifteen years before, Newman scorned the Protestant idea of the all-sufficiency of Scripture when that term is taken to mean that the Bible contains a workable and systematic program of conduct. To ignore the precedent of the Ancient Church is a momentous decision, because it involves giving up the Scripture altogether or else reducing it to a sort of magic manual wherein a man fumbles for confirmation of ideas which have come to him out of his own wickedness or the wickedness of the world.

II

The other Tracts published between January and November of 1834 may have been several cuts below Newman's both in style and substance, but except for three of them they made a solid contribution to the common cause. The exceptions were the work of Arthur Perceval. His "Churchman's Manual," the subject of so much tedious conversation at Hadleigh, was now in print and being circulated, much to the perplexity of the Tractarians, who did not know quite what use to make of it.[15] Perceval's Tracts—Numbers Twenty-three, Thirty-five and Thirty-six— were more of the same: empty rhetoric and bombast, with hardly a cliché missing, appeals to rally to something or other and to face obstacles squarely, lists of enemies—ranging from Unitarians to Roman Catholics—who, "obeying Satan's bidding, are endeavouring to do that together which they have failed to do singly, namely, to overthrow and destroy our branch of the catholic and apostolic Church."[16] Perceval's eagerness to help grew increasingly pathetic, as more and more the impatience of Keble and Newman became apparent. Perceval was doomed to the role of the well-intentioned but ineffectual Parson Blimp.

Dramatic dialogue was a mechanism used in two Tracts by Bowden and in three by the Keble brothers. Bowden's imaginary conversation took place (Tracts Twenty-nine and Thirty) between John Evans, a young layman who has left the Church of England for a dissenting sect, and his former parson, Dr. Spencer. John feels that the intensity and earnestness of the dissenting minister's preaching is better for him spiritually than Dr. Spencer's rather chilly, matter-of-fact presentation. After a bit of talk, however, during which Dr. Spencer enlightens John with the standard arguments in defense of the visibility of the Church and apostolical succession, John sees the light: "The true liberty," says John (with his hand, one must suppose, on his heart), "wherewith Christ has made us free, is theirs alone who, in reverencing his ministers, walk the way of his commandments."[17]

The Keble dialogues were in a series called "Richard Nelson" (Tracts Twenty-two and Forty-three by Thomas Keble, Tract Forty by John). Richard is an honest country mason, a sort of Tractarian Adam Bede, who talks to his parson about various ecclesiastical matters. He takes always the highest Apostolical view. While building a wall to protect his garden, Richard muses (Number Twenty-two) on the utility of the Athanasian Creed, which is "a fence or bulwark, set up to protect the Truth against all innovations and encroachments."[18] Later, in Tract Forty, Richard's nephew was going to marry an unbaptized girl, but Richard's opposition postponed the event. The bride's father, an unsettled and wild man politically, and something of a Baptist, scorned the idea of the sacredness of Christian marriage and so was unconvinced about the necessity for his daughter's baptism. Says Richard: "He has picked up this notion among others, which, I understand, the French are very full of, as well as our Frenchified newspapers."[19] Though he is called cruel and hardhearted by the prospective bride, Richard sticks by his guns and prevails in the end. Tract Forty-three finds Richard opposing the shortening of the liturgy, which, the proponents of such a scheme say, "need not altogether take up thirty-five or forty minutes at the outside, allowing fifteen or twenty for the sermon." To achieve this brevity would involve leaving out the creeds, absolutions and three fifths of the scriptural lessons which, Richard learns to his horror, are being called superstitions. "Well," Richard says, "whatever effect such a measure might have on the *Establishment*, I am confident it would deeply injure the *Church*."[20] The Richard Nelson series was a very effective one. It flowed smoothly and made its points in a charming way. From the consistency in style it would appear that the Keble brothers worked together on it. There was one slightly jarring note: Richard, horny-handed son of toil though he is, talks nevertheless like an Oxford don.

Except of course for Newman, the best writer the Tract party ever produced was Benjamin Harrison, Student of Christ Church and later Archdeacon of Maidstone. During the early days of the Movement he and Newman were very close, though the intimacy did not last. He contributed four Tracts, one of which, Number Twenty-four, appeared in January 1834. Harrison's thesis in this tightly reasoned essay was that the exercise and (prior to that) the existence of apostolical authority is a universal concept and only incidentally related to the age of miracles. It was an attempt to answer the objection often raised—by Thomas Arnold, for example—that one's contemporary religious practice cannot be determined by an era in the Church's history so far removed from one's own. Harrison skillfully combined rhetoric and a commentary on the Pauline epistles to show that regard for the Primitive Church is not simply a species of antiquarianism. He concluded on a note which was both light and shrewd: It is true that the present-day successors of the apostles cannot be as sure as were the apostles themselves "that in the commandments which they give they have the Spirit of God." But "neither can the people feel so sure as in those days of miraculous gifts that *they* have the Spirit of God with *them*; and thus the *relation* between the two parties remains unaltered."[21]

The Tractarians never concealed the fact that they were trying to breathe new life into a theology which had flourished in England during an earlier time. It was therefore not surprising that they incorporated into the Tracts some of the writings of the Caroline divines. The first of these reprints to appear—published as Tract Twenty-five—was a sermon by the seventeenth-century bishop named William Beveridge who pleaded with his own contemporaries for daily service, morning and evening, which, though prescribed by Scripture, patristic example and English statute, was yet "shamefully neglected all the kingdom over." The neglect was no less widespread in the 1830s and it was one of the practical faults the Tractarians were most anxious to correct. They felt strongly too about a related matter, the due place in Christian piety of the sacrament of the Eucharist. Tract Twenty-six was another extract from Bishop Beveridge, on "The Necessity and Advantage of Frequent Communion." To clear themselves of any possible charge of Roman sympathies in this area, Tracts Twenty-seven and Twenty-eight reprinted the attack of Bishop John Cosin (1594–1672) on transubstantiation; Cosin maintained that there was a spiritual but nevertheless real presence of Christ in the Eucharist. This Eucharistic emphasis—a constant theme with the Tractarians—was testified to also by an original Tract (Number Thirty-two) written by a young Oriel don named Charles Eden, who rather stiffly made his own appeal for more frequent celebration of the Lord's Supper.

Finally, two reprints (Tracts Thirty-seven and Thirty-nine) pointed out that the English Church had, in the seventeenth century, practiced a form of excommunication and thus demonstrated its basic independence of the state. Here, in the judgment of the Tractarians, was one more subject which the contemporary Church ought to take up. Surely an important criterion of an organization's freedom is its ability to determine who will be members in good standing. One wonders if, somewhere in Oriel, lists of naughty people, fit for excommunication, were wistfully drawn up.

III

Getting the Tracts written was the first hurdle but by no means the only one. If they were to serve their authors' idealistic purposes, they had to be read, pondered and then, hopefully, acted upon. "Our object," said Newman, "is to scatter information," and to do this effectively involved setting up some kind of circulation mechanism across the country. This proved to be more easily said than done.

By the beginning of 1834 a strangely inconsistent pattern had emerged. The Tracts were selling fast enough to necessitate reprints. They were being widely discussed in clerical circles and they had become notorious enough to have been adversely commented upon in the press. Newman was especially cheered by the request of the British Museum for copies of the Tracts to be placed in the Museum's collection. Even so, the publishers or booksellers—including Parker in Oxford—hesitated to stock them. Penny leaflets of a highly partisan nature apparently did not yield a percentage to the booksellers worth the trouble. Part of the difficulty was the inefficiency of Turrill, the London outlet, who offered to handle the Tracts exclusively—and guarantee their circulation—if they were converted into a periodical. Newman did not like this notion, but growing more impatient at having "to write, correct press, distribute all the Tracts" by himself, he was sorely tempted to accept.

John Bowden acted as Newman's London agent and pressed Turrill as hard as he could, but Bowden was an amateur at the publishing business and he had personal preoccupations of his own. In March 1834 Turrill entered into negotiation with the Rivington firm, which had already published the first volume of Newman's sermons, and this gave Newman hope that together the two booksellers might solve the circulation problem. "But," he observed to Bowden, "they have been slow about it, and meanwhile I have been undecided whether to wait for it or not."[22] In the end Turrill gave up the Tracts altogether and Rivington took them over. This change, however, made little practical difference.

Shortage of adequate funds was of course the real obstacle. The writers of the Tracts paid for the printing costs themselves, and though they were none of them poor men there was a limit to their financial resources. The publisher—Turrill or Rivington as the case may have been—was the seller, but not necessarily the printer, and outside his main shop in London he had only the scantiest connections, usually with other publishers in other cities. Advertising in the modern sense was unknown in the 1830s, and so many people did not read the Tracts because they did not know where to get them. "We are in want of money for the Tracts," Newman told Henry Wilberforce early in 1834, money to set up depots around the country, money to pay for sending the Tracts from London to the provinces in regular and predictable cycles.[23] Many of the Tractarians themselves contributed sums beyond what they already paid for printing—notably the ever-generous Bowden—and no doubt much of Newman's income went the same way.[24] But not for six or seven years, not till the Tracts had become book-sized treatises instead of throwaway leaflets, did they see much fruit of their extra investment.

Throughout 1834 and 1835 Newman racked his brain to find a way to circulate the Tracts more effectively. At first, as we have seen, he hoped the federation of churchmen's societies would serve as a network of distribution. When this came to nothing, he tried to contact individual clergymen in various parts of the country who might take upon themselves the responsibility of maintaining Tract centers. The results of this plan were very uneven. In Kent there were seven clergymen who responded favourably, including Robert Wilberforce and Charles Golightly, the latter of whom Newman described as "zealous" in the cause. In Oxfordshire, as one might expect, there were all kinds of willing participants, but in Cornwall there was only one. Archdeacon Froude ordered fifty copies a month, and Newman hoped that more response would ultimately come from Devon. In Gloucestershire only two participating clergymen could be found, besides of course the Keble brothers. Young Tom Mozley was "very zealous" in Northamptonshire. Most counties had no more than two or three voluntary centers and some had none.[25]

The circulation of the Tracts received something of a boost when

Rivington published the first forty-seven of them in a bound volume in November 1834. Newman wrote a preface for the new publication in which he outlined the intent of the Tract writers and the dangers they were trying to combat. "The neglect of the daily service, the desecration of festivals, the Eucharist scantily administered, insubordination permitted in all ranks of the Church . . . lead the feverish mind, desirous of a vent to its feelings and a stricter rule of life, to the smaller religious communities, to prayer and bible meetings . . . on the one hand,—on the other, to the solemn and captivating services by which popery gains its proselytes."[26] The volume had as its motto, "If the trumpet give an uncertain sound, who shall prepare himself to the battle?" The collection was no doubt a useful one, and brought Tractarian ideas to a new audience, but both by reason of its expense and its bulk it could not sound the trumpet in the sharp tone which Newman had in mind.

The appearance of the bound volume of Tracts did not prevent the basic circulation problem from getting worse. It reached its most acute stage in the summer of 1835. In August Rivington wrote to Newman to say that he wanted to cease being the publisher. Newman, obviously hurt and chagrined, wrote grimly to Bowden, "So I suppose we shall end at once."[27] Bowden hoped that the series could be carried on long enough to provide enough Tracts for a second bound volume. "At any rate, do not close abruptly or as it were fly from the field. March off with drums beating and colours flying in a farewell tract. . . . Make it appear that the work which you had undertaken has been accomplished, not given up."[28] When Harrison heard the news he asked, not too tactfully, "Could you not strengthen [the Tracts] by a little more *originality*?"[29] Pusey, who was in the process of writing a tract, suggested that perhaps "they might have done their work, and they might be resumed less offensively under another name, i.e. that we might gently let down the persons who have ignorantly declared against them."[30] Hugh Rose sent his regrets and promised to write a "strong" article in the *British Magazine* "as to the stupid folly which could not understand or value them."[31]

Throughout the autumn the fate of the Tracts hung in the balance. At one point it was decided that Keble should be editor of a periodical of Tracts which would appear monthly or perhaps every other month. Keble was willing enough. "Newman sends me word," he wrote to his brother Tom, "I am to be editor of the Tracts. If so, one of the first must be, 'Doctrines preacht by Mr. T. K. and excepted against by Mr. J. K., the 4th of October, 1835.' "[32] Newman, however, could not take such a light tone. It is clear that he did not want to give up the editorship, but he would never agree to a periodical format. "I am quite decided that I cannot be editor of the Tracts if they come out once a month. . . . It is the way to make them mere trash."[33]

Rivington, like Turrill before him, felt that a monthly journal was the only salvation for the Tracts. "Rivington says he does not sell two hundred copies of them," Newman reported glumly, and "I myself take thirty."[34] But Newman was convinced that the publisher himself was principally to blame for the poor circulation. Not only did Rivington fail to get the Tracts sent down to the country, but even his London shop gave spotty service. Bowden's well-intentioned attempt to keep the publisher on his toes had not been enough. "We must have a vigilant London superintendent," someone who will press Rivington in more than a casual way. "A year since I urged [Rivington] to put the business of the Tracts into the hands of one of [his] clerks or shopmen, and offered to pay for doing it, but [he] would not." Newman also pleaded with Rivington to let a Fleet Street publisher sell the Tracts and divide the publisher's percentage, but Rivington showed no enthusiasm for this idea either.[35]

In October 1835 Newman put together a detailed plan to get more distribution for the Tracts in the country. The plan involved circularizing clergymen who were asked "to cooperate in the promotion of Church principles" by ordering from Rivington in Newman's name and "without payment, a supply of the Tracts for the Times, so many copies of each Tract, to be sent down to you by coach quarterly, that is, on the first days of January, April, July and October." The clergyman should next "engage a publisher or other fit person in the nearest considerable town" to sell the Tracts on a percentage basis. Once a suitable merchant was found, the clergyman ought to "provide him with a board painted 'Tracts for the Times against Popery and Dissent,' and . . . see that it occupies a conspicuous place in his window." At the end of the year the clergyman was requested to send Newman an account of the number of Tracts received, of those still on hand, and the money earned by sales. As a kind of desperate afterthought, Newman urged that "*real* friends" of the Church be enlisted to do the same everywhere.[36]

Whether or not this plan was responsible, the Tracts began to sell better in 1836 and the upward curve continued in succeeding years. Rivington changed his mind and stayed on as publisher. The bound volumes of Tracts made their regular appearance in his London shop until eventually there were six of them. The Tracts now became longer, "much more treatises than sketches," as Newman put it, and this may have helped sales. Pusey's Tracts on Baptism (Numbers Sixty-seven, Sixty-eight and Sixty-nine) initiated this new trend; they formed together a dissertation of more than two hundred pages.

Newman had survived a crisis of sorts. He had won his main points, that the Tracts would not appear in contemptible "monthly dribblets," and that he himself would continue as editor. Keble perhaps sensed that Newman, for all his diffident talk, did not really want to resign. At any rate, by the middle of November 1835 Keble confessed second thoughts about his own position; though he would not refuse the post, he would not, for the moment, accept it either.[37] Keble had just been married, a step of which Newman sternly disapproved, and communication between the two was not at its cordial best. Meantime, Newman was hard at work on the circulation plan. And anyway Keble was not indispensable for the Tracts; only Newman was. And it was not reprehensible of him that he knew it.

In due time literally thousands of Tracts were in circulation, but these early reverses nevertheless had a permanent effect upon the Oxford Movement. The first Tracts, particularly the brilliant set published in 1834, laid the foundation for the later ones, a foundation at once doctrinal and psychological. To take the most obvious example: Tract Ninety sold ten thousand copies in a few weeks; it was in the hands of everyone and was discussed everywhere. It produced profound shock in the minds of many for whom it was an introduction to Tractarian views. But the basic ideas of Tract Ninety had been part of the public domain since 1834, almost seven years earlier, when Newman's two Tracts on the Via Media appeared. It is at least arguable that had the Tractarians succeeded better in circulating their little pamphlets in 1834 and 1835, much of the tragedy of 1841 could have been avoided.

CHAPTER 9

Conflict and Loss

Pusey sent a copy of his Tract on fasting to Thomas Arnold. The Headmaster of Rugby read it, pondered it for some weeks, and then sent its author a courteous but firm dissent. "My dear Pusey," he wrote, "I consider it very kind of you to send me the little tract. . . . I am sure there must be many points of unison still between us, without ascending to the highest of all; though by the form in which your tract appears I fear you are lending your cooperation to a party second to none in the tendency of their principles to overthrow the truth of the gospel." Arnold absolved Pusey of the "intolerance" and "folly" which marked the other Tracts, but he thought that Tract Eighteen shared the shallow antiquarianism which the new Oxford party appeared intent on erecting into a principle of orthodoxy. "The system pursued in Oxford seems to be leading to a rivival of the Non-jurors, a party far too mischievous and too foolish ever to be revived with success. But it may be revived enough to do harm—to cause the ruin of the Church of England first—and as far as human folly and corruption can to obstruct the progress of the Church of Christ."[1]

Arnold's letter was written in February 1834, the same month that the clerical address was presented to the Archbishop of Canterbury. One of those who had not signed the address was Renn Dickson Hampden. Newman had presented a copy to him and had invited his signature, and it was to Newman that the Principal of St. Mary Hall sent his chilly and contemptuous reply. "I am very sorry to say that I have not had time as yet to give due consideration to the proposed address from the clergy, which you have been so kind as to send me. There are so many things before me just at present which I am forced to attend to that I readily pass over what is not equally imperative. I trust, therefore, that you will excuse my only acknowledging it with my thanks."[2]

From another quarter came a different kind of reaction. Hurrell Froude, waiting to board the ship which was to take him to the West

Indies, penned a heated note to Newman. "I would not have had a hand in printing that address. . . . You should not have admitted that our system is in any respect defective now, in which it was ever anything but defective."[3]

And a little later, during the spring of 1834, Dr. Richard Whately, sometime Fellow of Oriel College, and now Archbishop of Dublin, paid a visit to Oxford. One Sunday while he was there, Dr. Whately received Holy Communion in the Oriel chapel. It was noted at the time that Mr. Newman was not present at this Communion service, and the archbishop was told by various people that Newman had absented himself because he could not share the Eucharistic cup with a man of Dr. Whately's heterodox views.[4]

As the Tract Movement shifted unevenly into high gear, everyone began to notice it and some began to fear it.

I

A topic which occupied the thoughts and filled the writings of the Tract party, from the beginning of its existence to the end, was the Thirty-nine Articles of 1563. These Elizabethan statements of doctrine smacked of a Protestantism much too strong for men who wanted the Church of England to conform to a primitive catholicity. Or rather, as the Tractarians themselves would have expressed it, the Articles reflected the passions of the Reformation era during which they were written, and therefore they *appeared* too Protestant, when in fact they were merely anti-Roman. For most Englishmen this distinction was overly subtle; being anti-Roman meant, they thought, the same as being Protestant. The Tractarians strenuously objected to this point of view. We have seen how Newman in the Via Media Tracts of 1834 attempted to put the Articles in their proper place; they were not, he argued, on a par with the primitive creeds and formularies as proclaimed in the Prayer Book. The Articles were useful because they combated certain Roman corruptions, but they did not compromise, they could not compromise, the essential catholicism of the Church. The Church of England, said the Tractarians, was not just a nice balance between the Protestantism of the Articles and the catholicism of the Prayer Book, she was rather the reincarnation in this time and place of the ancient Christian community which spurned both Roman decay and Protestant nihilism.

Ever since Queen Elizabeth's days the Articles had been used as a mechanism to ensure an ecclesiastical uniformity which was judged to be a condition for the nation's stability. Every Englishman in public life at some time or other had to accept the Articles in a solemn and public fashion and thus make avowal of his support of the Church as defined by the Elizabethan and succeeding governments. The Articles could be construed in a way that both the highest and lowest churchman could accept—"subscribe" to them was the technical expression—in good conscience, but they did effectively classify Roman Catholics and left-wing Protestants and exclude them, which of course was their original purpose. Among those obliged to subscribe to the Articles were the students at the universities; indeed, at Oxford the undergraduate had to subscribe twice, first at matriculation and again just before he took his degree.

By 1834, however, the political conditions which had prevailed when the Articles were drawn up had radically changed. Neither the Roman Catholic community, now small, isolated and inconsequential, nor bellicose Puritans any longer threatened the Establishment. But the Dissenters, their numbers growing swiftly and with new energies born of the Wesleyan reformation of a generation earlier, found subscription to the Articles a galling thing and an obstacle to the pluralistic society which they quite understandably desired. And they possessed some political leverage. In 1828, with the repeal of the Test and Corporation Acts, the Dissenters had received practically total political enfranchisement, and their support had contributed to the Whig victory at the polls in 1831 and to the passage of the Reform Act a year later. They had a right to expect some reward.

One of the matters which concerned the Dissenters most was the Establishment's monopoly of higher education. It was all very well to be able to vote, but a Dissenter could not hope that his son might achieve high station in politics or the professions so long as he was kept out of the universities. The London University was still in its infancy. That left only Oxford and Cambridge where subscription to the Articles, and hence formal acceptance of Anglicanism, was a requirement. On April 21, 1834, a member of the House of Commons, and a Dissenter, named G. W. Wood, brought in a bill which would make it "lawful for all His Majesty's subjects to enter and matriculate in the universities of England, and to receive and enjoy all degrees in learning conferred therein (degrees in divinity alone excepted) without being required to subscribe to any Articles of religion or to make any declaration of religious opinions. . . ."[5]

At about the same time an effort similar to Wood's (but apparently unconnected to it) was launched by a small group of liberal Cambridge dons. They petitioned both houses of Parliament for a reexamination of the question of religious tests in the universities and, specifically, the use made of the Thirty-nine Articles as an instrument of exclusion. The reaction at Cambridge was swift. Counterpetitions were signed by the majority of dons, the Heads of Houses and the undergraduates. These too were presented to Lords and Commons and were debated on the very day that Wood introduced his bill.[6]

By coincidence it was also the same day that the first of many meetings was convened by a self-appointed committee to organize resistance within the Oxford academic community. In attendance were Newman, Pusey and William Sewell, Fellow of Exeter. At Oxford, where neither liberals nor Evangelicals were so numerous as at Cambridge, the opposition to admission of Dissenters—for that is what the issue boiled down to—was overwhelming. The committee took upon itself the task of giving the university an opportunity to express itself. A declaration was first drawn up and submitted to those immediately concerned with instruction and discipline, that is, the professors, deans of colleges and public tutors. Within a few days the declaration was published with eighty-two signatures; only six refused to sign it. In the following weeks the declaration was widely circulated, printed in a half-dozen forms, incorporated into various magazines and newspapers. The committee then issued declarations of agreement and offered them to the various Oxford publics. The results were gratifying. Signatures were secured from the Proctors and 25 Heads of Houses, from 1900 members of Convocation (out of about 2500 total), from more than 2000 parents of undergraduates and from 1200 or so students.

The declaration was unequivocal. It maintained that "the University of Oxford has always considered religion to be the foundation of all education," and it protested against the idea "that religion can be taught on the vague and comprehensive principle of admitting persons of every creed." Therefore, "uniformity of faith upon essential points is absolutely necessary" and "the admission of persons who dissent from the Church of England would . . . unsettle the minds of the younger members of the university [i.e. the undergraduates], would raise up and continue a spirit of controversy which is at present unknown, and would tend to reduce religion to an empty and unmeaning name. . . ."[7]

The excitement over the Dissenters' issue was intense during the spring and early summer of 1834. Pamphlets spilled from the press at a rate of about three to one against admission. Keble wrote jauntily from Fairford that if Wood's bill passed he, Keble, would refuse obedience. Sewell described himself as "ready for martyrdom," which expression exaggerated somewhat the explosiveness of the question.[8] On July 28th, Wood's bill passed the Commons, but three days later it was thrown out by the Lords.

II

The universities had spoken—Cambridge a little more falteringly than Oxford—and the remnant of aristocratic power had supported them. For the moment the danger had passed. But the debate over the Dissenters' admission to English institutions of higher learning remained a lively one until 1871, when all religious tests were done away with.

The arguments on both sides had merit. The conservatives made the technical point that the universities and the colleges within the universities were private corporations and therefore had an inalienable right to govern their own internal affairs without intervention of Parliament. The liberals countered this by saying that whatever the original nature of the universities may have been they were now national institutions, whose graduates received certain automatic advantages in, for instance, the professions of law and medicine. To deny Dissenters these advantages simply because they would not subscribe to the Thirty-nine Articles was a form of naked discrimination.

Perhaps more overriding, however, was a question of fact. Did acceptance of the Articles indeed form part of the universities' educational system? The conservatives maintained it did, because much of the instruction given by the college tutors was strictly theological while some was tangentially so. Thus, for example, a student learned Greek by studying the New Testament texts, which could not be treated philologically without some reference to religious doctrine. The liberals scoffed at this assertion and pointed to the notorious religious laxity in the universities which had been widely deplored for generations. It would seem that the liberals had the better of this exchange, for although religious standards were much higher in 1834 than, say, twenty years earlier, it was still the rare college tutor who went to a great deal of trouble over his pupil's religious instruction and practice. We have already seen what happened to the attempt at Oriel by Newman, Froude and Robert Wilberforce to give the tutors a more definite religious role.

It may seem strange on the surface that the Tractarians should have rallied so strongly to the cause of subscription. They constantly warned that the Articles should not be taken too seriously and yet two out of three of the organizers of Oxford resistance to the admission of Dissenters were Tractarians. Of course, Newman and Pusey would automatically be opposed to any alteration of the religious status quo, especially if it threatened to water down even more the tepid theological mixture already inside the Established Church. They saw the value of subscription as a mechanism which would protect their students against such eccentricities as Unitarianism and Methodism. One task at a time, they seemed to be saying; once the Church of England is properly catholicized, then we can turn to the extreme Protestants.

But the Tractarian thought on the matter went deeper than that. Newman's mature views on the importance of subscription are worth quoting at some length. The basic value of subscription, he wrote to Arthur Perceval at the beginning of 1836, is

its witnessing to the principle that religion is to be approached with a submission of the understanding. Nothing is so common, as you must know, as for young men to approach serious subjects as judges—to study them as mere sciences. Aristotle and Butler are treated as teachers of *a* system, not as if there was more truth in them than in Jeremy Bentham. The study of the Evidences as now popular (such as Paley's) encourages this evil frame of mind—the learner is supposed external to the system. Our Lord is "a young Gallilean peasant," his apostles "honest men, trustworthy witnesses," and the like. Milman's [*History of the*] *Jews* exhibits the same characteristic in another department: Abraham is a sheik, etc. etc. In all these cases the student is supposed to look upon the system from without, and to have to choose it by an act of reason before he submits to it—whereas the great lesson of the gospel is faith, an obeying prior to reason, and *proving* its reasonableness by making experiment of it, a casting of heart and mind into the system, and investigating the truth by practice.[9]

What any religious system demands, Newman continued, is a "prompt and frank submission in the first instance," and in this fact lies the importance of subscription for university undergraduates. "In an age . . . when this principle is scouted, subscription to the Articles is a memento and protest—and again actually does, I believe, impress upon the minds of young men the teachable and subdued temper expected of them." The principle at stake did not depend upon "the degree of accuracy, the wisdom etc. of the Articles themselves. I am no great friend of them— and should rejoice to be able to substitute the Creeds for them. . . ."[10] Until the Church found a better mechanism of exclusion and a more suitable manner of encouraging student docility, subscription would have to do the job.

III

The first assault upon the Articles had come from outside Oxford— from the Dissenters in Parliament and from a minority group at Cambridge. When the fight started again late in the summer of 1834, the enemy was within the gates. "Hampden," Newman told Hugh Rose, "has just published a pamphlet [in which] he calls all articles impositions of human authority and advocates their removal as a test on matriculations—and assures his reader that all this is in no wise inconsistent with his being partner to the Declaration [of professors, deans and tutors] of May last. Do not take my word for it, since I have not read his effusion."[11] R. D. Hampden's effusion was entitled "Observations on Religious Dissent," and what Newman had heard about it was substantially correct. Hampden claimed to raise a point which "does not appear to have been attended to at all hitherto in any discussions of the subject of Christian dissent." He put his thesis in the form of a rhetorical question: "What is dissent in religion but difference of opinions arising out of the different conclusions drawn by different minds out of the same given elements of Scripture?" Roman Catholics, said Hampden, solve the problem by inventing tradition as an instrument to explain Scripture. Protestants, with their love of freedom, refrain from such a travesty, and so to discover the roots of their differences one must go back and investigate the various first steps which sects took from the common scriptural base. When one does so, one sees "that they differ in fact more in what is matter of human opinion and speculation than in their acceptance of divine truth."

In almost every word of his pamphlet could be heard the echo of Hampden's Bampton Lectures of 1832–33. "No conclusions of human reasoning," he argued, "however correctly deduced, however logically sound, are properly religious truths." They are merely, as he had said in the pulpit of St. Mary's, instances of "scholastic philosophy." "The principles of expediency . . . alone justify the separation of Christians into distinct communions." Arguments about religious truth all end nowhere. "If the alleged point cannot be proved out of Scripture, it is no truth of revelation." The converse of this principle, however, is false. "It by no means . . . follows that what can be proved out of Scripture must *therefore* be truth of revelation. To assert this would be to give an opening to every ingenious arguer—every skillful commentator or expositor—to pass off his own conclusions for the dictates of Scripture."

Hampden did not agree, for example, with the Unitarian theology, but he was consoled that the Unitarians received both Testaments and therefore deservedly bore the name Christian. "Who indeed is justified in denying the title to anyone who professes to love Christ in sincerity?" Theological opinions abound, and who is to say one is better than the other? "It seems *practically* impossible to check the tendency of the mind to speculate on such subjects, however *theoretically* unsound such speculation . . . must be."

What then about the admission of Dissenters to the universities? Hampden answered, with less than rigorous logic, that, though controversy over religious differences is pointless, yet education of the young in Anglican formularies is defensible because it is "strictly within our own province as a distinct communion." So it may well be that Anglicans cannot countenance "admission of Dissenters from our communion *as Dissenters.*" But he could not see why they should not be admitted precisely "*because* they are Dissenters." If they want to "come amongst us, and conform to our discipline, and receive instruction from us, knowing that we are members of the Church of England," what harm would there be? In short, the religious test involved in subscription to the Articles should go, for the Articles "may be very useful for ascertaining the competence of teachers or official persons in the university, but can be of no service to those who are to be taught."[12]

Hampden's "Observations" appeared first in August 1834. The pamphlet sold well enough to necessitate a second edition which came out

the following November. Hampden sent a copy of this edition to Newman, who replied in a note which, he noted later, "was the beginning
of hostilities in the university."

Dear Mr. Principal [Newman wrote], the kindness which has led to your presenting me with your pamphlet encourages me to hope that you will forgive
me if I take the opportunity it affords to express to you my very sincere and
deep regret that it has been published. . . . While I respect the tone of piety
in which the pamphlet is written, I feel an aversion to the principles it professes as (in my opinion) legitimately tending to formal Socinianism. And also
I lament that, by its appearance, the first step has been taken towards an inter-
ruption of that peace and mutual good understanding which has prevailed so
long in this place.[13]

Hampden immediately responded in a good-humoured though rather
condescending manner that he was ready "to hear any arguments that
may be alleged against my notions, to examine any such with freedom—
and admit my error if I can be proved to be wrong."[14] Before the dust
settled, R. D. Hampden was to hear many arguments, most of which he
did not like.

Even before the subscription controversy began, little love had been
lost between Newman and Hampden. Their paths had already crossed
on at least two occasions which could not but have left some personal
animosity. In the midst of the tutorial controversy at Oriel, Hawkins had
invited Hampden to give college lectures in place of the tutors he had
sacked, the chief among whom, of course, was Newman. This event
had scarred both men, because while Newman was annoyed at Hampden's
cooperation with Hawkins, Hampden for his part was chagrined (and
Newman somewhat wryly amused) at his failure to substitute adequately
for the dismissed tutors.[15] Then, early in 1834, Newman decided to stand
for election to the university professorship of moral philosophy. Despite
his usual diffident talk—"I have very little earnestness for the office."
"I have no especial wish for it"[16]—Newman understood the prestige
attached to a professorship, even to this "sinecure of trouble," as he called
it because of its bankrupt endowment. The influence would in his judgment have been worth the small trouble, and since no one else appeared
interested his election seemed secure. He was "floored" when at the last
moment Hampden declared himself available, and the electors—the Vice-
chancellor, the Proctors, the Dean of Christ Church, the President of
Magdalen and the President of St. John's—promptly elected him.[17] The
Oxford power structure had more in common with Hampden than with
the earnest, perhaps slightly fanatical young Oriel don.

Even so, the relationship between Newman and Hampden had remained up to this time formally correct. St. Mary Hall and St. Mary's
Church were related to one another through Oriel; the principal and the
vicar were bound to have some common dealings, which, in fact, went

smoothly enough. Indeed, at one point Newman as vicar played a small and consoling role in a Hampden domestic tragedy. Two Hampden infants died and were buried at St. Mary's, and on the second sad instance Newman presided at the funeral. "Mrs. Hampden always remembered the manner in which the funeral service [was] read on this occasion by Mr. Newman. . . . His remarkable power of giving expression to the grand words of the burial service was long recollected."[18]

Hampden's part in the subscription controversy had a practical as well as a theoretical side. As Principal of St. Mary Hall, he was a member of the Board of Heads of Houses, the body in the university which had the right of initiating legislation for the approval of Convocation. On November 10, 1834, the Board voted to present to Convocation a declaration of conformity to the Anglican usages of Oxford as a substitute for undergraduate subscription. The resolution passed the Board by a majority of one and this, in the minds of its opponents, made Hampden twice a villain. In making its proposal the Board showed how far out of touch it was with university opinion. "Dr. Hampden and his supporters," Henry Wilberforce observed, acted like "some child meddling with a piece of machinery, . . . trifling with a power the force of which he little suspected—the deep conscientious convictions of the mass of the younger graduates."[19] The Heads of Houses were evidently anxious to head off parliamentary action on Dissenters' admission by getting the university to mitigate the subscription statute itself. They asked the Duke of Wellington's opinion and the Duke, never one to bog himself down in theological niceties, urged them to go ahead.

The resistance committee of the preceding summer—Newman, Pusey and Sewell—sprang into action once more. Pusey worked all through one night to prepare a list of twenty-three "queries" to be presented to the Board, each one challenging the cogency of the resolution. Actually, this was a pamphlet whose object was to stir up opposition to the Board's decision; within a couple of days it was printed and circulated all over Oxford. Newman meanwhile drew up a petition of protests which was signed by fifty M.A.'s. Sewell also wrote a strong attack upon the substitute plan, but before it appeared, on November 17th, the Board met again, and, quite alarmed at the furor raised over the resolution, voted to rescind it and to drop the matter of subscription, at least for the present term.

But the battle was far from over. During the months which followed a veritable flood of pamphlets poured from the presses and inundated the Oxford common rooms. The position taken by most of them reflected the fact that the great majority of Oxford men, Apostolicals, High Churchmen and Evangelicals alike, stood together in firm opposition to any tinkering with the requirement of subscription. The Tractarians took a leading part in this literary effort. Pusey celebrated his recovery from an illness which had afflicted him through much of 1834 by writing several circular letters and pamphlets, and before long he was engaged in a lengthy and painful controversy with his old friend, Hawkins of Oriel. Newman did not write anything himself, but many of his friends and disciples did, including Bowden, Harrison, Charles Marriott, Charles Eden and Henry Wilberforce.

IV

Newman refrained from attacking Hampden perhaps because he feared that his past personal differences with the Principal of St. Mary Hall might be interpreted as the cause of his present doctrinal disagreement. Nevertheless he actively supported the work of his friends and in at least one instance he promoted it. On March 23, 1835, Newman wrote Henry Wilberforce and asked him to write a pamphlet on the danger of religious indifferentism at Oxford. It ought to be an anonymous pamphlet, said Newman, and should include citation from the works of Arnold, Whately, Hampden, Hawkins and Blanco White. Hawkins had just published his reply to Pusey, in which, Newman reported, he "sneers" at the idea that removal of subscription would mean a rise of infidelity in the university. Hawkins writes "from the purest motives," but he is "one of the same school and one who is tainted with certain notions of that school." The events pointed to the existence of a real plot. "Who can doubt, with the facts before him, that the movement at Oxford is but the *advanced guard* of a black host and that it desires to achieve the first of a series of changes."[20]

Wilberforce went to work, and ten days later he received more advice from Newman, plus the assurance that the cost of Henry's pamphlet would be absorbed by the Tracts for the Times.[21] Early in May Wilberforce published "The Foundation of the Faith Assailed in Oxford." It was a forty-page attack upon Hampden almost exclusively, with long quotations from the Bampton Lectures and from "Observations on Religious Dissent." This pamphlet Wilberforce called "the manifesto of the party by whom this proposal [to suppress subscription] is introduced,"[22] and he emphasized that Hampden was a member of the Board of Heads. All in all, Wilberforce's effort was not very exceptional nor could it be construed by the casual reader as a personal attack. Hampden thought otherwise. Newman liked it, though he was taken aback by Henry's free use of his adversaries' names. This, Newman said, normally an anonymous author should not do, though such restraint "does not apply to you who are more or less a stranger to them."[23]

Newman kept a close eye on the pamphleteering of his friends, and in the spring of 1835 he edited and wrote a preface for a collection of their short works on Hampden, subscription and related topics. Meanwhile, the fight was warming up again. On April 1st, the Board of Heads, again reacting to parliamentary pressure, formally proposed to Convocation the enactment of the following declaration as the statutory substitute for undergraduate subscription. "I declare that I do, so far as my knowledge extends, assent to the doctrines of the United Church of England and Ireland as set forth in her Thirty-nine Articles; that I will conform to her liturgy and discipline; and that I am ready and willing to be instructed in her Articles of religion, as required by the statutes of this university."[24] The Board clearly was trying to meet at least some of the objections of its opponents and still satisfy the Whig-dominated parliament. In the process, the original movers of the question, the Dissenters, had been lost sight of, for they could no more agree to the declaration than subscribe to the Thirty-nine Articles. The struggle had indeed moved onto new ground, where the Dissenters' claims were forgotten. It was now the Anglican liberals—what one day would be called the Broad Church—ranged against an unlikely alliance of Tories, Tractarians and Evangelicals.[25]

Through the spring of 1835 the pamphlet warfare continued. William Palmer pondered a short work against Hampden, reconsidered and then decided to concentrate his efforts on organizing the electoral defeat of the resolution.[26] So also did the Tractarian leaders. They spent much of April and May urging non-resident members of Convocation to come to Oxford for the vote. Pusey wrote young William Gladstone, soliciting his support, and when Gladstone replied, voicing some moral doubts about excluding Dissenters from the universities, Pusey assured him, "I have never thought of this question as with relation to Dissenters. . . . Subscription, in these days, I look upon as a decided benefit to the Church by promoting both a dutiful and teachable frame of mind." It may be that in theory no Anglican objection can be raised against offering the Dissenters a "civil education" in the universities, but the practical state of the Church and the attitude of the Dissenters themselves would make such a concession very dangerous at this moment. "The solid improvement of Oxford within man's memory is said to be far greater than that of the rest of the country, and we have, I trust, every ground to look for far richer increase, unless in impatience at some remaining evil we break up the system instead of endeavouring to act up to it."[27]

From Fairford Keble kept up a similar correspondence. He wrote a clerical friend in Bristol and suggested the circulation of anti-resolution petitions. "You see," said Keble, "those wise acres, the Heads of Houses, are quite determined not to let us alone."[28] And to Robert Wilberforce he sent a short note accompanied by the formal printed notice of resistance: "I shall be much [sur]prised if you do not view the matter in the same light as we do, viz., as a contest between faith and rationalism."[29]

Wilberforce did not disappoint Keble, nor did the assembled members of Convocation, when, on May 20, 1835, they rejected the recommendation of the Heads of Houses by a vote of 459 to 57. Frederic Rogers sat with a mob of undergraduates in the gallery of the Sheldonian Theater where the poll was taken and described the tumultuous scene to his sister.

The voters (the M.A.s) were in the area (which would be in a playhouse the pit but without benches), and just as they were beginning to give their votes, which they usually do by going up one by one to the proctor and whispering in his ear, one of the anti-reformers cried out, "Non placet!" (the form of negativing) and walked to one side of the theatre. It seemed from the gallery . . . as if the whole crowd were following him. You just saw a few spots here and there stationary in the midst of the great current, and rather struggling not to be carried away in it, as little bits of dirt do when you are pouring water out of a basin; and after a short settling we saw about forty gentlemen left alone with their glory in the middle of the room, looking very foolish and hardly knowing whether to stand boldly forth or not, to bear as best they might the shoutings of the opposite party and the undergraduates. . . . It is rather curious that these very young gentlemen whom people are so anxious to liberate from the yoke of subscription are the most noisy and vehement opponents of any "relief bill" that are to be found. I only wish they had confined themselves to applause, whereas they took the liberty of hissing our respectable provost [Hawkins] who is the great patron of change.[30]

The defeat by a plurality of slightly more than eight to one was a bitter pill for Hampden to swallow, and he reacted violently. He wrote the same day a stinging letter to Henry Wilberforce in which he demanded that the pamphlet Henry had written be acknowledged publicly by the author, so that "the connexion of his name with the pamphlet, as notorious as the pamphlet itself, . . . may in some measure at least carry its own antidote . . . [to] the mischief of his anonymous slanders."[31] Hampden also insisted that the name of the "assistant" whom Henry had mentioned in his pamphlet also be made public. Hampden of course knew perfectly well that Newman was behind Wilberforce's effort, but the charadelike rules of controversy which English gentlemen took so seriously prevented him from saying so until the anonymous parties admitted it themselves. The latter were for their part obliged to do so when reasonably requested. Thus, Hampden had found out the fact of Henry Wilberforce's authorship simply by leaving word at Parker's bookstore that he wanted to know.

But Wilberforce refused to give up the name of his "assistant," on the grounds that he, Wilberforce, was alone responsible for whatever appeared in the pamphlet. So Hampden tried another tack. On May 22nd he wrote directly to Newman "as the person through whom the pamphlet in question was conveyed to the Oriel common room." Newman, Hampden said, almost hysterically, must confess the identity of Wilberforce's "accomplice." "It is but right that society should have its eye on persons who can so unfeelingly scatter their venom under a mask; that at least one may not mistake them for *friends*."[32] Newman answered the same day in a single line in which he said "that he has placed [the matter] in the hands of Mr. Henry Wilberforce," but at the same time he authorized Parker to give his name on request to the collection of pamphlets on the subscription question which he had edited earlier in the spring. This collection had included Henry's "The Foundation of the Faith."

Hampden brooded for a month, and then exploded. He headed his letter with a frigid "Sir," instead of the customary "My dear Newman." "I have ascertained to my great disgust" that Newman edited the collection of pamphlets and wrote the offensive preface. "I say . . . disgust, for no other feeling, I am sure, is so due to the conduct of a person who can act with the dissimulation and falsehood and dark malignity of which you have been guilty." Dissimulation, "because you have worked the machine but hid yourself behind it"; falsehood, "because you have sent out to the public what you knew to be untrue," that is, the allegations in Wilberforce's pamphlet; malignity, "because you have no other ground of your assault on me but a fanatical persecuting spirit." There was much more of the same, but in substance the heated charges were woefully weak. For some reason the usually self-possessed Hampden imagined that opposition to his published views was itself an assault upon his person. The wild anger displayed in this letter did not, however, prove the fact. Wilberforce's pamphlet was like a dozen or a hundred others of the same genre; it was neither better nor worse than most. But whatever its merits or lack of them, it did not indulge in personal attack. What Hampden professed to see in it simply was not there, and it is hard to understand how he could have written to Newman in such scathing terms: "I should be sorry, sir, to bear in my heart such a practical refutation of my religious views as you have evidenced by your conduct."[33]

Newman responded in the third person. "Mr. Newman observes, in answer to the Principal of St. Mary Hall's letter received yesterday, that he cannot enter at length into the details of it without doing violence to his own feelings of self-respect." He went on to examine the specification of charges and, as one might expect, it took little space to refute them. There was, however, no oil for troubled waters if that should involve compromise of the essential issue: "[Mr. Newman] observes that he should rejoice at nothing more than a return to that state of good understanding with Dr. Hampden which he has before now enjoyed, and that he shall ever be watchful and eager to discern any approach to the removal of differences which separate him from Dr. Hampden. At the same time he certainly does recognize as conceivable the existence of motives for approving or disapproving the conduct of another distinct from those of a personal nature."[34]

When he heard of the confrontation, Hurrell Froude wrote merrily that Hampden, to prove himself a Christian, wanted to fight a duel with Newman.[35] It would seem that Froude was not far wrong. In any case, the bad blood between Newman and Hampden from this time on was a major theme of the Oxford Movement, for the little doctor may have lost the battle of 1835, but the war had just begun.

V

Among those who shouted *"Non placet!"* loudest at the Convocation of May 20, 1835, was Hurrell Froude. He had landed after the voyage from Barbados only three days before and had come directly to Oxford to vote. Tom Mozley's young sister Anne happened to be in the coach office the day he arrived and saw him being greeted by his friends. "He was terribly thin," she recalled, "his countenance dark and wasted, but with a brilliance of expression and grace of outline which justified all that his friends had said of him. He was in the theatre the next day, entering into all the enthusiasm of the scene. . . . While he lived at all he must *live* his life."[36] Rogers saw him too and was appalled at the sight. But like all of Froude's friends he hoped against hope. "They say . . . that no one ever gains flesh in the West Indies, but that it tells when they get back. I most certainly trust it may be so."[37]

In fact Froude was dying. He had left England eighteen months before—in November of 1833—and the time spent in the West Indies had done nothing to help him. His tubercular lungs continued their slow, relentless disintegration. He found the climate at Barbados "most delicious," with an average temperature of 83 degrees. The sudden squalls of rain reminded him of home, for which he longed with all his heart. It was a tedious, frustrating time, optimism about his health alternating with dark despair. "Sometimes," he wrote wistfully in September 1834, "I think I am much better than when I left England, and sometimes I can't tell why I think so."[38]

By Christmas, he had convinced himself that he did indeed feel better, though he had to admit an irregularity in his pulsebeat and a growing shortness of breath. He was plagued by insomnia and by the swarms of fat, semitropical mosquitoes which were as much part of the islands as the scenery. He stopped eating meat and he was consoled that the abstinence "has cooled me without weakening me." Most of all he missed his friends and the great adventure on which they had all embarked together. He complained bitterly of hearing nothing from them for months at a time. "When I come home I mean to rat and be married, i.e. if I can hook in any one to be such a fool. The great difference between a wife and a friend is that a wife cannot cut one and a friend can." In the days when sailing vessels formed the only link across the

Atlantic, mail delivery was capricious at best. As a matter of fact, his family and friends, especially Newman, did their best to keep the invalid informed. Still, the long silences from England served to heighten the depression which was a natural concomitant of Froude's fatal malady.[39]

But Froude remained irrepressibly Froude. He plunged insofar as he could into the life of his place of exile. He accompanied the Bishop of the West Indies on a month-long confirmation tour around the islands. They traveled on a 46-gun Royal Navy frigate, no less, which delighted Froude despite his radical views about the union of Church and state. By August of 1834, he had become a part-time don at the local Anglican college in Barbados. "I give two lectures a day which is an amusement and helps me to avoid thinking which is ruination I am sure. Some of the youngsters are very stupid, some passable, and one rather clever, so that the work is not monotonous." There were only fourteen students altogether. "People here seem to have found out that the Church is a bad speculation and send their sons into trade."[40]

Froude also observed and commented upon the great West Indian social question of the hour, the emancipation of the slaves which had gone into effect in 1833. The Negroes he thought "fat and merry and lazy; in a religious point of view I should think they were for the most part either methodistical or brutish; morality seems to be as rare among women here as among men in England." Yet he congratulated a parson who had integrated his communion rail in the face of opposition from the whites in his congregation. Froude himself promptly received Holy Communion with the blacks.[41]

The Tractarians always insisted on a reverence for the concrete at the expense, if need be, of the abstract. Probability, not certitude, was the aim of their argumentation; hate the sin, love the sinner. Froude in his attitude to the Negroes of Barbados provided a case in point. "I have felt it a kind of duty," he reported in November 1834, "to sustain in my mind an habitual hostility to the niggers and to chuckle over the failure of the new system [i.e. emancipation]; as if these poor wretches concentrated in themselves all the whiggery, dissent, cant and abomination that have been ranged on their side." The liberals have freed the slaves, Froude seemed to be saying, and the liberal cause is a bad cause, filled with "cant and abomination." "How whiggery has by degrees taken up all the filth that has been secreted in the fermentation of human thought! . . . They have it all now, and good luck to them." In much the same spirit, the gentle Pusey's voice would tremble, a few years later, when he spoke of "vile socialists" and "wicked chartists." It was a weakness of the Tractarian movement to view ameliorative social legislation as evidence of anti-Christ. Perhaps neither Froude nor Pusey nor any of their friends had seen enough of the harsh side of life.[42]

Froude, in any case, cheerfully approached the communion rail with a Negro, whereas, say, a fastidious Whig member of Parliament who had voted for emancipation might perhaps have remained in his pew. Religion was Froude's obsession, and the notion of the Eucharist was much on his mind. He came to think "it to be the most indispensable of all the duties of external religion that everyone should receive the Communion as often as he has the opportunity, and that if he has such opportunity every day of the week, it is his duty to take advantage of it every day of the week." He pored over the Tracts hungrily whenever they arrived and then wrote to Newman "pointing out wherein I think him too conservative." He read a great deal of Pascal, and suggested a series of publications dealing with the "Jansenist saints, Francis de Sales, the nuns of Port Royal, Pascal, etc., who seem to me to be of a more sentimental, imaginative cast than any of our own. . . ." His dislike of the Protestant reformers increased. "I think worse and worse of them. Jewell was what you would in these days call an irreverent Dissenter. . . ." And just before he sailed for home, in the spring of 1835, he remarked: "I have attacked Newman for some of the Tract Protestantism." Then, with a wan smile, he added: "However the wise acres are all agog about our being papists."[43]

After the victory over Hampden in May, Froude left Oxford never to return. Yet he held tight to his will to live. "I believe I have now almost entirely got rid of the cough I caught in landing and, though it has weakened me, that I am in a fair way to get back in a day or two to my average state." He was at Dartington, it was June, and he reveled in the loveliness of his last English summer. "The country is indescribably beautiful and the weather so fine that it seems determined to give me a fair chance."[44] This sentiment brought tears to the eyes of his friends, who knew now that Froude had no chance at all. Newman went down to visit him for several weeks in the autumn, and when he left, on a Sunday evening in the middle of October, Froude's "face lighted up and almost shone as if to say that in this world we were parting forever."[45] They continued to correspond with all the old treasured familiarity, though often Froude's letters were short and the intervals between them grew longer. But even as he approached the end, Froude could now and then show a spark of his former rueful humour. "My dearest Newman," he wrote once, "I am afraid you will be grumbling in your heart at me for putting off writing so long. But really I am not to blame, as I have not put pen to paper for a fortnight, except yesterday, when I began a letter to you upside down."[46]

By November Froude's condition had worsened, though he seemed to rally a little around Christmas. Early in the new year of 1836 Frederic Rogers visited Dartington, and he reported encouragingly to Newman. But Froude himself knew better. "I don't gain flesh in spite of all the milk," he wrote Newman towards the end of January. "Indeed, I suspect that in the last six weeks I have lost a good deal. . . ." A week later he could no longer write, and Archdeacon Froude sadly advised Newman, "Hurrell wishes me to say that he has nothing particular to say just now, but that you will hear from him in three or four days."[47]

Richard Hurrell Froude died on February 28, 1836. The archdeacon's letter reached Newman in Tom Mozley's rooms at Oriel. He read it, handed it to Tom, and left without a word. Later Henry Wilberforce found him in tears because "he could not see Froude just to tell him how much he felt that he had owed to him in the clearing and strengthening of his views."[48] Keble heard the news just as he was preparing to celebrate the Holy Communion. Much to the bewilderment of his parishioners, halfway through the service he broke down and wept.[49]

And so passed the restless spirit of the man whom Harriet Newman called "the bright and beautiful Froude." In Devon, where his mortal remains were buried, they remembered him as a fearless rider and a sailor who loved the wild and unpredictable sea and a young gentleman who quipped to hide the pain and the doubt which never ceased to assail him. At the end of 1837 Newman wrote a brief note in his diary: "Vale dilectissime. Farewell, most loved, so much missed, until that day which shall make you, known to so few, manifest to all as you were."[50] For his part Froude had already written his epitaph, although it was not carved on the simple stone over his Devon grave:

> Lord, I have fasted, I have prayed,
> And sackcloth has my girdle been;
> To purge my soul I have essayed
> With hunger blank and vigil keen.
> O Father of mercies! why am I
> Still haunted by the self I fly?[51]

CHAPTER 10

The Oxford Malignants

W HEN Pusey's mentor, Charles Lloyd, died in 1829, he was succeeded as Regius Professor of Divinity in the University of Oxford by
Edward Burton. Dr. Burton, though a young man, was an old-fashioned
scholar with wide and not very deep interests, whose rather unexceptional
published works filled five good-sized volumes. During the controversy in
1834–35 over undergraduate subscription to the Thirty-nine Articles, he
had stood solidly with the minority headed by Hampden and Hawkins.
On January 19, 1836, Burton suddenly died. He was only forty-two.

His body was hardly cold before the speculation and rumours began
to race through the Oxford common rooms. There were two university
professorships of divinity, the regius and the Lady Margaret, and both
of them were crown appointments, which meant in this instance that the
Whig Prime Minister, Viscount Melbourne, would have the first and last
word as to who would take Burton's place. Attached to the professorship
was a canonry in Christ Church and a rich Oxfordshire parish at a place
called Ewelme, so that the king's professor need never worry about money.
More than that, though its duties were not onerous—a few public lectures
a week which might or might not be delivered—the post had great
prestige. The Professors of Divinity were considered the semi-official
guardians of the university's Anglican orthodoxy. This status was confirmed in small but significant ways; the professors, for example, were
always consulted in the choice of university preachers, and whenever a
board was formed to investigate the theological opinions of a university
member, the professors were always on it. The regius professor also presided over the formal exam given to candidates for the Bachelor of
Divinity degree.

That this important appointment was in the hands of a Whig government filled the Tractarians with foreboding. But Hurrell Froude, in one
of his last letters, stated the political realities candidly: "Perhaps the

conservatives would not have done anything really better for us."[1] The
liberal enemy was not just a Whig; Peel in his own way was as dangerous
as Melbourne. What really bothered the Tractarians was the most persistent rumour of them all, that Renn Dickson Hampden would be the
new regius professor.

I

Edward Pusey, whose great heart ached for anyone in sorrow, went
down to Ewelme for Burton's funeral and offered what solace he could
to the grieving widow. But his thoughts, like the thoughts of all Oxford,
were on the appointment of Burton's successor. "Everything everywhere
seems dark," he confided to Newman on the day of the funeral. Hugh
Rose was already breathing fire and had written Pusey that it might be
wise to mount an attack upon Hampden immediately, to "bell the cat,"
as he put it, so that the government might hesitate if it were considering
such a fateful choice. Pusey found the prospects of still another battle
distasteful. "I am weary of reading in order to censure; it is a hurtful
office. . . . Yet," he continued, "if you think it advisable I could put
something in my preface [to the reissue of Tracts Sixty-seven, Sixty-eight,
and Sixty-nine] of Dr. H's views of the sacraments."[2]

Newman tried to cheer Pusey up. "I do not look at things so sadly as
you do. . . . As error is brought out, the good will not only be disengaged
and move freely and healthily but be propagated by the agitation." Even
if the worst should happen, even if Hampden should be appointed, the
air at least would be cleared. "The Heads of Houses do not see the
difference between H[ampden] and orthodoxy. Very well! Then H. is
not so far from representing their opinions. The authorities of the place
virtually speak out if he is made professor, what before was latent in their
opinions and feelings."[3] Yet Newman too hoped that the crisis would
not come. "I think," he told Henry Wilberforce, "the ministry will not
be so unwise as to run their heads against a wall by appointing Milman,[4]
Arnold or Hampden."[5] The best solution would be to give the professorship to somebody in the "middle party," neither liberal nor Tractarian.
A few days later, when he wrote to Tom Mozley, he was in a more somber
mood. "Burton's death is remarkable as tending to obliterate the middle
party of which he was the great hold in Oxford." This is why Newman
thought the regius professorship vacancy had fallen at such a crucial
moment. "Our persecution is on the eve of beginning. The first stroke
will have fallen if Hampden or other such precursor of Antichrist (for
it does not do now to mince matters) be placed in the divinity chair."[6]

The government was already moving. On January 25th, the day of
Burton's burial, Lord Melbourne wrote to Archbishop Whately and
Bishop Copleston and enclosed the list which Howley, Archbishop of

Canterbury, had submitted to him and which contained the names of those whom Howley believed should be considered for the regius professorship. There were nine names altogether, including Pusey, Newman and Keble and six others who were members of what Newman called the "middle party." In terms of preference, Pusey stood first on the list, Newman fourth and Keble fifth. The episcopal Noetics lost no time in advising the Prime Minister to reject these recommendations and to present Hampden to the post instead. Melbourne probably expected such a proposal and he was not at all adverse to it. Hampden was the kind of churchman an old-line Whig like Melbourne could appreciate, and anyway the government owed Hampden a favour for his part in the subscription controversy a year earlier. Melbourne hesitated long enough to consider the possibility of appointing Thomas Arnold, only to reject the idea because of the Headmaster of Rugby's notorious rashness. Accordingly the Prime Minister informed Archbishop Howley of his intention, Howley supinely agreed, and the addled old King William IV was told that his new Professor of Divinity in the University of Oxford would be Dr. R. D. Hampden.[7]

All of this was more or less public knowledge by the end of January, but until the final decision was formally announced rumours still flew and hope still sprang. Newman urged Keble to accept the post if it were offered to him, even though he might sternly disapprove of the source from which the offer came. "Some years since, in Robert Wilberforce's case, I certainly thought he ought not to have taken a living from Lord Brougham, yet I recollect insisting . . . that the question was not whether a Tory in the abstract should in the abstract receive a favour from a Whig but whether R. W. should receive one from H. B[rougham]." Keble, Newman argued, should not look upon the offer, if it came, as a favour to himself but rather as a chance to serve the common good. "This is a king's office—as a lawful subject can you abandon him to H[ampden]?" Keble's position was so firmly established and so well known that office from the Whigs could not possibly compromise it. Newman must have been aware that the same arguments held good for himself.[8]

But these speculations came to nothing in the face of the advice of Whately and the decision of Lord Melbourne. On February 8, 1836, Pusey was host at a dinner party at Christ Church attended by some of the leading opponents of Hampden's candidacy. The question which went round the table was whether the appointment could still somehow be headed off. Newman left the party convinced that it was time to break his self-imposed public silence on Hampden's heterodoxy. He worked furiously for the next several days, and on February 13th the result was published in the form of a pamphlet called "Elucidations of Dr. Hampden's Theological Statements."[9] Though published anonymously, everybody knew who had written it.

Newman in "Elucidations" followed a simple procedure. He quoted various works of Hampden (but mostly from the Bampton Lectures) and grouped the quotations under such headings as the Trinity, the Incarnation, Sacraments, and Atonement. At the end of each section he commented on the general drift of the citations. The title Newman chose was itself an attempt to score a controversial point, because he maintained that the real and, as far as he was concerned, the monstrous meaning of Hampden's teaching had been obscured by the muddled way in which it had been stated. So he concluded the pamphlet with one grand elucidation.

Dr. H.'s views then seem at length to issue in the following theory: that there is one and one only truth; that the truth is the record of facts, historical and moral, contained in the text of Scripture; that whatever is beyond that text, even to the classifying of its sentences, is human opinion and unrevealed; that a thoughtful person cannot help forming opinions and theories upon the Scripture record, . . . yet he has no right to identify his own opinion on any point, however sacred in itself, with the facts of the revealed history; . . . that though he considers he cannot be more sure of being right than another, and does not hold his opinions to be more pious than another's, and will not pronounce heretical opinions (so-called) to be dangerous to any being in the world, except to those who do *not* hold them, yet he himself firmly believes the Church's dogmatic statements concerning the Trinity, etc., and at a proper season would contend as zealously against Arian or Socinian doctrines as those who think that . . . belief in them is of importance to eternal salvation.[10]

There was more and all of it was devastating to the logic of Hampden's position. How could a man who held that all speculative theology was nonsense, that such statements of revelation as the Nicene Creed had no necessary connection with the "facts" of Scripture, that Anglicans were pledged to the defense of the Trinity even though they could not be sure that trinitarian interpretation of the Bible was truer than unitarian—how could such a man be an official teacher of theology in the most important center of Anglican studies? But it did no good to ask. Melbourne said in his maddeningly superior way that he found "Elucidations" to be "abstruse." Interestingly enough, he read the pamphlet in bed.[11]

Every other avenue also led to a dead end. Pusey wrote an exceedingly strong letter to Melbourne, but without effect. On February 10th, a protest meeting was held at Corpus Christi College. A petition to the king was drawn up and by the next evening, when it was sent to Archbishop Howley, it had the signatures of almost all the resident M.A.'s in Oxford. Melbourne responded to this move by telling the academic gentlemen that the next time they wanted something done they ought to apply to someone who could do it—that is, to himself and not to the king. When the matter came up in the House of Lords, the Prime Minister said: "I do not think there is anything to be condemned in the writings of Dr. Hampden. . . . I know very little on the subject, and yet I believe

I know more than those who have opposed the doctor's nomination. . . .
They are upon points of extremely recondite and difficult scholastic
learning; very few of your lordships indeed have the means of forming
any sound opinion on such extremely difficult, abstruse, and obscure
points as these."[12] One wonders if Melbourne delivered this last remark,
and with it a sardonic smile, to the assembled successors of the apostles,
the lord bishops. On February 17, 1836, the court *Gazette* announced the
king's pleasure that Dr. Hampden should occupy the divinity chair at
Oxford.

II

The government had spoken and nothing now could prevent Hampden
from succeeding to the post. But other weapons were being forged at the
very moment when Melbourne was disdainfully brushing aside the
pressures applied to him. The meeting at Corpus Christi on February 10th
established a committee of six—four moderates, led by Vaughan Thomas
of Corpus, plus Newman and Pusey—which was to carry the fight to the
Board of Heads of Houses and from there to the university Convocation.
If the politicians did not care about the views of the mass of Oxford
men, the university power structure might have to care. And so it turned
out.

Hampden won the first battle, but narrowly. The Corpus committee's
agent on the Hebdomadal Board, A. T. Gilbert, Principal of Brasenose
College, moved that official notice be sent to Lord Melbourne to the
effect that any candidate for the regius professorship would be preferable to Hampden. It was a scene of great embarrassment and bitterness,
for Hampden, as Principal of St. Mary Hall, took his place as usual at
the meeting.

When all stood awkward enough, the Dean of Christ Church broke silence by
saying, "Do you mean to stop here, Dr. H.? We are going to talk about you."
On his answering in the affirmative, Shuttleworth [Warden of New College]
asked him if he meant to vote. He said he should be guided by circumstances.
Gilbert and Symons [Warden of Wadham College] conducted the attack.
H. turned to the Vice-chancellor as "head of this present inquisition" and told
him he would find as bad things in the sermons of Pusey, Newman or [Walter F.]
Hook. He ended by voting for himself and just turning the scale thereby.[13]

During one of the anguished silences which marked this meeting, the
Dean of Christ Church got up to poke the fire. The chill of late winter
had intensified the emotionally frozen atmosphere. "Will you go on now,
Hampden," asked Shuttleworth mockingly, "or will you wait till it burns
up?"

Hampden could muster just enough support on the Board to avoid the humiliating appeal to the government, but he did not have the votes to stop a censure within the university. The Heads were not notably courageous men, and they could sense all around them the overwhelming anti-Hampden sentiment organized by the Corpus committee. After all, each of them had to share a college common room with fellows whose black looks spoke eloquently the almost unanimous judgment about Hampden and his views. Newman took some malicious pleasure in the fact that among those leading the charge against Hampden were the Vice-chancellor and the Dean of Christ Church, who, in 1834 when Newman and Hampden had competed for the moral philosophy chair, "were afraid of me as being ultra and thought Hampden the safer man."[14]

A few days after the official announcement of Hampden's appointment on February 17th, the Hebdomadal Board met again, and this time an anti-Hampden measure was passed. It proposed for the ratification of Convocation that the new regius professor, because of his past theological publications, did not possess the trust of the university and that therefore he should be deprived of the functions of selecting preachers and of examining the orthodoxy of any sermon delivered in the university. Such a statute would not materially affect Hampden's position, but it would be a humiliating repudiation of him as a teacher and a gesture of defiance to the government. The vote was thirteen to ten, and Convocation was summoned for March 27th. Among the minority on the Board supporting Hampden was his ever-faithful friend Hawkins of Oriel and, more significantly, the two Proctors, who, it will be remembered, had the right of veto over the acts of Convocation.[15]

Hampden appealed to the Duke of Wellington, as Chancellor of the university, to institute an inquiry into the legality of the measure. The Duke replied with the terseness of a battlefield dispatch. "You are a member of the Board of Heads of Houses; I . . . have no voice at that Board."[16] Meanwhile the Corpus committee whipped up enthusiasm among resident and non-resident members of Convocation. William Palmer, who took a leading part in the agitation, remarked that "all divisions and jealousies were forgotten in this noble effort." The committee would have preferred a condemnation of Hampden's specific errors rather than the roundabout and somewhat personal measure which the Heads proposed, but they took what they could get, judging it "neither unjust nor unprecedented."[17]

On March 5th the six members of the Corpus committee published a signed report in which they drew up their indictment of Hampden. "After a most careful and systematic research," they closed their investigation by calling upon all Oxford men to remember that

the present controversy is not so much concerned with an individual or a book, or even an ordinary system of false doctrine, which (after corrupting all soundness of Christianity in other countries) has at length appeared among us, and, for the first time, been invested with authority within the University of Oxford. This principle is the philosophy of rationalism or the assumption that uncontrolled human reason . . . is the primary interpreter of God's word without any regard to those rules and principles of interpretation which have guided the judgment of Christ's holy catholic Church. . . . It is the theory of rationalism (as set forth systematically in the Bampton Lectures of 1832 and still more recently asserted in lectures addressed to students) which is to be considered the root of all errors of Dr. Hampden's system.[18]

The report was followed up a few days later by a Declaration of Residents which among other things asserted that "we hereby declare our steadfast resolution to oppose . . . a philosophy which in other countries has poisoned the very fountains of religious truth, which for a long time reduced Protestantism in its original seat [i.e. in Germany] almost to an empty name, and changed the religion of the cross into the theology of deism."[19]

The report and declaration of the Corpus committee, the latter with eighty-two signatures of resident members of Convocation attached, were circulated in the thousands, and still the relentless assault upon Hampden went on. March 12th witnessed the publication of still another pamphlet, this one by Pusey, who followed the pattern set by Newman's "Elucidations." He took extracts from Hampden's works, some of them designed to demonstrate an erroneous phraseology, and others, by use of parallel columns, contrasted with the language of the Thirty-nine Articles. Pusey disclaimed in his preface any personal bias, and doubtless all who knew the gentle Professor of Hebrew would have believed him. But the method of short quotation out of context employed both by Newman and Pusey was raising some doubts. Those who had not read anything of Hampden's (and their number was legion) began to wonder if he were being fairly treated. "No charitable mind," one country clergyman was heard to say, "has a right to pick and choose parts of sentences and give them a colouring not belonging to them."[20] Such sentiments, however, were rare among Oxford men in the spring of 1836, however frequently they might have been heard in other circles. And in the long and acrimonious quarrel over Hampden, no one ever proved that Newman or Pusey misrepresented his views.

III

But Dr. Hampden was not without his supporters, few though they may have been in Oxford itself. Several prominent newspapers combined to defend him against his tormentors. On February 15th, the *Morning Chronicle* editorialized: "Nothing can be more disgusting to every friend of truth and religion than the system which has of late been adopted by a party who exclusively appropriate to themselves the title of friends to the Church and religion." And the *Sun* the same day: "Oxford is determined to maintain its well-earned character for civil and religious bigotry. As the rest of the world becomes enlightened, the shades of darkness concentrate themselves around this chosen spot as a final rallying point." By the end of February the *Chronicle* was convinced that "we are about to have a revival of the Inquisition at Oxford." The *Coventry Herald* of March 4th saw the "furious torrent" of "ecclesiastical toryism" directed against Hampden as an attack upon the British Constitution.[21]

Feelings on both sides had reached a high pitch by Thursday, March 17th, when Hampden, before a mixed crowd of well-wishers and curious onlookers, delivered his inaugural lecture as Professor of Divinity. His speech was a masterful one. Without really drawing back from the positions taken in the Bampton Lectures, Hampden blunted much of his opponents' attack by a forthright and almost lyrical protestation of his faith in the Trinity, the atonement and other basic Anglican doctrines. As far as the Trinity was concerned, "I reverentially appeal to the Searcher of hearts as a witness that I have never for one moment swerved from this true faith of the gospel, but that the more I have enquired into Scripture, . . . the more I have been convinced that the trinitarian doctrine professed by our Church is the true one, that it cannot be denied without expunging the Scriptures themselves, and unlearning every lesson which inspired prophets and evangelists and preachers have taught us." He admitted that frailty of expression may have caused some confusion about his views. "I will not pretend always to have stated my conviction in the fullest, clearest manner. . . . I will not claim to have been invariably accurate in the use of words, or to have anticipated every possible objection that could be raised against particular modes of statement." But surely misunderstanding over such a "recondite track of observation" should not lead to condemnation. "If . . . I am candidly judged by . . . my real intention, it will be found that in nothing have I departed from the true catholic faith of the Trinity."[22]

Hampden had summoned the court of fair play. If he had erred, it was because of a lack of artfulness, because of a typically English straightforward manner which despised wily and subtle argumentation. Newman and Pusey might point to the skepticism of his published works, but Hampden brushed this aside by the simple expedient of appealing to fair-minded men to judge him on the basis of his "real intention." This tactic was all the more effective when one remembers how few, inside or outside Oxford, had bothered to study the Bampton Lectures.

Hampden also chose his ground shrewdly when he came to speak of Scripture as "the sole supreme authority of all revealed truth." He knew perfectly well, of course, that his enemies had formed a temporary alliance against him, but that deep differences divided them from one another, and none deeper than the place of the Bible in the intellectual life of the Christian. Unblushingly Hampden made his appeal directly to the Evangelicals. "I cannot admit any other authority as approaching at all to the weight and sanctity of the evidence of Scripture. I should feel myself untrue to the great principle of Protestantism, which broke the seals of the Bible and opened wide its pages to the reading of every Christian man; I should feel myself also untrue to the teaching of the Church of England which so strongly declares that Holy Scripture containeth all things necessary to salvation." The Church's greatest service has been to "put the Bible into our hands." On the point in the Bampton Lectures which had raised such a storm, that only historical and moral (as opposed to speculative) "facts" could be found in Scripture, the regius professor remained tactfully silent.

Hampden concluded with an eloquent flourish.

That I labour under very great disadvantages in commencing the duties of my office is known to you all. . . . I come before you under a cloud of prejudice and clamour which, however easy for the feeblest among us to raise and diffuse, it is the hardest thing in the world to remove or even diminish. For one who has examined into the ground of an objection there are at least twenty who repeat it without examination; for one again who can comprehend the force of an objection there are at least twenty who never hear the answer, twenty who have not power or leisure or inclination to attend to or comprehend the answer. . . . Nothing again is easier than to detach sentences from the context and general scheme of an author's observations and to found on them almost any charge which an objector's own views may suggest. . . . I am at all times ready to meet fair and free discussion, but to misrepresentation and clamour and violence, with God's help, I will never yield. I pray God to forgive those who have employed such weapons against me, and to turn their hearts, and to grant them more of that mind which was in Christ Jesus.[23]

The indefatigable Pusey immediately set to work to confute Hampden's inaugural lecture. A pamphlet appeared on March 21st—"Dr. Hampden's Past and Present Statements Compared"—in which Pusey charged, quite correctly, that Hampden had in his lecture given a kind of popular sermon and had either implied a contradiction of the Bampton Lectures or had passed over silently the questions in controversy. More important, and Pusey in the simplicity of his heart did not evidently grasp this fact, Hampden had treated the whole matter as though it had nothing to do with religious doctrine and was purely a personal attack upon himself. What was perhaps a weakness in his own psychological armour proved in the long run to be a great benefit for Hampden's cause.

The issue remained in some doubt up to the last moment. The Proctors, on March 19th, indicated their intention to veto the censure statute, but when Convocation assembled, on Tuesday afternoon, March 22nd, the

Corpus committee still hoped to ram the measure through. They had plenty of votes, though there is little doubt that many of them were tainted by an appalling ignorance of the matter at hand. Tom Mozley recalled the non-residents pouring into Oxford and begging their resident friends to tell them what the Bampton Lectures were all about, and the residents knowing little more than what a casual fifteen minutes with Newman's or Pusey's pamphlets could teach them.[24] A friend of Hampden's described the scene as similar to "a Spanish town at an *auto da-fe*. . . . Early in the course of yesterday (March 21) the inns began to be filled with comfortable-looking gentlemen in white neckcloths and black gaiters, and countenances in which a general depression . . . was somewhat enlivened by the hope of inflicting in the meantime some vengeance on Lord Melbourne's appointee."[25]

Assured of an overwhelming majority, the Corpus committee hoped to place on record the university's judgment that Hampden deserved censure, no matter what the Proctors did. "I do not think they meant it unfairly," said Frederic Rogers, referring to the Proctors' statement of March 19th, "but they did not *pledge* themselves [about a veto] to act certainly one way or another, and of course nothing less than a distinct pledge would have made it safe for us to countermand the voters on our side."[26] The actual limitations placed upon Hampden by the proposed statute were trifling, to say the least; if the Proctors vetoed and thus killed the proposal, then the regius professor would be able to help select university preachers and to investigate charges of heterodoxy within the university. The anti-Hampden forces cared nothing about these formalities; what they aimed for was a manifestation of the university's disapproval of Hampden's views, and this could be achieved if a vote were taken before the Proctors intervened with their veto. The opening of Convocation was delayed for two hours while the Heads wrestled with the procedural problem of when precisely, whether before the vote or after, the Proctors' *non placet* took effect.

Meanwhile, pandemonium ruled the Sheldonian Theater. Undergraduates crowded the gallery and down below the Masters of Arts milled back and forth, caught up, most of them, in the fierce emotion of the moment. The prevailing spirit seemed to combine a revival meeting with a college reunion. As Pusey went up to take his seat several of Hampden's adherents hissed him and a voice called out that there passed a man who had betrayed his friend. The gentle Pusey was no doubt startled to be labeled Judas to a man he hardly knew. But such sentiments were soon drowned out; for every supporter Hampden could count on in the theater that day, he had six or seven enemies. The uproar hardly subsided when the Vice-chancellor, accompanied by the Heads and the Proctors, finally made his appearance. A dignitary read the proposed statute, and then the Vice-chancellor, shouting as best he might in the teeth of the noise, asked for the opinions of the house with the ancient formula, *"Ecquis sententiam vulgo proferre vult?"* Frederic Rogers described what happened.

At the last moment, when it was quite clear we should be vetoed, a rather important question arose, whether the proctors' veto *stopped* proceedings or only *nullified* them (as the king's refusing assent to a bill in parliament), or, in other words, whether the veto was interposed *before* the division or after; and, to the surprise of all persons present, Mr. Vaughan Thomas, a very grandiloquent and pompous gentleman, chairman of our meeting [i.e. of the Corpus committee], as the question was about to be put [delivered] a long Latin speech to show that they could not prevent us from dividing [i.e. from voting]; which, could he have got his point, would have almost made the veto a dead letter, as the division would have been in itself a declaration of the opinion of the university.[27]

Very few of those present understood Thomas' speech: The Latin was a barrier for many and the racket in the theater for all. One hostile witness observed acidly that the speech was "in good middle ages Latin," and, though "rather absurd, . . . was not a bit the worse as regards sense, or rather the want of it, than half the conversation of this place."[28] Somebody tried to address the chair in English: "Mr. Vice-chancellor, I trust that we shall have no modern liberalism or whiggery here!" But the Vice-chancellor shouted back over the tumult that in these sacred precincts all thoughts must be expressed in Latin. The statute was then read once more, after which the Vice-chancellor turned to those members of Convocation who held the doctor's degree: *"Placetne vobis, Domini Doctores?"* The statute did please a large majority of the assembled doctors. Then came the crucial moment. *"Placetne vobis, Magistri?"* intoned the Vice-chancellor. The Masters of Arts roared out a mighty *"Placet!"* but at the same moment two of the masters, scarcely to be heard even by the Vice-chancellor, who stood close to them, said with the solemn sanction of five centuries, *"Nobis Procuratoribus non placet."* The Proctors had spoken, and "the Vice-chancellor got up, dissolved Convocation, and was half way out before anyone knew what was going on," but not before the undergraduates saw him scuttling towards a rear entrance and threw jeers and catcalls after him.[29]

The rest was anticlimax. As they pushed their way out of the theater, Keble was overheard saying to Newman that when it came to a veto "others too might play at that game." The Sheldonian emptied within ten minutes, and the bulk of the anti-Hampden M.A.'s paraded to Brasenose College where, Rogers reported, "some very bad speeches" were given by a couple of London politicians; "electioneering kind of claptrap speeches, quite out of place." A petition, which had been prepared before by "sensible people," was proposed to the gathering, approved and immediately received 380 signatures.[30] The petition called for carrying the fight against Hampden to Convocation again next term when new Proctors would be in office.

IV

The new term began on April 13th, and a week before that the petition approved at Brasenose was presented to the Hebdomadal Board. The Heads debated the matter and they decided to summon Convocation once more on May 5th and to submit to it the same statute as the one vetoed on March 22nd. This time the Proctors voted with the majority of Heads and against Hampden. It seemed very unlikely as a result that the censure could be avoided.

Meanwhile the newspaper and pamphlet war grew in intensity and virulence. The *Leamington Chronicle* of March 23rd described the "distinguishing features" of the anti-Hampden forces as "the fury with which they attack the objects of their hate, a blind and infatuated zeal in carrying on their persecutions, and a reckless disregard of the means which they may adopt to accomplish their ends. . . . The proceedings at Oxford . . . have been marked by envy, hatred and uncharitableness. . . ." Next day, the *Standard*, which took the opposite side with equal violence, commented on the veto: "The triumph will be a short-lived one. The proctor's office is but temporary—the tenure of the present proctors will soon expire. We should despair of the university if it could furnish two others like them."

The journalists, however, besides their loud and inflammatory denunciations, also on occasion made sense. The *Times*, usually Tory and High Church in sympathy, wondered editorially if the agitation against Hampden had not descended to the level of personal attack. The Convocation of March 22nd, in the opinion of the *Times*, had shown despite the veto the university's judgment on the doctrinal matter. It was now time to call a halt. "We do supplicate our reverend brethren that they will suffer the heartburnings and deplorable animosities of which Oxford has of late been the focus to die away and at least among the ministers of our holy religion to be forgotten. . . ." And on April 1st the *Coventry Herald* raised a question which troubled many across the country who watched the fascinating struggle over Hampden. "If there is any truth in this charge of unsoundness in the faith, as drawn from the character of Dr. Hampden's published works, it is clear that he has hitherto been advanced from one preferment to another either very carelessly or else as the reward of his heterodoxy."[31] The *Herald* had its own pro-Hampden solution to the puzzle, but that mattered less than the universal wonderment which the chronology of the Hampden case provoked. The Bampton Lectures were delivered in 1832; Hampden became Principal of St. Mary Hall in 1833; and he was elected Professor of Moral Philosophy in 1834. If indeed the Bampton Lectures were filled with heresy, how was it that their author had advanced, after their publication, from one post of trust in the university to another? And how was it that the same people who had supported him in 1833 and 1834 now suddenly found him a heretic? Was it because he had written a pamphlet befriending the Dissenters and had been appointed to office by a Whig Prime Minister?

Other friends of Hampden raised other points. An anonymous pamphlet was circulated which parodied Newman's "Elucidations" and tried to demonstrate, by extracts from his, Pusey's and Sewell's works, the manner in which Hampden had been misrepresented. About the same time (April 1836) there appeared a vicious attack on the Tractarians, called "A Pastoral Epistle from his Holiness the Pope to some Members of the University of Oxford," in which the Tracts were quoted and misquoted to give them a Roman Catholic flavour. The attack on Hampden, said the pamphlet in effect, amounted to a popish assault upon the Reformation. Archbishop Whately's hand could be discerned in this production which came from the pen of one of his chaplains, and the Tractarians probably would have done well to ignore it. But Pusey fidgeted over the "dishonesty" and "irreverence" of the "Pastoral Epistle" and decided some kind of public answer was necessary. Accordingly, on April 25th, he published an "Earnest Remonstrance" which ultimately reappeared as Tract Seventy-seven.[32]

But these verbal exchanges were as child's play when compared to the thoughts that were taking shape in the mind of the Headmaster of Rugby. Thomas Arnold and Hampden were not well acquainted, but they shared the basic point of view of the old Oriel Noetics. They were both liberals politically and theologically. Arnold was ready at all times to make clear where his sympathies lay. "Hampden's Bampton Lectures," he wrote to a friend, "are a great work, entirely true in their main points, and I think most useful." And as for Hampden himself: "Hampden is a good man, and an able one; a lover of truth and fairness; and I should think that the wholesome air of such a man's lectures would tend to freshen men's faith and assure them that it had a foundation to rest upon, when the infinite dishonesty and foolery of such divinity as I remember in the lecture rooms and pulpits in times past would be enough to drive a man of sound mind into any extravagances of unbelief."[33] Arnold tried to take a detached view about being beaten in Oxford Convocation. "Oxford now is like Oxford in the sixteenth century," he said to Hampden, "and will never be reformed effectually except from without. I often think of the instructive fact that the Reformation was carried by a reforming government supported by a small minority of the clergy against the majority of the clergy, the country gentlemen and the populace."[34]

The Convocation of March 22nd, however, drove Arnold into a state of absolute fury. The moral earnestness which had burned away the dross of schoolboy sin at Rugby burst into flame at the Oxford persecution of Dr. Hampden. Impelled by this hot indignation, Arnold sat down and wrote a bitter denunciation of the anti-Hampden forces. Appearing in the April issue of *The Edinburgh Review* and entitled (by the editors of the *Review*) "The Oxford Malignants and Dr. Hampden," Arnold's article purported to be a review of Hampden's inaugural lecture, Newman's "Elucidations" and two of Pusey's pamphlets. In reality it was Arnold's unique contribution to the controversy: an essay which appealed by its sincerity while it repelled through its extravagance and harshness. "The Oxford Malignants" added no new light to the discussion, except perhaps in the emphasis it gave to a constitutional consideration. Oxford, Arnold charged, had surrendered to "lynch law."

If a clergyman's preaching be at variance with the tenets of the Church, the bishop of his diocese may take cognizance of it; or if the alleged offence be committed in Oxford, the university statutes have provided that the Vice-chancellor, with the assistance of six doctors of divinity, shall enquire into the truth of the charge and pass sentence accordingly. If Dr. Hampden had really published anything in opposition to the Articles of the Church of England, there was a ready way of substantiating the charge and obtaining a censure upon him from a competent authority. But the course of truth and honesty was not suited to the . . . conspirators. They thought they had a secure majority in Convocation which would vote for anything that they proposed to it. A *vote* they knew might give them what they could never hope from a *verdict*.[35]

Not justice but faction held the balance on March 22nd, and, Arnold argued, holds it still. And who are these "authors whose censure was to be coveted by every good Christian minister? A few obscure fanatics," Arnold answered. "The *individuals* indeed are sufficiently insignificant; nor shall we, by naming them, confer on them that notoriety for which nature has not designed them." The High Church party—"the party of Oxford Conspirators"—has two parts to it: "on the one hand, the mere low worldly clergy, careless and grossly ignorant, ministers not of the gospel but of the aristocracy, who belong to Christianity only from the accident of its being established by law"; and, on the other hand, "the formalist Judaizing fanatics . . . who have been the peculiar disgrace of the Church of England; for these High Church fanatics have imbibed, even of fanaticism itself, nothing but the folly and the virulence."[36]

So Arnold went on, striking out in every direction. He poured scorn upon Oxford itself: "Opinions and prejudices of one sort only found admission to it. It stood aloof from the great mass of the intelligence of the nation, neither influencing it nor influenced by it." Drawing a dark comparison between a Non-Juror of the seventeenth century and "one or two of the Oxford conspirators," Arnold sneered at the "pretended holiness of his life," a reputation gained "because he used a sentimental style of excessive religious feeling in his prayers and other compositions."[37] Nobody could have missed the allusion to Arnold's old friend John Keble.

Arnold raised the substantive issue of the Bampton Lectures only to dismiss Newman's "Elucidations" as fraudulent, while at the same time showing a curious inability himself to understand precisely what Hampden had said. What did it matter anyway, Arnold asked with an odd lapse of logic. "It is manifest that the real nature of a man's religious views and feelings is to be collected most perfectly from his general pastoral preaching to his own congregation; and not from a set of sermons preached on a particular subject and when that subject is in itself of an abstract and unimpassioned character." This is perhaps the most significant sentence in the whole of "The Oxford Malignants." For Arnold religion meant passionate concern, a kind of masculine assertiveness which had little to do with truth or falsity. And so for the opponents of Dr. Hampden Arnold had only the stern judgment and manly abhorrence that he might have had for a Rugby boy caught writing naughty words on the wall. "The attack upon Dr. Hampden bears upon it the character not of error but of *moral wickedness*. . . . And for such persecution the plea of conscience is not admissible; it can only be a conscience so blinded by wilful neglect of the highest truth, or so corrupted by the habitual indulgence of evil passions, that it rather aggravates than excuses the guilt of those whom it misleads."[38]

Arnold's public gnashing of teeth changed nobody's mind. On May 5, 1836, the scheduled Convocation came together. This time, however, decorum was maintained by excluding B.A.'s and undergraduates. Five Latin speeches were given in behalf of Hampden and two, one of them by Keble, against. Arnold was present in the theater, and one wonders what his thoughts were as he listened to Keble, a man presumably "corrupted by the habitual indulgence of evil passions." The vote to censure Hampden was 474 to 94, a majority of 380.

Whatever the worth of his theological views, Renn Hampden throughout the controversy of 1836 proved himself a brave and stubborn man. After it was over he showed that he could be a petty man as well. He took his little vengeance on the university by refusing to give up the principalship of St. Mary Hall even though he was now, as regius professor, Canon of Christ Church and Rector of Ewelme, Oxfordshire. Such flagrant pluralism was the source of considerable embarrassment to his supporters, who, with Edward Hawkins and Thomas Arnold in the lead, had chosen high moral ground on which to fight his battle. During 1837 the Duke of Wellington inquired formally whether Hampden intended to vacate St. Mary Hall. A fitful correspondence followed, and nothing in the end was done. Hampden summed up the affair by remarking about the Duke, "I wish he could have not destroyed my illusion as to his being a magnanimous person."[39]

But another noble lord understood. Hampden in 1837 met Melbourne for the first time, and Hampden, who always found conversation difficult, tried to blurt out all at once to the Prime Minister his thanks for the professorship and his sense of outrage against his enemies. The charming old sinner laid a kindly hand on the arm of the Regius Professor of Divinity. "Be easy," he said. "I like an easy man."[40]

CHAPTER 11

The Vicar of St. Mary the Virgin

NEWMAN occupied two rooms at Oriel, across the quadrangle from Provost Hawkins' lodgings and next to the chapel. There was a passageway which led out of the bedroom and into the gallery of the chapel and which could be used, depending on the tastes of the occupant, as a pantry, an oratory or a catch-all closet. Richard Whately, when he lived briefly in the same rooms, used to keep dried herrings hung on a string in this little corridor, and, according to a story told by the college servants, the future Archbishop of Dublin customarily began his day by broiling a herring over the coals of his fire and consuming it without benefit of salt, pepper or ceremony. Newman, who was at once more fastidious and more pious than Whately, often said his private prayers in the passageway and he had a shower bath installed at one end of it.

The sitting room was small but comfortable, with a window on each side. A crucifix, with the corpus removed, hung over the fireplace, and the walls were decorated with prints, one of them of the Anglo-Catholic Martyr King Charles I. The room was so jammed with books that there was scarcely space for more than two people to sit down. Included among the books, after 1836, was a set of Roman breviaries. They had belonged to Froude, a keepsake which the archdeacon had urged on Newman after Hurrell's death. These stubby little volumes were to be Newman's lifelong companions, and though from this time onwards he recited the office regularly he carefully abstained from anything in them—like invocations to Our Lady—which seemed out of tune with Anglican usage.[1]

The spring of 1836, the spring of Froude's death and the university's censure of R. D. Hampden, was what Newman called "a cardinal point of time." Though no one knew it then, what followed was the last summer of pre-Victorian England. For Newman personally it was a turning point in many ways. On April 28th Jemima Newman married John Mozley of Derby. Less than three weeks later Mrs. John Newman died, and in September Harriet Newman married Tom Mozley. Thus within a few months Newman was relieved of the family burdens which had taken up so much of his time and energy since the death of his father.

His two brothers continued along their eccentric ways. John Henry tried to keep in touch with both Charles and Francis but with the passing years the relationship grew more strained and fitful. Ultimately the strongest link with the elder brother came to be the dislike the two younger Newmans had for each other. A curious letter survives from the summer of 1836 in which Charles Newman left behind some evidence of the provocative and peculiar behaviour with which John had to contend. Charles wrote to accept his brother's invitation to meet in London on July 20th. Evidently John intended to give Charles a watch as a present, for Charles said, "If you really have one, I will accept it with thanks." However, he added that it had been foolish to purchase a watch in Oxford when London prices were so much lower. "I dare say you are aware that you constantly give four times the price Francis does—in books, for instance, and furniture. . . . Your plan [i.e. manner] may be accordant with your standing and place in life, but then it requires a larger fortune than you have."

After this patronizing advice, Charles moved on to greater issues. He airily thanked John "for the information you give me respecting your opinions." Whether the Tractarian system were true or not, Charles neither knew nor cared; he did consider it "utilitarian" during an era in which the wisdom of the past received scant attention. "Now since I suppose the claim of 'apostolical succession' affords a means of union to the Church and to conservative interest, I am very favourable to it. But the claim has seemed monstrous to almost all people." Charles suggested that John read the attack on *History of the Arians* published in *The Edinburgh Review*. "Either you or the reviewer (with whom Francis agrees—*I* think he says some things very true) is a great pretender."[2] Perhaps Newman, as he put down this letter with a mutter of impatience, thought of the old truism about the prophet's acceptance in his own familiar circle.

But the rest of the world did not look upon the Vicar of St. Mary's with such a jaundiced eye. He was thirty-five years old that summer, strong and vigorous, "almost daily striding along the Oxford road, with large head, prominent nose, tortoise-shell spectacles, emaciated but ruddy face, spare figure whose leanness was exaggerated by the close-fitting tail-coat."[3] He had tasted both victory and bereavement and they had left him tougher than before. He had come into the fullness of his powers. He was the leader of a cause whose righteousness made his seemingly endless exertions worthwhile. Now and then, however, especially after the loss of Froude (which he described as a kind of widowhood), he was overwhelmed by a sense of loneliness. But he could explain that too. "God intends me to be lonely," he said to Jemima.[4]

I

Across the High Street from Oriel College stands the university church of St. Mary the Virgin. The history of Oxford can be traced in its weathered stone. The spire which rises from a cluster of pinnacles and gargoyles is all that remains of the twelfth-century church, but every era since has left an imprint upon the church's material fabric. The Lady Chapel, also called Adam de Brome's Chapel, dates from 1328, and the Old Congregation House, long the university's legislative chamber, was built and attached to the church at about the same time. The front portico with its twisted Italian-style pillars was added under the patronage of Archbishop Laud in 1637. When Cromwell's Puritans brought that High Church prelate to trial and ultimately to death, one of the subjects of indictment against him was the "idolatrous" statue of Virgin and Child which Laud had set in the niche over the rear center of the porch.

The connection between Oriel and St. Mary's went back, as we have seen, to Adam de Brome himself. When Newman became vicar in 1828 many of the concrete reminders of the past had been recently swept away by the industriousness of his predecessor. Hawkins, when he was elected provost, handed over to Newman a refurbished St. Mary's. The nave had been renovated with a new wood pulpit (which is still there), new pews and other fittings. Hawkins also installed as his personal gift to the parish a new stone baptismal font to replace the wooden one the Puritans had put in. The seventeenth-century organ had received a thorough overhauling.[5]

St. Mary's had the mixed character of a university and a parish church. University functions, both academic and religious, centered there, and the Vice-chancellor had his own stall. Undergraduates and dons were expected to attend chapel in their own colleges, though they could make use of St. Mary's too if they liked. The families of the Heads of Houses usually worshiped there, as did university men who for one reason or another lodged outside college. The rest of the parish was made up mostly of college servants and the shopkeepers along the High Street. Among those who had a special statutory right to pews in St. Mary's Church were those connected with St. Mary Hall. In 1833 or 1834 Newman had to arbitrate between Dr. Hampden, who insisted on this right, and other parishioners of St. Mary's who evidently wished to exclude the St. Mary Hall people. In this minor altercation, Newman felt that Hampden was in the right, and he was pleased to see the Principal of St. Mary Hall emerge victorious.[6]

Newman had had a smattering of parochial experience at St. Clement's, Oxford, early in the 1820s. By the time he came to St. Mary's he was convinced that every clergyman must take a directly pastoral view of his vocation. There was no better way to accomplish this than to serve in a parish. This conviction, which grew upon him with the passing years, he shared with the other leaders of the Movement. Keble deserted Oxford early in his career for the parochial life in Gloucestershire, and Pusey, though more an academic animal, more typically a don than either of the other two, often took the Sunday service and preached at the parish church near his family home in rural Berkshire. This same pastoral preoccupation was what had got Newman in trouble with Hawkins over the proposed reform of the Oriel tutorial system. The frustration of this scheme, and the resulting loss of contact with undergraduates, served to confirm Newman in his devotion to his duties at St. Mary's.

These duties were as onerous as a vicar cared to make them. Newman, as one might expect, took a very serious view of his obligations. As an instance, take the matter of catechizing. In preparing a group for the reception of Confirmation he held three meetings a week for more than two months. He began by talking to each candidate individually and making notes about the reaction of each: "backward," "dull in appearance," "quick," and so on. The formal lectures which followed were built upon the Prayer Book, moving from a study of the Baptism service through Holy Communion to Confirmation. Collateral reading from Scripture and standard Anglican divines, as well as the catechism, was assigned to the pupils to be read between meetings. The class was usually a mixed bag to say the least; an average one, in 1832, contained twenty-six candidates ranging in age from fourteen to twenty-seven and almost entirely made up of domestic servants and apprentices. Some of these pupils studied, more did not, and others were so hopelessly stupid and ill prepared that many a teacher would have given up on them.

Not so Newman. He kept track of the progress of each and when one or another fell behind he gave individual lessons after the rest of the class had gone home. It must have been disappointing when only four or five of the class appeared. Once, in 1828, only one girl came, but the vicar devoted to her the full class time. He did not hesitate to mix moral exhortation with instruction. "C. Hillier," he noted in 1828, "has not been able to come this fortnight. He was much affected when I talked to him about his sinfulness and need of a new heart and Christ's sufferings, as I have observed before in him." And in 1832: "A[nne] Carpenter talked to and reproved most seriously."[7]

The financial administration of St. Mary's was not particularly burdensome to the vicar, because it was handled in the age-old fashion determined by the endowment. Yet some moneys did pass through his hands, and this Newman took special pains with. He kept an account book of the "sacrament money," the public collection taken up in church and destined to be used as alms. The collection on Christmas 1831 totaled three pounds and seventeen shillings, which sum the vicar dispensed to the worthy poor. He maintained also what he called "St. Mary's *private* charity fund." Included here were stole fees which the vicar received and also any donations which individuals might care to give. Thus, for example, when Provost Hawkins on one occasion wished to aid someone anonymously, he gave one pound to the private charity fund, and Newman passed his benefaction on. This was a lively account, with small sums (four to six shillings usually) coming and going and all of them carefully entered into a separate ledger by the vicar. Following Hawkins' example, he never threw away a receipt, and shopkeepers soon realized that Newman was a man no easier to get round than his predecessor. When he paid eight shillings for a large watering can, he made this notation: "They used to fill the [baptismal] font by means of an old slop pail. So I bought a can." In 1831 "I took up the pebbles in the church yard of St. Mary's and sowed grass at the Vice-chancellor's request." The bill for eight pounds and seven shillings was presented to and paid for by the bursar of Oriel College.[8]

These seemingly petty details help to draw a picture of Newman as parish priest. However great his absorption in the folios of the Fathers of the Church, however much strength he expended on reconstructing the subtle arguments of Arians and semi-Arians, he still had energy to concern himself over buying a proper watering can. He was never too busy to instruct and reprove some lout of a boy who would not study his catechism, even though, at the same time, he was writing tracts, treatises and sermons by the score, leading a politico-religious agitation of nationwide proportions, and trying to build an inner castle of religious mysticism. The sheer variety of his work, his tireless devotion to the needs of people and, no less, to the decorum of the house of God, laid the foundation to the vast influence he enjoyed as Vicar of St. Mary the Virgin. He gave of himself constantly and endlessly and yet he kept something back, something unique and mysterious. He reminded James Antony Froude, Hurrell's younger brother, of Julius Caesar. "I have often thought of the resemblance, and believed that it extended to the temperament. In both there was an original force of character which refused to be molded by circumstances, . . . a clearness of intellectual perception, disdain for conventionalities, a temper imperious and wilful, but along with a most attaching gentleness, sweetness, singleness of heart and purpose."[9] In 1838 a freshman undergraduate, just arrived in Oxford, was walking with a friend past St. Mary's. "My companion seized my arm, whispering to me, 'Look, look, there, that is Newman.' I looked and then I saw him passing along in his characteristic way, walking fast without any dignity of gait, but earnest like one who had a purpose; yet so humble and self-forgetting that you would not have thought him, at first sight, a man remarkable for anything."[10] Simple, unlettered people came to have the same awe of him. Once, as he walked at the upper end of the High Street, near Carfax, he encountered a drunk who was spewing out obscenities and blasphemies. Very quietly the vicar said to him, "My friend, if you thought of the meaning of your words you would not say them." The man, a big, brawny butcher, twice Newman's size, blinked in surprise, and then touched his cap and ambled away.[11]

Such, in its proletarian aspect, was what Oxford came to call "Newmania."

II

In a routine report to the Bishop of Oxford in 1832, Newman described as follows the liturgical life in his parish: "There is a service in my church twice on every Sunday, and on Christmas day, and on Good Friday; once on the first day of Lent, on each day during Passion Week but Good Friday, and on all saints days and holy days. . . . The Sacrament of the Lord's Supper is administered twelve times in the year. . . . I have one sermon on a Sunday, and a lecture on all holydays excepting four." Given the practice of the times, this was a full schedule, and it represented an expansion over what Hawkins had performed in his time as vicar. In 1830, Newman had inaugurated a service on those saints' feasts which the Book of Common Prayer listed, rather vaguely, as of special importance. Altogether there were about twenty-five of these (as distinct from movable feasts like the Ascension and Easter Monday and Tuesday), and they included the days honouring the apostles (for example, August 24th, St. Bartholomew's Day), St. Mary Magdalen (July 22nd), St. Michael (Michaelmas, September 29th), and so on.

Newman carefully put down in a notebook the numbers of those who attended the saint's-day services. The first entry was dated Lady Day, March 25, 1830: "Besides minister and clerk, seventeen; called in consequence on Dodd, Hayes, Hickman, Sykes and Lenthall to signify my approbation of their going." Here is an intriguing picture: the earnest young vicar calls upon some rather startled parishioners to tell them of his approval of their going to church on a weekday. Newman continued to record the attendance figures: "May 1, [1830]. St. Philip and St. James. Very few." "June 29, St. Peter. About eight." "August 24, St. Bartholomew. Between thirty and forty." He soon discovered what so many pastors discover, that the numbers varied little over the years, the average running to about twenty, and that though there were sometimes more and sometimes less than this, the same people composed the congregation, day after day, year after year. At the end of the little chart he kept on the subject he noted, "And so the enumeration goes on through 1836 and 1837, with no increase of the numbers and no diminution."[12]

Newman's attempt to expand and intensify the liturgical life of St. Mary's was perfectly consistent with the aims of the Tractarian Movement. The Tracts, for all their abstract argumentation, never lost sight of the simple concrete objective of making the doctrines and practice of the Prayer Book central to the Anglican's Christian witness. We have already noticed the stress the Tractarians gave to the notion of the Eucharist as the Christian's practical means of coming into contact with God. Indeed, Keble explained the importance of the apostolical succession in terms of its guaranteeing the valid celebration of the Lord's Supper. To elevate worship and to give the average man's life a sacramental orientation, these were the matters dearest to Tractarian hearts, far dearer than any of the polemics which might contribute to those ends. Newman did no more than practice what he preached when, in 1834, he introduced daily Morning Prayer at St. Mary's and, three years later, weekly Holy Communion.

Yet Newman never had much interest in rubrics as such. When he was a very old man he observed, "I don't think I made any innovation of ritual at St. Mary's, down to a surplice for preaching in. I found the stationary communion with its napkins or tablecloths, . . . and so I left it. Hawkins, my predecessor, I have heard say again and again that it was a remnant of Puritan times."[13] There was a custom at St. Mary's of distributing Communion to the worshipers as they knelt in their choir stalls; such a practice seemed highly indecorous to the more fervent ritualists among the Tractarians, but Newman never bothered to change it. The ritualists also insisted that the minister should take an eastward direction when he led the congregation in worship. This practice was based on a patristic precedent and it had some symbolic interest (Christ, the Orient, through whom prayer is directed, shall at his second coming appear in the east), but Newman treated it with cool pragmatism. He did not take an eastward position at the altar, but when he began the daily Morning Prayer he told Hurrell Froude, "I shall have a desk put near the altar facing south, from which I shall read the psalms and lessons, kneeling, however, towards the east. It seems to me that the absurdity . . . of Tom Keble's daily plan is his praying to *empty benches*."[14] John Keble's brother had started daily Morning Prayer in his parish in 1827. Tom was no ritualist, and he forthrightly ignored direction, putting his back to the altar and his face to the congregation, even when there was no congregation and perhaps no human being besides himself in the church. To Newman such a posture seemed absurd, but no more absurd than the faddist absorption in ritual detail which attracted others of his friends.

Newman did not dawdle over liturgical functions. He read the Anglican services quickly, much too quickly for some. Francis Newman had an Evangelical friend who concluded from the pace set at St. Mary's that Francis' brother must have had another service to conduct elsewhere.[15] But most of those who worshiped at St. Mary's were too struck by the vicar's almost mystical rendering of the Scripture passages ever to

notice the amount of time it took. Dr. Gilbert of Brasenose College (the
same Gilbert who had led the attack on Hampden in the Hebdomadal
Board) had a blind daughter who, to the end of her life, used to say that
she could not listen to the reading of Isaiah without hearing Newman's
voice.[16] Frederick Temple, an undergraduate at Balliol in 1839 (and
sixty years later Archbishop of Canterbury), recalled Newman's reverent
simplicity as he read the lessons—"as if he were giving a message to which
he himself was listening."[17] Frederick Oakeley expanded on this point.
"[Newman] succeeded in imparting to the Anglican service . . . an
indescribable charm of touching beauty and a wonderful power of instructive efficacy." His reading of Scripture

was a sermon in which you forgot the human preacher; a drama in which the
vividness of the representation was marred by no effort and degraded by no art.
He stood before the sacred volume as if penetrating its contents to their very
centre. . . . He brought out meanings where none had ever been suspected,
and invested passages which in the hands of the profane are often the subject
of unbecoming levity, with a solemnity which forced irreverence to retire
abashed into its hiding places.[18]

Long after Newman had left St. Mary's an old lady put the same thought
more succinctly: "Mr. Newman used very often to wear a rather dirty
surplice, but when he read the lessons we thought he was in heaven."[19]

III

Nothing Newman did in his long life, no book or campaign or pronouncement, had quite the sustained effect as the sermons he preached
in St. Mary's on Sunday afternoons between 1828 and 1843. Old men
who had heard them as boys remembered them with a reverence which
neither years nor sharp divisions could efface. Thomas Arnold's son
Matthew, who as an undergraduate at Balliol often listened to his father's
deadly enemy, recalled the scene.

Who could resist the charm of that spiritual apparition, gliding in the dim
afternoon light through the aisles of St. Mary's, rising into the pulpit, and then
in the most entrancing of voices, breaking the silence with words and thoughts
which were religious music, subtle, sweet and mournful? I seem to hear him still
saying: "After the fever of life, after weariness and sickness, fightings and
despondings, languor and fretfulness, struggling and succeeding; after all the
changes and chances of this troubled unhealthy state—at length comes death,
at length the white throne of God, at length the beatific vision.[20]

Newman's style of delivery in the pulpit belied the impact which his
sermons universally produced. It was simplicity itself. He used no ges-

tures. He stood in the pulpit thin, frail and apparently passionless, and read the sermons, carefully refraining from any ostentation, in a clear, tenor voice. The only rhetorical mechanism he employed was an occasional pause between sentences, which, it seemed to the listeners, was meant really to sustain the reflection of the preacher himself rather than to affect them. But the result was electric and dramatic. "There were times," said Henry Wilberforce, "when in the midst of the most thrilling passages he would pause, without dropping his voice, for a moment which seemed long, before he uttered with gathered force and solemnity a few weighty words." It was always an unforgettable moment. "The great church, the congregation all breathless with expectant attention, the gas light just at the left of the pulpit, lowered that the preacher might not be dazzled; themselves perhaps standing in the half darkness of the gallery, and then the pause."[21]

St. Mary's, when Newman preached, was usually jammed by five or six hundred people, mostly undergraduates and younger dons. They watched him spellbound and saw "no movement of the body, scarcely a movement of the hand."[22] There was not the slightest attempt to impress or to dazzle, and that very artlessness was realy the center of his art. The sophisticated congregation, which would have despised histrionics or mere cleverness, was caught up in swirl of the deepest feeling, traceable to a sense shared by all that the preacher was striving so hard to contain himself.

I used to go regularly on Sunday afternoons to listen to his sermons at St. Mary's, and I have never heard such preaching since. . . . He always began as if he had determined to set forth his idea of the truth in the plainest and simplest language. . . . But his ardent zeal and fine poetical imagination were not thus to be controlled. As I hung upon his words, it seemed to me as if I could trace behind his will, and pressing, so to speak, against it, a rush of thoughts and feelings which he kept struggling to hold back, but in the end they were generally too strong for him, and poured themselves out in a torrent of eloquence all the more impetuous from having been so long repressed. The effect of these outbursts was irresistible and carried his hearers beyond themselves at once.[23]

In content Newman's sermons were never directly controversial. They reflected, indeed, the tenets of the positions he argued so brilliantly in his tracts and books, but they appealed to the heart rather than the head and hence to an audience wider than his intellectual disciples. "His power," remembered J. C. Shairp, "showed itself in the new and unlooked-for way in which he touched into life old truths, moral and spiritual, which all Christians acknowledge but most have ceased to feel."[24] And Samuel Wilberforce testified to much the same thing: "He reached the heart of young Oxford; man after man, in whom was the receptive faculty, received the living force of his words and reproduced so far as he was able the Master's spirit in himself."[25] "He laid his finger," said Shairp, "—how gently, yet how powerfully!—on some inner place in the hearer's heart, and told him things about himself he had never known till then. . . . After hearing these sermons you might come away still not believing the tenets peculiar to the High Church system; but you would be harder than most men if you did not feel more than ever ashamed of coarseness, selfishness, worldliness, if you did not feel the things of faith brought closer to the soul."[26]

Yet however effective they were, Newman's sermons were not simply a cry of the heart. Though he did not argue in the pulpit or even, strictly speaking, instruct, he nevertheless framed his sermons in a strikingly original and incisive way. "His illustrations were inexhaustible," wrote J. A. Froude. "He never exaggerated; he was never unreal. A sermon from him was a poem, formed on a distinct idea, fascinating by its subtlety, welcome—how welcome—from its sincerity, interesting from its originality."[27] Newman's insights into scriptural passages, his limpidly clear but nicely balanced practical applications, his closely reasoned theses even when they denigrated, as they often did, the place of reason in religious life: all this was calculated to draw out the sympathy of his listeners, who were, after all, mostly stripling intellectuals.

Perhap the quality which contributed more than any other to the success of Newman's sermons was his sure grasp of the character of his congregation. Newman did not preach as though his listeners were profligates. He understood them, and they sensed immediately that he did. He understood that they were good, sensible, respectable men, who loved comfort and praise and power, who often indulged their appetites because that seemed the natural thing to do. They were young and full of life, and when they listened to Newman they never failed to hear a challenge to their better selves, an invitation to venture for the faith, a call to a noble ideal which the cynical years had not yet obscured. "He seemed," said Froude, "to be addressing the most sacred consciousness of each of us—as the eyes of a portrait appear to look at every person in the room."[28] He did not cater to them, but as he spoke, in the lengthening shadows of the late afternoon, he showed them the stark contrast between themselves and the "white throne of God." The demonstration was without extravagance or showiness; it throbbed instead with a genuine benignity and interest in them as they really were which made religion suddenly pertinent even to these rich young men, "even to those who were careless of religion, and to those who wished to be religious but had found religion dry and wearisome." More than one man found his life profoundly changed by his Sunday afternoon encounter with the Vicar of St. Mary's; it proved to be not one more tedious service but "like the springing of a fountain out of a rock."[29]

Between 1834 and 1843 Newman published eleven volumes of sermons, most of them first preached at St. Mary's. So it was that thousands who never attended a Sunday afternoon service could also share in the Newman pulpit magic. It was a different kind of magic indeed; the immediacy was gone, the blessed vision of peace which seemed to fill the church as Newman spoke could only be guessed at through the printed word. Yet the sermons are such perfect works of art that they stand even without the sound of the voice which first uttered them. It would have been an incomparable experience to have heard the blind Homer chanting the verses of the *Iliad* in some great Ionian hall; yet even without that one can still grasp something of the music and the wonder and the thrilling pathos of a line like "Such were the funeral rites for Hector, tamer of horses." Newman's Anglican sermons have passed the same test.

Because of the impact they had upon the contemporary generation of Oxford men, and because they were eagerly read by thousands of people who would not have bothered about tracts and treatises, Newman's sermons proved to be the most influential product of the Oxford Movement. Maria Pusey remarked to her husband with touching candour that while she found some of Edward's writings difficult and perplexing, "there are some things that come to one as truth as soon as they are proposed, and those are the things one really believes unhesitatingly. Mr. Newman's . . . sermons are full of truths of [this] sort, and perhaps that is one reason why I so like them."[30]

It was not, however, only the finely sculptured sentences or the partially veiled intensity or the shrewd insights which made people believe Mr. Newman "unhesitatingly." Something else enforced the credibility of the sermons, and this was the preacher's calm consistency. One will look in vain in them for a process of development. Neither the progress of the Tract Movement nor the personal doubts which began to assail Newman in 1839 altered the tenor of his sermons. To parody the famous line in the *Apologia*, what he preached in 1828, he preached in 1836, and he preached it to the end. It is true that the earlier sermons have a directly Evangelical flavour—a preference, for example, for Calvinist expressions about the human condition—which became more refined later on. But the substance remained the same, so much so that when he published the eighth volume of the *Parochial and Plain Sermons* in 1843, he included in it sermons first delivered in 1825, three years before he went to St. Mary's. On the doorstep of Rome he did not hesitate to give to the world the expression of his teaching when he was still a fervent Evangelical. And what was that message which spanned the decades and survived drastic changes of allegiance? Preaching in St. Mary's on May 9, 1830, Newman put it as well as (but no better than) he did on many other occasions.

Great perils just now encompass our branch of the Church; here the question comes upon us, as a body and as individuals, what ought we to do? Doubtless to meet them with all the wisdom and prudence in our power, to use all allowable means to avert them; but after all, is not our main duty this: to go on quietly and steadfastly in our old ways, as if nothing was the matter? . . . What is the use of these feverish exertions on all sides of us to soothe our enemies, conciliate the suspicious or wavering, and attach to us men of name and power? Rather, let our resolve be, if we are to perish, it shall be at our post of duty. We will be found in the circle of our sacred services, in prayer and praise, in fasting and almsdoing. . . . At length our deliverance will come, when we expect it not; whereas we shall lose our own hope and disorder the Church greatly if we presume to form plans of our own by way of protecting it.[31]

IV

Newman appended the following note to the report he sent in 1832 to his bishop: "A portion of St. Mary's parish lies in the hamlet of Littlemore, situated between two and three miles from Oxford across the Henley road, with no chapel upon it. Part of the year I have been residing not in Oxford but close upon this portion (there being no house belonging to me or suitable *within* it). I am in the practice of having a weekly lecture at Littlemore through the year."[32] No gentleman lived in Littlemore where the population was made up almost entirely of poor labourers. In 1830 Newman settled his mother and sisters not far away. This served several purposes at once. It gave Newman proximity to the women in his family for whom he alone among the three Newman brothers seemed to assume any responsibility. It also gave Mrs. Newman, Harriet and Jemima a chance to perform good works of mercy and in-struction to the portion of his parish most in need of such ministrations. Apparently they took up the role of angelic ladies with alacrity and considerable effectiveness.[33]

Newman estimated the number of his Littlemore flock at about two hundred in 1831, and it seems to have risen rather sharply during the next four or five years. He gave them the best service he could, consider-ing that there were no facilities in Littlemore itself. Almost from the moment he became Vicar of St. Mary's he began to plan for the day when Littlemore could be detached from the mother parish and thus receive the direct parochial attention it needed. His first idea, in 1829, involved giving the Littlemore mission to Robert Wilberforce, his colleague at Oriel, but nothing came of this. Meanwhile, Newman walked out to Littlemore almost every day. He visited the sick and the poor, did his best to alleviate the hardships which many of them had to contend with, and spent a good part of his time giving the most basic catechism lessons to their practically illiterate children.

There was a kind of relief for Newman in his work at Littlemore. Here he encountered the most simple of mankind whose elemental needs seemed a world apart from those of sophisticated Oxford society. In Littlemore the differences between High and Low Church amounted to little, and subtle argumentation had no place at all. Fresh from tilting with Hampden or with the religious doubts of some precocious undergraduate, Newman took his fiddle out to Littlemore, taught the children some hymns and then played along with them as they sang. He was never too much the don to appreciate what was really important in bettering the lot of the rural poor. "I have effected a great reform in the girls' hands and faces," he wrote on one occasion. "[I] lectured with unblushing effrontery on the necessity of their keeping their work clean, and set them to knit stockings."[34]

The original idea to detach Littlemore legally from St. Mary's and to form a separate parish out of it came up again in the early 1840s when Newman, in the unhappy dusk of his Anglican career, considered retiring from St. Mary's and settling himself in Littlemore as pastor. Before that, however, he put to himself the task of building a church in Littlemore. Pastoral ministrations were fine as far as they went, but people needed, in Newman's judgment, a permanent sacramental reminder of God's presence. What had happened in Littlemore (and indeed in different ways all over England) was the gradual withering away of allegiance to the Church for lack of a place to worship. People either frequented the Dissenters' chapel or stayed away from services altogether. Certainly the best-intentioned man in Littlemore would not have dreamed of walking into Oxford on Sunday afternoon and joining the university smart set at St. Mary's.

The main problem Newman faced in this project was, of course, raising the money to pay for it. The poverty of the Littlemore inhabitants ruled out the possibility of any substantial donations from them. So Newman had to turn to his friends and interested benefactors. He was not disappointed; cordial endorsement came from all sides. Harriet and Jemima began the formal campaign by contacting all the householders in Littlemore and gathering 295 signatures for a petition which stated the nearly unanimous desire of the villagers for a church of their own. Newman took this to Oriel in the spring of 1835 and asked for permission to build, arguing that St. Mary's Church was too far from Littlemore, that funerals held in churches other than St. Mary's were too expensive for the people of Littlemore (double fees were charged to non-parishioners), and that many, especially the elderly and infirm, were attending the Dissenters' chapel. The provost and fellows, who, it will be remembered, as a corporation were the Rector of St. Mary's, agreed to donate a plot of ground and a hundred pounds besides.[35]

In July of 1835 Newman's mother laid the cornerstone of the church in Littlemore. During the following months the appeal for funds went out and Newman kept careful account of receipts and expenditures. The church and its furnishings cost more than a thousand pounds, and most of this sum was raised in the course of 1835–36. Joshua Watson's Church Building Society gave 150 pounds, and Watson added a personal donation of 10 pounds. The Tractarians all contributed lavishly: Newman himself headed the list with 50 pounds; Pusey donated 25, Rogers 10, each of the Keble brothers 10, and Tom Mozley, who could hardly have afforded it, gave 5. The donors also included people of very different views. Hawkins contributed 25 pounds, and from far away in his bleak Welsh diocese Bishop Copleston, the oldest Noetic of them all, sent 10 pounds.[36]

The humbler people of Littlemore did what they could to help build their church. Newman carefully tabulated their donations, keeping track of their names and the sums they gave. The gift of two pennies from a Littlemore child was entered as solemnly into the ledger as the magnificent communion plate, worth more than 30 pounds, which came from John Bowden and his wife. Notations of the following kind tell the tale: "Received of Mr. Greening, this 11th of November, 1835, the sum of eight pounds, six shillings, subscriptions from persons in Littlemore towards the building of the new church."[37]

Dr. Bagot, Bishop of Oxford, consecrated the chapel of St. Mary the Virgin and St. Nicholas, Littlemore, on September 22, 1836. The plain gothic building, "like a barn with a pointed roof and narrow lancet windows,"[38] was crowded with Oxford society on one side and villagers on the other. There was some concern among Newman's friends about the bishop's possible reaction to what he saw. Frederic Rogers, that shrewd observer of men and events, was present and recorded the scene.

Newman's church, now finished, is certainly one of the most perfect things for its size I ever saw. The altar is beautiful and the rest is so well kept under that when you come in you seem to see nothing but the altar. The builders etc. are extremely puzzled at the capricious and unseemly (as to them appears) way in which his ornament is spent: no cushions in the armchairs by the altar, mere rush hassocks for the priest to kneel on there, no cushion to support the prayer book on the altar, no cushions *or hangings* on the pulpit *at all*, and instead of a reading desk the kind of stand that a person plays the violin before, with a bran hassock to kneel on when necessary; while the altar was carved stone, with seven very pretty early English arches, surrounded by a three-lighted window in the style of those of Christ Church chapter house, all very expensive. We were all in fear as to what the bishop would say; in the first place, [the] stone altar, and in the second, crosses over [it]; these are papistical, . . . [and] so was the ceremony of priests turning to the east to say the prayers. . . . Moreover, there was no vestry for the bishop to robe in and the pulpit was even illegally destitute of appurtenances. However, his Lordship was highly pleased and complimentary, and everything went off in the greatest style.[39]

The bishop apparently saw nothing popish about the decoration of the new church, and he was especially charmed by Newman's sermon.[40] Despite the recent bereavements and exertions—the death of Froude and of his mother and the Hampden affair—the consecration day turned out to be one of the happiest of Newman's life. His heart was now closer than ever to Littlemore, and it was to become ever more so.

V

Newman regularly employed a curate to help him with his parochial duties in Oxford and Littlemore. His choice invariably fell upon a younger don who shared the vicar's basic intellectual positions and for whom no special provision of board and lodging had to be provided. Isaac Williams, a delicate Welshman who was Fellow of Trinity and a close friend of both John and Thomas Keble, became Newman's curate in 1833. A shy, gentle, otherworldly man, Williams wrote poetry (which Newman did not much care for)[41] and later on he wrote two of the most famous Tracts, which brought a storm of trouble down on his head. Though entirely devoted to Newman and the cause, Williams drew back from the more extreme forms of "Newmania." He was the officiating clergyman at the funeral of Newman's mother and at the consecration of Littlemore chapel.

In 1837 Williams gave place in the curacy to a thirty-year-old Fellow of Magdalen named John Rouse Bloxam.[42] Bloxam was a rubrical enthusiast, an antiquarian and an amateur architect. He kept Newman *au courant* in matters ceremonial, about which the Vicar of St. Mary's knew very little. Bloxam took a special interest in the flock at Littlemore. He resided there with the village blacksmith for part of every week. He started a day school at Littlemore, designed stained-glass windows for the new church, and won the hearts of all with his sweet and simple disposition.

Bloxam eventually got into trouble with the Bishop of Oxford when he visited a Roman Catholic country house, attended Mass, and allegedly bowed down at the elevation of the Species. Newman managed to smooth the matter over, but Bloxam was shattered by the experience and resigned the curacy.[43] His successor, in 1840, was William Copeland, a brilliant, self-effacing don at Trinity. Copeland, like his close friend Isaac Williams, became a Tractarian workhorse, involved in every facet of the Movement and yet shunning publicity like the plague. Both he and Bloxam, it is interesting to note, went on to serve Anglican parishes with great distinction, and long before they died they renewed their former happy relationship with the vicar who had left them for Rome.

But this trio of devoted curates was overshadowed by an eccentric man who almost but never quite became one. We have already noticed the fierce support given to the Tract Movement in its first faltering steps in 1833 by Charles Portalis Golightly. This wealthy graduate of Oriel had served in a couple of country parishes, but by 1834 he had drifted back to Oxford and had taken up residence there. The next year, when he was planning the Littlemore church, Newman discussed with his

friends the possibility of giving the curacy and the direct superintendence
of things at Littlemore to Golightly if, as appeared likely at the time,
Williams planned to resign. It seemed a particularly good idea since
Littlemore was of course without endowment and Golightly had all the
money he would ever need. Newman thought Golightly a "safe" man as
far as his views went, though admittedly their friendship had been on a
more or less casual and social level.

In May 1835 the offer was made. Golightly was delighted but cautious.
"I am very much obliged to you," he wrote, "for your offer of Littlemore
and shall be very happy to accept it as far as I at present see." He
presumed he would not have to reside in Littlemore, "and you would not
send me about my business for anything short of heresy." Golightly did
not want the situation to blow up in his face: "I am very anxious that I
should be in my next station a fixture. A rolling stone gathers no moss."[44]
A few weeks later he wrote again. "Do you think," he asked Newman,
"that you are acting quite prudently in offering Littlemore to one of
whose religious sentiments you know nothing except from casual conversation? . . . How do you know you would like my sermons? . . . Supposing that some fine day Mrs. Newman and your sisters should . . . say,
'O John! what a Peculiar [i.e. Evangelical] you have got at Littlemore!' "
Golightly offered to send Newman a few of his sermons. "The question
is, do our sentiments sufficiently coincide for you to feel justified in en-
trusting part of your parish to me?" Once settled at Littlemore Golightly
wanted to stay there, while Newman, if he then discovered that he
disapproved of his curate's opinions, might want to turn him out—
"which," said Golightly, "I should not like."[45]

Newman very foolishly refused to look over Golightly's sermons. Instead he reiterated his confidence, sight unseen, and pressed the curacy
upon Golightly. So the matter stood until later in the year when Golightly
preached a sermon somewhere in Oxford which amounted to an attack
against Pusey's Tract on Baptism. Pusey went to Newman and insisted
that the offer to Golightly be revoked. Newman, reluctantly, agreed, and
he informed Golightly of his decision early in 1836. As Newman mournfully noted later, "He never got over it. We were never friends again."[46]
Indeed, that was a mild way of stating things. Golightly became at that
moment, and remained for the rest of his life, the Tractarians' most bitter
and relentless enemy. It did not matter very much in 1836, but five years
later Golightly's enmity would matter a great deal. Tom Mozley described the affair aptly: "It was a case of downright folly all round."[47]

VI

Newman's disastrous rupture with Golightly underscores the importance of personal relationships in that small world where the Oxford

Movement took root and grew. This was particularly true with regard to Newman, who came more and more to be identified with the Movement. His books and sermons explain this to some extent, but much of the "Newmania" which so annoyed the Heads of Houses (to the point that some of them scheduled college supper on Sunday to conflict with the afternoon service at St. Mary's) was simply the effect of Newman's face-to-face charm. The time indeed came when the phrase *"Credo in Newmanum"* was no joke to large numbers of Oxford men. Yet this influence manifested itself in different ways to different people, and it operated within the framework of a closed society which has long since passed away. And it was complicated further by Newman's own intense and sensitive temperament. Therefore the color and dimension of Newman's personal influence are not easy to draw.

To sketch the background is to say a word about the closely knit upper-class men who attended the University of Oxford. These youngsters came either from the right preparatory schools or else they had been tutored privately, usually in some country rectory. In either case they represented, as their fathers before them, a ruling class which was bound together by marriage, sentiment, and the habitual if unconscious assumption that to them belonged the burden of leadership in the realm. Nobody came to Oxford unless he was a little Anglican gentleman. This does not mean he had to be rich; arrangements could be made (as they were for Newman) to take care of little impoverished Anglican gentlemen. But most of the time he was rich or at least comfortably off, and certainly he did not matriculate without bearing on himself the mark of social acceptance. When he heard of young John Newman's acceptance at Trinity, the Headmaster of the school at Ealing commented, "Trinity? a most gentlemanlike college."

This social homogeneity was intensified by the identical classical training which they all received at Oxford. Or to put it another way, they were further alienated from the rest of mankind and driven, so to speak, to lean upon each other by the nature of their education. It was an exclusive prerogative of the gentleman to know Greek, and the English a gentleman spoke was scarcely intelligible save to another gentleman. Add to this the fact that Oxford was a clerical enclave, a place where professional religiosity (whatever its intrinsic value) was not only a condition of entrance but was entrenched by centuries of custom and by millions of pounds of invested capital, and one sees something of the psychological climate within which the famous Newman charm moved and had its being.

The closeness and interrelations of the ruling class formed a chain which bound together London office to Sussex country house to Oxford college. Parliament, Whitehall, the Board of Trade, all the centers of power and corners of culture were the preserves of gentlemen and their ladies. The Reform Act of 1832, together with succeeding legislation which would reflect profound social change, would in the end change all this, but it had not done so yet. Meanwhile, there still flourished a kind of masonry, with a set of symbols and language all its own, with a value system and mode of conduct that passed over the masses on a horizontal plane and joined parsons in Berkshire with civil servants at the Exchequer. When therefore one speaks of Newman's influence (or indeed that of any other influential man), one must understand it within the conditions imposed by this living chain.

Let us take one example. Perhaps Newman's dearest friend in the 1830s was Henry Wilberforce, the great emancipator's youngest son. Henry had two brothers: Robert, who had been tutor in Oriel with Newman, and Samuel, who had been an Oriel undergraduate but never a don. Samuel and Henry married sisters, two of the Sargent girls, while Henry Edward Manning, son of a London banker and sometime Fellow of Merton, married another, and George Dudley Ryder, whose father was Bishop of Lichfield and Coventry, still another. The Sargent family, like the Wilberforces, had been leading lights in the Evangelical revival. The girls' father, the Reverend John Sargent, had been Henry Wilberforce's tutor.[48]

All five of these young men became clergymen. Henry Manning succeeded his father-in-law as Rector of Lavington in Sussex and in 1840 was named Archdeacon of Chichester. Samuel Wilberforce became rector of an Anglican parish on the Isle of Wight, and later Archdeacon of Surrey, and still later Bishop of Oxford. Robert Wilberforce, after he left Oriel, served first as a parson at East Farleigh in Kent, and then went to the north of England as Archdeacon of the East Riding in Yorkshire. George Ryder was a parson in Hampshire, and Henry Wilberforce eventually followed his brother to East Farleigh. Natural ties of blood and affection were strengthened in this family group by common professional interests and the ever-present if unseen class solidarity. All the members of it felt profoundly the influence of Newman, but of course in different ways. Henry Wilberforce and George Ryder (and to a lesser extent their wives) might be called simply disciples, while Robert Wilberforce, as brilliant in some ways as Newman himself, might be better termed an intellectual colleague. Samuel Wilberforce, on the other hand, reacted against Newman's influence. With his shrewd insight into men and affairs, Sam saw long before most, long before Newman himself, the direction his thought was taking, and he fought to keep himself and the members of his family from being enchanted by the Vicar of St. Mary's magic. Manning swerved back and forth, now a Newmanite and then not, now endorsing the Tractarian cause and then lashing out at it, and whichever stance he took there always appeared to be a measure of calculation in it.

All these people not only read Newman's books and listened to his sermons, but they also knew him personally, and one of them, Henry

Wilberforce, on terms of the greatest intimacy. When they corresponded with each other, which they did with the fervour and at the enormous length typical of the nineteenth century, they argued out among themselves the virtues and deficiencies of Tractarianism. They corresponded as well with Newman himself, and the mutual cordiality showed itself at times of joy and sorrow. When Sam Wilberforce planned a holiday gala on the Isle of Wight in 1836, the guest list made the occasion look like a Tractarian camp meeting: Sam's own family of course were to come, and with them John Keble, Frederic Rogers and, Samuel hoped, Newman too: "We have a clerical meeting here, and you might be of great avail in instilling sentiments into our insular understandings."[49] And in 1837, when Caroline Sargent Manning died, Newman was among the first to whom her anguished husband turned for consolation.

This Wilberforce-Sargent group also had friends and associates upon whom the same influences played. Manning, for example, confided in his two closest friends, James Hope and William Gladstone, and the young lawyer and the rising politician discussed with the Rector of Lavington the state of the Church and the principles which Newman was advocating. So the shadow of St. Mary's fell across the Inns of Court and the halls of the House of Commons. Hope in turn had a lawyer friend named Edward Badeley who found himself touched by the same pervasive atmosphere. Newmanism was in the air which he and others of his class breathed.

And so went the waves of Newman's influence, out along the invisible lines which connected these literate, leisured, ambitious, talented people to each other. The end result had a curious and poignant aspect to it. Henry Wilberforce had a curate at East Farleigh, one Ambrose St. John, who was to be as close to Newman in his Catholic days as Henry had been in his Anglican; St. John lies buried in the same grave with Newman at Rednal. Henry himself and his wife Mary Sargent followed Newman to Rome, as did George Ryder. In the 1890s one of Ryder's sons succeeded Newman as superior of the Oratory in Birmingham. Robert Wilberforce also went to Rome, in his own time and way indeed, but not without the pull of Newman's teaching and example. Manning and Hope became Catholics on the same day, and Badeley shortly afterwards, but Gladstone stayed behind and an old friendship was broken forever. Newman kept a picture of Hope near the altar in his private chapel, but with Manning he kept up a running war which lasted till they were both old and withered men, both wrapped in the scarlet of Roman cardinals. Samuel Wilberforce grieved to see his family, his brothers and then a dear child, take the fatal Romeward step, while he moved up and up in the Anglican hierarchy. His bitterness broke through when once by chance he met Manning on a railroad platform. Said the Bishop of Oxford to his brother-in-law, the Roman Catholic Archbishop of Westminster: "Manning, I understand you are now an archbishop"; and then gesturing to the porter carrying Manning's bags, "And this gentleman, is he an archbishop too?"

VII

But we have got ahead of our story. We must return to the Vicar of St. Mary the Virgin in the middle of the 1830s.

The quality of Newman's friendship could be very strained. It depended a great deal upon who the friend was, of what sex and what age. He had no more than a handful of women friends throughout his life. He and Maria Pusey were on a first-name basis, but this gesture of familiarity was exceptional and apparently a bit awkward for them both. Then there was a lady whom John Henry had met through his sisters. "In all this goodly array," Tom Mozley remembered, "there was not a grander or more ornamental figure than Maria Rosina Giberne. She was . . . the prima donna of the company. Tall, strong of build, majestic, with aquiline nose, well-formed mouth, dark penetrating eyes, and a luxuriance of glossy black hair, she would command attention anywhere."[50] She commanded poor Frank Newman's heart, and he pursued her relentlessly for years, but in vain. She was a remarkably good portraitist and left behind many touching sketches of the characters of the Movement. She was entirely devoted to Newman—perhaps in love with him—who responded to her vivacious temperament with sensible caution. Though they had more than one serious quarrel, she remained through thick and thin his fervent disciple. She entered a convent after she became a Catholic and died in France a few years before Newman, his spiritual daughter to the end.

Perhaps the woman of whom Newman grew to be the fondest was John Bowden's wife, Elizabeth. It was a friendship which took many years to ripen and did not really flower until after Bowden's death when his widow was faced with the burden of raising her children alone and as Catholics, against the wishes of her family. She turned to Newman increasingly for advice and direction. Though he signed his letters to her "affectionately," he never called her by her Christian name. She, like Maria Giberne, shared many of his confidences, but there was never any doubt that she followed him rather than walked side by side with him.

Newman's pattern of action here stemmed not simply from the prudence of a man who had pledged himself to a celibate life. There was at stake something deeper and much more crucial. No one ever really took Hurrell Froude's place. From 1836 there was no one with whom Newman shared the give-and-take relationship of equals which, the ancients tell us, is the essence of friendship. Some commentators have hinted at an unhealthy, even unnatural possessiveness.

But it seems more likely that the real reason lies as much in the environment of Oriel as in the hidden places of Newman's temperament. By the "environment of Oriel" is meant the Noetic tradition of creative intellectuality which Copleston had given to Whately and Whately had handed on to Newman. The mind's business was not to absorb but to create, and the dialectic of the Oriel common room, where Newman shed the awkwardnesses of his youth, had been designed to sharpen rather than to fill the mind. This set of attitudes and practices fit Newman's gifts perfectly so that in one sense he was the last of the Noetics. Like them he wrote and talked more than he read, constructed more than he observed. The gravest intellectual criticism of Newman was that he never seemed to read important books.[51] His keen senses and his mathematical preciseness combined to provide him with an unusual perception which could go to the root of any intellectual problem and lay it bare. It did not, however, carry him to wide horizons. Newman took infinite care with detail, but he left vast stretches of knowledge untouched and, evidently, unconsidered. For example, though he often fidgeted himself about it, he never bothered to learn German, even though he knew that German theology and biblical criticism were having and would have profound effect upon Christian thinking everywhere. Yet to know a lot about German thought (as Pusey did) was something that did not appeal to him, indeed, probably never occurred to him. Such a dispersion of effort would amount, for him, to a dissipation of intellectual energies.

This same intense and narrow creativity Newman brought into his personal relationships. Whether or not it is useful to suggest that sublimation of his sexual drives also played a part will depend upon one's understanding of that term. But it is not too much to say that the more affection Newman felt for an individual the more eager he was to make that individual over. Manning late in life used to say that it was temper which had "ruined" Newman, that it was temper which led to the many bitter disagreements and estrangements of his personal life. This judgment misses the mark; indeed, it is typical of Manning's practical but often superficial pronouncements. Rather, what Newman suffered from was a frustration consequent upon the failure of people to be and to act as he wanted them to. The list of those who fretted him is very long; it spans both his Anglican and Catholic periods and includes names like Manning himself, Hawkins, Frederic Rogers, Ryder, Dalgairns and many, many more. One might argue that had these people been what Newman wanted them to be, they would have been better for it; such is the unconscious drift of much that has been written on this matter. But surely the answer is obvious: If these people had been made over to suit Newman, they would have ceased being themselves.

Here then is one key to that much-discussed and perplexing phenomenon, Newman's sensitivity. Newman at heart was a creative artist, and as he worked out the ideal of the Christian Church in his mind, so he constructed the ideal of the Christian man and to this image he expected his friends to conform. This explains why, after Froude died, Newman's closest friends were always men younger than himself, men to whom he was primarily a great master rather than a boon companion. He gave them himself fully, but he gave, as it were, from on high, not from their own level. Or perhaps it might be said that he reached down to them from on high and tried to lift them up. Time and time again he was disappointed, yet he never stopped trying and hence he never stopped suffering.

He could not share with Keble the intense sympathy that he did with younger men, because Keble already sat secure atop a height of his own. The same was true of Pusey, for Pusey already lived and worked like a saint and anyway possessed a catalogue-like mind which Newman really was incapable of appreciating. These two, as much as he loved and revered them, could not be made over, because, though less gifted than he, they did not need him. And so, in 1839, when he felt the first twinges of doubt over the Anglican position, Newman turned not to Keble and Pusey, but to Rogers and Henry Wilberforce.

The Platonic friendships with Elizabeth Bowden and Maria Giberne revealed the same quality. So did the weekly tea parties Newman began to give in 1837, at which congregated the bright young men of Oxford. "Last night went off very well," reported Tom Mozley's young brother James. "Conversation flow[ed] continuously and everyone [was] at his ease."[52] Mozley remarked that Newman was better able to carry off this sort of thing than Pusey, who would be stiff, preoccupied and probably sermonizing. James Froude recalled what a brilliant conversationalist Newman was on these occasions; he talked about everything with a verve, humour and naturalness which delighted the company. The only subject he steered clear of was Tractarian apologetics; he would not attempt to score intellectual points at the expense of his young guests.[53] If his kindness and cordiality predisposed them to read the Tracts with a friendly eye, well and good. But what they were at this stage mattered more to him than what they thought.

VIII

But the full intensity of Newman's aesthetic compulsion to remake his friends was never reached in these more or less casual relationships. The dearer a person was to him the more necessary it seemed that the friend conform to the ideal in Newman's mind. That is why the case of Henry Wilberforce's marriage, although in some ways a childish business, is nevertheless useful and instructive.

The essentials of the quarrel can be quickly stated. Henry was the youngest of the Wilberforce brothers. He tended to be insecure and unsettled; perhaps the famous family name and two brilliant older brothers overawed him. In any case, at Oriel he came under Newman's influence, and the ideal of a celibate dedication to the Church was given him with all the fervour that Newman could summon. No doubt this further agitated Henry's already ambivalent feelings, because, as Tom Mozley recalled, Henry came to Oxford untrained in the rough celibacy of a public school, and being a very charming fellow himself he found the absence of pretty faces and sweet voices a real trial.[54] As late as 1832 Henry was still undecided about a career but he had apparently made up his mind on one point. "O that I knew whether I ought to be a lawyer or not!" he wrote to Newman. "The more I think of it the less I like it. On the other hand, I think it right to tell you that I do expect to marry, and this perhaps will make you think me less fit for the Church."[55]

Theoretically Newman never insisted upon celibacy as a condition for fit service of the Church. In fact, he used to say that a country clergyman's life was such that perhaps he ought to marry. Yet as a practical means of accomplishing the renewal of the Church—which after all was the object of the Oxford Movement—celibacy held particular attraction for him. It combined imitation of ancient Christian practice with fleshly mortification; it was a sacrament, an outward sign of an interior and wholehearted dedication to the cause. Newman did not mind if Parson X or Y decided to marry Miss A or B, but for those who wanted to be closely associated with himself, he made celibacy a norm. This requirement extended even to Keble, who, when he planned to marry, did not mention the fact to Newman even though the two corresponded a couple of times a week. When he finally found out the truth, Newman was in anguish: "I heard yesterday what gave me the most piercing pain—I have felt sickish ever since—an authentication of the report that Keble is to be married."[56]

Late in 1833 Henry Wilberforce proposed to Mary Sargent. Around Christmastime he stayed at Oxford and evidently told everyone about his plans except Newman. Instead he asked Harriet to tell her brother the news. But Henry made matters even worse by suggesting that he did not tell Newman because he, Newman, would end their friendship the moment he learned of Henry's marriage. For some reason Harriet failed to inform Newman, who in the middle of January 1834 was busily "spreading my incredulity, and contradicting [the report] in every direction, and [I] will not believe it, though I saw the event announced in the papers, till he tells me."[57] At this point Frederic Rogers gently intervened and told Newman that Henry was indeed to be married: "He is hesitating about the best way of breaking it [to Newman], and hoping someone else will save him the pain."[58] The result of Henry's petty cowardice was pain all round. Newman was exceedingly angry, and understandably so, for Henry's failure to be candid had made him out a fool as well as an unnatural ogre.

There followed almost two years of coolness between Newman and Henry Wilberforce, and in the midst of it occurred a revealing correspondence. Newman's feelings are recorded in a draft of a letter he did not send.

When have I ever questioned the propriety of your marrying or dared to interfere with your Christian liberty? . . . It may be as well to remind you that the single thing I said was I thought you would be better to wait awhile—not that here I did more than state my opinion when asked. But you surely are inconsiderate; you ask me to give you my heart, when you give yours to another, and because I will not promise to do so, then you augur all sorts of ill treatment towards you from me. . . . My dear H., you really have hurt me. You have made a difficulty in the very beginning of our separation. You should have reflected that to remove it you would not only have to justify it to yourself but explain it to me.[59]

Perhaps if Newman had sent this effusion it would have cleared the air and deeper misunderstanding might have been avoided later on. However, he did not, and the correspondence between the two stayed away from the touchy question. Much of their mutual interest concentrated on the Dissenters admission affair and on Henry's pamphlet against Hampden. But early in 1835 Newman was upset again. Wilberforce, he said, had misrepresented him all over Oxford and to members of the Newman family. Apparently Henry had asked Harriet to intercede for him with her brother, unaware that Newman was still smarting over the fact that Harriet had known of Henry's marriage plans in 1833 while Newman was still in the dark. Throughout the spring of 1835 Newman composed letters to Henry which reflected his hurt feelings and which he kept tearing up. Finally, on June 8th, he sent one:

I am surprised and hurt at the inconsiderateness which has led you, in spite of the unkindness I experienced last year from you and my sister, to make me the channel of messages to her and her to me, as if to force upon me the recollection of what I fain would forget. I think this is indelicate to say the least and accordingly I have not read her letter. Had I been you or she, I should (I think) at once have been frank and wiped out the offence by owning it and regretting it. As it is it remains for me to beg that I may be suffered to have nothing to do with your intimacy [with her]. This I do, both to show you my feeling about the matter and to relieve for myself feelings which, if pent up within me, may do me harm. So for three years from the date of the offence [i.e. Christmas 1833] I shall bind myself to a definite line of conduct as regards you which I the less mind doing because for what I know it may inconvenience myself.[60]

This strange outburst, with its unspecified "definite line of conduct" for a three-year period already half over, received no answer for more than six weeks. Then, at the end of July, Henry wrote from the Isle of

Wight where he was staying with his brother Sam. "I never answered your last letter," he began, "and I do not know whether I ever should, but that I want to write you on another subject." The other subject was the announcement of the birth of a son. He maintained that he "was seldom more astonished" than by the suggestion that he and Harriet were conspiring against Newman. Rather he had thought that his hopes of healing the old wound would prosper by "urging the request of one who had unhappily given you offence through one who had not," but, he went on, there is another side.

I cannot help observing that here is one instance out of several of the practical evil which springs from your habit of refusing either to state what the conduct you complain of is, or to hear any explanation of it. I am sure but for this you would long ago have been convinced that although mistaken in what I did (a mistake which gave you pain, which I have therefore deeply regretted, and have acknowledged it, and asked your forgiveness for it), yet that nothing could be further from my intentions than any degree of unkindness to you. But when I tried to explain what I had done and why, you refused to hear a word. And as it now appears I was altogether ignorant of a large part of your ground of complaint and thus from mere ignorance as to what your feelings were was led again to wound them.

Henry then turned to the three-year "line of conduct," whatever exactly Newman meant by it. "I have some difficulty in writing at all about it, because I may seem to be deprecating it on my own account. I feel that I have already done as much that way as I can do without degrading myself (most men, I imagine, would say I had done more)." What Newman ought to do, said Henry with some boldness, is to take seriously the distinction between stern attitudes towards unbelievers and the same towards those who have offended one personally. He closed the letter by telling Newman that mother and child were doing well, and asking for prayers in their behalf.[61]

Newman answered immediately and frostily. He is always obliged when people offer him advice about himself; "though not useful in the way intended, it must always be of some use or other—if it were only to humble one. In the present case you are altogether wide of the mark, certainly—and every word you say has in my view of things an unreality which makes it, however kindly meant, quite unserviceable for the direct object intended." He has decided to forgo the three-year penalty and the protest against Harriet and Henry which it was to symbolize: "not however withdrawing one jot (of course) my expressed sense of it, but wishing to be released of the necessity of thinking or hearing of the subject any more." Explanations, he went on, only tend to feed misunderstanding, "and for this reason I always whether [sic] hear or give them with a heavy heart. . . . The true Christian way is to forgive and forget, not to prove yourself right—though there is no harm in showing you have an opinion." Above all he wanted no more argument. "Now I have said and wished again and again that I was speaking the last word on the subject. I hope I am now at length. We have made mutual accusations. Do let us forget them." And then, at the end, came this indescribably cold reference to Henry's new son: "You may be sure that you and all you are interested in are ever in my prayers."[62]

Henry overcame whatever revulsion that last sentence raised in him. He answered promptly, amicably, but stubbornly maintaining his basic contention: "I am sincerely obliged to you, though [your letter] brought tears to my eyes at seeing that I had given you pain. To speak plainly I am sure that I do not quite understand you as neither, I am certain, do you me, and added to this you have heard reports of sayings attributed to me which I unhesitatingly repeat are false." With magnanimity surely beyond the call of duty, Henry concluded by granting Newman the greatest favour in his power; he asked him to be godfather to newly-born John Henry William Wilberforce.[63]

That was the substance of the quarrel. Whatever explanations of it might be offered, for present purposes this will suffice: It demonstrated the kind of agony which entered into Newman's close friendships. It showed too his concern for the literal, precise defense of his own righteousness. Henry's rejection of celibacy and his consequent foolishness and then his quite admirable independence all did damage to the ideal Henry which Newman had in his mind and which he wanted to form into living flesh. The thrashing about in recrimination must have been Newman's own strange punishment of his artistic failure.

Yet how trifling such sensitivity seems when measured against the genius and holiness of the Vicar of St. Mary the Virgin. Or perhaps that sensitivity was the price which had to be paid for the gifts of mind and heart which transfigured Newman and set him apart from ordinary men. This, at any rate, is what appeared to be the case to Henry Wilberforce and a host of his contemporaries. To live with a saint is a joy and a privilege; but it is never easy.

CHAPTER 12

Dancing Days

IN 1836 Parliament passed an Act setting up a permanent board of
Ecclesiastical Commissioners who formed a corporation with power to
oversee and, if necessary, to alter the system of distribution of revenues
within the Church of England. This momentous piece of legislation
followed the precedent established by the Irish Church Temporalities
Act of 1833, which had moved John Keble to cry "national apostasy" and
which had united churchmen of all persuasions against the "aggression"
of the state. But by 1836 the climate of opinion had changed. To be sure,
there was wide opposition to the Commission, and its opponents ranged
across the whole ideological spectrum. Pusey and Henry Manning both
wrote pamphlets critical of the new law and its operation, and Sydney
Smith, one of the liberal founders of *The Edinburgh Review*, grumbled
at the creeping bureaucracy: "The whole world," said he, "is, in fact, in
commission."[1] Yet the passionate outrage of a few years before was
notably missing this time. However much it was disliked, nobody thought
that the Commission spelled imminent disestablishment and ruin.

A corner had been turned. The Church had survived one more crisis.
And with the survival came the end of the *ralliement* of 1833. It may
have been that the universal fear of churchmen, and hence the possibility of rallying all factions to a single cause, had reached its peak with
the Hampden affair at Oxford, during which men of all points of view—
High and Dry, Evangelical and Apostolical—had joined together to
censure the Regius Professor of Divinity. Prayer Book men and Articles
men had closed ranks to battle theological and political liberalism. The
result of that confrontation between government and Anglican Academe
had been a standoff, whereby the state's appointee kept his job only at
the cost of a no-confidence vote by the university. Hampden stayed in
Oxford, but not even the busiest of his enemies imagined that he posed
much of a threat any longer. He was an object of gossip now, rather than

an object of fear and hatred. It is "currently reported," John Keble wrote to his brother in mid-1836, that "Dr. H. has 70 persons at his lectures; and it is also said that they are a good deal taken with his unctuous way, and spend their time making odorous comparisons betwixt him and Dr. Faussett [the other university divinity professor]."[2]

The voice of Anglican normalcy began to be heard again in the land. Armageddon, it said, was still a long way off. Temporary alliances must give way to the old pattern of competing parties. For the Tractarian Movement this altered consensus had large implications. Born in a fever of universal apprehension, it reached maturity only when the sense of immediate danger had passed. This change in circumstances expressed itself in various ways. The Tracts themselves ceased to be impassioned appeals for action (in the spirit of Tract One, with its call to "Choose your side!") and became instead long, involved treatises. Presumably a parson could now take his time and ponder one of Pusey's immense collection of texts and not worry that tomorrow the Whigs might come and close his church. Newman, Keble and their friends no longer spoke, either in public or private, of an impending persecution; they concentrated rather on drawing out the consequences of the Caroline divines' ideas of catholicism without the pope and reformed religion without Lutheran and Calvinist aberrations. Their party platform was the Via Media between the excesses of Protestantism and Romanism. So it was that in 1836 Newman gave the Tracts a new title: "Tracts for the Times, against Popery and Dissent."

These late 1830s, before doubt and distrust began to gnaw at them, marked the Tractarians' happiest and most productive days. They were brimming over with confidence. From the pulpit of St. Mary's, from Pusey's cluttered study at Christ Church, from Keble's vicarage at Hursley, the lines of influence went out across the land. The Tracts sold briskly, and so did the flood of Tractarian sermons, poems, books and pamphlets which poured endlessly from the presses. More significant perhaps was the acceptance by many idealistic young people of what the Tractarians called their "ethos," by which they meant a combination of sacramental practice, private prayer and penitential austerity. Proper ethos not only reflected the ascetic ideals of the Ancient Christian Church; it was also a moral condition without which no one could receive apostolic truth.

They rejoiced above all in each other. Bound together by the exhilaration of a crusade, convinced beyond doubt that they had been called by God to a special work, they could still take lightly the slowly but steadily rising tide of criticism and partisan hostility. Pusey delighted his friends by telling them about the lady he encountered in the Oxford coach who, unaware of his identity, confided to her fellow passengers the fact that Dr. Pusey sacrificed a lamb every Friday. "Madam," said the Regius Professor of Hebrew, "I am Dr. Pusey, and I assure you I do not know how to kill a lamb."[3] But fittingly enough it was John Keble who, quite unintentionally, gave a name to this swiftly passing, joyous time. "My dearest Thomas and Betty and all," he wrote to his brother and sister-in-law, "these are the joys of our dancing days."[4]

I

The Hampshire village of Hursley lies four or five miles south and a little west of Winchester in the dead center of a kind of topographical saucer, with the countryside round about sloping gently down towards it. Its main street is also the road to Romsey another ten miles or so to the southwest. Most of the neat, sturdy cottages stand on the east side of this road, while on the west side, set upon a little knoll, is the Anglican parish church of All Saints. Another couple of hundred yards to the west, on higher ground still, is the vicarage, separated from the church by a high hedge and a low, tumbledown wall with brick posts. This wall encloses the churchyard where a luxuriant growth of weeds blends with the eighteenth-century headstones to produce a scene not, surprisingly, of neglect but of serenity. In the southwest corner of the churchyard is the only grave which appears to receive any care. Indeed, the brass on its monument shines as brightly as though it had been fixed there only yesterday. Beneath it lie the mortal remains of John Keble.

Keble came back to Hursley in 1836 and he remained there as vicar until his death exactly thirty years later. His earlier sojourn, as we have seen, was a brief, sad interlude, marked by disappointment in love and by the death of his beloved sister Mary Anne. Duty to an aging father had taken him back to Fairford, fifty miles away in Gloucestershire, and it was only when that duty was removed that he felt free to pick up again the reins of an independent life.

He found Hursley little changed during the decade of his absence: the same lush and lovely green country, the same swarms of small, twittering birds, the same brick houses, now and then painted yellow, peaked at either end, with the inevitable flowerpots in the windows. A stand of pollard limes still guarded the main street and the same tall elm shaded the blacksmith's shop at the end of the row of cottages. Lanes led like dark green tunnels through the foliage up into the countryside where pink, gold and red flowers grew wild next to amber-coloured wheat fields and where fat black-and-white cows lumbered across hilly pastureland. Hursley was pretty much the same and it was pretty much what Fairford had been, a corner of rural England, a place where John Keble could feel physically and spiritually at home.

The senior John Keble died after a lingering illness in January 1835.

A few months later, Sir William Heathcote, baronet and squire of Hursley Park, once more offered the Hursley living to his old Oriel tutor. The offer came as a godsend for Keble, who now technically was out of work. Even so, he hesitated to accept and fidgeted over a decision in what his friends recognized as a typically Kebleian manner. He had to consider his crippled sister Elizabeth, for whom he continued to be responsible. But he had to consider even more carefully the wishes of another lady. Charlotte Clarke was the sister of Tom Keble's wife Betty. For some time an "understanding" had existed between her and John Keble to the effect that marriage would take place as soon as the old Mr. Keble had gone to a better world. It was the rumour of this union in the summer of 1835 that had made Newman sick to his stomach.

Charlotte Clarke, in her early thirties in 1835 and thus ten years younger than her fiancé, was a lively and attractive woman. "Everything about her," observed novelist Charlotte Yonge, "had a choiceness and simplicity of its own."[5] She had a delicate complexion, hazel eyes and fine features. She dressed fashionably, most often in the bright colours which delighted Keble. She liked parties and entertaining, although she understood that a certain amount of sobriety was the lot of a parson's wife. "John and I didn't dance anything but minuets," she reported of one gala at Hursley Park.[6] What people most often remarked about her was her kindness and her facility for setting shy people at their ease. James Mozley thought her "decidedly pretty and interesting looking, very agreeable; I should think clever."[7] And Frederic Rogers found her "one of the most taking persons I ever met."

Mozley, however, also noticed that she appeared "delicate," and the more discerning Rogers described it more fully: "It is most painful to see how very weak and ill she is, and from what H[enry] W[ilberforce] says, I am afraid getting weaker and weaker fast."[8] Precisely what variety of complaints Charlotte suffered from remains unclear, though it seems that asthma was chief among them. In any case, her charm, everyone agreed, was enhanced by her fragility. She loved children, though they quickly tired her. She bore none of her own. Keble no doubt regretted this, but he loved Charlotte and cherished her, not least, perhaps, because she was a semi-invalid. Perhaps Keble needed Charlotte's ill health, as he had needed his father's—each a convenient escape from the larger world and its responsibilities. Countless times during the three decades of their married life his wife's health permitted Keble to excuse himself from the rough and tumble which, in the judgment of some,[9] he rather freely recommended to others.

By the autumn of 1835 Keble had reached the obvious conclusion: Hursley would be ideal. Charlotte Clarke agreed wholeheartedly, so Keble informed Heathcote that he would accept the living gratefully. Heathcote for his part agreed to see to the repair of the vicarage, which was ready early in 1836 to receive Keble, his sister and his bride. The wedding took place in Tom Keble's church at Bisley on October 10, 1835. Keble turned up a grotesque-looking groom: He had fallen off his horse the day before and broken his collarbone. But he was romantic enough, despite his discomfort, to send Charlotte on the morning of the wedding two short poems and a handful of late violets.[10] The newlyweds went off for a honeymoon in Wales, where they spent most of their time walking along the seashore and consulting doctors of medicine. Charlotte's ever-present cough seemed to improve, and John's arm too, though the sling and the bandages made him look, he said, like "the queerest hog in armour."[11] By November they had settled at Southampton, an easy ride from Hursley. In January 1836 they moved into Hursley vicarage.

And so Keble entered into what Newman called his "humdrum marriage." Of course it was no such thing for Keble. Though he may frequently have used his wife's bad health as a form of escape, this was no greater a fault than the similar use he had made of his father's. Moreover, Hursley became in its own way a center of the Oxford Movement precisely because Keble made his home there as master and not as his father's helper. Charlotte presided over that home, gave it substance and personal meaning, and she helped John Keble make Hursley the ideal Apostolic parish. Newman, who never really had a home of his own, could never have appreciated the importance of this. Yet Keble was anxious to mollify Newman, while at the same time making clear that the Vicar of St. Mary's views on celibacy were not, and need not be, shared by the Vicar of Hursley. Newman had written Keble sometime after the wedding and had rudely not even adverted to the existence of the new Mrs. Keble, of whom, sight unseen, he sternly disapproved. Keble replied on November 15, 1835. "A thing about which I have been . . . anxious, viz., my wife is much better than she was. And I must tell you that she is so pleased at your having written to me that she does not seem to feel at all affronted at your not mentioning her in your letter."[12] Keble was capable of a deft and delicate thrust.

II

Hursley parish covered about eight thousand acres altogether, with the village in the exact center. Included within the parochial boundaries were congregations at two nearby hamlets—Ampfield and Otterbourne—which the vicar had to attend to. Keble's predecessor, a cousin of Squire Heathcote, had employed two curates, but it seems that none of the three of them did much work. Keble at first employed one curate and later two, whom he kept as busy as himself. One of his earliest plans was to detach the Ampfield district and make a separate parish out of it. Then, as he

explained to Newman, the "duties of assistant curate of Hursley . . .
will be anything but burthensome."[13] Apparently nothing came of this
idea, however, and the burdens continued to be heavy. Among other
chores of administration which faced Keble was the construction of new
churches at Otterbourne and at Hursley itself.

The sleeping parish came awake at Keble's touch, and no one was
happier about it than the patron, Sir William Heathcote. During the ten
years he had lived at Hursley Park—the squire's 450-acre estate which
lay in luxuriantly wooded country west of the village—he had fretted
over the low level of religion which prevailed under Keble's predecessors.
The squire himself had imbibed the highest Apostolical principles and
he was anxious that the people of his district—most of whom were his
tenants or dependent upon him in one way or another—would come to
share those principles. Indeed, he was ready to ram them down their
throats. There was a story widely believed that Sir William would rent
neither land nor house to anyone who refused to go to church every
Sunday. And it was a fact that he preferred empty farms to farmers who
were Dissenters. Just within the rather narrow ambit of his principles,
tireless, tyrannical, Sir William Heathcote formed an effective partner-
ship with John Keble and nowhere was it truer than at Hursley that
squire and parson together shaped the character of the local population.

Sometimes, however, Hursley's number one parishioner was himself
a problem. Sir William suffered chronically from bouts of deep depression, which were accentuated after the death of his wife (Arthur Perceval's sister) early in 1835. Keble spent much of his time at Hursley Park
offering the consolation of religion to his former pupil, who had grown
up to be his patron, friend and ally. The gentle, sympathetic Keble,
himself no stranger to illness and bereavement, was particularly good at
this kind of ministration.[14]

The humbler members of the parish found it out too. The parson's
personal touch with the suffering and the ignorant came to be a living
legend. "The villagers of Hursley," observes Keble's latest biographer,
"grew familiar with the sight of a lantern bobbing down lanes and across
field paths late at night when wise people were comfortably resting by the
fireside."[15] The sometime Fellow of Oriel College (which he ceased to be
upon his marriage) and the Professor of Poetry in the University of
Oxford (a post he kept until 1841) was never too much the detached
intellectual to understand that a parish priest's effectiveness was largely
proportionate to his personal, concrete presence among his people.

Kind Keble was, but soft never. "Mr. Keble, he were a very stern
gentleman," recalled one who as a youth, guilty of some impertinence
or another, had felt the parson's stick across his shoulders. The Vicar of
Hursley modified not one whit his principles or his contempt for the
indulgences of this world. "It would be a gain to this country," he told

his parishioners, "were it vastly more superstitious, more bigoted, more gloomy, more fierce in its religion than at present it shows itself to be."[16] Discipline, he maintained, was what the Christian man needed more than anything. And when he made his parish rounds, or when he taught (as he did daily) in the village school, Keble took care lest apostolic visitation degenerate into an exchange of small talk.

He was a fierce defender of what he regarded his people's integral faith, and he did not hesitate to employ the strongest possible means to thwart those who might threaten it. "Those dreadful socialists," he reported in 1840, "have commenced an establishment within five miles of Romsey, and I hear that they have *sermons* every Sunday expressly to mock and blaspheme the text which they select."[17] The vicar pondered what measures might best be used against the socialists, whether to call in the magistrates or to urge his people to shun them. Ultimately, he selected the latter course, because it would help teach the people of Hursley "the meaning of excommunication."

Over the thirty years of his incumbency Hursley came to be regarded as the type of Tractarianism in action. The sacramental emphasis, the notion that liturgy was a service due to God rather than an occasion for stimulating faith, showed the catholic orientation which Keble had grown up with and which his studies of the Caroline divines and Christian antiquity confirmed. He introduced daily service, morning and evening, and greatly increased the celebrations of the Lord's Supper. Keble was no more a ritualist than Newman, and if anything he was even more reserved about any kind of outward show. But his intense devotion to the sacramental life as the ordinary means of the Christian's sanctification, and his notion of the Church as the living depository and channel of grace, led him to set great store on the worship habits in his parish. They never met his exacting ideals; he was often discouraged over the sparse crowds which came to weekday service and to Holy Communion.

Keble was not a strong speaker. His sermons were carefully put together, but they lacked the spark of genius which set Newman's sermons apart. Keble, needless to say, shrank from any homiletic tricks which he thought demeaning to himself and to the doctrine he proclaimed. The result was a performance far below the Evangelical standard of rhetorical fireworks. No one who listened to Keble was particularly moved by what he said. But this too was consistent with Keble's whole attitude towards religion. People should come to church not to be excited into an emotional (and probably transient) heightening of faith but rather to perform their sacred duty of prayer and praise to God. In this sacramental experience their faith would indeed be strengthened in a manner far more powerful than any at the disposal of a clever pulpit orator. The sermon, Keble believed, was an adjunct to the service only because it provided instruction. It was part of a larger catechetical program to which he gave his best energies for thirty years at Hursley. At Sunday Evensong, at the very moment when Newman spoke to the hushed throngs at St. Mary's, Keble did not preach at all. Instead he catechized, the boys one week, the girls the next, and at the end of the session he summarized the questions and answers for the benefit of the adults present. The landlord of the village inn, when asked in later years whether Keble was a great preacher or not, answered in the name of the whole parish: "Well, I don't know what a great preacher is, but he always made us understand him."[18]

One considerable part of John Keble's charm was his gaiety. Deadly serious though he remained about his pastoral vocation, he was never puritanical. Indeed, he quite shocked some of his Hampshire neighbours by introducing a cricket game for men and boys after Sunday Evensong. When protests came in (and eventually he had to bow to them as far as the cricket was concerned), he responded that Sunday was meant to be a day of joy as well as of prayer, that an innocent game could not be confused with servile labour. Later he opened a reading room for the same men and boys, also a Sabbath operation; here among various works of edification he included Scott's novels, and this in turn became the occasion for scandal. Charlotte Yonge has left a short memoir which indicates how deep an impression John Keble's Christianity, with its mixture of discipline and joy, made upon the young people of Hursley parish. The occasion was the annual gala for the combined Sunday schools of Hursley and Otterbourne. After games and a great feast, eaten out of doors, the day ended with singing.

How exquisite [wrote Miss Yonge] it used to be to stand on the terrace in the fresh evening scents of early summer, the grey church tower rising among the flowering shrubs, . . . the stars gradually gleaming out, or a round full moon rising, and the children's voices, softened in the open air, pealing out in "God save the Queen" and finally in Ken's Evening Hymn; the universal hum of "Thank you, Ma'am," Mr. Keble's public "Good night," and the cheers of the boys dying away with the trampling feet in the distance.[19]

III

Keble's transfer from Fairford to Hursley did not alter his position of special leadership within the Movement. He was of course farther away from his Oxford friends than before, but this made little difference since his visits to Oxford had never been very frequent anyway and the mail coaches traveled as regularly to Hampshire as they did to Gloucestershire. There was more work to do at Hursley; the parish was larger and the administration more demanding. And as vicar of a large parish, Keble was expected to take more interest in county affairs than he had when curate of a small one. Tom Mozley felt that at Hursley Keble allowed himself to be "a little smothered in the embrace of a not very large-minded or open-minded section of the aristocracy."[20] It is true that Heathcote and the Hursley Park set did occupy much of his attention, but some of it was traceable to Heathcote's peculiar difficulties and the rest to the fact that Keble, born and bred a gentleman, naturally sought his recreation among his equals.

Keble still acted as second reader for all the Tracts, though after he came to Hursley he wrote only one himself (Number Eighty-nine). He also went over all of Newman's works before publication. He engaged in an immense correspondence with Newman, Pusey and others and thus kept his finger on all aspects of Tractarian business. His intimacy with his brother Thomas if anything deepened after his removal to Hampshire. The two of them corresponded several times a week, and though often the burden of the letters consisted of gossip or family business (for example, the settling of old Mr. Keble's estate), the Movement and its fortunes absorbed a good deal of their energy. As Newman published nothing without first showing it to John Keble, so John did not publish without submitting first to Tom's judgment.

This relationship had a further dimension. There grew up around Tom Keble a group which came to be known as the Bisley School (the name taken from Tom's Gloucestershire living). The most notable among the half dozen or so clergymen who formed the group were George Prevost and Isaac Williams. Williams, as we have seen, had once served as Newman's curate at St. Mary's, but his connection with the Keble brothers was much older and deeper. The Bisley School tended to be suspicious of what it considered the subtleties of Newman and Pusey. Williams, indeed, claimed that the practical usefulness of Newman's early sermons came really from Thomas Keble through conversations which Newman had with him, Williams.[21] It was soon apparent that one of John Keble's tasks was to act as a bridge between the Bisley wing of the Movement and the Newman-Pusey wing.

Besides now and then pouring oil on troubled waters, Keble contributed in a variety of other ways to the prosperity of the Movement. For example, in conjunction with Newman and Pusey, he operated a kind of clerical employment agency. Keble's job was to keep his eye open for vacant livings and when he got news of one to send word to Oxford where some young clergyman, with the proper Apostolic views, might be put on the track. In October 1838 Keble inquired whether anyone in Newman's knowledge would be interested in the living at Portsmouth—seven thousand souls and five hundred pounds a year.[22] A few months later he was looking for a curate to serve at Tutbury, Gloucestershire; the parish counted three thousand people and the curate's stipend was a hundred pounds, plus a house. "They would like an active person," wrote

Keble, "such as my friends in Oxford may perhaps know." Nor did Keble refrain from vetoing candidates. In the instance of the curacy just mentioned, he dismissed one name suggested to him on the ground that "I am a little afraid of his being infected by Arnold."[23]

More important in the long run was the intellectual work of the Vicar of Hursley. The Tractarian ethos demanded a consistent dedication to scholarship and publication. This obligation went beyond the Tracts, even after they had evolved into long, learned books. To edit the writings of an obscure fourth-century author or of a seventeenth-century Caroline divine was an accomplishment doubly valuable in Tractarian eyes: it enriched the mind of the man who did it and it widened the area of Apostolic influence. Sermons which were really treatises and book reviews which were really essays fifty or sixty pages long appeared at the drop of a Tractarian hat. It may have been true that except for Newman's these productions "were stuffing and makeweights, learned, wise and good, but not calculated to take hearts by storm."[24] Yet it is undeniable that their weight, to say the least, was felt.

Keble possessed neither Newman's originality nor Pusey's stamina, and so his contribution in terms of brilliance and bulk was much less than theirs. Still, his influence remained unique. Part of this was due to his temperament and part to the fact that he was the oldest Apostolical of them all, a father figure, one might say. No plan could be settled at Oxford without first sending off a dispatch to Hursley to find out Keble's views. The various literary projects crossed his desk: to write a joint Church history; to translate and edit a Library of the Greek and Latin Fathers; to establish a multi-volume collection of the English Catholic divines; to provide a continuing series of Tractarian sermons. A few of these and similar proposals came to nothing, but most of them bore some fruit; and Keble, in far-off Hursley, had a hand in them all.

Shortly after he arrived at Hursley Keble finished a scholarly work which was to be of great moment to the Tractarian Movement and to the Christian Church at large. "I have this day," he wrote a friend on March 17, 1836, "sent my last sheet of the Hooker preface to the press." The three-volume edition of Richard Hooker's *Laws of Ecclesiastical Polity* (with some of Hooker's sermons and fragmentary remains bound at the end of Volume III) took Keble more than five years to prepare. The editing was a genuine piece of critical scholarship. The text, collated with manuscripts at Oxford and Dublin, was established with an integrity never before approached; extraneous material was excluded from the last two sections of *Laws*, and one whole section was proved by Keble to have been written by Hooker but not as part of the original work. Keble split the text up into paragraphs, verified the references, added a running paraphrase, and supplied some manuscript notes which Hooker himself had written in answer to contemporary Puritan objections to the book. In his lengthy preface (more than a hundred pages) Keble placed Hooker in the historical context without which his work could not be understood. And at the same time the editor kept his eye upon the present:

Bold must he be who should affirm that great as was then [the Church's] need of such a defender, it at all exceeded her peril from the same quarter at the present moment. Should these volumes prove at all instrumental in awakening any of her children to a sense of that danger, and in directing their attention to the primitive, apostolical Church as the ark of refuge divinely provided for the faithful, such an effect will amply repay the editor.[25]

Keble's edition of Hooker has remained a standard ever since its first appearance. It was a labour of love, since Hooker was the founder of that Anglo-Catholic school of theology which Keble and his friends were striving to resurrect. Indeed, it would not be too much to say that most of the Tractarians were men of only two books, Hooker's *Laws* and Bishop Butler's *Analogy*. Perhaps Robert Wilberforce escaped the long, narrow shadow of Oriel and of Whately and developed into an independent thinker; and Pusey, with his Teutonic thoroughness, may in his own way have done the same. Not so the rest. They dipped into other authors, they rooted industriously through the Fathers. But Hooker and Butler remained their staples and provided them with the criteria by which all other authors were judged. This made Keble's edition that much more directly important, and John Bowden expressed to Newman the universal Tractarian judgment: "Keble's preface is most glorious."[26]

On the heels of his Hooker triumph came another of Keble's more remarkable efforts. He and Charlotte vacationed in August 1836 with the Wilberforce clan on the Isle of Wight. Shortly after their return, John traveled the few miles to Winchester Cathedral and preached his sermon, "Primitive Tradition recognized in Holy Scripture." The occasion was the archdeacon's visitation, and Keble was selected as preacher simply because he was the most recently appointed incumbent in the archdeaconry. The clergy of the Winchester diocese were notoriously divided over apostolicity and the catholic claims; the Bishop of Winchester, C. R. Sumner, was an Evangelical. So Keble approached the assignment with some trepidation. Both Newman and Tom Keble went over the text, and as John reported to Newman after the event, "Your and my brother's approbation gave me so much courage that I thundered it out more emphatically almost than ever I did anything in my life."[27] He harangued the Winchester clergy for an hour and a half and gave great offense to many in the congregation, both liberals and Evangelicals. When he was finished, a clerical delegation asked him—"to my great surprise"—to publish the sermon. By the end of November it had been widely circulated and Newman commented, "What a magnificent sermon Keble's is.

I think it the boldest and most powerful composition we have yet put out."[28]

The sermon on Tradition stated perhaps in its clearest form the Tractarian view on non-biblical teaching authority. The perplexity of the times, said Keble, is rooted in the challenge to Anglicanism from the civil power, from the aggressive theology of Rome and from the tension between voluntary associations of churchmen and the bench of bishops. The best way to meet the problem is the reassertion of the primitive Christian regard for Tradition, "not as overriding the sole and paramount claim of the Holy Scripture as a rule of faith but as supplementing it." Scripture itself has recognized the unique importance of Tradition and indeed historically speaking it was anterior to the formation of the biblical canon. To Tradition the Christian owes the articles of faith in the creed, the proper mode of biblical interpretation and many practical points like the method of administering the sacraments. And the traditional guarantee of orthodoxy the English Church still possesses in the apostolic succession of her bishops. "Of the two texts, Tradition and Holy Scripture, either suffers if the other is neglected." The usefulness of Tradition, Keble warned, depends upon our willingness to rediscover the Ancient Christian Church at its purest and best and the courage to apply the lesson to our own troubled times.[29]

IV

Keble's visitation sermon brought down on him a storm of criticism. More than a year after it was delivered rumours reached Oxford "that 200 and more of the Winchester clergy are petitioning the Archbishop [of Canterbury] to call a provincial council to censure the Rev. John Keble for laying waste the diocese by his sermon on Tradition."[30] The story turned out to be unfounded, but anyway such alarms troubled the Tractarians very little in 1837. Their mood was one of sublime confidence which opposition tended only to reinforce. These were their dancing days. So much was this the case that Keble and Newman had in the meantime embarked upon another literary venture, never dreaming that it would ultimately damage the Movement beyond repair. Evidently in their childlike enthusiasm they did not yet realize that it was possible to go too far too fast.

The preparation of Hurrell Froude's manuscript papers for publication occupied Keble and Newman (as joint editors) for the better part of two years. The idea apparently came to them in October 1836, when Archdeacon Froude sent them "all your letters to him that I can find. . . . With the latter I must confess I have not parted without regret. They are memorials of your affectionate friendship with one whose image is ever before me."[31] Other odds and ends—unpublished essays (some quite long), poems and the like—were also among Hurrell's papers, enough of them to fill several printed volumes. One problem arose in connection with the private letters. In them Froude, as had been his custom, employed the strongest language about such matters as the Real Presence in the Eucharist and the evil work of the Protestant Reformers. Would this prove too tough a meat for the reading public? Newman and Keble thought not, and after consulting at some length with Isaac Williams and Frederic Rogers, and after securing the endorsement of Archdeacon Froude, they decided in the spring of 1837 to publish Froude's *Remains*.

Through the rest of the year parcels went back and forth between Oriel and Hursley, with detours often to London, where Rogers was studying law at Lincoln's Inn. Rogers was a good choice as a consultant. He had known Froude very well, he combined sensitivity with a worldly wisdom which should have made him a better than average judge of possible public reaction. By the end of May 1837 Rogers was advising publishing Froude's manuscripts "as soon as they are ready; unless of course there is anything which on consideration he as a clergyman of the Church of England had no right to publish." This advice clearly begged the question, but then Rogers knew how perilous it was to give Newman advice. Even so, he urged discretion upon Newman; do not, he said, "throw away your character for judgment and moderation." He added that he found nothing objectionable in Froude's expressions about the Eucharist.[32]

A month later Newman sent Keble a transcription of Froude's "Private Thoughts." "I am sanguine that the volume will take with university men. . . . The 'Thoughts' present a remarkable instance of the temptation to rationalism, self-speculation etc. subdued. . . . If you say 'yes' and send them to me, I propose to go to press almost immediately."[33] Keble said "yes" with enthusiasm. This process of cross-checking and mutual veto was typical of the whole Froude venture. It was carried on entirely by mail, except for a week or so in October 1837 which Newman spent at Hursley.

As the work of sifting through Froude's letters and other manuscripts for suitable extracts went on, Keble and Newman elaborated certain rules of thumb. For example, they decided to omit "those passages which seemed at all to reflect on anyone"; there were several, for example, which poked fun at some of the more eccentric Oriel dons. Other critical references, if they stayed in, might be switched within the narrative in such a way that nobody could guess what people were meant. "May we not suppose," Keble asked, "it is what he would recommend if we could ask him?"[34] Newman was more concerned about the emergence of the genuine Froude. The extracts must show, he insisted, Froude's "unaffectedness, brilliancy, playfulness," how "he disdained all *show* of religion," "the interesting *growth* of his mind," "his utter hatred of pretence and humbug."[35]

In the middle of August 1837 Archdeacon Froude sent Newman his son's "Private Journal" for the years 1826–27 and with it the letter his wife had sent Hurrell shortly before her death. We have already noted the anguish which his mother's letter caused Hurrell and also the connection between her judgment of him and the keeping of the Journal. That morbid document, short as it was, still was the most striking manuscript Froude had left behind. It laid bare the vein of self-contempt as well as the painful and sometimes grotesque attempts at self-mastery which had clouded Froude's early and mid-twenties. Newman had not known of its existence before. He excitedly told Rogers that the entries in the Journal were "more interesting than anything I have seen except, perhaps, his letters to Keble."[36] One would have expected the intimate character of the Journal to have made the editors pause and ask themselves what effect such revelations would have upon the bluff English gentlemen who would read them. Instead Newman asked, "Does it not seem as if Providence was putting things into our hands for something especial? There is so gradual and unexpected an accumulation."[37]

The Journal also confronted the editors with a new problem which both of them, but especially Keble, felt acutely. Why was it that Froude, in the midst of the spiritual torments of his young manhood, as he thrashed around in prodigious fasts and prayer exercises; why was it that the exceedingly pious Froude did not, in the Journal, advert at all to the person of Christ? Newman noticed this omission immediately and brought it to Keble's attention. At first reading, Keble thought that Froude's rapturous expressions about the Eucharist would dissipate any doubts the public might have on this score.

I can vouch for this [wrote Keble], that he seemed to me to look on the manifestation of our Lord's human nature in the gospel with more awe and reverence than almost any person I ever knew; and that many, many years ago. This and a deep sense of his own (what he calls) imbecility and dread of saying more than he meant, seem to me generally to have been the causes of his instinctively avoiding the name of our Lord even when he was most completely talking, as it were, to himself.[38]

It was not much of an explanation but it was the only one available if the editors intended, as the events proved they did, to attach a permanent importance to the introspective diary of a religious young man passing through a stage of scrupulosity. When the Journal was published in the first volume of the *Remains*, the following footnote was supposed to settle the matter: "The truth is that a mind alive to its own real state often shrinks to utter what it most dwells upon, and is too full of awe and fear to do more than silently hope what it most wishes."[39]

Froude's *Remains* were published in two sets of two volumes each in 1838 and 1839. Newman wrote a preface to the first set and Keble to the second, though of course each man approved the other's work. Newman's preface was the more crucial because it appeared in the volume which was calculated to give more offense. By the time Keble's preface appeared, the fat was already in the fire. A strain of arrogance runs through Newman's preface. Thus he explained the project itself: "Though posthumous publication, particularly of private letters and journals, is hazardous and delicate," nevertheless the editors feel justified in this case because both the executors and the friends "on whom [Froude] was known chiefly to rely, unanimously and decidedly judged publication most desirable." If Froude spoke intolerantly, his language is no more fierce than that of the ancient Christian writers against "unbelievers and corrupters of the faith." The reader furthermore should take care not to call this in the *Remains* petty or that paradoxical, because the editors have had "such an error continually before their eyes and have not, to the best of their judgment, inserted anything which did not tell, indirectly perhaps but really, towards filling up that outline of [Froude's] mind and character which seemed requisite to complete the idea of him as a witness to Catholic views." And the seemingly "dangerous tendency toward Romanism" was dismissed in the preface as "perhaps the vaguest of all charges."[40] This cool tone pervades the preface, and it is astonishing when one remembers he is reading the justification of two sensitive men who are about to strip their dearest friend naked and hang him up in full public view.

Only Frederic Rogers seems to have sensed the possible trouble which the *Remains* might give rise to, and only he was in a position to do anything about it. Unfortunately, he spoke much too softly. Newman, it will be recalled, consulted Rogers throughout the editing process, and then he asked Rogers to review the book for a magazine of which Newman (to use modern parlance) was an associate editor. (This was extraordinary practice, judged by present-day standards: a reviewer who acts at the instance of an editor who is also editor of the book in question, who received substantial aid in the work done from the reviewer, and to whom the reviewer gives final right to take anything he dislikes out of the review.) Rogers was sent the proofs and he found the going slow and difficult. Writing towards the end of November 1837, he raised several minor points which, presumably, could still be altered in the final version. (All but one of them were ignored.) At the end of his letter, he turned to the larger issue. "According to my present light," Rogers wrote, "I cannot quite think that all the unqualified consequences F[roude] draws from a theory are true in practice." Rogers felt that Froude "pushes sometimes too boldly, or that perhaps he does, or that some people may possibly think that he does. I shall put it in and you can cut it out if you like. It seems to me ludicrous and somewhat unfair to pledge the orthodox B[ritish] C[ritic] to an unqualified puff of such a book as F[roude]'s, bones and all."[41] Newman replied frostily, "As to your criticism of R. H. F.'s text, some of the things you object to were already altered in the proof. . . . You need not make your review a mere panegyric."[42]

It might have been better for all concerned—and not least for the memory of the "bright and beautiful Froude"—had the optimism at Oriel and Hursley been less manic in 1836 and 1837.

V

Keble's flights of optimism had to be paid for with periods of depression. He suffered chronically from this condition and though it certainly never reached pathological proportions, it did affect him seriously, at least in Newman's opinion, during the early 1840s.[43] From this distance it is impossible to say what occasioned his dark moods. Keble himself connected them to what he ruefully called his indolence. This seems odd because Keble worked very hard and produced a great deal. Yet he did tend to procrastinate; letters were not answered as promptly as they might have been and he was never able to concentrate on any project with the single-minded fury of Newman or Pusey. His Christmas greeting to Newman in 1834 expressed the feeling of relative inadequacy. "A comfortable Christmas to you, dear Newman, and much success in all your good undertakings; in which I wish I could be more a *pars major* than I am; but then you see, I am *I*, and you are you."[44]

Froude's death was a case in point. With a new wife and a new parish in the spring of 1836, Keble had put off writing Froude until it was too late. He never ceased to reproach himself for that failure of friendship, and perhaps it partly explains why he threw himself so intensely into the work of editing Froude's *Remains*. But the trouble with depression is that it feeds upon itself. The desire to do tardy justice to Froude led Keble to all sorts of agonizing doubts of his own powers. Early in 1838 Newman sent down to Hursley a copy of his preface to the first part of the *Remains*, which Keble promptly misplaced. He found it again stuck among some notes for a lecture he was preparing. "I very much fear," he wrote Newman, "I have annoyed you and done harm to the publication by the delay of which I have been guilty."[45]

When it came time for him to write his own preface to the second part of the *Remains*, similar problems arose. "I do hope I shall not cause any more delay now, but that it may go to the press with your and R[ogers]'s corrections. I feel more than ever that I cannot do justice to [Froude]—not even tolerable justice."[46] In September 1839 he lost some extracts which were to be included in the volume. "As usual, I am at fault. I only hope that it will not put things out too much, but there it is." To find the extracts will mean more delay, "for which I cannot enough apologise." As to the preface, "I am not of course satisfied with it; one could not be on this subject and I fear I have said many foolish things."[47] Nothing seemed to go right. He had been working at the same time on an essay about St. John Chrysostom and had just finished a metrical version of the Psalms. With regard to the Chrysostom, "I fear I shall betray great unpreparedness. It is no use making apologies, but Wilson [the curate] has been away and there has been a good deal of illness of late. Really, I am disgusted with myself in re typographica. I thought the Psalms had been done so carefully and here I see that foul blot you mention in the new edition."[48] Newman's sharp eye had betrayed poor Keble as a careless proofreader.

It was not just in the Froude venture that this unhappy side of Keble's temperament showed itself. Time and again he blamed himself for not doing more and then, in the next breath, he protested he could do no more. Thus as University Professor of Poetry he had to come to Oxford each term and give a Latin lecture. In the spring of 1838 Pindar was his subject and he found himself two thirds finished and swamped with other work. And in 1836: "I must seem to you to have deserted the cause; I do not know how it is, but week after week passes away and nothing ever done but a few parish sermons. I have not yet half finished my lecture."[49] This latter protestation was a response to Newman, who kept pressing Keble. "I hope you will not forget your promise of a volume of sermons. I put it on this simple ground. *We are raising a demand for a certain article, and we must furnish a supply.* Men are curious after apostolic principles, and we must not let the season slip."[50]

Keble plugged along but with no more confidence than before. "The stuff I send you," he wrote, in reference to a book review, "is poor and prosy enough, but if it does no good I hope it will do no harm."[51] And some months earlier: "I am rather in despair, seeing that every day convinces me more and more of my great inability to write or say things persuasively." What it all amounted to, Keble feared, was a failure to "our" cause. "But what right have I to say 'our,' who contributes just nil to the firm? I am really ashamed to think how little I have done while you have been slaying the slain."[52] During the autumn of 1837 some of Isaac Williams' books and papers turned up missing either at Hursley or Oriel. Newman asked Keble about them. "I cannot light upon Isaac's papers," he answered, "and it makes me sometimes quite uncomfortable."[53] Newman, much to his chagrin, eventually found the articles mislaid in his own study, and Keble sent him a word of melancholy consolation: "Touching Williams' books, I am sure you would be amply recompensed for the disgust you talk of could you know the satisfaction

I have in not being guilty. You can abundantly afford it, but I had no character to spare."[54]

Frederic Rogers spent a holiday with the Kebles on the Isle of Wight and at Hursley late in the summer of 1836. He saw something of both sides of Keble's disposition.

I never saw so much of Keble before [he wrote his sister], and am delighted to have done so now. . . . Most delightful people they all are most certainly. I never could have conceived a person keeping as Keble does his boyish spirits till I had seen him pelting his young nephew into his lessons in the most reckless way. At the same time, *I* am very much afraid of him, I confess, from not being able quite to understand him always, or to make myself always understood by him; and in talking of serious subjects he has a disconcerting way of keeping silence sometimes, which may mean either that he thinks you have been over forward or are talking sillily, or that what you say is new to him and he has no answer to make. I sometimes wonder how two men so very unlike as Newman and he have got to understand one another so perfectly as they do. I suppose they hardly could have done so unless they had had Froude as an interpreter at first.[55]

Rogers had not been entirely candid with his sister. His holiday with the Kebles was designed also as an opportunity to press Keble on certain matters close to Newman's heart. This project did not go very well. "Keble is so slow and undecided about diverse things," Rogers reported to Newman, "that I cannot answer one half your [questions] yet; but I write just to say what I can about him and other things." Keble "seems very little inclined to send his parochial sermons up to you. He says, 'Newman has been troubled enough with things that won't do.' However, he says, 'sometime' he will select some for publication himself." Newman was anxious that Keble write an attack on the Ecclesiastical Commission; "he says he is sure that if you are not up to it he is not."[56] And so the discussion went, back and forth.

Two years later, in the spring of 1838, another of Newman's young disciples was quite put out at his first experience with the Vicar of Hursley. The famous Keble charm completely eluded James Mozley. "Keble does not exhibit the *Christian Year* in his outward air or manner; and people who come with the idea would be rather floored and perplexed, and not know what to make of him. It is neither amiable, nor civil, nor courteous, nor engaging, nor anything of the kind, but he leaves you pretty much to yourself, and speaks just when he likes and what."[57] No sense of self-importance is so tender as that of the young intellectual, and Mozley, it appears, had been snubbed by Keble. It must have been one of those black, indolent days at Hursley.

James Mozley's brother Tom saw it another way. Keble "had not the qualities for controversy or debate which are necessary for any kind of public life. He very soon lost his temper in discussion." This, in Tom

Mozley's view, explained the retirement first to Fairford and then to Hursley, and in each case to the bosom of congenial friends and relatives. "There was really no getting on with Keble without entire agreement, that is submission." The same quality betrayed him more than once into fantasy. One time, for example, he held forth on the ancient beauty of the west front of Lichfield cathedral and was very angry at Mozley for disabusing him—the work was cement, produced on an assembly line only a year before. Keble was annoyed to know the truth, which robbed him of happiness based on an error honestly held.[58]

Yet Mozley remembered too, as they all did, that Keble was "the sun of this little world." His whole disposition, his attitude towards life and towards his own limitations, his understanding of the Christian gospel, all of these were expressed by a habit he had "of suddenly rousing himself, shaking himself rather, throwing his shoulders back and raising his head," a kind of physical "sursum corda."[59] Keble saw it as his duty to rouse himself continually from the dark slough of self-distrust, to throw back his shoulders and lift up his heart. But he could do this only in his own way and from a remote refuge like Hursley. Despite Newman's complaint that Keble's was "a light too spiritual and subtle to be seen unless put upon a candlestick,"[60] the Vicar of Hursley would not be other than himself; if something, as a result, were lost, it could not be helped.

CHAPTER 13

A Question of Affection

"APOSTOLICITY is growing so fast in Oxford," wrote Newman in the spring of 1837, "that I trust it is not too fast." At Balliol College, for example, "Oakeley is growing prodigiously. . . . At Exeter right opinions are strong. At Magdalen, Trinity, University and Oriel nucleuses are forming. Marriott goes the whole hog."[1] Some of the interest in Apostolic principles reflected an aesthetic-ritualist preoccupation which frankly puzzled Newman, but he rejoiced if such externals indicated the presence of inner conviction. He told Henry Wilberforce about two Magdalen men who had begun to wear stoles with St. Andrew's crosses embroidered on them, and evidently the same people were using genuflections at certain points in the celebration of the liturgy. "I cannot conceive what it means," Newman commented. "But all sorts of reports are current. I heard the other day that I worshipped the holy elements in the Service, and what was more strange, that I did so before the consecration."[2]

As their cause prospered during the late 1830s the Tractarians were often confronted with this double effect: a measurable increase in numbers and fervour among their followers, and an accompanying flurry of rumours about the Romish character of the Tractarian enterprise. It is curious how little the rumours bothered Newman so long as he felt himself secure in his Anglicanism. There was a certain insensitivity in this, parallel to his indifference to the attractiveness of Rome for others until he himself, in 1839, began to feel that attraction. His friends, sometimes, took it upon themselves to fill the gap. Keble was given the testimony of "some young gentleman, fresh from Oxford," who went "the other day into Littlemore Chapel and saw wax candles burning before the altar, and understood that there they burned night and day; the which, when I heard, I desired the informant to tell the gentleman, with my compliments, that he is an abominable liar. Should I," he asked Newman, "have

[252]

spoken more mildly?"[3] Newman tended to take such stories much too lightly, and Keble offered him a bit of advice: it might be better to decline "openly receiving such presents as candlesticks at present. . . . I mean of course for the sake of the weaker brethren."[4]

Newman fretted himself more over other side effects of the Movement's progress. He met Mrs. Barbara Wilberforce at Southampton late in the summer of 1837. The emancipator's widow, a more narrow and unyielding Evangelical than her husband had ever been, was frankly concerned about some of Mr. Newman's views and about the influence he was exercising over at least one of her sons. There was an unpleasant exchange. "It is one great distress I feel," Newman reported to Henry Wilberforce, "the unsettling people; yet I do not know how it is to be helped. It has pained me a good deal."[5] And there was more pain to come, more estrangement, more cutting and being cut. Newman listed for Bowden in 1838 those Oxford personages who had ceased speaking to him: "Baden-Powell has lately commenced cutting me—why, I know not. Also Shuttleworth. So has Daubney, though I believe in him it is mere awkwardness."[6] But the process of exclusion worked both ways, and among those left behind by the Tractarians were one who had helped launch the Movement and another whom Newman had tried, without much success, to recruit: "I lament about [William] Palmer, but good fellow as he is, he never has been one of our own. Samuel W[ilberforce] is so far from anything higher than a dish of skimmed milk that we must hope nothing from him."[7] Barbara Wilberforce might have been reassured by that judgment that her darling Sam had escaped the net which had ensnared her other boys, for she no doubt agreed with Sam's mother-in-law—who was also Henry's mother-in-law—Mrs. John Sargent, that Newman was "a confirmed old papist."

I

But Mrs. Sargent's charge was premature. In 1837 it had not crossed Newman's mind, had not entered his wildest dreams, that the papal system stood for anything more than dreary corruption. What made him sound like a papist, at least to the committed Protestants of the Church of England's Evangelical wing, was his insistence that though "Romanism may be considered as an unnatural and misshapen development of Truth," yet "Rome retains the principle of true Catholicism perverted; popular Protestantism is wanting in the principle." Or, as he expressed the same thing in the form of a paradox: "The best Dissenter is he who is least of a Dissenter; the best Roman Catholic is he who comes nearest to being a Catholic."[8]

The problem was the same one which had plagued the followers of the Anglican Via Media since the seventeenth century. The promotion of Catholicism means, for most people, the promotion of popery. The only refuge from Rome in the popular mind was Protestantism. Newman was well aware of this ancient national prejudice and by 1836 he felt the time had come to tackle it. "My writing against the Church of Rome" took up much of his time and energy during the late 1830s; it was a measure of the confidence he had at that moment in the strength of his own position.

Newman's assault upon Rome came chiefly in three Tracts and one lengthy treatise. Tract Seventy-one, which appeared at the beginning of 1836, was titled "On the controversy with the Romanists." It aimed not so much at examining the large issues which divided Rome from England as suggesting certain lines of attack for the Anglican to follow. The best method of combating a rising Roman influence, argued Newman, is to concentrate upon the "practical grievances to which Christians are subjected in the Roman communion"; instances of these grievances include denial of the Eucharistic cup to the laity, unwarranted condemnations of non-Roman Christians, and image worship. The high ground of Trinity and Incarnation should be avoided because there is no disagreement in those areas, and the Eucharist is not a proper matter for controversy either, because Eucharistic arguments, said Newman, so easily disintegrate into irreverence. But in other practical matters Roman assertions, though often appealing, are specious, and one is most easily saved from them by recalling that the burden of proof rests upon him who insists that his communion has a monopoly of the truth; no Anglican makes such a presumptuous claim.

The Roman Church, Newman continued, can be hit hardest by stressing that it is "one whole system, written and unwritten, defined indeed and adjusted by general statements, but not limited to them or coincident with them." Roman Catholics brush away the scandal and abuses of image worship by invoking the canons of the Council of Trent on this subject; but what about the practical system which is permitted by those canons and which in some sense emerges from them? In looking at the Roman Church as it really is one sees the corruptions intertwined into her essential fabric, and appeal to paper judgments, like the canons of Trent, cannot alter the final, unhappy picture.

The Church of England, for her part, defends herself best by admitting that she is incomplete, that she has sinned by omission, that she has been "surrounded by political influences of a highly malignant character." Her great strength lies in the fact that despite her failings she still possesses all the elements of Catholic life, the faith and the sacraments. Her failure to go far enough has not created an insuperable obstacle to her communicants attaining "the perfect development of the Christian temper."[9]

So Newman proposed that the Roman menace be met head on. It was not a method likely to endear him to the likes of Mrs. John Sargent, who identified the Via Media with a drift towards Rome. In Tract Seventy-two Newman took a specific instance of how to counter a Roman pretension without falling into the opposite error of Protestant minimizing. The Tract was a reprint of an Anglo-Catholic defense of prayer for the dead written by a seventeenth-century Archbishop of Armagh named James Ussher. Newman made his point in a short preface. The Roman Church, he wrote, constantly gives the false impression that because her doctrines resemble superficially those of the Ancient Church one must either accept the Roman view or else disclaim the primitive Christian testimony. Thus Roman Catholics propose the reverence of the Fathers for the Blessed Sacrament as an argument supporting transubstantiation, which in reality is a medieval corruption. Perhaps there is no more striking instance of this procedure than the invention of Purgatory and its justification by Roman controversialists in the ancient practice of prayers for the dead. Archbishop Ussher in his learned exposition proved that prayers for the dead and Purgatory are not indissolubly linked; the early Christians did indeed pray for the dead, but they did not believe in Purgatory. In presenting this new edition of Ussher to the public, Newman was insisting on a basic Tractarian position: Anglicans tended to fly too quickly to the refuge of Protestantism. They seemed eager in their controversies with Rome to give up too much; by agreeing, for example, that prayers for the dead imply Purgatory, they were in effect forced to renounce a practice which went back to the second century.

In Tract Seventy-nine, "On Purgatory," Newman wrote a kind of commentary on Archbishop Ussher. He began by emphasizing once more the difference between Roman theory and practice. "Romanism in theory may differ little from our own creed; nay, in the abstract type, it might even be identical, and yet in the actual framework, and still further in the living and breathing form, it might differ essentially." Purgatory provided the perfect instance. "The pictures of Purgatory so commonly seen in countries in communion with Rome, the existence of Purgatorian societies, the means of subsistence accruing to the clergy from belief in it, afford a strange contrast to the simple wording and apparent innocence of the decree [of Trent] by which it is made an article of faith. It is the contrast between a drug in its lifeless seed and the same developed, thriving and rankly luxuriant in the actual plant."

In the sequel Newman did what few others could do so well; he set down a thorough, accurate, dispassionate account of his opponents' position. The Roman Catholic doctrine on Purgatory was carefully drawn, the classical arguments for it advanced. But at the end of the exposition he dismissed the scriptural and patristic arguments in a couple of pages of withering scorn. None of the scriptural citations brought forward by the Roman controversialists meant anything more than Archbishop

Ussher said they meant, that prayers for the dead are indeed beneficial. And the patristic evidence betrayed, in Newman's judgment, a common Roman flaw: The witness of the Fathers is measured not by its own worth but in the light of present Roman practice or definition. The Council of Florence defined Purgatory thus and so, and therefore this is what the Fathers *must* have meant. "How hopeless then is it to contend with the Romanists as if they practically agreed to the foundation of faith."

Newman spent the rest of Number Seventy-nine examining the roots of the modern "legend" of Purgatory. Some of them, he admitted, did lie in the sayings of certain early Christian intellectuals, notably Origen and St. Augustine, but such remarks fit just as smoothly into Ussher's explanation. More pertinent, however, in Newman's view, was what might be called the doctrine's emotional context. There is a measure of plausibility and attractiveness in the idea of a halfway house between heaven and hell. People do commonly ask the question, what happens after they die to the great mass of people who are neither very good nor very bad? "Such speculations," said Newman, voicing a favourite Tractarian theme, "are dangerous when indulged; the event proves it; from some of these in fact seems to have resulted the doctrine of Purgatory."[10] Once a few isolated scriptural texts, mentioning purification by fire, are applied to this common curiosity, it takes on a doctrinal framework which in turn provides the key to more obscure texts and also to the primitive practice of praying for the dead. In essence, the Romanists do what the Protestants do: They erect a private judgment into a condition for salvation.

II

In the introduction to Tract Seventy-nine, Newman expressed that confident serenity which marked the Tractarian dancing days: "We are in no danger of becoming Romanists and may bear to be dispassionate and (I may say) philosophical in our treatment of their errors." No doubts crowded in yet, no fears that a corner might be some day turned and a specter have to be faced. "Whoever be our opponent, papist or latitudinarian, it does not seem to be wrong to be as candid and conceding as justice and charity allow us."[11] The important thing, in Newman's mind, was to convince the Church of England that she need not become Protestant in order to escape the dank embrace of Rome. There was another choice.

The cause of truth was of course the major concern, but Newman did not ignore the pragmatic uses of an anti-popery campaign. "We have determined to commence a series *against popery*," he explained to Bowden. "Many advantages will follow from this. Two years since the cry was against the Dissenters. This helped us. Now popery is the popular alarm, and we shall be able to convey the very same doctrines and in all parts of them under this economy. Also, we show we're not papists."[12]

This last consideration was no mere afterthought. Newman considered the "notion of my being a papist absurd, for it argues an utter ignorance of theology." Yet he knew the charge was being made and that to refute it would demand more than a few Tracts. "True it is, every one who by his *own wit* [has] gone as far as I *from* popular Protestantism . . . might have been in danger of going further," that is, in danger of drifting Romeward. But he thought such a drift a very unreal threat to him, precisely because he had discovered the Via Media in the Ancient Church and in the best Anglican divines and not in his "own wit." "No one who either had learned his doctrine *historically* or had tolerable clearness of head could be in more danger than in confusing the sun and moon."[13] To demonstrate clearly that he suffered from no such confusion, he brought out in the spring of 1837—about the same time as Tract Seventy-nine—his *Lectures on the Prophetical Office of the Church viewed relatively to Romanism and Popular Protestantism.*

The *Prophetical Office* grew out of some weekday lectures Newman had delivered at St. Mary's and also out of a controversial correspondence he had had with a French Catholic priest during the early 1830s. It was more, of course, than an attack upon Rome; it stated, perhaps in its clearest form, the Tractarian idea of what the essence of the Church was. And indeed it struck harder in the long run at "popular Protestantism" than it did at Rome. But it contained the harshest language about Rome that Newman ever used and so it became an instant hit with the chronically anti-Roman English public.

In the beginning of the book Newman insisted on the superficiality of the charge that the Via Media conspired to create sympathy for Rome. He granted that the Roman Church occupies a position which has some merit. "It has preoccupied the ground, and we cannot erect our own structure without partly breaking down, partly using what we find upon it." The real danger lies among the Protestants who have no ground at all and therefore can be, ironically, much more easily seduced by the blandishments of popery. "Viewed politically, Protestantism is at this day the rallying point of all that is loyal and high minded in the nation." Yet intellectually it is barren and empty. "To what theology can the serious Protestant, dissatisfied with his system, betake himself but to the Roman, unless we display our characteristic principles and show him that he may be Catholic and Apostolic, yet not Roman?"

The controversy with Rome, Newman went on, is long and hard, and it is not open to the unlearned, because in the last analysis it deals with a question of fact: Do current Roman beliefs and practices square with those of the Ancient Church? The answer must depend upon a work of research, a lengthy and exhaustive inquiry into the past and into the

present. "We must meet [the Roman Catholics], and may do so fearlessly, on the ground of antiquity to which they betake themselves." For
they maintain, and rightly, that written revelation cannot be understood
outside the framework of tradition. But do they in fact remain faithful
to tradition? Newman's answer of course was negative.

Instead of standing "pertinaciously and immovably fixed on the ground
of antiquity," Roman Catholics swerve aside and really place their reliance upon infallibility as a present and living force in the Church. This
explains the Roman Church's "bold speculation" and "bold exactness."
A gesture indeed is made to the primitive Christian community, but
really Roman Catholics hanker after more information than knowledge
of the Ancient Church can provide. So they interpret the past by the
demands of an insatiably curious present, and prayer for the dead turns
into Purgatory, the Real Presence into transubstantiation. Rome says too
much, and so leads to an oversystematized brand of Christianity which
tends to water down the austere Christian teaching revealed in the
Ancient Church. "It provides us with a sort of graduated scale of devotion and obedience, and, so far, tends to engross our thoughts with the
details of a mere system, to a comparative forgetfulness of its professed
Author." Rome, argued Newman, has abandoned antiquity, because she
has tried to remove all obscurity from religious life and thus hand to the
believer a certainty over a wide extent of matters which antiquity cannot
provide. Witness, for example, the detailed directions involved in gaining an indulgence, based upon an abstract doctrine sealed by infallibility,
whereby the Christian can measure out the punishment due to his sins.
Where in such a practice is that regard for the factual—as opposed to the
abstract—which one gains by simply imitating the Ancient Church?

The *Prophetical Office* is a profound and subtle book, and it would not
do to oversimplify its conclusions. Yet one might say that Newman's
target was private judgment as practiced both by Roman Catholics and
Protestants. The Via Media was a narrow, difficult road which steered
between the unproved infallibility of Rome and the unproved personal
competence of Protestantism. The Protestant reliance upon an untrained,
emotional, contextless reading of Scripture results, said Newman, in a
mindlessness not much different from Rome's. "There is neither natural
probability nor supernatural promise that individuals reading Scripture
for themselves, to the neglect of other means when they can have them,
will, because they pray for a blessing, be necessarily led into a knowledge
of the true and complete faith of a Christian." Newman made no concessions to democracy. The mass of men are unable to discern doctrine
from Scripture and until they can consult the Fathers they will continue
to be led this way and that by any clever preacher.

Why should the Ancient Church have the power of authoritative teaching denied to every other institution and individual? Newman replied

that though it may be that the ideal Church should be blessed with infallibility, yet, following the analogy of ancient Jewish history, it seems probable that the sins of the Church have rendered such a gift forfeit. And the worst of these sins is disunity. "The Church Catholic, being no longer one in the fullest sense, does not enjoy her predicted privileges in the fullest sense. And that soundness of doctrine is one of the privileges thus infringed is plain from the simple fact that the separate branches of the Church do not agree with each other in the details of faith." All branches contain the outline of the truth, but not the details, and therefore "it would follow that the Ancient Church will be our model in all matters of doctrine, till it broke up into portions and for Catholic agreement substituted peculiar and local opinions." "The Church Catholic is unerring in its declarations of faith or saving doctrine." This means in effect that the Christian must abide by the ancient creeds. The Roman Church has added to the deposit of antiquity and has come to rely instead on the indefectibility of the Roman see. The Via Media, on the other hand, turns to antiquity, because then the Church was still undivided, and unity is a condition of the full privileges promised by Christ.

If this is the case, then it follows that a careful distinction has to be drawn between what is essential in the Christian life—that which can be clearly discerned from undivided ancient Christianity—and that which is only accidental. Newman, in making this distinction, brought his argument to its climax. There is in the Church, he argued, an Episcopal Tradition and a Prophetical Tradition. The first of these is the expression of the essential, "a collection of definite articles set apart from the first, passing from hand to hand, rehearsed and confessed at baptism, committed and received from bishop to bishop, forced upon the attention of each Christian and thus demanding and securing due explanation of its meaning."

Prophetical Tradition, on the other hand, is a "certain body of truth, pervading the Church like an atmosphere, irregular in its shape from its very profusion and exuberance; at times separable only in idea from Episcopal Tradition, yet at times melting away into legend and fable." Prophetical Tradition can be "corrupted in its details, in spite of its general accuracy and its agreement with Episcopal." The Prophetical Tradition may indeed be accidental in that it does not lay claim to the same sort of assent as does the Episcopal, expressed, say, in the Athanasian Creed. But accidental, insisted Newman, does not mean unimportant or indifferent.

The primitive Church . . . was simple and precise in her fundamentals to include all classes. . . . However, while thus considerate, she has not forgotten her high office as the appointed teacher of her children. She is "the pillar and ground of the truth;" of all truth, Christian truth in all its developments, in

the interpretation of Scripture, in the exposition of doctrine, in the due appointment of ordinances, in the particular application and adjustment of the moral
law. . . . And, in consequence, such being her office towards her children, they
are bound, if they would remain her children, as far as their minds attain to
her doctrine, to take it on the ground of her Catholicity."

This is the Prophetical Office of the Church. And, as might have been
expected from Newman, it possesses an explicitly moral dimension. "A
child comes to his mother for instruction; she gives it. She does not
assume infallibility, nor is she infallible; yet it would argue a very unpleasant temper in the child to doubt her word, to require proof of it
before acting on it. . . . Sometimes, perhaps, she mistakes in lesser
matters and is set right by her child; yet this neither diminishes her
prerogative of teaching nor his privilege of receiving dutifully." The
genuinely catholic Church "asks for a dutiful and simple-hearted acceptance of her message growing into faith, and that variously, according to
the circumstances of individuals, . . . without imposing any yoke after
the manner of Rome, or repressing the elastic or creative force of their
minds. She makes her way by love, she does not force a way by violence.
All she asks is their *confidence*, which will practically preserve them from
all difference from her, except in minor matters." He who scorns the
Church's Prophetical Tradition "is excluded on a moral offence; not only
because he believes amiss, but because he acts presumptuously. The
Church Catholic is more likely to be right than he."

What, in the light of all this, must the Anglican do? Stand firm,
answered Newman, in the confidence that the Church of England possesses the Episcopal Tradition, and "follow the Prayer Book, instead of
following preachers, who are but individuals." For the Prayer Book is a
genuinely catholic thing, filled with both the Episcopal and Prophetical
Traditions; we must "embrace and act upon the doctrine of our services,
and, if anywhere we differ, differ in silence."[14]

In the *Prophetical Office* Newman drew out in its most persuasive form
the consequences of the Via Media. It was a beautiful and impressive
theory, enough, really, to take one's breath away. If it lashed out at Rome
or at popular Protestantism, it did so in no carping way and certainly
in no unfair way. It assumed a lofty ground and never descended to the
level of polemics. Only one thing about it seemed to bother its author;
is the Via Media but a dream? "Protestantism and popery are real re-
ligions; no one can doubt about them; they have furnished the mould in
which nations have been cast; but the Via Media, viewed as an integral
system, has never had existence except on paper." Yet the Via Media
displays "a critical fastidiousness, trifling with them both and boasting
to be nearer antiquity than either. What is this but to fancy a road over
mountains and rivers, which has never been cut?" Newman admitted
ruefully that this was a plausible objection. "But if this be so, if the

English Church has the mission, hitherto unfulfilled on any considerable stage or consistent footing, of representing a theology, Catholic but not Roman, here is an especial reason why her members should be on the watch for opportunities of bringing out and carrying into effect her distinctive character."[15]

III

The *Prophetical Office* cost Newman an unusual amount of toil. "I have re-written some parts an incredible number of times." He claimed nothing new for it; it was "but a systematizing, consolidating, supplying premises, etc.," all under "the highest authority of our [Anglican] writers." Still he knew it was "strong" compared to his earlier writings: "it is all the difference between drifting snow and a hard snowball."[16] And he confided to Rogers, "I am very anxious about this book. I cannot conceal from myself that it is neither more nor less than hitting Protestantism a hard blow in the face."[17] He had described the book as an attack upon Romanism, and yet he judged that the Protestants would take offense from it.

For Protestantism remained the real enemy; Rome, as far as England was concerned, was as far away as the moon, and Newman did not hesitate to say, in reference to the *Prophetical Office*, "I frankly own that if in some important points our Anglican ethos differs from popery, in others it is like it, and on the whole far more like it than Protestantism."[18]

A strikingly poignant statement of this attitude came from Frederic Rogers in the autumn of 1837. Rogers' sister Emily died late in September. Newman wrote a letter of condolence to her parents, and Frederic described the reception of that letter at the Rogers home in London.

I must tell you a thing which struck me a good deal when your letter arrived. My mother read it to my father, and I observed him point to a passage in it and say, "You see, he says so without scruple." It turned out that both he and my mother had felt a desire to ask Emily to pray for them, if possible, hereafter, but had stopped themselves not knowing whether it would be right. Does this not make one indignant with Protestantism? My [deceased] sister too, I find, that when she got to Catholic views she seemed as if she had found a "haven," having been *very* much distressed at thinking herself bound to find truth for herself when she felt herself unequal to it. I never before appreciated the cruelty of Protestantism.[19]

What Rogers called "cruelty" was rooted in the Protestant attitude towards justification which, as he saw it, left the individual alone to face God without the healing mediation of the Church. It may have been sweetness to discover Christ as one's personal saviour, but it could be a hellish experience—and of course Rogers was thinking of frail, dying

Emily—to wander through life looking and never finding. Rogers had learned this point of view from Newman, who, when the news of Emily Rogers' death reached him, had already turned his furious energies to an analysis of this key Protestant doctrine.

Newman's *Lectures on the Doctrine of Justification* grew out of a newspaper controversy. The *Christian Observer*, an Evangelical magazine, had bitterly attacked Pusey's Tracts on Baptism (Numbers Sixty-seven, Sixty-eight and Sixty-nine) and had directed the most scathing sarcasm at Pusey himself. "Professor Pusey," the *Observer*'s editor wrote, among other things, "teaches that the sacraments are the appointed instruments of justification. The learned professor ought to lecture at Maynooth [the Roman Catholic seminary in Ireland] or the Vatican, and not in the chair at Oxford, when he puts forth this popish doctrine."[20] Newman had sometime before put on record his total commitment to Pusey personally and his endorsement of Pusey's Tracts.

If you knew my friend Dr. Pusey [Newman wrote in April 1836] as well as I do, . . . you would say, I am sure, that never was a man in this world on whom one should feel more tempted to bestow a name which belongs only to God's servants departed, the name of a saint. Never a man who happened unconsciously to show . . . entire and absolute surrender of himself, in thought, word and deed to God's will. And this being so, I shall battle for him when his treatise is attacked, and by whomsoever.[21]

Newman kept this promise literally. His estrangement from Charles Golightly and from Samuel Wilberforce began when they spoke out publicly against Pusey's views on Baptism. And as for the editor of the *Observer*, Newman put him through the verbal meat grinder which he reserved for particularly noxious opponents. In January 1837 Newman sent a letter to the *Observer*, which published it in two sections occupying altogether about seven pages of large type. The editor's rejoinder appeared next, and this was sixty pages long, printed in small type. Newman took up the cudgels again in March, but after that the controversy ceased, because, Newman claimed, the *Observer* insisted on suppressing part of his next letter out of concern for "pounds, shillings and pence."[22] Presumably the editor, for economic reasons, denied Newman the space he wanted.

In any case, the correspondence had brought the pressing subject to his attention, and so at this point Newman decided to write a full-length treatise on justification. He saw the problem in terms of the denial or at least the misunderstanding of essential Christian truths, like baptismal regeneration and the sacramental idea generally, based on the widely held Protestant view of justifying faith. It would do no good of course to invoke the Fathers or the Caroline divines in the debate over justification, because the Protestants—whether Dissenters or Evangelical Anglicans—

would accept only the scriptural approach. Newman described the venture as a bold voyage, undertaken "with sun, stars, compass and a sounding line, but with very insufficient charts." Then, mixing his metaphors, he added, "It is *terra incognita* in our Church, and I am so afraid, not of saying things wrong so much as queer and crotchety, and of misunderstanding other writers. For really the Lutherans, etc., as *divines*, are so shallow and inconsequent that I can hardly believe my own impressions about them."[23] By Christmas 1837 he had sent the first section of the book to the publisher in London, and early in 1838 the complete *Lectures on the Doctrine of Justification* came off the press.

In the history of the Oxford Movement, *Justification* is significant because it tackled the basic Protestant position (as Newman saw it) upon which Protestant practice was based. The emphasis upon internal conversion, "serious religion," "spiritual mindedness" which were the hallmarks of the Evangelical revival within the Church of England stemmed from the notion of justification by fiduciary faith as Luther had first proposed it. This was why from the beginning all varieties of Protestantism had exaggerated the sermon as the instrument of redemption, because through the proclamation of God's Word the sinner was led to confront God or kept from turning away from him, and therefore the sacramental path of internal regeneration was useless or even dangerous. The Via Media, with its sacramental bias, could not but see this as a perversion of the Bible's call for universal trust in the saving power of the gospel.

Newman kept carefully away from patristic argument. The whole book was what might be called scriptural apologetics, and it leaned heavily on verbal analysis: that is, Newman was constantly asking rhetorically what this or that passage in the Bible really meant. As always, it was the Tractarian (and Caroline) Via Media which he offered, this time between faith alone and formalistic obedience to the law.

Justification by faith only, thus treated [i.e., as a leading idea in a theological system], is an erroneous, and justification by obedience a defective view of Christian doctrine. The former is beside, the latter short of, the truth. The former legitimately tends to the creed of the rigid Lutherans; . . . the latter to that of . . . extreme writers of the Roman school. That we are absolutely saved by obedience, that is by *what we are*, has introduced the proper [i.e., intrinsic and therefore false] merit of good works; that we are absolutely saved by faith, or by *what Christ is*, the notion that good works are not conditions of our salvation.

Perhaps the most important insight Newman expressed in *Justification* came in the third lecture. There he dealt with the primary sense of the term justification and broke through the old forensic idea—i.e., a man is rendered technically just in God's eyes by an external decree of forgiveness of his sins with no accompanying internal sanctification—with an illuminating distinction. "I would explain the distinction I am drawing thus: to 'justify' *means* in itself 'counting [i.e., considering] righteous,' but includes *under* its meaning 'making righteous'; in other words, the sense of the *term* is 'counting righteous,' and the nature of the *thing* denoted by it is making righteous. In the abstract it is a counting righteous, in the concrete a making righteous." If God says I am righteous, then, no doubt, I really am.

Newman believed that a distinction of this kind could reduce the old Protestant-Catholic quarrel to manageable proportions. He did much the same thing in dealing with the sanctified term "faith only." There is no need to sacrifice the expression, he argued, so long as we understand it properly. Faith "justifies only in two ways: as the only inward *instrument*, and as the only *symbol*. Viewed as an instrument, it united the soul to Christ through the sacraments; viewed as a symbol it shows forth the doctrine of free grace." Needless to say, this notion would hardly please the Evangelical, but it could give solace to a young Tractarian clergyman, say, who was worried about subscribing to the Articles. He could do so with a clear mind, even if Article XI did say that "we are justified by faith only is a most wholesome doctrine and very full of comfort."

Actually what Newman attempted in *Justification* was parallel to what he tried to do in the *Prophetical Office*. An Anglican must not be frightened into an extreme Protestant position, any more than into a Roman, by semantics. Prayer for the dead does not necessarily mean Purgatory; and justification by faith alone is a perfectly intelligible idea without giving it the meaning Luther gave it. The argument boiled down ultimately (as Pusey had maintained in his Tracts) to the relation between faith and Baptism. Newman took the part of the unequivocal sacramentalist.

Faith, . . . being the appointed representative of baptism, derives its authority and virtue from that which it represents. It is justifying because of baptism; it is the faith of the baptized, of the regenerate, that is, of the justified. Justifying faith does not precede justification; but justification precedes faith and makes it justifying. And here lies the cardinal mistake of these [Protestant] views of the subject which are now in esteem. In those views, faith is considered as the sole instrument, not after baptism but before; whereas baptism is [in fact] the primary instrument, and causes faith to be what it is and otherwise is not, giving it power and rank. . . . Viewed in its theological aspect, . . . the Protestant account will be found to give a character and vagueness to the whole system built upon it. What indeed can be expected but arbitrary distinctions and unreal subtleties in the conformation of a theology which has a flaw in its leading principle, which starts with maintaining that faith is what nothing ever was or can be, an abstraction in actual existence.

There was hardly a word in the Tractarian vocabulary as disagreeable as "abstraction." The Christian's practical working out of his salvation was in the end all that mattered. And the greatest obstacle to doing so was the doctrine that began and ended in the air. A faith which did not bring into existence the new man was vague, shadowy, ethereal. "It is as unmeaning to speak of living faith . . . being independent of newness of mind, as of solidity as divisible from body, or tallness from stature, or colour from landscape." The Protestant's contempt for sacramental forms, said Newman, and his insistence upon the religious experience produced by the fiery preacher, are the measure of his unreality. And perhaps they create something more, something worse, even, than the neo-paganism of Rome: "This is the idolatry of a refined age in which the superstitions of barbarous times displease, in consequence of their grossness."[24]

IV

Newman suffered occasionally from toothache, and throughout his life he was subject to fits of temporary deafness if he stayed too long at his desk. But the prodigious amount of work he did between 1836 and 1838 apparently agreed with him. "I rejoice to say," he told Keble in April 1837, "I am better than I have been for years."[25] The writing of two full-length books, of a half-dozen Tracts and numerous incidental pieces, the supervision, financial and literary, of the whole Tract venture, the parochial preoccupations at St. Mary's and Littlemore, the sermons, the daily burden of an immense correspondence, the editing of Froude's *Remains*, and, as we shall see, the editorship of a quarterly magazine: such activities shaped the pattern of these incredibly busy years. Their variety and magnitude testify also to the importance to the Oxford Movement of the leisured independence available to a university don.

The busy years were also satisfying ones. Although he could not see it at the time, Newman was approaching the zenith of his influence within the Church of England. Evidence abounded of the prosperity of the Apostolic cause. The future looked bright and if the battle had not yet been won, it seemed unlikely that it would be lost. In the midst of this accomplishment and energetic confidence, how out of tune must have sounded the voice urging restraint and caution. It was a voice out of the past, and it must have seemed almost from the dead.

By 1836 Hugh James Rose had severed his connection with the University of Durham and had accepted the position of Principal of King's College, in the new University of London. He still edited the *British Magazine*. His health was no better and indeed he was within two years of his premature death. His relations with the Tractarians were still cordial, though a decided strain was beginning to show. One cause of it was his hesitancy to publish an article of Newman's—"Home Thoughts

Abroad," first written when Newman and Froude were on their Italian visit in 1833—because he thought it granted too much to the Roman position. He eventually did publish it, but not before Froude lashed out at him, "As to propitiating Rose, he is much in our debt and ought to make propitiation himself. I am quite out of patience waiting month after month for 'Home Thoughts Abroad.' "[26] These words were written only weeks before Froude's death.

Rose had never enjoyed the full confidence of Froude or Keble, and the public quarrel with Pusey over German theology in the late 1820s left scars that probably never healed completely. As early as the spring of 1834 Keble felt that Rose was drawing back from the fight he helped to initiate. Keble complained that Rose was erratic, that he vacillated even on so key an issue as the Irish Bishoprics Act, writing about it with commendable fury in 1833 and then moderating his tone markedly in 1834. Rose annoyed Keble particularly by editing a strong paragraph out of a letter Keble had sent to be published in the *British Magazine* and by adding a prefatory note to the letter which further softened Keble's argument. "It is quite plain," said Keble, "that [Rose] forgets from month to month what he wrote the number before." Keble recognized that Rose, as an influential editor and as a man with friends in high places, "is a delicate subject, and I would not pain him if I could help it." Nevertheless, Rose had let himself be guided too much by his emotions; Keble did not charge him with lying "but only with having said a little more than he meant at first. But I dare say by this time he is more comfortable from the mere act of writing out his feelings."[27] For Rose had written to Newman complaining about Keble's lack of cooperation. Keble himself never deviated from his basic estimate of Rose: "I have always thought him too much attached to an Establishment."[28]

Keble hoped that Rose could be persuaded to resign the editorship, or at least to take a partner, because he knew that the *British Magazine* would never be an organ in the Apostolic campaign under Rose's moderate and perhaps temporizing direction. Most of the Tractarians agreed, including Newman, who wrote to Bowden late in 1834: "How Rose (entre nous) has backed out of the Mag[azine]. I suppose he fears to commit the archbishop. You will observe he gives no opinion of his own. Except the correspondence, the Mag[azine] is actually stupid. Keble wishes (among other Utopian plans) that you should become editor—which I suppose is as impracticable on your side as on the side of the publishers."[29]

Yet Newman kept a regard for Rose personally as well for his position in the Church which few of his friends shared. It was a moment of some significance, therefore, when Rose, in the spring and summer of 1836, held up a warning hand. The occasion was his reading of Pusey's Tracts on Baptism, and it was to Pusey that he sent his first remonstrance. The liberals and Evangelicals, he wrote April 30, 1836, have in their different ways brought the Church of England to such low views that the possibility of deliverance seemed remote. "The first real ground of hope which has been *visible* has been the existence of a body of men at Oxford, with many close friends through the country, whose characters and reputation stood high, whose learning could not be doubted, and who have fearlessly stood forward *in combination* to speak the old truths." But all the good done can be forfeited, he went on, if the Oxford men should adopt extremist views. "I can hardly describe my own sense of the importance of your movements just now. If you leave our present *standing-point*, very many from fear, very many from conviction will break away. The enemy will have the best possible handle to use *against* you and *for* himself and his own ends; i.e., the increasing his strength and scattering to the four winds of heaven all united elements of opposition to it."[30]

Pusey forwarded this note to Newman, who wrote to Rose the next day: "I conjecture thus much—that you are not satisfied and are afraid, yet have nothing very definite to say."[31] Rose agreed that this was the case, and in a letter written on May 9th he told Newman "the *sort* of feeling which I have on the subjects we have been discussing." He pointed out first of all that the English nation and its clergy were an "eminently anti-reading" people for whom, therefore, the vision of the Primitive Church, so often evoked by the Tractarians, could be a danger as well as a blessing. "I will frankly confess that I am a little apprehensive of the effects of turning the readers, such as they are, out to grass in the spacious pastures of antiquity without very strict tether. *All* that is in antiquity is not good, and much that was good for antiquity would not be good for us. . . . If *such* minds are led to search out *all* the opinions and practices of antiquity as of great value, *because* they are derived from antiquity—where they and we shall get to it seems hard to tell." In Rose's view, the Tractarians were giving too much away. Apostolicity, for example, should not be explained "as a thing to which we were to recur as a sort of ancient novelty, a truth now first recovered," when in fact the Church of England had always held, sometimes obscurely to be sure, the doctrine of apostolic succession. "We must find out what is really fit to be taught and teach it as of *authority*—as a doctrine which has always been held, not as a thing which [our readers] are to go and look for, and find out, and prove by themselves." Rose insisted on scholarship, prudence and patience. A grave danger existed, he believed, in whimsically setting out the contrast between the ancient and the contemporary Church for the consideration of the masses. "If they are once impressed with the notion that we are *imperfect*, and require *improvement* and *change*, they have not the means of knowing or discovering how *much* or how *little*, and are merely converted into *ignorant* reformers."[32]

Rose wrote again a few days later, very much in the same strain. He spent most of his letter elaborating his view that Newman and Pusey were too hard on the contemporary Anglican Church in the name of an abstract antiquity and that this emphasis could be very damaging to the faith of their readers. He had just finished reading the first of Newman's anti-Roman Tracts (Number Seventy-one) and here he found something else to wonder at and to sorrow over.

I have been reading your first Number against Romanism, the last half of which is admirable. Towards the first [half], I feel somewhat as towards part of your "Home Thoughts Abroad" and several other papers and letters. . . . I would say that the impression which they would produce on my mind, *if I did not know you*, and therefore which I cannot but suppose they will produce on others is this nearly: "The *hearts* and *affections* of these writers are not with us. Their *judgment*, arising from deep learning, thought and piety, is *against* Rome decidedly, while still they think that she has much which we want. In this unhappy state they feel that in the Church of England—and there alone— is safety; but they feel that there is *nothing more*. A good deal *to tolerate*, a good deal *to deplore*; something no doubt to be *thankful for*, on the principle of regard for the bridge which carries you over; but little or nothing to *love*. They join her on the principle of *any port in a storm*. . . . They can find nothing better, nay, nothing else—and therefore they *are* thankful that there is any port where they can be moored in perfect safety."[33]

This was a shrewd stroke, and Newman felt the sting of it. "You have spoken the truth," he replied, "not that I would go and tell everyone at Charing Cross. I do *not* love the Church of England."

The Anglican Church [he continued], the old Church of 1200 or 1600 years, the Church of the builders of our cathedrals, the Church again of [the Caroline divines], . . . so far forth as they agree together and are lights shining in a dark place, the Church discriminated by the imposition of hands, not a tyrant's jurisdiction, I love indeed—and the later not a whit less favourably than the earlier. . . . I love the Church as embodying the good characteristics of the English ethos; I love it for its human traits as sanctified into the Church apostolical.

The Church of the Reformation, however, the Church established by law in England, that was something else, and the mention of it altered for Newman the whole question of affection.

But I cannot endure, except by patience and resignation, the insults of the world which she has worn now three hundred years. I cannot love the "Church of England," commonly so designated; its very title is an offence (though it were absurd to insist on this), for it implies that it holds not of the Church Catholic, but of the state.

If, Newman protested, we had been born thirty years earlier, we might have remained quiet.

But the times will not allow of this. They force us to speak our opinion, and I cannot so economize as not to speak in *substance* what I wish. . . . Again, outward circumstances are changing, the state is deserting us. We have [therefore] a *reason* for being bolder. . . . Why may I not in my heart deplore the hardheartedness . . . of those, whoever they were, who gave up (practically) to the Church of Rome what we *might have kept*? . . . My heart *is* with Rome, but *not as* Rome but as, and so far as, she is the faithful retainer of what we have practically thrown aside.

The task now, he concluded, was to show the "impossible barriers" between England and Rome—Mariolatry, for example—and this the series of anti-popery tracts can do. Even more important was to demonstrate that "what captivates in Rome might be ours."[34]

Rose did not answer for two months, and when he finally did (July 10, 1836) he wrote a sad, gentle note which for the most part avoided the whole tortured question of affection. "I did not answer your last very interesting (painfully so in some points) letter, for I think we now understand one another pretty well."[35] So they did. And so another bridge was burned, another link to the palmy days of 1833 severed. Newman, always sensitive to such things, noted a "coolness" between himself and Rose, though apparently there was a warming trend in 1837.[36] Towards the end of the next year Rose died, and Newman wrote feelingly to his widow.

I will only say that in sorrowing for the loss the Church has sustained in Mr. Rose I am sorrowing particularly for one who was always a kind, considering friend to me. In fact it was he who brought me into notice; he was the first to induce me to write on theological subjects and then to praise me when I had written. So generous, so noble minded and warm-hearted in all he did: this I have ever kept in mind, and may I never forget it.[37]

V

The estrangement from Hugh Rose carried with it an important practical consequence. If the *British Magazine* would not serve the Movement's purposes, then perhaps some other periodical would. "Rose, . . . with his ten thousand excellencies," concluded Newman, "yet has not the firmness for these times."[38] Early in 1836 Newman was already seriously thinking of an alternative to Rose's magazine. He went to London and met with High Church leader Joshua Watson, who was the financial angel of a journal called *The British Critic, Quarterly Review and Ecclesiastical Record*, and also with the magazine's editor, James Shergold Boone. The meetings were cordial; Rose, who was to attend them, fortunately was detained. Newman tersely reported the results to Keble: "I have bargained to supply Boone with four sheets quarterly for the *British Critic*."[39] A "sheet" included sixteen pages, and so the bargain meant that the Tractarians made themselves responsible for sixty-four pages per issue. This would amount to about one quarter of the *Critic*'s total space. No doubt the most attractive feature of this arrangement from the point of view of the magazine's management was that the Tractarians agreed to write without fee.

The *British Critic* had been founded in 1793. Watson began to subsidize it in 1814. Intended originally to be a general review appearing monthly, it had been reduced to a theological quarterly, mostly because it could not compete for good writers with the likes of the *Edinburgh*. Boone[40] was the latest in a series of less than successful editors. He had taken his degree at Christ Church, Oxford, where his brilliant performance had given promise of a great future. After a brief tenure as a prep school master, he took his M.A., received orders and became the pastor of a London parish. His youthful precocity seemingly failed to mature, and perhaps he saw the *British Critic* venture as his last chance to make a literary name for himself. If this is so, it helps explain why he jumped at the chance to add Newman and his talented friends to his stable of writers. Within two years, they had replaced him.

Newman's agreement to supply regular contributions to the *British Critic* did not mean that he bound himself to write any given quantity. "When he did write," recalled Tom Mozley, "he did not give himself over much time. He desired to make the review the means of introducing his friends and supporters and of giving them the opportunity to try their hands and acquire confidence." Most of those whom Newman enlisted wrote well but with the common Tractarian failing: "Even they who could say or write a short thing very well indeed wrote a long thing, not ill perhaps, but so as no human being was ever likely to read it through."[41]

Boone soon realized that by formally bringing the Tractarians into the *British Critic* he had allowed the camel to get a nose in the tent. The more the editor came to rely on the articles submitted by Newman and his friends, the more he was at their mercy. In effect the magazine had two editors, because the Tractarian contributions reached Boone's desk only after they had crossed Newman's. By December 1836 Boone saw how untenable his position had become. He complained bitterly to a friend of one of Newman's disciples, Samuel Wood, at the anti-Protestantism contained in an article Newman himself had written. Wood's report to Newman displayed the coldly calculating line the Tractarians had taken.

[Boone] declares that if another [article] of the same kind is sent he will throw up the editorship. . . . Now this is more probably a mode of expressing anger than a real expression of purpose; still, anyhow, it is an indication of his state of feeling and of what things may be tending to, against which one should be forearmed for the purpose of dictating terms. . . . I should be sorry to see *you* hampered and engaged by review editorship; but in case of your thinking proper to undertake it, we must all, of course, do our best, and I think we could manage it.[42]

Boone did not resign at that moment, but his days were numbered. In mid-July 1837 Newman wrote Boone "in disgust" at an article the editor had written and chided him for accepting contributions from a notorious Evangelical. "We must prepare for dropping him," Newman told John Bowden.[43] And six weeks later he added: "About Boone something must be done. Do not let it go the round of our friends, but I am going to write Joshua Watson to see if it be impossible quite to dispense with him." Newman was sure he could work out an arrangement with Rivington, who was his own publisher as well as publisher of the *British Critic*. "We could easily afford to pension him (if he would consent) because if we had [the *British Critic*] in our hands we might put aside for that purpose part of what Rivington now pays to the writers. But I fear he will stick."[44] Watson apparently agreed at least that the anomalous situation could not continue; in October he informed Keble that "Boone must resign the B.C.," but he, Watson, said "nothing of who will come in except that it will be hard to find a good one."[45]

Rumours swirled around Oxford and London through the autumn of 1837 as to who would succeed Boone. On December 12th Newman told Bowden, "*Entre nous*, I think the editorship of the B.C. will be offered to *Manning*, but this is *quite* a secret. Then I shall try to get Wood as sub-editor."[46] The Manning story proved unfounded, however, and early in the new year it was learned that a moderate High Churchman named Samuel Maitland had taken the editorship. "Nothing could be better," Newman observed, "*unless* he were under Rose's eyes, for he is going to live in [London]; but we must be quite decided and if he will not put in our strong articles we must retire."[47]

Though he appeared ready to accept Maitland under these strict terms, Newman's thinking really ran along the lines suggested a few months earlier by Henry Wilberforce. "My own feeling and wish is strongly that you should either let the [British] Critic drop and set up a new review, or, what would perhaps be better, become editor yourself, as Boone offered." The exact nature of Boone's "offer" is unclear, though it seems fair to surmise that it came as a result of severe exasperation. In any case Henry was not above playing on Newman's vanity to persuade him to make the move: as things stand, said Henry, the situation remains "anomalous," with everyone thinking that Newman "in some way [plays] second fiddle to Boone, and this hurts your name." A practical advantage would accrue to Newman's editorship, too: the money left over after expenses—"however small it may be matters not"—could be put in a general fund or else used to pay writers of Newman's choice, instead of being "divided only among Boone's people."[48]

Frederic Rogers, on the other hand, when he heard a rumour that

Newman was dissatisfied with the Maitland appointment, offered advice of a different kind: "I cannot help being half glad that they have not given the *B.C.* to a nominee of yours; it seems almost as if one ought to wait till F[roude]'s *Remains* come out before accepting anything from the Zs [i.e. the Watson–High Church party], lest they think afterwards that we got it under false colours."[49]

But Newman had no intention of waiting. By the end of January 1838 Maitland had changed his mind. He had just been appointed librarian at Lambeth (the Archbishop of Canterbury's London headquarters), and, said James Mozley, he "was frightened by an article of Pusey's on the Church Commission which he thought went too far for him in his present situation of librarian to the archbishop."[50] So apparently Maitland edited only the January issue, and Newman, though he did not formally assume the editorship till July, took care of the April and succeeding numbers. In March he wrote to Henry Wilberforce, "As to the *British Critic* I want your assistance by all means." Then, referring to Henry's monetary preoccupations, he added merrily, "I fear you will find the pay bad, only five pounds or guineas a sheet."[51] Keble received the news with a notable lack of enthusiasm: "I'm sure I wish I could help you in the *B.C.* which I am on some accounts gladder for you to have than not."[52] Keble's reaction not only reflected the black mood which at that moment possessed him; it was also in some measure prophetic. The *British Critic*, in Newman's hands, proved to be a mixed blessing at best, and once he gave its direction over to his disciples, it turned into a huge albatross hung around the neck of the Oxford Movement.

VI

A literary project of much more lasting value began its long and honourable progress about the same time. This was the Library of the Fathers, the first volume of which appeared in 1838. The idea for the series was Pusey's, who soon associated Newman and Keble with himself as joint editors. Keble predictably hesitated before committing himself to the project, but ultimately he agreed: "I am sincerely rejoiced and am proud to have my name inserted; at least I should be proud if I were not conscious of my knowledge of the Catholic fathers being too limited by far to justify such a step had I been [able] to choose for myself."[53]

The Library of the Fathers was published fitfully over a period of forty-seven years. By the time the last volume appeared, in 1885, Pusey had been dead three years, Keble almost twenty, and Newman had become an aged Roman Catholic cardinal. The series comprised forty-eight volumes and brought to the English reading public the works of thirteen ancient Christian writers. The bias shared by both Newman and

Pusey for the fourth century was reflected in the fact that of the total thirty-three volumes were devoted to writings by SS. John Chrysostom, Augustine and Athanasius.

The squad of editors and translators who laboured on the Library included scholars from two generations. But no one worked harder or more faithfully than did Charles Marriott of Oriel. Pusey wrote shortly after Marriott's death (in 1858) that the Library had "for some years wholly depended" upon the editorial labours of the frail, eccentric don whom Oxford undergraduates nicknamed "the veiled prophet."[54] The Library, and the devotion of Marriott and many others to it, survived all the vicissitudes which the Movement suffered; it stands as a permanent monument to the transfigured band of men who wanted more than anything else that modern Christendom might be patterned faithfully to its ancient foundations.

Another Pusey-inspired activity during the late 1830s was that of the Oxford Theological Society. Beginning late in 1835 this group met weekly or bi-weekly, on Fridays at 8:00 P.M., in Pusey's rooms at Christ Church. Newman and Keble were of course included in this project too, though it was originally Pusey's hope that the Society might function under a rather broader board of governors. He invited the two Professors of Divinity to be ex-officio members, but they both declined as did William Palmer. (It seems unlikely that R. D. Hampden was invited to join after he succeeded to the regius professorship in 1836.) Palmer attended one meeting and came away dissatisfied at "the wisdom and expedience of the design"; he noted that "discussion was encouraged at first but was afterwards discouraged."[55] This remark of Palmer's inferred that the Society was a closed, Tractarian operation, as it indeed became when all the non-Tractarians refused to take part in it; but in fairness he might have added that Pusey intended the Society's sessions to be the occasion for the delivery of a long and learned paper and not for random conversation. Thus his own inaugural lecture took an hour and twenty minutes to deliver, and Keble spoke to the Society no less than eight times over several years on ancient Christian mysticism. A condensation of Keble's papers was eventually published as Tract Eighty-nine.

Audiences of fifty and more B.A.'s and M.A.'s (undergraduates were excluded) gathered to hear the lectures given before the Theological Society. Besides Pusey and Keble, they listened frequently to the likes of Newman, Marriott and Benjamin Harrison. Many of the lectures were published, either as Tracts or as a preface to a volume in the Library of the Fathers.

In terms of their ultimate consequences, possibly the two most momentous Friday meetings of the Society ever held were those during which Isaac Williams addressed the eager young men on the subject of "Reserve in Communicating Religious Knowledge." This title was suggested by Newman, who had touched on this subject in *Arians* and who, like Williams, was apparently unprepared for the howls of protest which arose when Williams' lectures were published as Tract Eighty.

Williams had been drawn to this subject both by way of patristic study and by the long and worshipful association with his heroes, John and Thomas Keble. While reading Origen's commentaries on the gospel, he noticed "how much [Origen] alluded to a mysterious holding back of sacred truth, such as I had always been struck with in the conduct of the Kebles." Williams, always a careful, reflective man, wrote down his thoughts on reserve and ultimately showed them to John Keble, "who wished [them] to be one of the Tracts."[56] Newman agreed, Pusey asked Williams to deliver them first as two lectures before the Theological Society, and the fat was in the fire.

Tract Eighty appeared in the autumn of 1837. A careful analysis of Scripture, wrote Williams, and especially of the gospels, reveals that revelation is filled with obscurities and metaphors—"a very remarkable holding back of sacred and important truths, as if knowledge of them were injurious to persons unworthy of them. . . . What is much to be observed with regard to these expressions of Our Lord is that the not understanding of them was considered as a matter of reproof, as implying something morally deficient, not intellectually." Williams gave several instances of what he meant, including Christ's remark about the "leaven of the Pharisees" (Mark 8:17) and the often repeated gospel paradox, "He that hath ears to hear, let him hear." Jesus' use of parable confirmed the point, in Williams' judgment, as did the often unexpected impression created by the public miracles.

Williams argued that this practice of Christ carries through in the spiritual striving of the Christian. As Jesus gave knowledge of himself only to those who were prepared, and only to the extent of that preparation, so in the Christian, God, in a manner of speaking, hides his presence. There is therefore in the man of God a holy reserve, which neither pure speculation nor religious enthusiasm can penetrate. Ignorance of God—in the usual Tractarian sense of practical ignorance rather than speculative—is not outside the divine plan: "The fact I allude to is that this blindness of heart and darkness which is superinduced as the natural consequence of an evil life is variously, yet consistently, throughout the whole of Scripture attributed to the agency of God." Therefore, the pure food of revelation must not be thrown to dogs but must be kept in reserve and given piecemeal to those who are able little by little to digest it.

As Our Lord disclosed the greatness of his divine power and person to a chosen few obedient and teachable spirits, limiting even that disclosure more and more: first to twelve, then to four, then, still further, to three (as in the garden of Gethsemane and at the transfiguration, etc.); so does it appear that in morals, both when considered as separate from and also when considered as including religion, there is something, which is called knowledge, which is infinitely great and good, which is concealed from all others, who are universally represented as being in a state of darkness and ignorance, and is thus disclosed to these alone.

Radically, said Williams, reserve is a condition of Christian life insisted upon by Jesus himself. The Ancient Church practiced it in various ways, but most importantly in her sacramental and ascetic life. What has happened since, and particularly from the time of the Reformation, has been a gradual desertion of reserve as a principle and the substitution of

a new principle, unknown to former ages, prevailing throughout the world, in the shape not only of an article of faith but as the one and only article, indeed as one so important and requiring to be received with such authority as to supersede the very fabric of the Church; dispensing with her sacraments, her creeds, her liturgies, her discipline; and the principle is that the highest and most sacred of all Christian doctrines is to be brought before, and pressed home to, all persons indiscriminately, and most especially those who are leading un-Christian lives.

Williams was referring to the fundamental Protestant notions of the Atonement and the unique instrumentality of faith, which left such matters as sacraments and creeds in a position of minor importance. He was quite aware that people who differed on reserve would differ also in the practical promotion of religion. The building of churches, for instance, as well as the indiscriminate distribution of Bibles appeared to Williams as an attempt to make human means serve God's ends, and therefore they were in themselves fruitless enterprises. "For if the erection of church, which, from commodiousness and easiness of access are to invite and from their little cost partake more of a low contriving expediency than of a generous love of God, is to do the work of religion, then it is more easy to win souls than Scripture will warrant us in supposing." Williams did not oppose building churches; he opposed rather the idea that providing a place to give a sermon to lots of people (like passing out Bibles to all and sundry), because then lots of people would experience the Atonement and accept Christ as their personal saviour, would in the end promote the Christian life. The fact is, he maintained, that "these unhallowed approaches to our blessed Saviour, which these principles indicate, will . . . in some manner lead to a disbelief in his divinity, the knowledge of which . . . was that which he kept from the unworthy."[57]

James Mozley used to say that "there must be something harsh in Pusey's statements, as they offend people so mightily—more than the same view expressed by other divines."[58] Though there was nothing harsh about Williams' writing, yet his explanation of reserve earned him the same kind of reproach that the Tracts on Baptism brought upon

Pusey. Part of the trouble can be attributed to Williams' style: it wandered, it repeated, it was fuzzy, and still at times it achieved a certain majesty. The reader is lulled along for a while and then suddenly he finds that Williams has got his point across, and if the point is one with which the reader violently disagrees (as would have been the case with most Anglicans in the 1830s), he may think that he has been deceived. It is not without significance that in later life Williams judged that he wrote Latin better than English.[59]

Thomas Mozley believed the cause of Williams' difficulties lay with himself and his associations. "Isaac Williams was the simplest of men," observed Mozley. He lived among friends whom he admired and who agreed with him. "In some respects this was the common temptation and the common fault of all the [Tract] writers. Moving in a phalanx, with a certainty of support, they all said with tenfold freedom and fulness what they would have thought a good deal more about had they been called on to do it singly on their own separate account."[60] What Mozley suggested, in other words, was that Williams failed to practice the reserve he preached.

But Mozley also oversimplified the rather subtle point Williams was trying to make; he dismissed Tract Eighty as creating "a duty of not telling people all we believe and know, be it ever so necessary to be believed or known."[61] This was the common accusation at the time, and Williams deeply resented it. Early in 1839 he published Tract Eighty-seven, which he hoped would clarify as well as continue his original argument. This effort was somewhat blunted by the same stylistic faults which flawed its predecessor; it was also twice as long as Number Eighty. Yet in his peroration Williams put clearly, beautifully, and with all the candour one could want, his basic position.

This reserve by which God discloses himself . . . proves the entrance to be narrow and confined. . . . It is not by speculative enquiry, nor learned research but by deepest humiliation of soul and body that we must feel after him, and expect pain and trouble in doing so, knowing that he is "a consuming fire," and therefore will burn up what is human about us as we approach him. . . . Such reflections should encourage in us habits of reverence, reserve and fear, as considering the awful dispensation under which we walk. . . . If we wish to do good to the world we must not look to it but unto God; the bad instruments of the world (such as the daily periodical) must not be ours; the platform is not our strength, nay even in the pulpit itself is not our chief strength; in these we must yield to others if they wish it; but our chief strength must be the altar; it must be in sacraments and prayers and a good life to give efficacy to them; and in secret alms to the poor to buy their prayers which have great power with God. Our strength must be in secret where God is.[62]

It can be argued that Williams' Tracts on reserve brought the Oxford Movement's program to its climax. All the essentials of it can be discerned in his exasperatingly diffuse pages. There was first of all the accent on interior religion; understanding, said Williams, followed upon a clean heart. To want to know everything at once, to want to experience the touch of God in the emotional aftermath of a fiery sermon is at best an illusion and at worst a grave sin of presumption. Related to this idea was Williams' view of the sacramental aspect of the Christian dispensation; the Church's chief vehicles of grace are themselves an instance of reserve—that is, one cannot in the sacraments see or sense or grasp the whole reality signified, but one moves step by step, day by day, towards communion with God as he is in himself.

Williams also insisted upon the importance of practical as opposed to speculative knowledge. This was always a basic Tractarian tenet; it was, in a sense, Keble writ large. And around this idea swung not only Williams' argument but the whole Tractarian ethos. Reserve does not mean the absence of speculation but rather the situating of speculation within its proper sphere. Therefore, the objection that reserve was a means to muzzle the full impact of revelation missed Williams' main point: that knowledge for the Christian is not abstract but concrete—knowledge almost in the biblical sense of intercourse. Williams claimed that he was not saying, Thou shalt not teach such and so, but rather, My knowledge of Christ and my life of virtue are correlative, feeding one another, and it is wrong to think that one can safely outstrip the other.

Nor should it be overlooked that reserve fitted nicely the tastes and attitudes of the Tractarians. Reserve automatically ruled out display—whether of the ranting Protestant preacher or the papist flagellant—and it inculcated austerity of speech and action, reserve, that is, in the ordinary sense of the word. Understatement was the atmosphere at Bisley and Hursley, the places Williams loved most. To him and the other Tractarians self-containment was naturally congenial. They were mostly country gentlemen to whom flamboyance smacked of the vulgar. Reserve, on the other hand, whether natural or religious, suited them perfectly.

The Bishop of Gloucester condemned the Tracts on reserve without reading them. Their title was abhorrent enough as far as his lordship was concerned. This episcopal reaction proved to be an omen of the wrath to come. In the summer of 1838, when the Movement stood at its zenith, that wrath was very close. But at least this had been accomplished: with Williams' Tracts on reserve the Tractarian position had been stated fully; all that could be said had been said, and anyone who, unlike the Bishop of Gloucester, wanted to know what it was all about, could find out. In all likelihood, however, Tom Mozley spoke for many of the most ardent spirits when he recalled that moment: "Certainly very few of us could say where we meant to stop or what we had in view as the future of the Church of England. For my own part, I never knew where it was all to end, except somewhere in the first three centuries of the Church and I have to confess that I knew very little indeed about them."[63]

PART III

The Parting of Friends
1839–45

CHAPTER 14

"What a Squall Has Overtaken Us!"

Frederic Rogers was still a Fellow of Oriel, but as the 1830s progressed his law career kept him more and more in London. There, at his club or in the courts or while passing by chance through St. Paul's Churchyard, he often heard people who did not know of his Oxford connections discussing the thriving Tract Movement. He took understandable pleasure in this and reported it happily to Newman as an omen of prosperity. On at least one occasion, however, he added a monitum: "I hear people talk of the desirableness of some systematic or at least compendious, statement of what you really do teach."[1]

Rogers usually gave sound advice and this time was no exception. The Tractarians by 1838 had already produced an immense literature, and still there was no one source to which the curious and the misinformed might go to find out precisely what essential tenets they shared. And Rogers knew, no doubt better than his Oxford friends, that the ranks of the misinformed were growing fast. This failure to provide a "systematic or compendious statement" of Tractarian doctrine stemmed to a large extent from the original genius of the Movement which resisted formal instruments of control and relied instead on the integrity and freedom of the individual contributor, responsible only, in Keble's phrase, by reason of his canonical obedience. To be sure, an informal directorate had inevitably developed in the place of the board of censors which William Palmer had wanted in 1833. The triumvirate of Newman, Pusey and Keble for all practical purposes determined what the Movement stood for and, perhaps more important, they decided who could speak for it. But none of them had come up with a Tractarian manual.

It is possible that Rogers was thinking of William Palmer when he made his suggestion. During 1838 Palmer, now more or less estranged from the Tractarians, had published his *Treatise on the Church of Christ*. These two volumes contained a methodical presentation of what has come to be called the "Branch Theory"—the notion that the one Church of Christ may include several distinct branches (Roman, Greek and English), each one genuine, though at odds with the others, so long as it maintains the primitive faith and the apostolic succession. Nothing could have been more systematic than Palmer's high and rather dry statement, and though it expressed some common views with the Tractarian position, in its rigid and speculative character it was quite different. Palmer, Newman had said, "was never really one of us"; and when he had scanned the book he confided to Bowden, "Have you seen Palmer's book? It is quite overcoming—his reading—and makes one feel quite ashamed. It will do a great deal of good, for just at this moment we need ballast."[2] With this faint praise, Palmer was dismissed. Events had carried everyone concerned a long way from Hadleigh.

Of the four who had met at Hadleigh in that far-off summer of 1833, Froude was dead, Rose was dying, Palmer had taken his own tack, and Arthur Perceval had come to the correct conclusion that nobody paid any attention to him. He quarreled first with Rose,[3] and though his relations with Newman and Keble remained cordial enough, it was clear that they were less than interested in his views. This was especially true of a pet project of Perceval's, the revival of Convocation. This legislative body of the Anglican clergy (not to be confused with the assembly of M.A.'s at Oxford) had been an empty formality since early in the eighteenth century, and Perceval among many others thought that if revived it might serve as an instrument of saving the Church from the Whigs. He pressed this point with Keble and Newman over several years, but to no avail. The Tractarians took the position that Convocation threatened the apostolic prerogatives of the bishops and therefore would have no part in it. Now and then Perceval, who desperately wanted to be counted among Tractarian policy makers, threatened to speak out independently, especially on the Convocation issue. He hoped thereby to get a hearing for his ideas at Oxford or Hursley. Instead he received bland assurances that he should of course say anything he pleased. The implication was that what he said could not matter less.

Towards the end of 1838, Perceval's sense of isolation reached a height, driven there perhaps by Williams' Tract on reserve and the publication of Froude's *Remains*. He complained bitterly to Keble and apparently told him of an article he had written critical of the Tractarians. Keble replied in kind. "Whatever you have said," Keble wrote, "I am sure you have said in a kind and courteous spirit and manner." Anyway such a statement from Perceval was bound to do good if it only showed that those who agreed on many great matters were not borne "slavishly along in anybody's wake."

But I don't quite understand what you allude to when you say that private remonstrance has failed. Do you mean that neither Pusey nor Newman has published a recantation of their supposed errors? Or that the Tracts are not stopped? Or what reasonable expectation have you failed in which makes you thus speak like a person in authority who had been treated with less respect than he ought to be?

We cannot recant, Keble concluded, unless we are convinced we are wrong or unless we are told to do so by ecclesiastical authority. In the meantime, "we must take our chance of reproof and exposure, and be thankful when it is administered in so friendly a spirit as yours no doubt will be."[4]

I

The trouble really started with Tract Seventy-five. It was titled "On the Roman Breviary as embodying the Substance of the Devotional Services of the Church Catholic." The bulk of this lengthy Tract was a translation of excerpts from the breviary's temporal and sanctoral cycles. Newman wrote an historical introduction, drawing chiefly on William Palmer's *Origines Liturgicae*. In the breviary, he maintained, as in so many other matters, the Roman Church took to herself and corrupted what was once the common Christian heritage. Yet, though corrupted, the prayer service of the Ancient Church was less mutilated in the breviary than elsewhere, and since the Romish interpolations and legends were easily discernible, Newman argued that the breviary remained useful for study and private devotion.[5]

The point made in the introduction to Number Seventy-five echoed Newman's complaint to Rose that affection for the Church of England was hard in the light of all that England had by default given up to Rome. And it understood too that in Newman's mind what had been given up was primarily an organized devotional life. The ascetic preoccupation of the Tractarians cannot be overemphasized. Their speculative arguments never ranked in importance with their pleas for prayer, self-denial, sacramental practice and the whole apparatus which for Roman Catholics was a systematic approach to a supernatural vocation. The Ancient Church was to be studied indeed, but above all it was to be imitated.

Tract Seventy-five appeared in late June 1836, shortly after Newman had been given Froude's breviaries as a memento of his dead friend. The recitation of the breviary—stripped of course of its Marian and other "exaggerations"—became from that time on a part of Newman's daily schedule. Nor did he hesitate to recommend its use to his friends and disciples. He told Henry Wilberforce early in 1837, "The breviary devotions take up from three to four hours a day, a time which may be easily redeemed from the world. I like them uncommonly. They are very unexciting, grave and simple."[6] To Newman's "astonishment," Tract Seventy-five's first edition (750 copies) was sold out within a few months.[7]

It was a small step from Tract Seventy-five to the idea of a complete edition of the Roman breviary for use by Anglicans. Newman encouraged several of his disciples to undertake this task and offered to translate the breviary hymns himself. By Lent of 1837 Samuel Wood and Robert Williams, a young alumnus of Oriel and since 1835 a member of the House of Commons, were hard at work on the translation. But the Tractarian ranks were far from agreed on the matter. Charles Marriott by chance met Williams in London and he wrote to Newman in some alarm: "I hope [Williams] will not get too much loose from his Anglicanism in his breviary work. I am sure we must not only take care of ourselves but keep close under our good mother's care or we shall get into mischief." Williams had been quoted to Marriott as dismissing William Palmer's work as "mere Anglicanism etc. Now I cannot help," observed the mild Charles Marriott, "being a little angry at this, for I hope Anglicanism is Catholicism in England, though it be something short of Autocatholicism. I cannot help liking to see Palmer clamber up into the camp of the Philistines like Jonathan and set them all cutting their own throats."[8]

Keble too seemed uneasy over the breviary project. In publishing a translation he thought it imperative to insert some caution or warning about objectionable parts; otherwise, he said, it "seems to me disrespectful to God and his saints and uncharitable to many persons—I do not mean Protestants but ill-informed persons generally."[9] Part of Keble's hesitancy could be traced to Bisley where his brother and especially George Prevost, his brother's close associate, had grave reservations about the prudence of the whole idea.

Keble was worried about something else, too. If the Tract on the breviary sold astonishingly well, the same could not be said for Froude's *Remains*. By August 1838, after five months on the market, only 360 copies had been sold. Keble could not understand it, "considering how everyone everywhere seems to be talking of the book—but I presume they talk without reading."[10] This presumption was doubtless correct, as it indeed would have been a year or two before with regard to Hampden's Bampton Lectures. Keble discovered that many of his friends among the country clergy were put off by the *Remains*, even when they admitted the "beauty" of the book. John Miller, a venerable High Church parson and a longtime associate of Joshua Watson, wrote Keble that he wanted nothing more to do with the Tractarians. "I do not see," sniffed Keble, "that he speaks from conviction. No doubt he will think better of it one of these days." Closer to home, George Moberly decided to withdraw his name from the list of translators for the Library of the Fathers. "He gives all manner of reasons, but I suppose he thinks it would hardly suit his present position to embark so openly (so people might represent it) in our bout."[11] Moberly, once a don and tutor at Balliol, had become increasingly intimate with Keble since his appointment as Headmaster of nearby Winchester Preparatory School. Though Keble was chagrined by Moberly's attitude, he took consolation from old Archdeacon Froude's firmness. A visit to Dartington convinced Keble that the archdeacon was weathering his trials well and did not seem to mind "the things that are said and written" about the *Remains*. His sister, Hurrell's aunt, gave Keble the impression that the book "was the greatest comfort to them."[12]

But it was small comfort to most people, including some of the Tractarians' most cordial admirers. An instructive example of the reaction raised by the publication of the *Remains* was that of the Reverend Edward Churton. An elegant, scholarly clergyman, Churton had been a friend of Pusey's at Christ Church and had endorsed the aims of the Movement ever since its beginning. After reading the *Remains*, however, he was badly shaken. The book, he told Pusey, "was an error of friendship and . . . has laid open your friends and you to attacks which you might have, not dishonourably, declined."[13] He quarreled with both Pusey and Newman over the matter during the summer of 1838, and then wrote Pusey shortly afterwards: "I have often thought of our last interview. If, in the strong feeling of regret which the first reading of poor Froude's *Remains* excited I expressed myself beyond the licence of a friend, let it be considered unsaid. I must still own that there are sentences and even pages of that book which I could wish almost to have lost my right hand sooner than have seen published." Yet Churton was more sad than angry, and he hoped that the *Remains* resulted from a momentary aberration that could be swiftly forgotten. What he feared was that the Tractarians were about to embark upon a new extravagant line which would leave the Apostolic cause at the mercy of liberals and Evangelicals. "I think I see something of the false principles, and wide ramifications of false principles, by which this age is misguided, and I wish to be more and more in heart and hand with those who are applying the true correction."[14]

Churton was laying down a threat as much as he was offering an olive branch. Still, his position was essentially friendly and his complaints private. Not so the organs hostile to the Movement. The *Edinburgh* published a savage review, and other voices across the land took up the cry that Froude, in his exaggerations and scrupulosity, in his contempt for the Reformation and for the ideal of liberal progress, betrayed the latent Romanism of the Tractarian system. Perhaps the shrillest condemnation of all came from that place so closely connected with the fortunes of the Oxford Movement, the pulpit of the Church of St. Mary the Virgin.

On May 20, 1838, Dr. Godfrey Faussett, Lady Margaret Professor of Divinity, preached a university sermon on the "Revival of Popery." His immediate target was Froude's *Remains*. This "offensive publication," said

Dr. Faussett, not only contained "startling and extravagant passages" which themselves might have been excused, but it also propagated a hatred for Protestantism and a sickly hankering after "rigid mortifications and painful penances." He then widened his indictment to include the "formidable conspiracy" of Froude's friends who represented "an increasing aberration from Protestant principles," "a disposition to overvalue the importance of apostolical tradition," and "a tendency to depreciate the principles of Protestantism" and to "palliate" the "errors of popery."[15]

The day after Faussett's sermon appeared in printed form, Newman, in the white heat of an energy of which, when roused, he was capable all his life, wrote a reply. It left Faussett's hysterical argument in shreds. Froude had indeed expressed strongly his distaste for Protestantism but he had not by that fact committed himself to Rome. Quite to the contrary, he had spoken of desiring the "total overthrow" of the Roman system, and when a friend had spoken of Romanists as schismatics in England and Catholics abroad, Froude had replied, "No, they are wretched Tridentines everywhere."[16] Newman quoted these sentiments from the *Remains* and others like them to counter Faussett's charge of popery. The bulk of the pamphlet dealt once more with the distinction which the Tractarians had to make endlessly, that Catholicism meant the sacramental system and not the corruption of Rome. Faussett, for example, had sneered at the use of the word "altar." "The body of the English Church has for three centuries past called the Lord's table an altar," Newman fired back, "though the word is not in our formularies. I think a man wrong who says it is not an altar, but I will not denounce him; I will not write in a hostile tone against any person or any work which does not, as I think, contradict the Articles or the Prayer Book."[17]

Faussett was no match for Newman as a controversialist. He asserted without proving his assertions and down on top of him fell the wrathful combination of learning, literary skill and restrained passion which were Newman's rhetorical stock-in-trade. An amusing confirmation of this was the statistic that Newman's answer outsold by half Faussett's original charge. "I have sold *at the same time* 750 to his 500. Who would have thought," Newman asked James Mozley, "persons would buy an *answer* without a *question*?"[18]

Keble meanwhile continued to fret at Hursley that the *Remains* did not sell. "The more I look at the *Remains* the more I wonder at their not selling. They seem to be so very interesting. No doubt papers like the *Edinburgh*, Faussett's sermon etc. have a certain effect."[19] After some hesitation, however, it was decided—despite second thoughts by Archdeacon Froude—to forge ahead and publish the second part of the *Remains*, which appeared, with Keble's preface, in 1839. Curiously, it sold well right from the beginning. Rumbles were heard from the direction of the Lady Margaret Professor, but Newman did not take them seriously. "Old Faussett," he told John Bowden, "started half off his seat when he heard of the new volumes [of the *Remains*], as if he should say, 'Why, I annihilated Mr. F.'s writings last year. What is meant by the absurdity of continuing them?' "[20]

II

The stir caused by the publication of Froude's *Remains* was not, however, limited to sedate literary and academic circles. Towards the end of July 1838 Lord Morpeth delivered a violent speech in Parliament in which he decried the popish tendencies he discerned at Oxford and singled out specifically the villainy of Newman as editor of the *Remains*. In the House of Commons young William Gladstone offered a defense of the Tractarians, while Sir Robert Harry Inglis, member for the university, insisted that Oxford was not becoming a less loyal child of the Reformation. "Over hasty Sir Robert!" commented Frederic Rogers jauntily.[21]

Newman did not care what the politicians said, and he was confident that he could successfully repel any attack from the likes of Faussett or *The Edinburgh Review*. But given his principles there was one person whose disapproval he could not sustain. That person was his bishop. The whole Tractarian edifice, as Newman had helped to shape it, rested upon acceptance of the bishops as the lineal successors of the apostles. As Newman once expressed it, he had no vicar of Christ save his bishop. "To suffer my bishop to breathe a word against me would be to put myself in a false position. Depend upon it our strength (as of every thing or person, political, religious, philosophical) is *consistency*."[22]

The Lord Bishop of Oxford, Richard Bagot,[23] was a mild, courteous, friendly man whose lack of activity earned him the nickname "King Log" among his clergy. He was a nobleman who had passed through Rugby and Christ Church at the turn of the century, had held a fellowship at All Souls for a brief time, had married a daughter of the Earl of Jersey, and then had begun his climb up the ladder of ecclesiastical preferment. His first living—a parish in Staffordshire—was the gift of his father. He became successively Canon of Worcester, Canon of Windsor, Dean of Canterbury, and, in 1829, upon the death of Charles Lloyd, Bishop of Oxford. In 1838 he was fifty-six years old.

Bishop Bagot was a High and Dry Tory who disliked the Whig-liberals as much for their bad manners as for their evil tenets. He denounced the Ecclesiastical Commission of 1836 as an act of aggression against the Church and the English constitution. These and similar views, which were occasionally proclaimed at the episcopal palace at Cuddesdon, made it safe to assume that the bishop was basically in sympathy with Tractarian aims, at least in the beginning. Perhaps he was startled by the vehemence with which the Tractarians exalted his office and that of his colleagues on the episcopal bench; but then he may rather have liked being called a successor of the apostles even if he could not imagine anyone understanding the term literally. He would have been dismayed had he known just how literally John Newman took the title and how the thought of it moved him: "Sometimes when I have stood by as [the bishop] put on his robes, I felt it would have been such a relief if I could have fallen at his feet and kissed them."[24]

Happily for Bishop Bagot's composure the Vicar of St. Mary's successfully resisted this impulse. Meanwhile, the bishop said nothing whatever about the Movement; he neither praised it nor condemned it. He was unfailingly kind to the Tractarians whenever he happened to meet them. In 1836, when the church at Littlemore was consecrated, Newman's friends were uneasy that the bishop, who presided at the ceremony, might find certain features of the new building "papistical," like the stone altar with crosses over it and the pulpit illegally destitute of appurtenances. "However, his Lordship was highly pleased and complimentary, and everything went off in the greatest style."[25] Bagot on this occasion praised especially Newman's sermon, which, he said, gave him "sincere delight."[26] A little more than a year later Newman dedicated his volume on *Justification* to the bishop, who once more responded graciously if noncommittally. On the whole, though the Tractarians might have wished for more active support from the Bishop of Oxford, they could at the same time console themselves that he did nothing to obstruct them.

Then, in 1838, the bishop decided to break the silence of five years. He delivered that summer a kind of pastoral letter to his clergy called a Charge in which he discussed various concerns of the diocese, including the Tracts. As was usually the case, the Charge was given orally first, as part of a formal diocesan visitation, and then afterwards published. Some bishops charged their dioceses annually, but Bagot was more inert in this regard as in many others, and the very infrequency of his public policy statements lent them added interest.

But the Tracts were by no means the primary business on his mind. In the general realignment of dioceses undertaken by the Ecclesiastical Commission, Bagot to his distress found his jurisdiction doubled by the addition of the whole county of Berkshire. "I am visiting an altered diocese," he cried, "altered in every way!" The bulk of the Charge was taken up with a denunciation of the Commission—"a power as irresponsible as it is gigantic, . . . which before long must supersede all other authority in the Church, and whose decrees are issued in such a manner as to render expostulation and remonstrance unavailing. . . . Their acts . . . seem to me to be every way full of peril to the Church."[27]

Only towards the end of the Charge did Bagot leave the subject of administrative problems to touch upon other matters.

With reference to errors in *doctrine*, which have been imputed to the series of publications called the *Tracts for the Times*, it can hardly be expected that, on an occasion like the present, I should enter into or give a handle to anything which might hereafter tend to controversial discussions. But, generally speaking, I may say that in these days of lax and spurious liberality anything which tends to recall forgotten truths is *valuable*; and where these publications have directed men's minds to such important subjects as the union, the discipline and the authority of the Church, I think they have done good service.

Yet the bishop felt it necessary to add a word of caution.

But there may be some points in which, perhaps from ambiguity of expression or similar causes, it is not impossible but that evil rather than the intended good may be produced on minds of a peculiar temperament. I have more fear of the disciples than of the teachers. In speaking therefore of the authors of the Tracts in question, I would say that I think their desire to restore the ancient discipline of the Church most praiseworthy; I rejoice in their attempts to secure a stricter attention to the rubrical directions in the Book of Common Prayer; and I heartily approve of the fasts and festivals of The Church. But I would implore them, by the purity of their intentions, to be cautious both in their writings and their actions to take heed lest their good be evil spoken of; lest in their exertions to re-establish unity they unhappily create fresh schism; lest in their admiration of antiquity they revert to practices which heretofore have ended in superstition.[28]

Bagot probably congratulated himself at the nicely balanced moderation of his statement. He had been besieged by anonymous letters calling upon him to check a revival of popery in his diocese. He had found no substantiation for such charges but he asked those against whom they were made to tread cautiously lest they invite evils which the bishop was sure they did not intend.

But Newman, who heard the Charge on August 14th, thought otherwise. He was stunned at Bagot's ambiguity, particularly because rumour around Oxford had had it that the bishop intended to come down squarely on the Tractarian side. Newman wrote immediately to Keble and described the relevant passages, concluding with weary disappointment:

Now does it not seem rather hard that he should publicly attack things in the Tracts without speaking to me about them privately? Again, what good does it do to fling an indefinite suspicion over them when in the main they are orthodox? Then again, it seems hard that those who work and while working necessarily commit mistakes, instead of being thanked for that work, which others do *not* do, are blamed. It is very comfortable to do nothing and to criticize.[29]

A few days later Newman explained to Henry Wilberforce the line of action which the Charge had led him to take. "The bishop has been delivering a very strong and good Charge, but while taking a number of good things *from the Tracts,* as *we* would say, he has given the said Tracts a leetle, very leetle wipe [*sic*]. He has said there are expressions in them which may be of disservice to certain minds; and by not saying what, he has thrown a vague suspicion over them all." Perhaps, Newman went on, the bishop considers this a most gentle check, but "he does not seem to understand that by my principles, and still more by my professions as exhibited in the said Tracts, I cannot be party to anything he censures in cathedra, ever so slightly." Therefore Newman wrote Bagot and asked him to state which Tracts were objectionable, and if the bishop should refuse to specify, then all the Tracts would have to be suppressed "with as much speed as is convenient."[30]

Keble endorsed this general strategy. "I quite agree with you that it would be *impossible* to go with this kind of indefinite censure." But he pointed out to Newman that in all likelihood the bishop had meant nothing definite, simply because bishops seldom did. "It seems a pity to make him commit himself. . . . You see, he will hate to be driven into responsibility, at least if he is like most of his station." As for Newman's complaint about those who criticize without doing anything themselves, it "is too just. But," Keble gently reminded him, "you had counted the cost before and knew it would be so."[31]

Keble proved to be quite correct. A few days later, after the offer had been made to him, Bishop Bagot wrote to Newman in astonishment that anyone could have construed his remarks as a censure. "Certainly no person whom *I* have met, or who heard my Charge, viewed that part of it in the light in which it appears to have struck you. . . . Although I should not have been surprised at dissatisfaction expressed by those who differ widely from the Tracts at my *approbation of so much,* I little thought that I could have given pain to the other side by the caution I gave them to avoid the possibility of misrepresentation." The bishop went on to protest that withdrawal of the Tracts would not be "quite fair to me, as it would make me appear to have said or done that which I really have not."[32] Poor Bagot had not expected so relentless an interpretation of his rather obscure admonition. And what made it all the more embarrassing and perplexing to him was that it was done for the sake of and out of respect for his own apostolic position.

The crisis passed as quickly as it had risen. Pusey persuaded Newman to draw back from pressing the matter, and the bishop assured everyone how happy he was at the tone of the discussion. Keble summed up the furore succinctly: "The bishop has clearly fallen into the error of which you suspected him," he wrote to Newman, "using words of course without any definite application; and moreover, seeing how little most of us care for the sentiments of our diocesan, he has naturally enough assumed that his words would not be taken as they were uttered and is now startled to find that they are so."[33] When the Charge appeared a few weeks later in printed form a footnote had been added to the section in which the Tracts were discussed. "As I have been led to suppose," wrote the Lord Bishop of Oxford, "that the above passage has been misunderstood, I take this opportunity of stating that it never was my intention therein to pass any *general censure* on the Tracts for the Times."[34]

III

The storm cloud raised by Bishop Bagot's Charge of 1838 sank behind the horizon. But all the world knew that it still hovered there, and the Tractarians soon grew aware of the rise of a cold, shifting wind which made Newman exclaim a few months later, "What a squall has overtaken us!"[35]

Prominent among the dark signs of trouble was the business of the Martyrs' Memorial. "They talk," Pusey told Benjamin Harrison on October 10, 1838, "of building a Church of the Martyrs here [in Oxford], which, emanating from Golightly, . . . is nothing but a cut at us. So we [Anglicans] too have begun canonizing! Only instead of being done by the Church it is done by one or two individuals. And we are to have churches of St. Latimer, St. Cranmer and St. Ridley."[36]

The project to erect a monument to the memory of the three leading English Protestants executed during Queen Mary's reign had indeed come from the nimble brain of Charles P. Golightly. A small group which met at Golightly's home early in the autumn of 1838 decided that such a tribute to the Reformation would serve a double purpose: First, it would enkindle renewed devotion to the Protestant character of the Church of England, and second, it would neatly catch the Tractarians on the horns of a dilemma. Those who subscribed to the monument would thereby detach themselves from the anti-Protestantism published, for instance, in Pusey's and Isaac Williams' Tracts and particularly in Froude's *Remains*. If, on the other hand, they refused to subscribe, they would open themselves to accusations of Roman sympathies.

It is no comment on the fervour of Golightly's Protestantism to recall his quarrel with Newman over the Littlemore curacy. And that quarrel in turn had risen out of Golightly's public denunciation of Pusey. To take a good swipe at the Tractarians therefore was a deed which could give Golightly personal as well as ideological satisfaction. He pursued his objective relentlessly and, though the idea of a martyrs' church was eventually abandoned, a widespread subscription brought in enough to pay for an addition to the Oxford Church of St. Mary Magdalen and for the ornate monument which still stands just to the west of Balliol College.

Nobody doubted that Golightly's prime target was the editors of Froude's *Remains*, but as it turned out it was Pusey who bore the brunt of the attack. Newman remained adamant from beginning to end; he would have nothing to do with the subscription, which he judged to be simply a trap. Keble, though more open to discussion on the matter, ended up in basically the same frame of mind. "I am not at all prepared," he told Pusey, "to express a public dissent from Froude in his opinion of the Reformers *as a party*."[37] Pusey for his part would not have dreamed of dissociating himself from his colleagues at a moment of public excitement.

But the pressures put upon him were considerable. They came first from friends and allies like Harrison, Sewell and Edward Churton, who urged that the Tractarians must give evidence of their genuine anti-Roman feelings unless they wanted to forfeit the trust of the country. To endorse the Martyrs' Memorial was an ideal way to accomplish this, because what it involved was a gesture which denounced the Roman fanaticism of Bloody Mary without involving the acceptance of the offensive tenets of the Reformers whom she burned to death. Churton put this argument in a letter to Newman: "The only difference between us and the ultra [-Protestants] ought to be that we both honour the martyrs, but we think we know why and they do not. I live out of the way of these jars, but I am disgusted to see the quantity of small abuse current against men that I esteem, and [I] pray you, by the public cause in which we are all engaged, not to give such blockheads an advantage when there is no occasion."[38]

Newman remained unmoved by Churton's esteem and by his categorization of Golightly and his friends as "blockheads." Pusey, however, attempted to find some means of accommodation. He suggested various alterations of the plan which would not commit subscribers to anything more than regard for the providential part played by the sixteenth-century Reformers in the life of the Church. But by November 1838 he had pretty well given up. "It has been altogether a very unfortunate business," he wrote to Harrison, "as was likely since it originated in wrong and unkind feelings."[39] To Bishop Bagot he explained that "this plan of a monument was *devised* only to serve as a party purpose: it was in fact (as some of themselves avow) a counter movement against Froude's *Remains*, or, as one of them said, 'it will be a good cut against Newman.' . . . I regret the plan because it has seemed to me . . . the great blessing of our Reformation that we are not (as the Lutherans and Calvinists are) connected with any human founder or bound up with his human infirmities. We are neither Cranmerites nor Ridleyites but an apostolic branch of the Church Catholic; and I fear lest this plan should tend to increase the vulgar impression that we were a new Church at the Reformation instead of being the old one purified."[40]

The bishop, however, was alarmed by the rift which the memorial project was causing in his diocese. Just after the new year, he called on Pusey informally at Christ Church and asked him to reconsider, saying "in his kind and painfully diffident way" that the Tractarians' adhesion to the project "would be *invaluable* to the Church at this moment." Pusey countered by proposing to let his name appear as a subscriber if it was made clear that he did so in deference to the bishop's wishes. He could not, of course, commit Newman and Keble to do even this much. Bagot not unnaturally refused an offer with such strings attached. It would, he said, "neither be satisfactory to yourself or to me, nor would it tend to do good. . . . Let me entreat you, then," the bishop added with unusual vigour, "by the love which (in spite of the assertions of your opposers in these days of misrepresentation) I am convinced you feel for our reformed Church, if you cannot approve the memorial, to make some declaration . . . such as shall stop the accusations of your being in any degree hostile to the Reformation [and] enable your friends to defend you from such charges."[41]

The bishop's appeal led Pusey to suggest a fanciful plan for an alternate memorial, a church to be built in honour of the Holy Trinity "and in humble acknowledgment of the Good Providence of Almighty God over his Church in this land, and of his manifold blessings vouchsafed to her at the time of the Reformation." He cheerfully estimated that a subscription of ten thousand pounds could pay for such a monument, which, he thought, would detach people from Golightly's project. Keble agreed to contribute one hundred pounds though he thought Pusey's hopes extravagant to say the least. When Pusey applied to the bishop for endorsement, Bagot patiently explained to him that to support two competing fund drives would only contribute to the partisanship he was trying to avoid.[42] So Pusey dropped his idea and contented himself with a pamphlet—"A Letter to the Bishop of Oxford"—in which the same old ground of the catholicity of the English Church was gone over once again.

By February 1839 Golightly's project had achieved its purpose, and Keble wrote Newman from Hursley with a mixed sense of relief and apprehension. "I am heartily glad [Pusey's idea for a church] is put by if it was to have the effect you seem to apprehend, of separating us more or less from the *Remains*. On some accounts I caught at it, but always with the feeling you expressed, that 'our strength is to sit still.' I really sometimes feel sorry for the self-blame which people like Harrison, Miller etc. must suffer when they come to see that history [of the Reformation] in its true light."[43]

IV

Perhaps Keble might have spared some sympathy for Bishop Bagot, who remained patient and courteous in the face of Tractarian subtleties, which he could not possibly have understood, and of wildly grandiose schemes to build monumental churches in his diocese. For that matter, Keble might have felt a bit sorry for himself, because at the same time the Martyrs' Memorial was pending a gale was blowing up within the Movement itself, and Keble stood right in the middle of it.

The trouble had been brewing for some time, but it did not reach a head until after the publication of the *Remains* and the proposal to publish the Roman breviary. The Bisley group—Thomas Keble, Isaac Williams, George Prevost and one or two others—had long been suspicious of their Oxford allies and especially of Newman. They considered themselves, with good reason, as representative of the country clergy who would have to be the backbone of any English Catholic renewal. Newman, they thought, because he lived in a more rarefied academic atmosphere, did not appreciate the hard realities of the ordinary parochial ministry which was their daily lot. He was too cerebral, too subtle and he moved too fast. Perhaps they thought also that he dragged along their hero, John Keble, too freely in his wake.

It is impossible to say how much of their resentment came from personal pique, but one direction it took can be discerned in what Williams told Pusey in August 1838. Williams had received a letter from Frederic Rogers in which it was proposed that a hundred pounds be raised to commission a marble bust of Newman. Tom Keble owned himself "proud and happy to subscribe," but Williams had his doubts and so he sought Pusey's advice.

For I have myself quite shrunk from it in a way that I hardly thought would have been possible with any opinion of Rogers'. Prevost takes the same view of it as myself. I need not mention to you any of the many thoughts which occur to one in the way of objection, for you will at once understand them— as, for instance, are we helping each other in the attainment of that humility which we know will have the highest place hereafter by a thing of this kind.[44]

Williams claimed that he was interested in Pusey's "unbiased" opinion, and such no doubt was the case. He may also have hoped to head off the project by enlisting Pusey's opposition to it. If so, his efforts were in vain. By 1840 the bust was completed, and Williams had to console himself as best he could with the knowledge that the work had been done without Newman's cooperation.

While Williams was bewailing this assault upon humility, Tom Keble was in the midst of an increasingly acrimonious correspondence with Newman. It had begun with Tom's objections to a passage in Newman's pamphlet against Faussett and then had widened into other areas. When Bishop Bagot's Charge appeared and Newman threatened to withdraw the Tracts, Tom wrote him an irritatingly contradictory admonition in which he recommended both that Newman should "go out of Oxford somewhere or other for a time and forget Faussett, etc.," and that he should not cease publishing the Tracts.[45] Other letters passed between the two which deepened the misunderstanding.

Then early in November Prevost wrote Newman "protesting in strong terms against the Breviary being published." It was a harsh letter and Newman answered in a similar spirit. Then he wrote John Keble to say "that though I did not feel that Prevost's opposition was an insurmountable objection, I could translate no more hymns without your leave."[46] The whole breviary project, he added, would be canceled if Keble gave the word. Shortly afterwards Newman shot off another missive to Hursley. "I wish parties would seriously ask themselves what they desire of me. Is it to stop writing? I will stop anything you advise. Is it to show what I write to others before publishing? It is my rule already."

Now this being understood [Newman continued], may I not fairly ask for some little confidence in me as to what, under these voluntary restrictions, I do? People should really put themselves into my place, and consider how the appearance of suspicion, jealousy and discontent is likely to affect one who is most conscious that everything he does is imperfect, and therefore soon begins to suspect everything he does to have no heart and little power to do anything at all. . . . Is such conduct kind towards me? . . . If I ought to stop, I am ready to stop, but do not in the same breath chide me (for instance) for thinking of stopping the Tracts, and then be severe on the Tracts which are actually published. . . . I feel that if I am met with loud remonstrances before gentle hints are tried, and if suspicions go before proofs, I shall very soon be silenced whether persons wish it or no.[47]

John Keble moved more swiftly than was his custom, but his first attempts to heal the wounds were not very successful. He passed on to Newman a letter of Tom's in which the Bisley group's objections to the breviary project were more clearly drawn. Newman answered by protesting that, though he wanted to smooth things over, his "view about Prevost's letter is *substantially* what it was. . . ." Tom Keble also apparently suggested that a board of ten revisers be set up to pass on Tractarian publications, and to this plan, so reminiscent of William Palmer's proposal back in 1833, Newman claimed to have "no objection except what seems to me its impracticability." Then he added, somewhat stiffly: "Will your brother allow more than one or two out of all our friends [to sit on the board]? . . . Are *all* the articles in the *British Critic* to have a second reviser after myself?" In Newman's mind there was no illusion as to what Tom Keble's plan involved: "It is virtually enjoining silence, which if it is to be done had better be done openly."[48]

And so the old question, wrestled with so many times before, came up again. Was responsibility within the Movement to be an individual or a corporate affair? John Keble's basic sympathies lay with Newman and the individual approach. Keble had helped fight off Palmer's attempt at joint censorship five years before, and it was he, after all, who first employed the sanctified phrase "canonical obedience" to describe the Tractarian mode of operation. Yet at the same time he realized with his brother that the situation had drastically changed since 1833 when all the writers so to speak began even. The country clergy in 1838 could not prevent Newman (or Pusey) from printing anything; whatever it was it became immediately identified as Tractarian material. Newman exer-

cised an informal but practically complete control over Tractarian publishing ventures, which meant in effect that Newman could commit large
numbers of people without consulting them. Newman might protest, as
he did, "that your brother knows the country clergy and makes their
feelings his standard, . . . but I do not write for them. . . . I write for
those I do see, namely the generation . . . rising into active life, particularly at Oxford. . . . I do not consider that for them I am going too
fast."[49]

John Keble's problem was compounded by the affection he felt for
both the principals of the quarrel. No one in the world, except his wife,
was dearer to him than his brother and Newman. But since no one else
could possibly bring the two together, it was up to John Keble to speak
out candidly. He gently chided Newman for his lack of respect for the
country clergy, for his failure to grasp how important the parsons of
England were if the hopes of the Movement were to be fulfilled, and in
the typical Keble manner he suggested that the "fidget" from which
Newman presently suffered would soon pass away. Newman must recognize, Keble went on, that he is "naturally very sensitive," and "on reflection" he will see "that nothing unfriendly could be intended" by Tom
or Prevost. There are some disagreements "as to the amount of deference
due to primitive antiquity in those points in which the English Church
does not expressly follow it," and as a result "we said and thought"
some things which "appear extravagant" to others. Finally, said Keble,
Newman should be prepared to take these remonstrances from the Bisley
group as warnings that perhaps other people were not going so far as he.

To his brother he spoke rather more forcefully.

I want you to consider [John wrote Tom, November 28, 1838] whether you
and Prevost . . . are quite doing justice to Newman in the sort of exceptions
which for some time past (I think ever since the *Remains*) you have made about
his proceedings. You have talked generally about not trusting him, about going
railroad pace, etc. But when particular points were mentioned you avoided any
discussion of them. . . . This rather hurts and embarrasses him. He feels as
if he was looked [at] with suspicion, without any frank and quiet explanation
of the cause, and declares that it is so painful to him that he thinks he could
not go on long writing with that sort of [impression] on his mind. He puts
himself entirely in my hands, offers to stop the Tracts entirely, to put an end
to his Tuesday night parties or anything else which I recommend.

Newman indeed is "sensitive . . . to an extreme," and "such very clever
persons must submit to be[ing] misconstrued by us middling ones." Still,
no one can deny that such sensitivity is the heavy cost of a genuinely
creative mind. Therefore, said John Keble, if Tom should be moved to
object again,

perhaps for some little time to come you had better bring your objections to
my shop, and I will promise to deal more civilly with them than I have some-

times done, I fear, and if I think best, I will state them fairly and quietly to [Newman]. I wish he was not so keen in his feelings, but I suppose it goes along with his keenness of perception. I have observed it of him always, at times, but he veils it wonderfully. . . . [You might] naturally say, "Well, if he is so touchy I will just leave off admonishing him altogether." But I do not think you will in fact say it, because you know too well what sort of person he is. I feel for him extremely, and the more because in general he is so reserved about his own feelings that one supposes nothing but strong pressure would make him cry out in this way.[50]

Tom Keble replied sharply to this admonition, but his brother refused to be drawn into further argument. "I am very much obliged to you for your last letter," John wrote on December 10th, "on which I could say a good deal, all in an amicable way; but I think it will be better to go on thinking and chewing the end of it a little longer."[51] For his part Newman had calmed down sufficiently by Christmas to accept what appeared to be a compromise. "I am quite ready," he told John Keble, "that all Tracts should undergo the revision of two persons whom your brother chooses, though I do not understand *whom* you mean. Isaac Williams of course is one; is Prevost the other? Nothing you said . . . annoyed me in the least. You have a way of saying things which does not annoy."[52]

Keble's quiet strength made it possible for them all to weather the storm, but it did not pass away without leaving behind a damaging resentment on both sides. Nothing much came of the two-man board of censors. Eighty-five Tracts were already published by the autumn of 1838, and only five more were destined to appear: two by Isaac Williams, one by John Keble, a translation by Newman and the fateful Number Ninety. The board apparently never functioned, though to have agreed to it at all was a considerable concession for Newman. The dispute also involved him in a quarrel with Frederic Rogers, who sided with the Bisley group on the breviary matter. They were quickly reconciled, but not before Newman cried out in pain to his oldest friend, John Bowden: "I am so bothered and attacked on all sides by friends and foes that I had much rather say nothing and . . . write nothing more. . . . It is just like walking on treacherous ice: one cannot say a thing but one offends someone or other—I don't mean foe, for that one could bear, but friend."[53]

And while they argued, the Tracts were selling at a sixty-thousand-a-year pace.

V

As 1839 began, Newman seemed to experience a revival of spirits. "What a great thing it is that our bishop is for us!" he exclaimed. This sanguine judgment he based upon various rumours he had heard about

Bagot's "speaking kindly of us."[54] But more than anything else Newman was impressed by the bad notices the bishop was receiving in the Evangelical and liberal press. "I confess I was not fully reconciled till I saw the poor bishop had got into trouble, and now I begin to feel very grateful to him."[55] Even the success of Golightly's Martyrs' Memorial did not appear to bother him. "I could fancy worse things," he told Frederic Rogers cheerfully. "I think it may do good."[56]

Another thing which might do good occurred to Newman in January 1839. This was a collection of anti-Roman extracts from his own works and from those of Pusey and Keble. He suggested that these statements be stitched into some of the Tracts reprinted and circulated in February. Pusey agreed that such a move might quiet the suspicions of those who feared that Tractarianism led to Rome. Keble agreed too but he never got round to it. "Another instance of idleness," he said woefully, "is that I have not got ready any quotations from my own works against popery."[57] Though "indeed on looking" he "found little or nothing," still, when his friends' extracts appeared without his, he felt the familiar nagging sense of inadequacy. "I half-wish now," he told Newman in mid-February, "that I had added my anti-popish extracts to yours. I don't like to be separated from you and Pusey."[58]

By the spring of 1839 this was a quite natural sentiment for Keble to express, for Pusey had by that time assumed first-rank leadership within the Movement; the place in the triumvirate left vacant by Froude was now his. His gifts of course differed spectacularly from Froude's; rather than brilliant, Pusey was dogged, thorough, persistent and stubborn. He worked until he collapsed, and then, after a convalescence spent, say, at Brighton, he went back to work until he collapsed again. He was a dull lecturer. He sat amid the chaos of his Christ Church study and talked from notes written on "odds and ends, slips and backs of letters and so on."[59] But in the pulpit it was another story; there was a magic in Pusey's delivery despite an utter lack of style. "I can see him," recalled the Oxford chronicler Tuckwell, "passing through the crowds which overflowed the shabby, inconvenient, unrestored [Christ Church] Cathedral, the pale, ascetic, furrowed face, clouded and dusky always as with suggestions of a blunt or half-used razor, the bowed grizzled head." In his "harsh, unmodulated voice" he spoke of "high-pitched devotional patristicism" like "a man inhabiting his message," with "now and then the search-light thrown with startling vividness on the secrets hidden in many a hearer's heart."[60] Only Newman was his peer in attracting the young men of Oxford.

And yet something in his relentless nature repelled at the very moment it attracted. "There must be something harsh in Pusey's statements," observed James Mozley, "as they offend people so mightily—more than the same view expressed by older divines."[61] Mozley was in a good position to know, because for a time he lived with Pusey. In 1836 Pusey took into his home several young Apostolicals who had taken their B.A. degree but had not been elected to fellowships. The young men paid no rent and had free use of Pusey's immense library. The only condition imposed upon them was that they must study theology. In the summer of 1838 the arrangement was altered because of Mrs. Pusey's precarious health. Pusey bought a house in St. Aldate's Street where the young men paid only "a very small sum a week for our frugal diet," as one inmate remembered. Here the work done was more directly in assistance to Pusey's many projects, especially the Library of the Fathers. Ultimately the inmates were elected to fellowships and the house on St. Aldate's closed, but not before the young men had become fashioned by the Puseyite regimen. Years later one of them, after he had lost his faith, described his life in those years as "a great deal of degrading superstition, of fasting and attending endless religious services."[62]

In May 1839 Pusey had to pass through the most fiery of his many trials. On Trinity Sunday, his wife, Maria Barker, died after a lingering illness. No love had been deeper or more single-minded than Pusey's and no grief was more inconsolable than his. She had shared everything with him, not excluding his scholarly pursuits. With her his shy, narrow disposition never failed to find solace. What was rough and disorderly in him, she softened and smoothed. As he watched her slowly dying he remembered how he had first seen and loved her and how he had braved his tyrant of a father to have her. The whole sad story is perhaps best told in a short note Pusey wrote Keble just after Maria's funeral. "God has been very merciful to me in this dispensation, and carried me on, step by step, in a way I dared not hope. He sent Newman to me . . . in the first hour of sorrow, and it was like the visit of an angel. I hope to go on my way lonely, not forlorn."[63]

Pusey, who had always been too preoccupied to pay much attention to the world around him, now consciously retired from social life. He devoted some time to his children, who were frail like their mother, but most of his energy he reserved for the Apostolic cause. It is from this time that the common picture of Pusey emerges: "his exceeding slovenliness, . . . buttonless boots, necktie limp, . . . unbrushed coat collar," combined with "the almost artificial sweetness of his smile, contrasting as it did with the sombre gloom of his face when in repose."[64] Early in 1840 James Mozley reported to his brother Tom: "They have got a most frightful portrait of Pusey out, which is stuck up in all the shop windows. He looks wretched enough *propria persona*, but this portrait quite makes one wretched to look at it—it presents such a picture of intense misery, age and infirmity."[65] Tom's sensible wife, Harriet Newman, thought they all looked terrible: Her brother, she said, "is shockingly thin. . . . Mr. Keble *does* get so old. Mr. [Isaac] Williams look[s] sadly ill."[66]

CHAPTER 15

Roman Specter

Harriet Newman Mozley's fretful observation about the disintegrating appearance of the leaders of the Movement reflected perhaps more than her feminine concern about their health. She knew now, along with the rest of the world since the publication of the *Remains*, how savagely Froude had racked his weak body with fasting and sleeplessness, and she may have suspected that Froude's friends had similarly let their ascetic practices get out of hand. Harriet was a direct, outspoken girl for whom such activities could not but suggest the morbidity of Rome. And no doubt she worried about the rising chorus of rumour and criticism which cried out that the Movement was indeed drifting Romeward.

Her brother was anxious to reassure her. "I am glad H[arriet] is not very much disgusted at Tract 85," Newman wrote to her husband early in 1839. "Every arrow has its mark." The Tract was Newman's own, and it was a brilliant elaboration of the favourite Tractarian theme, which echoed Edward Hawkins' "Tradition" sermon of twenty years earlier, that the scriptural bases of the Church can be discerned only within the framework of patristic practice. It has done some good already, Newman told Tom Mozley; it has "brought over" one man and "put a spoke in the wheel" of another. "Persons who think we are doing good on the whole must give us a little confidence and not be criticizing us every step."[1]

Keble in turn sought to reassure Newman. "I think," he wrote about the same time, "some of those who started at your last Tract [Eighty-five] are beginning to see that they were wrong."[2] That may have been true, but the rumours continued nonetheless. "I heard yesterday," Newman reported to Henry Wilberforce on January 22, 1839, "that the Master of University [College, Oxford] has been assured by a lady at Cheltenham that we offered sacrifices every morning. He explained it by morning

[300]

prayers. No, she said, it was not that; she knew for certain we killed *something*, she did not know what. Qu., little children? or each other? or frogs? spiders? What?"[3]

The charge of popery had been leveled at the Movement ever since its beginning. It had never bothered Newman and it did not bother him now. He was more confident than ever in the rightness of his Via Media in the spring of 1839 (he had reached, he said later, the zenith of his influence within the Church of England), and silly tales told at the Evangelical center at Cheltenham could not shake him. But had people known generally that the leaders of the Movement had begun to hear private confessions, they would have been convinced that the worst rumours were true. Nothing raised the hackles of popular English anti-Romanism as did the confessional. It was not that the Tractarians thought in terms of judicial absolution as a Roman priest did; insofar as they had a clear view they regarded confession as a species of spiritual direction or, at most, as a sacramental intervention of God analogous to Baptism in which the minister's part was that of a minor instrument. This distinction, however, was too subtle for the average Englishman who recalled among his nursery bogeymen the wicked Jesuit confessors who had whispered iniquities into the ears of the Stuart kings.

Newman and Keble apparently began the practice reluctantly, but when troubled young academics at Oxford or guileless farm labourers at Hursley asked to confess, neither vicar refused them.[4] Newman, who listened to the self-revelations of young men at the north end of the altar rails in St. Mary's, would not hear women's confessions. Pusey seemed to become a confessor with a good deal more zest; his clientele grew quite large and included both men and women. Long years afterwards the embittered Mark Pattison recalled that as an undergraduate "I once and only once got so low by fostering a morbid state of conscience as to go to confession to Dr. Pusey."[5] Pattison accused Pusey of having broken the confidence of the confessional on that occasion, but he offered no proof for this allegation made in his agnostic old age.

Private confessions, severe lenten fasts, plans for implementing Froude's idea for colleges of celibate clergymen to serve the new industrial towns: these and similar matters occupied Tractarian minds as the 1830s merged into the '40s. If they had a Roman sound to them, that could not be helped. They were in fact the only real antidote to Romanism. So argued Newman in an article in the *British Critic* for April 1839, entitled "State of Religious Parties." "The spirit of Luther," he wrote, "is dead, but Hildebrand and Loyola are still alive. Is it sensible, sober, judicious to be so very angry with those writers of the day who point to the fact that our divines of the seventeenth century have occupied a ground which is the true and intelligible mean between extremes?" The widespread success of the Movement in recalling catholic principles indicates that it has spoken to something deep in human consciousness as well as to an abiding English religiosity. The final choice, Newman concluded, will not lie between Romanism and Protestantism. "Would you rather have your sons and daughters members of the Church of England or of the Church of Rome? That is the real alternative, if we follow things to their results, and the Romanists feel this. . . . Do they not thus recognize in us their real and most formidable opponents?"[6]

Henry Manning took a continental tour during the summer of 1839. He wrote to Newman that he saw signs on every side of the imminent collapse of the Roman Church. He poured scorn on the "smooth duplicity" of Rome which put a brake on doctrines like Purgatory and indulgences in England and allowed these same superstitions full rein in Italy. Indeed, Manning remarked, "their smoothness in England is worse than their bitterness abroad."[7] The Tractarians thought that Manning was a pretty smooth article himself: "very respectably revolutionist," as Rogers shrewdly expressed it.[8] Yet they agreed with Manning on one thing, that despite superficial appearances their own program had no Roman strings attached to it. What they forgot was the advice Hugh Rose had once given Keble: "The world is ruled by *seems*, not is, by *words* and *appearances*, not by *things* and *realities*; . . . if you once give an obnoxious name to a book or a man, *no power* can rescue them, no power can make them sufficient for good."[9]

1

When it came to Roman Catholicism, the Tractarians dealt at first exclusively in books and theories. They belonged to a class and generation of Englishmen for whom the Roman Catholic Church was little more than a vast abstraction. They had no acquaintance with it as a working system except when they viewed it disdainfully, as Henry Manning did, while traveling in such benighted lands as Ireland or Italy. They knew no Catholics. When Newman was curate at St. Clement's during the mid-1820s, he once chided a parishioner who consistently stayed away from the Anglican service. He had no idea that the man was the Oxford Catholic priest.[10] The Tractarians were much like novelist George Eliot, who recalled that in her girlhood she would have been more startled to meet a Roman Catholic in the flesh than a creature from another planet. Frederick Oakeley, with charming exaggeration, described the fairly common impression. As a youth, said Oakeley, he believed that there were perhaps eighty or a hundred Catholics in all England, "who were distributed in certain great families over the midland and northern counties. I thought that each of these families lived in a large haunted house, embosomed in yew trees and surrounded by high brick walls. . . . I fancied, of course, that there reigned around and within these abodes a preternatural silence, broken only by the flapping of bats and the screeching of owls."[11]

The penal laws had done their work. In 1830 there were perhaps 160,000 Catholics in England—hardly 1 per cent of the population— served by about 400 priests and organized into four vicariates apostolic. But not even these statistics indicate how inconsequential Catholicism really was in the country. Generations of persecution and disability had not only shrunk the Catholic numbers but they had also isolated the tiny remnant from the mainstream of English life. Though there had been no bad anti-popery riots since 1780, the small pockets of Catholic villagers in Lancashire and the stubborn segment of the gentry which had held on to the old faith were not about to assert themselves. They had learned to keep their heads down and to stay to themselves; they were satisfied that their second-class citizenship was a distinct improvement over what their ancestors had experienced.

Anti-Romanism was part of an Englishman's birthright. It was as much a patriotic sentiment as a religious conviction. Almost three centuries of conflict with the continental Catholic powers, together with unrelenting propaganda, had made it so. The pope stood for all that was treacherous, superstitious, tasteless and bizarre. The pope smelled of garlic, and his politics were devious while his religion was a mummery fit only for in- ferior peoples like the Italians and the Irish. The pope had once sent the Armada to destroy English liberties, and he had burned helpless Protes- tants at Smithfield and had tried to blow up the houses of parliament. All these elements were jumbled together in the Englishman's mind and became a subconscious (and hence irrational) principle of discernment. Popery was falling down before idols, it was the torture chamber of the Spanish Inquisition, it was the antithesis of everything good and English.

Such was the hard-core popular attitude, enshrined in the yearly observance of Guy Fawkes Day, November 5th, when a special service in the Anglican Prayer Book celebrated the nation's deliverance from popery. The ruling classes did not, to be sure, encourage the grosser aspects of this prejudice, but down deep they shared the lower orders' horror of Rome, even if they did so in a more genteel manner. Though they had tended to admire the Catholic refugees from the French Revo- lution and even to lionize Pius VII for his brave resistance to Napoleon, the common enemy, their basic antipathy remained. During the agitation prior to the passage of Catholic emancipation in 1829, the prevalent liberal philosophy tempered anti-popery sentiment only to the extent that it called Catholicism not dangerous but absurd. Wrote Sidney Smith: "As for the enormous wax candles and superstitious mummeries and painted jackets of the Catholic priests, I fear them not. . . . Tell me any other thing absurd or incredible, but, for love of common sense, let me hear no more of the danger to be apprehended from a general diffusion of popery. It is too absurd to be concerned over; every man feels it is nonsense when he hears it stated, and so does every man while he is stating it."[12]

II

The passage of Catholic emancipation was an Irish-liberal victory. Indeed, O'Connell found so much hostility to himself among English Catholic society that he said his only regret at the triumph of 1829 was the inclusion of his English co-religionists in the provisions of the Act. Emancipation did of course alter the status of English Catholics, but until the beginning of massive Irish immigration in the late 1840s the social and political improvement was enjoyed mostly by the handful of Catholic nobles and gentlemen.

Prominent among these was the sixteenth Earl of Shrewsbury.[13] The Talbot family traced its lineage back to a Lord Chamberlain of Edward III and its earldom to the middle of the fifteenth century. With but few lapses it had remained steadfastly Catholic, to its great cost, all through penal times. John Talbot, who succeeded to the title on the death of his uncle in 1827, inherited vast holdings in land which made him wealthy, though not so wealthy as popular rumour estimated. The earl was a shy man, dedicated to the Church for which he and his ancestors had suffered and sensitive to his position as the premier Catholic nobleman in England. But he was hardly robust enough for the rough and tumble of an active political life. He found it more congenial to be a builder of churches and a patron of the gothic revival in architecture. His seat at Alton Towers in Staffordshire became in time the center and rallying point of refined English Catholic life.

The building of Alton Towers, on the site of the family's old hunting lodge, had been begun by the earl's predecessor on a grandiose scale. To complete the project, Lord Shrewsbury in 1832 hired a young architect named Augustus Welby Pugin.[14] The result was a magnificent mansion of turrets and stained glass set like a jewel in the midst of formal gardens and a lush green park. Here the gentle earl lived with his family in comfortable piety and played host to what Catholic dignitaries there were in England. Here also, in the sumptuous chapel, was celebrated the Roman liturgy in neo-gothic splendour for the edification of any lady or gentleman who cared to witness it.

Pugin developed eventually into the brilliant, eccentric, often violent apostle of the neo-gothic style. Shortly after his association with Lord Shrewsbury began, he joined the Catholic Church, and he devoted to his new religion the same wild energy which made him a great artist and which burned out into madness and death before he was forty. The Tractarians knew something of Pugin, for though he was no university man and hardly a gentleman, his gifts as well as his oddities secured him a welcome at Oxford dinner parties. "Pugin has been here," Newman told Henry Wilberforce, "and I cannot help liking him, though he is an immense talker."[15] But James Mozley observed that in Newman's presence Pugin "was not quite so vigorous." Otherwise "everything moves his wrath, especially in architecture. Such a one ought to be hanged for building such a steeple" was an ordinary Pugin judgment.[16]

Pugin and Lord Shrewsbury helped literally to change the face of the English Catholic community. The earl's generosity and the artist's genius together set in motion the flurry of church construction which gave Catholics for the first time since the Reformation decent and even beautiful facilities for their public worship. This was not simply a matter of satisfying fastidious rubrical tastes; it meant that Catholics could once more have the important support which came with respectable buildings they could point to and be proud of.

The leadership in this modest Catholic renewal of the 1830s and 1840s grew into a triumvirate with the coming of age of Ambrose Phillipps.[17] Son of a wealthy Leicestershire landowner, Phillipps shocked his family when, at age fifteen, he announced that he had become a Roman Catholic. Neither five terms at Cambridge nor a severe physical breakdown could budge his youthful decision. In July 1833 he brought his bride, a daughter of the old Catholic aristocracy, to Grace Dieu Manor, which his father had made over to him together with an allowance of twelve hundred pounds a year. From that time Grace Dieu as much as Alton Towers hummed with genteel Catholic activity.

Phillipps soon was on intimate terms with Lord Shrewsbury and Pugin. Though the three did not always agree, their common commitment to Catholicism and gothic beauty overcame most differences and they worked harmoniously together. The Tory earl was by far the most conservative of the three, but he was also the most easily led. Phillipps held a unique position. Like the earl he was rich and a gentleman; like Pugin he was a convert. But he had been brought up as a son of the Establishment, had a member of Parliament for a father and an Anglican bishop for an uncle, and had gone to a university (Lord Shrewsbury had been educated by the Jesuits at Stonyhurst). In short, Phillipps could build a bridge to the Tractarians, something the other two could never do.

Though he had only a hazy notion of it at first, Phillipps found such a role very much to his taste, and he urged his friends down the avenues which led to the Oxford men. Lord Shrewsbury was for a long while reluctant; he thought Pusey especially distasteful: "There never was a more deluded mind," said the earl.[18] But Phillipps, who had an awesome regard for Pusey and Newman and was sure that their Movement would, with a little encouragement, bring them eventually to mother Rome, prevailed over his noble friend's objection, and soon small but significant contacts were made. Letters passed with growing frequency between Grace Dieu and Oxford; young dons came as guests to Alton Towers where as often as not they attended Mass in the chapel. Phillipps meanwhile arranged for the Trappists and Italian Passionists to establish houses in England; he was sanguine that the contemplative and active religious orders would hasten the conversion of England. Lord Shrewsbury, though again somewhat dubious, paid most of the bills for these Apostolic ventures.

Phillipps, Pugin, and Lord Shrewsbury turned an abstraction into a reality. This was the basic influence they had on the Tractarians. For at Oxford Roman Catholicism was either a total unknown or else it was, in the minds of Oxford men, simply the opportunism and wicked liberalism of Irish politicians. Phillipps particularly endeared himself by his sturdy opposition to O'Connell. Newman noted approvingly that Phillipps was "so attacked by his own party as to be a sort of confessor."[19]

Different aspects caught the attention of different minds. Some Tractarians were impressed by the splendid liturgical services in Lord Shrewsbury's chapel. Others, raised on Scott and Wordsworth, went into romantic raptures over the neo-gothic setting of that liturgy. The more thoughtful could not but be attracted by the sacramental emphasis which prevailed among these Romanists, the same emphasis, indeed, they had heard from Keble and Newman. Similarly, they discovered ascetic ideals —the living cycle of feast and fast—worthy of Dr. Pusey himself. The difference was that here these things were accepted with calm unanimity by people of their own rank and much like themselves. There was no vulgarity at Grace Dieu and Alton Towers, but there was no doubt or compromise either. And there were no Dr. Hampdens or Archbishop Whatelys.

III

Perhaps this contact of Tractarians with Roman Catholics would have remained a polite interlude had it not been for Nicholas Wiseman.[20] The son of an Irish merchant settled in Seville, Wiseman had gone to English Catholic schools—a dull, gawky, lonely boy whose ordinary companion was a book—and then, in 1818, to the newly reopened English College in Rome. He blossomed in his new environment and grew into an urbane young ecclesiastic, clever at languages, eloquent, industrious and pious. He was ordained priest in 1825 and spent the next several years doing philological research in the Vatican Library. In 1829, when he was but twenty-six years old, Wiseman was named Rector of the English College.

For the next twelve years, besides his academic duties, he acted as a kind of unofficial host of English dignitaries who visited the eternal city, and all the time he was dreaming a very great dream.

The early nineteenth century witnessed a significant revival of the fortunes of Catholicism among European intellectuals and the upper classes generally. The names of Döllinger, Montalembert and Lacordaire come to mind as typical of the new vitality which surged through the Roman Church from top to bottom. Wiseman lived at the exciting center of this phenomenon; he cultivated the rising continental thinkers, who in turn thought of him as one of themselves. And he dreamed that England too might have a Catholic revival. The task would be harder there, because it would have to start almost from nothing. Yet the passage of emancipation had cleared the political path, and in 1833, when Newman and Hurrell Froude during their Mediterranean holiday called on him in Rome, Wiseman began to suspect that the ecclesiastical barriers were not insuperable either. If these young dons, so genuinely devoted to the Christian Church's catholicity, represented the next Oxford generation, then perhaps the fullness of time had come. "From the day of Newman's and Froude's visit to me," he wrote later, "never for an instant did I waver in my conviction that a new era had commenced in England. . . . To this grand object I devoted myself. . . . The favourite studies of former years were abandoned for the pursuit of this aim alone."[21]

Some years passed before Wiseman's vision assumed any practical shape. But he kept a careful eye on the progress of the Oxford Movement, maintained a polite contact with its leaders and rejoiced in its program to un-Protestantize the English Church. In the meantime he fretted about the problems within the Roman Catholic body itself. Timid, unassertive, leaderless, the English Catholic community, as it stood, could never be the foundation for a religious revival. In 1835 Wiseman decided to intervene personally. He took an extended leave from his duties at the College and, with the blessing of the Roman authorities, came home to England full of plans to found a learned journal and, perhaps, a Catholic university. Nothing came of this latter idea, but, thanks to the help of Daniel O'Connell, Wiseman succeeded in launching the *Dublin Review*, the first issue of which appeared in 1836.

The *Dublin*'s polished prose and respectable scholarship made an immediate impression in the little world of theological magazines. It avoided high-pitched controversy and politics, and concentrated on those issues of direct interest to the Tractarians. One of the early numbers contained an analysis of Keble's Tradition sermon, and though Keble did not like some of the reviewer's observations he still admitted cautiously, "There is certainly a great deal of eloquence and acuteness in the paper, and, if one could believe it sincere, a good spirit."[22]

But even more influential was Wiseman's personality and tireless

energy. He went everywhere and saw everyone. He lectured to London
society audiences at the Sardinian embassy; he crisscrossed the country
to meet all the leading Catholics (one lengthy visit was made to Alton
Towers); he charmed O'Connell, Lord Brougham and other liberal politicians. His "tall, slight, apparently long-necked" figure was a familiar sight
all over the kingdom, and though he seemed to some "a little pompous
in manner," yet his cheerful nature and essential simplicity soon dis-
armed the most critical.[23] He hoped to put some heart into his fellow
Catholics as well as win a measure of acceptance by the nation at large,
and by the time he returned to Rome, in the autumn of 1836, it was
clear he had made progress in both areas. What is more, he had made
himself the indispensable man: he was Roman to his fingertips and yet
Irish enough to be on good terms with O'Connell; he handled the English language with verve and style; he shared none of the inhibitions of
the present Catholic leadership, clerical and lay, and he stood securely
above their quarrels; he was an intellectual with the best continental
credentials who yet moved easily through drawing room and marketplace.
No one doubted, after a year's exposure in England, that the tattered
Catholic remnant of eccentric country gentlemen and timorous vicars
apostolic had found a leader.

Back in Rome Wiseman did not forget the Tractarians. He approached
them primarily in the pages of the *Dublin*. From 1836, in a series of
articles which ranged from a discussion of the Hampden controversy to
a review of Froude's *Remains*, he examined in a carefully moderate tone
England's claim to the apostolic succession. Needless to say, he found the
claim wanting. His point was a technical one, and though he argued it
persuasively, it did not make any particular impression in Oxford.

But then, in the summer of 1839, Wiseman published an essay which,
as he put it, lifted the argument "to a higher level."[24] The article turned
on a learned comparison between the position of the Donatist schismatics
in fifth-century Africa and that of the Tractarians. Wiseman advanced
much patristic evidence to bear out his thesis, but essentially it came
down to this, that the Tractarians like the Donatists pretended to a
share in catholicity on the grounds of a common catholic antiquity. But
other bodies, which the Tractarians (and in their time the Donatists)
recognized as catholic, have rejected the Tractarian (Donatist) bid. Thus
the Archbishop of Canterbury, if he were sufficiently High Church to be
concerned about such things, might grant the pope a share in catholicity
to the degree that the Roman Church has maintained at least some of
the common doctrine of the first several centuries; but the pope will not
return the favour nor, for that matter, will the humblest missionary
bishop. A local catholicity, said Wiseman, is a contradiction in terms
whether in the fifth century or in the nineteenth.

What is at issue, he continued, is not a right but a fact. The Church of England is not in fact recognized as catholic by the rest of the catholic world, and no erudite argument from the Fathers nor fervent devotion to the rights of the English bishops can alter that reality. Moreover, again as a matter of fact, Rome stands now in the nineteenth century precisely where she did at the time of the Donatists. Rome, the source of unity, holds together the local churches all over the world and guarantees their catholicity. Wiseman quoted St. Augustine, who had debated the question with the Donatists and had stated the principle in the form of a Latin slogan: *"Quapropter securus judicat orbis terrarum, bonos non esse qui se dividunt ab orbe terrarum, in quacumque parte orbis terrarum."* ("The world as a whole speaks safely and authoritatively when it condemns those, wherever they may be, who cut themselves off from unity with itself.") The slogan is awkward in any language; but its application becomes clear if "universal Christian Church" is allowed to stand for "world as a whole" *(orbis terrarum)*.

Wiseman in effect cut through the elaborate defenses of the Via Media with an ethical rule of thumb. He confronted the Anglican, who admitted that the true Christian Church must have the universality proclaimed in the Nicene Creed and reiterated in the Prayer Book, with the question whether this catholicity could really have a unique existence in one little island. It was a moral question with all the practical overtones which the Tractarians considered so important. At the same time Wiseman's use of the sweeping *"securus judicat"* contrasted sharply with much of the theoretical and often petty argumentation to which the Tractarians had been driven in order to shore up their abstract catholicism. Thomas Arnold, speaking for the enemies of the Via Media within the Church of England, dismissed it contemptuously as "a dress, a ritual, a name, a ceremony." And Newman himself had confessed in the *Prophetical Office* that the trouble with the Via Media lay in its abstract character. Nobody could say whether it would work or not because it had never been tried in practice. It was a paper theory found in books but not in life. If Wiseman's application of *"securus judicat"* was correct, then Arnold and his friends were right too in calling the Oxford Movement a fatuous and trivial venture.

Newman did not read the *Dublin* article until mid-September 1839, when his London friend, Robert Williams, pointed it out to him. It made no impression on him at first; he had studied the literature of the Donatist controversy some years before and he had not seen any parallel in it to the Via Media. But Williams, pacing anxiously up and down Newman's rooms at Oriel, kept repeating over and over, *"Securus judicat orbis terrarum,"* and after he had gone, Newman could still hear the phrase ringing in his ears. Suddenly its cogency struck him "with a force which I never had felt from any words before." Wiseman's article, he confided to Frederic Rogers a week later, "has given me a stomach ache."[25]

IV

It seems strange and even extravagant that an obscure wrangle of the fifth century should have shaken the confidence of a nineteenth-century reformer and abruptly altered the direction of the Movement he led. Yet so it was. "Securus judicat," Newman recalled years later, "decided ecclesiastical questions on a simpler rule than that of antiquity; nay St. Augustine was one of the prime oracles of antiquity; here then antiquity was deciding against itself. What a light was hereby thrown upon every controversy in the Church!" It occurred to Newman literally for the first time "that the deliberate judgment, in which the whole Church at length rests and acquiesces, is an infallible prescription and a final sentence against such portions of it as protest and secede." By the *"securus judicat"* of St. Augustine, "the theory of the Via Media was absolutely pulverized."[26]

The painful impact which Wiseman had produced on Newman's mind probably would never have happened had the ground not been carefully prepared. Newman did indeed give up the Via Media after the summer of 1839, but the *"securus judicat"* article came to him only after grave doubts over the theory had already arisen. Newman, in typical Tractarian fashion, had set a course of theological study for himself during the long vacation. The subject he chose was the Monophysite controversy. This was another fifth-century ecclesiastical quarrel, which, however, had nothing to do with the Donatists. The Monophysites were a sect which denied the genuine humanity of Christ. They insisted that what appeared human in Jesus of Nazareth had been merely an illusion, a veil, so to speak, to hide his divinity. Such a theory had obvious ramifications in the practicalities of Christian life, for if Christ were not in fact human, the economy of salvation, the role of Christ as unique mediator, the functioning of the sacraments, all these would be drastically affected. Monophysitism was condemned at the general Council of Chalcedon in 451; the Fathers of that Council adopted as their own the doctrinal statement of Pope Leo I in which the relationship between the divine and human natures in Christ was spelled out.

Newman began his investigation about the middle of June 1839. The general area was already familiar to him; the Christological controversies had been his special study ever since he had done the research for *Arians* almost a decade before. But he had not until now gone carefully through the Monophysite phase of the problem. "It was during this course of reading that for the first time a doubt came upon me of the tenableness of Anglicanism. I recollect on the 30th of July mentioning to a friend . . . how remarkable the history was; but by the end of August I was seriously alarmed."[27]

The tangled details of the Monophysite controversy lie outside the scope of these pages. Once more, as in the case of the Donatists, what matters is the parallel to the nineteenth-century situation, because it is this parallel which hit Newman so hard. The Monophysites, he discovered, appealed to antiquity in their protest against Pope Leo and the Council of Chalcedon which followed the pope's lead and adopted his formula to define the relation between the human and divine in Christ. That formula involved the invention of new terms and consequently, the Monophysites charged, constituted an addition to the primitive creed. Another party was active too, which, though it steered clear of Monophysitism, was suspicious of Leo's formula and preferred to leave the matter undefined and thus avoid a confrontation. The Roman imperial government supported this latter group, because it seemed more likely to preserve harmony; comprehension of as many divergent points of view as possible within one institutional framework was the government's policy.

As early as July 12th, Newman had noticed "two things [which] are very remarkable at Chalcedon—the great power of the pope (as great as he claims now almost), and the marvelous interference of the civil power, as great almost as in our kings."[28] And so the seed of alarm had been sown, and in the weeks following it grew swiftly. How similar was the attitude of the imperial government in the fifth century to that of English governments from Queen Elizabeth to Lord Grey and Robert Peel. Even more striking was the fact that all Christian bodies—Protestant, Roman, Greek—agreed that Pope Leo's formula and Chalcedon's decree were true to revelation while the Monophysite view, sophisticated as it was, was not. Why did Rome always end up on the right side? And if she were right at Chalcedon, was it not possible that she had also been right at the Council of Trent? The decrees of Trent stuck like a bone in Tractarian throats. "Wretched Tridentines everywhere" had been Hurrell Froude's blanket indictment of Roman Catholics. At Trent, so the Tractarian argument ran, the Roman Church had formally invented the doctrines patently at variance with primitive Christian teaching. But what if Trent, Newman asked himself, had done only what Chalcedon had done before, that is, had stated primitive teaching in a clearer and more developed form?

The rejection of the Council of Trent was an absolute necessity to the Via Media. Only if Trent and Rome had been untrue to antiquity would the Tractarian alternative to Protestantism stand up. Newman had never hesitated to affirm that his theory had more in common with Rome than with Protestantism, but he maintained that it was still an essentially different and truer catholicism, because it avoided the corrupt additions which Rome had made to antiquity. Now, in the long shadow of the fifth century, he was not so sure. "My stronghold was antiquity, now here, in the middle of the fifth century, I found, as it seemed to me, Christendom of the sixteenth and nineteenth centuries reflected. I saw my face in that mirror, and I was a Monophysite."[29]

This was Newman's state of mind when Robert Williams walked into his rooms at Oriel with a copy of the *Dublin Review* under his arm.

Only two people were let in on Newman's secret. "We are not," he told Rogers, "at the bottom of things. At this moment we have sprung a leak. . . . It is no laughing matter. I will not blink the question, so be it; but you don't suppose I am madcap to take up questions suddenly—only there is an uncomfortable vista opened which was closed before."[30]

At the beginning of October 1839 Newman visited Henry Wilberforce at the latter's parish near Southampton. One day, as the two took a walk in the New Forest, Newman told Henry how the Monophysites and *"securus judicat"* had combined to raise grave doubts in his mind. He thought it likely that once he returned to Oxford and set to work he could find a satisfactory answer to them. Yet, he said, "I cannot conceal from myself that for the first time since I began the study of theology a vista had been opened before me to the end of which I cannot see."[31] Henry, thunderstruck, said that he hoped Newman would die rather than go to Rome. Newman nodded gravely and answered that such would be his own preference if it were the will of God.

Newman told no one else. He urged his friends to read Wiseman's article but he confided nothing of his own uneasiness. To Bowden, who was on a Mediterranean holiday, he wrote, "Dr. Wiseman's last article against the Tracts in the *Dublin Review* is the only good thing which has been written against us. You should read it, it is worth your while."[32] Newman hoped Keble would write an answer to Wiseman but he found the Vicar of Hursley more than usually lackadaisical. "I shall send for Wiseman's review," he replied. "The mere statement about the Donatists is not very alarming; it sounds too absurd, but I suppose he knows how to work up such things."[33]

This offhand remark of Keble's, written perhaps the very day that Newman walked with Henry Wilberforce in the New Forest and told him the terrifying news, leads to a question of crucial importance in the history of the Oxford Movement. Why did not Newman, at this moment, confide in Keble? A year earlier, at the time of Bishop Bagot's Charge, Newman had maintained that Keble was the only person upon whom he could rely. And yet, at the outset of his greatest crisis, he turned to two young men, as much disciples as friends, and left Keble in the dark. Hursley was not far from Henry Wilberforce's; indeed, the letter in which Keble promised to send for the *Dublin* was addressed to Newman in care of Henry. And he had begun that letter by saying, "I wish you could have come here."[34] But Newman did not go.

Froude had boasted that his most significant accomplishment was bringing Keble and Newman together. This was true certainly on several levels, but it may never have been true as far as a real meeting of minds was concerned. An analysis of the Keble-Newman correspondence bears out this contention. The two men rarely discussed intellectual matters.

It was as if they agreed that by 1833 the whole party platform had been decided upon and that no substantive issues remained to be debated. Their letters were personal, often intimate, but mostly they dealt with practicalities: editing, correction of proofs, errands to be run and the like. They shared rumours and sympathy, they bucked one another up, they commented on personalities, but they never discussed such things as the meaning of the Monophysite controversy of the fifth century.

Perhaps Newman thought Keble too shallow intellectually to be of help in such an area. Or maybe he feared that telling Keble might trigger one of his friend's dark, desponding moods. Or again, perhaps Newman was simply too proud to lay his new doubts before Keble, who never had any doubts of his own. Whatever the answer, not until a year later (as we shall see) did Newman open his mind even partially to Keble, and when he did, in the fall of 1840, he put the problem in its practical rather than its intellectual form. He asked Keble whether he should resign St. Mary's, just as he had asked in 1838 if he should suspend publication of the Tracts. By that time his doubt had turned into a certainty that the Via Media had been all along an illusion.

V

But when he returned to Oxford for the beginning of the new term, in October 1839, Newman recovered some of his former serenity. His doubts for the moment "vanished" and his "old conviction remained as before."[35] He found that Wiseman's article was causing a considerable stir among his friends and so he determined to write an answer. The result was a long essay published in the British Critic in January 1840. Called "The Catholicity of the Anglican Church," the article confronted the Anglican with the Roman claims, and in doing so it reflected the new tension within the author's own mind. As usual Newman stated the view he was opposing with keen insight: "The objection [to Tractarianism] is this, . . . that unity is the tenure of divine favour; that communion with our brethren is the means of communion with our Lord and Saviour; that the Church is not only apostolic but catholic; and that . . . our Church is emphatically in a state of estrangement, having intercourse with no other Christian body in any part of the world, excepting her own dependencies and offshoots."

The real conclusion of the article came in the first part of it where Newman set up a dialogue between Anglican and Roman. Says the Roman: "Our teaching is the true, for it is everywhere the same; yours has no warrant, for it is but local and private." Responds the Anglican: "We go by antiquity, that is, by the apostles. Ancient consent is our standard of faith." And the Roman: "We go by catholicity. Universal consent is our standard of faith." The article was written with all the old

Newmanesque verve, but there was a new note in its argument. When it turned to Wiseman's use of *"securus judicat"* it seemed to falter and to fall back upon a negative position. If the Anglican is not the catholic Church in England, asked Newman, is there a catholic Church in England? Surely the Romanists can make no such claim when "we see [them] associated everywhere with the low democracy, pandering to the spirit of rebellion, the lust of change. . . . We see [Rome's] grave theologians connecting their names with men who are convicted by the common sense of mankind of something very like perjury, and its leaders in alliance with a political party notorious in the [world] as a sort of standard for liberalism and infidelity."[36] The reference to Wiseman and O'Connell was clear enough ("I had an unspeakable aversion to the policy and acts of Mr. O'Connell," Newman recalled in later years),[37] but for all its indictment of Rome's "political, scheming, grasping spirit," the article failed to resolve the riddle of Anglicanism's insular "catholicity." Indeed, it seemed as though Newman felt ready to desert that ground altogether.

Keble must have sensed this. After reading the article before publication, he said, "I cannot see anything to criticize in this paper except one or two mere verbal matters which I have marked in pencil." However, he added, "I wish you to consider whether p. 77 [in the proofs] is not *almost* in contradiction to that place in the Via Media [i.e., in the *Prophetical Office*] where you say that popular views now are lower than those of the Reformers."[38] This was a key departure and Keble had seen it as such. The Tractarians always distinguished between formal Roman doctrine and the corrupt popular practices which that doctrine permitted or encouraged. The Roman system, they had consistently argued, was as wrong in its own way as its Protestant opposite number, but it was more sophisticated. Its theoretical statements about the veneration of the Virgin Mary, for example, might be unobjectionable and could, if one did not look sharp, lull one into overlooking the vulgar Mariolatry which was its ordinary practice. Romanism must be judged as a whole, and once it is the true Christian will see that he must steer a middle way between it and Protestantism. Indeed, Keble remembered that not so long ago Newman had asserted that the popular corruptions among the Romanists were worse than the aberrations of the Protestant Reformers. He was not saying this any more, and perhaps Keble, though not privy to Newman's disturbing secret, nevertheless guessed that his friend had followed the Via Media to a dead end.

VI

During the same autumn of 1839, while he tried to ward off the Roman specter through speculative inquiry, Newman was embroiled in two embarrassing incidents which indicated that the same ghost haunted the streets of Oxford. A young Hebrew scholar and Fellow of Exeter named John Brande Morris had substituted for Newman in the pulpit at St. Mary's during the latter's holiday. An eager and somewhat extravagant practitioner of Tractarian "ethos," Morris had especially strong views on the value of fasting—so much so that he was nicknamed Simeon Stylites after the legendary Egyptian hermit who sat on a pillar and ate practically nothing. On St. Michael's day (September 29th), Morris preached on his favourite subject and suggested, among other weird things, that as angels feasted on liturgical festivals, so the animal kingdom ought to be made to fast on fast days. Among his startled congregation sat the Vice-chancellor.

Then, on the following Sunday, Morris preached at St. Mary's again, and this time he proclaimed that anyone who denied the Roman Catholic notion of the Eucharist as a sacrifice gave evidence of a carnal and un-believing mind. "This," as Newman observed to Bowden, "was too much for any Vice-chancellor," who summoned Morris, had his sermon officially examined and then censured him. Newman was very annoyed at Morris, whom he had explicitly warned to avoid bizarre statements at St. Mary's. "May he . . . have a fasting horse," said Newman grimly, "the next time he goes steeple chasing."[39] More ominous, however, was the fact that the Vice-chancellor had said nothing to Newman about the matter one way or another and had removed his family from services at St. Mary's. "The Heads of Houses are getting more and more uneasy," Newman told Jemima. "I should not wonder if the bishop got uneasy, in which case I suppose I should resign my living."[40]

The Vice-chancellor had brought Bishop Bagot into the Morris affair by sending him a copy of the objectionable sermon. Perhaps the bishop would like to have reminded Newman of his remark in the Charge of 1838: "I have more fear of the disciples than of the teachers." Instead he courteously asked Newman for a formal opinion of the sermon, and when Newman responded by roundly condemning it the bishop let the matter rest.

This little tempest was swiftly followed by another. In mid-November 1839 Newman heard rumours that his curate, John Bloxam, while on a visit to Alton Towers the previous August, had gone to Mass in Lord Shrewsbury's chapel and had with the other worshipers prostrated himself at the elevation of the Host. Newman, seriously disturbed this time, went to Bloxam for an explanation. During the several days he stayed at Alton Towers, said Bloxam, he had gone each morning to the chapel gallery and recited privately the Anglican service from the Prayer Book, after which he customarily knelt and prayed for some longer time. One day Mass was celebrated while he was thus kneeling in the gallery; he had remained as he was and had not participated in the slightest way.

Newman immediately wrote to Bishop Bagot, told him of the rumours, and quoted in full Bloxam's side of the story. The bishop responded with unusual testiness that he regretted the news and regretted even more that Newman had brought it to his attention. "I feel," he said, "that it is a matter . . . resting between yourselves." If Newman wished to be rid of Bloxam, and Bloxam refused to resign his curacy, only then "the bishop's aid or interference would be necessary."[41]

Several more letters passed between Newman and the bishop until Bloxam, sick with worry and pressed by a family emergency, did resign his curacy. By the time the correspondence closed Bishop Bagot had resumed his kindly demeanour: "I am quite satisfied and very much regret to find this business has had so uncomfortable effect upon [Bloxam's] health and spirits." More significant in the long run was the revelation through the Bloxam affair of how little sympathy there was between the Vicar of St. Mary's and his bishop. Newman insisted on treating Bagot as a successor of the apostles who by reason of his office should provide clear doctrinal and disciplinary leadership. Bagot reacted like a harried administrator who recognized that he had little real power and who therefore evaded problems he could do nothing about anyway. But whatever his shortcomings Bishop Bagot's concern was geniune. "My dear sir," he wrote to Newman, "let me entreat you to exert your own high and influential name among a numerous body of clergy and young men destined for orders who look up to you—to discourage by every means in your power indiscretions similar to Mr. Bloxam's, or any little extravagances, the results of youth, harmless perhaps in themselves, but which . . . tend to retard the progress of sound and high Church principles which you would inculcate."[42]

As for Bloxam, he soon recovered his equanimity, and within six months he had entered into correspondence with Ambrose Phillipps on the subject of possible union between the Roman and Anglican churches. Newman in March 1840 wrote him a letter of gratitude: "What a loss I have in you, my dear B. I feel it most acutely. . . . You have inspired a great reverence for religion and love of the Church, and I see it in more ways than I can name."[43]

One immediate effect of Bloxam's resignation was that Newman began to spend much more of his time in Littlemore. At the beginning of Lent 1840 Newman moved into the rooms vacated by Bloxam while the new curate, William Copeland of Trinity College, took the duty at St. Mary's.

Newman fasted rigourously that Lent. On Wednesdays and Fridays he ate nothing until six in the evening, and on other weekdays he abstained from tea, wine, butter, coffee, fish, fruit, pastry and all meat except bacon. On Holy Thursday and Good Friday he had only bread and water. Without friends and books, he plunged into the parochial life of the place. Among the simple people of Littlemore he found none of the perplexing problems of Oxford society; he found instead ignorance, dirt and the mundane concerns of the rural poor. Much of his time went to catechizing the children and supervising the school, whose mistress, he discovered to his horror, was a drunk.[44] On March 10th he wrote to Henry Wilberforce, "For several days I have been saying to myself, O that Henry would bring his wife here to put my school to rights! I see indeed that the girls' hair wanting [sic] combing, but I cannot get farther in my analysis of the general air of slatternness which prevails."[45] It is a touching picture: The great Mr. Newman puzzles over little girls' lack of cleanliness and dreams that the Sargent woman who had lured Henry away might come to his aid. Mary Wilberforce responded by sending the pinafore patterns which the girls made themselves in time for Easter. Newman apparently had some success in teaching the children some religious music, for when Keble visited Littlemore late in the fall of 1840 he heard them sing "the Magnificat and Nunc Dimittis to one of the Gregorian chants, and I liked it much."[46]

The interlude at Littlemore was a happy one, but it did not completely relieve Newman's mind. He still worried over *"securus judicat."* "As to Dr. Wiseman's article," he wrote John Bowden the last week of February 1840, "I do not think you have hit the point of it. It made a very great impression here, and to say what of course I would only say to such as yourself, it made me for a while very uncomfortable in my own mind."[47] And, despite all he had to do in the parish, Newman felt the sharp pangs of loneliness at Littlemore, pangs more intense perhaps because of sheer hunger. On March 25th, he wrote a memorandum about his illness in Sicily seven years earlier and then added a pathetic postscript:

The thought keeps pressing on me while I write this, what am I writing it for? For myself I may look at it once or twice in my life, and what sympathy is there in *my* looking at it? Whom have I, whom can I have, who would take interest in it? I was going to say I have only found one who ever took that sort of affectionate interest in me as to be pleased with each detail, and that is H[enry] W[ilberforce]. And what shall I ever see of him? This is the sort of interest a wife takes and none but she—it is a woman's interest—and that interest, so be it, will never be taken in me. Never, so be it, will I be other than God has found me. All my habits for years, my tendencies are toward celibacy. . . . Shall I have in my old age spiritual children who will take an interest? How time is getting on![48]

A few days before he had written playfully to Tom Mozley, "I think I shall build a monastery here [in Littlemore] and shall come to you for architectural hints, which will be better than your personal ones through H[arriet]."[49] There was, however, nothing playful about the monastic intention. It was something Newman had thought about for a long time. The idea of living close by a rule had always attracted him, and now, with the new long shadows all around him, the notion of retirement from the present stress and activity to a life of prayerful study had a special appeal. In May, using Bloxam as his agent, he quietly bought ten acres of land near the Littlemore chapel. He dropped the bombshell almost casually to his sister Jemima: "What a beautiful spring this has been. . . . We have bought nine or ten acres of ground at Littlemore, and . . . in due time shall erect a monastic house upon it. This may lead ultimately to my resigning my fellowship."[50]

Back at Oriel and Oxford, the doubts and perplexities, the thoughts of resignation continued through the summer and fall of 1840. Finally, in October, Newman wrote the long letter to Keble, referred to above, in which he sought advice as to whether he ought to resign, if not his fellowship, then St. Mary's. He advanced first the technical reason that his work in the parish had practically no impact upon the townsmen of Oxford who were really his parishioners; instead, members of the university, graduates and undergraduates, flocked to his sermons, services and lectures. "It seems . . . I am using St. Mary's to the neglect of its direct duties for objects not belonging to it; I am converting a parochial charge into a sort of university office."

Then he got to the heart of the matter. "I cannot disguise from myself that my preaching is not calculated to defend that system of religion which has been received for 300 years and of which the Heads of Houses are the legitimate maintainers in this place. . . . I am leading my hearers to the primitive Church, . . . but not to the Church of England."

But this is not all. I fear I must allow that whether I will or no I am disposing them towards Rome. First because Rome is the only representative of the primitive Church besides ourselves; in proportion then as they are loosened from the one they will go to the other. Next because many doctrines which I have held have far greater or their only scope in the Roman system. . . . The *arguments* which I have published against Romanism seem to myself as cogent as ever, but men go by their sympathies, not by argument; and if I feel the force of this influence myself, who bow to the arguments, why may not others still more who never have in the same degree admitted the arguments? Nor can I counteract the danger by preaching or writing against Rome. I seem to have shot my last arrow in the article on English Catholicity. It must be added that the very circumstance that I have committed myself against Rome has the effect of setting to sleep people suspicious about me, which is painful now that I begin to have suspicions about myself.[51]

Keble was, needless to say, alarmed. On October 30th, he wrote to his brother Tom about Newman's "enquiry which (*between ourselves*) he has been very seriously making of me: whether he ought not to give up St. Mary's. I am inclined to think on consideration no; but I should like to know your impression, if I could, even before I write to him. The Heads of Houses discouraging him as they do is one reason and there are several others; but from some things I have sometimes heard you say,

I should like to know what your first impression is." It seemed as though Keble could not get himself to put down black on white the real problem Newman had raised, because only towards the end of his note to Tom did he say, delicately, "Newman is rather getting out from an apprehension that though his arguments tell strongly against Romanism, yet the sympathies he encourages are more strongly in favour of it."[52]

With or without advice from his brother, John Keble sent his answer to Newman on November 3rd. He dismissed the first of Newman's worries out of hand. "My feeling[s] about the parishioners of St. Mary's are that you would have just the same matter of complaint in any other place where your lot was cast among the same class of people, town tradesmen, I mean, and such like. So that if it were your duty to retire on that ground, it would be equally the duty of almost all town clergymen." With regard to the Heads of Houses, Keble admitted that Newman's position was "unpleasant," to be sure. Since the Heads had not authority over Newman as parish priest, their animosity, so long as it was not coupled with some overt act, was not in Keble's judgment sufficient warrant for resignation.

"The only one of your topics," he continued, "which moves me is the last—the greater power of the sympathies you excite in favour of Romanism than of your arguments against it." Now even if this is literally true, said Keble, retirement from St. Mary's is not so crucial as is desisting from writing and editing. "At Oxford you are on the spot to be consulted and are presently made aware of any exuberance. I cannot well conceive a situation in which [the danger of Romanism] is more mitigated and repressed than at Oxford while you and Pusey and [Isaac] Williams are there." Indeed, retirement might effect the very things Newman wants most to avoid: drive people Romeward and disenchant or destroy the catholic elements within the Church of England, under the impression that Newman had given up the battle. At the end of his letter, Keble added a word of comfort: "I suppose no honest man, having been instrumental in setting a great power in motion, can help feeling anxious and responsible as to whether it moves in the right or wrong direction. I am prosing away at a great rate and tiring you with truisms."[53]

Keble's advice prevailed, and Newman stepped back from the brink and stayed on at St. Mary's. His mood seemed to brighten towards the end of the year. He wrote to Bowden, "I do not think that people here are in a dangerous way. They are very *good-humoured* as far as I know; and if they criticize me, it is in fun, meaning nothing by it."[54] And to Rogers (who was in Italy), "On the whole, though I cannot draw out my reasons, I am more comfortable than I was. . . . I do not fear at all any number of persons as likely to go to Rome, if I am secure about myself. If I can trust myself, I can trust others."[55]

CHAPTER 16

Number Ninety

NEWMAN celebrated his rising spirits as 1841 began by engaging an old foe. At the ceremonial opening of a reading room at Tamworth, Sir Robert Peel had given a speech in which he lauded secular education as the best means of promoting moral improvement among the masses, social unity and a host of other admirable objectives. It was a rather humdrum pronouncement, but coming as it did from the leader of the conservative party it attracted a good deal of attention. It also irritated the editor of the *Times*, who thought it smacked too much of the liberalism of Bentham and Lord Brougham. The editor's son, just down from Oxford and an enthusiastic Newmanite, suggested that Newman would be the very one to expose Peel's radical leanings in the columns of England's most prestigious newspaper.[1]

Accordingly, on February 5, 1841, the *Times* published the first of seven letters signed "Catholicus," the pseudonym Newman employed. He found the task a congenial one; he could level his attack against the enemy of 1833, the liberal enemy which reduced religion to emotion and party feeling. For the most part he took a lighthearted approach and poked fun at Peel's high-flown phrases. Peel, for example, had grown rhapsodic over the prospect that "virtuous women" would be able to congregate the Tamworth library. "What does this mean?" asked "Catholicus," tongue in cheek. "A very emphatic silence is maintained about women not virtuous. Does it mean to exclude them while bad *men* are admitted? Is this accident, or design, sinister and insidious against a portion of the community? What has virtue to do with a reading room?" The answer to Newman seemed clear: "If virtue be a mastery over the mind, . . . we must seek it in graver and holier places than libraries and reading-rooms."[2]

The "Catholicus" letters caused quite a stir. Peel himself was furious at them, and Lord Morpeth thundered away at them in the halls of Parliament. Though the secret of Newman's authorship was well kept, the Tractarian bias of the letters, which attacked the Tory leader in a Tory newspaper, was obvious enough for the liberal press to suspect a plot. The *Chronicle* editorialized "on one of the strangest novelties of the nineteenth century," the antagonism between the "iron mace" of Puseyism and the "rope of sand" which was Toryism. The Puseyites, said the *Chronicle,* "have all the marks of the most right-down [*sic*] earnestness that the world has seen in religion since the time of the Puritans and the Reformers." They might have been ideal allies for the Tories in those days when the Tories had principles, a time, in the *Chronicle*'s judgment, which had long since passed.[3]

At least "Catholicus" did not have to worry about the problem of Rome versus England. But even as he composed his letters for the *Times,* Newman could not banish the perplexity from his mind. Frederic Rogers, one of only two who were aware how deeply Newman was disturbed, was vacationing in Italy, and he seemed intent on trying to dislodge the Roman poison from his mentor's mind by reciting all the mummery and superstition he saw—like the seventy soldiers who, after an eight-day retreat, threw themselves down, sobbing and groaning, in front of a picture of the Virgin.[4] Newman gently chided him for his violent reaction and suggested that "such prejudice and suspicion . . . disqualify you as a witness of facts against [Rome]."[5]

When he replied, Rogers pulled no punches.

I quite own [he wrote] that I am disposed to fix upon the faults of Rome. I know I have long felt so, ever since I began to feel that the controversy between Rome and ourselves was really pressing and since I have fancied that high estimate of her advantages was leading to a scorn of our own Church. And I cannot complain of being distrusted on that account; I distrust myself. I know I am very likely not to observe their merits or to give them proper weight. But I do think you are a little hard on my honesty when you set me aside as simply "disqualified to be a witness of facts against her." And again I think you are mistaken in thinking that it is their demureness or their minute ceremonial merely that is setting me against them. However, I will not inflict justifications on you, particularly as I have just plucked a letter which I had nearly finished to you containing nearly two pages of them.[6]

On February 21st, in the midst of the uproar over "Catholicus," Newman observed his birthday. "I never had such dreary thoughts," he told Jemima, "as on finding myself forty. Twenty-one was bad enough."[7] Six days later Tract Number Ninety came off the press.

I

Tract Ninety was the climax of the Oxford Movement; everything else led either up to it or away from it. Hence its intellectual genesis is important. Newman always maintained that he wrote Number Ninety for the sake of those disciples of his who otherwise would have drifted off to the embrace of Rome. There is no reason to disbelieve this assertion nor, on the other hand, to credit those critics who at the time and later insisted that Number Ninety proved that Newman all along intended to betray the English Church. But no man was so acutely conscious of his own inner feelings as was Newman, and certainly he would never have written the tract had not he hoped also to resolve something of his own perplexity.

Much has been written about Newman's sensitivity and about his ability to get inside the minds of others. In the light of this undeniable fact, it is astonishing indeed that Newman apparently never thought anybody with a good Tractarian background would be seriously or honestly troubled by the Roman claims until he himself had been struck by them. From the fall of 1839 an entirely new note appeared in his correspondence. Thus, on October 23, 1839, he wrote to Bowden that he feared "breakers ahead" in the form of secessions to Rome. "If a [national] convocation were now to meet, I think there would be a schism."[8] To Jemima, on November 17th: "I never can be surprised at *individuals* going off to Romanism, but that is not my chief fear, but schism in the Church."[9] And to Tom Mozley, a few weeks later: "I think the tide is turning, and we shall be left on the beach. . . . I should not be surprised to see conversions to Romanism somewhere or other."[10]

What is remarkable is that the Tracts, sacramentality, the breviary, Froude's *Remains*, indeed antiquity itself pointed towards a catholic religiosity which, as Newman himself had said, was without Rome a paper theory. Yet he could not see the danger to others until he had himself felt the "hit" (to use his own word) from Rome. Perhaps this indicates how intensely personal the Movement was to those who shared in it, how much one's own "ethos" dominated the directions it took. The prudent man examines his conduct with a thought as to how it will affect others—whether it is expedient in the Pauline sense. Newman seems not to have done so. He told Bowden that Wiseman's article was the "only good things which had been written against us." Yet roughly the same things had been said before, but because Newman had not himself felt their force, he could not imagine that others might have been struck by them.

Number Ninety then was written to head people off from Rome, but it was written also to make it possible for Newman himself, now that the Via Media was dead, to remain within the Church of England. The tract was not, needless to say, addressed to Bowden, Keble or Pusey, nor to the likes of Rogers or Henry Wilberforce. It was meant for men still younger, if not in years, then in exposure to Tractarian ideas. Included among these were the breviary enthusiasts, Robert Williams and Samuel Wood; also the Mozley brothers, James because he was young and Tom because he was scatterbrained. William Palmer of Magdalen (not to be confused with Palmer of Worcester), Bloxam and Morris, with their liturgical and aesthetic emphases, formed another susceptible group. There were others with similar preoccupations scattered across the country, and to all of them Newman, after 1839, felt a kind of duty. He tried to fulfill it in Number Ninety.

The people he had most under his eye, those whom he called "the *now* rising generation at Oxford," were, he said, "Arnold's youths. Much depends on how they turn out."[11] He did not refer only to those who had been at Rugby Preparatory School and hence had felt the personal touch of Thomas Arnold's magic, but also to a whole generation of Oxford graduates who testified to Arnold's influence by their contempt for humbug, by their serious dedication to a humane, undoctrinal brand of Christianity which fitted well with radical ideas in politics. Many of these young men came to the startling conclusion that Tractarianism was a perfect complement to what they had learned from Arnold, and soon, much to the surprise and disappointment of the Headmaster of Rugby, they were hanging on every word from the Vicar of St. Mary's. This phenomenon was in a way history repeating itself; as the first Tractarians had been largely formed by the Evangelical revival, so the new breed came by one route or another from Rugby.

The most prominent of "Arnold's youths" were Arthur Stanley and William George Ward. Indeed, in September of 1839, when Newman experienced his first doubt about the Via Media, he remarked, "The worst of it is that those sharp fellows Ward, Stanley and Co. will not let one go to sleep upon it."[12] Both Ward and Stanley were from Balliol, which in the late 1830s had just about overtaken Oriel as the leading college in Oxford. Balliol was an exciting place in those days, filled with inquiry and spirited debate, where inferences were driven hard towards conclusions. A clever, diffident, somewhat fearful youth—Tuckwell said he arrived at Oxford somewhere between a girl and a man—Stanley[13] had gone to Rugby where Arnold's massive masculinity had left a permanent impression upon him. During his undergraduate days he felt the pull of Tractarianism. It was not fatal in his case; he survived to become Arnold's biographer and ultimately Dean of Westminster. But he went to listen to Newman at St. Mary's mostly out of curiosity, and came away, for a time at least, a fervent convert.

W. G. Ward[14] was a Fellow of Balliol (elected 1834) and mathematics lecturer in the college. Though never at Rugby, he was an ardent disciple of Arnold's and of Whately's and Bentham's too. He avoided Newman at first like the plague. When someone asked Ward if he attended St. Mary's, he retorted, "Why should I go and listen to such myths?" But in 1837 Stanley persuaded Ward to go with him to hear Newman lecture. The two Balliol men sat in the front row and nudged one another and as Newman spoke, whispered asides like "What would Arnold say to that?" After several weekly demonstrations of this kind, Newman had the benches turned to face each other, like choir stalls, and thus eluded the distraction. Ward, for his part, heard no myths, but rather a consistent and, to him, deeply moving confirmation of Arnold's call to personal holiness. By May 1839 Newman could write, "The only real news is the accession, I trust, of Ward of Balliol to good principles. He is a man I know very little of, but whom I cannot help liking very much, in spite of his still professing himself a radical in politics."[15]

Ward was a fat, ungainly mathematical genius, blessed with a magnificent singing voice and boundless good humour. He resembled Whately not only in appearance but in the relentlessness of his argument based upon very few principles. If a subject appealed to him, his intellect devoured it; if it bored him, he left it completely alone. Ward never minded admitting ignorance: "Quite out of my line," he would say cheerfully. "I'm far too stupid in such matters to be of the slightest use." "Intellect," he once said to Henry Wilberforce, "is a wretched gift, my dear Henry. Absolutely worthless. Now my intellect is in some respects almost infinite, and yet I don't value it a bit."

Moral idealism had made Ward a disciple of Arnold's, and the same thing brought him to the feet of Newman. He scarcely knew Pusey or Keble; he did not care about the carefully balanced positions which the Tractarians had constructed. The Via Media or, indeed, any moderate stance, was unreal to him. He grasped the principles of sacramentality as the basis of moral perfection and antiquity as the criterion of Christian truth. And he saw both of these ideas better expressed in Roman than in Anglican formularies. So he kept demanding, in his blunt, narrow way, that England conform to Rome; anything else, he said, was quite absurd.

Ward was for this reason a difficult disciple. Despite his unflagging devotion to Newman, he had not the slightest sympathy or understanding for the agony of indecision which afflicted his mentor from 1839 onwards. For Ward never had a doubt about anything. This quality infuriated his friends and colleagues at Balliol, where the common room arguments went on into the night. But Ward never lost his temper as he pressed his opponents with his devastating wit and immense dialectical skill. He pressed Newman the same way: If Rome is better, more catholic, more tuned to the Primitive Church, then why not go to Rome? To Ward it all seemed so simple.

Yet no one could be angry for long with Ward. His goodness was as unaffected as that of a child and his jovial spirits cheered everyone who came into contact with him. Years later, Benjamin Jowett, who was at Balliol with Ward, remembered an occasion which in a way sums up Ward's whole life. On a summer evening Ward was to preach at Newman's chapel in Littlemore. He took Jowett with him. "The sermon which he preached was a printed one of Dr. Arnold's, but with additions and alterations which, as he said, it would have driven the author mad to hear." As they walked home at twilight along the Iffley road, Ward sang arias from *Don Giovanni*.[16]

Another Fellow of Balliol for whom Tract Ninety was intended was Frederick Oakeley.[17] Though ten years older than Ward, Oakeley was an indecisive man, "very impressible and impulsive," Tom Mozley remembered. Ward's unshakable self-confidence gave him the intellectual mastery over Oakeley soon after their friendship began. At Oxford Oakeley had outgrown his Evangelical upbringing and had become deeply interested in liturgical matters. "Years before the Movement a clever but cynical Oriel friend described him as so impressed by worship and devotion that if he should come upon a temple filled with a multitude prostrate before an idol, he would throw himself down among them."[18]

Isaac Williams thought Oakeley's "abilities were rather showy, from an elegant and pleasing style, than either acute or deep."[19] Another observer noted that though he possessed "a facile and elegant pen," he was "without much learning."[20] Yet Tom Mozley admired his selflessness: "Nobody cared less for himself or took less care of himself."[21] Until Ward came along, Oakeley found little of an intellectual nature to interest him in the Movement. "In truth," he recalled, early Tractarianism "never presented any features of attraction either to my own mind or to that of others whom the Movement eventually absorbed into itself. I can confidently assert that the hardest trial to which my faith was ever exposed was that of being asked to see in the Anglican bishops the successors of the apostles."[22]

In 1839, Oakeley, without giving up his Balliol fellowship, became pastor of a small London parish. From that time on, until he left the Anglican Church six years later, Oakeley made Margaret Street Chapel the metropolitan center of avant-garde liturgy. Ward was a frequent visitor to Margaret Street, and he helped Oakeley minister to an ever-growing crowd of fashionable Londoners. Despite their incongruous appearance—the stout and awkward Ward, flailing the air with irreverent sallies, and the fastidious Oakeley, who walked with a limp and whose greatest joy was fussing with rubrical niceties—they were two of a kind. In 1839, Ward pounced upon Froude's *Remains*, and the very things which disturbed moderate readers delighted Ward. Said Frederic Rogers, "He found in Froude's *Remains* a good deal of his own radicalism, . . . and it seemed *literally* to make him jump for joy."[23] In the summer of 1840, Oakeley spent two weeks in Normandy, and, as he reported to Pusey, he was "much pleased altogether" by Roman Catholicism, and "saw and heard a good deal of the Church which was interesting."[24] In the spring of 1841, Newman produced Number Ninety to satisfy Ward, Oakeley and the new Tractarians who had sprung up around them.

II

Tract Ninety was titled "Remarks on certain Passages in the Thirty-nine Articles." It was eighty-seven pages long. It bore the date January 25, 1841, but it did not appear until February 27th. Though the author of Number Ninety, as with all the Tracts, was anonymous, very few in Oxford did not know that Newman had written it.

The Tract was a bold attempt to give comfort to Anglo-Catholics who feared that subscription to the Thirty-nine Articles involved them automatically in a denial of catholic truth. Newman, always a stout defender of subscription to the Articles—as he had proved in the Hampden case—had covered some of the same ground in earlier works, and he quoted freely from them throughout Number Ninety. But never before had he examined the Articles so minutely and, of course, never before had their anti-Roman emphasis been so much on his mind. He stated his objective in the introduction: "That there are real difficulties to a catholic Christian in the ecclesiastical position of our Church at this day, no one can deny; but the statements of the Articles are not in the number, and it may be right at the present moment to insist upon this."[25]

The Articles, promulgated early in Elizabeth I's reign, were a Reformation document. They showed in almost every line that they intended to keep Rome out of the English Church. Nevertheless, they also tried to be as comprehensive as possible, for at the moment when they began their juridical existence (1563), the queen and her ministers still hoped to bring the masses, so recently Catholic, into the national Church. Thus, for example, much latitude was allowed in expressing the pivotal matter of justification (Article XI): "We are accounted righteous before God only for the merit of our Lord and Saviour Jesus Christ by faith, and not for our own works and deservings; wherefore, that we are justified by faith only is a most wholesome doctrine and very full of comfort." Here was a statement which most people could accept so long as each could emphasize what he chose. Indeed, Newman had accepted it and had written a book explaining in what sense he did accept it.

There was then a certain conscious looseness about the wording of the Articles, and during the three hundred years that they had been imposed as a test of orthodoxy, Anglicans of various parties had taken advantage of this. Newman could not be blamed if he followed a path so often trod before; Evangelicals and liberals had construed the Articles in such a way that they could subscribe to them, even though they seemed to contradict, for instance, the Evangelical-liberal view of baptismal regeneration. But nobody before Tract Ninety had attempted to interpret the Articles in a manner which clashed with the deep national prejudice against Rome. Generally, and somewhat thoughtlessly, it was taken for granted that as the Prayer Book represented the catholic, so the Articles proclaimed the Protestant, side in the grand Anglican compromise. Newman, however, had never acceded to this notion. The Articles, in his judgment, had to have a catholic interpretation because, among other reasons, they had to be in harmony with the Prayer Book, wherein the primitive Christian creeds and liturgy were enshrined. And besides, "the Articles," he said, "are evidently framed on the principle of leaving open large questions on which the controversy hinges. They state broadly extreme truths and are silent about their adjustment." Moreover, the sixteenth-century framers of the Articles "constructed them in such a way as best to comprehend [i.e. include] those who did not go so far in Protestantism as themselves. Anglo-Catholics then are but the successors and representatives of those moderate reformers."[26]

So Newman felt free to interpret the Articles in a catholic sense, even though it was clear that the framers intended a Protestant sense. If violence were not done to the actual meanings of the words themselves, then it mattered little what the framers may or may not have intended. They, after all, protested against the abuses of their own time, while the catholic creeds were for all time. Up to a point there was nothing new in this approach, as anyone familiar with the Tracts was quite aware. But Tract Ninety did add something new by its obvious preoccupation with the Roman problem. Thus Newman explained Article XXVIII, which condemned transubstantiation, as affirming a Real Presence in the Eucharist while it rejected a cannibalistic theory of that Presence. If Roman transubstantiation were indeed cannibalistic (and no doubt some Roman Catholics treated it so), then the Article did condemn it. But was it cannibalism, as a matter of fact?

Newman insisted throughout Number Ninety that the Articles dealt with what might be called an existential rather than with an essential situation. That is, the damnatory clauses in the Articles were aimed at an actual condition with which the framers were familiar and not with the doctrinal basis of that condition. The two indeed might go together, but the Articles did not necessarily encompass both. So Article XXII called the "Romish doctrine" of Purgatory, images, relics, and invocation of the saints "a fond thing vainly invented" and "repugnant to the Word of God." But, Newman asked, what precisely is "Romish doctrine?" Only "Romish doctrine" is "fond" and vain according to the Article. Romish doctrine is not that of the Primitive Church, which used images, relics and the like and prayed for the dead. Nor is it (and this was the crucial point) the doctrine of the Council of Trent, which condemned the same kind of superstitious corruption as the Article did. And anyway the decrees of Trent were published after the Articles and therefore could not fall under the latter's scope.[27]

This was the sort of reasoning which brought out the wrath of the average English reader of Number Ninety. It was all very well to inter-

pret the Articles in a way which would include various English points
of view, but to him it was monstrous to open a way, through the Articles,
for a rapprochement with Rome. He thought he knew perfectly well what
Romish doctrine was and he resented any attempt to explain it away.
Article XXXI said it clearly enough for him: "The sacrifices of Masses
in the which it was commonly said that the priest did offer Christ for
the quick and the dead to have remission of pain or guilt were blasphemous fables and dangerous deceits." But Newman replied: "Nothing
can show more clearly than this passage that the Articles were not written
against the creed of the Roman Church, but against actual existing
errors in it, whether taken into its system or not."[28] That last phrase
should be noted; Newman was arguing that whether or not Rome had
fostered a deceitful notion of the Eucharistic Sacrifice was beside the
point, because the Article specified a particular kind of corrupt practice.
Therefore, an Anglican who believed the Roman Mass to be truly a
mysterious share in Christ's original sacrifice (as the Council of Trent
had taught) could still swear to the Article in good conscience.

Enough has been said to suggest the drift of Number Ninety and
perhaps to indicate the measure of fury it was bound to provoke. But its
impact cannot be fully appreciated without the challenge with which
Newman concluded it: "The Protestant confession was drawn up with
the purpose of including Catholics; and Catholics now will not be excluded. What was an economy in the Reformers is a protection to us.
What would have been a perplexity to us [in the sixteenth century] is a
perplexity to Protestants now. We could not then have found fault with
their words; they cannot now repudiate our meaning."[29]

III

Newman was surprised at the violent outburst caused by Number
Ninety. One reason perhaps was that, as usual, he had shown the Tract
to Keble before publication, and Keble had reacted without any particular enthusiasm and certainly without alarm. "My dear N.," Keble wrote
on February 19th, "these [enclosed] are all the notes which occur to me,
except one or two errata which I have marked in the [proof] sheets. I
am much obliged to you for the Tract and should think it very likely to
answer its purpose with such as can be content to take what is given
when they cannot have the best."[30]

W. G. Ward, on the other hand, prophesied trouble, and he proved
to be right. By Sunday, March 7th, Newman had begun to hear the
rumbles. "I have just published a Tract, Number Ninety," he told Tom
Mozley, "which people fear will get me into a scrape—it is on the Articles. It has been sent off by enemies to various bishops, and is selling very
fast here. I think people are *sick* of the subject and will in weariness let

us rest. They have cried wolf till they have no voice. The Tract was necessary to keep our young friends from stumbling at the Articles and going to Rome."[31]

But there was to be no rest from the agitation of the Movement's ancient enemy, Charles P. Golightly, who mounted a very skillful campaign. He began by talking about Tract Ninety all over Oxford, describing it as a "curiosity" and urging all and sundry to read it. Then he turned his attention to the country at large; he bought such quantities of the Tract that Parker, the Oxford bookseller, had difficulty keeping it in stock. Among those to whom Golightly sent a copy were all the bishops. Next he looked for a way to arouse the Oxford power structure against the Tract. He tried to enlist the Rector of Exeter first, and failing this (for Richards of Exeter was friendly to the Tractarians) he succeeded with the Warden of Wadham. Now, with an agent on the Board of Heads of Houses, Golightly canvassed for allies among the college tutors who, unlike himself, had official status in the university and could therefore raise an official protest. He was rebuffed in several colleges— Oriel and Christ Church among others—but his persistence was rewarded by the adherence of four senior tutors: T. T. Churton of Brasenose, John Griffiths of Wadham, H. B. Wilson of St. John's and Archibald Campbell Tait of Balliol, "gentlemen," observed one of Newman's friends, "who had scarcely the happiness of each other's acquaintance till Golly's skill harnessed them together."[32]

All this activity took place during the first week of March against the background of the newspaper war occasioned by the "Catholicus" letters in the *Times*. Then, on Monday, March 8th, there appeared in Oxford, in printed form, the famous Letter of the Four Tutors. The two Evangelicals—Churton and Griffiths—and the two liberals—Wilson and Tait —addressed themselves to the editor of the Tracts for the Times because of the "painful impression" they had received from the contents of Number Ninety. As college tutors, they said, it was their statutory duty to use the Articles as a "text-book . . . in their theological teaching," and they discerned in Tract Ninety "a highly dangerous tendency from its suggesting that certain very important errors of the Church of Rome are not condemned by the Articles." As specific instances, they listed Number Ninety's treatment of Purgatory, indulgences, veneration of images, invocation of the saints and the Mass. The tutors denied that they wished to inhibit due liberty, "but this Tract puts forward new and startling views as to the extent to which that liberty may be carried." If the views of the Tract's author were to prevail, the tutors were afraid "the most plainly erroneous doctrines and practices of the Church of Rome" might be taught "in the lecture rooms of the university and from the pulpits of our churches." The tutors demanded, finally, that the author of Number Ninety make himself known.[33]

Newman, as editor of the Tracts, did no more than acknowledge receipt of the tutors' letter and added with icy politeness that he received it "as expressing the opinion of persons for whom he has much respect and whose names carry great weight." But meanwhile the letter was being widely circulated and the lines were being drawn for a fight. On Tuesday Newman wrote in alarmed tones to Harriet: "I have got into what may prove a serious mess here. I have just published a Tract which I did not feel likely to attract attention. I sent it to Keble before publishing; he too made no remark upon it. But people are taking it up very warmly— thanks, I believe, entirely to Golightly."[34]

But if forces were marshaling against Newman, others were rallying to him. On that same Tuesday he received a strong endorsement from William Palmer of Worcester; and considering the strained relations which had long existed between the two men, Palmer's letter was a magnificent gesture indeed. "My dear Newman," Palmer wrote, "though I have taken no part in the discussions relative to the Tracts, I yet feel it my duty to express to you, under present circumstances, the gratification which I have derived from Number Ninety just published. While I should hesitate to commit myself to every statement contained in it, I have no hesitation in expressing an opinion that it is the *most valuable* of the series of Tracts that has come under my observation." Palmer added that he would gladly assume this stance publicly: "If my opinion can be of any service to you I do not wish to conceal it."[35] And a day or two later came a similar statement from the other survivor of the Hadleigh conference. "I think [Tract Ninety] one of the most important papers that has been put out and calculated, under God's blessing, to do much good. . . . If I can be of any service I will not fail you. . . . Yours in heart and affection, Arthur Perceval."[36]

It must have seemed to Newman like the good old days of 1836 when differences were forgotten for the sake of bringing down the impious Hampden. George Moberly, Keble's friend from Winchester who had been so annoyed at the *Remains*, sent word that "on the whole the Tract in its main design and 19/20ths of its execution appear to me *most valuable*. We want to be taught that we have a higher and holier origin than the Reformation and the Articles."[37] From Leeds Walter Hook, a High Churchman of spotless credentials, took a belligerent line: If they force us into a party, said he, then we must act like a party, "by which I mean that in any ulterior proceedings little minor points of difference must be forgotten, and we must act as one man in asserting our general principles."[38]

The "ulterior proceedings" Hook spoke of went on apace. The Board of Heads of Houses held its weekly meeting on Wednesday, March 10th, and the Vice-chancellor, Dr. Wynter, formally brought Tract Ninety and the Letter of the Four Tutors before the Board for its consideration. Richards of Exeter reported that though few of the Heads had yet read the Tract, "they were very fierce against it and against the Tracts in general, against which they seemed to have declared 'War to the knife.'" Richards had gone to the meeting armed with the letter from Palmer, but he had sensed that the feelings of the Heads were so roused that to have read it to them would have been like throwing "cold water on a red hot iron." The Heads adjourned without taking action and agreed to meet again the following Friday.[39]

Newman, at Littlemore, wondered whether he should come forward and acknowledge authorship of the Tract. His friends persuaded him to wait; "it is better to remain quiet," one of them advised, "and not give up your name till it is officially called for."[40] Meanwhile, Golightly carried his indefatigable crusade into the common rooms. On Thursday morning he was closeted so long with the Provost of Oriel that Dr. Hawkins missed his breakfast. During the days following he received letters of congratulation from four bishops. "Do you know," Newman wrote Henry Wilberforce on Thursday, "I am in a regular scrape about that Tract Ninety? *All* through Golius, who has solely, proprio motu, stirred up the world which else would have slept."[41]

It was not quite fair to say "*all* through Golius," because if there had not already existed a reservoir of animosity towards the Tractarians Golightly could have accomplished little. This was apparent when the Heads met again on Friday afternoon, March 12th. The vast majority of them had long hoped for an opportunity to bring Newman and the Tracts into disrepute, and Tract Ninety—with or without Golightly— seemed to provide the golden opportunity. But as they wrangled through their meeting it became increasingly clear that they were, for the most part, timid, compromising men. They were frankly afraid to put the matter before a university Convocation, which alone could administer a university repudiation—as it had done to R. D. Hampden. When news of this hesitancy reached the outside, there was a sigh of relief among Newman's friends, who were convinced that had the Heads summoned Convocation they would have won a smashing victory.

Instead the Heads appointed a committee to look into the matter and to report back to the full Board the following Monday. Newman meantime spent the same Friday writing a pamphlet which attempted to vindicate the Tract from the accusations of the four tutors. He wrote with furious speed and by nightfall the work was done. Following the literary etiquette of the time, he used the epistolary form and addressed it to Dr. Richard Jelf, Pusey's old friend, now Canon of Christ Church. Jelf saw and approved the pamphlet on Friday evening, and on Saturday, March 13th, it went to press.[42]

Over the weekend Keble wrote worriedly from Hursley and suggested that Newman appeal to the bishop "whether there is not something scandalous in letting [Evangelical and liberal] books pass while [the Heads]

censure a Tract which at any rate touches on no fundamentals. Might
he not fairly say to the Heads, 'Let me see you censure some of your
anti-regeneration sermons, etc., and then I will consider what you say
about [Tract Ninety].' " Even so, Keble was having some second thoughts
and he was bothered that perhaps he had read the proofs of Number
Ninety too quickly. If the Tract were ever reprinted he had in mind
several substantive changes which he sent along for Newman's perusal.
Thus, for example, "in the matter of indulgences . . . and images, the
Article, I suppose, meant to condemn *both* the doctrine (and here a
tangible one existed) and the bad practice flowing from it; and I suppose
the same would hold in all these things: they meant the doctrine from
which the bad practices legitimately flowed."[43] But worried or not, Keble
wrote directly to the Vice-chancellor and assumed equal responsibility
for the Tract. Pusey wrote also, but with a heavy heart and more out of
loyalty than conviction.

On Saturday morning, Pusey called on the Provost of Oriel and asked
him to move for a delay in the Board's action until the "Letter to Jelf"
could be published. Newman wrote the provost to the same effect the
next day. Years later, when they were both old and the fires of their
enmity had long burned out, Newman and Hawkins tried to remember
exactly what had happened. Newman recalled only "that together with
others I thought there was a kind of race between the Board and myself
which should get into print faster."[44] Hawkins' memory was a little more
precise. After receiving Newman's letter of March 14th, in which he
learned that a short defense of Number Ninety was in the press and could
be expected on Tuesday or Wednesday, Hawkins "accordingly moved
the Board on [Monday] the 15th that everything respecting the Tract
should be suspended till the promised defence appeared."[45] His motion
was defeated by the panicky, angry Board of Heads, which instead passed
overwhelmingly a censure motion, for which, to his credit, Hawkins did
not vote.

On Tuesday morning, March 16th, the censure appeared in the form
of a printed broadside. "Resolved," it said, "that modes of interpretation
such as are suggested in . . . Tract [Ninety], evading rather than explaining the sense of the Thirty-nine Articles, and reconciling subscription to
them with the adoption of errors which they were designed to counteract, defeat the object and are inconsistent with due observance of . . .
[University] Statutes."[46] The ground taken by the censure was exactly
that of the four tutors. And Newman's answer to the four tutors, the
"Letter to Jelf," was delivered from the printer at noon. The race had
been lost. But Newman remained marvelously cool and self-possessed.
He sat down and wrote a courteous note to the Vice-chancellor, in which
he acknowledged the authorship of Number Ninety. "I hope it will not
surprise you," he said, "if I say that my opinion remains unchanged of

the truth and honesty of the principle maintained in the Tract, and of the necessity of putting it forth."[47]

IV

When he broke the news of the censure to his sister Harriet, Newman managed a cheerful aside: "I have quite enough, thank God, to keep me from inward trouble; no one ever did a great thing without suffering."[48] Harriet, in a delightfully intuitive manner, had already made up her mind about Tract Ninety: "Though I shall take a long breath before I read it, I will continue to believe that it does not go too far."[49]

The censure by the Heads, though a blow, was not in itself a disaster. Anyone familiar with the legal subtleties of Oxford knew that the Heads, acting without Convocation, did not speak for the university. And besides, the vulgar speed with which the Heads had moved and their obvious personal bias had caused disgust in many an Oxford common room where there was no sympathy for Tractarianism. The problem remained, however, that the world at large, untutored in academic law, might presume that the censure of Number Ninety had been administered by the university itself. Keble saw a silver lining in that the Heads had not addressed the censure to the tutors, which, had they done so, would have made Number Ninety a matter for controversy in the day-to-day teaching of the colleges. Nor had the censure mentioned the rest of the Tracts. All may yet be well, he told Pusey, if the Oxford authorities "and the bishops will not lay their heads together and contrive something more stringent."[50]

At Oriel, Dr. Hawkins was also eager to point out the limited scope of the censure. As Head of Newman's college where a good many of the fellows were ardent Tractarians, Hawkins was in an awkward position. He had honourably tried to delay the censure until the "Letter to Jelf" was published but he nevertheless believed that in substance the censure was good and necessary. For the sake of peace in his own house, however, he defended the Board's action on the ground that the censure was "logical," not theological. "It was aimed against *an evasive and sophistical* mode of reasoning, applied to what is *part and parcel of our Statute Book,* the Articles. [Hawkins] felt himself that neither the Board nor Convocation had any business to meddle with theology" and that "the resolution was drawn up so as to avoid the appearance of a theological censure." This struck more than one Fellow of Oriel as "evasive and sophistical" and hardly calculated to soften the effect of the censure in the popular mind.[51]

But on Wednesday, March 17th, the affair of Number Ninety took a new turn, which, given Tractarian principles, was bound to be more crucial than the badgering of the Heads of Houses. The Bishop of Oxford decided to intervene. The mail that day brought two letters from Bagot, one to Pusey and the other to Newman. Both were worded with the bishop's habitual kindliness, but they also revealed how sorely alarmed he was at the present state of things. Newman he simply asked to guarantee that no further discussion of the Articles would appear in the Tracts. He suggested to Pusey that Newman might be persuaded, by Pusey, to publish a statement avowing his acceptance of both the letter and the spirit of the Articles. Bagot insisted in both letters that what he cared for most was peace in the Church.[52]

Newman immediately agreed to the bishop's desire that the Articles not be discussed in future Tracts. But with regard to the statement about the spirit of the Articles, he would say only, "I am most desirous of saying in print anything which I can honestly say to remove false impressions created by the Tract."[53] Bagot meanwhile sought the advice of the Archbishop of Canterbury. The primate assumed a predictable stance, summed up best perhaps by this line from a letter to Bagot dated March 22, 1841: "It would I think be unadvisable that your Lordship's name should be connected in any way with the discussion on this matter." Forthrightness was not the episcopal bench's strong suit. But the archbishop did offer one positive recommendation: "It seems most desirable that the publication of the Tracts should be discontinued forever."[54]

While these negotiations were going on, Newman continued to receive pledges of support, though not all of them were unqualified. Oakeley sent word that the people attached to Margaret Street Chapel—and not extremists, he added—were indebted to Tract Ninety for making it possible for them to subscribe to the Articles.[55] Oakeley did not append his definition of extremist. Keble liked the "Letter to Jelf" much better than he had the Tract: "I am sure this must do good, and I trust the whole affair will be over-ruled [sic] to do so." He still hoped for the best, but he continued to fret over Number Ninety's treatment of the Roman doctrine on Purgatory, and he warned Newman not to fight with or threaten the Heads.[56] Bowden wrote from London on March 23rd and suggested a formal Address by the M.A.s to the Chancellor (the Duke of Wellington), "praying him to check the assumption by the Heads of an authority inconsistent with the constitution of the university." But Bowden, like Keble and Pusey, had not liked some of Tract Ninety, and he thought that Newman, "*having* alluded to men's 'straggling in the direction of Rome,' should . . . express [a] sense of the serious nature of the sin which they would commit in leaving the particular position in the spiritual temple in which God has placed them." "I may misread you," Bowden added, "but my impression is that a Romanizing youth—from what you say—might understand you to mean that under certain circumstances he might justifiably straggle."[57] That indeed was what

Newman was saying, and such a sentiment indicated how far his ideas had drifted from those of his oldest friend.

On the same day that Bowden wrote Newman from London, Bishop Bagot invited Pusey to the episcopal palace "for a little private conversation on this painful position of things." Pusey accordingly went to Cuddesdon the next morning, Wednesday, March 24th. The bishop asked Pusey to act as intermediary in proposing three steps to Newman: that the Tracts be discontinued, that Number Ninety be suppressed (that is, not reprinted), and that Newman should make it publicly known that such action was taken in deference to the bishop's wishes. Pusey brought the message to Newman in the afternoon. He left little doubt that he thought the bishop's proposition, considering the pressures being exerted from London, was a reasonable one. Newman agreed to the first and third requests, but he balked at the second. To suppress Number Ninety and then to publish that this was done at the bishop's bidding was tantamount to an episcopal censure, which, in Newman's judgment, was far worse than privately withdrawing the Tract from circulation. Probably Bagot did not appreciate this fine point nor the bitterness it aroused in Newman: "I am pained to see," he told Pusey, "that authorities in London have increased their demands according to my submissiveness. When they thought me obstinate they spoke only of not writing more in the Tracts about the Articles. When they find me obedient, they add the stopping of the Tracts and the suppression of Number Ninety."[58]

Newman sought advice from Keble and Walter Hook. The essence of Keble's reply was that Newman should try to persuade the bishop not to suppress Number Ninety and if he failed he should obey but also resign St. Mary's.[59] Hook recommended resistance even to the courts if necessary. "Let Dr. Bagot act as your *bishop* and all will be right. If he condemns you it will be in his court and by his proper officers, but he cannot condemn you before you have obtained a hearing. . . . A regard to the proper forms will interpose that delay which may prevent the bishop from acting rashly."[60] There was much to what Hook said, but Newman preferred Keble's line, and perhaps he knew that his threat to resign St. Mary's in the middle of the fuss would have more weight with the bishop than any appeal to the courts of law.

On Friday, March 26th, Pusey brought Bagot Newman's answer, and the bishop yielded on the issue of suppressing Number Ninety. He would. be satisfied, he said, if Newman "will not shrink from a frank and generous avowal that I had expressed my opinion that the Tract was objectionable and likely to disturb the peace . . . of the Church, as well as to state . . . my advice that the Tracts for the Times should be discontinued."[61]

So Newman went to work on still another pamphlet. He wrote it at one long sitting on Monday, March 29th, and since he sent each manuscript page to the printer as he finished it, the "Letter to the Bishop of Oxford" was through the press and available to the public by Tuesday afternoon. The bishop was delighted. He sent Newman an expression of "satisfaction" and "gratification," and he said, "Now that calm has, as I hope, succeeded the threatened storm, . . . you will never regret having written that letter to me."[62] Newman too was happy enough with what he called "a very fair bargain. . . . I am quite satisfied with the bargain I have got, if this is all—as I suppose it will be."[63] And on April 1st he sent reassurances to Keble: "We are all in very good spirits here."[64]

V

Tract Ninety was a best seller. Twenty-five hundred copies were sold in the first two weeks and ten thousand by May 25th. It also set off a veritable orgy of publication during the spring of 1841 as pamphlets and remonstrances, attacks and counterattacks tumbled off the presses. Nicholas Wiseman—now a bishop and residing in England—addressed a "Letter" to Newman, which was answered by a "Letter" to Wiseman from Palmer of Worcester, which in turn was answered by "Remarks" from Wiseman to Palmer. Hook wrote a "Letter" to the Bishop of Ripon defending Number Ninety, and Golightly gleefully responded with "New and Strange Doctrines extracted from the Writings of Mr. Newman and his Friends." Golightly professed himself annoyed that Hook should find the Tract writers guilty only of having expressed themselves incautiously, and so he, Golightly, proposed a list of awful Tractarian heresies. Then followed twenty-seven shabby pages of quotation out of context from the Tracts, Froude's *Remains* and various of Newman's books.[65]

One of the four tutors, Wilson of St. John's, composed a "Letter" to T. T. Churton, another of the four. Wilson complained about Tract Ninety's imprecise language and "want of definiteness." He shrugged away Newman's plea that Number Ninety or something like it was necessary to keep men from going to Rome: "Surely there are other arrows within the quiver of a well-furnished theologian" so that one need not give the Articles a Roman flavour nor introduce "a scheme of reconstructing our Church according to some ideal primitive model."[66] W. G. Ward answered Wilson with "A Few Words in support of Number Ninety," which disposed of Wilson's charge that using the principles of Tract Ninety a Unitarian could subscribe to Article II (on the Trinity). A young politician named Robert Lowe attacked the honesty of the Tract writers in a pamphlet called "The Articles construed by Themselves," and this brought Ward back into the field with "A Few more Words in support of Number Ninety."

Frederick Oakeley submitted eighty-four pages of defense to the public, and Arthur Perceval thirty-three. Perceval's pamphlet was called "A Vindication of the Principles of the Authors of the Tracts for the Times." He admitted that there was much in Number Ninety that he did not understand, but he did not "see how any member of the Church of England can be blamed for doing what Mr. Newman has done."[67] In a shriller tone was "Puseyism Unmasked," by an anonymous author who (the advertisement stated) had earlier written "God is Love." Whoever he was, this gentleman explained unequivocally that all the trouble stemmed from "the undue and semi-popish exaltation of the power and dignity of the episcopal and ministerial office. . . . *We are not contending for trifles,*" he warned in italics.[68] And then there was S. R. Maitland, for a brief moment in 1838 editor of the *British Critic,* who wrote "A Letter to a Friend on Tract . . . Eighty-nine." "Perhaps, like the rest of the world," said Maitland, "you are so engrossed by Number Ninety that you have paid little or no attention to Number Eighty-nine." Keble's Tract on mysticism is "a very injurious publication" which "may be quietly stealing into circulation while everybody is looking another way."[69]

But of course the most important of the post-Tract Ninety publications were Newman's own. The "Letter to Jelf," his answer to the four tutors, plunged immediately into the thorny question of whether the Articles, in condemning the corruptions of the Roman system, also contained a condemnation of the authoritative teaching of the Roman Church on these points (Purgatory, etc.). Newman maintained that they did and, vehemently, that he had not said otherwise in Number Ninety. "The simple question is whether taken by themselves in their mere letter [the decrees of Trent] express [the corruption]; whether in fact other senses, short of the sense conveyed in the present authoritative teaching of the Roman Church will not fulfill their letter and may not even now in point of fact be held in that Church." In other words, as Newman treated the Articles, so would he treat the decrees of Trent. Their precise meaning did not necessarily involve the corruptions of the Roman system. Unhappily, "Romish doctrine" was too often "authoritative doctrine." "If there ever was a system which required reformation," said Newman, "it is that of Rome at this day." Indeed, he went further: given the existent corruption, the decrees of Trent have perhaps intensified it and will continue to do so "while these decrees remain unexplained in any truer and more catholic way."

But Newman maintained that there were signs within the Roman Church of a closer adherence to the letter of Trent's decrees, and to the extent that this was the case it was a cause for rejoicing, for it meant that an undeniably genuine branch of the Church catholic might yet approach its true fulfillment, despite its corrupt "traditionary system." The Church of England, on the other hand, has developed a traditionary system of its own which, in the name of the Articles, has given a false Protestant orientation. "To this exclusive modern system I desire to oppose myself; and it is as doing this doubtless that I am incurring the censure of the four gentlemen who have come before the public."

Newman concluded the "Letter to Jelf" with a kind of appeal. The Church, he said, is on the verge of a deeper life than she has known for more than a century. A multitude of signs point to this, not least among them the literary revival associated with the names of Wordsworth, Coleridge and Scott. "The age is moving towards something, and most unhappily the one religious communion among us which has of late years been practically in possession of this something is the Church of Rome. She alone, amid all the errors and evils of her practical system, has given free scope to the feelings of awe, mystery, tenderness, reverence, devotedness and other feelings which may be especially called Catholic. The question then is whether we shall give them up to the Roman Church or claim them for ourselves, as well we may, by reverting to that older system which has of late years indeed been superseded, but which . . . is . . . congenial . . . [and] even necessary to our Church."[70]

The "Letter to the Bishop of Oxford" was, as we have seen, a command performance. In it Newman fulfilled the bishop's direction to state that he, Bagot, was disturbed at the friction caused by Number Ninety and that he wished the Tracts discontinued. But more than this, Newman offered a general defense of the Tractarian activities over the preceding eight years. The Tracts, he protested, do not "betray a leaning towards Roman Catholic error and a deficient appreciation of our own truth." Nor have the Tractarians, in trying to breathe new life into the Primitive Church, been irresponsible; this, said Newman, is an "odious charge." The cause of dissension has largely arisen because patristic evidence is "uncongenial to our present ideas of religion." Oxford itself has been a source of trouble; that is, young intellectuals have grasped principles and pressed them to conclusions which Newman and the other leaders of the Movement were not prepared to grant. All of this has been troublesome, but it has not been irresponsible.

Newman protested that his loyalty and reverence for the Church and for Bagot personally were unflagging, and he defended himself further by citing his record at St. Mary's: His sermons had been non-controversial ("far more practical than doctrinal"); he had not tinkered with the liturgy ("I have altered nothing that I found established"); he had avoided any agitation for Church union ("Our business is with ourselves"). At the end, he referred to the condemnation of the Board of Heads and observed only his "pain" at having received the disapprobation of "persons in station." He carefully denoted their action as an "opinion."[71]

The old-line Tractarians found more to cheer about in the two "Letters" than they had in Tract Ninety itself. On the Friday after Easter, Keble told Pusey, "I cannot but think that N.'s coming out as he has in this whole business will do the cause a great deal more good than any fresh stir, of which this Tract has been made the pretence, is likely to do it harm. People quite unconnected write to one as if they were greatly moved by it."[72] And Pusey told James Hope, "You will be glad to hear that the immediate excitement about Tract Ninety seems subsiding, although I fear . . . into a lasting impression of our Jesuitism. On the other hand, they who have read what Newman has written since on the subject must be won by his touching simplicity and humility. I should hope too that a good deal will have been incidentally explained which people thought to be done gratuitously."[73] And Robert Wilberforce, now an archdeacon in Yorkshire, told Newman himself: "Respecting the prudence of publishing Number Ninety I do not speak, but I am well satisfied that nothing can be more unjust than the attacks made upon it. Its main principles are proved beyond controversy. But your letter to the bishop is written in a tone so calm, Christian and convincing that I am satisfied it will have great weight with all good men."[74]

Pusey and Keble posed a special problem. Though they both rushed loyally into print with "Letters" of their own, their hearts were not with Tract Ninety. Newman tried in vain to get both of them to refrain from publication. "We have got the principle of our interpretation admitted, in that it has not been condemned. Do not let us provoke opposition."[75] Pusey particularly did not enter into Newman's view of the Articles; "[he] considers what has been done [by the Tract] a pure evil (in his heart) and only wishes to soften and remedy it; of course my argument would not tell with him."[76]

And so the battle over Number Ninety came to an end. To outward appearances it seemed that the Tractarian forces, though scarred, still stood firm and undivided. The reality, however, was something else, and Newman recognized the fact if no one else did. What was needed now, as the summer of 1841 began, was quiet.

Don't let us have any more discussion about the Articles [he wrote Tom Mozley on June 18]. Go on with your history or doctrine or architecture etc., etc. which is your particular *line*. Number Ninety was intended to set you at ease, so that you might do that in safety. No one now will attack you, depend upon it, upon the ground of the Articles. Whereas if you begin to speak of the Articles, they will. . . . The Hebdomadal Board has been too cautious to attack doctrines or historical views, but an *interpretation* of the Articles. The bishop has only spoken of a particular Tract. There is nothing to hinder your lives of St. Anselm, your doctrines of etc. etc. [sic]. Before there was an appeal in terrorem, now there is not. *Drop* the subject of Number Ninety, but *use* it.[77]

CHAPTER 17

Threats and Alarums

DISASTER followed in the wake of Number Ninety. During the months after the uproar of March 1841, blow after blow fell upon the Tractarians in swift succession. Newman thought he had purchased peace through his negotiated submission to Bishop Bagot, but the events proved him quite wrong. A sword had been unsheathed which was about to cut through old and treasured bonds.

Newman later used to say that his most intimate friendships seemed to last seven years. First there had been Froude, whom he had come to know intimately in 1829 and who died in 1836. Then there was Frederic Rogers, who in his devoted candour and playfulness was a shadow of Froude. By 1843, as things turned out, Rogers too had served his seven-year term and had gone, not through death but through estrangement. The reason was Tract Ninety and all that Tract Ninety involved. A hint of Rogers' uneasiness appeared very early in the game. In April 1841 he wrote Newman from Rome, where he was vacationing with several young Oxford friends: "We hear terrible rumours about what is going on at Oxford—[Arthur] Stanley with active curiosity, . . . [James] Hope with a manly anxiety and I with a stomach ache."[1] A month later, back in London, Rogers had not yet mustered enough courage to read the Tract: "I shall be anxious to hear many things, and have been just setting to work on the lighter literature that hangs about No. 90 before attacking the great work itself."[2]

But then Tract Ninety had not been written for the likes of Rogers. He did not need it, as did Ward, Oakeley and a whole phalanx of young and troubled spirits. And Newman, who had needed it too, inevitably turned away, little by little, from those who had not felt as he had the "hit" from Rome. Rogers was not the only casualty. Pusey, increasingly bewildered by the direction Newman was taking but as ever stubbornly loyal, had eventually to be instructed by W. G. Ward as to Newman's real state of mind. Keble's enlightenment in this regard was less humiliating but no less painful. Newman was a man who had never dealt easily with his equals (with the exception of Froude), and after the affair of Number Ninety there is no escaping the conclusion that he preferred disciples to friends. Consequently he lived his last years in the English Church caught in a strange cross fire of vituperation from pigheaded enemies and adulation from followers, most of whom were neither very intelligent nor very stable. Even for the loftiest of spirits this is an unhealthy psychological climate.

There were, however, among the young men whom Newman perhaps too hastily dignified with the name friend, one or two of a superior sort. Richard Church,[3] for example, later the renowned Dean of St. Paul's and the chronicler of the Oxford Movement, began his close association with Newman about the time of Number Ninety. Born the year of Waterloo, Church had been raised an Evangelical and had matriculated at Wadham, one of the few Oxford colleges with an Evangelical flavour. His first exposure to Apostolical views came with the reading of Keble's *Christian Year*. George Moberly and Charles Marriott influenced him in their different ways, and by 1835, when he met Keble and Newman for the first time, he was able to describe them to his mother as "men to whom I have looked up with great interest and veneration." In 1836 Church took his B.A. with First Class Honours, and the same year, after having long avoided the Sunday afternoon service at St. Mary's because he "thought it rather a fashion of a set who talked a kind of religious philosophy," he heard Newman preach on the "Ventures of Faith." He ever afterwards considered that occasion the turning point of his life. In 1838 he was elected Fellow of Oriel and before long he was working for Pusey in the Library of the Fathers. By the spring of 1841 he was close enough to Newman to act as the latter's chief agent and informant during the early stages of the Tract Ninety controversy.

As Rogers temperamentally resembled Froude, so Church was something like Rogers, only younger and, for a while, more pliable. James Robert Hope,[4] with whom Newman began to grow friendly about the same time, had a more accidental similarity to Rogers. Hope, three years older than Church, was, like Rogers, a lawyer. A graduate of Eton and Christ Church, he had held a fellowship at Merton briefly and had considered becoming a clergyman. He was instead called to the bar in 1838, but his religious interests continued and led him to specialize in ecclesiastical law. In 1840, as counsel for clergy lobbying against a proposed piece of legislation, he gave a three-hour speech in the House of Lords; the brilliant manner if not the High Church content moved the liberal Lord Brougham to remark after hearing it, "That young man's fortune is made."

Hope moved in a circle which included Gladstone, Manning, Edward

Badeley and other young men out of Oxford indeed but still tied to the university by Apostolical sentiment. All of them, in various degrees, looked for intellectual leadership to Newman. Hope, as genuinely selfless, benign and dedicated a man as the Oxford Movement produced, came into ever greater prominence in the years after Number Ninety, as the Tractarians, harried on every side, leaned increasingly on the services of an ecclesiastical lawyer.

I

The first case was that of Keble's curate, Peter Young, over whom the storm broke in the middle of July 1841. Young was in deacon's orders, but Keble looked upon him more as a son than as an associate in parochial duty: "If one man is more blameless and devoted than another," he once observed of him, "I should say from what I see of him that Peter Young is that man. . . . He seems to me such a *very* superior person—so full of thoughtfulness, thoroughly self-denying and humble."[5] Young professed all the proper Tractarian views, and besides he was a suitor of Charlotte Keble's cousin (whom he later married), which romance endeared him even more to the Vicar of Hursley and his wife. "He is the sort of person," said Charlotte approvingly, "who must be made to think about himself or he would quite forget."[6]

On Thursday morning, July 8, 1841, the inoffensive Mr. Young traveled the few miles from Hursley to Farnham Castle, the residence of the Bishop of Winchester, to take the canonical examination prior to his ordination as priest. There were several other candidates present also, and all of them, no doubt, looked upon the occasion as a mere formality, which indeed it usually was. But the bishop, Dr. Sumner, was an Evangelical and his distaste for the Tractarians was notorious. Apparently he had decided to make a test case of Young's application for orders, because "it was plain from the moment that Young went into the house that a dead set was to be made at him. Questions were put to him which were not put to the others, the first being, 'What is your mode of interpreting the Thirty-nine Articles?' "[7]

This question, and the ones which followed it, had to be answered in writing. The last on the list dealt with transubstantiation and the Real Presence. Young answered it by drawing the usual Tractarian distinctions and denying that Christ's Presence in the Eucharist was either corporeal in the Roman sense or simply figurative. Next morning, on Friday, the bishop summoned Young for an oral interview. Flanked by his two chaplains, Dr. Sumner demanded that Young explain his answer on the Eucharist. Young began to quote the Articles and the catechism, but Sumner interrupted and told him sharply to use his own words. Though he was by this time badly rattled, Young stuck to his position and continued to deny that the Presence was strictly figurative. The bishop finally ended the unpleasant confrontation by recommending "Young to go away and get clearer views on the subject" and intimating that there were other sections of the written exam with which he was displeased.[8]

Keble was stunned when, on Friday night, the disconsolate Young brought the news to Hursley that he had been refused ordination on doctrinal grounds. Such an episcopal veto was almost unheard of. The canonical inquiry had long been a most casual affair; Keble himself had been ordained without a prior examination of any kind. Bishop Sumner had conferred deacon's orders on Young in 1840 without hesitation and "without a word of reference to any particular school." But that of course was before Tract Ninety. Earlier in 1841, when the bishop had come to Hursley to administer Confirmation, Keble had told him of Young's intention to apply for priest's orders and had asked the bishop if "there was any particular line of reading which he would recommend to Mr. Y., and he said no." "On the whole," Keble told Pusey, "it looks more like a deliberate beginning of serious vexation on the part of authority than anything I have met with yet."[9]

Keble immediately wrote the bishop and offered to come to Farnham if he "could be of any use in clearing up matters." Sumner replied coldly that he saw no good reason for an interview with Keble. He also refused to return Young's examination papers, though he had previously agreed to do so. One rumour had it that when one of the bishop's advisers said that Keble would resign his living if he saw how mild Young's answers had been, his Lordship of Winchester, taken aback, responded, "Then I shall not send them back."[10] Instead he dispatched them to one of his chaplains, who was supposed to explain their unsuitableness to Young. Eventually, however, Young secured copies of the papers from the chaplain. Keble in turn showed them to Newman and Pusey, and though they both endorsed Young's answers, Newman did so with much more enthusiasm than Pusey.

Keble meanwhile hustled Young off to Ireland for a holiday. "You may imagine," he told his brother Tom, "how sweetly and humbly [Young] takes it all, though of course it is very trying to him."[11] During the weeks following there was time for all concerned to ponder the obvious fact that the Bishop of Winchester's real target was not the insignificant Young but John Keble himself. Though Sumner might not have yet been willing to force Keble's resignation from Hursley, he would not hesitate, if he got the chance, to isolate the dean of the Tractarians. Young had presented him with that chance. "How far it may go on," said Keble, "seems impossible to say. It appears the beginning of a regular plan."[12]

And so it probably was, though it is doubtful that the Bishop of

Winchester had sorted out the details of the plan. What the Heads at Oxford had done to Newman, Sumner now proposed to do to Keble— to place him, that is, in a position where his devotion to the Church of England could be called into question. For Keble had a few months before laid down a kind of abstract challenge which Sumner took up and turned into a hard practicality by denying orders to Peter Young. It will be recalled that Keble contributed to the flood of literature occasioned by Tract Ninety. His pamphlet, the "Letter to Justice Coleridge," offered a general defense of Newman and also elaborated on one point. What should be the course, Keble asked, of a clergyman who has sworn canonical obedience to his bishop and then finds that the bishop will not allow the catholic interpretation of the Articles? To continue the ministry under such circumstances would be unthinkable; it would be an act of patent dishonesty and an implicit endorsement of episcopal heresy. What the clergyman must do, Keble said, is either to appeal over his bishop's head to the metropolitan archbishop, or to a synod of the bishops, or else to resign his living and retire to lay communion. And since the former line of action would be too scandalous, "it seems on the whole" that resignation, "painful and trying as it must be in most cases, both in a temporal and spiritual sense, would be the only [course] open to us."[13]

The "Letter to Coleridge" had been privately printed (250 copies circulated) early in April 1841. Now, in July, Keble found he had crawled out on a limb. The Bishop of Winchester may not have felt strong enough to saw off the limb, but he could strike at Keble through Young and perhaps maneuver the Vicar of Hursley into some imprudent act. It was this latter possibility which worried Keble's family and friends. "For heaven's sake," appealed one of them, "stand your ground in quietness and confidence. . . . Put yourself into no bother and all will come right. . . . If you fidget the bishop into a false position, he will fast do something he does not mean and does not know the meaning of."[14]

The crucial moment was to come on September 23rd when the bishop made his formal visitation and read his Charge. Shortly before, Keble wrote Sumner and took upon himself any error in protocol or procedure. "I do not expect any notice to be taken of this letter, but I am easier now I have sent it."[15] No notice was taken of Keble's communication, though Sumner did agree to an interview with Young on September 23rd. Commented Keble: "If it was the merest formality, instead of a grave point of doctrine and a young clergyman's character at stake, it could hardly be treated more lightly."[16]

Keble awaited the day with great apprehension. The earlier Charge of the Bishop of Gloucester, in whose diocese both Tom Keble and George Prevost held livings, though it attacked the "sophistry" of Number Ninety and abused the Tracts generally, nevertheless absolved any of the Gloucester clergy who approved them. John Keble told Prevost that he would gladly exchange such sentiments for what he expected from his own bishop. The events of September 23rd bore him out. The Charge sounded very severe to Keble. Yet he remained calm. He promised Pusey to do nothing until the printed version of the Charge appeared. "I fear it will be necessary to write the bishop, but you may depend on my not resigning unless he actually tells me he wishes me to do so. And I will be as careful as I can to drive him up to no such point."[17] He sent the news to Tom in a grimly humorous vein: "Prevost, it must be allowed, exercised a sound discretion in declining to take our Charge in the bush for yours in the hand; for surely as far as I can hear it was the difference between whips and scorpions."[18]

Keble took what consolation he could from the fact that Bishop Sumner was kind enough to Young, whom he acquitted of any malice at their interview of September 23rd. But the bishop did not budge on the question of ordination and agreed only to talk to Young again after a few months. This was an excruciating time for Keble, for while he fretted over his youthful protégé and over the effect this controversy would have on the Church, he had at the same time to wait for the printed version of the bishop's Charge, which did not appear until the end of November. He was determined to take no action until he had read that document carefully, but he knew that then he would have to act. Keble did not want to resign Hursley and yet he felt that "my unlucky printed Letter [to Coleridge]"[19] pledged him to do exactly that in the circumstances which Sumner had now precipitated. If Sumner were like Bagot or even like the Bishop of Gloucester, a personal appeal might settle matters. But he was "jealous of interference to such a degree," said Keble, "that it might rather induce him to make the [printed] Charge more stringent."[20]

All Keble's friends urged him not to resign, but Newman told him not to appeal either, because if he did there was a danger of a near-unanimous rejection of catholic interpretation by the episcopal bench. "There are many men who only want as much as some synodical false step to give up the English Church."[21] For Keble, who had committed himself in the "Letter to Coleridge" either to resignation or at least appeal, such advice was gall and wormwood. "I am in doubt every way," he cried, "and I cannot trust my own judgment at all."[22]

II

Judgment, or the lack of it, brought about another crisis that same July when the summer issue of the *British Critic* appeared. This was the first number of the review to be published under the direction of its new editor, Thomas Mozley. It had hardly reached its readership when howls of protest were heard on all sides.

For some time Newman had contemplated turning the *British Critic* over to other hands in the spring of 1841. The preceding October he had told Tom Mozley of his intention and Mozley replied, "Half a dozen people have mentioned to me within the last twelve months that you had some idea of giving it up."[23] Tom was Newman's own choice as a successor, and in some ways this made sense. Mozley wrote with a pleasant style, he had considerable experience in composing for magazines, and he possessed a breadth of interest which could be useful for an editor. But on the other hand he was a notoriously careless, lazy fellow, without much depth or perception. His parish was off on the Salisbury Plain, twenty miles from the nearest railroad, a fact which would provide him with an automatic excuse for missing deadlines or failing to do library research. Though of course Mozley was Newman's brother-in-law, nobody would charge that nepotism played a part in the new editor's appointment. Two other explanations, however, are credible: first, that Newman, always anxious to re-create his friends and disciples, thought that the *British Critic* might serve the purpose of turning Tom Mozley into a responsible adult; and, second, that Newman really intended not to give up supervision of the journal, only to rid himself of some of the busy work.

In all his dealings with Mozley on the *British Critic* Newman never failed to employ the tone of a patron. Thus several months before Mozley assumed his duties, Newman was giving him detailed advice. "You must be more punctual than you are when you are editor. Pray do not leave things to the last minute, else you will get into a regular scrape."[24] He promised to send a list of writers, "all of whom, I think, will write for you; but there are some . . . who must be left to communicate to me and to send their compositions to me." Tom should immediately write to "some of them by way of introducing yourself, viz. to H. Wilberforce, Wilson [Keble's other curate], Rogers, Oakeley, R. Wilberforce, Keble, Bowden, I. Williams and Moberly." Also Newman wanted Tom's brother James to become a regular contributor. Indeed, since Tom lived so far from the intellectual center of things, perhaps James, Oakeley, Henry Wilberforce and Newman himself could be a good stable of four—they "are very different writers"—to contribute one article per quarter, and then Tom Mozley would have to find three or four more. "Do begin and write some articles yourself at once—there's a good fellow."[25]

Another bit of Newman's advice—disastrous as it turned out—came a little later. "Ward is *full* of ideas of writing and it would be a great point to *expand* him. He is most desirous to be moderate."[26] W. G. Ward, in the second of his two pamphlets defending Number Ninety, had recommended what he called the "non-natural" sense of the Thirty-nine Articles and this piece of imprudence had cost him his mathematics lectureship at Balliol. Newman admitted that Ward "has said things *in it* very strong,"[27] but he could not help but feel some responsibility for Ward's loss of position. Therefore he pressed Ward upon Mozley and the *British Critic*. When Ward in the summer of 1841 proposed to do an essay on Thomas Arnold, Newman sight unseen endorsed it. "I have no doubt it will be a good one," he said.[28]

Ward, however, did not appear in the July 1841 issue of the *British Critic*, though his friend Oakeley did. So also did Newman, Bowden, Henry Wilberforce and James Mozley. Tom Mozley celebrated his new eminence by contributing two articles. These two, and Oakeley's, were the ones which caused the clamour. Tom's first piece was a fifty-page attack on Sir Robert Peel and the Tamworth Address. It was straight Tractarian dogma spiced by the sarcasm for which Tom Mozley had a great gift. Peel he indicted as a shifty politician whom no "man on earth can venture to say what he will do next." Surely, he told his readers, "though the writer be the leader of the Conservative party in the House, and has great weight in questions of malt registration and sugar—surely by this time his name is a nullity in any question in the smallest degree connected with religion."[29]

But this was mild compared to Tom's second effusion, which dealt with that ancient Tractarian enemy, Dr. Godfrey Faussett, Lady Margaret Professor of Divinity in the University of Oxford. Faussett, it will be recalled, had much to his sorrow clashed with Newman in 1838. In the wake of Number Ninety he decided to try again. On June 3rd, Newman wrote to Mozley: "Faussett this very day is firing against [Tract Ninety] and glorying that the university is at length beginning to persecute."[30] The occasion was a lecture in the Divinity School where the Margaret Professor indeed rejoiced at the censure of Number Ninety and heaped abuse upon its author. Newman, with his pledge to the bishop, could not answer himself, and his first instinct was to suggest an article in the *British Critic*. "If you could have an article, not arguing, but taking the moderate, sensible line and expressing sorrow at [Faussett's] violence, picking out choice phrases etc. from him (he will publish of course)," or something "in Keble's line" alluding to dangerous precedents in restricting the meaning of the Articles, this, thought Newman, would be the very thing, "but I do not think it well to enter into a *defence* of the Tract."[31] A few days later Faussett's attack was still on his mind. "If you write on it, what say you to showing up Faussett's great indolence and incapacity *as a professor*? He comes out merely to bark at those who are doing something. I have no good opinion about it, but I think he deserves severity."[32] Yet he wanted Tom to take care: "As to Faussett, I think you can be strong and yet *bland* and *temperate*."[33] And on June 21st he sent a last playful word of caution: "I will not see Faussett's execution but deliver him with a recommendation of mercy to the secular arm."[34]

But Tom Mozley showed no mercy. His essay in the July issue was as strongly personal as was Faussett's lecture. Tom seized upon Newman's suggestion about Faussett's sloth and raked the Margaret Professor with savage sarcasm. Faussett, he said, has indulged in a "theological triennium"; three years ago he attacked the Tractarians and now he does so again, because it takes him "three years to write a pamphlet." The average undergraduate stays about three years at Oxford and so gets one chance to see Dr. Faussett: "A person of rather striking appearance, and displaying his doctor's robes to great advantage, ascends the pulpit and with a countenance and gestures fully wrought up to the occasion delivers sentence or punishment or whatever else it is called. His style is round, wordy, full of antithesis," but all it produces is a "fury of negation." "Society justly expects that men shall *earn* their right to censure their neighbours. They must not cry down their neighbours unless they *do* something themselves. The best course indeed is . . . to *do one's own work,* and let the works of others alone. But to do nothing oneself and merely rail at those who . . . are more in earnest and active than oneself is intolerable." Tom concluded by taking Newman's cue and describing Faussett as "Growler," the lazy watchdog who lay in his kennel sleeping with his nose "out in the sunshine" and only stirred to chase away another dog who was resisting the thieves.[35]

Oakeley's article was of a different character altogether. It was a review of a reprint of Bishop Jewel's *Apology of the English Church,* a sixteenth-century Protestant classic, which of course gave occasion for Oakeley to express his views of the Reformation. "That deplorable schism," he called it, "far too much of intrinsic evil to be a legitimate subject of triumph." But Oakeley went further than the historical context when he described the Church of England as pervaded with Protestantism and "comparatively uninfluenced by the efforts of a few to elevate it" to a more catholic ground. And when one bears in mind, said Oakeley, that Protestantism is "in its essence and in all its bearings . . . characteristically the religion of corrupt human nature," and that "Protestant tone of doctrine and thought is essentially anti-Christian," then one can grasp how perilous is the state of the Anglican Church.[36]

Newman reported his own reaction to the article to Tom Mozley on April 6th. "Oakeley has written a very able one on Jewel, but when it got into type I was scared, considering the present row [over Number Ninety]. I will send it to you. It struck me whether it *might* do. . . . But after all I really do not know."[37] Thirty years later, Mozley reread the article and found some of it "impudent." Then he searched his unreliable memory. "The chances are," he said in his *Reminiscences,* "that I did not read the article carefully, except here and there." He trusted instead that Oakeley, "a singularly gentle, modest, humble minded man," would not go too far.[38] And so he printed it.

On July 25th William Palmer of Worcester, who had so gallantly come to Newman's defense at the time of Number Ninety, now rode to the attack against Oakeley. Whoever wrote the article (it was of course unsigned), he said angrily to Newman, shows "a spirit of hostility to the Reformation generally . . . and anything but a friendly spirit towards the Church of England." The author seemed to Palmer poised between Rome and England: "It appears to me indeed that a man has no right to speak *doubtfully* on such important questions; if he cannot firmly say where the true Church is, he ought to remain silent until further study has enabled him to speak decidedly on a point of such great importance and on which it is deeply criminal to unsettle the minds of others without necessity." Palmer hinted darkly that such articles "compromise the character of a Review so important from its well known connexions."[39]

William Palmer was only one of a chorus. Keble was deluged with complaints, and he protested to Newman: "Has not our friend [Mozley] gone beyond the just limits of Christian and (if it may be said in the same breath) gentlemanly severity in several parts, I fear, to be honest, I must say in the general condition and execution of that paper [on Faussett]?"[40] Keble thought an apology should be printed in the next issue. "Would it not be well to put a drag on T. M.'s . . . wheels? Else he will get us all into a scrape."[41] And he added a little later, after the Peter Young affair had begun: "It becomes now more needful than ever that we should take no false step, and I want the matter of the *B. C.* to be very gravely considered. I am afraid almost to say it, but I must say I do not think T. M. a safe editor. His wit quite runs away with him." Sir William Heathcote has canceled his subscription, and "Wilson wishes we were entirely rid of [the *British Critic*]."[42]

Newman's reaction to the outcry was curious. To Keble and the other complainants he was quite testy. "As to T. M.," he said to Keble, "will you please state more at length what you think best. The Review is Rivington's; we cannot change about editors at our pleasure. . . . If we give it up I suppose it will get into the hands of our opponents, but I assure you *I* have not the slightest personal wish to keep it in our hands. My only feeling would be that we were all rather hasty with T. M., but this is a thing which neither he (I am sure) nor I shall trouble about."[43] To Mozley, on the other hand, Newman sent only consolation: "Depend upon it, this will blow over and you have no cause to be discouraged. . . . I fear there is a consensus against the article on Faussett, and we must, I think, banish satire from the Review for a long while."[44]

Mozley cared nothing for any opinion but Newman's, and so quite predictably he showed no sorrow over the storm he had raised. "I am sorry to say," he wrote, "I do not as yet feel the slightest compunction for the Faussett article. If it has tended to produce a correct impression of its subject, that is all I care for."[45] Newman was in no position to complain, since Tom had followed his lead on Faussett and had printed what

Newman called Oakeley's "able" article. Moreover, Tom Mozley, as editor, was Newman's creation; no man readily admits that his judgment about other men is faulty.

In the weeks and months which followed, Newman continued to buck up Tom Mozley and to defend him against all comers. He had to remind the bumptious Tom that his critics were widespread, for Tom shut tight his eyes and pretended that only one or two wicked enemies conspired against him. Rivington asked the editor to be more prompt in delivering the material to the printer and informed him that many prestigious people were complaining about the *British Critic*'s Romanizing tendencies; so far, said Rivington in November, the circulation has not been affected.[46]

The October issue appeared and occasioned only sighs of relief from the general body of Tractarians. There was nothing in it of a controversial nature, not even Ward's rambling remarks about Arnold, which nobody could understand anyway. But the doubts raised by the July *British Critic* did not dissipate and continued to be a source of trouble and anxiety to Newman's friends. As late as January of 1842 Keble had to write to a friend, "I think it is a hard measure to condemn and proscribe a number of persons, some of them old and dear friends, without having read any of the writings which are ground of the sentence except one number of a Review, which number many of the condemned persons themselves earnestly protested against, and for which in fact the editor only is answerable, and he not one of the writers of the Tracts."[47]

But, unhappily for Keble, the editor of the *British Critic* was not in fact solely responsible for its contents.

III

While Keble contemplated various dreary prospects, another blow was struck at him and the other Tractarians. This was the affair of the Jerusalem bishopric. On October 5, 1841, Newman received a communication from his young friend at the *Times* and immediately sent it on to Keble with a covering note.

I enclose what will be no consolation to you, but think you ought to see. It really does seem to me as if the bishops were doing their best to uncatholicize us, and whether they will succeed before a rescue comes, who can say? The Bishop of Jerusalem is to be consecrated forthwith, perhaps in a few days. M. Bunsen is at the bottom of the whole business, who, I think I am right in saying, considers the Nicene Council the first step in the corruption of the Church.[48]

The idea for a bishop at Jerusalem to care for the non-Roman and non-Greek Christians originated with the King of Prussia. In the summer of

1841 he dispatched Christian Karl Bunsen to England as a special envoy in hopes of persuading the English government and Church to join the scheme. James Mozley described Bunsen as "a short, corpulent man with a bright red face and sharp eyes, decidedly clever-looking. . . . He is an immense talker—literally talks unceasingly and has a most amusing way of silencing others by lifting up his finger."[49]

Bunsen was a career diplomat and an amateur theologian whom Newman and Froude had met at Rome in 1833 when Bunsen headed the Prussian legation there. His powers of persuasion were considerable and among his early converts to the Jerusalem bishopric idea was the simple-hearted Pusey. "I was led to imagine," Pusey explained later, "that there was already a Church of Jewish converts and of English at Jerusalem and that the bishop was to be sent over primarily for their sakes."[50] The sharper eye of James Hope saw the situation more clearly, and already in mid-July he was warning his Oxford friends about the mischief Bunsen was up to.

The Prussian plan called for a bishop to go to Jerusalem and take charge of Anglicans, German Protestants and any others who might care to acknowledge his jurisdiction. The bishop would be nominated alternately by the British and Prussian governments, his endowment would come equally from the two countries, he would be consecrated according to Anglican rites, and he would be free to ordain Lutherans who accepted the Thirty-nine Articles as well as the Confession of Augsburg.

There was widespread support for the idea. The politicians regarded it as a means of asserting British presence in the Near East, where France and Russia had long enjoyed special prestige as protectors of the Roman Catholic and Orthodox Communions respectively. The Evangelicals were delighted at the obvious strengthening of the Protestant connection, while the theological liberals rejoiced at the doctrinal compromise such a link was bound to involve. High Churchmen, though perhaps not so enthusiastic, nevertheless were ready to make the best of it, and many of them discerned the possibility that the scheme might lead to the conversion of Prussia to episcopacy. Among these were some who had rallied to Newman at the time of Number Ninety, including Hook, Benjamin Harrison, Edward Churton and even William Palmer of Worcester.

To the Tractarians the Jerusalem bishopric was an abomination. Bowden called it "horrible, monstrous";[51] Gladstone confessed that "I almost reel and stagger under it."[52] The reasons for such reactions are clear enough. The very things which appealed to others appalled the Tractarians: The Jerusalem bishopric was Erastian, Protestant, undoctrinal, anti-sacramental, liberal and a wholesale surrender of the apostolicity of the bishops. Keble, whose beloved curate languished without priest's orders, now saw the Church cheerfully admitting Lutheran preachers to ordination. He wrote a fierce letter to Harrison, once a close ally, "merely to disburthen my mind. . . . [I] received an answer from him which did not at all satisfy me, as I shall explain to him before long, for although one's remonstrances are too late, . . . I suppose it is worth while making them from time to time with statements of principles which they wish one day they had attended to."[53] Keble was quite correct; remonstrances were too late. On November 7, 1841, Michael Solomon Alexander, a Jewish convert to Anglicanism, was consecrated the Anglo-Prussian Bishop of Jerusalem by the Archbishop of Canterbury and the Bishop of London.

Newman, who had remained strangely detached at the Peter Young crisis—"I suppose," he had said to Keble in July, "this may be henceforth the case in some dioceses, but I cannot understand its taking place on a large scale"[54]—was driven almost into frenzy by the Jerusalem bishopric. "Here I am," he wrote to Hope, "labouring with all my might to keep men from Rome and as if I had not enough trouble a new element of separation is introduced." Immediately he planned a formal Protest. "I think I shall introduce it as a preface or appendix to every book and every edition of a book I print. If people are driving me quite against all my feelings out of the Church of England, they shall know that they are doing so."[55] And to Samuel Wood a few days later:

Have you heard of this deplorable Jerusalem matter? I do dread our bishops will convert men to Rome, Dr. Wiseman sitting still. There is not a single Anglican at Jerusalem, but we are to place a bishop (of the circumcision expressly) there, to collect a communion of Protestants, Jews, Druses, Monophysites, conforming under the influence of our war steamers, to counterbalance the Russian influence through Greeks and the French through Latins.[56]

The acceptance by high authority of Bunsen's plan hit Newman at a particularly vulnerable moment. During the summer and fall of 1841 he had returned to his study of the Arians of the fourth century; for several months prior to the announcement of the Anglo-Prussian bishopric he had been working up to ten and twelve hours a day on a critical edition and translation of St. Athanasius. In the midst of these studies the doubts of 1839 had appeared again, this time stronger than ever. Added to this internal agony was the rising tide of episcopal condemnation of the Movement. During 1841 seven bishops' Charges appeared which attacked Number Ninety, its author and, by implication, all the Tracts. The bishops indeed spoke as individuals, but what frightened and depressed Newman was that the accumulation of these hostile Charges would in fact constitute a unanimous judgment of the bishops in the only manner such a judgment could be expressed in the nineteenth century.[57] There was little doubt by the fall of 1841 that virtually all the bishops, one after another, would disown the Tracts. And what happened then to the contention that the Church of England possessed genuine catholicity through the apostolic succession of her bishops? To James Hope Newman said: "When friends who rely on my word come to me and say, 'You *told* us that the English Church was catholic,' what am I to say to this reproach?"[58]

So the Jerusalem bishopric was a last straw, and Newman, who could do nothing about the episcopal Charges, determined to use his waning strength in protest against it. He consulted with Hope about the legal implications, and both Pusey and Keble saw and somewhat reluctantly approved the Protest's final form. All his friends tried to calm him. Bowden employed colourful imagery: if the two archbishops and the Bishop of London should get drunk every night, he wrote, this fact "would not alter my duties toward the Church which they unworthily governed." And even if all the bishops should "unchurch—so to say— the Church under their charge, it does not follow *necessarily* that men should go to Rome."[59]

Keble wrote two letters to the Bishop of Oxford, one, he said, "more impudent" than the other, "imploring" Bagot to disown the Jerusalem bishopric. The bishop replied that he had not been consulted about the matter and he knew only what he read in the newspapers.[60] Keble urged caution on Newman, and he wrote with some annoyance on November 15th that "I suppose any advice which I might offer would come too late. . . . Mind, I am not saying it ought not to be done. I cannot judge of the call there is for it as you can." But "if not too late" Keble hoped that Newman would soften the tone of the Protest and perhaps include "a little expression of reverence to those whom you are censuring," that is, the bishops. "The step you are taking," Keble added astutely, "seems a new kind of thing, for a presbyter formally to protest against an act of his metropolitan [Canterbury] and, I suppose, by construction against his diocesan."[61]

Keble's advice did come too late. Two days before he sent it Newman submitted his Protest to the Bishop of Oxford and the Archbishop of Canterbury. It was at the same time printed and circulated. "I, in my place," wrote Newman, "being a priest of the English Church and Vicar of St. Mary's, Oxford, by way of relieving my conscience, do hereby solemnly protest" against the Jerusalem bishopric and "disown it," as a virtual recognition of heresy. Keble was right: it was a new step, and it was a long one too.[62]

Newman's Protest was a short, non-argumentative document. Several others like it were also printed, notably one by young William Palmer of Magdalen, whose insolent tone gave offense to many erstwhile Tractarian allies. James Hope took another tack in a long pamphlet on the Jerusalem bishopric published late in 1841. Hope's argument was an ingenious legal brief which showed, through an analysis of Acts of Parliament going back to Henry VIII, that English law either "excludes

Prussian Protestants from Bishop Alexander's communion at Jerusalem"
or else "cuts Bishop Alexander off from the unity of the Anglican
Church. Under either conclusion, it seems to me that the position of the
Church of England remains unaltered by the erection of this new diocese
and that on this score we need feel no anxiety." Indeed, Hope saw reason
for restrained optimism: "If the policy of our ecclesiastical superiors
should be such as by wise moderation to allow our Church, now troubled
and cast to and fro, to settle down by free discussion into a gradual
consent, the time may not be far distant when instead of a clandestine
and unlawful attempt at union in a distant country, we may . . . stand
forth . . . to call men from both extremes of error, . . . and in joining
together those bodies which are still churches, raise into that unity those
which are not."[63]

IV

Hope's able pamphlet suffered from its similarity to Tract Ninety.
Anglo-Catholics, it argued in effect, need not despair over the Protestant
connection implicit in the Jerusalem bishopric, because, despite the clear
intention of the authorities, that connection can still be explained away.
It was problematical through how many crises such an argument could
carry the party. Meanwhile from another quarter came a call for Hope's
legal skills.

In December 1841 the Peter Young case approached its climax. The
Bishop of Winchester's Charge was now published and it contained the
same strong condemnation of Tractarian views as when Sumner preached
it several months earlier. On December 7th, the bishop interviewed
Young once more and again declined to ordain him priest. Keble there-
upon sent all the relevant documents to Hope.

There were several possible courses open to Keble. He could first of
all resign Hursley, but this he had definitely decided not to do. Secondly,
he could appeal either to the Archbishop of Canterbury as metropolitan
or to the Anglican clergy as a whole through Convocation. Both of these
appeals would have the effect of publicizing his intention to remain in
his living despite a doctrinal disagreement with his bishop. Theoretically,
such action in itself would amount to an appeal from a lower court—
the Bishop of Winchester's—to a higher, but in fact it would be a bold
formality, since the archbishop would not act on an appeal and Convocation, reduced for more than a century to complete legal impotence,
could not.

Another more complicated possibility was to force Bishop Sumner's
hand by way of the Church Discipline Act of 1840. This legislation
empowered a bishop to establish a commission to investigate a clergy-

man's doctrine and ritual practices and to transmit the case for judgment directly to the archbishop's provincial court. The Act provided that conviction of irregularities could lead to the clergyman's suspension or deprivation from his living. The advantage of this course was that a clear decision would be forthcoming, but its difficulty lay in getting Bishop Sumner to initiate such a proceeding. Keble was perhaps too apolitical to see that the bishop was too shrewd to make a martyr of the Vicar of Hursley.

Many of those closest to Keble, including his brother Thomas, wanted him to do nothing at all, to sit still and let the crisis pass. But Keble, given his commitment in the "Letter to Coleridge," felt he must do something. His own instincts led him to favour appeal to Canterbury as "quieter, more respectful" and just as likely to be influential as any other action.[64] Hope, however, at first advised appeal to Convocation, which would mean circularizing the clergy generally. Keble rejected this idea until Newman, who was increasingly gloomy about episcopal reaction, seconded Hope. Keble accordingly changed his mind, only to change it again a few weeks later. Hope and his lawyer friend Edward Badeley suggested the alternative provided by the Church Discipline Act, and this advice Keble decided to follow. When Thomas Keble urged him to give up thoughts of lawcourts and appeals and to be satisfied with a formal Protest, John answered, "As the appearances of heresy on the Protestant side are so strong that I cannot act on my 'Letter' to Judge Coleridge by resigning, I must take this other alternative that 'Letter' suggests, viz., that of an appeal to ecclesiastical law."[65]

In mid-January 1842 Keble wrote Bishop Sumner and asked for what he called a "dispensation," that is, a public statement from the bishop to the effect that, despite the recent Charge, Keble and people of like mind may still function in the Diocese of Winchester. He also once again protested against the treatment of Peter Young. The demand for a dispensation was a maneuver; if Keble differed from the bishop so much in a doctrinal matter, then perhaps the bishop would be moved to invoke the Church Discipline Act. And this is what Keble wanted, for as he told Tom, "[Newman] says, and I can easily believe [it], that a favourable decision from Sir H. Jenner [the presiding judge in the provincial court] would do more towards quieting matters and keeping people from Rome than anything else."[66]

But when the bishop answered on January 22nd, it was clear he had no intention of being lured into the ecclesiastical courts. With regard to Young, said Sumner, he had not changed his mind and therefore Young was "at liberty for the present to continue as a deacon in his curacy." As for a dispensation, Keble was not going to get one. The bishop had given his views in the Charge about doctrines "extensively promulgated" which, in his opinion, were dangerous to the Church. It had been a hard duty,

Sumner said, but he had done it and he did not intend to back away. "I can give you no authority," he continued, "to furnish a private inter-pretation—being liable to misconstruction when repeated, according to your avowed purpose—of sentiments delivered by me publicly and ex-pressed in as plain and unambiguous language as I know how to adopt."[67] The bishop, in other words, rested with the Charge; he would neither prosecute Keble nor offer him any face-saving escape. If Keble were uncomfortable because he thought Charles Richard Sumner was a suc-cessor of the apostles, that was Keble's lookout. Charles Richard Sumner was burdened by no such opinion.

If the bishop would not accuse Keble of heresy, was there some other way to force the issue? Edward Badeley thought there was, and he recom-mended that "the *tolerability* of catholic views generally" might be estab-lished if one of the Movement's legion of enemies would accuse Keble of false doctrine, "upon which the diocesan (B[adeley] says) *must* issue a commission under the Church Discipline Act, and it must come before our friend Sir H. Jenner."[68] "Surely," Keble told Newman with a strange wistfulness, "there must be some . . . fanatical enough and sincere enough to accept such a challenge if it were offered them."[69]

Either Badeley was mistaken or else no accuser could be found. Keble meantime worked on a formal Appeal to be lodged with the Archbishop of Canterbury—which, as will be recalled, was his intention in the first place. By March 5, 1842, after endless revisions based on advice from all sides, Keble had the document printed and sent first, out of courtesy, to Farnham Castle. Bishop Sumner acknowledged receipt and said that if Keble thought this was the best way to proceed, he, Sumner, would do nothing to deter him. Then at the end of his note the bishop added a sentence of stiff but kindly sentiment about Keble's good motives, which, Keble admitted, was "a great comfort to me."[70]

Keble's Protest and Appeal (he used both words) was an extremely severe indictment of the Bishop of Winchester, who had denied Young the priesthood "avowedly and solely on the ground of his declining positively to deny all mysterious presence of our Blessed Lord's Body and Blood in the Holy Eucharist, excepting in the faithful receiver." Keble listed twenty-one heads under which Sumner had acted frivolously or maliciously, and he built up a very strong case. It was curiously weak-ened, however, by the twentieth and twenty-first points, in which Keble implied that Sumner was a heretic on the Eucharist instead of Young. This was a bold thrust, but a foolish one. It need not have been made, and therefore under the circumstances should not have been. The charge would have been much more effective had it remained implicit.

During the next six weeks or so Keble distributed copies of his Protest-Appeal around the country. He sent fifty to Newman and asked him to give them to Isaac Williams and Copeland, who in turn might pass them around; "I think you have more work to do than they," he said delicately to Newman. Every copy left Hursley with an accompanying letter from Keble "to tell its story." Keble was consoled to hear that the Bishop of Exeter approved "every word of it."[71] As for his own bishop, Keble met him on diocesan business in April and "found him, as I expected, cool, civil and distant."[72] Keble did not remain long under any illusions. Early in April he wrote Newman, "Now my bolt has been shot at the bishop and archbishop nothing seems likely to come of it."[73] And nothing did come of it, except Peter Young continued a deacon (and stayed at Hursley until 1857 when he was ordained for the Bishop of Exeter) and John Keble drained his inner self in fury and despair until his friends grew alarmed. Judge John Coleridge urged upon him what was hardly necessary, "a distrust of your own judgment in this matter," with a reminder "of the serious consequences to the Church for which *you will be responsible.* . . . The very circumstance that you are always brooding over these matters in some measure makes a bye-stander's opinions more entitled to weight with you."[74]

V

When Keble married in 1835 he forfeited his Oriel fellowship but he kept the university professorship of poetry, an office which had no celibate strings attached to it. The chair of poetry involved only small burdens; the professor had to give a Latin lecture each term and a ceremonial oration in alternate years. The tenure of office was five years and the occupant normally served for two terms. Keble, on the strength of *The Christian Year*, had been unanimously elected Poetry Professor by university Convocation in 1831, and so his second term expired in 1841, on December 13th to be exact. During the last week in October, Keble delivered his final lecture and at the same time quizzed Newman about the protocol involved in giving up the professorship. Did the tenure expire automatically or had the occupant to submit a formal resignation before December 13th? "You know," he said, "the Chancellor might die and a new one be elected before that time, and it would be hard on me to lose the profit and pleasure of composing his installation ode."[75] Keble's ode for the installation of the Duke of Wellington in 1834 had been one of the triumphs of his university career.

At least two months before, a movement was afoot to elect Isaac Williams to the chair as Keble's successor. Williams possessed undoubted qualifications for the post: He was a sound scholar, he had published a good deal of poetry, he was a resident don (of Trinity College) and a thoroughly respectable man. No one, not even Williams' friends, pretended he was a great poet; Newman thought his work "obscure," if not "soft" or "effeminate."[76] But then it was not an age of great poets; certainly nobody on the Oxford horizon could claim to have better credentials than Williams. And his own rueful admission that he wrote Latin better than he did English could have been considered another circumstance in his favour.

But Williams was also a leading Tractarian, a disciple of the Keble brothers, a former curate of Newman's, and, above all, the author of the Tracts on reserve. In the charged atmosphere of Oxford in the autumn of 1841, these things weighed much heavier than Williams' poetic skill or lack of it. It is only fair to say that they seemed more important to his supporters as well as to his opponents.

The spearhead of the drive for Williams came predictably from Bisley. Thomas Keble and George Prevost spent the latter part of the summer sounding out opinion, and they soon discovered, to their surprise, that the first obstacle to the candidacy was Newman. "I am a little staggered by what you say about Isaac's being a candidate for the professorship," Tom wrote to Newman on September 6th. "[I] wish I had known you so decidedly disapproved of it. For I understood from Copeland that you only were in doubt." As will be recalled, there was a history of tension between Newman and the Bisley School and this showed clearly in Tom's next sentence: "But perhaps it is not too late for him to withdraw his name if the majority of his friends so advise." Tom and Prevost were not about to give Newman a veto over Williams' candidacy; they would yield, Tom said, to the judgment of "more experienced persons, and especially to that of Dr. Pusey, Copeland and yourself and my brother. Isaac himself is I think disposed to be quite passive in the matter, but would, I dare say, feel a defeat, though more on account of the cause than for his own sake."[77]

Both Newman and Thomas Keble were concerned about the effect a defeat would have upon the Tractarian cause, and it was on this intangible point that they differed. Tom felt that it was a matter of principle for Williams to run, especially if the ground for opposing him would be "his being the author of Tract so and so." And since Williams was obviously the best candidate on non-doctrinaire grounds—that is, as poet and scholar—then even "if he is defeated," argued Tom, "the world will know that it [is] for his principles, and I should have thought good would come from this—almost as much as if he were successful."[78]

Newman for his part was against Williams' running "from a great dread of Convocation." The timidity of the Heads had saved the Tractarians from a test of strength in the university at the time of Tract Ninety. But a contested election in Convocation, with one candidate a Tractarian, might amount to the same thing. Yet Newman, though he felt the danger keenly, was diffident in the case of his colleagues' determination. "Considering I am the cause of opposition [in the university]

by Number Ninety, it would have been ungenerous to press my view."[79]
And though still unconvinced of the wisdom of the course, he did his
best to rally the troops. "A great struggle is being got up against Williams
for Garbett," he wrote to Tom Mozley on October 29th. "*We must
strain every nerve*," for if Williams is defeated by a large majority, "it
will hasten the catastrophe of men going to Rome."[80]

The formal sponsors of Isaac Williams' candidacy were the president
and fellows of his college, Trinity. When they submitted their confrere's
name for the consideration of the Convocation to be held early in 1842,
the opposition was ready. On November 16th a circular appeared an-
nouncing that the Reverend James Garbett of Brasenose College would
also stand for the professorship. "There is another candidate," read the
circular, "the Rev. I. Williams, Trin. Coll., a writer in the 'Tracts for the
Times,' and more particularly of the well-known tract on 'Reserve in
Religious Teaching.' The election of Mr. Williams in Mr. Keble's room
would undoubtedly be represented as a decision of Convocation in favour
of his party."[81]

Garbett was an ideal candidate in an election which had nothing to
do with qualifications for the post contested. He was an amiable Evangelical parson with a living in the Chichester diocese, who had won a
First Class as a Brasenose undergraduate and who was entirely innocent
of the poetic arts. Williams may not have been a particularly significant
poet, but Garbett was not a poet at all.

From November 1841 through the following January the strange campaign was fought. Each candidate, besides his Oxford headquarters at
his own college, had an active committee working in London. The
canvass for votes was carried on furiously on both sides. The first Tractarian salvo was fired off by Pusey, who on November 17th sent an ill-
advised letter to every member of Convocation in which he appealed for
support of Williams, "whose earnest desire and aim it has for many
years been to promote the sound principles of our Church according to
the teaching of her liturgy." This was an oblique reference to Williams'
poetry, much of which had a liturgical flavour. "On the other hand,"
said Pusey, "it is a known fact that Mr. Garbett would not . . . have been
brought forward except to prevent the election of Mr. Williams."[82] No
doubt it was a "known fact," but Pusey unfortunately could not prove
it, and the Principal of Brasenose, Dr. Gilbert—the same Dr. Gilbert
who had led the anti-Hampden forces in 1836 and as Vice-chancellor had
censured J. B. Morris three years later—categorically and persuasively
denied the accusation in a letter to the *Times*. Whereupon Pusey retired
in some confusion from the public field.

But he like all the Tractarians kept up a feverish private canvass for
votes. They soon found that their opponents had already been working
with great effect. On November 23rd Keble sent the disquieting word

that Henry Manning, recently appointed archdeacon and a very influential man, was going to vote for Garbett. "It might make a great difference if M. could be made aware that it is made a party question on the other side," said Keble.[83] A week later from London Roundell Palmer, the lawyer brother of William Palmer of Magdalen and a member of Williams' London committee, wrote Newman: "I suspect some who are put down as promises cannot be relied upon. . . . Is it possible that Archdeacon Manning is *certainly against* us? So I read it, but I can scarcely believe my eyes."[84]

Pusey took it upon himself to try to recapture Manning. On November 25th he wrote, "We are surrounded by sorrows. . . . Williams, whom you must know too, is the very ideal of a peaceful, reverential member of our Church; all his influence is for good." The Low Church and the liberals have mounted "an active canvass against him, directed through him at us all and all our principles; any decisive majority will be looked upon as a rejection of them, and the more so because Williams is so very quiet and excellent a person." But desertion by friends, said Pusey, is worse than the attacks of enemies. "The greatest sorrow would be that you too were going to take part against us. Yesterday it was told me positively; today doubt is thrown upon it. If it is not so, it will be a great relief to us all to know it."[85] Manning replied a few days later that he intended to abstain because he was a friend and neighbour of Garbett's, but he promised smoothly and not very convincingly that "if anything induces me to vote in the election, it will be to protect [Williams] from what I consider unjust."[86]

It is hazardous ever to describe Manning's reactions as typical, for Manning always played his own game. Yet his refusal to support Williams did reflect a current opinion shared by other Tractarian allies. Blunt Judge Coleridge probably expressed the common frame of mind with more directness than Manning did. It is clear, he told Keble, that the Garbett supporters mean the election "to be a contest between the pro- and anti-tract men, and that the result of it is to be the Oxford judgment on the question." Coleridge thought this monstrous and he wanted nothing to do with it. If Williams' friends were doing the same thing—and Coleridge suspected that at least the London committee was drifting in that direction—if they were "trying the question and pledging opinions on the Oxford *controversy*" as a whole, "I will be no party to that; honestly, I cannot be."

The judge voiced another common feeling when he added, "Your young friends at Oxford positively shock and alarm me. They give abundant excuse, if not reason, for the general offence and alarm."[87] What troubled him was the possibility that in supporting Williams' candidacy he was at the same time giving aid and comfort to W. G. Ward and Oakeley. "I own to you," wrote an acquaintance to Newman, "what I do not own to others that I feel very uneasy about the line which Ward has taken." This uneasiness had led the man in question to recommend the withdrawal of both candidates from the election.[88]

All through December this idea gained favour. Coleridge and Robert Wilberforce were among those who proposed it and Keble toyed with it for a while because he thought mutual withdrawal might "strengthen our hands against any future move of the Heads."[89] But he changed his mind as soon as he considered how such a sign of weakness might effect the bishops as they composed their Charges. Roundell Palmer reported the climate in London: "Some of our friends here would be glad even now to see both the present candidates withdrawn. . . . This (in my judgment) would be weak and inexpedient."[90]

Ironically, as the doubts and defections mounted, Newman, who had not wanted Williams to run in the first place, was thrust into the role of party manager. During the whole of December letters poured into Oriel from members of Convocation who pledged themselves to follow Newman's lead entirely. Given his unsettled state of mind, this must have been a galling burden indeed. He received almost daily reports from the committee in London, one of whose members wrote just after Christmas, "I place myself *entirely* and *unreservedly* in your hands, as one of the most intimate friends of Williams, and in the fullest and most unqualified reliance on your judgment to do whatever you think best."[91] Luckily, enough of the old spark remained for Newman to provide a measure of effective leadership, especially so since Keble was absorbed in the Peter Young affair and Pusey, after his unfortunate open letter, seemed to have little heart for the campaign. On January 3, 1842, Newman could write almost cheerfully to Hope: "Are we really to be beaten in this election? I will tell you a secret. . . . We have 480 promises. Is it then hopeless? . . . I don't think our enemies would beat 600; at least it would be no triumph."[92]

But next day came a momentous intervention. William Gladstone asked for an interview with Frederic Rogers, who was active in the Williams cause. "I found him obviously set on getting the matter finished quoquo modo," reported Rogers, "if not by the withdrawal of both, by the withdrawal of one." Gladstone argued that five of the seven bishops who belonged to Oxford Convocation had signed the proposal for mutual withdrawal. "He seems to have got them (especially the Bishop of Oxford) to sign by the notion . . . that their *authority* would put an end to the contest." (The other two bishops—including old Copleston—refused to sign because they preferred to see Williams overwhelmingly defeated in Convocation.) Gladstone insisted that Williams should withdraw whatever Garbett did for the sake of peace in the Church and out of respect for the episcopal office.[93]

So once more the Tractarians were shattered upon their own cornerstone. Garbett's supporters, confident of victory, rejected the Gladstone proposal. Williams, who built his whole intellectual position upon the apostolic succession, could not ignore, as Garbett easily did, the bishops' wishes. By January 11th Roundell Palmer had received a letter from Gladstone, "inclosing a letter and a portion of another from the Lord Bishop of Oxford to him (Gladstone) simply urging the unconditional withdrawal of Williams." The London committee met next day and authorized Palmer to reply that any such proposal should be made directly to Trinity College and to Williams himself. The committee also urged the bishop in fairness to state publicly that his request that Williams retire should not be construed as a censure of the Tracts or of Williams' theological views. Bagot answered, again through Gladstone, and agreed to say only that he had no personal objection to Williams. The committee met once more on January 17th, declared the bishop's communication "not satisfactory," and sent it back to him.[94]

But this was a futile gesture. In Oxford a spokesman for Trinity College said that "with certain statements on the part of Bishop *Bagot*, [the President and Fellows of Trinity] would yield to him *as* Bishop *Bagot*, not as Bishop of Oxford."[95] The President of Trinity was furious at Bagot for what he considered unwarranted interference in the affairs of the university: "it is the one point for which he says he would go to the stake."[96] On January 20th Isaac Williams formally withdrew from the contest, even though, as he told Tom Mozley, "certainly Newman and some others are most strenuous against comparison of votes or any compromise."[97]

It was Garbett's party which pressed for a comparison of votes, because they expected a majority of up to seven hundred or even eight hundred. But when the poll of Convocation was taken it showed that Garbett had pledged to him 921 votes and Williams 623. Newman maintained that if the formal election had taken place Williams might have won, because many of his opponents would not have bothered to come up to Oxford for the vote. Roundell Palmer, though he did not agree with this view, found a silver lining of his own: "The substantive advantages of letting all the world know that we had 623 supporters will remain. . . . And as I suppose we could not have *won* had it gone on to a poll, there is perhaps as much advantage in having a large *positive number* as there is loss in having a less proportionate number."[98]

Isaac Williams himself said the last word on the election, more in sadness than in bitterness: "Certainly these are most trying times. Our friends [i.e. the Tractarians] have bolstered up the bishops and made their words to be as weighty as gods, and all we get by it is . . . their condemnation, which otherwise would have been as light as feathers. It is very trying to one's patience."[99]

It was more than just trying; it was the signal of a great approaching catastrophe. And men of equal integrity looked at it from different points of view. Newman saw it as one more sign that "the English Church is not part of the Church Catholic, but only visited with overflowings of grace and that God may *call* some persons on to what is higher. . . . I have no call at present to go to the Church of Rome, but I am not confident that I may not some day. . . . The bishops are sowing the seeds of future secessions. They all speak against us or are silent. We have no thanks given us for what is well done. For eight years not a word of direct praise has been granted. . . . All sorts of irregularities have been committed on the other side. All sorts of heresies are promulgated."[100]

Edward Churton, on the other hand, blamed Newman, Pusey and Keble for arrogantly failing to take advice and supinely allowing their juniors to push them towards the brink.

It is perhaps useless to write more to you [he said to Pusey on December 9, 1841] or to other friends whom I love when I have found all my poor advice so often rejected and when neither you nor they have ever asked advice of me. But surely, according to the common rules of humanity, in a time of great public excitement against you and your views, you should reasonably suppose that you may not be your own best counsellors. . . . I should say that every man, however comparatively a fool may give good advice in a matter on which he is well-informed, and often the wisest persons want [i.e. need] advice when discretion sleeps at wisdom's gate.

The crux of the problem, Churton continued, is a lack of control over the young firebrands. Here, for example, is Palmer of Magdalen, age thirty-two, tilting over the Jerusalem bishopric with the Archbishop of Canterbury, age seventy-six: "A strange sympathy with semi-barbarous communions of Christianity seems to have destroyed his duty and affection to his Mother." (Churton's reference was to Palmer's interest in the Russian Orthodox Church.) "Sir Robert Peel has been insulted in a way that he will not forget." The Heads of Houses, Professor Faussett, now the bishops themselves have all become targets of youthful impetuosity.

You have let them get ahead of you and drag you after them. Hence your proposal of reviving monastic life. . . . Hence Number Ninety, written not to express Newman's own views, but theirs who would needs venture to the edge of the precipice to show how bold they were and how little they cared for the opinion of the cold and prudent, which youth regards as timidity. . . . Hence the rash publication of the rough notes of poor Froude; hence the encouragement of Oakeley, a man destitute of all self-control; hence the assignment of the *British Critic* to Mozley; hence Warde [*sic*] was suffered to publish what for his own sake, as well as the public interest, he ought to have been compelled to suppress.[101]

Churton's indictment, harsh though it was, was not unreasonable or undocumented. If it did not touch Newman's argument, that was because it moved on a different plane than his. So also did the analysis of Judge

Coleridge, delivered to Keble a few days before Churton wrote Pusey. To Coleridge the present troubles stemmed from a basic betrayal of the Movement's first principles.

One piece of worldly-looking wisdom has not unmeritedly done you great harm—I mean the sort of organization that you have assumed. It gave you the air of a party and of course exposed you to all the prejudices and just censures which exist against any party in religion. The having a review at all was, in my opinion, unwise, and the allowing it to be conducted as the B[ritish] C[ritic] has latterly been ruinous. *Everyone* agrees in this and wishes it abandoned. Merely to conduct it modestly would now be not enough. Those were your days of real strength when you acted more independently of each other, when you were not established—the saeculum ante-Constantineum.[102]

Those palmy days before Constantine, back in the summer of 1833, seemed now as far off as another world.

CHAPTER 18

Collapse

TUCKWELL, the gossipy chronicler of mid-nineteenth-century Oxford, once drew an intriguing picture of what the university might have been like had Newman and Thomas Arnold resided there together. "It was unfortunate for [Newman] . . . that he should have reigned without a rival; his only opponents on the spot—Faussett, Golightly and the rest—men *impares congressi*." How different if Arnold had lived at Oriel instead of at Rugby. "Who can tell what consequences might not have issued from the immediate and continued contact of the two great gladiators; . . . how many divergences might have been reconciled by the mutual respect and the recognition of fundamental community which close collision must have produced on two so noble natures, the hurricane of opposing passion hushed by the still small voice of sympathy which vibrates between all good men."[1]

There was a brief time when Arnold did come to the center of the stage where Newman had held sway so long. Late in 1841 Arnold was appointed university Professor of Modern History and on December 2nd, in the midst of the Williams-Garbett election campaign, he delivered his inaugural lecture. A professor seldom attracted an audience of more than thirty or forty, and since none of the usual lecture rooms could accommodate the crowd of up to five hundred which wanted to hear Arnold, the Sheldonian Theater was used for the occasion. "And there," as Arthur Stanley described the scene, "its whole area and lower galleries entirely filled, the professor rose from his place . . . and in that clear manly voice, which so long retained its hold on the memory of those who heard it, began, amidst deep silence, the opening words of his . . . lecture."[2]

Arnold's series, which continued into 1842, was a great success, so much so that Newman could not resist a mildly snide comment. "Arnold is giving lectures," he told Henry Wilberforce on January 31st, "which all the intellectual of the Heads of Houses attend."[3] Three days later the two gladiators, as Tuckwell called them, came face to face. Hawkins brought Arnold to dinner at Oriel, and Newman, as senior fellow, sat next to the Headmaster of Rugby throughout the evening. They got on well enough by conversing about neutral matters: "I recollect the productions of North Africa was a fruitful subject." Arnold's composure was in marked contrast to Hawkins' obvious nervousness—"The Provost so dry and unbending," Newman said, "and seeming to shrink from whatever I said, and Arnold who was natural and easy, at least to all appearance. . . . At last the Provost and Arnold rose up to go, and I held out my hand, which [Arnold] took, and we parted."[4]

Four months later Thomas Arnold was stricken by a heart attack and died at Rugby. He was barely forty-seven. Immediately it was proposed that a monument to Arnold's memory be established at Rugby, and the Tractarian leaders were in something of a quandary as to whether they should contribute. Pusey opposed the idea, because he thought that a contribution to the memorial would be an endorsement of Arnold's latitudinarian theology. Newman, however, drew a distinction between the Headmaster of Rugby and the liberal divine—"I am conscious of having always done justice to his great merits at Rugby, nay, having always defended him . . . as considering him widely different from . . . other persons with whom he is associated; as being more real and earnest than his friends; as having done a work while they are merely talkers."[5] Of the three only Keble had ever been close to Arnold personally, and so only he had felt the sharply personal pain occasioned by Arnold's venomous attack upon the "Oxford Malignants" five years before. "Ought I to give my name [to the memorial subscription] or no?" Keble asked Newman. "On private grounds of course I wish to do so, and I suppose from all I hear that poor Arnold really has done a great deal towards elevating the moral tone of the public schools." His first instinct was to decline "gently," but "I should be sorry if I found afterwards that you thought I might accede."[6] Ultimately the memorial money was used to build a library at Rugby and to endow the Arnold Historical Essay at Oxford. The Tractarians would have opposed the latter proposal, but by the time it came before Convocation (1850) they had lost all cohesiveness and power in the university.

Arnold's sudden death moved Newman to consider the disposition of his property in case he should die. On June 21, 1842, he wrote Tom Mozley about his estate. He owned ten acres of land in Littlemore in joint tenancy with Charles Marriott, Samuel Wood, William Froude (a younger brother of Hurrell's), Richard Church and John Bloxam. If he should die, his share in the real estate would revert to the other five, who, he said, "have been taken for good reasons which I need not enter into. The *purposes* they would put the property to you can conjecture without any great stretch of the imagination." Newman wanted his personal estate to revert to the same five men, but until he could decide between setting up a trust or establishing joint tenancy he intended to leave it to Mozley, who would do "as I should have done myself had I lived." His property—"as far as I can remember it at the moment"—consisted of copyright to his own works, to the Tracts and to the *Lyra Apostolica*, two accounts at the Old Bank in Oxford, the furniture at Littlemore and a thousand-pound government bond.[7]

I

The low ebb to which the fortunes of the Movement sank during 1842 and 1843 was due primarily to a collapse of leadership. Rebuffed in the Peter Young case, Keble grew increasingly depressed and withdrew more and more into the consoling activities of parochial and country life. In the spring of 1842 Newman left Oxford and took up permanent residence in Littlemore. A year later Pusey was formally censured and silenced by the university. And in September 1843 Newman resigned St. Mary's, and the *British Critic* closed down forever.

The *British Critic* provides the most striking instance of this leadership crisis. Newman continued to strike an ambivalent pose with regard to Tom Mozley's editorship. It was as though he could not decide whether to retire from all active controversy and let Mozley take complete charge of the magazine, or to keep his hand in the operation and make sure his brother-in-law did not commit some irreparable blunder.

The *British Critic*'s central problem during the last eighteen months of its existence was what to do about those candid Romanizers, W. G. Ward and Frederick Oakeley. Early in 1842, Ward wrote a review of the recently published *Essays* of Archbishop Whately. He showed it to Newman, who in turn sent it on to Mozley with a warning that it was extremely strong. Mozley, without seeing the article, wrote to Ward at the end of January and suggested, "Perhaps it would be possible, by some slight alterations, to convey all your meaning without very seriously committing the *B.C.* . . . Pray have mercy on the poor *B.C.* and its editor whom people will persist in holding solely responsible for all the strong things that have been said in it these later numbers." Then Mozley put his finger on the painful spot.

You confess a readiness to join Rome under certain circumstances whether Rome continues as she is or not; i.e. you really would be *glad* of the excuse of the English Church being degraded by heretical communion to join Rome at once. Now it hardly seems fair that the *B.C.* should express such a feeling, considering what it has hitherto been and what it will probably remain for some time. As far as I can detect my own feelings, I am not *ready* to join Rome, though I admit there seems no other alternative if communion with the

English Church should become positively sinful. With regard to the reprobation of Whately, it is scarcely possible to go beyond the public taste. Very quiet people have said the book is shocking and that it is surprising No. Ninety has made such a stir and Whately's book remain unnoticed, as it destroys all idea of a Church.[8]

Given the fact that all the articles in the *British Critic* were unsigned and hence attributable in some measure to the editor, Mozley's plea for moderation, though expressed in his typically brash manner, does not seem unwarranted. All the more surprising then is the fury it roused in Newman. "I am very much hurt," he wrote Mozley, "at a note which you have sent to Ward." Ward himself did not seem to mind, but, said Newman, "anyone else but a person so singularly sweet-tempered as he (for this is his strong point, from being fat, I suppose) would have taken offence at it." Ward, he went on, has put

himself *simply* into your and my hands and would feel no annoyance though you rejected his article in toto.
I assure you he does not wish to have any dealings, good or bad, with the *B.C.* unless others wished him to have. He is *not* bent on agitating in the way you take for granted. . . . I confess to you, [if] a stranger had written to me thus, I should have written a cold, dry answer that I would have nothing to do with the *B.C.* Furthermore, you state his *opinions* in a repulsive form which I think unjust—but this I do not go into.[9]

This was a strange performance, and perhaps it can be understood only as a measure of Newman's own internal distress. He thought Ward's Roman tendencies basically right, and yet he resisted being pushed along at Ward's speed. At the same time, he wanted Mozley to act like an editor, and yet resented it when he did.

Mozley replied to this outburst with puzzled humility. "If my note to Ward seemed to express what you say, you must set it down to my awkwardness." He was "anxious" to have Ward's assistance in the *British Critic*. Then, referring to his own ill-defined position, he remarked wistfully, "I really thought when I was writing to Ward I was carrying out your wishes."

Ward nevertheless remained a source of worry, first of all because of his provocative conversation. "I must have heard twenty times, e.g., that Ward says he is only waiting for you [Newman] to join Rome and he will. . . . Now . . . I will confess that going over to Rome seems to me the most awful and most painful step I can conceive, except perhaps coming over to the Church of England if I were now in the Roman communion." Yet Ward talked of such momentous matters in the most casual and uninhibited way, assuming a "triumphant tone" as he defended the worst of Roman fanaticisms. Furthermore, Ward's association with Oakeley compounded the danger. "Now I admire most exceedingly Oakeley's talents and singlemindedness. But I see in him a determination to commit us all to the very utmost. That he will go over to Rome very soon, without waiting for the contingency Ward speaks of, I have not much doubt." A question like the Jerusalem bishopric, said Mozley, means little to Oakeley. "He *prefers* the Roman communion and has got over all the difficulties of the case. . . . I have been fifty times startled by passages in his articles for the *B.C.*, but have always made it my rule to let everything pass that I thought *could be defended*, whether I liked the first blush of it or not."[10]

Newman calmed down soon enough and even managed an apology of sorts: "I know I told you Ward's article was very strong, though I dare say I did not bring out my meaning." He warned Mozley not to confuse Oakeley and Ward. "Oakeley I am suspicious of. I think *at present* he would do nothing without me. . . . Ward I see much of, O[akeley] little. In confidence I tell you I have only lately been speaking to W. about O." Mozley should not let Ward's strong expressions bother him: "recollect echoes last long after the sound. . . . I assure you W. is very different from what you fancy. I wish you knew him better. I do not mean to deny that he has said things he ought not to say, and that he does *in his heart* continue to wish to be put out of the . . . perplexity in which the English Church is." Newman thought Ward an admirable person. "I know of no one who has so consciously wished to correct the faults imputed to him, who is so thankful to be told of them, so encouraged by being told of improvement in him, so vexed [at himself] at charges brought against him."[11]

It is worth noting that Newman admitted Mozley's basic charge against Ward, that is, that Ward "in his heart" hoped for some crisis which would give him reason to end his "perplexity" and join Rome. But Newman admired Ward, while he was "suspicious" of Oakeley, even to the point of warning the former against the influence of the latter. Ward "wished to correct the faults imputed to him" and was "thankful to be told of them," doubtless told by Newman himself. Oakeley, on the other hand, consulted Newman rarely and was capable, apparently, of making up his own mind. (It was ironical that when all three became Roman Catholics in 1845 the order of their going was Ward, Newman and then Oakeley.) Newman, the consummate artist and the heir to the creative teaching method of Copleston and Whately, always judged his intimates according to their willingness to conform to the ideal image in his mind.

Meanwhile the *British Critic* drifted. Ward and Oakeley became the major contributors, so much so that Pusey, a few years later, described them as having taken over the magazine. Tom Mozley, though he fretted, lacked the wit and courage to assert real control over them. "I will not say," he recalled in later years, "that I hesitated much as to the truth of what they wrote, for in that matter I was prepared to go very far, at least in way of toleration." He found Oakeley easy enough to deal with, but "it was otherwise with Ward. I did but touch a filament or two in one of his monstrous cobwebs and off ran he immediately to Newman to complain of my gratuitous impertinence." Ward gave the editor practical headaches too, with his "minute and detestable" handwriting and his habit of submitting manuscripts in "bundles of irregular scraps of paper." Yet Tom admitted that Ward's articles were popular, "much to my surprise."[12]

Out of just over fifty articles published in the *British Critic* between April 1842 and October 1843 Oakeley and Ward each wrote eight. This in itself would not justify Pusey's thesis that they had taken control, but it must be said in addition that their articles gave the magazine its tone. And others of Newman's young friends were also contributors; some of them, like James Mozley and Richard Church, were moderate enough, but others—notably J. F. Christie and J. D. Dalgairns—were more wild and woolly than Ward at the top of his form. So Mozley complained bitterly to Newman about the antics of Christie, who submitted his article late and held up publication of the whole number and who rejected any editorial changes even though his content was manifestly silly. But—and here Tom Mozley revealed his lamentable weakness—he published Christie's article anyway.[13]

Dalgairns' article in the October 1842 issue caused universal offense, but Newman, who had inserted it, was of little help to the embattled editor of the *British Critic*. "You must look reality in the face," he told Mozley. "If the *B.C.* persists in its Romanism you will gradually have one indignant cry against it from all parts of the Church and you will lose your position. You may think it good [i.e. ironic], my writing this, who approved Dalgairns' article, but I am writing you to realize facts, whether I am involved in the fault or not."[14] And then, with curious inconsistency, he said two weeks later, "I am very sorry you should have thought D.'s article strong."[15]

In the midst of criticism and conflicting device, Tom Mozley, in September 1842, was confronted with a hostile Charge from his bishop, Denison of Salisbury. Dr. Denison spoke with great harshness of the *British Critic*, which he described (Tom informed Newman) as sitting "in the critic's chair placed somewhere in the vague region of an imaginary Catholicism."[16] Newman immediately advised Mozley to write the bishop and tell him that "with such an unmitigated censure it would be impossible for you to do *what he would wish*, viz., get men *he would like* to write for you (for it stands to reason did you wish e.g. Pusey or Hope or Manning to write, how *could* they when the bishop has given such a character to the review?)"[17]

But Tom did not agree. An interview with Denison, written or oral, would do no good. Bishop Denison, Tom said, *"has no power of managing a difficult affair*. He would be short and bluff, and so should I."[18] Then, countered Newman, Mozley must consider resignation or, on the other hand, "If you keep the review, I think you must discharge Oakeley and

Ward, and if you think so I will take the responsibility. Depend on it, they *cannot* write without bringing in their notions."[19] Tom did not want to do either. "I think," he said, "there is no need to do anything at present about Oakeley and Ward. *I wish them still to write* for the B.C."[20]

So the wrangle went on. Newman's subtle intelligence thrust upon him all the crosscurrents and purposes. If Bishop Denison could be pacified "merely by excluding Oakeley and Ward from your pages, it is what I should most like you to do. . . . I so dislike row and agitation, constitutionally, that I should be glad if the review could get more humdrum. I am sure our principles will spread eventually, and they will spread better for going slow." And yet he added in the next breath, "I agree in the main with W. and O., and at all events think they are doing a *work* by breaking down prejudices etc., and if I do not write like them it is only because it is not my way. I could not say what they say without unreality or, sometimes, without offending my ideas of taste and propriety. But still I am sure they are doing good."[21]

Tom Mozley's simpler mind, however, fastened on one objective. When Newman insisted that he take some action with regard to Bishop Denison's Charge—"No one is respectable who does not act on principle. Consistency is better than truth, i.e. in the eyes of people. Take what theory you please, but act upon it."[22]—Tom answered almost petulantly, "I say that of course a measure of obedience in some shape or other must be rendered to [the Charge], and as far as I am concerned I would rather not give up the B.C."[23] The *British Critic*, storm center that it was, had given Mozley an importance in the world he had never had before. He did not intend to sacrifice it.[24]

Finally, to satisfy Newman, Tom decided to compose a short piece on the bishop's Charge and insert it in the January 1843 number. He showed it of course to Newman prior to publication, and Newman thought it "very good but rather hard" and a bit too long.[25] In the end it was Oakeley who reviewed the Charge (along with three others), and, as might be imagined, he gave small comfort to Bishop Denison: "In each successive peril that assails the most essential being and welfare of the Church of England," proclaimed Oakeley, "they who take their stand on the Catholic system will be found her truest and most constant defenders."[26]

Oakeley's piece was not so much an answer as it was one more provocation. And thus the *British Critic* plunged towards its final dissolution.

II

Except in the issue of July 1841, most of which was arranged for by Newman, not one of the old-line Tractarians wrote for the *British Critic* through the whole of Thomas Mozley's editorship. That only the work of the young and mostly extreme appeared in its pages tended to confirm the charges of coddling the immature leveled by Edward Churton and Judge Coleridge at the end of 1841. Newman's hold on his young men was hesitant at best, and this reflected his own inner uncertainty. But one thing he was convinced of: if they and he were to be saved for the Church of England, the ideals of 1833 would not suffice. How far he had drifted from those ideals he expressed in a remark to Tom Mozley in September 1842: "I am not commonly fond of Via Medians."[27]

By that time Newman had been living for some months in an L-shaped row of converted stables on his property in Littlemore. The move from Oriel, which involved a kind of semi-retirement from St. Mary's, had been immediately occasioned by all the troubles since Tract Ninety. With the growing consensus of bishops' Charges against him, he felt particularly isolated and uncomfortable in St. Mary's pulpit. "I cannot be a demagogue," he said.[28] Settling at Littlemore gave Newman a temporary respite while he thought out a more drastic step: the resignation of St. Mary's and retirement to lay status.

The foundation at Littlemore did in the end prove to be a halfway house, but the root idea for it antedated any particular Tractarian crisis. As early as March 1840 Newman wrote Tom Mozley from Littlemore, "I think I shall build a monastery here."[29] Froude had often talked of employing colleges of celibate clergymen as a means of Christianizing the new industrial centers. Newman, however, especially after he began to doubt the tenableness of the Via Media, put his emphasis more on the contemplative than on the active apostolate. He envisioned his monastery primarily as a place of austere and prayerful retreat, removed as far as possible from the temptations to respectable self-indulgence which enticed every Oxford don. For he was aware of that aspect of the Tractarian image which Tom Mozley drew so colourfully many years later:

The authors of the Movement lived in a university, in the midst of cheerful and educated, if not always congenial society, libraries, magnificent buildings, frequent services, and, it must be added, all the comforts and elegancies of life. Something amounting to an appreciable sacrifice could be taken out of this superabundance and yet leave a large and solid reminder. Even a saint, not to say a confessor, might enjoy life at a university.

Tom recalled traveling to Oxford on *British Critic* business one Wednesday in Lent.

My principal apprehension on going there was that my incurable worldliness would clash with the serious and saintly tone I imagined to be inspired by the Movement. I felt guilty of irreverence by intruding on one of the contributors, the largest contributor I may say [W. G. Ward?]. . . . He was observing the fast no doubt honestly and in a true sense, but he was still in bed at 11 A.M., and a large dish of mutton chops was keeping hot for him at the fire. The scout [servant] informed me this was his custom.[30]

Newman, however, wanted not only to flee academic Babylon. By the end of 1841 talk was common in Oxford that many junior men would go over to Rome if Newman did. "These are real cases," Newman told Henry Wilberforce. In October 1841 an eccentric Fellow of Magdalen named Sibthorpe, neither young nor a disciple of Newman, did become a Roman Catholic. The Sibthorpe case caused a brief sensation in Oxford (where the converted don dined ostentatiously on fish) and a flurry of anti-Tractarian feeling around the country, even though Sibthorpe admitted that only the Tracts kept him from going to Rome sooner than he did. Bishop Wiseman, who received Sibthorpe into the Roman Church, looked on the event as a portent, and the bishop's ally, Ambrose Phillipps, said that he had "the greatest hopes" from Oxford of "a speedy reunion" of the churches, and he expected numerous conversions at Oxford "soon."[31]

These events were in Newman's mind when he wrote Hope, in December 1841, "I am almost in despair of keeping men together. The only possible way is a monastery. Men want an outlet for their devotional and penitential feelings, and if we do not grant it, to a dead certainty they will go where they can find it."[32] But at the same time he received a stern warning from an old friend. "Knowing you, my dear Newman, as I do," wrote Archdeacon Robert Wilberforce, "feeling all my obligations to you, being aware of your extraordinary powers, I know that it would be hopeless for me to turn you from any course which you had resolved upon." Wilberforce was talking about the same young men, one of whom had told him that Newman had denied the presence of holiness in the Anglican Church. "I cannot and will not believe that in the bottom of your heart you have more idea of an union with Rome than you had when we used to take our quiet walks on the banks of the Isis." Wilberforce protested that though Newman had suffered "personal injustice," yet this was not enough to abandon "what you yourself taught five years ago. . . . What change is there which has come over your spirit which has made men venture to speak of you as inclining towards the schismatical and idolatrous mother of so many divisions in the Church of God?"[33]

To Newman, however, such questions no longer had meaning. Rome, though perhaps idolatrous, was assuredly catholic while England—what was England but a shadow and a memory? The monastic life was one of those necessary institutions which England had left to Rome and the only way, in Newman's judgment, to keep men from Rome was to offer them a taste of it within the English Communion. Littlemore was to fulfill that function. Tom Mozley, beset with his troubles at the *British Critic*, suggested monasticism as a solution to his own greatest problem. "Froude's colleges for larger towns have only been *talked* of. Why should not those who are very dissatisfied and who despair of success—why should not Ward . . . and Oakeley and others attempt such societies?"[34] But Mozley, as we have seen, did not escape so easily; Ward and Oakeley were not the stuff of which monks are made.

Indeed, when Newman first settled permanently in Littlemore he was alone. Almost immediately distorted accounts of what he intended appeared in the press, and spies from Oxford—not excluding Heads of Houses and Professors of Divinity—hovered around the shabby little cottages. Bishop Bagot wrote and asked him to state his reasons for the move, and when Newman replied with spirit—"What have I done that I am to be called to account by the world for my private actions in a way in which no one else is called? . . . I feel it very cruel . . . that very sacred matters between me and my conscience are made a matter of public talk"[35]—the bishop hurriedly backed down. But a few weeks later, in May 1842, the good but harassed prelate issued his Charge, in which he labeled Tract Ninety as establishing "a system of interpretation which was so subtle that by it the Articles might be made to mean *anything or nothing*."[36] Newman was thunderstruck by the bishop's breach of trust; he had unwillingly written the "Letter to the Bishop of Oxford" at the time of Number Ninety on the guarantee that that document would contain Bagot's only public pronouncement on the Tract. Now the bishop had gone back on his word. "The tide was too strong for him," was Newman's later, and no doubt accurate, judgment.[37]

At least there was a measure of peace in Littlemore. Late in the spring Newman was joined by John Dobrée Dalgairns, twenty-three years old and immature for his age, a graduate of Exeter College whose Catholic leanings had prevented his election as a fellow. In July came William Lockhart, a relative of Sir Walter Scott, whose family sent him to Newman in hopes that the young man might be dissuaded from his intention to become a Roman Catholic. Lockhart, who was barely twenty-two, promised Newman to delay his decision for at least three years. Frederick Bowles, a B.A. of Oriel, followed in December; like Dalgairns, he was twenty-three. A riper man was Ambrose St. John of Christ Church, Henry Wilberforce's curate, who joined the community in the summer of 1843 at the age of twenty-eight. St. John was destined to be Newman's closest friend and confidant for the next thirty years.

This was the nucleus of the monastery, though others came and went, notably James Antony Froude and Mark Pattison. It was Pattison who left behind a summary of the daily horarium. Built around the common recitation of the breviary, the day began at 5:00 A.M. and ended a little after 9:00 P.M. The food was sparse and simple; every man was expected to clean up after himself. Silence was maintained between 2:00 and

8:00 P.M. Newman told his young friends that their life was one of prayer and study, not of discussion.[38] There was recreation, however, and much laughter, and on occasion Newman could be prevailed upon to play his fiddle. Meantime, he still had his parish to look after, though curates assumed most of the formal and liturgical duties.

Pattison wondered how Newman could be "content with a society of men" so limited as Bowles, Lockhart and Dalgairns. One might well wonder the same with regard to the young Pattison. Even so, he had a point. There was a lack of intellectual quality among the men of Little-more, and even the brightest of them, Dalgairns, was too romantic and immature to allow his considerable mental powers full scope. A packet of letters from Dalgairns to his friend William Gresley survives as testimony to the characteristic tone of life at Littlemore. Just before he entered, Dalgairns wrote: "I believe idleness will work wonders with me. With all my pretence to monasticism, I do think that I love home as heartily as most men; nay, I do think I could fall in love as well as my neighbours if I could find anybody fool enough to have me, but these are not times when young women are disposed to run the risk of ejection which thorough-going apostolicals seem likely to incur."[39]

Dalgairns quickly became an expert on Newman's state of mind. He assured Gresley that Newman had not considered seceding to Rome: "He never allows his thoughts to wander beyond today."[40] "My great comfort in all these rows is that nothing is done by Newman and Pusey which does not arise out of circumstances, and naturally, so that it is not they who act but Providence."[41] With regard to the Littlemore establishment itself: "This is really the whole mystery of our pseudo-monastery: it is intended to be a place where a man may be silent and pray and read and (if he will) be more austere than he can be in the world."[42] Yet the "world" retained some of its allure: a trip home at Easter 1843 upset him with its "excitement" and, he complained, has "undone the work of Lent." A similar visit six months later left him distracted by sisters and cousins. He admitted that to marry was the "natural thing to do," but he rejoiced that he had been kept so far free of "infatuation."[43]

On the issues of the day, Dalgairns no doubt reflected Newman's Little-more views while adding nuances of his own. "Dread of Evangelicals," he proclaimed, "has made us cold and heartless, which Anglicanism has always been."[44] The Via Media was dead: "Persons must soon come to see . . . that Catholicity without union or unity with Christendom is absurd."[45] Dalgairns was refused priest's orders in October 1842, and about the same time he lost another bid for a fellowship. "You see," he told Gresley, "I am destined to remain at Littlemore," though he wished it were a real monastery instead of an Anglican "shadow."[46]

Dalgairns' pretentiousness and posturing lend some confirmation to Mark Pattison's adverse judgment about the quality of Newman's Littlemore companions. It would seem that Dalgairns saw no more deeply into his monastic experience than the exceptional status it gave him and the special relationship he thereby had with a great man. He thrilled to the idea that what he was doing was dangerous; on one occasion he spoke of the necessity to curb his pen, lest Gresley should burn his letters without reading them, because of the shocking and perhaps subversive material they contained. For some temperaments there is a delicious and bizarre satisfaction in just being different. The atmosphere at Littlemore must have been, to say the least, a far cry from the old days in the Oriel common room.

Early in 1843 Newman determined to set his young men to work on a definite project. This was the *Lives* of the English saints, which, Dalgairns announced to Gresley with delightful solemnity, would enlist "all the rising talent" in Oxford to compose "regular long lives with historical research and so on." Once these works are published, he added, English ecclesiastics will not be able "to go on humbugging about our being just like the primitive Church when they have plainly set before them what the Church of England was from the first."[47] Newman himself took a more modest line in explaining the proposed series, and he invited, besides the Littlemore coterie, people like Richard Church and Bowden to participate. "I mean the work to be historical and devotional," he told Bowden, "but not controversial."[48] He asked Keble to prepare a life of Bede the Venerable. Keble accepted with his usual reluctance and in doing so displayed a surprising ignorance of literary history: "Is not [Bede's] History in Saxon? I do not know a word of Saxon."[49]

But Keble never got around to writing the biography of Bede, and the series of saints' *Lives* had an ill-starred passage from the beginning. If Newman hoped that the project would turn the public mind to a greater sympathy with medieval Catholicism, he was no doubt disappointed. Six volumes of *Lives* eventually appeared, but by the time they were completed Newman had given way as editor to Oakeley. The young enthusiasts who wrote the *Lives* had trouble distinguishing past fact from past legend, and Newman's own reputation as an historian suffered from the venture.[50]

III

In May 1842 Harriet Mozley visited her brother at Littlemore. She liked what she saw—"Inside it is very pretty and neat—just my fancy. I do not wonder at John's present enthusiasm." She described the setting to Jemima: "There are four or five sets of rooms—sitting and bedroom—all on the ground floor—the door opening into the verandah which runs all along. . . . The kitchen is in the middle—a pretty little garden before the verandah. At right angles is the library, a large pretty room with a nice roof, the sides covered with books." Dalgairns was Newman's only companion at the time, and he might have winced had he heard Harriet's shrewd description: "He was reading in the library, a modest looking blushing youth, all the *men* again talking of his beauty and fine eyes. I thought him nothing but a boy, with no harm about him and particularly cleanly looking!"[51] Later in the summer Newman declined an invitation from Jemima: "There is no chance, I fear, of my getting to Derby this year. I am a family man and cannot leave home."[52]

Newman's old friends reacted variously to his preoccupation with the monastery at Littlemore, which involved a gradual abdication of leadership within the Movement and a drift into what they considered a narrow and dangerous orbit. Some of them, like Robert Wilberforce, remonstrated strongly with him. Others hoped against hope and grasped at any straw which seemed to bind him even lightly to former times. Thus Keble went out of his way to praise articles in the *British Critic* whenever he could—which was not often.[53]

But the most forlorn figure during these troubled days was Pusey. Ever since Tract Ninety it was clear to almost everyone that a major divergence of view had developed between him and Newman. Pusey, however, refused to see it—out of kindness, Newman said, but also out of a failure to attend to the obvious. "Then again he has been unwilling to see it; when I have mentioned differences he has either explained them away or seemed annoyed at the notion." Indeed, Pusey did more than that. In February 1842 he published a public "Letter" to the Archbishop of Canterbury in which he set himself squarely with his friend and against the episcopal Charges. Newman was touched but troubled. "What shall I say about Pusey's pamphlet?" he wrote to Henry Wilberforce. "I think it the most magnificent thing he has written. He quite justifies what I used to call him, Ho megas Pousaios, when we used to ride together. But it commits him, dear fellow; he cannot bear to be left behind."[54]

Later in the same year Pusey and Newman engaged in what was their first acrimonious correspondence. It turned around one of Newman's Littlemore companions (probably Lockhart), who had been on the verge of joining Rome. Pusey asked with his usual moral earnestness whether the young man were willful or self-indulgent or whether the use of the breviary at Littlemore had had a corrupting effect on him. Newman in calmer times might have received such queries amiably enough, but his present anxiety led him to put a bad construction on Pusey's well-intentioned though awkwardly phrased expressions. The upshot was a brief but unpleasant exchange, at the end of which Newman tried to explain to Pusey where he stood with regard to the Tractarian new breed. The attempt was not very successful. He said he thought the differences between Oakeley and Ward on the one hand and Pusey on the other were historical rather than doctrinal, but he did not draw out what he meant. He confessed he did not see things as clearly as others and that he resented being pushed along at others' pace. But on the crucial question of approval of Ward's and Oakeley's position, Newman took refuge in a painful double negative. "In certain cases I have *not dis*approved it. . . . I must add that I had never been myself *pained* at W.'s or O.'s writings, which I know you have been. As to my being entirely with Oakeley and Ward, I think my sympathies *are* entirely with them; but really I cannot determine whether my opinions are. I do not know the limit of my opinions."[55]

All this perplexed poor, good Pusey. His mind, that vast catalogue of facts, could not enter into the tangle of subtleties and cross-purposes which obscured the path of his more poetic friend. At the beginning of 1843 came another agonizing shock. Newman publicly retracted the harsh expressions he had used about Rome ("lost Church," "papal apostasy," "cause of Anti-christ" and the like) in his writings between 1833 and 1837. The retraction, which appeared without signature in the February *Conservative Journal*, "bears every mark of belonging to you except your name," Jemima Mozley told her brother, and "is making a great hubbub in the world. It seems a rather mysterious document."[56] It was mysterious because it left without apology many doctrinal arguments against Rome which Newman had stated before and after 1837. The retraction gave the impression that the author did not know at the moment whether he considered those arguments still valid or not. "I have said *nothing* of course on doctrinal points," Newman explained to Pusey, "but only as to *abuse. You* stand on very different ground and have nothing to unsay."[57] As a matter of fact, Pusey had never employed the abusive language about Rome which had been almost habitual with Newman. But to stand on different ground from Newman was precisely what Pusey found most painful. Yet he put the best face on it he could. "Altogether," he said to Keble, "I do not see that people ought to be disturbed about it."[58]

But of course he was gravely disturbed, and so were many others, most notably Frederic Rogers. The break between Newman and Rogers is difficult to reconstruct because of the limited nature of the evidence. And what evidence there is has been curiously misinterpreted by writers whose chief aim has been to exonerate Newman from any blame for the quarrel.[59] This excessive moralism has led them to adopt the nonsensical proposition that every personal crisis in Newman's life was traceable solely to the perfidy or insensitivity of others. The attempt to apply it in the case of the estrangement with Rogers has resulted in a distinct injustice to a luminously honourable man. As a matter of fact there was nobody to blame in this tragic affair, unless one is prepared to charge it against an inscrutable Providence.

As we have seen, Rogers, eager apostolical that he was, had a strong anti-Roman bias which, after 1839, annoyed Newman more than once. At the time of Tract Ninety Rogers began to worry about the course the Movement appeared to be taking, and no doubt his uneasiness was intensified by the knowledge (shared at that time only by Henry Wilberforce) that Newman had been seriously "hit" by Rome. When the July 1841 issue of the *British Critic* caused such a fuss, Newman apparently suggested that Rogers assume some active role in the management of the magazine. Rogers' reply testified to his perplexity. "As to the *B.C.*," he wrote on July 22nd,

I confess myself out of heart. A line which shall satisfy Oakeley, Ward, Keble and Wilson [Keble's curate] permanently seems hard to find independently of the particular difficulties about Mozley. I am afraid your notion of my getting "general influence" in the review is rather hopeless. I feel far too perplexed and mistrustful myself to have any chance of keeping together half-a-dozen different sets of writers, all pulling in directions which I don't understand.[60]

The steady deterioration of sympathy went on during the following months. Rogers' legal career kept him in London most of the time, and the lessening frequency of his meetings with Newman was itself a cause of gradual estrangement. Newman felt Rogers' absence keenly, because he had long depended on the young lawyer's sensible, man-of-the-world advice about practical problems. Rogers, for his part, gave that advice with a candour seldom approached by Newman's other friends.

Throughout the poetry professorship campaign Rogers acted as one of Isaac Williams' chief London agents. During this time—the winter of 1841–42—he was in frequent communication with Newman. But then about Easter 1842 the two men had some kind of confrontation in which Rogers told Newman that the Romeward direction the Movement appeared to have taken made the old footing of intimacy between them no longer possible.

Exactly what Newman's reaction to this was remains unclear. But on April 3, 1843, almost a year later, Rogers wrote a letter in which he referred to the "painful restrictions which I have understood you to impose." The whole letter deserves study. "My dear Newman," Rogers began, "I do not like meeting you again without having said, once for all, what I hope you will not think hollow or false. I cannot disguise from myself how very improbable—perhaps impossible—a recurrence to our former terms is." He went on to express his consciousness of how much he stood to suffer by the loss of Newman's friendship. "I know that it is in great measure by my own act that I am losing this, and I cannot persuade myself that I am substantially wrong, or that I could have long avoided what has happened."[61] Then, after having expressed beautifully his debt of gratitude to Newman, he continued:

One thing more I wish to say, as in one point (unfortunately indeed unimportant) I *may* have been (I think) misunderstood, and in a way which I should be pained to think—and by my own fault I may have seemed designedly to neglect openings which you gave me, and to keep things perversely on their present footing. If I have done so, it has been, as far as I know myself, partly from awkwardness, partly from not knowing what I was meant to do, and partly from a weak and unwise—sometimes involuntary—shrinking from intercourse under the painful restrictions which I have understood you to impose. If any irritation has mixed itself with these feelings, I am sorry and ashamed of myself for it in this as certainly in other cases as unjust, ungrateful and misplaced.[62]

One can only guess at what "painful restrictions" Newman imposed after the quarrel in the spring of 1842. Judging from the answer to the letter just quoted, it may be that they involved some sort of distinction between Rogers' public endorsement of the Movement and his private advice to a friend. "I never have assumed," Newman wrote sharply, "you acted on the notion that you agreed with me. . . . You never have told me your opinions. What did more than pain me was first and chiefly your refusing me that advice which I had a right to ask as a friend . . . and next your refusing to receive my confidence. I hope you will not refuse to continue to me the benefit of your prayers."[63]

Rogers responded immediately. "I must have explained myself ill both now and last Easter to leave you with the impression that I misunderstood you, unless indeed I misunderstand you still." He did not misunderstand Newman's distinction between advice and agreement; he denied its validity.

You have been in the habit of asking for my opinion not only in matters merely personal but as the conductor of a great Movement in the English Church. And I fancy that in cases of this kind I have been of use to you as habitually showing you in my own person what ordinary men would think of this or that course of conduct and enabling you to adapt your course to their notions. I cannot feel myself at liberty to occupy this place in a Movement which, *I* feel, is tending to a secession from England to Rome. I think it would, *in me*, be a treachery to the English Church to which I belong and to which I feel more and more contented to belong; and that I could do nothing but what I have done. If I had acted in the same way in any simply private matter, I should have felt myself unjustifiable.

With regard to Newman's chilly request for continued prayer, Rogers commented sadly: "I do not know how to speak of the last sentence of your letter. I must indeed be changed if I were to forget you. I am sure you will sometimes remember me."[64]

Newman scribbed some notes for a reply he never sent. They were cold, even bitter. "Will you let me add without offence that it has been growing on me for some time that there is a trait of suspiciousness (the nearest word I can find) in your character. . . . Another person once remarked to me what I think meant the same thing. May you find others as *reverential* in their feelings towards you as I have been."

So ended one of the grandest alliances of the Oxford Movement. Twenty years were to pass before a reconciliation was effected between Newman and Rogers and then, needless to say, it was too late for the old intimacy to be revived. The tragedy of broken friendship touched them both profoundly, but it is hard to see how it could have been avoided. Rogers knew Newman better perhaps than anyone alive, and he knew that, despite protestations, there was really no distinction between private advice and public commitment when dealing with Newman. In trying to force the distinction Newman had put upon Rogers an intolerable burden. "You never have told me your opinions," Newman had said, and this was simply untrue. Nobody could be closely associated with Newman, nobody could be his confidant, unless he were prepared to give the same wholehearted devotion to the cause as Newman himself gave. The trouble was that the cause had changed for Newman and had remained static for Rogers.[65]

But Newman did not grasp this, and so the estrangement with Rogers became that much harder to bear. He even told Keble that Rogers had "peremptorily refused"[66] to advise him on ecclesiastical matters. Yet in fact there was nothing peremptory about Rogers' decision, which had been mulled over and argued over for at least a year. It was simply part of the inevitable grief and pain to which the Movement was hurrying its major participants.

About the same time as the final break with Rogers, Newman learned of the death of his friend Samuel Wood, and he confided to his sister in a couple of bleak lines his sense of loss. It is no irreverence to Wood's memory to suggest that as he penned them Newman was thinking more of Frederic Rogers: "I have lost a great friend in Wood. . . . God makes me new friends when I lose old; to be sure, they are younger, but there are compensations even then. My dear Jemima, my life is done before it seems well begun."[67]

IV

Richard G. Macmullen, aged twenty-eight and an ardent Tractarian, was a Fellow of Corpus Christi College. According to the statutes of Corpus, every fellow within a certain time after his election had to secure the Bachelor of Divinity degree. According to the statutes of the university, the B.D. was earned by a formal disputation presided over by the Regius Professor of Divinity. Whatever intrinsic merit this procedure may once have had, by the summer of 1842, when Macmullen applied, it

had been long an empty formality. It amounted really to a conversation
on some theological subject between the candidate and anyone who chose
to "dispute" with him in the presence of the professor, who then automatically recommended that Congregation grant the degree. As is
apparent from this description, the B.D. had escaped the reforming provisions of the Examination Statute of 1800 and remained (like the M.A.)
a medieval shadow without substance. How lightly the whole thing was
taken can be gathered from the fact that when Thomas Arnold earned
his B.D., just before he went to Rugby, Newman, as a favour, played the
part of Arnold's "opponent" in the disputation.

No one imagined that the B.D. degree was a test of Anglican orthodoxy.
But in 1842 R. D. Hampden was Regius Professor of Divinity, and a
Tractarian candidate might therefore expect a certain amount of difficulty. As the long vacation began, Hampden was still smarting over a
recent failure to reverse the censure of 1836. He and his allies on the
Board of Heads had judged that the disarray of the Tractarians and the
Bishop of Oxford's anti-Tract Ninety Charge might have meant a
favourable reconsideration of Hampden's position by Convocation. They
were, however, mistaken, and the censure was confirmed on June 7th.
At that very moment the young and vulnerable Macmullen applied for
permission to dispute for the B.D.

He was vulnerable because the degree was a condition of his keeping
his fellowship and hence his livelihood. Whether Hampden fully appreciated this is unclear. He did know of course that Macmullen was one of
the enemy and he had at hand a procedural weapon with which to smite
him. During the professorship of Dr. Burton, Hampden's predecessor,
an attempt had been made to reform the manner of earning the B.D.
Nothing had come of this, except that Burton as a matter of practice
eliminated the disputation and substituted instead "two exercises [writ-
ten] in English upon subjects regularly announced to the university," or
else, if the candidate preferred, upon two subjects specifically chosen for
him by the professor.[68] Hampden had followed the same procedure since
1836 and though strictly speaking it was not justified by the letter of the
statutes, apparently the B.D. was not taken seriously enough for anybody
to complain.

A theoretical objection to the new procedure was that it altered what
had been essentially public debate between equals to a written exam
submitted by candidate to professor, and thus enhanced to a considerable
degree the professor's power in the matter. Macmullen, with views so
distasteful to Hampden, was bound to be at a greater disadvantage than
he would have been under the older system. Yet he probably did not
realize how much trouble he was in for until the professor assigned him
the two subjects upon which he was to write: first, "The Church of
England does not teach, nor can it be proved from Scripture, that any
change takes place in the elements at consecration in the Lord's Supper."

And second, "It is a mode of expression calculated to give erroneous views of Divine Revelation to speak of 'Scripture and Catholic Tradition' as joint authorities in the matter of Divine Revelation." These two theses were obviously designed to put a Tractarian on the spot.

Hampden probably intended no more than petty vengeance upon Macmullen (whom he did not know) and through him upon the Tract party. But he made a serious miscalculation by basing himself upon an extra-legal custom barely ten years old. Macmullen responded first by offering to dispute on the subjects the professor had chosen but as worded in the Thirty-nine Articles (in effect, what Peter Young had offered to do in his quarrel with the Bishop of Winchester). Hampden declined and insisted that the candidate treat the subjects in the wording assigned. "And so," reported Provost Hawkins of Oriel, "matters slept for a long time."

Then, in the late autumn, Macmullen, after consultation with Pusey, "applied again, flatly repudiated Dr. H[ampden]'s subjects and claimed the right of naming his own." When Hampden declined once more, Macmullen appealed to the Vice-chancellor, who in turn brought the matter to the Board of Heads. Those gentlemen, though they may have sympathized with Hampden and believed him "substantially right" (in Hawkins' phrase), were annoyed at the fuss this most unpopular colleague of theirs had raised, and they tried to escape their quandary by instructing the Vice-chancellor to inform Macmullen that "no appeal could lie under the existing circumstances, the *practice* in question [i.e. the substitution of written exercises for oral disputation] being mere matter of convenience between the professor and the candidate for a degree and unknown to the statutes." In other words, Macmullen would have to satisfy Hampden in one way or another.

In the state of high excitement which prevailed in the university in 1842 and 1843, the Macmullen affair was not so insignificant as it may now appear. Hawkins probably expressed the general feeling when he told Bishop Copleston that "it is a *party quarrel* and may easily involve all Oxford in the flame." This fear seemed especially warranted when Macmullen interpreted the Vice-chancellor's statement as an invitation to proceed judicially against Hampden if the latter failed to allow him to dispute. Macmullen accordingly published a Latin disputation subject, appointed two formal opponents—Charles Marriott and James Mozley—and gave Hampden two days to agree to preside. Hampden, tough as ever, refused. Macmullen then asked the Vice-chancellor to take the professor's place, a shrewd if impertinent maneuver which led the Vice-chancellor to ask Hawkins to negotiate with Hampden. There was no doubt in Hawkins' mind that Macmullen and his friends intended "to bring the subject before the Congregation or the Convocation, or by some means or other to unseat the regius professor and place Dr. Pusey or someone else in the divinity chair."

They did not succeed, but then, on the other hand, neither did Hampden. The case went through various stages of adjudication without reaching Congregation and at last, in 1844, Macmullen got his degree. Three years later he became a Roman Catholic and Hampden was named Bishop of Hereford. These eventualities perhaps convinced Hawkins that the judgment he had made in the midst of the controversy was the right one, though it may be hard now to see how a fair-minded man with an elevated sense of legal niceties could have arrived at it. "I cannot think," he wrote on December 31, 1842,

the questions wrong *in themselves*. And if not, surely Dr. H[ampden] ought to be supported, or the professor is no longer to act for the university and attest to the fitness of candidates for divinity degrees. And all D.D.s must . . . become professors and watch over each individual degree. And I confess it appears to me that if the professor were in this instance defeated, I should think myself bound, having known Mr. M[acmullen]'s case from his own statement, to oppose his degree if it came before the Congregation.

Macmullen's appeal to the pre-Burton practice, endorsed by the university statutes, seemingly made no impression upon Hawkins. But there was an explanation for this odd lapsus: "After all," he said, "Dr. H[ampden] is only in *his* office *resisting Tract Ninety*."[69] And that for Hawkins was enough.

V

Hawkins and the other Heads, however, were bent upon greater game than the obscure Macmullen. In May 1843 they got their chance, and this time without the albatross of Hampden hung about their necks. Pusey wrote the simple fact to Newman in a short note, dated May 18th: "You will be very sorry to hear that the storm has at last reached me. God guide me through it, for it may be a heavy one, not for myself, but for its effects on others."[70]

On the Sunday before, May 14th, Pusey delivered at Christ Church a sermon titled "The Holy Eucharist, a Comfort to the Penitent." The occasion was one of those formal services at which theoretically the whole university was present and at which clerical members of the university took their turn in the pulpit. Pusey's sermon was a fearlessly forthright statement of the high Tractarian Eucharistic doctrine which, in Pusey's systematic mind, was closely akin to his much-discussed views on post-baptismal sin. Afterwards Pusey commented, "When people said that I had scared them about post-baptismal sin, I was led to preach a course of sermons on comforts to the penitent. Of these the sermon on the Holy Eucharist was one."

As might have been expected from Pusey, the sermon was immensely learned; it bulged with allusions, quotations and images drawn from Scripture and the Fathers. What made it a hard saying for the non-Tractarian hearers was its bold enunciation of the sacramental principle at the expense, so it must have seemed, of the fundamental Protestant notion of justification. Pusey was saying in effect that the sacramental system, climaxed in the Eucharist, was the real refuge of sinful man, and this meant at least implicitly a denial of the unique instrumentality of faith. So there it was once more, the old Protestant-Catholic quarrel.

Pusey employed some very strong and lofty language. To the penitent, he said, the Eucharist's "special joy is that it is his Redeemer's very broken Body, it is his Blood, which was shed for the remission of his sins. In the words of the ancient Church, he 'drinks his ransom.' " And a little later in the sermon: "This may have been another truth which our Lord intended to convey to us when he pronounced the words as the form which consecrates the sacramental elements into his Body and Blood, that that precious Blood is still, in continuance and application of his one oblation once made upon the cross, poured out for us now." Finally, Pusey pointed to the practical consequences of Eucharistic piety: "It implies a life so different from this our commonplace ordinary tenor, a life so above this world as knit with him who hath overcome the world, so angelic as living on him who is the angels' food, a union with God so close that we cannot mostly, I suppose, imagine to ourselves how we could daily thus be in heaven and in our daily business here below."[71]

Yet there was nothing so extraordinary in Pusey's sermon to explain the storm which broke upon him because of it. He had said and written all these things before. As James Mozley put it, "The audience listened with the attention it always does to Dr. Pusey, and then the audience went away. There were the usual effects of edification and admiration produced. . . . It was of course said to contain high doctrinal views on the subject treated of; but as all Dr. Pusey's sermons contain high views, there was nothing to draw attention in this remark."[72]

But among the audience which went away from Christ Church that Sunday morning were the Vice-chancellor and the Provost of Oriel. These two potentates walked together and discussed the sermon they had just heard. "We both expressed ourselves startled and dissatisfied with the statements made with regard to the Eucharist," said the Vice-chancellor later, "but we both agreed that it would be inexpedient to take any public notice of it, being convinced that the writer would be able by ingenuity to evade any direct charge of heterodoxy." As the day wore on, however, the question of expediency—the only question apparently of any interest to the Vice-chancellor and the Heads—began to be seen in a different light. The next day unfavourable comment about the sermon continued, and on Tuesday, Dr. Faussett, Lady Margaret Professor of Divinity and the gentleman so mercilessly lampooned by Tom Mozley in the *British Critic*, formally demanded an investigation. It is impossible to say how much of this resulted from conscious conspiracy, but certainly neither Faussett nor the Vice-chancellor nor any of the Heads would have dared to tackle Pusey two years or even a year before. Evidently, in the judgment of the Oxford power structure, the fullness of time had come.

On Wednesday, May 16th, the Vice-chancellor informed Pusey that his sermon had been delated as contrary to "the doctrines of the reformed Church of England." The Vice-chancellor then created a special panel of six doctors of divinity to examine the sermon. To this extraordinary court he appointed Faussett, Pusey's accuser, and Hawkins, a man who had already stated that he thought the sermon heterodox. What is more, if one excepts Hampden (who by terms of the censure of 1836 could not sit on such a panel), the Tractarians had no more bitter and violent enemies in Oxford than Faussett and Hawkins. Justice for Pusey, or even a temperate examination of the issues raised by his sermon, was impossible with a board of judges so constituted. But the wily Vice-chancellor found a way to neutralize the bad image his panel might deservedly have; as a sixth member he appointed Dr. Richard Jelf, Pusey's intimate since their school days together at Eton, the man who had officiated at Pusey's wedding.

Pusey stood no chance in the face of his worldly-wise enemies, whose intention was to destroy his influence in the university. Jelf hoped that his presence on the panel instead of a stranger or *"perhaps* an enemy" might do his friend's cause some good, but Jelf's High and Dry views were far removed from Pusey's, and when the six doctors met on May 27th the best Jelf could do was to protest that though the sermon expressed "much that is objectionable in tone and language and tendency," there was nothing in it contrary to Anglican teaching. He was outvoted six (including the Vice-chancellor) to one.

There followed a series of shabby maneuvers. The sermon was condemned because of "certain things" in it which the doctors agreed were contrary to the Anglican formularies. These "things" were never stated publicly. Instead the Vice-chancellor moved on quickly to the matter of punishment. University statute provided an alternative between recantation and suspension, of which the former was considered less severe. But what the Vice-chancellor and his advisers—chiefly Hawkins—dreaded above all was a confrontation with Pusey himself. Indeed, it had taken a callous disregard for every principle of justice as well as for Oxford precedents of three centuries to have denied Pusey a hearing before he was condemned. Now that he was condemned, without having had a chance to defend himself, his accusers still refused to hear him. "Foreseeing," explained the Vice-chancellor airily, "that if I should summon Dr. Pusey before me . . . in the presence of those who had adjudicated upon the sermon, it might happen that he would refuse to recant, and

thus an interview painful to all parties might be productive of no beneficial result, I determined upon endeavouring to ascertain privately
whether or not it would be likely that he might be induced to recant the
offensive doctrine." Denied the simple justice of a hearing, Pusey would
be offered escape through secret negotiations.

Only a man as simple and otherworldly as Pusey would have fallen
into the trap thus laid for him. On Tuesday, May 30th, the Vice-chancellor sent Jelf to inform Pusey that his sermon stood condemned and
that his only hope of reprieve was a recantation. If Pusey would sign
certain statements of doctrine which would be presented to him, the
sentence might be reversed. But, Jelf added, even before Pusey was
allowed to see the statements he must agree to absolute secrecy about
"the fact of . . . receiving these statements"; he "was to make no copy
of them, . . . to consult no friend about anything in them." "For the
sake of the peace of the Church," Pusey said afterwards, "I accepted
even these conditions."

It is problematical whether Pusey was lulled by his oldest friend acting as messenger boy for his enemies. In any case, by accepting the
Vice-chancellor's conditions he sealed his fate. When the statements were
presented to him on May 31st—they were the work of Hawkins—he
could not sign them. They were vague, tendentious and did not at all
conform to the procedure dictated in such cases by university statute.
"The statute speaks of certain definite statements which shall be retracted," Pusey told the Vice-chancellor, while Hawkins' propositions
were merely snippets of the sermon which might or might not bear a
Roman interpretation. "I should consider any ulterior measure . . .
without exhibiting to me what I have asked for, [namely] . . . definite
propositions of my own and not *adhering to our formularies*, as un-
statutable as well as harsh and unjust."

Such a plea did not move the six doctors. The smell of blood was
too strong in their nostrils. They met on June 1st, rejected out of hand
Pusey's request for specifics and sent Jelk back with a fresh recantation
form not materially different from the first. Pusey would not sign this one
either, and for the same reasons. He once more insisted that his inquisi-
tors abide by statute and present him with definite propositions, clearly
at variance with Anglican teaching, if they expected a recantation. The
same evening the six doctors met again and advised the Vice-chancellor,
now that Pusey had twice refused to "recant," that the Regius Professor
of Hebrew should be suspended from preaching within the university
for two years. It was so determined and formal notice of the sentence
was given to Pusey the next day.

The world at large knew nothing of these goings-on. Pusey had not
even been able to consult with his friends, though he of all men alive
needed advice on practical matters. The six doctors, for their part, were

not anxious to reveal their own ignorance and vindictiveness. But they were badly shaken when Pusey published a Protest which caused rumbles all the way to London. It was true, as Hawkins at least had no doubt foreseen, that Pusey's case suffered from not being able to speak of the secret negotiations carried on through Jelf, for in those negotiations, which included the two recantation statements, were displayed the incredibly weak grounds upon which the Vice-chancellor had acted.

Even so, Pusey was still able to make another point which suddenly showed the six doctors that their imposition of silence was a two-edged sword. The fact that he had consistently demanded and just as consistently been refused a hearing of any kind moved fair-minded people of all theological persuasions to sympathy for Pusey and some of them to outrage. Hawkins, the guiding genius behind the whole sordid business, recommended to the Vice-chancellor that he might neutralize the impact of this damaging revelation by stating the fact, if not the contents, of the secret negotiations and inferring that they were themselves a kind of hearing. This clumsy and dishonest stratagem was tried but without much effect.

It is strange how adamantly Hawkins maintained this indefensible position. Some months afterwards he quarreled over it in the Oriel common room with the usually imperturbable Charles Marriott. Marriott described the whole proceeding of the six doctors as "absurd." Hawkins immediately bristled and, as Marriott told the story, "complained of my saying so to him, but I really could not in conscience withdraw it. . . . He then referred to the mysterious 'communications' [i.e. with Jelf], of which I said I judged from the Vice-chancellor's message to Pusey that they did not constitute a full hearing. He still maintained that they had, but didn't tell me what they were."[73]

Throughout the summer protests and petitions poured in to the Vice-chancellor. Edward Badeley was particularly active, and he, with Gladstone and Judge Coleridge, led an aroused High Church laity to increasingly strident demands that justice be done Pusey. Nothing of course was done, except that the Vice-chancellor grew more strident himself; he acts, said James Mozley, "as if he were the Vice-chancellor of the universe."[74] In the long run it may be that the Oxford power structure, through its star-chamber tactics in the persecution of Pusey, damaged itself as much as it did the Tractarian cause. Less than a decade later, as the need to reform the university was debated in the parliament, many powerful men remembered the affair of the six doctors as a case in point.

But in 1843 Pusey's suspension was primarily a blow to the leadership of the Movement. Now its enemies could claim a clean sweep: Newman, Keble (in the Peter Young case) and Pusey had all been authoritatively censured or silenced. This accumulation of adverse sentences was bound to have a depressing effect, and there were many who judged the time had come to cut bait. Henry Manning, for example, sent Pusey in the middle of July a letter filled with tortured prose like the following: "On the sermon itself I feel as yet unwilling to say more than that I can see nothing that is not capable of a sound meaning and covered by the Fathers and our own divines." He refrained from speaking with "more decision," because he had only read the sermon once "and that aloud."[75]

Isaac Williams, on the other hand, spoke warmly for the ever-shrinking Tractarian circle: "We have to thank you for your sermon. I do not like saying much to you about it as you may be so tired of the subject that you are glad to get away from it. But I may just mention that John Keble exclaimed on reading the Preface, 'Any annoyance or mischief about the matter is a mere nothing compared with the immensity of good this will do.' And on reading the sermon he said it was not so strong as Hooker, and it has left the very same impression on his mind that it did on mine, which I will not venture to repeat to you." Williams added that it was "a high privilege" to proclaim God's truth and one must expect to suffer for it.[76] Coming from Williams, who had suffered more than his share for the Movement, this sentiment was perhaps a consolation to Pusey, who was ill and depressed most of the summer.

Keble also had intervened to prevent a gesture of defiance which Pusey had considered. Pusey should not, he said, dedicate the published version of the sermon to Newman because it "might rather seem to be saying to the Heads, I take the opportunity of your attacking me to show how little I care for your attacks by expressing my sympathy with your last victim."[77] Pusey reluctantly agreed and the sermon was published without dedication.

As for that last victim, he brooded over the affair from Littlemore. "Matters are looking very grave," he wrote to Tom Mozley on June 19th. "The Vice-c. and co. find they have an arbitrary and more than military power and seem well disposed to use it and to put down Catholicism at all risks." Newman still showed a spark of the old party manager when he added a warning to Tom: "James [Mozley] says you are writing [on the six doctors] in the *B.C.*: *be very sure of your facts*; do not rely on Pusey's Protest and *beware of libel*. . . . Recollect, Badeley said that your Faussett article was indictable."[78]

But ten days earlier he had given Henry Wilberforce an indication of his deeper frame of mind with reference to Pusey's plight and indeed to that of the whole Movement. After telling Henry of the latest rumours about the six doctors, he said wearily, "Keep your eyes and ears open as to what is going on, but I have neither time nor will to meddle with these dirty matters."[79]

CHAPTER 19

The Spring Goes Out of the Year

IN the second week of July 1843 Harriet Newman Mozley returned from a round of visits to her home in Cholderton, on the Salisbury Plain. The high-strung Harriet, who, like her brother, experienced occasional fits of deafness, had suffered from acute insomnia for months, and she had gone on holiday in hopes that a change of scene might bring some relief. But it had not, and at home again, with her intense, witty, shallow husband, she found the same measure of confusion and distress as before, symbolized perhaps by the gaunt skeleton of the church Tom had been trying to build for years and could not seem to finish. Harriet indeed had not been well since the previous September when she sat with her husband and listened to the Bishop of Salisbury condemn the *British Critic* in his Charge.

"She desired to try a more thorough change," Tom remembered, and since neither he nor she had ever been out of England, "I provided for my [parochial] duty, borrowed fifty pounds from my principal tithe-payer, . . . and drove to Southampton, whence we crossed to Havre."[1] Their progress across Normandy was at first a delightful one, and Harriet was especially pleased by the high regard in which her brother was held by French Roman Catholics. *"Quoi!"* cried one curé when he discovered Harriet's relationship. "M. Newman! *Celui qui est l'homme très célèbre."* But she was a little disturbed by another of the priest's remarks—*"il est un de nous-mêmes"*—because, though she discovered much to admire in French Catholicism, there was also much which to her sedately English temperament appeared flamboyant if not idolatrous.[2]

Harriet had not the slightest suspicion of what was passing through her impulsive husband's mind on the same subject. About September 1st, Tom, pleading the press of *British Critic* business, left Harriet in Normandy and fled back to England. He sat down in his study with "my huge unfinished church before my windows" and wrote Newman that he intended to become a Roman Catholic immediately. Newman hurried off to Cholderton and spent a whole day talking Tom out of his snap decision. He urged Tom to concentrate on completing his church, "which seemed providentially designed to compel deliberation." Though surprised and disappointed by this advice, Tom in the end agreed to wait two years before he took any decisive step. In the course of the conversation Newman revealed to Tom for the first time his own grave doubts about Anglicanism. Presumably his argument was that if he, Newman, could wait until he was absolutely sure, Tom could do the same. Unhappily for domestic tranquillity Tom told the other members of the family of Newman's deep unsettlement; the news left Jemima upset and Harriet fiercely angry.[3]

Forty years after that breathless moment Thomas Mozley wondered what it was he had been seeking. Perhaps he had been affected by his "runaway horses, Ward and Oakeley." More likely he sought relief from the ceaseless controversy in the Church of England where there reigned "ten thousand popes—the lay popes ten times more arrogant, unreasonable and bitter than the clerical, and the female popes a hundred times worse than either."[4] Though he did not say so, he may well have had one popess in mind. On September 9, 1843, when Harriet discovered what had happened, she wrote her husband from Normandy, "It seems to me the most treacherous thing in the world to have persuaded me to stay here against my will and then to go home and in my absence without a word of preparation to take so grave a step. . . . I feel it more bitterly than words can express. . . . I shall not rest till I have something from you to reassure me."[5] Harriet got her way, as the Newmans usually did. Tom never strayed again.

I

Two days before Harriet thus put her irresolute husband on a short leash, her brother got his own way too. On September 7, 1843, he informed Bishop Bagot of his intention to resign the vicarage of St. Mary the Virgin, Oxford. "I shall give your lordship much pain I fear," he wrote, but then Bagot should not be surprised at such a step "when so many bishops have said such things of me, and no one [has] undertaken my part in respect to that interpretation of the Articles under which alone I can subscribe to them."[6] To Harriet the explanation, though not essentially different, was more sharply focused: "I do so despair of the Church of England, I am so evidently cast off by her, and on the other hand I am so drawn to the Church of Rome, that I think it *safer* as a matter of honesty *not* to keep my living."[7]

The bishop replied gently and regretfully and reminded Newman of the legal formalities necessary for resignation. These he fulfilled before a notary in London on September 19th.

But the decision of September was preceded by a strange duel between mismatched antagonists which had begun in March. On March 14th Newman wrote Keble and raised once more the question of resignation. He reminded Keble of the reasons he had advanced in 1840—undue influence over undergraduates instead of over his proper parishioners, and unintentional creation of sympathy for Rome among the most sensitive of his hearers. These reasons, he said, were no less strong in 1843, and added to them was "the gradual advance . . . to a unanimous condemnation of Number Ninety on the part of the bishops." And the method employed by the bishops rendered Newman's position uniquely difficult: "they condemn it without specifying *what* they condemn in it. This gives an opening to every reader who agrees with it on the whole to escape the force of their censure. I alone cannot escape it."

Newman admitted that resignation might "imply a great dissatisfaction with the Church of England" and thus amount to a species of scandal. But this could be avoided by detaching Littlemore from St. Mary's parish and allowing Newman to serve as parson of the former. The legal rector of St. Mary's was Oriel, and the college had refused such a separation before—"but," said Newman, "I think some arrangement of the kind might be managed."[8]

From the evidence available it is hard to avoid the conclusion that when Newman first broached the subject of resignation to Keble, in October 1840, he had wanted to be talked out of it and he was. Now, two and a half years later, he had no intention of being diverted from the act, no matter what Keble said. Of course much had happened since 1840, but one thing had remained constant on both occasions: Newman had made up his mind to a course of action and he wanted Keble not so much to advise as to confirm. This time he did not get that confirmation.

On March 14th Newman told Keble that he would not in any event resign before the autumn. An immediate answer therefore was not necessary, "indeed, from the nature of the case I do not wish a speedy one." Keble did not reply until May 3rd. He said he thought "the time is come when there will be nothing wrong in your retiring if your own feelings prompt you to do so." But he attached a definite condition: "I am not sure that I should say this if it involved your retiring from the exercise of the ministry; but, if you can manage to keep Littlemore, there will be no appearance of that kind." Then Keble added a word of gentle, between-the-lines remonstrance at which he was so adept: "I do not think so much of bishops' words in their Charges as you do, and as I did myself, now that I have found out how they might act on them and do not, thereby proving themselves not in earnest. But without saying that it is your duty to retire one may very well think that it is perfectly open to you to do so. Whichever way you resolve, I do not see that you can do very wrongly."[9]

Newman answered the next day, and now, for the first time, he told Keble of the doubts which had begun in the summer of 1839 and had grown ever since. It is enough perhaps to quote the ringing climax of his account: "I am very far *more* sure that England is in schism than that the Roman additions to the primitive creed may not be developments, arising out of a keen and vivid realizing of the divine depositum of faith."[10]

Newman had also found out that the college would not detach Littlemore from St. Mary's. The next Oriel don to be vicar, if Newman resigned, would be C. P. Eden, who had written one of the early Tracts but who sternly disapproved of recent developments in the Movement. Indeed, Eden told Newman quite candidly that if he were vicar "and had not daily service [at Littlemore], he [was] not prepared to let *me* read the service on the ground that it would be investing me with a sort of authority in the place."[11]

Keble read this bitter news in an abandoned chalk pit near Hursley where he had gone on a walk with that day's letters. It seems likely that he had already guessed something of Newman's state of mind, even though till now he did not know the particulars. His answer showed neither surprise nor the faintest hint of reproof. But at the same time neither did it encourage resignation. "Your withdrawing from the English ministry under the present circumstances will be a very perilous step, not so much in itself but because of its bringing you, as I fear it would, in every respect nearer what I must call the temptation of going over."

Keble suggested Newman was perhaps being precipitous: "You speak . . . of our Church showing no signs of repentance, no yearning after catholicity; but is not the time too short for any one to be acting on this impression? . . . From bishops one could hardly look at present for more than toleration, and that I consider myself to have from my diocesan [Sumner], much more you from yours [Bagot]. Are you sure that some of your feeling on this head is not owing to a natural reaction from having had too eager expectations at some time? . . . Do you not think it possible that you may have overestimated the claims of Rome in your later studies from a kind of feeling that your earlier expressions had done her wrong?" Resignation, he went on, might indeed have a bad effect upon others, but Keble feared it would have a worse effect upon Newman. "You see my deep feeling about your withdrawing from your ministerial place refers almost wholly to what I fear might come after." Keble finished by insisting, in his typical self-deprecatory fashion, that Newman "not in the smallest degree depend on my advice or opinion in this matter."[12]

This contest went on, with several interruptions, through the spring and summer of 1843. On June 9th Newman told Henry Wilberforce that "Keble has more than permitted me to resign St. Mary's, though this is a secret."[13] This appears a rather free interpretation of what Keble wrote on May 30th: "I really do think the position so very difficult a one that I dare not press your retaining St. Mary's. . . . You see therefore that on the whole my leaning is towards your retiring as quietly as you can." But then he added, "You yourself allow that if the tone of the bishops . . . was favourable to Number Ninety instead of adverse, you should not think yourself guilty of any breach of trust in remaining. And I am not prepared to give so much weight as you seem to do to the *un-enacted* leanings and tendencies of a particular generation."[14]

By late July Keble was recommending absorption in parochial work as a possible antidote and an accompanying withdrawal "for awhile from theological study and correspondence." Or maybe "unreserved confidence in some *really worthy* confessor might be a great help to you at times."[15] Newman did not acknowledge these suggestions immediately. Instead, about August 1st, he began to keep a detailed journal "which would do to show anyone in confession and give him a sort of idea of my present state." For the next ten days he set down with minute care in this spiritual diary all his inner thoughts and tensions. On August 20th he wrote Keble and asked him to take the journal and study it. As for Keble's advice about parochial preoccupation, Newman simply dismissed it: "If I were to have any thing more directly *practical* it should be an hospital. I fear the more parochial duty I took the more I should realize, and the greater temptation I should be under to give up, our present defective system, which *seems* to be without the capabilities of improvement."

In a long postscript Newman pressed Keble still further. He had preached four sermons during the past couple of years which had quieted the restlessness of several young Anglicans who had "felt unsettled as to Rome. . . . It has struck me that the fact of publishing sermons just now would be a sort of guarantee to people that my resigning St. Mary's (to which I am more and more strongly drawn) did not involve an ulterior step—for no one could suppose that I should be publishing today and leaving the Church tomorrow."[16]

Keble's reply, written on August 25th, was short and betrayed for the first time some irritation at the pressure Newman was applying. "I should think on the whole," he wrote, "that unless you feel very strongly drawn towards showing me your journal I had better not see it; your own feelings in such a matter must be the only criterion." As to the sermons, "the only objection to publishing, I suppose, would be from a fear of being or seeming insincere; and this again must depend on the nature of the sermons."[17] Keble's note crossed one written by Newman the same day in which he announced that William Lockhart, one of the Littlemore monks, had broken his promise and was about to be received into the Roman Church. "Would *this*," Newman asked, "be a good excuse for giving up St. Mary's?"[18] But once more Keble refused that sanction which Newman so desperately wanted. "I confess I do not quite see how it smooths matters for your resignation. I should have thought the quieter things were at the moment the better for that step; and therefore that this, causing alarm, would rather defer it."[19]

Through the last day of August and the first days of September, Newman bombarded Keble with no less than five notes and letters.[20] On September 1st he said, "I am ready still to keep St. Mary's if you think best," and then he listed the reasons why the secession of Lockhart— "decidedly the greatest prize I have heard of their [i.e. the Roman Catholics] making"—left him no choice but to resign. Later the same day he wrote again to say that another person, more important than Lockhart, was on the verge of going to Rome. "Apparently I was right in saying this morning that it is useless waiting for a quiet time." And on September 5th still again: "*Another* person, still more important, as I should say, than the last mentioned has surprised me by telling me he must go over to Rome. . . . Really I cannot keep St. Mary's on."

But Keble, on September 4th, had for all practical purposes said his last weary word on the subject: "As to St. Mary's, I cannot say anything against such feelings and considerations as you allege; and after all what right have we to expect to see our way clearly in respect of consequences? You can but do what seems right for the time, taking care not to act from impulse, and there is Another to be trusted with the results."[21]

"You can but do what seems right . . ." The day after he received Keble's letter Newman sent his resignation notice to the bishop. And so ended this shadowy game of charades. Newman had intended since the preceding Lent to resign St. Mary's in the autumn,[22] and he did as he intended. He told Henry Wilberforce in May that he had informed Keble of his difficulties "in honesty and propriety" and that he would abide by Keble's advice. But as a matter of fact he did not do so, or rather he extracted from Keble a reluctant agreement "to do what seems right." There was no conscious deceit in this; Newman really thought he was doing what Keble wanted.

Another factor adds still more unreality to this conflict of wills. Over and over Newman protested his sorrow at causing Keble "pain" about the matter of resignation. And just as consistently Keble fretted that he did not feel enough pain. "Your letters," he wrote on September 7th, "as you may suppose make me rather giddy and put me out of breath; but I wish I felt your distress more keenly than I do. For instance, I got your . . . note in Winchester yesterday, and brooded over it during my walk home; and yet I lost none of my night's rest by it; whereas, if one felt it more, one might perhaps be able to say or do something that might be of use to you."[23]

September 25, 1843, marked the seventh anniversary of the dedication of Littlemore Chapel. It turned out to be a mournfully festive occasion. Many of Newman's friends attended the service, which was conducted by Edward Pusey. Newman himself preached the last and in many ways the most memorable of his Anglican sermons. It was published under the title "The Parting of Friends."

And O, my brethren, O kind and affectionate hearts, O loving friends, should you know of anyone whose lot it has been, by writing or by word of mouth, in some degree to help you thus to act; if he has ever told you what you knew about yourselves, or what you did not know, has read to you your wants or feelings and comforted you by the very reading; has made you feel that there was a higher life than this daily one and a brighter world than that you see; or encouraged you, or sobered you, or opened a way to the enquiring, or soothed the perplexed; if what he has said or done has ever made you take interest in him and feel well inclined towards him; remember such a one in time to come, though you hear him not, and pray for him that in all things he may know God's will and at all times he may be ready to fulfil it.[24]

A witness recalled that by the time Newman had finished, everyone in the church was weeping. When he came down from the pulpit he took off his ecclesiastical robe and tossed it across the communion rail. He received Communion from Pusey's hand and did not otherwise officiate at the service.

II

Thomas Mozley in later years paid tribute to the courtesy and forbearance of Francis Rivington, publisher of the *British Critic*. Occasionally Rivington had had to complain about Mozley's tardiness;[25] yet on the whole, considering the widespread criticism of the journal, Rivington maintained a remarkable composure. Perhaps it was because, as Newman once suggested, that controversy is a good magazine salesman.[26] But in any case, about the time of Newman's resignation from St. Mary's, Rivington was finding the pressure too much for him. On September 15, 1843, he wrote to Tom about an article, scheduled for the October issue, in which the writer stated an explicit preference for the Roman over the English Church: "It appears to me that we cannot consistently express such an opinion in a review which professes itself an organ of the Church of England."[27]

Rivington's was a mild expression of a sentiment which burned fiercely within the breast of William Palmer of Worcester. During the thirty months since Tract Ninety, when he had come gallantly to Newman's defense, Palmer had watched aghast as, in his judgment, the situation went from bad to worse. He had been particularly distressed by Ward's pamphlet "A Few More Words," which, he thought, not so much defended Number Ninety as wildly misapplied the principles of that subtle document. And when Ward's became the paramount influence on the *British Critic*, Palmer resolved upon attack.

First he consulted Newman. "I pressed upon him the great offence such things had given and urged him to use his influence . . . to suppress such teaching." Newman replied, with what Palmer described as "evident excitement," that he was editor of the *British Critic* no longer, that the bishops and university officials had silenced him and destroyed his influence, and so those potentates "would now have to deal with younger men whom it was not in his power to restrain."[28]

This conversation must have occurred in the summer of 1843 when Newman was distracted almost to the point of obsession over the timing of his resignation from St. Mary's. Some further correspondence passed between Newman and Palmer on the *British Critic* matter—all of it courteous and unconstructive—and Palmer also took his case to Keble. "I have a long letter from Palmer of Worcester, urging the necessity, on the part of other people, of some such protest against the B[ritish] C[ritic] etc., as he is going to make himself."[29] Keble of course did nothing.

Palmer's protest, *A Narrative of Events connected with the Publication of the Tracts for the Times*, appeared in September 1843 to a chorus of approval from the High Church party and to the considerable discomfort of publisher Francis Rivington. "It is the design of the following pages," wrote Palmer in his preface, "to clear those who uphold Church principles from the imputation of approving certain tendencies to Romanism." The Movement of 1833, he went on, had had no Roman tendencies, but recent developments had sullied the original aim and impetus of the Movement. Said Palmer: "The injury which has been inflicted by [the *British Critic*] cannot be repaired by any mere change of management."

The purpose of Palmer's *Narrative* was to distinguish in the public mind the *British Critic* writers from those High Churchmen who had been to a greater or less degree allies of the Tractarians—people like Palmer himself, Perceval, Hook, Edward Churton, Manning, Rose (had he lived) and scores of others. To accomplish this he retold the history of 1833 and 1834 when Newman's Tracts had conflicted with Palmer's grand design for a nationwide association. For the most part Palmer's account was soberly objective, although a snide or resentful tone now and then crept in. Thus, in speaking of the early Tracts, he said that "at first" he aided in their circulation, "because their general tendency seemed good, though I confess that I was rather surprised at the rapidity with which they were composed and published without any previous revision or consultation." And remembering the cold shoulder he had received from the Oriel men in 1834 Palmer had trouble avoiding bitterness in 1843: On that occasion, he said, "I did not . . . entirely relinquish the hope of being of some use."[30]

But Palmer reserved his harshest attacks for Ward and the *British Critic*. Page followed page of citations to demonstrate that for two years the magazine had been "under the influence of those who are uncertain in their allegiance to the Church of England."[31] When he had finished there was not much left for Rivington to do but close the magazine down. This he did. October 1843 marked the final issue of the *British Critic*.

Palmer's deeper objective in the *Narrative* appears to have been two-fold, one a noble aspiration and the other not so noble. He wanted first to save what could be saved for the apostolical Anglo-Catholic cause as he understood it. Nobody could have blamed him for this and for his consequent effort to shoot down the likes of Ward and Oakeley. But he was moved also by bitterness and jealousy and even rage at the thought of his Movement snatched from him at its birth and brought to the shambles of 1843 by the intransigence of Newman. Throughout the pamphlet he employed the most exaggerated and affected phrases with regard to Newman's part in the tragedy; it was as though he did not trust himself to use straight English sentences lest the distaste he felt by this time for Newman should become too apparent.

With Palmer's *Narrative* the Movement had come so to speak full circle and had begun to consume itself. Newman's comments on the *Narrative* made to Bowden at the end of October leave the same impression. "Palmer, I suppose, has written his pamphlet under the idea that he can keep the bishops from ultra-protestantizing by separating catholic views and imprimis the Movement of 1833 from Romanism. But this seems to me moonshine. They *are* ultra-protestant, they have nothing else in them, i.e. speaking of them as bishops."[32] And William Copeland, Newman's sometime curate, dismissed the *Narrative* as a political tract. "The strong language," he told Keble, "used by Palmer in the beginning of the 'Narrative' shows his sense of panic at the political aspect of affairs which he viewed with an Irish eye."[33] It was ironic that even at this late hour poor Palmer could not escape the stigma of his birth.

The light of the *British Critic* flickered briefly once more before it went out forever. Frederick Oakeley reported that "a strong wish has been expressed" that the magazine continue under his editorship. If Rivington should object he could sell his interest in the magazine's name. "I confess," said Oakeley, not very convincingly, "that I have no very strong feeling in the matter."[34] Newman opposed the idea and nothing came of it. Instead Rivington in 1844 began publication of a new High Church magazine called the *Christian Remembrancer* which Newman condemned without reading. "They say," he told Bowden, "the new review is very stupid. I have not seen it. I expected the first number or two to be brilliant. My anticipation and malicious wish was that Palmer would go to Cambridge for contributors, fall into the hands of the Camden men[35] and like Phaeton be hurried across the sky by a much more unruly team than ever perplexed the course of the *British Critic*." People have told him, he added—people probably like Dalgairns—that the *Remembrancer* has "the calm of dulness, unmitigated and hopeless."[36]

Another immediate result of Palmer's *Narrative* and the closing of the *British Critic* was a production which brought the fortunes of the Movement, if that were possible, to an even more critical stage. This was the publication of W. G. Ward's enormous and disorderly book called *The Ideal of a Christian Church*. Ward wrote it in a couple of months (it was published in June 1844). As an answer to Palmer it was like a deluge in answer to a prayer for rain. Abstract, rambling, intense, awkwardly written, *Ideal* possessed all of Ward's virtues and all of his faults. It was read by few and understood by even fewer. It purported to be an elaboration of Ward's *British Critic* articles (which Palmer had attacked so fiercely) and specifically his notion that ethical concern was the center of genuine religion. Perhaps it was, but to most readers, then and now, it seemed more like a flood of words which meant, as Bishop Bagot had said about Number Ninety, everything and nothing. One assertion, however, stood out sharply clear: Ward's "ideal" was the Church of Rome and in the English Church he found nothing but decay.

"A dimness of spiritual vision," wrote Ward, has characterized the Church of England since the Reformation. "So powerless has our Church been to train her children in these most essential of all requisites, an obedient life and an orthodox faith," that the ordinary run of Anglicans "show themselves to be . . . spiritually blinded by the carnal and worldly atmosphere of our Church-system, by the foul atmosphere of Lutheranism which as some pestilential vapour overspread us. . . . We cannot learn doctrine from the English Church if we would, for she *teaches* no uniform doctrine to be learned." And passages like the following summed up Ward's impudent and yet somehow innocent estimate of his place in the sun.

We find, oh most joyful, most wonderful, most unexpected sight! we find the whole cycle of Roman doctrine gradually possessing numbers of the English Church, numbers even of those who are as yet unconscious how much of truth they hold. . . . And this work has been done with no help whatever from without. . . . *It has been done under God by the inherent vitality and powers of our own Church*. Whether at the present time "High Church" doctrines are increasing or diminishing in numerical strength I am unable even to guess; but that *Roman* sympathies and doctrines are making the most rapid strides among "High churchmen," this no one . . . can for a moment doubt. . . . No argument has appeared of any force against these positions; and, what is more to the purpose, no condemnation of them by any authoritative tribunal. Three years have passed since I said plainly that in subscribing to the Articles I renounce no one Roman doctrine; yet I retain my fellowship which I hold on the tenure of subscription and have received no ecclesiastical censure in any shape.[37]

Those who had already brought down Pusey and Newman were not likely to let such a challenge pass.

III

Retirement into lay communion took Newman a long step towards Rome, but it was not the final step. Though he was no longer an official teacher in the Church of England, he was still a Fellow of Oriel, still intent upon keeping his young men faithful to their Anglican allegiance, still not sure that the intellectual claims of Roman Catholicism, which seemed stronger to him every day, were enough to move his will. But much indeed had happened in the year since Pusey had told Henry Manning, "I do think persons near Newman do him injustice. They fasten their own corollaries upon his principles, and because Newman cannot deny that they may be plausibly drawn, though he does not see them or appropriate them, they assume he is with them."[38] Pusey, though he did not yet know all, knew better now.

And so did Manning. The prudent archdeacon made inquiries as soon as he heard of the resignation of St. Mary's. "My dear Newman," he wrote on October 8, 1843, "I had intended to come to Littlemore yesterday to see you; but I was in so much pain from a cold in my face that I most unwillingly gave it up at the last moment." More likely Manning, who was spending the day as guest of the Bishop of Oxford, suffered from a cold in the feet. But however that may be, Newman told Manning the whole story—the doubts of 1839 and everything that had followed—in three letters written between October 14th and October 31st. Manning, greatly alarmed, sent them on to Gladstone, who reacted excitedly: "My first thought is, 'I stagger to and fro, like a drunken man, and am at my wits' end.' "[39] Manning reacted by delivering a violently anti-Roman sermon in Oxford on Guy Fawkes Day, November 5th.

Pusey, leading from a strength Newman had lost, did not hesitate to tell Manning that his performance had been dishonest. "I can only marvel . . . how you could preach the sermon, so abstracting from your own feelings. I know with what end you did it—to regain people to their allegiance to our Church. I doubt its efficacy. But this is expediency only."[40] Newman, though annoyed at first, took a milder line with Manning, to whom he wrote on Christmas eve: "It is no pleasure to me to differ from friends—no comfort to be estranged from them—no satisfaction or boast to have said things which I must unsay. Surely I will remain where I am as long as I can. I think it right to do so. If my misgivings are from above, I shall be carried on in spite of my resistance."[41]

But Manning was only one of many who came now to share what had been once a secret known only to Frederic Rogers and Henry Wilberforce. To some Newman gave only a hint; thus he said to Charles Marriott that he—Newman—should not be trusted too far. Marriott replied: "It is probably well for us that we do not know too much of one another, but, if I must not trust you, I must take leave for the present to trust the Power that I believe watches over you."[42]

Such a sentiment must have been gall and wormwood to Newman. His greatest burden during these last Anglican years was the knowledge that many of his friends intended to base their own decisions upon his. If he moved, so would they; if he stayed, so would they. As it turned out his decision had less impact than he or they expected. But throughout 1844 and 1845 Newman continued to be tortured by the thought that what he did or did not do might have eternal ramifications for others. "I hope I am not wrong," he said to Keble in January 1844, "but I have lately been praying that if *I* am right, Pusey, Manning, etc. may be brought forward; but if Pusey, Manning, etc. are right, I may be brought back— that nothing, if it be possible, may separate us."[43] He remembered Sicily and his near-fatal illness in 1833, and how he had cried out, "I have not sinned against the light."

And now at the end of eleven years from that time, [what] is my own state? Why, that for the last five years (almost) of it, I have had a strong feeling, often rising to an habitual conviction . . . and growing more urgent and imperative continually, that the Roman Communion is the only true Church. . . . And then another terrible thought strikes me. We hear of physicians thinking they have cured a complaint when they have but thrown their patient into a contrary one—and enough has happened to make me fear greatly lest a sort of latitudinarianism and liberalism *may* be the end of them . . . whom I am keeping from Rome. I am quite sure there is this *danger*. I dread it in particular persons. The time may even come when I shall beg them to join the Church of Rome and they will refuse.[44]

He was plagued by rumours. In March 1844 a Manchester clergyman announced in a public speech that "Mr. Newman has been obliged to leave the Church of England and go over to Rome." In November a bogus letter to Isaac Williams was quoted in London newspapers to the same effect. "A splendid myth," Newman commented; he had not written a line to Williams for months.[45] Yet he found it necessary to reassure a half-dozen intimates that the story was untrue. The simply curious put down one account of his apostasy only to pick up another, and his enemies kept repeating that his hesitancy and silence were deceitful means he used to subvert the loyalty of his disciples. "What I feel most at present as to the attacks made on me," he told Keble, "or rather the only thing which I *feel*, is the charge of dishonesty. Really no one but [Daniel] O'Connell is called so distinctly and so ordinarily a liar as I am. I think nothing tends to hurt my spirits but this. I am not treated merely as a gentleman, and that by educated people."[46]

He was deluged too by communications from friends or even from people he scarcely knew who heard the rumours and wondered at them. One unidentified friend wrote, "If on the strength of old associations, and the unvarying kindness which you have shown me for so many years, I may make any suggestion to you, I do so most earnestly and . . . most affectionately implore you to *pause* before you take this most fearful step."[47] This correspondent, like many others, promised his prayers in Newman's behalf. A former schoolfellow added his plea: "O my very dear friend, to whom I am so deeply and eternally obliged, not so much for private acts of friendship but for the reality and consistency which your writings with others have imparted to my religious views—can you think of leaving us, so many as we are that have benefited by your exertions. I entreat you not to forsake us."[48] There was also another kind of letter, not a plea but a presumption, like the one from the young clergyman whom Newman had never met. He was about to become a Roman Catholic and wrote jauntily to inform Newman of the fact, since Newman's writings, he said, had been instrumental in his decision. He went on in an argumentative and pretentious way and concluded on a particularly painful note: "But it was at the bed of the dying that I felt most deeply the failure of the English system. There I was quite bewildered and weighed down with grief to think of the awful responsibility I had taken on myself. . . . An Anglican death seems a practical refutation of the Anglican Church."[49] Such words must have reminded Newman of the deathbed of his sister Mary, and of Hurrell Froude, and most forcibly at that moment of John Bowden.

Bowden had suffered from tuberculosis for years, and in the summer of 1844 his condition took a sudden turn for the worse. Newman made several trips to Roehampton and Clifton to see his dying friend. He found Bowden, as ever, calm and uncomplaining, dividing what scant energy he had between devotions in the Bible and breviary and the completion of a pamphlet in which he argued against segregated seating (between the rich who paid pew rent and the poor who did not) in parish churches. It was a typical Bowden point of view and one which hearkened back to the beginning of the Movement when so much emphasis had been placed upon the common man's role in revivifying the Church.[50]

On Sunday, September 15th, at four o'clock in the morning, Bowden died, and Newman found his body laid out in the familiar drawing room of the Bowden house in London. Newman recalled later that he "sobbed bitterly over his coffin to think that he had left me still dark as to what the way of truth was and what I ought to do in order to please God and fulfill his will." And to Jemima he said, "There lies now my oldest friend, so dear to me—and I, with so little faith or hope, as dead as a stone and detesting myself."[51] There was another dimension to the death of Bowden: "He is my oldest friend. . . . He is the link between me and Oxford. In losing him I seem to lose Oxford."[52]

1844 was a sad year altogether, and it saw the snapping of more than one of the "cords of silk"[53] (to use Gladstone's phrase) which bound Newman to the English Church. About Eastertime Lucy Pusey, not quite fifteen years old, died and was buried beside her mother in the nave of Christ Church. It was a devastating blow to Pusey but hardly less so to Newman, who had held the little girl on his lap in earlier, happier days. As she lay dying her father asked her if she had a message for Mr. Newman. "Give him my respectful love," said Lucy, "and thank him for all his kindness to me."[54]

The news of Lucy's death reached Hursley on April 25th, Keble's fifty-second birthday. He wrote a moodily introspective letter of condolence: "While recollections stare me in a manner in the face, now on my . . . birthday, which ought to make me feel more than most others, somehow I seem to feel very little. I know that what I say is true, but it does not oppress me as it ought. Do you pray for me that I may truly repent, now that my time for repentance is growing so short."[55]

IV

1844 was a sad year, but the early part of it was quiet enough. Pusey busied himself both before and after Lucy's death with his project of translating Roman Catholic devotional books for English use. It was a strange activity for an aging Tractarian in the midst of private sorrows and the swirling rumours about Newman's imminent secession, and only the stubbornly innocent Pusey, with his utter contempt for what has come to be called public relations, would have done it. He denied in any case that the works were Roman; as he edited them, he said, they were genuinely catholic.

Keble's spirits meanwhile sank even lower when, early in the summer, he read Arthur Stanley's *Life and Correspondence of Thomas Arnold*— "which book," he told his brother Tom, "if I had not grown far harder and more unfeeling than I could wish, would distress me, I really think, more than anything that has been published for years, and that in a great variety of ways." The author was that same Stanley who had once accompanied W. G. Ward to hear Newman preach at St. Mary's. What distressed Keble was the memory of Arnold at Corpus Christi College and of a friendship that had gone sour, and the conviction that Arnold's religious faith had deteriorated into an empty humanism. But beyond all these considerations and yet mixed in with them as Keble brooded through the summer was the feeling that if he, Keble, were a better man, perhaps Arnold could have been saved and Newman too; he was obsessed with the "sad depressing thought that if one were or had been other than one is, the anguish might have been averted or mitigated."[56]

By the end of September, however, Keble had to turn to face another kind of danger. "The Symonians," he wrote Tom, "are summoned for the eighth [of October]. I find Pusey is very earnest for this move and that makes me resolve to try to be there at any sacrifice, whatever I may think of the policy of the move."[57] The reference was to the election of a new Vice-chancellor for the university. Normally the office was filled without contest by a prearranged succession among the Heads of Houses. But in 1844 the new Vice-chancellor was scheduled to be Dr. Symons, Warden of Wadham College, an Evangelical and one of the six doctors who had censured Pusey's Eucharist sermon. Most of the Tractarians, including Keble, did not consider it expedient to oppose Symons, but Pusey insisted that Symons' condemnation of the doctrine in the sermon had been a virtual declaration of heresy. So out of loyalty to Pusey it was decided to contest Symons' candidacy. The result was an electoral disaster much worse than the one over the poetry professorship twenty months earlier. Dr. Symons was nominated by a vote of 882 to 183.

Symons' victory demonstrated how shattered the Tractarian party had become, and no one was surprised when it proved but the prelude of a full-scale assault upon W. G. Ward and of a final attempt by the Heads to crush the Movement once and for all. On December 13, 1844, the Vice-chancellor announced that the Board of Heads would propose to Convocation, scheduled to meet the following February 13th, these three resolutions: that Ward's *Ideal of a Christian Church* contained passages at variance with Anglican belief and made a mockery of his subscription to the Thirty-nine Articles when he took his B.A. and M.A. degrees; that therefore Ward should be stripped of those degrees; and that persons suspected of "unsound opinions" should, in place of subscription, submit to a test which would commit them to acceptance of the Articles as they had been originally conceived and as they were now accepted by the university.

"As usual," Richard Church commented years later, "the Board entirely mistook the temper of the university, and by their violence and want of judgment turned the best chance they ever had, of carrying the university with them, into what their blunders really made an ignominious defeat."[58] Church was referring to the inquisitorial third resolution; it was presumptuous to assign a particular intent to the framers of the Articles, three hundred years dead, and it was madness to suppose that there was any one sense in which the mixed bag of nineteenth-century Oxford now understood those delicately worded phrases.

If the Heads had been content to destroy Ward, and in the process to deal what was left of the Tractarians a severe blow, they could have done it. But even here they invited ridicule (with which Ward was not slow to gratify them) by moving for degradation instead of expulsion—in effect, they would reduce Ward to a walking contradiction in terms: an undergraduate Fellow of Balliol. The third resolution, the odious and ridiculous new test, raised the hackles of all parties and guaranteed that the Heads should lose whatever small shred of reputation they retained for equity and common sense. Archibald Tait, a leading young liberal, one of the four tutors of Tract Ninety fame, and Arnold's successor as Headmaster of Rugby, published a blistering indictment of the third resolution. Tait was candid in stating his affection for Ward—they had been dons together at Balliol—his extreme dislike for Ward's views, and his agreement with Ward that everybody subscribed to the Articles in a "non-natural sense," that is, everybody interpreted as he subscribed. "There is no need," said Tait, "of our narrowing the limits of the Church of England because some amongst us wish to make it too wide."[59]

Pusey followed the shorter course of writing an open letter to a newspaper in which he served notice that he would never under any circumstances takes the new test. A score of others publicly proclaimed the same thing, but the rising crescendo of protest reached its peak with a brilliant fortissimo from Ward himself. If, Ward wrote in an open letter to the members of Convocation,

after the most labourious endeavours to separate off the *opinions* of my work from the *wholly distinct* question you have to consider, and after an anxious, calm, judicial study of our formularies in their whole extent, you come to the opinion that my mode of subscription to them is so different from your mode in its degree of laxity that it amounts to a difference in *kind*, then come up and vote against me.[60]

On January 23, 1845, a few days after this broadside appeared in Oxford common rooms and country parsonages, the Heads withdrew the third resolution. Now Ward was to be condemned not on a principle of subscription, which even before a vote was taken had been universally repudiated, but because he had written a disagreeable book. Many fairminded men, who had no sympathy with Ward or Tractarianism, argued that the first two resolutions should also be withdrawn, since, in principle, they were based on the third. So, for example, thought Garbett, Professor of Poetry, who wore plenty of scars from his war with the Tractarians. "Certainly I for one," he told the Bishop of Chichester, "shall refuse to make a victim of Mr. Ward on a principle which Convocation rejects."[61]

But the Heads had not yet run the course of their collective madness. "Kindly, generous, good-natured men in private life, but implacable in their fierce fanaticism," Richard Church described them.[62] Was it not still possible, they asked each other, to recoup for the loss of the test and at the same time to humble the mightiest of their enemies, now in retirement and suspicious silence? Could they not, given the rising anti-Tractarian sentiment, do what they had not dared to do four years before—brand the former Vicar of St. Mary's with a university condemnation? Showing the same spitefulness with which some of them had once scheduled the Sunday supper hour to conflict with the service at St. Mary's, the Heads, on February 4th, announced that they would submit a new third resolution. It was a censure of Tract Ninety.

Only nine days were left until the meeting of Convocation. Newman himself never stirred at Littlemore, but the printing presses, even in that short interval, rumbled in his behalf. One of the most touching and persuasive defenses came from Frederic Rogers. Another was the work of the new Vicar of St. Mary's, C. P. Eden, whom Newman considered "a jealous and capricious fellow,"[63] yet who never lacked the courage to speak up against manifest injustice. The disgust at the Heads was almost universal, and men as different as Gladstone, Stanley and Jowett urged the Proctors to veto the resolution. One of the two Proctors that term was a Trinity don named Guillemard. The other was Richard Church.

February 13th dawned wet and snowy. By mid-morning upwards of twelve hundred voting M.A.'s jammed the Sheldonian Theater. Only Newman was missing. Pusey was there, to give Ward what support he could. Hampden too took his place next to Faussett and not far from Hawkins. Gladstone, Manning, Hope, Tait, George Moberly, the Squire of Hursley, Sir William Heathcote, were among the prominent non-residents present, together with an ample collection of lords and baronets. Bishop Copleston came from Llandaff. The Fellows of Balliol stood together, unanimous in their support for their difficult but enchanting confrere. And in a particularly apt gesture of solidarity, on the rostrum with Ward stood Frederick Oakeley.

The first resolution was called, and a university functionary read out the objectionable passages from *Ideal*. Then Ward was given leave to speak and, by special permission, in English. The speech went on for an hour, and in the middle of it Arthur Stanley, who had helped Ward compose it, poked Jowett and said, "They never would have let him use English had they known how well he can speak." But well or ill, the result was a foregone conclusion. Ward retracted nothing; he denied the legality of the whole proceeding; he repeated over and over his adherence to the complete cycle of Roman doctrine; and "his whole defence . . . expressed as its sole ground the unwelcome assumption of the hopelessly illogical character of the English Church." The first resolution was carried 777 to 341. The second—stripping Ward of his degrees—passed also, but by the sharply reduced margin of 569 to 511.[64]

Then came the third resolution, the condemnation of Tract Ninety. The Vice-chancellor read it, and as the mixed chorus of "placets" and "non placets" began to rise and echo, the Proctors stood up in their places, and Guillemard intoned the formula, *"Nobis procuratoribus non placet."* A great shout went up all round the theater and pandemonium reigned as dignified doctors and masters jostled one another for a chance to shake the hand of Guillemard and Church. The scene was not unlike that played in the same cavernous room almost exactly nine years before, when the Proctors had vetoed Convocation's first attempt to censure R. D. Hampden. On that occasion, as they pushed their way out of the theater, Keble had said to Newman, "Two can play the veto game." And so indeed it had turned out.

Throughout his two-month ordeal Ward had maintained his irrepressible good humour, and after the meeting of Convocation, when he appeared on the steps of the Sheldonian arm in arm with Tait (who had voted for the first resolution) he received the reward of a massed cheer from the undergraduates. At the same time the Vice-chancellor, hurrying back to Wadham, was pelted with snowballs. Later in the day Ward called on Pusey at Christ Church to thank him for his support. Before long Ward was entertaining the gloomy assemblage in Pusey's rooms with a hilarious description of his new position as an undergraduate fellow. "They can't expect me to wear an undergraduate's cap and gown," he said; "I suppose I must wear my beaver." Manning, who was present, thought Ward guilty of shocking levity, and he told Pusey later that despite eighteen months' effort "to form a fair and charitable opinion," he concluded that Ward was "a light-minded man, . . . less censurable for his opinions than for the moral habits which appear to govern him. . . . His manner of asserting has in it the restlessness and wilfulness of a schoolboy."[65]

Ward, however, was not to be put off by a dour archdeacon, even when that gentleman represented an important reservoir of support. After February 13th he delighted in sending out notes which were signed, "W. G. Ward, Undergraduate," and he entertained his close associates by composing appropriate jingles like this one:

> A system has now been devised
>   Which cannot be evaded;
> And those don't to it conform
>   Will forthwith be degraded.[66]

The refrain repeated the word "degraded," and Ward, an expert mimic, recited it each time with a different voice, first that of the Vice-chancellor, then the Master of Balliol and down the list of the Heads of Houses.

In a more serious vein, Ward published a short "Letter" to the Vice-chancellor, once more protesting Convocation's incompetence in his case, and he approached legal friends in London with the thought of pressing his claim through the civil courts. But these moves went up in smoke, along with most of the sympathy Ward had gained during his struggle with the Heads, amid the shock, consternation and merriment which greeted the news, early in March, that the Reverend W. G. Ward, champion of clerical celibacy on the Roman model, had been engaged since the preceding December and would be married in a few weeks' time. Those for whose judgment Ward had most respect—Newman, Oakeley, Arthur Stanley—had cordially endorsed his plans but had advised delay in the announcement until after the meeting of Convocation. Many others who had put themselves on the firing line on February 13th were in various degrees upset: Keble was "much pained," Church "decidedly cool,"[67] and Archdeacon Manning absolutely livid. It was not the marriage to which he objected but the timing. "I confess I did not expect so unscrupled an absence of sensitiveness, shrinking delicacy and self respect," said Manning. "God forbid that this ethos should spread among our younger men." He would rather they signed the Articles as full-blown Romans than that they sacrifice those moral virtues "which appear to me to be the foundation not only of saintly but of a manly character."[68]

On March 31, 1845, William George Ward took to wife Frances Mary Wingfield, a parson's daughter and an ardent Tractarian. In so doing he solved the problem of his status as an undergraduate don, because his marriage necessitated his resignation from Balliol. The newlyweds settled in a cottage near Oxford, and, as far as it is possible in this valley of tears, they lived happily ever after. A small irony lies in the fact that one of their closest friends in later years was Cardinal Manning.

V

The day after Ward and his book were condemned by Convocation, Frederick Oakeley published an open "Letter" to the Vice-chancellor in which he declared his unequivocal agreement with Ward. He too held the whole cycle of Roman doctrine, and therefore if Ward deserved punishment so did he. It was a chivalrous act, fully consistent with Oakeley's character, but it was an unnecessary provocation too, which kept the pot boiling at the very moment when the tattered Tractarian remnant needed peace and quiet to regroup. Oakeley compounded the trouble by issuing another, similar statement a few days later, this one addressed to the Bishop of London. Oakeley, it will be recalled, was Fellow of Balliol and also officiating minister of a chapel of ease on Margaret Street in London, and evidently this was why he felt compelled to fire off a double blast.

It gained him little sympathy, even in quarters where he expected support. Keble called the maneuver "imprudent" and "unnecessarily frank."[69] Pusey wrote Oakeley a strong letter of remonstrance which the latter described as "cruel."[70] And on March 1st Keble told Pusey, "I wonder that a person of Oakeley's experience should be so much hurt and astonished at not carrying everyone along with him in so very delicate and critical a move. He writes as if one blamed his motives or as if it were inexcusable to question his judgment."[71]

Apparently Oakeley had not expected the authorities to accept his challenge, but Blomfield, the Bishop of London, called his bluff by asking for his resignation from Margaret Chapel. Oakeley was literally prostrated by this maneuver; as Ward said, "Margaret Chapel has been to him so thoroughly his one strongest . . . earthly tie that the idea of parting from it . . . is like a person losing his nearest and dearest friend or relative."[72] The matter hung in abeyance for several months, during which the nervous Oakeley was more often ill than not. Then, on June 9th, an action was initiated against him in the ecclesiastical courts. Oakeley did not contest and on June 30th the decision was handed down which revoked Oakeley's license to perform any ministerial office in the Province of Canterbury until such time as he satisfied his bishop as to his orthodoxy.

Thus one more Tractarian stronghold was overrun. Margaret Chapel, since Oakeley had come there in the summer of 1839, had been the Movement's spiritual center in London. Its prestigious congregation had included Gladstone, Hope, Badeley, Judge Coleridge and a bevy of fashionable ladies who found Oakeley's ministrations a unique source of spiritual strength. In this Oakeley was much like Newman as Vicar of St. Mary's. He may, like Ward, have held the whole cycle of Roman doctrine, but he did not try to teach it. Or rather in the pulpit and at the altar of Margaret Chapel he carefully avoided the controversy he reveled in when writing for the *British Critic*. His aim, he said, was not to "dissatisfy Anglicans with the system in which they found themselves, but rather to give that system all the advantages of which it seemed capable, and leave Divine Providence to work out the conclusion."[73]

Oakeley prided himself that Margaret Chapel's services, Sunday and weekdays, were "quiet, orderly and reverent." The music was "of a more ecclesiastical and varied character than was then usual even in cathedrals." Newman, who first visited the place in the autumn of 1843, reported that "the Gregorian chants are certainly very good."[74] Oakeley described the preaching at Margaret Chapel as propounding "a somewhat more earnest and consistent view of religious truths than in the ordinary Protestantism of the day." There was a great deal of opposition to the Margaret Chapel ministry, and Oakeley doubted whether "two or three, if so many," of the London clergy could have been invited to the pulpit there without the "certainty of an anti-Catholic protest." He fell back upon "unrepealed though obsolete rubrics" as a defense against his critics, but never did he permit the "sham" of conciliating opposition by balancing rubricism with a good Protestant sermon.[75]

Oakeley accomplished more than most Tractarians in making the sacramental principle a living reality for the people he served. Among the leaders of the Movement only Keble and Newman were his peers in the practical apostolate. Oakeley's compulsive, mercurial temperament gave him much personal agony, but it also drove him to overcome great obstacles and create a Tractarian parish in the heart of London. Years later he could smile over some of those obstacles. When he arrived in 1839, "the chapel . . . was a complete paragon of ugliness, . . . low, dark and stuffy, . . . begirt by a hideous gallery filled on Sundays with uneasy school children." The congregation "bore the change with more equanimity than might have been expected," but the same could not be said for the parish clerk, a hard-line Protestant who had been at Margaret Street for fifty years. Oakeley's liturgical ideas left little scope for the clerk, whose reading desk was demolished in the course of a re-arrangement of the chancel. The old man, reduced to the pews, took revenge for his vanished eminence "by reciting the responses with vociferous obtrusiveness."[76]

But the summer of 1845 was still too early in time for Oakeley to look back without anger. All he could see at that moment was the destruction of his work, and indeed of himself as an Anglican, by the engines of the Establishment. The battle was over and the time to disengage had come. During the months after February 1845 Oakeley passed through a series of emotional tempests, but by September he was calm and self-possessed. It is true, he wrote to Pusey, that there are instances of great spiritual goodness in the Church of England. He did not deny that God's grace is conveyed "in certain cases through ordinances external to her [i.e. the Roman Catholic] communion." On the other hand, Newman's grounds, if they are valid, must apply to all people: a person does not have a special call to the Church of Rome but to the true catholic Church, and if the Church of England is the catholic Church (or part of it), "*no one* ought to move, not Newman more than another. If it be right for him to go on the supposition of the negative of that hypothesis, it is also right for others to go, who have either arrived independently at his conclusion or take his view upon trust." Oakeley counted himself among the latter: "I for one have not the learning necessary to determine for myself the question of our position as Church, but I do find an inward response to the doctrine which comes to me upon N[ewman]'s authority."[77]

VI

Everyone knew that it was now only a matter of time. Pusey, the last of his intimates to admit the possibility, now accepted it as inevitable.

"Poor fellow," Newman wrote of Pusey, "he has this morning got [a letter] from me which I do trust must break the neck of all incredulity in him once for all. I have been thinking all the morning about him."[78] This was at the end of the summer of 1844. During the following months nothing occurred to alter the direction of things. Indeed, the last savage, senseless attack of the Heads upon Number Ninety was calculated, if anything, to speed the process. But Newman had reached a point beyond caring about the gyrations of Hawkins, Golightly and their ilk. On February 5, 1845, the day after the censure resolution was announced, he observed, "I have not heard the result; and be it strange or not, I feel little or no interest about it. I have no curiosity."[79] In the ensuing struggle over Ward and Oakeley he took no part.

At the turn of the year 1844–45 Newman finished his labour of love, a critical edition of the works of St. Athanasius, and began the famous *Essay on the Development of Christian Doctrine*. He determined to make no move until he had finished it. It was a complex literary and historical venture, and there were many false starts before he got into the rhythm of the argument. His monks at Littlemore remembered the hours he stood at a tall desk writing and rewriting until the weariness and pain were etched in the lines on his face. Rumours circulated that he was composing a piece of Roman propaganda. In fact the essay proved to be Newman's intellectual justification for his secession to Rome and, more important, his interpretation of the genuine destiny of the Movement of 1833.

Newman's ideas on doctrinal development had been a long time forming. He had fought them off at first, tried to compromise with them in Tract Ninety, and finally surrendered to what he considered their cogency. There was much sophistication and subtlety in them, but essentially they were reducible to a simple principle: There was in fact no other existential realization of the Ancient Christian Church except the Roman system. If so, then the manifest additions Rome had made to the old creeds—Purgatory, transubstantiation, papal power and the like—were not corruptions of Christian tradition, as the Tractarians had always maintained, but developments, based upon a deep and even supernatural understanding of that tradition.

There will always be a great deal of debate about the validity of Newman's theory, but Professor Chadwick is probably right in seeing this as the fundamental tenet: "Among many developments claiming to be the authentic developments of primitive Christianity, you must choose that structure of development which comes nearest, in resemblance, to the ancient and undivided Church. Then, when you have found the face which is *most* like the face in the portrait, you must ask yourself, how is it, that in spite of these resemblances the face bears such important marks of difference from the portrait?"[80] In other words, Newman's is not an historical argument if by historical argument you mean a progress from sources. Rather Newman's argument, like W. G. Ward's, is an ethical argument. The Ancient Church was a force for sanctification fifteen hundred years ago, and the contemporary Church must be the same. Therefore true development must follow a course of genuine practical accomplishment.

Newman never thought himself inconsistent with the spirit of the Oxford Movement because he underwent a momentous change of mind about the actual location of the true Christian Church. The Tractarians had always emphasized the practical, ethical and ascetic aspects of Christianity. When they studied the literature of the primitive Christian community they did so to find patterns of conduct. And it was precisely here that the Via Media went to dust in Newman's hands. It was a theory and nothing more, a beautiful theory if you like, but it bore no resemblance to the real state of things in nineteenth-century England. Dean Church commented many years later that it was the life of the New Testament that Newman was seeking as an Anglican and as a Roman Catholic. He left the Church of England because it was too "respectable," had made too many compromises with the world.[81] He went to Rome because there was nowhere else to go, given the contemporary facts as he saw them.

Keble and Pusey thought him too impatient, and Keble especially felt that he hankered after a measure of certainty which was presumptuous in a mere mortal. Almost a decade later Keble said in effect that Newman had been betrayed by his own mathematical sense of neatness. When he was desperately trying to prevent Robert Wilberforce from following Newman's road Keble argued that "if we are to accept the R. C. view, . . . we must not expect . . . that candid judges will account us altogether logical; they will say, such [a] one gave way to his feelings (his love of system and exactness, his longing after a perfect, visible polity etc.)."[82] To Keble, such longing was the trap and the snare which caught a disillusioned Newman. "Nor indeed," he said a little earlier to Wilberforce, "will I quite believe until I am forced to do so that you can have so given up your old faith in antiquity for a philosophical dream about development."[83]

What Keble thought a dream, Newman (and later Wilberforce) considered the only significant reality. "Time is short, eternity is long," intoned Newman at the end of *Development*. And whether Keble's judgment was right or wrong, this fact remains. Newman waited more than five years before he entered into the scientific exploration of the doubts of 1839. During these five years he prayed, fasted and suffered with almost superhuman intensity. The words he formed for *Development* were chiseled out of his living flesh. Every human consideration prompted him not to go to Rome, and when he went it was only because he thought his eternal salvation depended upon it. The Church to Newman was the vehicle of salvation, really and truly, and if it was not that it was nothing. He never liked Ward's book, not even the title; the Church, he said, is not an "ideal," it is a fact.

"Where am I to stop?" he asked Pusey in the middle of March 1845. "What to believe? Each has his own temptations. I thank God that he has shielded me morally from what intellectually might easily come on me—general scepticism. Why should I believe the most sacred and fundamental doctrines of our faith if you cut off from me the ground of development. . . . I cannot hold precisely what the English Church holds and nothing more. I must go forward or backward, *else* I sink into a dead scepticism, . . . into which too many in Oxford, I fear, are sinking."[84]

The book on development occupied Newman throughout the spring and summer of 1845. But his thoughts were not exclusively on this intellectual statement of his decision. On March 20th he wrote to Henry Wilberforce, "I wished to have waited seven years from my first conviction which would bring it to the summer of 1846. But really my mind is getting so much more made up that I don't think I shall last so long. As a great secret, I wish to say that my expectation is that some move will take place with the end of the year, but what extent or whom it will embrace I do not know. I expect to resign my fellowship in October term at latest."[85]

A month later he wrote Henry again, this time expressing the deep anguish through which he was passing. His thoughts had been turned back to the old days at Oriel by the posthumous publication of Blanco White's autobiography. It was "the most dismal, horrible work I ever saw." Blanco White, the Spanish ex-priest, once an honourary member of the Oriel common room and intimate of Archbishop Whately, had died a pantheist, with no belief in an ultra-mundane God, doubting the immortality of the soul, "meditating from Marcus Antonius [*sic*]." He denied that Christianity was anything more than a collection of moral duties. "I have heard him say this but was shallow enough not to see its drift." Then he turned to his own situation: "When a man feels he cannot stand where he is, and has dreadful feelings lest he should be suffered to go back, if he will not go forward, such a case as Blanco White's increases those fears. For years I have had an increasing intellectual conviction that there is no medium between pantheism and the Church of Rome. If intellect were to settle the matter, I should not be now where I am."

Poor old Blanco White, Newman went on, "sincere and honest. He gives up his country and his second home, Spain, Oxford, Whately's family all for an idea of truth or rather for liberty of thought."

But then the thought forcibly comes upon me, why may not the case be the same with me? I see Blanco White going wrong, yet sincere; Arnold going wrong, yet sincere. They are no puzzle to *me*. I can put my finger on this or that point in their character and say, *Here* was the fault. But they did not know their fault; and so it comes upon me, How do I know that I have not my weak points which occasion me to think as I think? How can I be sure that I have not committed sins which bring this unsettled state of mind upon me as a judgment?

The memory of Blanco White stirred other sad, harassing thoughts.

I am nearly the only person he speaks of with affection [in the book]. . . . It seems as if people were just now beginning to praise me when I was going away. It seems an omen of my going away that they praise me. Their praises are valedictions, funeral orations: Rogers [in a pamphlet defending Number Ninety in 1845], James Mozley [in the *Christian Remembrancer*, April 1845] and now Blanco White. The truth is, I have had so little praise that I do not understand receiving it. . . . No one has spoken well of me; my friends who have had means of knowing me have spoken against me. Whately and Hawkins have both used opprobrious language about me till I began to think myself really deceitful and double-dealing as they said. . . . My prime of life is past and I am nothing. . . . It is all gone and over and there is no redress and no retrieving; and I say with Job, O that it were with me as in years past when the candle of the Lord shone upon me.[86]

Meanwhile, a kind of numbness settled upon Newman's friends as they awaited the inevitable blow. Manning and Coleridge suggested that Newman be persuaded to go to Rome "and there make the move instead of here. They think it would have perhaps rather less effect in checking the course of improvement which we hope is going on here." But Keble's marvelous delicacy vetoed this suggestion before it ever got to Newman: "It seems to me that in his place I should feel as if going there was making the step as public as possible—as if saying to the pope, 'Make haste and employ me.'" Yet Keble did agree that the step ought to be taken outside England; perhaps Newman might place himself under the wing of "some very good, retired, holy priest in the Tyrol or upper Germany or Lombardy."[87] Keble hoped that Pusey would suggest something like this to Newman.

When the blow actually came it was almost anticlimactic.[88] At the end of September Dalgairns left Littlemore and was received by the Italian Passionist Father Dominic (one of the community brought to England under the patronage of Lord Shrewsbury and Ambrose Phillipps). A few days later Ambrose St. John went to Prior Park and was received there. They both hurried back to Littlemore on October 3rd, the same day Newman sent the resignation of his fellowship to the Provost of Oriel. Hawkins replied coldly that he hoped Newman "may still be saved from some of the worst errors of the Church of Rome, praying to human mediators or falling down before images."

On October 8th, Father Dominic was to pass through Oxford on his way to the Continent. It was a wet, blustery day and the priest had sat on the top of the coach for five hours. But his spirits were warmed when Dalgairns met him with the news that Newman had asked him to come to Littlemore: "I wish him," Newman had told Dalgairns, "to receive me into the Church of Christ." The next day, at six o'clock in the evening, Newman and two other members of the Littlemore community made their professions of faith and received conditional Baptism. It had all been done so quietly and with so little fuss that not even Golightly knew about it.

On October 3rd, John Keble had begun a letter to Newman but his wife's severe illness had caused him to leave it unfinished. By the time he picked up his pen again, more than a week later, the hard blow had fallen. Nothing could improve upon the farewell he wrote, and perhaps nothing could express better than that farewell the romance, the nobility, the high aspirations of the Oxford Movement.

My dearest Newman, you have been a kind and helpful friend to me in a way in which scarce anyone else could have been, and you are so mixed up in my mind with old and dear and sacred thoughts that I cannot well bear to part with you, most unworthy as I know myself to be; and yet I cannot go along with you. I must cling to the belief that we are not really parted—you have taught me so and I scarce think you can unteach me—and, having relieved my mind with this little word, I will only say God bless you and reward you a thousandfold all your help in every way to me unworthy, and to so many others. May you have peace where you are gone and help us in some way to get peace; but somehow I scarce think it will be in the way of controversy. And so, with somewhat of a feeling as if the spring had been taken out of my year, I am, always, your affectionate and grateful, J. Keble.[89]

Epilogue

CHAPTER 20

An End and a Beginning

THE reactions to Newman's secession from the Church of England were various, even if one does not count those of his avowed enemies. Bishop Wiseman played the part of victor with civility and restraint; "the Church has not received at any time," he said simply, "a convert who has joined her in more docility and simplicity of faith than Newman."[1] Shortly after the *Essay on Development* was published, James Hope joked with a friend at a dinner party about what Hope called "the Extravagant of John."[2] Manning admitted to obscure fears for the future: "I still seem to see great difficulties before us. . . . Not the least part of the difficulty will be to show why principles are safe so far and no farther."[3] Less enigmatic was Archdeacon Robert Wilberforce: "I grieve over your notice of Newman," he told Pusey on October 13, 1845. "I had heard the event yesterday. The injurious effect upon the Church it seems to me hardly possible to estimate."[4]

Judge Coleridge worried over the damage that *Development* might do: "Can it be doubted that the forthcoming work will be a most moving and convincing argument for Rome—a raising of the deep questions of conscience as to the *necessity* of going to her (for nothing less than a conceived necessity I am persuaded would have seemed sufficient justification for the step [Newman] has taken). And if the book be such," he asked Pusey, "can you point out the man who is likely to meet its effect with any tolerable cogency? I own I cannot." Yet amid the darkness the judge discerned one ray of light: "What a deep comfort and strong support it is to me to perceive how you and Keble have received this stunning blow."[5]

Not everyone, however, was similarly consoled. Edward Churton declined to join any more Tractarian-sponsored projects, because, he said, "late events have so disheartened me for any public effort that . . . I could not answer to myself that I was doing what a sense of duty to the

Church of England at this moment most requires."[6] Walter Hook, the Vicar of Leeds, took a more violent line. He described Newman as "our poor, fallen, sinful friend. . . . Most persons," he predicted, "will regard Newman as a traitor; those who, like myself, supported him without agreeing with him consider ourselves most shamefully treated when we hear that for years he has entertained an intention to apostatize." Yet Hook did not intend to be "unkind about Newman, for I pity him, poor fellow, with all my heart. I suppose that now he *is* separated from the Church we cannot pray for him except for his being brought back. But there must be for some time a stigma of disgrace not only upon his friends but upon all who ever supported him."[7]

The disaster of Newman's secession had a special poignancy for Pusey and a special urgency as well. It was up to him, in the midst of personal sadness, to demonstrate that the Movement had not died with the departure of its greatest leader. "It is an exceeding mystery," he wrote in the October 16th issue of the *English Churchman*, "that such confidence as [Newman] had once in our Church should have gone. Even amid our present sorrows it goes to the heart to look at that former self and think how devotedly he worked for our Church, how he strove to build her up. . . . Yet since God is with us still, He can bring us even through this loss. We ought not indeed disguise the greatness of it. It is the intensest loss we have had."

But Pusey, who could always find a bright side, wondered whether God did not intend Newman to be a kind of mediator between Rome and England. After all, he said, "it is not what is true in the Roman system against which the strong feeling of ordinary religious persons among us is directed, but against what is unholy in her practice. It is not anything in our Church which keeps them from acknowledging us but heresy existing more or less within us." Newman might well prove to be a bridge: "If anything could open their eyes to what is good in us, or soften in us any strong prejudices against them, it would be the presence of such a one, nurtured and grown to such ripeness in our Church, and now removed to theirs."

Pusey knew, however, that in the crisis at hand it was not enough for him to mourn and eulogize his departed friend nor to speculate about a possibly happier day in the future. The times called for a manifesto to those whom Newman had left behind, depressed and dismayed.

It is of course a heavy thing to us who remain, heavy to us individually in proportion as any of us may have reason to fear lest, by what has been amiss in oneself, one has contributed to bring down this heavy chastisement upon our Church. But while we go on humbled, . . . surely neither need we be dejected. God's chastisements are in mercy too. . . . For myself I am even now far more hopeful as to our Church than at any former period—far more than when outwardly things seemed more prosperous. It would seem as if God in His mercy let us now see more of His inward workings in order that in the tokens of His presence with us we may take courage.[8]

A few days afterwards, Keble sent notice that for him too the fight would go on. "My dear Pusey, I believe I have not written to you since the thunderbolt fell. But I consider that I have heard from you through the letter in the *English Churchman*, and many thanks for the comfort it gave me in common with thousands more."[9]

About the same time Bishop Bagot called on Pusey at Christ Church and assured him of his unshaken confidence. If only ten communicants were left to the Church of England, said the bishop, he knew that Pusey would be one of them.[10]

Only days after his visit to Christ Church, Bishop Bagot was transferred, at his own request, to the Diocese of Bath and Wells, and not long after that he suffered the first in a series of mental breakdowns which were to trouble him until his death in 1854. Prime Minister Robert Peel appointed Samuel Wilberforce to take Bagot's place in Oxford. The contrast could hardly have been more striking. Whereas Bagot was gentle, kindly, weak and lazy, his successor was a veritable dynamo of energy, tough, efficient, even ruthless if the occasion called for it. Unlike his brothers Robert and Henry, he had been little touched by the Tractarian program; indeed, from 1837, he had been warning them and his brothers-in-law, Henry Manning and George Ryder, against Newman's personal and intellectual influence. Newman himself he regarded as a "pervert," guilty of that self-will "which has ever driven heretics and schismatics to the accomplishment of their lamentable end. May God give him the grace of repentance before he falls through Rome into infidelity."[11]

Samuel Wilberforce was not a theologian of stature like his brother Robert, but he possessed in great abundance the practical gifts of a leader of men. In this he was his father's son. He devoted to the Church of England the same kind of vigour his father had displayed in forty years of parliamentary life. As William Wilberforce had freed the slaves for God's sake, his son hoped to save the Anglican Church from what he considered the extremists of right and left. "My desire," he told a friend shortly after his appointment to Oxford, "will be in God's help to be in the position of father in God to all my clergy; to sympathize with their trials; to help, love, pray for, work with them; to be the same to all who love Christ, whether they verge to Tract or Low Church errors; to allow the full licence the Church allows, without ever compromising what seems to me wrong."[12]

In many ways Bishop Wilberforce represented the flowering of the Evangelical revival which his father had nurtured for so many years at Clapham. As Robert Wilberforce expressed it, that revival had been "the waking up of a whole generation" to an elevated sense of the Christian ministry, without, however, professing any "new principle or doctrine"; Samuel did not look "to any change in the Church's external circumstances but to the primary and irreversible principles of grace."[13] To him the early Tractarian notion of the Via Media was the natural outgrowth of the Christian seriousness he had been taught as a boy. He sought that middle way, was satisfied he had found it and followed it doggedly all his life. This involved him in many practical compromises and it demanded a certain amount of adroitness—so much so, that he was contemptuously nicknamed "Soapy Sam" and "Slippery Sam," and it is undeniable that at least some of the implied opprobrium was deserved. Nor can it be denied that he was an ambitious man who thought the salvation of the Church of England depended to a large extent upon his own advancement. But then there were many others who thought so too. William Palmer, the pioneer of 1833, said at the end of his life that Samuel Wilberforce had saved the Oxford Movement from Rome and from petty rubricism. Whatever one thinks of Palmer's judgment, the fact remains that Samuel Wilberforce was the greatest single force in the Church of England in the twenty-five years immediately after Newman's secession.

So the October of 1845, which saw Newman become a Roman Catholic and Wilberforce appointed Bishop of Oxford, was a climactic moment in the history of the Movement. It marked an end to be sure, but it was a beginning as well. Within the Anglican Communion the struggle to promote sacramental catholicity went on. Without Newman that struggle was bound to be a different kind of phenomenon, because Newman was unique and irreplaceable. His luminous intelligence and artistry, his controversial skill, the magic of his personality, his immense capacity for work, and (despite his own frequently stated denials) his considerable gift for organization and management—all these qualities were lost to Anglicanism and, after 1845, devoted to another cause.

Yet the Movement within the Church of England did not collapse. To be sure, without Newman it never again enjoyed intellectual prominence nor did it ever again possess the buoyancy and vigour of 1838 and 1839. It suffered further damaging losses to Rome, it splintered into conflicting groups, and for some it disintegrated into a petty fussiness over rubrics. If anything, the state grew more hostile towards it: In 1847 R. D. Hampden was created a bishop and three years later, in the famous Gorham case,[14] the privy council decreed that a clergyman need not believe in baptismal regeneration. But in the face of defeat and catastrophe—the Gorham decision was in some ways a worse blow than the condemnation of Tract Ninety—the ideals of a Via Media, of patristic tradition and monastic asceticism, of a catholicism without the pope were maintained, and, more than that, were promoted to a degree which has profoundly effected the worldwide Anglican and Episcopalian bodies.

Leaving aside the intrinsic merits of the case, this achievement was due largely to the stubborn efforts of people who have figured prominently in these pages—to Pusey and Keble, first of all, who, harassed though they always were, never weakened in their resolve. And there were others who in less spectacular ways contributed in their own measure. There was, for example, that trio of Newman's former curates —William Copeland, John Bloxam, Isaac Williams—each of whom spent his life as a pastor of souls and an embodiment of Tractarian ethos. Williams' intimates of the Bisley School, Tom Keble and George Prevost, remained as ever at their posts. Charles Marriott stayed at Oriel and served as Vicar of St. Mary's until 1854 when he was struck down by cholera, which he contracted while tending his sick parishioners during an epidemic; he lingered painfully for four years and then died as selflessly as he had lived. James Mozley eventually succeeded Hampden as Regius Professor of Divinity, while Richard Church developed into an elegant scholar and ultimately became the eloquent[15] Dean of St. Paul's Cathedral in London.

Among the laymen, Frederic Rogers maintained a close interest in the fortunes of the Movement to which he had contributed so much in its founding days; towards the end of his distinguished career in the colonial office he was created a baron. Roundell Palmer did ever better; he became the first Earl of Selbourne and was several times Lord Chancellor. And everyone knows to what heights William E. Gladstone ascended. "He is Pusey in a blue coat," commented John Keble. "And what can be said more for any layman?"[16]

There were other less happy results of the Oxford Movement's intense beginnings. That religious skepticism which Newman feared was the only genuine alternative to Rome did indeed afflict some of his erstwhile disciples, notably Mark Pattison, James Froude[17] and, most surprisingly, Thomas Mozley. Charles Golightly suffered in another way; at the time of Number Ninety he was obsessed by a fear that he was about to be beaten up by gangs of Tractarian thugs who he imagined were waiting for him round every corner. This illusion gradually faded, but he never completely regained his balance, at least not well enough to savour what must have seemed to him a great victory.

Newman once remarked that Golightly was "a man literally without bowels. I doubt whether he has any inside or is more than a walking and talking piece of mechanism."[18] For such a one the heavy exodus to Rome between 1845 and 1855 was at worst a healthy catharsis for the Church of England. But to those intimately associated with the Movement it was a keenly painful parting of friends, both for those who went and for those who stayed. Ward and Oakeley went, of course, and so did at least a hundred of the congregation of Margaret Chapel and six of the clergy who had served there.[19] Macmullen, who had quarreled with Hampden over his B.D. degree; Palmer of Magdalen (Roundell's brother), who had chided the Archbishop of Canterbury over the Jerusalem bishopric; J. B. Morris, who in 1839 had so annoyed the Vice-chancellor with his sermon on fasting; all of them went, as did the monks at Littlemore.

Many of the converted Anglican clergy were ordained to the Roman priesthood—Oakeley, for example—but those who were married could not be and necessarily reverted to the lay state where they had, many of them, a hard time of it financially. W. G. Ward was an exception since he inherited a large fortune. But Henry Wilberforce, after he became a Roman Catholic (in the summer of 1850), had to turn to journalism for a living. As might be imagined, Henry's conversion brought particular joy to Newman, who worked hard to bring it about. However, not until several months after his wife had done so did Henry make his move, and so it was in a way due to the Sargent woman's influence that Henry and Newman continued to share the same faith and their old intimacy. Mrs. Wilberforce must have taken some satisfaction in a note sent to her on the eve of her reception from her husband's friend and mentor, who no longer considered her a siren: "God and his mother and all saints and good angels be with you, my very dear Mary Wilberforce, is the prayer of yours most affectionately, John H. Newman."[20]

Also on the distaff side, Maria Giberne and Elizabeth Bowden followed Newman, but Jemima Mozley stayed sadly where she was and Harriet died in 1852 unreconciled to her brother. In the wake of the Gorham controversy, after 1850, there was another rush to Rome: James Hope and Edward Badeley were only two of a large and distinguished company. Manning made his profession of faith the same day as Hope, and since he was a widower he was soon after ordained a priest. He rose swiftly through the restored Roman Catholic hierarchy in England until he reached the highest rung as Cardinal Archbishop of Westminster. He was a great leader indeed, but often a hard taskmaster, and one disgruntled subordinate, after a harsh interview with his chief, said that he planned to go and weep at the grave of Caroline Sargent, whose death had made Manning's eminence possible.

In terms of sheer intellectual talent, Rome's greatest coup, next to Newman, was Robert Isaac Wilberforce. He had been badly shaken by the Gorham decision, but like Newman after Tract Ninety he waited four years before he could persuade himself to take the final step. During all that time he was under constant and relentless pressure, and his case perhaps more strikingly than any other demonstrates the agony of separation which the breakup of the Oxford Movement involved. Newman wrote him a long and brilliant statement of the development of doctrine thesis, and then added more playfully, "I have some little time since been saying Mass for you, and I heartily do wish that prayers and Masses would make you move faster. You are in the *way*, you are *coming*, why don't you trot on a bit? I don't ask you, with Froude of old, to go across country but do put your spurs into your horse, my dear Robert Wilberforce."[21]

On the same side, urging the same thing in their different ways, were Manning and Henry Wilberforce. Over against them stood Hook, Pusey, Gladstone and Keble, who had been Robert's tutor at Oriel thirty years before. This tug of war was filled with grief for all concerned but especially for Keble as he watched Wilberforce gradually detached from his Anglican moorings. When it was clear that Wilberforce had reached his decision, Keble wrote sadly, "I know it is what I have deserved— but these sheep, what have they done? I can but pray—would I might pray in earnest—that this burden may be in some way (if it pleases Him) taken off the Church and laid on me. Just as I have always felt concerning J. H. N[ewman]., so I feel now—that if one had been different from what one is this fearful blow might have been spared."[22] And he added shortly afterwards: "I feel, unable as I am to contend with you in learning, that I stand upon the right principle (please God) in this controversy. (Your own books greatly confirm me in thinking so.) And I pray God that I and all who are near and dear to me may sooner die a thousand deaths than do as you seem preparing to do."[23]

In the autumn of 1854 Robert Wilberforce resigned his parish and his archdeaconry and went to Paris, where he was formally received into the Roman Catholic Church. His brother Samuel, the Bishop of Oxford, to whom he had always been particularly close, promised that he would strive "with what little strength is given me for the rest of my life against the accursed abominations of the papacy."[24] Less than three years later Robert Wilberforce was dead.

Newman, in contrast, converted at the age of forty-four, lived as a Catholic for forty-five years. This second half of his life followed in many ways the pattern set by the first: It was highly productive from a literary and theological point of view; it was controversial; it was often dominated by Newman's special gift for friendship. It also brought him much suffering, disappointment and estrangement (notably from Dalgairns, W. G. Ward and Manning, all converts like himself). One basic difference between the Roman Catholic and Anglican halves of Newman's life was the essential peace of mind which he enjoyed after his conversion. "From the time I became a Catholic," he wrote in the *Apologia* (1864), "of course I have no further history of my religious opinions to narrate. In saying this I do not mean to say that my mind has been idle or that I have given up thinking on theological subjects; but that I have had no changes to record and have had no anxiety of heart whatever, I have been in perfect peace and contentment. I never have had one doubt."[25]

Newman was largely responsible for that renaissance of Catholicism in the English-speaking world to which he himself gave the happy name "the second spring." Such an achievement was no doubt reward enough for a man whose life in both its halves showed a remarkable and even heroic consistency to a lofty religious ideal. But there was to be something added. Despite his later battles with ecclesiastical authorities in Ireland, England and Rome—battles not unlike those he had fought with the Heads at Oxford and with the Anglican bishops—and despite unjust suspicion of his integrity which dogged him no less in his Roman Catholic than in his Anglican days, Newman in the end received a gesture of recognition of the kind which he had so much wanted from the kindly, muddleheaded Bishop Bagot. In 1879 John Henry Newman was made a cardinal. "The cloud," he said, "is lifted from me forever."

Most of Newman's Catholic years were spent in Birmingham, where he was founder and superior of the English Oratory. This meant in effect that he was pastor of a large factory-town parish and head of a small group of secular priests who lived together and divided their energies between the pastoral ministry and study. And so came to pass in some measure Hurrell Froude's dream of celibate colleges to serve the new urban masses. The Oratory, as ideal and practice, had been begun by the sixteenth-century St. Philip Neri, to whom Newman had a special devotion all his Catholic life. There was a haunting element of continuity in this as well: The gay and gentle yet tough-minded St. Philip reminded him, Newman said, of John Keble.[26]

Notes

TABLE OF ABBREVIATIONS USED IN THE NOTES

KP = The papers of John Keble deposited in the archives of Keble College, Oxford.

NP = The papers of John Henry Newman deposited in the archives of the Oratory, Birmingham.

PP = The papers of Edward Bouverie Pusey deposited in the archives of Pusey House, Oxford.

AM = Anne Mozley (ed.). *Letters and Correspondence of John Henry Newman During his Life in the English Church.* 2 vols. London, 1920.

OF = Fathers of the Birmingham Oratory (eds.). *Correspondence of John Henry Newman with John Keble and Others, 1839–1845.* London, 1917.

Liddon = Henry Parry Liddon et al. *Life of Edward Bouverie Pusey.* 4 vols. London, 1893–97.

NOTES

CHAPTER 1

1. *Remains of Richard Hurrell Froude.* Edited (anonymously) by J. H. Newman and J. Keble (London, 1838–39), Part I, Vol. I, 246.
2. Georgina Battiscombe, *John Keble. A Study in Limitations* (London, 1963), pp. 132–33.
3. Richard Church, *The Oxford Movement. Twelve Years, 1833–1845* (London, 1891), p. 29.
4. "George IV," in *The Four Georges.*
5. See the standard treatments in Elie Halevy, *England in 1815* (London, 1949), pp. 203 ff.; G. D. H. Cole and Raymond Postgate, *The Common People, 1746–1946* (London, 1961), pp. 190 ff.; and E. L. Woodward, *The Age of Reform* (Oxford, 1939), pp. 2 ff. and 56 ff.
6. In *Adam Bede.*
7. The Duke, however, was not above electoral manipulation. See Halevy, p. 142 f.
8. Norman Gash, *Mr. Secretary Peel* (Cambridge, Massachusetts, 1961), supersedes all earlier works on Peel.
9. Halevy, pp. 115 ff.
10. J. A. Reynolds, *The Catholic Emancipation Crisis in Ireland* (New Haven, 1954), p. 92.

11. See W. E. H. Lecky, *Leaders of Public Opinion in Ireland* (London, 1903), pp. 1–86; Denis Gwynn, *Daniel O'Connell* (Cork, 1947), pp. 76–180; and Reynolds.

12. Gwynn, p. 175.

13. *Ibid.*, p. 177.

14. Gash, p. 521, and Gwynn, p. 178.

15. Charles Greville, *A Journal of the Reigns of King George IV and King William IV* (New York, 1875), II, 155.

16. Gwynn, p. 182.

17. AM, I, 181. Newman to Harriet Newman, March 16, 1829.

18. Gash, pp. 560 ff.

19. AM, I, 177 f. Newman to his mother, March 1, 1829.

20. Gash, pp. 610 ff.

21. Donald Southgate, *The Passing of the Whigs* (London, 1962), pp. 3 ff.

22. T. B. Macaulay, *Speeches on Politics and Literature* (London, n. d. [Everyman Library]), pp. 10–14.

23. Spencer Walpole, *A History of England* (London, 1912), III, 227–30.

24. Greville, I, 156.

25. Froude's *Remains*, Part I, Vol. I, 429–30. The poem was written in 1833.

CHAPTER 2

1. Greville, II, 16–19. Greville exaggerated the casualties at Bristol.

2. Liddon, I, 266. Keble to Pusey, October 1832.

2a. Erastian and Erastianism refer to the ascendancy of state over Church in ecclesiastical matters, named for the Swiss theologian Thomas Erastus (1524–83). See *The Oxford Dictionary of the Christian Church* (London, 1958), p. 460.

3. The Articles are printed as an appendix to the Book of Common Prayer; in the 1928 revised edition on pp. 768 ff.

4. See the maps facing p. 514 in G. F. A. Best, *Temporal Pillars* (Cambridge, 1964).

5. Halevy, pp. 393 ff., and Best, pp. 46 ff.

6. Halevy, p. 398.

7. *Ibid.*, p. 391.

8. *Ibid.*, p. 396.

9. *Ibid.*, p. 398, and Best, pp. 276–277.

10. Diana McClatchey, *Oxfordshire Clergy, 1777–1869* (Oxford, 1960), p. 13.

11. Best, p. 545, and Halevy, p. 396. There are some slight divergences in the figures.

12. In *Barchester Towers*.

13. Halevy, p. 399. The proportion was no better in other cities.

14. For a succinct statement of the Anglo-Catholic position, see P. E. More and F. L. Cross (eds.), *Anglicanism: the Thought and Practice of the Church of England, illustrated from the Religious Literature of the Seventeenth Century* (Milwaukee, 1935), pp. xix–xl.

15. From Dinah Morris' sermon in George Eliot's *Adam Bede*.

16. The classic life of Wilberforce was written by his sons, Robert Isaac and Samuel, in five volumes (1838). See also F. K. Brown, *Fathers of the Victorians. The Age of Wilberforce* (Cambridge, 1961), and David Newsome, *The Wilberforces and Henry Manning* (Cambridge, Massachusetts, 1966), pp. 5–56.

17. The Evangelical lines stretched outside Clapham to other leaders of the revival like Hannah More and Charles Simeon.

18. G. O. Trevelyan, *The Life and Letters of Lord Macaulay* (New York, 1877), I, 74.

19. R. I. Wilberforce, "The Evangelical and Tractarian Movements" (London, n. d.), p. 5. This was Wilberforce's Charge as Archdeacon of the East Riding, Yorkshire, in 1851.

20. See Yngve Brilioth, *The Anglican Revival. Studies in the Oxford Movement* (London, 1925), pp. 25 ff.; also Best, 157–58, 275.

21. Woodward, pp. 331 ff.

22. AM, I, 389.

CHAPTER 3

1. Alexis de Tocqueville, *Journeys to England and Ireland* (London, 1958), p. 48.

2. *Ibid.*

3. *Ibid.*, pp. 49–50.

4. What follows is based on Strickland Gibson, "The University of Oxford," in *The Victoria History of the County of Oxford* (London, 1954), III, 1–39, and on C. E. Mallet, *A History of the University of Oxford* (London, 1924–27), I, 20 ff.

5. Thomas Hughes, *Tom Brown at Oxford.*

6. G. V. Cox, *Recollections of Oxford* (London, 1868), p. 25.

7. L. M. Quiller-Couch (ed.), *Reminiscences of Oxford by Oxford Men* (Oxford, 1892), pp. 119 f.

8. Mallet, III, 165.

9. *Ibid.*, 168.

10. Gibson, 30.

11. *Tom Brown at Oxford.*

12. John Morley, *The Life of William Ewart Gladstone* (London, 1903), I, 50.

13. Shane Leslie, *Life of Cardinal Manning* (London, 1921), pp. 19, 25 and 26.

14. Quiller-Couch, pp. 308 and 329.

CHAPTER 4

1. AM, I, 64–65, and A. D. Culler, *The Imperial Intellect* (New Haven, 1955), p. 26.

2. AM, I, 60.

3. Culler, pp. 29 ff.

4. See Richard Church's description of the Oriel examination in Liddon, I, 66–69. Church was Fellow of Oriel from 1838 to 1852.

5. Culler, p. 32.

6. What follows is based upon W. A. Pantin, "Oriel College," in *The Victoria History of the County of Oxford*, III, 119–31.

7. See A. R. Ashwell *et al.*, *Life of Samuel Wilberforce* (London, 1880), I, 27. Wilberforce matriculated as an undergraduate at Oriel in 1822.

8. See Mallet, III, 166, 183.

9. Mallet, III, 183. The remark was made by John Keble.

10. *Ibid.*

11. W. J. Copleston, *Memoir of Edward Copleston* (London, 1851). See Culler, pp. 37 ff.

12. Mallet, III, 185, and Culler, p. 38. The devoted student was Richard Whately.

13. Culler, p. 38.

14. AM, I, 65.
15. Thomas Mozley, *Reminiscences, chiefly of Oriel College and the Oxford Movement* (London, 1882), I, 80.
16. See E. J. Whately, *Life and Correspondence of Richard Whately* (London, 1866), 2 Vols.
17. Whately, I, 13.
18. Culler, p. 39. See also Whately, I, 20 and 31.
19. Culler, p. 57.
20. *Letters on the Church by an Episcopalian* (New York, 1837), pp. 10, 39–40, 59, 105–7, and 178.
21. William Tuckwell, *Reminiscences of Oxford* (London, 1900), p. 18.
22. KP, John Keble to Thomas Keble, n. d.
23. See A. P. Stanley, *The Life and Correspondence of Thomas Arnold* (New York, 1898), 2 Vols.
24. Stanley, I, 23. J. T. Coleridge to Arthur Stanley, September 1843.
24a. Battiscombe, p. 63.
25. *Tom Brown's School Days.*
26. Thomas Arnold, *Principles of Church Reform* (London, 1833), pp. iv, 29 and 32–37.
26a. KP, Hugh James Rose to John Keble, April 8, 1833.
27. See J. W. Burgon, *Lives of Twelve Good Men* (London, 1888), I, 194–241.
28. Stanley, I, 305.
29. Burgon, I, 203.
30. See AM, I, 152–53.
31. Burgon, I, 207. Keble to Hawkins, December 28, 1827.
32. *Ibid.,* 209.
33. *Apologia pro Vita Sua* (Modern Library ed.), p. 39.
34. Edward Hawkins, "A Dissertation upon the Use and Importance of Unauthoritative Tradition. . . ." (London, 1819), pp. 1, 3, 25, 22, 6, 69.
35. *Ibid.,* pp. 20 f.
36. H. Hampden, *Some Memorials of Renn Dickson Hampden* (London, 1871).
37. Mozley, *Reminiscences,* I, 380.
38. See J. H. Thom, *The Life of the Rev. J. B. White* (London, 1845), 3 Vols.
39. Mozley, *Reminiscences,* I, 56.
40. R. D. Hampden, *The Scholastic Philosophy considered in its relation to Christian Theology* (Oxford, 1833), pp. 13, 29, 53, 54, 77, 381, 390.
41. Battiscombe is the latest and best study of Keble. See also J. T. Coleridge, *A Memoir of the Rev. John Keble* (London, 1869), 2 Vols., which contains much useful correspondence; Walter Lock, *John Keble. A Biography* (London, 1894); and W. J. A. M. Beek, *John Keble's Literary and Religious Contribution to the Oxford Movement* (Nijmegen, 1959). Church, pp. 20–29, and Christopher Dawson, *The Spirit of the Oxford Movement* (London, 1945), pp. 16 ff., present thoughtful evaluations of Keble.
42. Mozley, *Reminiscences,* I, 220.
43. *The Christian Year* (New York, 1896), p. 209.
44. See H. P. Liddon *et al., Life of Edward Bouverie Pusey* (London, 1893–97), 4 Vols. Liddon's work is monumental and indispensable.
45. *Ibid.,* I, 32.
46. *Ibid.,* 5.
47. *Ibid.*

48. *Ibid.*, 23.
49. *Ibid.*, 42.
50. The description of Lloyd's manner is that of Frederick Oakeley, who also attended the lectures. See Quiller-Couch, pp. 327–29.
51. See Liddon, IV, 395 ff., for a complete list of Pusey's works.
52. AM, I, 163.
53. Old Mr. Pusey died very suddenly a few weeks earlier. This event did not seem to diminish his son's nuptial bliss.
54. The description is that of Frederic Rogers, in Church, pp. 50–51.
55. Froude's *Remains* contain some raw material for a biography which has never been written. The best analysis remains that of Church, pp. 30 ff.
56. Mozley, *Reminiscences*, I, 226.
57. Froude's *Remains*, Part I, Vol. I, 436.
58. *Ibid.*, 433.
59. *Ibid.*, 246.
60. *Ibid.*, 1–144.
61. *Ibid.*, 52.
62. *Ibid.*, 41.
63. *Ibid.*, 197.
64. *Ibid.*, 437.
65. Battiscombe, p. 75.
66. Froude's *Remains*, Part I, Vol. I, 433.
67. AM, I, 426.
68. Froude's *Remains*, Part I, Vol. I, 434.
69. *Ibid.*, 296.
70. *Ibid.*, 307–8.
71. Mozley, *Reminiscences*, I, 228.
72. Church, p. 44.

CHAPTER 5

1. In a letter of September 25, 1834. Froude's *Remains*, Part I, Vol. I, 377.
2. *Ibid.*, 438.
3. The literature on Newman is enormous. Among those books dealing specifically with his Anglican career is Wilfrid Ward, *Life of Cardinal Newman* (London, 1912), 2 Vols., of which only Chapter 1 of Vol. I deals with the years up to 1845. See also among others Maisie Ward, *Young Mr. Newman* (New York, 1948), Sean O'Faolain, *Newman's Way* (London, 1952) and R. D. Middleton, *Newman at Oxford* (London, 1950). The latest and best biographical study is Meriol Trevor, *Newman: the Pillar of the Cloud* (London, 1962). Miss Trevor has produced a beautifully and sharply drawn picture of the Anglican Newman; she has worked more extensively than anyone else with the vast deposit of papers at Birmingham. However, her book is somewhat less useful than it might have been due to a complete absence of citations. Also, Miss Trevor displays such a passionate partisanship that her account of Newman's personal relationships is sometimes distorted. A few instances of this flaw will be given below. (For a good analysis of Miss Trevor's book, see David Newsome, "Newmania," *The Journal of Theological Studies*, Vol. XIV, Part 2, 420 ff.)
4. Mozley, *Reminiscences*, I, 214.
5. *Apologia*, pp. 33 f.
6. See KP, Keble to Robert Wilberforce, September 10 [or 18], 1853.

7. Joseph Milner, *History of the Church of Christ* (London, 1794–1809).
8. *Apologia*, pp. 35 f.
9. *Ibid.*, p. 75.
10. *Ibid.*, p. 236.
11. *Ibid.*, p. 47, and AM, I, 63.
12. *Apologia*, p. 39.
13. *Ibid.*, p. 42.
14. Mozley, *Reminiscences*, I, 29.
15. *Apologia*, p. 39.
16. *Ibid.*, p. 34.
17. See the brilliant study of Robert Wilberforce in Newsome, *The Wilber-forces and Henry Manning*, pp. 39 ff., 71 ff. and 84 ff.
18. For the quarrel with Hawkins see Culler, pp. 64 ff.
19. AM, II, 242.
20. J. H. Newman, "Personal and Literary Character of Cicero" (1824), re-printed in *Historical Sketches* (London, 1920), I, 258.
21. J. H. Newman, "Poetry, with Reference to Aristotle's Poetics," in the *London Review*, 1829, reprinted in *Essays, Critical and Historical* (London, 1924), I, 21.
22. J. H. Newman, *The Arians of the Fourth Century* (London, 1924), p. 29.
23. *Ibid.*, pp. 234 f.
24. *Ibid.*, pp. 42, 71 f.
25. See AM, I, 363–78.
26. The application was made by Principal Shairp. See William Knight, *Principal Shairp and his Friends* (London, 1888), p. 37. Shairp actually transposed Arnold's original lines, which read:

> For thou art gone away from earth,
> And place with those dost claim,
> The children of the Second Birth
> Whom the world could not tame;

> And with that small transfigur'd Band,
> Whom many a different way
> Conducted to their common land,
> Thou learn'st to think as they.

They are from "Obermann" (1852).

CHAPTER 6

1. *Apologia*, p. 63.
2. The sermon was published as a pamphlet a few weeks later. The text will be found in Eugene Fairweather (ed.), *The Oxford Movement* (New York, 1964), pp. 37, 38, 39, 41, 42, 44, 47.
3. Battiscombe, p. 152.
4. AM, I, 384.
5. Liddon, I, 276.
6. William Palmer, *A Narrative of Events connected with the publication of the Tracts for the Times, with Reflections on existing Tendencies to Romanism. . . .* (Oxford, 1843), p. 5. Palmer reprinted this forty years later and though he added to it he did not alter the original composition. Unless otherwise indicated, the 1843 ed. is cited here.
7. KP, John Keble to Thomas Keble, n. d. (but clearly mid-July 1833).
8. See Burgon, I, 62–146. Burgon calls his sketch of Rose "The Restorer of the Old Paths."

9. Burgon, I, 77.
10. In *Vanity Fair*.
11. In the dedication of Vol. IV, *Parochial and Plain Sermons* (1838).
12. Burgon, I, 86.
13. *Ibid.*, 88.
14. *Ibid.*, 90.
15. KP, Keble to Newman, April 4, 1837.
16. From the preface of the anthology *Lyra Apostolica* (1836).
17. *Lyra Apostolica* (1836).
18. See Palmer's *Narrative* and *Dictionary of National Biography* (1895), XLIII, 168–70.
19. *Narrative*, p. 5.
20. William Palmer, *Origines Liturgicae* (Oxford, 1832), 2 Vols.
21. *Apologia*, pp. 67 f.
22. AM, I, 408.
23. Burgon, I, 92.
24. See A. P. Perceval, *A Collection of Papers connected with the Theological Movement of 1833* (London, 1842), and *Dictionary of National Biography*, XLIV, 368.
25. Mozley, *Reminiscences*, I, 311.
26. Apparently Tom changed the second *e* to an *i*. KP, John Keble to Thomas Keble, n. d. (but certainly July 1833).
27. Charles Greville, *A Journal of the Reign of Queen Victoria* (London, 1885), I, 101.
28. Perceval's *Collection*, p. 25.
29. Burgon, I, 93.
30. AM, I, 385. Froude to Newman, July 30, 1833.
31. *Ibid.*, 387. Newman to Keble, August 5, 1833.
32. *Ibid.*, 384 f.
33. Perceval's *Collection*, p. 20. The Manual is printed *ibid.*, pp. 51–64.
34. KP, Froude to Perceval, August 14, 1833.
35. Burgon, I, 93.
36. The sermon is printed in Perceval's *Collection*, pp. 38–43.
37. KP, Rose to Keble, August 19, 1833.
38. Burgon, I, 93.

CHAPTER 7

1. KP, Keble to Newman, August 8, 1833. The substance of this letter is in AM, I, 388 ff. but there are several significant omissions and alterations. See note 5 below.
2. AM, I, 384, Keble to Newman, July 1833.
3. AM, I, 387, Newman to Keble, August 5, 1833.
4. *Ibid.*
5. KP, Keble to Newman, August 8, 1833. The autograph letter reads as in the text. Miss Mozley's reproduction (AM, I, 388) reads as follows: "If the [instead of "we"] Hadleighans could not agree where *inter quatuor muros* will you find six men to agree [instead of "act"] together?" These alterations considerably weaken the force of Keble's question. Keble associates himself with the four who met at Hadleigh and he asserts that action must follow upon deliberation. This sort of thing is typical of Miss Mozley's work (as has often been observed in the past) and though her collection is still indispensable, it must be remembered that she omits and alters without any indication that she has done so.

6. Palmer's *Narrative*, pp. 13 ff.
7. KP, Froude to Perceval, August 14, 1833.
8. KP, John to Thomas Keble, August 16, 1833.
9. KP, Froude to Perceval, August 14, 1833.
10. KP, Keble to Newman, August 8, 1833.
11. NP, Newman to Thomas Mozley, August 5, 1833.
12. *Ibid.*
13. AM, I, 395 f., Newman to Rogers, August 31, 1833.
14. KP, Rose to Keble, August 19, 1833.
15. PP, Newman to Perceval, September 6, 1833. On the back of this letter Newman copied out Keble's manifesto.
16. *Ibid.*
17. AM, I, 393, Palmer to Newman, August 31, 1833. Rose's letter to Palmer is here quoted verbatim.
18. *Ibid.*
19. AM, I, 397, Newman to Froude, September 2, 1833.
20. The Tracts were first issued as penny pamphlets and ultimately in bound volumes (six altogether) in which the original pagination was maintained. They were all anonymous. For authorship, see the useful chart in Liddon, III, 473–80.
21. "The Catholic Church," 4 pp.
22. "Thoughts respectfully addressed to the Clergy on Alterations in the Liturgy," 8 pp.
23. KP, Keble to Newman, August 8, 1833.
24. AM, I, 394, Newman to Bowden, August 31, 1833.
25. Palmer's *Narrative*, pp. 21 ff.
26. AM, I, 403, Newman to Froude, September 18, 1833.
27. NP, Newman to Henry Wilberforce, September 3, 1833. "We are publishing Tracts in our society and perhaps may proceed to a quarterly periodical."
28. PP, Newman to Perceval, September 6, 1833.
29. Palmer's *Narrative*, pp. 21 ff., and AM, I, 402.
30. PP, Newman to Perceval, July 20, 1834.
31. AM, I, 399, Newman to R. F. Wilson, September 8, 1833.
32. *Ibid.*, 402, Froude to Newman, September 15, 1833.
33. KP, Keble to Newman, September 27, 1833.
34. Liddon, I, 279.
35. AM, I, 399, Rickards to Newman, September 6, 1833.
36. Palmer's *Narrative* (1883 ed.), p. 56.
37. *Ibid.*
38. Burgon, I, 95 ff.
39. *Ibid.*, 103, Rose to Newman, October 14, 1833.
40. AM, I, 409 ff.
41. *Ibid.*, 412 ff.
42. *Ibid.*, 404, Turrill to Newman, October 2, 1833.
43. Tract Ten, p. 5.
44. *Ibid.*, p. 6.
45. Palmer's *Narrative* (1883 ed.), p. 56. Cf. AM, I, 422.
46. *Ibid.*, 427, November 20, 1833.
47. *Ibid.*, 430, November 22, 1833.
48. *Ibid.*, Newman to Froude, November 13, 1833.
49. *Ibid.*
50. *Ibid.*, 426, November 17, 1833.
51. PP, Keble to Perceval, n. d. (but certainly mid-November 1833).

52. AM, II, 6, Newman to Froude, December 15, 1833.
53. AM, I, 419, Newman to Froude.
54. *Ibid.*, 433, Archdeacon Froude to Newman, November 25, 1833.
55. Palmer's *Narrative*, pp. 10 ff. The text of the address is printed here.
56. KP, Keble to Henry Richards, December 25, 1833.
57. Palmer's *Narrative*, p. 12.
58. See *Ibid.*, pp. 95–97, for a list of those present at Lambeth—Keble among them—and for the archbishop's acceptance speech.
59. *Ibid.*, pp. 13–16.
60. *Ibid.*, pp. 22 f.
61. Tract Eighteen, p. 18.
62. *Apologia*, p. 86.
63. George Prevost (ed.), *The Autobiography of Isaac Williams* (London, 1892), pp. 70 ff.
64. See Burgon, I, 153–93. Burgon calls his sketch of Marriott "The Man of Saintly Life."
65. See *Dictionary of National Biography*, VIII, 100 f.
66. AM, I, 391.
67. *Ibid.*, 421, Newman to Froude, November 13, 1833.
68. *Ibid.*, 424, Newman to Bowden, November 13, 1833.
69. NP, Rogers to Newman, December 18, 1833.
70. AM, I, 424.

CHAPTER 8

1. AM, I, 385, Froude to Newman, July 30, 1833.
2. NP, Spry to Newman, November 11, 1833.
3. NP, a notebook partially and fitfully filled with lists, ideas for Tracts, circulation plans and the like.
4. *Ibid.* This list of grievances is dated May 4, 1834.
5. AM, II, 13.
6. *Ibid.*, 14.
7. *Ibid.*, 15, January 3, 1834.
8. Tract Thirty-one, p. 4.
9. Tract Thirty-three, esp. pp. 5–7. Newman wrote a pamphlet on the subject of suffragan bishops in 1835. Cf. *Via Media* (1923), II, 53–90.
10. Tract Thirty-four, pp. 1 f.
11. Tract Thirty-eight, pp. 10, 11, 6, 12.
12. Tract Forty-one, pp. 3–4, 6.
13. Tract Forty-five, pp. 2, 4–5.
14. *Ibid.*, p. 5.
15. On September 6, 1833, Newman ordered two hundred copies of the Manual (PP, Newman to Perceval). About the same time, Keble told Newman that his brother Tom thought "Perceval's catechism too hard for the poor. I will try and get him to draw up something himself. I fancy he would do it especially well" (KP, Keble to Newman, n. d.). But in February 1834, when the Manual was published, Tom Keble ordered fifty copies and used them in his school at Bisley. On November 13, 1834 (PP, Newman to Perceval), Newman told Perceval, "We have not used your catechism yet, [John] Keble not having yet had his mind sufficiently disengaged to have a talk with me about it." "Used" in this context meant perhaps the inclusion of the Manual in the series of Tracts.
16. Tract Thirty-six, p. 7.

17. Tract Thirty, p. 7.
18. Tract Twenty-two, p. 4.
19. Tract Forty, p. 6.
20. Tract Forty-three, p. 8.
21. Tract Twenty-four, p. 10. With regard to Harrison's intimacy with New-
    man, the following notation is found in a collection of "Extracts of facts
    from letters of friends destroyed," in Newman's hand, among NP:
    Nov. 2, 1837 —"At this date I must have been very intimate with
    (Archdeacon) Harrison, for [in a letter of this date] Manning says, 'Pray
    send your answer through Harrison, as you are busy.' "
22. NP, Newman to Henry Wilberforce, March 10, 1834, and Newman to
    Bowden, March 14, 1834.
23. NP, January 7, 1834.
24. Froude gave over his income from his fellowship to the Tracts. See AM,
    II, 154.
25. NP, the notebook cited above in n. 3.
26. *Tracts for the Times*, I, iv.
27. AM, II, 107, August 3, 1835.
28. *Ibid.*, 108, August 4, 1835.
29. *Ibid.*, 119, Harrison to Newman, September 3, 1835.
30. *Ibid.*, Pusey to Newman, September 4, 1835.
31. Burgon, I, 105.
32. NP, Newman to Manning, September 8, 1835, in which announcement of
    Keble's editorship is made. KP, John to Thomas Keble, October 1835.
33. NP, Newman to Bowden, October 10, 1835.
34. *Ibid.*
35. *Ibid.*
36. NP, the notebook cited above in n. 3. Cf. also NP, Newman to Bowden,
    September 11, 1835.
37. AM, II, 127, Keble to Newman, November 15, 1835.

CHAPTER 9

1. Liddon, I, 282–83.
2. AM, I, 423, November 15, 1833.
3. Froude's *Remains*, Part I, Vol. 332, November 17, 1833. Newman summed
   up his final judgment about the address thus: "Much as I dislike the
   spirit, . . . yet it is better to agitate for it if possible. It will do for a
   beginning." NP, Newman to Henry Wilberforce, January 7, 1834.
4. The rumour was untrue, as Newman later explained to Whately (AM,
   II, 61–63).
5. Culler, pp. 102 ff.
6. *Ibid.*
7. *Ibid.*, p. 104. For Newman's part in the agitation see NP, Newman to
   Bowden, April 21, 1834.
8. Culler, p. 105.
9. PP, Newman to Perceval, January 11, 1836.
10. *Ibid.*
11. Culler, p. 109, August 20, 1834.
12. R. D. Hampden, "Observations on Religious Dissent" (Oxford, 1834), pp.
    5, 9, 20, 40.
13. AM, II, 69.
14. NP, November 28, 1834.

15. Mozley's *Reminiscences*, I, 230 and 353.
16. AM, II, 14, 24.
17. *Ibid.*, 25.
18. Hampden's *Memorials*, p. 22.
19. "Dr. Hampden and Anglicanism," *Dublin Review* (July 1871), XVII, 78. This article is a lengthy (66–108) review of Hampden's *Memorials*, recently published. It is unsigned, but the author was Henry Wilberforce, as is clear from correspondence from Wilberforce and from Hampden's daughter to Newman in NP. The article is a useful and lively account of Hampden's quarrel with Newman.
20. NP, March 23, 1835.
21. NP, April 3, 1835.
22. "The Foundation of the Faith Assailed in Oxford," p. 23.
23. NP, Newman to Henry Wilberforce, May 3, 1835.
24. Culler, p. 110.
25. For a description of the gradual elimination of the Dissenters' claims see *ibid.*, pp. 105 ff.
26. Palmer's *Narrative*, pp. 27 ff.
27. Liddon, I, 307, Pusey to Gladstone, May 5, 1835.
28. KP, Keble to Richards, April 7, 1835.
29. KP, Keble to Robert Wilberforce, April 2, 1835.
30. G. E. Marindin (ed.), *Letters of Frederic Lord Blachford* (London, 1896), pp. 23 f., Rogers to Katherine Rogers, May 21, 1835.
31. For this exchange see *Dublin Review*, XVII, 81 ff.
32. NP, Hampden to Newman, May 22, 1835.
33. NP, Hampden to Newman, June 23, 1835.
34. NP, Newman to Hampden, June 24, 1835.
35. NP, Newman to Bowden, July 7, 1835, in which Newman quotes Froude's remark.
36. AM, II, 95.
37. *Letters*, p. 24.
38. Froude's *Remains*, Part I, Vol. I, 374.
39. *Ibid.*, 385.
40. *Ibid.*, 369.
41. *Ibid.*, 380 ff.
42. I have profited from discussions on this point with my friend Father Richard Berg. The lack of social concern on the part of the Tractarians is traceable partly to the caste system to which they were conditioned but more, as Froude's case shows, to their preoccupation with the supernatural aspects of Christianity. They saw it as their business to help the poor through acts of charity without, however, committing themselves to the support of social change. Indeed, they viewed social change—at least the kind widely supported by their contemporaries—as hostile to Christianity. This gave rise to a curious indifference to many of the issues of the day. For example, repeal of the Corn Laws—the protective duty on imported wheat—was perhaps the most crucial political and social question of the 1830s and 1840s, and yet Newman could write: "As to the Corn Laws, everyone is certainly giving them up. The *Times* has long ago, but I do not understand the question at all myself." NP, Newman to Thomas Mozley, August 20, 1841.
43. Froude's *Remains*, Part I, Vol. I, 380, 395.
44. *Ibid.*, 410.
45. Trevor, pp. 179 f.

46. *Ibid.*
47. AM, II, 142 and 147.
48. *Ibid.*, 154.
49. Battiscombe, 184.
50. Trevor, 182.
51. Froude's *Remains*, Part I, Vol. I, 430. The poem was composed in 1833.

CHAPTER 10

1. Froude's *Remains*, Part I, Vol. I, 426. Burton was appointed by a con-
    servative government. For his attitude on subscription to the Articles,
    see PP, Newman to Perceval, November 13, 1834.
2. Liddon, I, 365–67.
3. *Ibid.*, 368.
4. Henry Hart Milman (1791–1868), Keble's predecessor as Professor of
    Poetry. His *History of the Jews* (1829) and later histories of Christianity
    earned him a reputation for latitudinarian views. He died as Dean of
    St. Paul's.
5. NP, January 21, 1836.
6. NP, January 23, 1836.
7. Liddon, I, 369–70. Cf. Greville, II, 462.
8. AM, II, 143 ff.
9. Liddon, I, 370–71.
10. "Elucidations," quoted in *Dublin Review*, XVII, 74 f.
11. See David Cecil, *Melbourne*, pp. 283–87.
12. *Ibid.*, and Liddon, I, 371 ff.
13. Mallet, III, 260. Shuttleworth later became a Hampden ally. See also
    Newman's account of the meeting, NP, Newman to Bowden, February
    17, 1836.
14. AM, II, 149.
15. See above, pp. 56 and 57.
16. Liddon, I, 374.
17. Palmer's *Narrative*, p. 29 n.
18. Liddon, I, 372 f.
19. *The Case of Dr. Hampden* (London, 1848), p. 2. This appeared as part
    of the controversy over Hampden's appointment as Bishop of Hereford
    in 1847.
20. Mallet, III, 259.
21. These quotations will be found in *The Oxford Persecution of 1836. Ex-
    tracts from the Public Journals* (London, 1836), pp. 4, 5, 18 and 27.
22. R. D. Hampden, "Inaugural Lecture, read before the University of Ox-
    ford, in the Divinity School, March 17, 1836" (London, 1836), pp. 8,
    10, 15.
23. *Ibid.*, pp. 16, 20, 25, 30.
24. Mozley's *Reminiscences,* I, 373.
25. Hampden's *Memorials*, p. 66.
26. Blachford's *Letters*, pp. 28 ff., Rogers to Katherine Rogers, March 30, 1836.
27. *Ibid.*
28. Hampden's *Memorials*, pp. 66 f.
29. Blachford's *Letters*, p. 30.
30. *Ibid.*
31. *The Oxford Persecution*, pp. 65–75.
32. Liddon, I, 379–80.

33. Stanley, II, 36.
34. Hampden's *Memorials*, p. 38, Arnold to Hampden, May 17, 1835.
35. "The Oxford Malignants," *The Edinburgh Review* (April 1836), LXIII, 229.
36. *Ibid.*, 233–35.
37. *Ibid.*, 237.
38. *Ibid.*, 238–39.
39. Hampden's *Memorials*, p. 92.
40. *Ibid.*, p. 57.

CHAPTER 11

1. Burgon, I, 201, and Trevor, 195.
2. KP, Charles Newman to John Newman, July 16, 1836.
3. Tuckwell's *Reminiscences*, pp. 182 f.
4. AM, II, 152.
5. See the descriptive pamphlet, "The University Church of St. Mary the Virgin, Oxford," available at St. Mary's.
6. NP, memorandum in Newman's hand, dated "1833 or 1834" and titled, "My arbitration between Dr. Hampden and the parishioners of St. Mary's."
7. NP, a notebook covering catechetical instruction over several years, beginning in 1828.
8. NP, an account book in Newman's hand.
9. J. A. Froude, "The Oxford Counter-Reformation," *Short Studies on Great Subjects*, p. 179.
10. William Lockhart, quoted in R. D. Middleton, *Newman and Bloxam* (London, 1947), p. 7.
11. *Ibid.*, p. 8.
12. NP, notebook in Newman's hand.
13. Middleton, pp. 15 f., Newman to Greenhill, March 1, 1887.
14. *Ibid.*, p. 13.
15. Trevor, p. 202.
16. Middleton, p. 12.
17. *Ibid.*
18. Frederick Oakeley, *Historical Notes on the Tractarian Movement* (London, 1865), pp. 25 f.
19. Quoted in Middleton, pp. 12 f.
20. *Ibid.*, pp. 9 f.
21. In the *Dublin Review* (April 1869), XII, 325–26.
22. Middleton, p. 9.
23. F. W. Doyle, *Reminiscences* (London, 1886), p. 145.
24. J. C. Shairp, *Studies in Poetry and Philosophy* (London, 1886), p. 248.
25. Quoted in Middleton, p. 8.
26. Shairp, p. 248.
27. Froude, p. 186.
28. *Ibid.*
29. *Ibid.*
30. Trevor, p. 208.
31. J. H. Newman, *Parochial and Plain Sermons* (London, 1891), III, 26–28.
32. NP, copy of a questionnaire from the Bishop of Oxford to his clergy on the subject of the requirement of residency. The note about Littlemore is added at the bottom.

33. See AM, II, 437.

34. *Ibid.*, 271, Newman to Jemima Mozley, April 1, 1840.

35. NP contains a copy of the formal petition. Cf. AM, II, 90.

36. NP contains several lists of subscribers to the chapel fund.

37. *Ibid.*

38. Trevor, p. 196.

39. Blachford's *Letters*, pp. 38 f., Rogers to Emily Rogers, September 24, 1836.

40. AM, II, 189.

41. AM, II, 225, Newman to Bowden, March 19, 1838. "I have not seen
    Williams' 'Cathedral,' but I fear it will be obscure. However, everyone
    has his line." Cf. *Autobiography of Isaac Williams*, p. 57.

42. See Middleton, who makes use of Bloxam's papers.

43. *Ibid.*, pp. 55 ff. More will be said about this affair in Chapter XV.

44. AM, II, 91.

45. *Ibid.*, 93.

46. *Ibid.*, 94. Cf. KP, John to Thomas Keble, n. d.: "Golightly has been slant-
    ing off from sound doctrine and is consequently not going to be N's
    curate at Littlemore. I don't mean anything very bad, only that he has
    talked in sermons in a vague way about new birth and against Pusey."

47. Mozley's *Reminiscences*, II, 108–14, contains an unusually sympathetic
    picture of Golightly.

48. See Newsome, *The Wilberforces and Henry Manning*, pp. 24 ff., for a
    genealogical chart of the Wilberforces, Mannings, Ryders and Sargents.

49. AM, II, 182.

50. Mozley's *Reminiscences*, II, 42.

51. See the very perceptive remarks of Professor Owen Chadwick, *From
    Bossuet to Newman. The Idea of Doctrinal Development* (Cambridge,
    1957), p. 111.

52. Anne Mozley (ed.), *Letters of J. B. Mozley* (London, 1885), p. 81.

53. See AM, II, 201 n.

54. Mozley's *Reminiscences*, I, 130.

55. NP, February 14, 1832.

56. NP, Newman to Henry Wilberforce, May 3, 1835.

57. AM, II, 18, Newman to Rogers, January 14, 1834.

58. *Ibid.*, 19.

59. NP, Newman to Henry Wilberforce, January 8, 1834 (not sent).

60. NP, June 8, 1835.

61. NP, July 24, 1835.

62. NP, July 28, 1835.

63. NP, August 3, 1835. Meriol Trevor treats the Henry Wilberforce marriage
    on pp. 158–64 more fully than it is treated here. Nevertheless, there is
    in her account a defensiveness which amounts to distortion. A full read-
    ing of the correspondence reveals that though Henry was pigheaded
    and inconsiderate, he still had some right on his side. Miss Trevor, by
    failing to quote adequately from Henry's letters of July 24th (p. 163)
    and August 3rd (p. 164), quite plainly creates a false impression.

CHAPTER 12

1. See Olive Brose, *Church and Parliament* (Stanford, 1959), pp. 120 ff.

2. KP, John to Thomas Keble, n. d. (but certainly June or July 1836).

3. Trevor, p. 197.

4. KP, August 8, 1839.

5. M. Mare and A. Perceval, *Victorian Best-seller. The World of Charlotte M. Yonge* (London, 1949), pp. 126 f.
6. Battiscombe, p. 166.
7. Mozley's *Letters*, p. 77, James to Anne Mozley, April 27, 1838.
8. NP, Rogers to Newman, August 18, 1836.
9. Mozley's *Reminiscences*, I, 223.
10. Battiscombe, p. 169.
11. KP, John to Thomas Keble, October 21 or 26, 1835.
12. KP, Keble to Newman, November 15, 1835.
13. KP, Keble to Newman, August 16, 1839.
14. Battiscombe, p. 172.
15. *Ibid.*, p. 178.
16. Quoted by Mare and Perceval, p. 122.
17. KP, Keble to Newman, January 31, 1840.
18. Battiscombe, p. 176.
19. Mare and Perceval, p. 126.
20. Mozley's *Reminiscences*, I, 221.
21. Prevost, *Autobiography of Isaac Williams*, pp. 49 f.
22. KP, Keble to Newman, October 15, 1838.
23. KP, Keble to Newman, December 4, 1838. See also KP, John to Thomas Keble, n. d. (but about 1837).
24. Mozley's *Reminiscences*, I, 312.
25. John Keble (ed.), *The Works of that Learned and Judicious Divine Mr. Richard Hooker* (Oxford, 1836), I, cvii f. See also Coleridge's *Keble*, I, 202.
26. AM, II, 177, Bowden to Newman, June 30, 1836.
27. *Ibid.*, 190, October 4, 1836.
28. *Ibid.*, 192, Newman to Maria Giberne, November 27, 1836.
29. See Coleridge's *Keble*, I, 246 ff., Lock's *Keble*, pp. 92 ff., and Battiscombe, pp. 193 ff.
30. AM, II, 219 f., Newman to Keble, November 3, 1837. Keble had a new edition with preface and appendices published the preceding summer. See KP, Keble to Newman, July 15, 1837.
31. AM, II, 191.
32. Blachford's *Letters*, p. 43.
33. AM, II, 211.
34. KP, Keble to Newman, August 31, 1837.
35. AM, II, 212, Newman to Rogers, July 5, 1837.
36. AM, II, 216 f.
37. *Ibid.*
38. KP, Keble to Newman, August 31, 1837.
39. Froude's *Remains*, Part I, Vol. I, 68.
40. *Ibid.*, v–xxii.
41. NP, Rogers to Newman, November 27, 1837.
42. AM, II, 221.
43. This is why Newman excised some passages in Keble's letters to himself. See his longhand statement in KP, dated August 24, 1878. Mrs. Battiscombe tried valiantly to recoup some of these passages by the use of infrared and ultraviolet photography, but in vain. See Battiscombe, p. x.
44. AM, II, 71.
45. KP, Keble to Newman, January 27, 1838.
46. KP, Keble to Newman, n. d. (but sometime in the summer of 1839).
47. KP, Keble to Newman, September 23, 1839.

48. *Ibid.*
49. KP, Keble to Newman, June 1836.
50. AM, II, 171.
51. KP, Keble to Newman, September 7, 1839.
52. KP, Keble to Newman, January 14, 1839 and August 7, 1838.
53. KP, Keble to Newman, September 12, 1837.
54. KP, Keble to Newman, December 31, 1837.
55. Blachford's *Letters*, pp. 35 f., Rogers to his sister, August 1836.
56. NP, Rogers to Newman, August 18, 1836.
57. Mozley's *Letters*, pp. 75 f., James to Anne Mozley, April 27, 1838. There is a partial about-face at the end of the letter.
58. Mozley's *Reminiscences*, I, 217–22.
59. *Ibid.*, 223.
60. AM, II, 145, Newman to Froude, January 31, 1836. The reference was to the possibility that Melbourne might appoint Keble Divinity Professor.

CHAPTER 13

1. NP, Newman to Henry Wilberforce, March 14, 1837.
2. NP, Newman to Henry Wilberforce, September 10, 1837.
3. KP, Keble to Newman, September 12, 1837.
4. KP, Keble to Newman, September 21, 1837.
5. NP, March 25, 1837.
6. NP, Newman to Bowden, September 4, 1838.
7. NP, Newman to Bowden, November 6, 1838.
8. J. H. Newman, *Lectures on the Prophetical Office of the Church*, reprinted in *Via Media* (London, 1918), I, 41 and 45.
9. Tract Seventy-one, pp. 9, 16, 32.
10. Tract Seventy-nine, pp. 1, 2, 3, 27, 31.
11. *Ibid.*, p. 3.
12. NP, Newman to Bowden, September 11, 1835.
13. AM, II, 206, Newman to Jemima, April 25, 1837.
14. *Via Media*, I, 37, 79, 95–98, 102, 119 f., 167, 201 f., 212, 249–51, 256 f., 258, 262 f.
15. *Ibid.*, 18–20.
16. AM, II, 192 and 197.
17. *Ibid.*, 198.
18. *Ibid.*, 206 f.
19. NP, Rogers to Newman, October 2, 1837.
20. Tract Eighty-two, p. v. This correspondence between Newman and the editor was placed at the beginning of the fourth volume of the Tracts (1837). For some unaccountable reason Roman numeral pagination was used, though the material did make up a separate Tract (Eighty-two). The editor's objection to Pusey's views on post-baptismal sin was a common one. If Pusey were right, it would seem necessary to posit a sacramental action involving absolution of some kind from serious sin committed after Baptism. This would mean in effect a sacrament of Penance which was a "good work" which no Protestant could admit.
21. AM, II, 172, Newman to Maria Giberne, April 19, 1836.
22. *Ibid.*, 205, Newman to Bowden, April 12, 1837. See n. 20 above.
23. *Ibid.*, 222, Newman to Bowden, January 17, 1838.
24. J. H. Newman, *Lectures on the Doctrine of Justification* (London, 1924), pp. 2, 65, 227, 251, 264 f., 265, 323.
25. AM, II, 206.

26. *Ibid.*, 142. Cf. *ibid.*, 138, for Newman's suggestion that "Home Thoughts" become one of the Tracts.
27. KP, Keble to Newman, April 1, 1834 and n. d. (but certainly autumn 1834).
28. KP, John to Thomas Keble, n. d. (but probably autumn 1833).
29. NP, Newman to Bowden, December 1, 1834. The reference to the archbishop had to do with Rose's appointment to the honourific post of Chaplain to the Archbishop of Canterbury.
30. Burgon, I, 108.
31. *Ibid.*, 109.
32. *Ibid.*, 109 ff.
33. *Ibid.*, 112.
34. NP, Newman to Rose, May 23, 1836.
35. Burgon, I, 115.
36. NP, Newman to Bowden, January 13, 1837.
37. NP, Newman to Mrs. Hugh James Rose, January 29, 1839.
38. NP, Newman to Bowden, March 16, 1837.
39. AM, II, 146.
40. See *Dictionary of National Biography*, II, 832 f., E. R. Houghton, "The *British Critic* and the Oxford Movement," *Studies in Bibliography* (Charlottesville, 1963), pp. 119 ff., and Mozley's *Reminiscences*, II, 200 ff.
41. Mozley's *Reminiscences*, II, 208.
42. AM, II, 195.
43. NP, Newman to Bowden, July 12, 1837.
44. NP, Newman to Bowden, August 25, 1837.
45. KP, Keble to Newman, October 28, 1837. See also KP, Newman to Watson, September 1, 1837, for a summary of Tractarian complaints against Boone.
46. NP, December 12, 1837.
47. AM, II, 223.
48. NP, Henry Wilberforce to Newman, November 2, 1837.
49. NP, Rogers to Newman, December 28, 1837.
50. Mozley's *Letters*, p. 71.
51. NP, March 15, 1838.
52. KP, Keble to Newman, January 27, 1838.
53. See Liddon, I, 409 ff.
54. Burgon, I, 166 ff.
55. Palmer's *Narrative*, p. 31.
56. Prevost, *Autobiography of Isaac Williams*, pp. 89 f.
57. Tract Eighty, pp. 3, 6, 36, 59, 62, 68.
58. Mozley's *Letters*, p. 73.
59. Prevost, *Autobiography of Isaac Williams*, p. 21.
60. Mozley's *Reminiscences*, I, 430–31.
61. *Ibid.*, 438.
62. Tract Eighty-seven, pp. 123–25.
63. Mozley's *Reminiscences*, I, 407.

CHAPTER 14

1. Blachford's *Letters*, p. 52.
2. AM, II, 225, March 19, 1838.
3. See Burgon, I, 112.
4. PP, Keble to Perceval, April 29, 1839.
5. Tract Seventy-five, pp. 1 f.
6. NP, March 25, 1837. Cf. AM, II, 274.

7. AM, II, 198, Newman to Rogers, January 7, 1837.

8. NP, Marriott to Newman, n. d. (but certainly spring 1837).

9. KP, Keble to Newman, September 7, 1839.

10. KP, Keble to Newman, August 7, 1838.

11. *Ibid.*

12. *Ibid.*

13. PP, February 22, 1839.

14. PP, Churton to Pusey, September 21, 1838. Churton was a close friend of Joshua Watson and later his biographer. He had been a master at Charterhouse where both Tom Mozley and W. M. Thackeray were his students.

15. Middleton, *Newman at Oxford*, pp. 134 ff.

16. Froude's *Remains*, Part I, Vol. I, 434.

17. J. H. Newman, "A Letter to the Rev. Godfrey Faussett, D.D.," reprinted in *Via Media* (London, 1923), II, 197 ff.

18. AM, II, 228.

19. KP, Keble to Newman, September 8, 1838.

20. NP, January 5, 1840.

21. Blachford's *Letters*, pp. 51 f., Rogers to Newman, August 1, 1838.

22. AM, II, 237, Newman to Bowden, September 4, 1838.

23. See *Dictionary of National Biography*, I, 871 f.

24. Trevor, p. 219.

25. Blachford's *Letters*, pp. 38 f., Rogers to Emily Rogers, September 24, 1836.

26. AM, II, 189.

27. R. Bagot, "A Charge on the Third Visitation" (London, 1838), pp. 6 f.

28. *Ibid.*, pp. 20 f.

29. AM, II, 231.

30. NP, August 19, 1838.

31. KP, Keble to Newman, August 15, 1838.

32. Quoted in Liddon, II, 56.

33. KP, Keble to Newman, August 23, 1838.

34. Bagot's "Charge," p. 21 n.

35. NP, Newman to Henry Wilberforce, January 22, 1839. Newman went on to cite instances of the "squall," notably the *Times* attack on William Gladstone's recently published pro-Establishment manifesto, *The State in its Relations with the Church* (1838). "It is impossible," wrote Newman, "they can overset so much of a man. Do they think to frighten him? for he has been counting the cost; yet I should not wonder if he was surprised. Does he expect such a tempest?"

36. Liddon, II, 64.

37. *Ibid.*, 71.

38. NP, Churton to Newman, December 20, 1838.

39. Liddon, II, 67.

40. *Ibid.*, 68.

41. *Ibid.*, 72.

42. *Ibid.*, 75.

43. KP, Keble to Newman, February 6, 1839.

44. PP, Williams to Pusey, August 1 [1838].

45. AM, II, 239, Newman to Keble, November 21, 1838.

46. *Ibid.*, 238. Newman's part in the breviary project was the translation of the hymns.

47. *Ibid.*, 240.

48. *Ibid.*, 241.

49. *Ibid.*, 243.

50. KP, John to Thomas Keble, November 28, 1838, in which John quotes his letter to Newman.
51. KP, John to Thomas Keble, December 10, 1838.
52. AM, II, 245.
53. *Ibid.*, 243.
54. *Ibid.*, 247.
55. *Ibid.*
56. *Ibid.*, 249.
57. KP, Keble to Newman, n. d. (early 1839).
58. KP, Keble to Newman, February 15, 1839.
59. Mozley's *Letters*, p. 73.
60. Tuckwell's *Reminiscences*, pp. 136 f.
61. Mozley's *Letters*, p. 73.
62. Mark Pattison, *Memoirs* (London, 1885), p. 189. For an analysis of Pattison's relations with Pusey see V. H. H. Green, *Oxford Common Room* (London, 1957), pp. 109 ff.
63. Liddon, II, 101.
64. Tuckwell's *Reminiscences*, p. 138.
65. Mozley's *Letters*, p. 120.
66. *Ibid.*

CHAPTER 15

1. NP, Newman to Thomas Mozley, February 11, 1839. Tract Eighty-five later gave rise to accusations of sophistry. See the penetrating analysis of this work "which carried the sceptical side of [Newman's] thought to the limit" in Owen Chadwick, *From Bossuet to Newman* (Cambridge, 1957), pp. 126 ff.
2. KP, January 14, 1839.
3. NP, January 22, 1839.
4. Trevor, pp. 203 f. and Battiscombe, pp. 178 f.
5. Pattison's *Memoirs*, p. 189.
6. See *British Critic* (April 1839), XXV, 395–426. The quotation in the text is taken from the reprint in *Essays Critical and Historical* (London, 1907), I, 306. Newman quoted at length from this article in the *Apologia* and remarked dramatically (p. 115) that "it contains the last words which I ever spoke as an Anglican to Anglicans."
7. NP, Manning to Newman, September 17, 1839 and January 15, 1840.
8. Blachford's *Letters*, p. 46.
9. KP, Rose to Keble, August 19, 1833.
10. This story was told by Bloxam. See Trevor, p. 360.
11. Oakeley, *Historical Notes*, p. 35.
12. Quoted in Wilfrid Ward, *The Life and Times of Cardinal Wiseman* (London, 1912), I, 209 f.
13. For what follows see Denis Gwynn, *Lord Shrewsbury, Pugin and the Catholic Revival* (London, 1946).
14. See *ibid.* and B. Ferrey, *Recollections of . . . Pugin* (London, 1861).
15. NP, January 1840.
16. Mozley's *Letters*, pp. 99 f.
17. E. S. Purcell, *Life and Letters of Ambrose Phillipps de Lisle* (London, 1900), 2 vols.
18. *Ibid.*, I, 274 f., Shrewsbury to Phillipps, November 2, 1842.
19. NP, Newman to Thomas Mozley, March 7, 1841.

20. Ward as cited above and also B. Fothergill, *Life of Wiseman* (London, 1963).
21. Ward's *Wiseman*, I, 119.
22. KP, Keble to Newman, September 12, 1837.
23. For Wiseman in England, see *ibid.*, 214 ff. Wiseman kept the curial officials in Rome apprised of the Oxford situation. See C. Dougherty and H. Welsh, "Wiseman and the Oxford Movement: an Early Report to the Vatican," *Victorian Studies* (September 1958), II, 149 ff. For this reference and for many helpful suggestions I am grateful to my friend Father James Reidy.
24. Ward's *Wiseman*, I, 322.
25. AM, II, 256, September 22, 1839.
26. *Apologia*, p. 135.
27. *Ibid.*, 132.
28. AM, II, 254 f., Newman to Rogers.
29. *Apologia*, p. 132.
30. AM, II, 256.
31. H. Wilberforce, *Dublin Review* (April 1869), XV, 327.
32. NP, October 20, 1839.
33. KP, Keble to Newman, October 2, 1839.
34. On the envelope is the direction "c/o H. Wilberforce, Bransgore, Ringwood."
35. *Apologia*, p. 135.
36. Reprinted in J. H. Newman, *Essays and Sketches* (London, 1948), II, 46, 47, 105, 104.
37. *Apologia*, p. 142.
38. KP, Keble to Newman, December 25, 1839.
39. AM, II, 260.
40. *Ibid.*, 261.
41. OF, p. 43.
42. *Ibid.*, p. 45.
43. R. D. Middleton, *Newman and Bloxam* (London, 1947), p. 58. The whole affair is treated here, pp. 55–58.
44. Trevor, pp. 231 ff.
45. NP, March 10, 1840.
46. KP, John to Thomas Keble, November 30, 1840.
47. OF, p. 54.
48. NP, a memorandum inserted in the Henry Wilberforce correspondence. See AM, I, 377, where a significant portion is omitted, and Trevor, p. 235.
49. NP, Newman to Thomas Mozley, March 20, 1840.
50. AM, II, 273. See Middleton's *Bloxam*, pp. 69 ff., for the purchase of the land in Littlemore.
51. Printed in *Apologia*, pp. 149 ff.
52. KP, October 30, 1840.
53. KP, November 3, 1840.
54. AM, II, 281, November 6, 1840.
55. *Ibid.*, 285 f., November 25, 1840.

CHAPTER 16

1. *The History of the Times* (New York, 1935), I, 406–409.
2. J. H. Newman, "The Tamworth Reading Room," *Discussions and Arguments* (London, 1924), pp. 261, 268.

3. See NP, for a transcription of the *Chronicle*'s articles.
4. Blachford's *Letters*, pp. 95 f., April 8, 1841.
5. AM, II, 289.
6. Blachford's *Letters*, p. 87, January 30, 1841. The April 8th letter (cited above, n. 4) indicates that Rogers kept pressing the point despite Newman's rebuke.
7. AM, II, 290.
8. NP, Newman to Bowden, October 23, 1839.
9. AM, II, 262.
10. NP, December 12, 1839.
11. AM, II, 225.
12. *Ibid.*, 256.
13. See R. E. Prothero, *The Life and Correspondence of Arthur Stanley* (London, 1893), 2 Vols. For a short sketch see Geoffrey Faber, *Jowett* (Cambridge, Massachusetts, 1958), pp. 116 ff.
14. Wilfrid Ward, *William George Ward and the Oxford Movement* (London, 1890).
15. AM, II, 252 and Ward's *Ward*, pp. 79, 83.
16. Ward's *Ward*, p. 113.
17. *Dictionary of National Biography*, XIV, 731 f. See also Oakeley's memoirs of his Oxford days in Quiller Couch, pp. 300 ff., and his *Historical Notes on the Tractarian Movement* (1865).
18. Mozley's *Reminiscences*, II, 4 f.
19. Prevost's *Autobiography of Isaac Williams*, p. 87.
20. Church, p. 321.
21. Mozley's *Reminiscences*, II, 4 f.
22. Oakeley, *Historical Notes*, p. 20.
23. Ward's *Ward*, p. 84.
24. PP, August 17, 1840.
25. Tract Ninety, p. 2. The pagination used here is that of Pusey's reissue in 1865. Newman's contributions to the controversy—the Tract itself, the "Letter to Jelf," and the "Letter to the Bishop of Oxford"—are reprinted in *Via Media*, II, 269 ff.
26. Tract Ninety, pp. 84 f.
27. *Ibid.*, pp. 38 ff.
28. *Ibid.*, pp. 61 f.
29. *Ibid.*, pp. 86 f.
30. KP, Keble to Newman, February 19, 1841.
31. NP, Newman to Thomas Mozley, March 7, 1841.
32. AM, II, 292 ff., Church to Rogers, March 14–21, 1841. Rogers was on holiday in Italy and Church's vivid description of events to him in this long letter is the best source.
33. Printed in *Via Media*, II, 359 f.
34. AM, II, 292.
35. OF, p. 77.
36. *Ibid.*, p. 81, March 10, 1841.
37. *Ibid.*, p. 80, Moberly to Church, n. d.
38. *Ibid.*, p. 88, Hook to Newman, March 17, 1841.
39. *Ibid.*, p. 78, Church to Newman, March 10, 1841.
40. *Ibid.*, p. 79, Church to Newman, March 11, 1841.
41. NP, March 11, 1841.
42. AM, II, 292 and OF, pp. 82 ff.
43. KP, Kreble to Newman, March 14, 1841.
44. NP, Newman to Hawkins, January 1, 1866.

45. NP, Hawkins to Newman, April 2, 1866.
46. *Via Media*, II, 362.
47. *Ibid.*, 363.
48. AM, II, 300, March 16, 1841.
49. *Ibid.*, 299.
50. KP, Keble to Pusey, n. d. (but about March 16, 1841).
51. Hawkins' views were reported in KP, Church to Keble, March 23, 1841.
52. Liddon, II, 185 ff.
53. *Ibid.*, 189.
54. *Ibid.*, 190, March 22, 1841.
55. PP, Oakeley to Pusey, March 14, 1841.
56. KP, Keble to Newman, n. d. (but after March 16, 1841).
57. NP, Bowden to Newman, March 23, 1841.
58. Liddon, II, 192 f.
59. OF, pp. 100 f., March 26, 1841.
60. *Ibid.*
61. Liddon, II, 199.
62. OF, p. 103.
63. AM, II, 305, Newman to Jemima Mozley, March 30, 1841.
64. *Ibid.*, April 1, 1841.
65. Golightly also published a "Letter" to Bagot.
66. H. B. Wilson, "Letter to T. T. Churton" (London, 1841), p. 29.
67. A. Perceval, "A Vindication" (London, 1841), p. 17.
68. "Puseyism Unmasked. Sketches for the Times" (London, 1841), p. 2.
69. S. R. Maitland, "A Letter" (London, 1841), p. 5.
70. J. H. Newman, "Letter to Jelf," *Via Media*, II, 368, 369, 378, 386.
71. J. H. Newman, "Letter to the Bishop of Oxford," *Via Media*, II, 400, 419, 423.
72. PP, Keble to Pusey, Easter Friday, 1841.
73. AM, II, 307 f.
74. OF, p. 108, April 8, 1841.
75. AM, II, 306, Newman to Keble, April 1, 1841.
76. *Ibid.*
77. NP, June 18, 1841.

CHAPTER 17

1. Blachford's *Letters*, p. 19.
2. NP, Rogers to Newman, May 10, 1841.
3. Mary Church, *Life and Letters of Dean Church* (London, 1894). For a more recent appraisal see B. A. Smith, *Dean Church* (London, 1958).
4. Robert Ornsby, *Memoirs of James Robert Hope-Scott* (London, 1844), 2 Vols.
5. PP, Keble to Pusey, July 17, 1841.
6. Battiscombe, p. 223.
7. AM, II, 313, Keble to Newman, July 19, 1841.
8. PP, Keble to Pusey, July 17, 1841.
9. *Ibid.* and KP, Keble to Perceval, August 8, 1841.
10. AM, II, 314.
11. KP, July 18, 1841.
12. *Ibid.*
13. John Keble, "Letter to Justice Coleridge" (Pusey ed., London, 1866), p. 21.
14. Battiscombe, p. 224.

15. KP, Keble to Newman, September 11, 1841.
16. *Ibid.*
17. Liddon, II, 234.
18. KP, John to Thomas Keble, September 25, 1841.
19. KP, Keble to Newman, September 30, 1841.
20. KP, Keble to Newman, October 7, 1841.
21. OF, p. 139.
22. KP, Keble to Newman, September 30, 1841.
23. NP, Newman to Thomas Mozley, October 21, 1840 and Mozley to Newman, October 24, 1840.
24. NP, Newman to Thomas Mozley, December 21, 1840.
25. *Ibid.* and NP, Newman to Thomas Mozley, April 6, 1841.
26. NP, Newman to Thomas Mozley, August 20, 1841.
27. NP, June 3, 1841.
28. NP, July 15, 1841.
29. *British Critic* (July 1841), XXX, 59, 47.
30. NP, June 3, 1841.
31. *Ibid.*
32. NP, June 7, 1841.
33. NP, June 12, 1841.
34. NP, June 21, 1841.
35. *British Critic* (July 1841), XXX, 216, 217, 225, 220.
36. *Ibid.*, 2, 28, 29, 37 f.
37. NP, April 6, 1841.
38. Mozley's *Reminiscences*, II, 244.
39. NP, Palmer to Newman, July 25, 1841.
40. KP, July 4, 1841.
41. *Ibid.*
42. KP, July 19, 1841.
43. OF, p. 136, July 20, 1841.
44. NP, Newman to Thomas Mozley, n. d. and July 15, 1841.
45. NP, Thomas Mozley to Newman, July 17, 1841.
46. NP, Rivington to Thomas Mozley, n. d. (but certainly after October 1841). Among those who had complained about the *British Critic*'s July and October issues were Hook, Perceval and Edward Churton.
47. KP, Keble to Mr. Cooke, January 10, 1842.
48. OF, p. 142.
49. Mozley's *Letters*, p. 87, February 11, 1839.
50. Liddon, II, 250.
51. NP, Bowden to Newman, October 11, 1841.
52. Ornsby's *Hope-Scott*, I, 302.
53. KP, Keble to Newman, October 19, 1841.
54. OF, p. 136.
55. OF, pp. 144 f.
56. *Ibid.*, p. 146.
57. Trevor, pp. 257 ff., an excellent analysis of the Charges.
58. *Ibid.*, p. 260.
59. NP, Bowden to Newman, October 11, 1841.
60. KP, Keble to Newman, n. d.
61. KP, Keble to Newman, November 15, 1841.
62. The text is in the *Apologia* and AM, II, 324.
63. J. R. Hope, "The Bishopric of the United Church . . . at Jerusalem" (London, 1841), pp. 56 f., 62.

64. KP, Keble to Newman, December 25, 1841.
65. KP, January 31, 1842.
66. *Ibid.*
67. KP, Sumner to Keble, January 22, 1842.
68. KP, Keble to Newman, January 23, 1842.
69. *Ibid.*
70. KP, Keble to Newman, March 6, 1842.
71. KP, Keble to Newman, May 18, 1842.
72. KP, Keble to Newman, April 4, 1842.
73. *Ibid.*
74. KP, Coleridge to Keble, February 8, 1842.
75. KP, Keble to Newman, October 23, 1841.
76. AM, II, 212, and Prevost's *Autobiography of Isaac Williams,* p. 57.
77. NP, September 6, 1841.
78. *Ibid.*
79. NP, Newman to Jemima, November 21, 1841.
80. NP, October 29, 1841.
81. Liddon, II, 262.
82. *Ibid.,* 263.
83. KP, Keble to Newman, November 23, 1841.
84. NP, R. Palmer to Newman, November 29, 1841.
85. PP, November 25, 1841.
86. PP, November 27, 1841.
87. KP, Coleridge to Keble, n. d.
88. NP, W. Trower to Newman, December 24, 1841.
89. KP, Keble to Newman, December 2, 1841.
90. NP, Palmer to Newman, November 29, 1841.
91. NP, N. Goldsmid to Newman, December 27, 1841.
92. Liddon, II, 266.
93. NP, Rogers to Newman, January 4, 1842.
94. NP, Goldsmid to Newman, January 13 and 17, 1842.
95. *Ibid.*
96. NP, Isaac Williams to Thomas Mozley, n. d. (mid-January 1842).
97. *Ibid.*
98. NP, Palmer to Newman, January 20, 1842.
99. NP, Isaac Williams to Thomas Mozley, n. d.
100. NP, Newman to Henry Wilberforce, November 8, 1841.
101. PP, Churton to Pusey, December 9, 1841.
102. KP, Coleridge to Keble, December 5, 1841.

CHAPTER 18

1. Tuckwell's *Reminiscences,* pp. 184 f. Cf. the comments of Dean Lake, quoted in AM, II, 359 n.
2. Stanley, II, 254.
3. NP, January 31, 1842.
4. AM, II, 394 f.
5. *Ibid.,* 359 f.
6. KP, Keble to Newman, September 7, 1842.
7. NP, Newman to Thomas Mozley, June 21, 1842.
8. NP, Thomas Mozley to W. G. Ward, January 25, 1842.
9. NP, Newman to Thomas Mozley, January 26, 1842.
10. NP, Thomas Mozley to Newman, January 28, 1842.

11. NP, Newman to Thomas Mozley, January 29, 1842.
12. Mozley's *Reminiscences*, II, 224–26.
13. NP, Thomas Mozley to Newman, March 30, 1842.
14. NP, Newman to Thomas Mozley, October 18, 1842.
15. NP, Newman to Thomas Mozley, October 30, 1842.
16. NP, Thomas Mozley to Newman, September 9, 1842. At one point in this letter Tom remarked, "Harriet heard the Charge."
17. NP, Newman to Thomas Mozley, September 14, 1842.
18. NP, Thomas Mozley to Newman, September 16, 1842. Part of this crisis over Bishop Denison's Charge was the alleged reaction of Keble's friend George Moberly, who was reported to have said: "I tell you, I will not be dragged through the mud by a set of writers whom I think so etc. etc." See NP, Newman to Thomas Mozley, September 17, 1842.
19. *Ibid.*
20. NP, Thomas Mozley to Newman, September 20, 1842.
21. NP, Newman to Thomas Mozley, September 26, 1842.
22. NP, Newman to Thomas Mozley, October 30, 1842.
23. NP, Thomas Mozley to Newman, St. Martin's Day [November 11 or 12], 1842.
24. Keble commented: "What will Mozley do [after Denison's Charge]? Will he follow Newman's example? I think not, for he likes the *B.C.* better than ever N. did the Tracts." KP, John to Thomas Keble, September 20, 1842.
25. NP, Newman to Thomas Mozley, December 26, 1842.
26. *British Critic* (January 1843), XXXIII, 281.
27. NP, Newman to Thomas Mozley, September 17, 1842. The reference was to George Moberly, whom Newman liked despite his Via Media views.
28. NP, Newman to Thomas Mozley, October 30, 1841.
29. NP, March 20, 1840.
30. Mozley's *Reminiscences*, I, 408–12.
31. Tom Mozley thus reported at second hand a conversation Phillipps had with the Bishop of Chester's son. "He said that he expected *soon* some conversions there [i.e. Oxford], and described himself as being on very intimate terms, *not* with *you* and *Pusey*, but another set of similar views. I thought of Bloxham [*sic*] but did not think of Sibthorpe as I do not realize his being much in Oxford." NP, Thomas Mozley to Newman, November 2, 1841.
32. OF, p. 172.
33. NP, Robert Wilberforce to Newman, December 9, 1841.
34. NP, Thomas Mozley to Newman, November 30, 1841.
35. AM, II, 351.
36. Richard Bagot, "A Charge . . . at the Fourth Visitation" (London, 1842), pp. 17 f. The tone of the Charge as a whole was, as one might expect, moderate and conciliatory. Here is the context of the phrase quoted in the text: "I am aware that the Articles of our Church were rather drawn up with the view of including than of excluding men of various shades of opinion, and I am further aware that if a precedent were wanted for—I will not say stretching—but for contorting the meaning of those formularies, nothing can exceed the licence which has been assumed by Calvinistic interpreters of the Articles—a licence which has often gone beyond what was attempted in the 90th Tract. Still I cannot persuade myself that any but the plain obvious meaning is the meaning

which as members of the Church we are bound to receive; and I cannot reconcile myself to a system of interpretation which is so subtle that by it the Articles may be made to mean anything or nothing."

37. *Apologia*, p. 223.
38. Trevor, pp. 270 ff. There is some discrepancy between the accounts of the horarium given by Pattison (*Memoirs*, pp. 190–93) and KP, Dalgairns to Gresley, May 10, 1842. See Trevor, p. 274.
39. KP, Dalgairns to Gresley, January 21, 1842.
40. KP, January 21, 1842.
41. KP, March 7, 1842.
42. KP, September 12, 1842.
43. KP, November 24, 1843.
44. KP, April 3, 1843.
45. KP, January 6, 1843.
46. KP, October 31, 1842.
47. KP, April 3, 1843.
48. AM, II, 369.
49. OF, p. 216.
50. See J. Derek Holmes, "Newman's Reputation and the Lives of the English Saints," *Catholic Historical Review* (January 1966), LI, 528–38.
51. Dorothea Mozley (ed.), *Newman Family Letters* (London, 1962), pp. 121 f., Harriet to Jemima, May 13, 1842.
52. AM, II, 356.
53. NP, Newman to Thomas Mozley, July 11, 1843. "Your article is superb. Keble thinks it the most powerful which has appeared in the *B. C.*" Tom's article dealt with Pusey's suspension, about which see below.
54. NP, Newman to Henry Wilberforce, February 19, 1842. On Pusey's pamphlet see Liddon, II, 272 ff.
55. OF, p. 199.
56. AM, II, 364.
57. Liddon, II, 298.
58. *Ibid.*, 302. The retraction made things a bit strained at Littlemore. See KP, Dalgairns to Gresley, March 10, 1843: "You wish to know what Newman's queer production in the *Conservative Journal* means. It certainly is most singularly abrupt; and if you ask me why it appeared in that form I can only answer that I am not a bit wiser than you on the matter. He is singularly touchy on the point and will not be questioned by anybody about it."
59. I refer particularly to Miss Trevor's treatment, pp. 288 ff.
60. Blachford's *Letters*, p. 106.
61. Up to this point the letter is published both in OF, p. 221, and Blachford's *Letters*, pp. 110 f. Miss Trevor says (p. 290) quite incorrectly that part of the letter "was printed by Anne Mozley, no doubt at [Rogers'] wish, as expressing his sense of what he owed to Newman's friendship. But by itself it gives little indication of what was going on." The reader may judge for himself whether or not the unpublished part of the letter indicated something of what was going on. Miss Trevor thinks that the unpublished part was simply "more in the same style." The inference that Rogers arranged with Anne Mozley to have only the first part of the letter printed is both unfactual (since Anne Mozley did not do so) and unfair.
62. NP, Rogers to Newman, April 3, 1843.
63. NP, Newman to Rogers, April 5, 1843. See Trevor, p. 290.

64. NP, Rogers to Newman, April 10, 1843. Miss Trevor quotes the substance of this letter (p. 290) which she describes as Rogers' attempt "to justify himself." However, she fails to notice Rogers' remark about "last Easter" and hence she confuses the chronology. The beginning of the quarrel with Newman could not have occurred in the Lent of 1843 as she says (p. 289), because Rogers speaks of "last Easter" in his letter of April 10, 1843. In 1843 Easter fell on April 16th. Therefore there was nothing sudden or peremptory about Rogers' decision to break off with Newman. Miss Trevor is at her worst when she concludes her account by saying that Rogers must have imagined that Newman all along was acting like a politician. "Perhaps this seemed natural to Rogers, now that he was living in the political world, but it is extraordinary that anyone who had been Newman's close friend could imagine that he looked at the Movement in such a light" (p. 291).

65. OF, p. 221 comments: "The hyper-sensitive Newman of fiction ought to have broken entirely with Rogers. The real Newman did nothing of the kind." The fact is exactly the opposite of this assertion.

66. OF, p. 220, May 4, 1843.

67. AM, II, 369, April 30, 1843.

68. This account is based on two long letters from Provost Hawkins to Bishop Copleston, NP, December 29 and 31, 1842.

69. NP, December 31, 1842.

70. This account is taken from Liddon, II, 306 ff.

71. E. B. Pusey, "The Holy Eucharist, a Comfort to the Penitent" (Oxford, 1843), pp. 18, 22 and 28.

72. Quoted in Liddon, II, 309.

73. NP, Marriott to Newman, October 11, 1843.

74. Mozley's *Letters*, p. 145.

75. PP, July 15, 1843.

76. PP, July 1, 1843.

77. PP, June 10, 1843.

78. NP, June 19, 1843.

79. NP, June 9, 1843.

CHAPTER 19

1. Mozley's *Reminiscences*, II, 273 ff.

2. *Newman Family Letters*, p. 130.

3. Trevor, pp. 300 f.

4. Mozley's *Reminiscences*, II, 392.

5. *Newman Family Letters*, p. 141.

6. OF, p. 262.

7. *Ibid.*, p. 268, and AM, II, 380.

8. OF, pp. 211–13.

9. *Ibid.*, pp. 215–17.

10. *Ibid.*, p. 219.

11. NP, Newman to Thomas Mozley, May 5, 1843.

12. OF, pp. 223 f.

13. NP, June 9, 1843.

14. OF, pp. 231 f.

15. *Ibid.*, p. 243.

16. *Ibid.*, pp. 245 f.

17. *Ibid.*, p. 248. The four sermons were published at the end of 1843 in

Sermons on Subjects of the Day. Keble went over them before publication and many of his suggestions were incorporated.

18. OF, p. 248.
19. *Ibid.*, p. 249.
20. *Ibid.*, pp. 249–59.
21. *Ibid.*, p. 255.
22. AM, II, 377.
23. OF, p. 261.
24. J. H. Newman, *Sermons on Subjects of the Day* (London, 1918), p. 409.
25. See for example NP, Rivington to Mozley, n. d. (early 1842).
26. NP, Newman to Thomas Mozley, September 17, 1842.
27. NP, Rivington to Mozley, September 15, 1843.
28. Ward's *W. G. Ward*, pp. 244 f.
29. OF, p. 249.
30. Palmer's *Narrative*, pp. 20 ff.
31. *Ibid.*, p. 50.
32. NP, Newman to Bowden, October 31, 1843.
33. A group at Cambridge interested in art and liturgy.
34. NP, Oakeley to Thomas Mozley, October 23, 1843.
35. A group at Cambridge interested in art and liturgy.
36. NP, Newman to Bowden, April 8, 1844.
37. W. G. Ward, *The Ideal of a Christian Church* (London, 1844), pp. 408, 326, 409, 565–67.
38. PP, Pusey to Manning, October 17, 1842.
39. OF, pp. 271, 278.
40. PP, Pusey to Manning, July 9, 1844.
41. OF, p. 293.
42. NP, Marriott to Newman, August 31, 1843.
43. OF, p. 301.
44. *Ibid.*, pp. 315–17, June 8, 1844.
45. NP, Newman to Thomas Mozley, November 7, 1844.
46. OF, pp. 349 f.
47. *Ibid.*, p. 339, November 4, 1844.
48. *Ibid.*, p. 342, November 11, 1844.
49. NP, unnamed clergyman (signature excised) to Newman, June 18, 1844.
50. See NP, Newman to Bowden, December 29, 1842.
51. AM, II, 392.
52. OF, p. 333.
53. Gladstone's phrase to Manning. See OF, p. 293.
54. Liddon, II, 385.
55. PP, Keble to Pusey, April 25, 1844.
56. KP, John to Thomas Keble, June 6, 1844.
57. KP, John to Thomas Keble, September 28, 1844.
58. Church, p. 237.
59. A. C. Tait, "A Letter to the Reverend the Vice-Chancellor" (London, 1845), p. 19.
60. Ward's *W. G. Ward*, p. 333.
61. *Ibid.*
62. Church, p. 329.
63. NP, Newman to Bowden, September 29, 1843.
64. Ward's *W. G. Ward*, pp. 338 ff.
65. PP, Manning to Pusey, March 5, 1845.

66. Ward's *W. G. Ward*, p. 345.
67. *Ibid.*, pp. 351 f.
68. PP, Manning to Pusey, March 5, 1845.
69. PP, Keble to Pusey, February 26, 1845.
70. PP, Oakeley to Pusey, February 27, 1845.
71. PP, Keble to Pusey, March 1, 1845.
72. PP, Ward to Pusey, n. d. (but certainly February 26, 1845).
73. Oakeley's *Historical Notes*, p. 65.
74. NP, Newman to Bowden, October 31, 1843.
75. Oakeley's *Historical Notes*, pp. 65 f.
76. *Ibid.*, pp. 62 ff.
77. PP, Oakeley to Pusey, September 10, 1845.
78. NP, Newman to Henry Wilberforce, August 29, 1844.
79. NP, Newman to Henry Wilberforce, February 5, 1845.
80. Chadwick, *Development*, pp. 143 f.
81. Richard Church, *Occasional Papers* (London, 1897), II, 471 f.
82. KP, Keble to Robert Wilberforce, September 20, 1854.
83. KP, Keble to Robert Wilberforce, September 3, 1854.
84. Liddon, II, 450. This is not to say that Newman did not consider or speak about development of doctrine before 1845.
85. NP, March 20, 1845.
86. NP, Newman to Henry Wilberforce, April 27, 1845.
87. PP, Keble to Pusey, August 14, 1845.
88. Trevor, pp. 358 ff.
89. OF, p. 386.

CHAPTER 20

1. Ward's *Wiseman*, I, 433.
2. *Memoirs of Hope-Scott*, II, 64. This was a legal historian's joke referring to a decretal of Pope John XXII.
3. Purcell's *Manning*, I, 310.
4. PP, October 13, 1845.
5. PP, Coleridge to Pusey, October 19, 1845.
6. PP, Churton to Pusey, October 13, 1845.
7. PP, Hook to Pusey, October 15, 1845.
8. Liddon, II, 460 ff.
9. *Ibid.*, 463 f.
10. *Ibid.*, 464.
11. Newsome, *The Wilberforces and Henry Manning*, p. 309.
12. *Ibid.*, pp. 306 f.
13. Robert Wilberforce's Charge of 1851, "The Evangelical and Tractarian Movements," p. 6.
14. See J. C. S. Nias, *Gorham and the Bishop of Exeter* (London, 1951), and G. C. B. Davies, *Henry Phillpotts, Bishop of Exeter* (London, 1954), pp. 230 ff.
15. Principal Shairp said (Knight, p. 423) that Dean Church as a preacher "was the only man who even could *remind* him of Newman."
16. KP, John to Thomas Keble, June 9, 1847.
17. But Newman denied flatly that J. A. Froude had ever been a disciple of his. See C. S. Dessain (ed.), *The Letters and Diaries of John Henry Newman* (London, 1963), XIII, 85 f.
18. AM, II, 397.

19. Oakeley, *Historical Notes*, p. 59.
20. Newman's *Letters and Diaries*, XIII, 475, May 23, 1850.
21. Newsome, p. 386.
22. KP, Keble to Robert Wilberforce, September 3, 1854.
23. KP, Keble to Robert Wilberforce, September 20, 1854.
24. Newsome, p. 401.
25. *Apologia*, p. 237.
26. Newman's *Letters and Diaries*, XII, 25.

Index

Index